Ethics

Ethics

Theory and Contemporary Issues

Concise Edition

Barbara MacKinnon
The University of San Francisco, Professor Emerita

WADSWORTH
CENGAGE Learning

Australia • Brazil • Japan • Korea • Mexico • Singapore • Spain • United Kingdom • United States

WADSWORTH
CENGAGE Learning™

Ethics: Theory and Contemporary Issues,
Concise Edition
Barbara MacKinnon

Publisher: Clark Baxter

Senior Sponsoring Editor: Joann Kozyrev

Development Editor: Ian Lague

Assistant Editor: Nathan Gamache

Editorial Assistant: Michaela Henry

Media Editor: Diane Akerman

Marketing Manager: Mark T. Haynes

Marketing Coordinator: Josh Hendrick

Marketing Communications Manager: Laura Localio

Associate Content Project Manager: Sara Abbott

Associate Art Director: Faith Brosnan

Print Buyer: Linda Hsu

Rights Acquisition Account Manager, Text: Roberta Broyer

Production Service/Compositor: Knowledgeworks Global Limited

Senior Photo Editor: Jennifer Meyer Dare

Cover Designer: Sarah Bishins, sarahbdesign

Cover Image: © L & M SERVICES B.V. The Hague 20091011

For product information and technology assistance, contact us at
Cengage Learning Customer & Sales Support, 1-800-354-9706
For permission to use material from this text or product,
submit all requests online at **www.cengage.com/permissions**
Further permissions questions can be emailed to
permissionrequest@cengage.com

Library of Congress Control Number: 2009940129

ISBN-13: 978-0-8400-3295-9

ISBN-10: 0-8400-3295-1

Wadsworth
20 Channel Center Street
Boston, MA 02210
USA

Cengage Learning is a leading provider of customized learning solutions with office locations around the globe, including Singapore, the United Kingdom, Australia, Mexico, Brazil, and Japan. Locate your local office at **international.cengage.com/region.**

Cengage Learning products are represented in Canada by Nelson Education, Ltd.

For your course and learning solutions, visit **www.cengage.com.**

Purchase any of our products at your local college store or at our preferred online store **www.CengageBrain.com.**

Printed in the United States of America
2 3 4 5 6 7 14 13 12 11 10

For Edward, Jennifer, and Kathleen

CONTENTS

PREFACE

This concise edition of *Ethics: Theory and Contemporary Issues* is the same as the sixth edition except that it does not include readings with the text. This concise edition is ideal for instructors who want a briefer text that nonetheless provides a comprehensive introduction to ethics with an emphasis on pedagogy through examples that interest students and study tools that help them to fully comprehend the content.

ADDITIONS AND CHANGES

Although the basic elements remain the same, this edition has the following additions and changes from the fifth edition. All introductions have been updated, with special attention paid to the chapters in Part II. These updates include recent statistics, relevant cases, and contemporary examples. Among the contemporary topics treated are:

- the Patriot Act and privacy,
- torture and Abu Ghraib prison,
- the Buddhist views of death,
- partial birth abortion,
- sex workers and the sex trade,
- same-sex marriage,
- the Tuskegee syphilis study,
- Guantanamo Bay and the Geneva Conventions,
- enemy combatants,
- health care,
- global warming,
- the war on terror,
- Wikipedia and Google,
- outsourcing and offshoring, and
- Earth democracy.

Bibliographies have been updated and expanded.

Key Elements

The following are key elements of this edition:

The theory chapters present moderately detailed summaries of the theories and major issues, positions, and arguments. The contemporary issues chapters present several different things, including overviews or summaries of:

- current social conditions and recent events that will interest the student in the topic and provide current information,
- conceptual issues such as how to define the key words on the subject matter of the chapter (for example, pornography, cloning, and terrorism), and
- arguments and suggested ways to organize an ethical analysis of the particular topic.

The presentations in the text often ask questions and are usually followed by possible answers or those that already have been given. The aim is to present more than one side of the issue so that students can decide for themselves what position they will take. This also allows instructors to put whatever emphases they wish on the material or direct the students' focus as they see fit.

Where possible throughout the text, the relation of ethical theory to the practical issues is indicated. For example, one pervasive distinction that is used throughout is the one between consequentialist and nonconsequentialist considerations and arguments. The idea is that if students are able to situate or categorize a kind of reason or argument, then they will be better able to evaluate it critically. References to treatments of related issues in other chapters are also given throughout the text.

Pedagogical Aids This text is designed to be "user-friendly." To aid both instructor and student, the following pedagogical aids are provided:

- clearly organized material by means of diagrams, subheadings, definitions, and word emphases;
- a real-life event or hypothetical dialogue or updated empirical data at the beginning of each chapter to capture students' interest;

- review exercises at the end of each chapter that also can be used as test or exam questions;
- discussion cases that follow each chapter in Part II and provide opportunities for class or group discussions;
- topics and resources for written assignments in the discussion cases and the selected bibliographies at the end of each chapter; and
- the appendix on how to write an ethics paper, which gives students helpful advice and brief examples of ethics papers.

The outline of the highlights of the history of ethics on page xvi is admittedly sketchy. It makes only a limited attempt to include twentieth-century ethics and notes only a couple of non-Western figures. However, for those who are interested in history or in placing figures mentioned in this text into an historical context, it should be useful.

Gender and Racial Concerns Although this is primarily a general ethics text, it does make extra effort to include writings from female authors in the reading selections as well as in the bibliographies. Moreover, feminist issues are also treated throughout the text. These include questions of sex equality and sexual harassment, abortion, pornography, ecofeminism, and gender discrimination in the developing world. Racial concerns are stressed not only in the chapter on discrimination but also in the chapter on economic justice and throughout the text, where possible.

International Concerns References to international concerns are found throughout the text and are prominent in Chapter 19 on global issues. Chapter 18 on violence, terrorism, and war is also heavily international in scope.

IN SUMMARY

Ethics: Theory and Contemporary Issues

- It is flexible by allowing instructors to emphasize the theory or issues or the textual material as they choose.
- It is user-friendly while at the same time philosophically reliable. This book is not "pop ethics." You cannot do that and at the same

time be philosophically accurate and adequate. On the other hand, it uses many pedagogical aids throughout and at the end of each chapter. This text often provides examples and up-to-date newsworthy events. I ask stimulating questions throughout the textual presentations. I give diagrams wherever I think they will help.

- This edition is current, although the most recent relevant events and statistics will wait to be included in the next, seventh, edition next year.
- It is pedagogically helpful by including several teaching aids that amplify its teachability.
- It is balanced in the ethical theories and contemporary sources on the issues.

Web-Related Elements

Online Student and Instructor Resources Many student and instructor resources are available online at www.cengage.com/philosophy/mackinnon/ethicsconcise. The student companion website for this text includes test questions, quizzes, and web references for various topics treated in the text. The password-protected instructor website includes these items as well as an Instructor's Manual and PowerPoint® slides for lecture and review.

Instructor's Manual Online

The Instructor's Manual (IM) is available online at www.cengage.com/philosophy/mackinnon/ethicsconcise. It is available on the password-protected instructor companion site so that only instructors will have access to it. Interested instructors should contact their local Wadsworth sales representative or Wadsworth directly for a password.

Premium Website

Wadsworth's Premium Website includes step-by-step learning objectives for each topic, assignments, tests, quizzes, and study tools. The text will also be accompanied by Wadsworth's interactive ethics simulations. These animated modules prompt students to apply the ethical theories they have learned to challenging "real-world" situations by making a series of ethical choices in response to an unfolding story.

ACKNOWLEDGMENTS

I wish to thank the many instructors who took part in the e-survey regarding the sixth edition, upon which this concise edition is based, including Kenneth Beals at Mary Baldwin College, Melvin J. Brandon at Spring Hill College, Barlow Buescher at Pierce College, Albert E. Cinelli at Sierra College, Brian Cooney at Centre College, David B. Dillard-Wright at the University of South Carolina Aiken, Thomas Ellis at Texas A&M University, Michael Emerson at Northwestern Michigan College, Ann Farley-Parker at Cedar Valley College, Robert Gall at West Liberty State College, Jason Glenn at Baton Rouge Community College, Tara Holman at Georgia Perimeter College, Christopher Hudspeth at the University of South Florida, Steven Jauss at University of Arkansas at Little Rock, John Jensen at Gonzaga University, Robert Franklin Johnson at Florida Southern College, Michael M. Kazanjian at Triton College, especially Sarah E. Kreps at Tidewater Community College, C. David Lisman at Community College of Aurora, David Lopez at American River College, Robert B. Mellert at Brookdale Community College, Sarah Bishop Merrill at Texas State Technical College-Harlingen, Patti Nogales at California State University—Sacramento, Marcella Norling at Orange Coast College, Lawrence Pasternack at Oklahoma State University, Craig Payne at Indian Hills Community College, Patty Seck at Century College, Justin Skirry at Nebraska Wesleyan University, Eric Sotnak at the University of Akron, Christina M. Tomczak at Cedar Valley College, Pamela Tranby at Riverland Community College, Elizabeth Tropman at Colorado State University, Abraham Velez at Eastern Kentucky University, Louise Walkup at Three Rivers Community College, and Kristen Zbikowski at Hibbing Community College. Many of their helpful suggestions have been incorporated into these editions.

The students in my classes at the University of San Francisco over the years also have contributed greatly to this text by challenging me to keep up with the times and to make things more clear and more interesting. I wish also to thank them here.

I wish to acknowledge the many professional people from Cengage Learning who have worked on this edition, especially Joann Kozyrev, Sr. Sponsoring Editor, Philosophy and Religion; Diane Akerman, Media Editor; Nathan Gamache, Assistant Editor; Michaela Henry, Editorial Assistant; and Sara Abbott, Associate Content Project Manager. I also am most grateful for the detailed and professional work done on the preparation of this text by S. M. Summerlight.

Finally, I greatly appreciate the support given me by my husband and fellow philosopher, Edward MacKinnon. To him and to our two wonderful daughters, Jennifer and Kathleen, this book is again dedicated.

Barbara MacKinnon
Oakland, California

Ancient

500 B.C.E.	400	300	200	100	0	100 C.E.	200

Sappho
637-577

Socrates
469-399

Zeno
351-270

Jesus
?4 B.C.E.–C.E. 29

Plotinus
205-270

Plato
427-347

Philo Judaeus
20 B.C.E.–C.E. 40

Buddha
557-477

Aristotle
384-322

Sextus Empiricus
60-117

Confucius
552-479

Marcus Aurelius
121-180

Medieval

C.E. 300	400	500	600	700	800	900	1000	1100	1200	1300

Augustine
354-400

Anselm
1033-1109

Aquinas
1224-1274

Boethius
480-524

Abelard
1079-1142

Scotus
1265-1308

Mohammed
570-632

Avicebron
1021-1058

Ockham
1285-1347

Maimonides
1135-1204

Avicenna
980-1037

Averroes
1126-1198

Modern

1500	1600	1700	1800	1900	2000

Bacon
1561-1626

Locke
1632-1704

Hume
1711-1776

Kierkegaard
1813-1851

Moore
1873-1958

Hobbes
1588-1679

Leibniz
1646-1716

Kant
1724-1804

Marx
1818-1883

Rawls
1921-2002

Spinoza
1632-1677

Hegel
1770-1831

Nietzsche
1844-1900

Habermas
1929-

Rousseau
1712-1778

Mill
1806-1873

Sartre
1905-1979

Wollstonecraft
1759-1797

DeBeauvoir
1908-1986

Bentham
1748-1832

James
1846-1910

Dewey
1859-1952

Part One

Ethical Theory

1

Ethics and Ethical Reasoning

WHY STUDY ETHICS?

We live in a dangerous world. Whether it is more dangerous than in times past is an open question. One can think, for example, of the thirteenth century when Genghis Khan and his successors swept across Asia, Europe, and northern Africa and threatened to destroy all of Arab civilization. We also can think of the bubonic plague in the mid-fourteenth century that wiped out one-fourth of Western Europe's population and still reappeared in the following three centuries. On the other hand, today's threats may be even more powerful and have the capacity to affect many millions more people. For example, we have recently been made only too aware of the extent and capacity of terrorist networks around the world. Unstable nations and rulers possess powerful weapons of mass destruction. Individuals promoting a cause, acting out of revenge or in frustration, or for no clear reason at all can randomly kill people who are simply going about the business of life. We question what we may rightly do to lessen these dangers or prevent great possible harm. In some cases, the only way to do so seems to involve threats to other important values we hold—for example, rights to privacy and our basic civil liberties.

These are matters not only of practical and political bearing but also of moral rights and wrongs. They are also matters about which it is not easy to judge. We do not always know what is best to do, how to balance goods, or what reasons or principles we ought to follow.

For example, on October 24, 2001, six weeks after the terrorist attacks on the World Trade Center, the U.S. Congress passed the Patriot Act. Among its provisions are "enhanced surveillance procedures." One of these is the "authority to intercept wire, oral, and electronic communications relating to terrorism." This act amended the 1978 Foreign Intelligence Surveillance Act (FISA) to include terrorism. Warrants to surveil were still required but could be delayed for a few days. Since that time, questions have been raised about whether such warrants are required. This is both a legal and an ethical matter. Whatever the legal conclusions, we can still ask whether the dangers are such that personal and private communications should be open to certain investigations without notification. How does one balance the supposed value of protection with the value of privacy?

Or consider academic cheating, such as buying and selling term papers or cutting and pasting pieces from Internet sites and passing them off as one's own work and ideas. One may admit that this is clearly dishonest, yet one might argue that if professors make it easy to do so by the assignments they give or by their lack of oversight, then it should not be considered morally wrong.

In this text, we will examine some of the moral dilemmas we face as individuals and as peoples. Hopefully, by an explicit focus on such dilemmas, the decisions we must make will be more well informed and, in fact, better decisions. At least that is the aim of this study of ethics.

WHAT IS ETHICS?

I have asked students on the first day of an ethics class to write one-paragraph answers to the question, "What is ethics?" How would you answer? There have been significant differences of opinion among my students on this issue. Ethics is a highly personal thing, some wrote, a set of moral beliefs that develop over the years. Although the values may initially come from one's family upbringing, they later result from one's own choices. Other students thought that ethics is a set of social principles, the codes of one's society or particular groups within it, such as medical or legal organizations. Some wrote that many people get their ethical beliefs from their religion.

One general conclusion can be drawn from these students' comments: We tend to think of ethics as the set of values or principles held by individuals or groups. I have my ethics and you have yours, and groups also have sets of values with which they tend to identify. We can think of ethics as a study of the various sets of values that people do have. This could be done historically and comparatively, for example, or with a psychological interest in determining how people form their values and when they tend to act on them. We can also think of ethics as a critical enterprise. We would then ask whether any particular set of values or beliefs is better than any other. We would compare and evaluate the sets of values and beliefs giving reasons for our evaluations. "Are there good reasons for preferring one set of ethics over another?" As we will pursue it in this text, ethics is this latter type of study. We will examine various ethical views and types of reasoning from a critical or evaluative standpoint. This examination will also help us come to a better understanding of our own and various societies' values.

Ethics is a branch of *philosophy*. It is also called *moral philosophy*. Although not everyone agrees on what philosophy is, let's think of it as a discipline or study in which we ask—and attempt to answer—basic questions about key areas or subject matters of human life and about pervasive and significant aspects of experience. Some philosophers, such as Plato and Kant, have tried to

do this systematically by interrelating their philosophical views in many areas. According to Alfred North Whitehead, "Philosophy is the endeavor to frame a coherent, logical, necessary system of general ideas in terms of which every element of our experience can be interpreted."[1] Other people believe that philosophers today must work at problems piecemeal, focusing on one particular issue at a time. For instance, some might analyze the meaning of the phrase "to know," while others might work on the morality of lying. Furthermore, some philosophers are optimistic about our ability to answer these questions, while others are more skeptical because they think that the way we analyze the issues and the conclusions we draw will always be colored by our background, culture, and ways of thinking. Most agree, however, that the questions are worth wondering and caring about.

We can ask philosophical questions about many subjects. In aesthetics, or the philosophy of art, philosophers ask questions not about how to interpret a certain novel or painting, but about basic or foundational questions such as, What kinds of things do or should count as art (rocks arranged in a certain way, for example)? Is what makes something an object of aesthetic interest its emotional expressiveness, its peculiar formal nature, or its ability to show us certain truths that cannot be described? In the philosophy of science, philosophers ask not about the structure or composition of some chemical or biological material, but about such matters as whether scientific knowledge gives us a picture of reality as it is, whether progress exists in science, and whether it is meaningful to talk about the scientific method. Philosophers of law seek to understand the nature of law itself, the source of its authority, the nature of legal interpretation, and the basis of legal responsibility. In the philosophy of knowledge, called *epistemology*, we try to answer questions about what we can know of ourselves and our world and what it even is to know something rather than just believe it. In each area, philosophers ask basic questions about the particular subject matter. This is also true of moral philosophy.

Ethics, or moral philosophy, asks basic questions about the good life, about what is better and worse, about whether there is any objective right and wrong, and how we know it if there is.

This definition of ethics assumes that its primary objective is to help us decide what is good or bad, better or worse, either in some general way or in regard to particular ethical issues. This is generally called *normative ethics.* Ethics, however, can be done in another way. From the mid-1930s until recently, *metaethics* predominated in English-speaking universities. In doing metaethics, we would analyze the meaning of ethical language. Instead of asking whether the death penalty is morally justified, we would ask what we meant in calling something "morally justified" or "good" or "right." We would analyze ethical language, ethical terms, and ethical statements to determine what they mean. In doing this, we would be functioning at a level removed from that implied by our definition. It is for this reason that we call this other type of ethics *metaethics, meta* meaning "beyond." Some of the discussions in this chapter are metaethical discussions—for example, the analysis of various senses of "good." As you can see, much can be learned from such discussions. The various chapters of Part Two of this text do normative ethics, for they are concerned with particular concrete issues and how to evaluate or judge them.

ETHICS AND RELIGION

Many people get their ethical or moral views from their religion. Although religions include other elements, most do have explicit or implicit requirements or ideals for moral conduct. In some cases, they contain explicit rules or commandments: "Honor thy father and mother" and "Thou shalt not kill." Some religious morality is found in interpretations of religious books, lessons such as, "In this passage the Bible (or Koran or Bhagavad Gita) teaches us that we ought to. . . . " Some religions recognize and revere saints or holy people who

provide models for us and exemplify virtues we should emulate.

Philosophers, however, believe that ethics does not necessarily require a religious grounding. Rather than relying on holy books or religious revelations, philosophical ethics uses reason and experience to determine what is good and bad, right and wrong, better and worse. In fact, even those people for whom morality is religiously based may want to examine some of these views using reason. They may want to know whether elements of their religious morality—some of its rules, for example—are good or valid ones given that other people have different views of what is right and wrong and given that that these are different times with different problems.

Moreover, if moral right and wrong were grounded only in religious beliefs, then nonbelievers could not be said to have moral views or make legitimate moral arguments. But even religious believers should want to be able to dialogue with such persons. In fact, even religious believers regularly make moral judgments that are not based strictly on their religious views but rather on reflection and common sense.

Thinking further about religious morality also raises challenges for it. A key element of many religious moralities is the view that certain things are good for us to do because this is what God wants. This is often referred to as the "divine command theory." The idea is that certain actions are right because they are what God wills for us. Plato's dialogue *Euthyphro* examines this view. He asks whether things are good because they are approved by the gods or whether the gods approve of them because they are good. To say that actions are good just because they are willed or approved by the gods or God seems to make morality arbitrary. God could decree anything to be good: lying or treachery, for example. It seems more reasonable to say that lying and treachery are bad, and for this reason the gods or God condemn or disapprove of them and that we should also. One implication of this view is that morality has a certain independence; if so, we should be able to determine whether certain actions are right or wrong in themselves and for some reason. (Further discussion of this issue may be found in Chapter 6's section titled "Evaluating Natural Law Theory.")

Religion, however, may still provide a motivation or inspiration to be moral for some people. They believe that if life has some eternal significance in relation to a supreme and most perfect being, then we ought to take life and morality extremely seriously. This would not be to say that the only reason religious persons have for being moral or trying to do the morally right thing is so that they will be rewarded in some life beyond this one. Rather, if something is morally right, then this is itself a reason for doing it. Thus, the good and conscientious person is the one who wants to do right just because it is right. However, questions about the meaning of life may play a significant role in a person's thoughts about the moral life. Some people might even think that atheists have no reason to be moral or to be concerned with doing the morally right thing. However, this is not necessarily so. For example, a religious person may disvalue this life if he or she thinks of it as fleeting and less important than the things to come or what lies ahead in another world beyond this one. And atheists who believe that this life is all there is may in fact take this life more seriously and want to do well in it. Furthermore, the religious as well as the nonreligious should be able to think clearly and reason well about morality.

For at least three reasons, we all must be able to develop our natural moral reasoning skills. First, we should be able to evaluate critically our own or other views of what is thought to be good and bad or just and unjust, including religious views in some cases. Second, believers of various denominations as well as nonbelievers ought to be able to discuss moral matters together. Third, the fact that we live in organized secular communities, cities, states, and countries requires that we be able to develop and rely on widely shared reason-based views on issues of justice, fairness, and moral ideals. This is especially true in political communities with some separation of church and state, where no religion can be mandated, and where one has freedom within limits to practice a chosen religion or practice no religion at all. In these settings, it is important to have nonreligiously based ways of dealing with moral issues. This is one goal of philosophical ethics.

ETHICAL AND OTHER TYPES OF EVALUATION

"That's great!" "Now, this is what I call a delicious meal!" "That play was wonderful!" All of these statements express approval of something. They do not tell us much about the meal or the play, but they do imply that the speaker thought they were good. These are *evaluative* statements. Ethical statements or judgments are also evaluative. They tell us what the speaker believes is good or bad. They do not simply describe what the object of the judgment is like—for example, as an action that occurred at a certain time or affected people in a certain way. They go further and express a positive or negative regard for it. However, factual matters are often relevant to our moral evaluations. For example, factual judgments about whether capital punishment has a deterrent effect might be quite relevant to our moral judgments about it. So also would we want to know whether violence can ever bring about peace; this would help us judge the morality of war and terrorism. Because ethical judgments often rely on such empirical or experientially based information, ethics is often indebted to other disciplines such as sociology, psychology, and history. Thus, we can distinguish between empirical or *descriptive judgments,* by which we state certain factual beliefs, and *evaluative judgments,* by which we make judgments about these matters. Evaluative judgments are also called *normative judgments.* Thus,

■ Descriptive (empirical) judgment: Capital punishment acts (or does not act) as a deterrent.
■ Normative (moral) judgment: Capital punishment is justifiable (or unjustifiable).

Moral judgments are evaluative because they "place a value," negative or positive, on some action or practice such as capital punishment. Because these evaluations also rely on beliefs in general about what is good or right—in other words, on *norms* or *standards* of good and bad or right and wrong—they are also *normative.*

For example, the judgment that people ought to give their informed consent to participate as research subjects may rely on beliefs about the value of human autonomy. In this case, autonomy functions as a norm by which we judge the practice of using people as subjects of research. Thus, ethics of this sort is called *normative ethics,* both because it is evaluative and not simply descriptive and because it grounds its judgments in certain norms or values.

"That is a good knife" is an evaluative or normative statement. However, it does not mean that the knife is morally good. In making ethical judgments, we use terms such as *good, bad, right, wrong, obligatory,* and *permissible.* We talk about what we ought or ought not to do. These are evaluative terms. *But not all evaluations are moral in nature.* We speak of a good knife without attributing moral goodness to it. In so describing the knife, we are probably referring to its practical usefulness for cutting or for impressing others. People tell us that we ought to pay this amount in taxes or stop at that corner before crossing because that is what the law requires. We read that two styles ought not to be worn or placed together because such a combination is distasteful. Here someone is making an aesthetic judgment. Religious leaders tell members of their communities what they ought to do because it is required by their religious beliefs. We may say that in some countries people ought to bow before the elders or use eating utensils in a certain way. This is a matter of custom. These normative or evaluative judgments appeal to practical, legal, aesthetic, religious, or customary norms for their justification.

How do other types of normative judgments differ from moral judgments? Some philosophers believe that it is a characteristic of moral "oughts" in particular that they override other "oughts" such as aesthetic ones. In other words, if we must choose between what is aesthetically pleasing and what is morally good, then we ought to do what is morally right. In this way, morality may also take precedence over the law and custom. The doctrine of civil disobedience relies on this belief, because it holds that we may disobey certain laws for moral reasons. Although moral evaluations are different from other normative evaluations, this is not to say that there is no relation between them. For example, moral reasons often form the basis for certain laws. For example, consider the copyright laws and downloading music from the Internet. In 2005, the U.S. Supreme Court ruled unanimously that this is a form of illegal piracy and that file-sharing services are engaging in copyright infringement.[2] There may also be moral reasons supporting such opinions—considerations of basic justice, for example. Furthermore, the fit or harmony between forms and colors that ground some aesthetic judgments may be similar to the rightness or moral fit between certain actions and certain situations or beings. Moreover, in some ethical systems, actions are judged morally by their practical usefulness for producing valued ends. For now, however, note that ethics is not the only area in which we make normative judgments. Whether the artistic worth of an art object ought to be in any way judged by its moral value or influence poses another interesting question that may arise here.

Thus, we can distinguish various types of *normative* or evaluative judgments (and areas in which such judgments are made) from *descriptive* judgments about factual matters (and areas or disciplines that are in this sense descriptive).

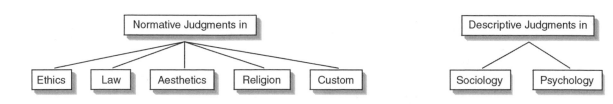

Ethical Terms

You might have wondered what is the difference between calling something "right" and calling it "good." Consider the ethical meaning for these terms. *Right* and *wrong* usually apply to action as in "You did the right thing" or "That is the wrong thing to do." These terms prescribe things for us to do or not to do. On the other hand, when we say that something is morally good, we are not explicitly recommending doing it. However, we do recommend that it be positively regarded. Thus, we say things such as "Peace is good, and distress is bad." It is also interesting that with "right" and "wrong" there seems to be no in-between; it is either one or the other. However, with "good" and "bad" there is room for degrees, and some things are thought to be better or worse than others.

We also use other ethical terms when we engage in moral evaluation and judgment. For example, we sometimes say that something "ought" or "ought not" to be done. There is the sense here of urgency. Thus, of these things we may talk in terms of an *obligation* to do or not do something. It is something about which there is morally no choice. We can refrain from doing what we ought to do, but the obligation is still there. On the other hand, there are certain actions that we think are permissible to do but we are not obligated to do them. Thus, one may think that there is no obligation to help someone in trouble, though it is "morally permissible" (i.e., not wrong) to do so and even "praiseworthy" in some cases. Somewhat more specific ethical terms include *just* and *unjust* and *virtuous* and *vicious.*

To a certain extent, which set of terms we use depends on the particular overall ethical viewpoint or theory we adopt. (See the following discussion of types of ethical theory.) This will become clearer as we discuss and analyze the various ethical theories in this first part of the text.

ETHICS AND REASONS

When we evaluate an action as *right* or *wrong* or some condition as *good* or *bad,* we appeal to certain norms or reasons. Suppose, for example, I said that affirmative action is unjustified. I should give reasons for this conclusion; it will not be acceptable for me to respond that this is just the way I feel. If I have some intuitive negative response to preferential treatment forms of affirmative action, then I will be expected to delve deeper to determine if there are reasons for this attitude. Perhaps I have experienced the bad results of such programs. Or I may believe that giving preference in hiring or school admissions on the basis of race or sex is unfair. In either case, I also will be expected to push the matter further and explain *why* it is unfair or even what constitutes fairness and unfairness.

To be required to give reasons to justify one's moral conclusions is essential to the moral enterprise and to doing ethics. However, this does not mean that making ethical judgments is and must be purely *rational.* We might be tempted to think that good moral judgments require us to be objective and not let our *feelings,* or *emotions,* enter into our decision making. Yet this assumes that feelings always get in the way of making good judgments. Sometimes this is surely true, as when we are overcome by anger, jealousy, or fear and cannot think clearly. Biases and prejudice may stem from such strong feelings. We think prejudice is wrong because it prevents us from judging rightly. But emotions can often aid good decision making. We may, for example, simply feel the injustice of a certain situation or the wrongness of someone's suffering. Furthermore, our caring about some issue or person may, in fact, direct us to think about the ethical issues involved. However, some explanation of why we hold a certain moral position is required. Not to give an explanation, but simply to say "X is just wrong," or simply to have strong feelings or convictions about "X," is not sufficient.

ETHICAL REASONING AND ARGUMENTS

We also should know how to *reason well* in thinking or speaking about ethical matters. This is helpful not only for trying to determine what to think about some questionable ethical matter but also for making a good case for something you believe is right as well as in critically evaluating positions held by other people.

The Structure of Ethical Reasoning and Argument

To be able to reason well in ethics, you need to understand something about ethical arguments and argumentation, not in the sense of understanding why people get into arguments, but rather in the sense of what constitutes a *good* argument. We can do this by looking at an argument's basic structure. This is the structure not only of ethical arguments about what is good or right but also of arguments about what is the case or what is true.

Suppose you are standing on the shore and a person in the water calls out for help. Should you try to rescue that person? You may or may not be able to swim. You may or may not be sure you could rescue the person. In this case, however, there is no time for reasoning, as you would have to act promptly. On the other hand, if this were an imaginary case, you would have to think through the reasons for and against trying to rescue the person. You might conclude that if you could actually rescue the person you ought to try to do it. Your reasoning might go as follows:

Every human life is valuable.
Whatever has a good chance of saving such a life should be attempted.
My swimming out to rescue this person has a good chance of saving his life.
Therefore, I ought to do so.

Or you might conclude that someone could not save this person and your reasoning might go like this:

Every human life is valuable.
Whatever has a good chance of saving such a life should be attempted.
In this case, there is no chance of saving this life because I cannot swim.
Thus, I am not obligated to try to save him (although, if others are around who can help, I might be obligated to try to get them to help).

Some structure like this is implicit in any ethical argument, although some are longer and more complex chains than the simple form given here. One can recognize the *reasons* in an argument by their introduction through key words such as *since, because,* and *given that.* The conclusion often contains terms such as *thus* and *therefore.* The reasons supporting the conclusion are called *premises.* In a sound argument, the premises are true and the conclusion follows from them. In this case, then, we want to know whether you can save this person and also whether his life is valuable. We also need to know whether the conclusion actually follows from the premises. In the case of the examples given above, it does: If you say you ought to do what will save a life and you can do it, then you ought to do it. However, there may be other principles that would need to be brought into the argument, such as whether and why, in fact, one is always obligated to save another when one can.

To know under what conditions a conclusion actually follows from the premises, we would need to analyze arguments with much greater detail than we can do here. Suffice it to say here, however, that the connection is a logical connection—in other words, it must make rational sense. You can improve your ability to reason well in ethics first by being able to pick out the reasons and the conclusion in an argument. Only then can you subject them to critical examination in ways we suggest below.

Evaluating and Making Good Arguments

Ethical reasoning can be done well or done poorly. Ethical arguments can be done well or poorly. A good argument is a *sound argument.* It has a valid form in that the conclusion actually follows from the premises, and the premises or reasons given for the conclusion are true. An argument is poorly done when it is fallacious or when the reasons on which it is based are not true or are uncertain. This latter matter is of particular significance with ethical argumentation, because an ethical argument always involves some *value assumptions*—for example, that saving a life is good. These value matters are difficult to establish. Chapters 4 through 7 will help clarify how to analyze value assumptions. The discussion below of the relation between ethical theory and ethical judgments also suggests how thinking about values progresses.

However, in addition to such value assumptions or elements, ethical arguments also involve conceptual and factual matters. *Conceptual matters* are those that relate to the meaning of terms or concepts. For example, in a case of lying we would want to know what *lying* actually is. Must it be verbal? Must one have an intent to deceive? What is deceit itself? Other conceptual issues central to ethical arguments are questions such as, "What constitutes a 'person'?" (in arguments over abortion, for example) and "What is 'cruel and unusual punishment'?" (in death penalty arguments, for example). Sometimes, differences of opinion about an ethical issue are a matter of differences not in values but in the meaning of the terms used.

Ethical arguments often also rely on *factual assertions*. In our example, we might want to know whether it was actually true that you could save the person. In arguments about the death penalty, we may want to know whether such punishment is a deterrent. In such a case, we need to know what scientific studies have found and whether the studies themselves were well grounded. To have adequate factual grounding, we will want to seek out sources of information and be open-minded. Each chapter in Part Two of this book begins with or includes factual material that may be relevant to ethical decisions on the particular issue being treated. Even though they are limited, these discussions show the kind of thing one must do to make good ethical decisions.

Notice that one can have an opinion about a matter of good and bad as well as an opinion about factual matters. For example, I might indicate that my opinion about whether random drug testing is a good thing is only an opinion because I do not feel adequately informed about the matter. This is an opinion about a moral matter. I can also have an opinion about the connection between passive smoking (inhaling others' tobacco smoke) and lung cancer. This would be an opinion about a factual matter. Because I can have an opinion about both values and matters of fact, I should not use this criterion as a basis for distinguishing

values and facts. To do so would imply that moral matters were always matters of opinion and factual matters were never such.

Those who analyze good reasoning have categorized various ways in which reasoning can go wrong or be fallacious. We cannot go into detail on these here. However, one example that is often given is called the *ad hominem* fallacy. In this fallacy, people say something like, "That can't be right because just look who is saying it." They look at the source of the opinion rather than the reasons given for it. Another is called "begging the question" or arguing in a circle. Here you use the conclusion to support itself. An example of this would be something like "Lying in this case is wrong because lying is always wrong." You can find out more about these and other fallacies from almost any textbook in logic or critical thinking, some of which are listed in the bibliography at the end of this chapter.

You also can improve your understanding of ethical arguments by being aware of a particular type of reasoning often used in ethics: *arguments from analogy.* In this type of argument, one compares familiar examples with the issue being disputed. If the two cases are similar in relevant ways, then whatever one concludes about the first familiar case one should also conclude about the disputed case. Thus, in a famous use of analogy that is summarized in Chapter 9 of this text, an argument about abortion by Judith Thomson, one is asked whether it would be ethically acceptable to unplug a violinist who had been attached to you and your kidney to save his life. She argues that if you say, as she thinks you should, that you are justified in unplugging the violinist, then a pregnant woman is also justified in "unplugging" her fetus. You would critically examine such an argument by asking whether or not the two cases were similar in relevant ways—that is, whether the analogy fits.

Finally, we should note that giving reasons to *justify* a conclusion is also not the same as giving an *explanation* for why one believes something. One might say that she does not support euthanasia because that was the way she was brought up. Or that she is opposed to the death penalty because she cannot stand to see someone die.

To justify such beliefs, one would need rather to give reasons that show not why one does, in fact, believe something but why one *should* believe it. Nor are *rationalizations* justifying reasons. They are usually reasons given after the fact that are not one's true reasons. These false reasons are given to make us look better to others or ourselves. To argue well about ethical matters, we need to examine and give reasons that support the conclusions we draw as well as we can.

ETHICAL THEORY

Good reasoning in ethics involves either implicit or explicit reference to an ethical theory. An *ethical theory* is a systematic exposition of a particular view about what is the nature and basis of good or right. The theory provides reasons or norms for judging acts to be right or wrong and attempts to give a justification for these norms. It provides ethical principles or guidelines that embody certain values. These can be used to decide in particular cases what action should be chosen and carried out. We can diagram the relationship between ethical theories and moral decision making as follows.

We can think of the diagram as a ladder. In practice, we can start at the ladder's top or bottom. At the top, at the level of theory, we can start by clarifying for ourselves what we think are basic ethical values. We then move downward to the level of principles generated from the theory. Moving next to conclusions about moral values in general, the bottom level, we use these principles to make concrete ethical judgments. Or we can start at the bottom of the ladder, facing a particular ethical choice or dilemma. We do not know what is best or what we ought to do. We work our way up the ladder by trying to think through our own values. Would it be better to realize this or that value, and why? Ultimately and ideally, we come to a basic justification, or the elements of what would be an ethical theory. If we look at the actual practice of thinking people as they develop their ethical views over time, the movement is probably in both directions. We use concrete cases to reform our basic ethical views, and we use the basic ethical views to throw light on concrete cases.

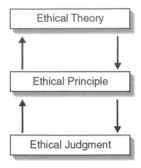

An example of this movement in both directions would be if we started with the belief that pleasure is the ultimate value and then found that applying this value in practice would lead us to do things that are contrary to common moral sense or that are repugnant to us and others. We may then be forced to look again and possibly alter our views about the moral significance of pleasure. Or we may change our views about the rightness or wrongness of some particular act or practice on the basis of our theoretical reflections. Obviously, this sketch of moral reasoning is quite simplified. Moreover, this model of ethical reasoning has been criticized by feminists and others, partly because it shows ethics to be governed by general principles that are supposedly applicable to all ethical situations. Does this form of reasoning give due consideration to the particularities of individual, concrete cases? Can we really make a general judgment about the value of truthfulness or courage that will help us know what to do in particular cases in which these issues play a role?

TYPES OF ETHICAL THEORY

In this first part, we will consider four types of moral theory: utilitarianism, Kant's moral theory, natural law, and virtue ethics. These theories exemplify different approaches to doing ethics. Some differ in terms of what they say we should look at in making moral judgments about actions or practices. For example, does it matter morally that I tried to do the right thing or that I had a good motive? Surely it must make some moral difference, we think. But suppose that in acting sincerely I violate someone's rights. Does this make the action a bad action? We would probably be inclined to say yes. Suppose, however, that in violating someone's rights I am able to bring about a great good. Does this justify the violation of rights? Some theories judge actions in terms of their *motive,* some in terms of the character or nature of *the act itself,*

and others in terms of the *consequences* of the actions or practices.

We often appeal to one or the other type of reason. Take a situation in which I strike a person, Jim. We can make the following judgments about this action. Note the different types of reasons given for the judgments.

That was good because you intended to do Jim good by awakening him—or it was bad because you meant to do him harm. (Motive)

That was good because it was an act of generosity—or it was bad because it violated the bodily integrity of another, Jim. (Act)

That was good because it helped form a sense of community—or it was bad because of the great suffering it caused Jim. (Consequences)

Although we generally think that a person's *motive* is relevant to the overall moral judgment about his or her *action,* we tend to think that it reflects primarily on our moral evaluation of the *person.* We also have good reasons to think that the results of actions matter morally. Those theories that base moral judgments on consequences are called *consequentialist* or sometimes *teleological* moral theories (from the Greek root *telos,* meaning "goal" or "end"). We also may think that what we actually do or how we act also counts morally. Those theories that hold that actions can be right or wrong regardless of their consequences are called *non-consequentialist* or *deontological* theories (from the Greek root *deon,* meaning "duty"). One moral theory we will examine is *utilitarianism.* It provides us with an example of a consequentialist moral

theory in which we judge whether an action is better than alternatives by its actual or expected results or consequences; actions are classically judged in terms of the promotion of human happiness. Kant's moral theory, which we will also examine, provides us with an example of a non-consequentialist theory according to which acts are judged right or wrong independently of their consequences; in particular, acts are judged by whether they conform to requirements of rationality and human dignity. The naturalistic ethical theories that we will examine stress human nature as the source of what is right and wrong. Some elements of these theories are deontological and some teleological. So, also, some goal-oriented or teleological theories are consequentialist in that they advise us to produce some good. But if the good is an ideal, such as self-realization, then such theories differ from consequentialist theories such as utilitarianism.[3] As anyone who has tried to put some order to the many ethical theories knows, no theory completely and easily fits one classification, even those given here. Feminist theories of care provide yet another way of determining what one ought to do. In Part Two of this text we will examine several concrete ethical issues. As we do so, we will note how these ethical theories analyze the problems from different perspectives and sometimes give different conclusions about what is morally right and wrong, better and worse.

CAN ETHICS BE TAUGHT?

It would be interesting to know just why some college and university programs require their students to take a course in ethics. Does this requirement rely on a belief that ethics or moral philosophy is designed to make people good and is capable of doing that?

On the question of whether ethics can be taught, my students have given a variety of answers. "If it can't be taught, then why are we taking this class?" one wondered. "Look at the behavior of certain corporate executives who have been found guilty of criminal conduct. They surely haven't learned proper ethical values," another responded. Still others disagreed. Although certain ideals or types of knowledge can be taught, ethical behavior cannot because it is a matter of individual choice, they said.

The ancient Greek philosopher Plato thought that ethics *could* be taught. He wrote, "All evil is ignorance." In other words, the only reason we do what is wrong is because we do not know or believe it is wrong. If we come to believe that something is right, however, it should then follow that we will necessarily do it. Now, we are free to disagree with Plato by appealing to our own experience. If I know that I should not have that second piece of pie, does this mean that I will not eat it? Never? Plato might attempt to convince us that he is right by examining or clarifying what he means by the phrase "to know." If we were really convinced with our whole heart and mind, so to speak, that something is wrong, then we might be highly likely (if not determined) not to do it. However, whether ethics courses should attempt to convince students of such things is surely debatable.

Another aspect of the problem of teaching ethics concerns the problem of motivation. If one knows something to be the right thing to do, does there still remain the question of why we should do it? One way to teach ethics to youngsters, at least, and in the sense of motivating them, may be to show them that it is in their best interest to do the right thing.

With regard to teaching or taking a course in ethics, most, if not all, moral philosophers think that ethics, or a course on ethics, should do several other things. It should help students understand the nature of an ethical problem and help them think critically about ethical matters by providing certain conceptual tools and skills. It should enable them to form and critically analyze ethical arguments. It is up to the individual, however, to use these skills to reason about ethical matters. A study of ethics should also lead students to respect opposing views, because it requires them to analyze carefully the arguments that support views contrary to their own. It also provides opportunities to consider the reasonableness of at least some viewpoints that they may not have considered.

In this opening chapter, we have questioned the value of ethics and learned something about what ethics is and how it is different from other disciplines. We have considered the relationship between ethics and religion. We have provided a description of ethical reasoning and arguments and have examined briefly the nature of ethical theories and principles and the role they play in ethical reasoning. We will examine these theories more carefully in the chapters to come, and we will see how they might help us analyze and come to conclusions about particular ethical issues.

NOTES

1. Alfred North Whitehead, *Process and Reality* (New York: Macmillan, 1929), 4.
2. *The New York Times,* June 28, 2005, p. A1.
3. I thank reviewer J. E. Chesher for this distinction.
4. Some issues raised in this selection can also be discussed in relation to relativism (see Chapter 2).

REVIEW EXERCISES

1. Determine whether the following statements about the nature of ethics are true or false. Explain your answers.
   a. Ethics is the study of why people act in certain ways.
   b. To say that moral philosophy is *foundational* means that it asks questions about such things as the meaning of right and wrong and how we know what is good and bad.
   c. The statement "Most people believe that cheating is wrong" is an ethical evaluation of cheating.
2. What is meant by the "divine command theory"?
3. Label the following statements as either *normative* (N) or *descriptive* (D). If normative, label each as *ethics* (E), *aesthetics* (A), *law* (L), *religion* (R), or *custom* (C).
   a. One ought to respect one's elders because it is one of God's commandments.

b. Twice as many people today, as compared to ten years ago, believe that the death penalty is morally justified in some cases.

c. It would be wrong to put an antique chair in a modern room.

d. People do not always do what they believe to be right.

e. I ought not to turn left here because the sign says "No Left Turn."

f. We ought to adopt a universal health insurance policy because everyone has a right to health care.

4. Discuss the relation between ethical theory and ethical reasons; between ethical theory and ethical reasoning.

5. As they occur in the following statements, label the reasons for the conclusion as appeals to *motive* (M), the *act* (A), or the *consequences* (C).

a. Although you intended well, what you did was bad because it caused more harm than good.

b. We ought always to tell the truth to others because they have a right to know the truth.

c. Although it did turn out badly, you did not want that, and thus you should not be judged harshly for what you caused.

Selected Bibliography

Antony, Louise, and Charlotte Witt (Eds.). *A Mind of One's Own: Feminist Essays on Reason and Objectivity.* Boulder, CO: Westview, 1992.

Art, Brad. *What Is the Best Life? An Introduction to Ethics.* Belmont, CA: Wadsworth, 1993.

Bassham, Gregory, et al. *Critical Thinking: A Student's Introduction with PowerWeb: Critical Thinking.* Burr Ridge, IL: McGraw-Hill Higher Education, 2004.

Becker, Lawrence, with Charlotte B. Becker. *A History of Western Ethics.* Hamden, CT: Garland, 1991.

Bishop, Sharon, and Marjorie Weinzweig. *Philosophy and Women.* Belmont, CA: Wadsworth, 1993.

Blackburn, Simon. *Being Good: An Introduction to Ethics.* New York. Oxford University Press, 2001.

Brandt, Richard. *Ethical Theory: The Problem of Normative and Critical Ethics.* Temecula, CA: Textbook Publishers, 2003.

Cohen, Stephen. *The Nature of Moral Reasoning: The Framework and Activities of Ethical Deliberation, Argument, and Decision Making.* New York: Oxford University Press, 2004.

Diestler, Sherry. *Becoming a Critical Thinker,* 2d ed. Upper Saddle River, NJ: Prentice Hall, 1998.

Frankena, William K. *Ethics,* 2d ed. Englewood Cliffs, NJ: Prentice Hall, 1987.

Halpern, Diane F. et al. *Thought and Knowledge and Thinking Critically about Critical Thinking.* Mahwah, NJ: Lawrence Erlbaum Associates, 2003.

Kourany, Janet, James Sterba, and Rosemarie Tong. *Feminist Frameworks.* Englewood Cliffs, NJ: Prentice Hall, 1992.

MacIntyre, Alasdair. *A Short History of Ethics.* New York: Macmillan, 1966.

May, Todd. *Moral Theory Poststructuralism.* University Park, PA: Penn State University Press, 2004.

Noddings, Nel. *Caring: A Feminine Approach to Ethics and Moral Education.* Berkeley: University of California Press, 1984.

Nussbaum, Martha. *The Fragility of Goodness.* New York: Cambridge University Press, 1993.

Pearsall, Marilyn. *Women and Values: Readings in Recent Feminist Philosophy,* 2d ed. Belmont, CA: Wadsworth, 1993.

Rachels, James. *The Elements of Moral Philosophy.* New York: Random House, 1986.

Rosen, Bernard. *The Centrality of Normative Ethical Theory.* New York: Peter Lang Publishing, 1999.

Rowan, John R. *Conflicts of Rights: Moral Theory and Social Policy Implications.* Boulder, CO: Westview Press, 1999.

Taylor, Paul. *Principles of Ethics.* Encino, CA: Dickenson, 1975.

Thomson, Judith Jarvis. *The Realm of Rights.* Cambridge, MA: Harvard University Press, 1990.

Toulmin, Stephen, Richard Rieke, and Allan Janik. *An Introduction to Reasoning,* 2d ed. New York: Macmillan, 1984.

Warnock, G. J. *The Object of Morality.* New York: Methuen, 1971.

Wellman, Carl. *Rights and Duties,* 6 vols. Hamden, CT: Routledge, 2002.

Williams, Bernard. *Ethics and the Limits of Philosophy.* Cambridge, MA: Harvard University Press, 1985.

Zimmerman, Michael J. *The Nature of Intrinsic Value.* Lanham, MD: Rowman & Littlefield, Publishers, 2001.

2

Ethical Relativism

For decades, anthropologists and sociologists have collected information on the diverse mores of different cultures. Some societies hold bribery to be morally acceptable, but other societies condemn it. Views on appropriate sexual behavior and practices vary widely. Some societies believe that cannibalism, the eating of human flesh, is good because it ensures tribal fertility or increases manliness. Some Inuit groups, the native peoples of northern Canada and Alaska, believed that it was appropriate to abandon their elderly when they could no longer travel with the group, while other groups once practiced ritual strangulation of the old by their children. Ruth Benedict has documented the case of a Northwest Indian group that believed it was justified in killing an innocent person for each member of the group who had died. This was not a matter of revenge but a way of fighting death. In place of bereavement, the group felt relieved by the second killing.[1]

Some societies believe in female circumcision; in other societies, it not only is regarded as wrong but also is illegal. In some countries, it is acceptable for women to wear short skirts; in others, women are expected to cover their legs and hair. You should be able to think of many other examples of such differences.

Before we begin to examine some ethical theories, we ought to consider whether the very idea of applying ethical theories is misguided because it assumes that we can use these to determine what is morally right and wrong. We commonly hear people say, "What is right for one person is not necessarily right for another" and "What is right in some circumstances is not right in other circumstances." If this were true, then it would seem that we cannot make any general or objective moral assessments. "When in Rome," should we not then "do as the Romans do"? In other words, would not morality be either entirely a personal matter or a function of cultural values? These are questions about ethical relativism. In this chapter, we will examine ethical relativism and its two basic forms and then present reasons for and against it. The last sections on "Moral Realism" and "Moral Pluralism" are more technical and not necessary for a basic understanding of ethical relativism, but they do introduce two key related issues addressed by philosophers today.

WHAT IS ETHICAL RELATIVISM?

There are various views on what is the best way to understand *ethical relativism* or what the term essentially means. According to some philosophers, ethical relativism is a theory that holds that there are no universally accepted ethical standards. This is surely true as one only needs to have a minimal understanding of various cultures to see this. But ethical relativism holds more than this. It is the view that there is no objective standard of right and wrong, even in principle. There are only different views of what is right and wrong. In saying they are "relative" to individuals or societies, we mean that they are a function of, or dependent on, what

14

those individuals or societies do, in fact, believe. *According to ethical relativism, there is no objective right and wrong.* The opposite point of view, that there is an objective right and wrong, is often called *objectivism,* or sometimes *nonrelativism.*

We can understand more about ethical relativism by comparing our views of the status of ethics and ethical matters with our ordinary beliefs about science. Most people believe that the natural sciences (biology, chemistry, physics, geology, and their modern variants) tell us things about the natural world. Throughout the centuries, and modern times in particular, science seems to have made great progress in uncovering the nature and structure of our world. Moreover, science seems to have a universal validity. No matter what a person's individual temperament, background, or culture, the same natural world seems accessible to all who sincerely and openly investigate it. Modern science is thought to be governed by a generally accepted method and seems to produce a gradually evolving common body of knowledge. Although this is the popular view of science, philosophers hold that the situation regarding science is much more complex and problematic. Nevertheless, it is useful to compare this ordinary view of science with common understandings of morality.

Morality, in contrast to science, does not seem so objective. The few examples of diversity of moral beliefs noted at the beginning of this chapter could be multiplied many times over. Not only is there no general agreement about what is right and wrong, but also we often doubt that this is the kind of matter about which we can agree. We tend, then, to think of morality as a matter of subjective opinion. This is basically the conclusion of ethical relativism: Morality is simply a function of the moral beliefs that people have. There is nothing beyond this. Specifically, no realm of objective moral truth or reality exists that is comparable to that which we seem to find in the world of nature investigated by science.

TWO FORMS OF ETHICAL RELATIVISM

In further exploring the nature of ethical relativism, we should note that it has two basic and different forms.[2] According to one version, called *personal* or *individual ethical relativism,* ethical judgments and beliefs are the expressions of the moral outlook and attitudes of individual persons. I have my ethical views, and you have yours; neither my views nor yours are better or more correct. I may believe that a particular war was unjust, and you may believe it was just. Someone else may believe that all war is wrong. According to this form of relativism, because no objective right or wrong exists, no *particular* war can be said to be really just or unjust, right or wrong, nor can *all* wars. We each have our individual histories that explain how we have come to hold our particular views or attitudes. But they are just that: our own individual views and attitudes. We cannot say that they are correct or incorrect, because to do so would assume some objective standard of right and wrong against which we could judge their correctness. Such a standard does not exist, according to ethical relativism.[3]

The second version of ethical relativism, called *social* or *cultural ethical relativism,* holds that ethical values vary from society to society and that the basis for moral judgments lies in these social or cultural views. For an individual to decide and do what is right, he or she must look to the norms of the society. People in a society may, in fact, believe that their views are the correct moral views. However, a cultural ethical relativist holds that no society's views are better than any other in a transcultural sense. Some may be different from others, and some may not be the views generally accepted by a wider group of societies, but that does not make these views worse, more backward, or incorrect in any objective sense.

REASONS SUPPORTING ETHICAL RELATIVISM

There are many reasons for believing that what ethical relativism holds is true. We will first summarize three of the most commonly given of those reasons and then evaluate their related arguments.[4]

The Diversity of Moral Views

One reason most often given to support relativism is the existence of moral diversity among people and cultures. In fields such as science and history, investigation tends to result in general agreement despite the diversity among scientists. But we have not come to such agreement in ethics. Philosophers have been investigating questions about the basis of morality since ancient times. With sincere and capable thinkers pursuing such a topic for millennia, one would think that some agreement would have been reached. But this seems not to be the case. It is not only on particular issues such as abortion that sincere people disagree, but also on basic moral values or principles.

Moral Uncertainty

A second reason to believe that what relativism holds is true is the great difficulty we often have in knowing what is the morally right thing to believe or do. We don't know what is morally most important. For example, we do not know whether it is better to help one's friend or do the honest thing in a case in which we cannot do both. Perhaps helping the friend is best in some circumstances, but being honest is the best in others. We are not sure which is best in a particular case. Furthermore, we cannot know for sure what will happen down the line if we choose one course over another. Each of us is also aware of our personal limitations and the subjective glance that we bring to moral judging. Thus, we distrust our own judgments. We then generalize and conclude that all moral judgments are simply personal and subjective viewpoints.

Situational Differences

Finally, people and situations, cultures and times differ in significant ways. The situations and living worlds of different people vary so much that it is difficult to believe that the same things that would be right for one would be right for another. In some places, overpopulation or drought is a problem; other places have too few people or too much water. In some places, people barely have access to the basic necessities of life; in other places, food is plentiful and the standard of living is high. Some individuals are more outgoing, and others are more reserved. How can the same things be right and wrong under such different circumstances

and for such different individuals? It seems unlikely, then, that any moral theory or judgment can apply in a general or universal manner. We thus tend to conclude that they must be relative to the particular situation and circumstance and that no objective or universally valid moral good exists.

ARE THESE REASONS CONVINCING?

Let us consider possible responses by a nonrelativist or objectivist to the preceding three points.

The Diversity of Moral Views

We can consider the matter of diversity of moral views from two different perspectives. First, we can ask, how widespread and deep is the disagreement? Second, we may ask, what does the fact of disagreement prove?

How Widespread and Deep Is the Disagreement?

If two people disagree about a moral matter, does this always amount to a moral disagreement? For example, Bill says that we ought to cut down dramatically on carbon dioxide emissions, while Jane says that we do not have a moral obligation to do this. This looks like a basic moral disagreement, but it actually may result from differences in their factual beliefs. Bill may believe that the current rate of such emissions will result in dramatic and serious harmful global climate effects in the next decades, the so-called greenhouse effect. Jane may believe no such harmful consequences are likely, because she believes that the assessments and predictions are in error. If they did agree on the factual issues, then Bill and Jane would agree on the moral conclusion. They both agree on the basic moral obligation to do what we can to improve the current human condition and prevent serious harm to existing and future generations. The table below illustrates this.

It is an open question how many of our seeming moral disagreements are not basic moral disagreements at all but disagreements about factual or other beliefs. But suppose that at least some of them are about moral matters. Suppose that we do

Basic Moral Agreement	Factual Disagreement	Different Moral Conclusions
We ought not to harm.	CO_2 emissions harm.	We ought to reduce emissions.
We ought not to harm.	CO_2 emissions do not harm.	We need not reduce emissions.

disagree about the relative value, for example, of health and peace, honesty and generosity, or about what rights people do and do not have. It is this type of disagreement that the moral relativist would need to make his or her point.

What Would Disagreement About Basic Moral Matters Prove? I have asked students in my ethics class to tell me in what year George Washington died. A few brave souls venture a guess: 1801, or at least after 1790? No one is sure. Does this disagreement or lack of certitude prove that he did not die or that he died on no particular date? Belief that he did die and on a particular date is consistent with differences of opinion and with uncertainty. So also in ethics: People can disagree about what constitutes the right thing to do and yet believe that there is a right thing to do. "Is it not because of this belief that we try to decide what is right and worry that we might miss it?" the nonrelativist would ask.

Or consider the supposed contrast between ethics and science. Although a body of knowledge exists on which those working in the physical sciences agree, those at the forefront of these sciences often profoundly disagree. Does such disagreement prove that no objectivity exists in such matters? If people disagree about whether the universe began with a "big bang" or about what happened in the first millisecond, then does this prove that no answer is to be found, even in principle, about the universe's beginning? Not necessarily.

Moral Uncertainty

Let us examine the point that moral matters are complex and difficult to determine. Because of this, we are often uncertain about what is the morally best thing to do. For example, those who "blow the whistle" on companies for which they work must find it difficult to know whether they are doing the right thing when they consider the possible cost of doing so to themselves and others

around them. However, what is described here is not strictly relativism but *skepticism.* Skepticism is the view that it is difficult, if not impossible, to know something. However, does the fact that we are uncertain about the answer to some question, even a moral question, prove that it lacks an answer? One reason for skepticism might be the belief that we can only see things from our own perspective and thus can never know things, even in ethics, as they are. This is a form of *subjectivism.* The nonrelativist could argue that in our very dissatisfaction with not knowing and in our seeking to know what we ought to do, we behave as though we believe that a better choice can be made.

In contrast, matters of science and history often eventually get clarified and settled. We can now look up the date of George Washington's death, and scientists gradually improve our knowledge in various fields. "Why is there no similar progress in ethical matters?" relativists might respond. Or have we actually made some progress in resolving some moral matters?

Situational Differences

Do dramatic differences in people's life situations make it unlikely or impossible for them to have any common morality? A nonrelativist might suggest the following. Suppose that health is taken as an objective value. Is it not the case that what contributes to the health of some is different than what contributes to the health of others? Insulin injections are sometimes good for the diabetic but not for the nondiabetic. Even though the good in these specific cases differs, there is still a general value—health—that is the goal. Or is not justice an objective moral value? It involves "giving to each his or her due." Yet what is due people in justice is not the same. Those who work might well deserve something different from those who do not, and the guilty deserve punishment that the innocent do not. (See the table below.)

Objective Value	Situational Differences	Different Moral Conclusions
Health	Diabetic	Insulin injections are good.
Health	Nondiabetic	Insulin injections are not good.
Justice	Works hard.	Deserves reward.
Justice	Does not work hard.	Does not deserve reward.

Absolute Value	Situational Differences	Same Moral Conclusions
Stealing is always wrong.	Person is starving.	Do not steal.
Stealing is always wrong.	Person is not starving.	Do not steal.

One reason situational differences may lead us to think that no objective moral value is possible is that we may be equating objectivism with what is sometimes called *absolutism*. Absolutism may be described as the view that moral rules or principles have no exceptions and are context-independent. One example of such a rule is "Stealing is always wrong." According to absolutism, situational differences such as whether or not a person is starving would make no difference to moral conclusions about whether they are justified in stealing food—if stealing is wrong. (See the table above.)

However, an objectivist who is not an absolutist holds that although there is some objective good—for example, health or justice—what is good in a concrete case may vary from person to person and circumstance to circumstance. She or he could hold that stealing might be justified in some circumstances because it is necessary for life, an objective good, and a greater good than property. Opposing absolutism does not necessarily commit one to a similar opposition to objectivism.

One result of this clarification should be the realization that what is often taken as an expression of relativism is not necessarily so. Consider this statement: "What is right for one person is not necessarily right for another." If the term *for* means "in the view of," then the statement simply states the fact that people do disagree. It states that "What is right in the view of one person is not what is right in the view of the other." However, this is not yet relativism. Relativism goes beyond this in its belief that this is all there is. If *for* is used in the sense "Insulin injections are good for some people but not for others," then the original statement is also not necessarily relativistic. It could, in fact, imply that health is a true or objective good and that what leads to it is good and what diminishes it

is bad. For ethical relativism, on the other hand, there is no such objective good.

FURTHER CONSIDERATIONS

The preceding should provide a basis for understanding and critically evaluating ethical relativism. However, each type of relativism and its opposite, nonrelativism, must overcome more problems.

One problem for the social or *cultural relativist* who holds that moral values are simply a reflection of society's views is to identify that society. With which group should my moral views coincide: my country, my state, my family, or myself and my peers? Different groups to which I belong have different moral views. Moreover, if a society changes its views, does this mean that morality changes? If 52 percent of its people once supported some war but later only 48 percent, does this mean that earlier the war was just but became unjust when the people changed their minds about it?

One problem that the *individual relativist* faces is whether that view accords with personal experience. According to individual relativism, it seems that I should turn within and consult my moral feelings in order to solve a personal moral problem. This is often just the source of the difficulty, however, for when I look within I find conflicting feelings. I want to know not how I *do* feel but how I *ought* to feel and what I *ought* to believe. But the view that there is something I possibly ought to believe would not be relativism.

A problem for both types of relativist lies in the implied belief that relativism is a more tolerant position than objectivism. However, the cultural relativist can hold that people in a society should be tolerant only if tolerance is one of the dominant values of their society. He or she cannot hold that all people should be tolerant, because tolerance cannot be an objective or transcultural value, according to relativism. We can also question whether there is any reason for an individual relativist to be tolerant, especially if being tolerant means not just putting up with others who disagree with us but also listening to their positions and arguments. Why should I listen to another who disagrees with me? If ethical relativism is true, then it cannot be because the other person's moral views may be better than mine in an objective sense, for there is no objectively better position. Objectivists might insist that their position provides a better basis for both believing that tolerance is an objective and transcultural good and that we ought to be open to others' views because they may be closer to the truth than ours are.

Relativism, or expressions that seem to be relativistic, may sometimes manifest a kind of intellectual laziness or a lack of moral courage. Rather than attempt to give reasons or arguments for my own position, I may hide behind some statement such as, "What is good for some is not necessarily good for others." I may say this simply to excuse myself from having to think or be critical of various ethical positions. Those who hold that there is an objective right and wrong may also do so uncritically. They may simply adopt the views of their parents or peers without evaluating those views themselves. However, the major difficulty with an objectivist position is the problem it has in providing an alternative to the relativist position. The objectivist should give us reason to believe that there is an objective good. To pursue this problem in a little more detail, we will examine briefly two issues discussed by contemporary moral philosophers. One is the issue of the reality of moral value—*moral realism;* and the other concerns the problem of deciding between plural goods—*moral pluralism.*

MORAL REALISM

If there is an objective morality beyond the morality of cultures or individuals, then what is it like? Earlier in this chapter, we compared science and ethics. I suggested that natural science is generally regarded as the study of a reality independent of scientists—namely, nature. This view of the relation of science and nature can be called *realism.*

Realism is the view that there exists a reality independent of those who know it. Most people are probably realists in this sense.

Now compare this to the situation regarding ethics. If I say that John's act of saving a drowning child was good, then what is the object of my moral judgment? Is there some real existing fact of goodness that I can somehow sense in this action? I can observe the actions of John to save the child, the characteristics of the child, John, the lake, and so forth. But in what sense, if any, do I observe the goodness itself? The British philosopher G. E. Moore held that goodness is a specific quality that attaches to people or acts.[5] Although we cannot observe it (we cannot hear, touch, taste, or see it), we intuit its presence. Philosophers such as Moore have had difficulty explaining both the nature of the quality and the particular intuitive or moral sense by which we are supposed to perceive it.

Some moral philosophers who want to hold something of a realist view of morality try to argue that moral properties such as goodness are *supervenient,* or based on or flow from other qualities such as courage or generosity or honesty. Obviously, the exact relation between the moral and other qualities would need further explanation. Others attempt to explain moral reality as a relational matter: perhaps as a certain fit between actions and situations or actions and our innate sensibilities.[6] For example, because of innate human sensibilities, some say, we just would not be able to approve of torturing the innocent. The problems here are complex. However, the question is an important one. Are moral rights and wrongs, goods and bads something independent of particular people or cultures and their beliefs about what is right and wrong or good and bad? Or are they, as relativism holds, essentially a reflection or expression of individuals or cultures?

MORAL PLURALISM

Another problem nonrelativists or objectivists face is whether the good is one or many. According to some theories, there is one primary moral principle by which we can judge all actions. However, suppose this were not the case, that there were instead a variety of equally valid moral principles or equal moral values. For example, suppose that autonomy, justice, well-being, authenticity, and peace were all equally valuable. This would present a problem if we were ever forced to choose between the more just resolution of a conflict and that which promoted the well-being of more people. For example, we may be able to do more good overall with our health care resources if we spend them on treating diseases that affect more people. However, there is some element of unfairness in this proposal because people who have rare diseases did not choose to have them. In such cases when values conflict, we may be forced simply to choose one or the other for no reason or on the basis of something other than reason. Whether some rational and nonarbitrary way exists to make such decisions is an open question. Whether ultimate choices are thus subjective or can be grounded in an assessment of what is objectively best is a question not only about how we do behave but also about what is possible in matters of moral judgment.

The issue of moral relativism is not easily digested or decided. The belief that guides this text, however, is that better and worse choices can be made, and that morality is not simply a matter of what we believe to be morally right or wrong. If this were not the case, then there would not seem much point in studying ethics. The purpose of studying ethics, as noted in Chapter 1, is to improve one's ability to make good ethical judgments. If ethical relativism were true, then this purpose could not be achieved.

The two major ethical theories that we will examine, utilitarianism and Kant's moral theory,

are both objectivist or nonrelativist moral theories. Naturalist theories also tend to be objective because they have as their basis human nature and what perfects it. As you learn more about these views, consider what their reasons are for holding that the objective good they specify really exists.

NOTES

1. Ruth Benedict, "Anthropology and the Abnormal," *Journal of General Psychology, 10* (1934): 60–70.
2. We could also think of many forms of ethical relativism from the most individual or personal to the universal. Thus, we could think of individual relativism, or that based on family values, or local community or state or cultural values. The most universal, however, in which moral values are the same for all human beings, would probably no longer be a form of relativism.
3. According to some versions of individual ethical relativism, moral judgments are similar to expressions of taste. We each have our own individual tastes. I like certain styles or foods, and you like others. Just as no taste can be said to be correct or incorrect, so also no ethical view can be valued as better than any other. My saying that this war is or all wars are unjust is, in effect, my expression of my dislike of or aversion to war. An entire tradition in ethics, sometimes called "emotivism," holds this view. For an example, see Charles Stevenson, *Ethics and Language* (New Haven, CT: Yale University Press, 1944).
4. These are not necessarily complete and coherent arguments for relativism. Rather, they are more popular versions of why people generally are inclined toward what they believe is relativism.
5. G. E. Moore, *Principia Ethica* (Cambridge: Cambridge University Press, 1903).
6. Bruce W. Brower, "Dispositional Ethical Realism," *Ethics, 103,* no. 2 (Jan. 1993): 221–249.

REVIEW EXERCISES

1. Explain the definition of *ethical relativism* given in the text: "the view that there is no objective standard of right and wrong, even in principle."
2. What is the difference between individual and social or cultural relativism?

3. What is the difference between the theory that people do differ in their moral beliefs and what the theory of ethical relativism holds?
4. What are the differences among the three reasons for supporting ethical relativism given in this chapter? In particular, what is the basic difference

between the first and second? Between the first and third?

5. How would you know whether a moral disagreement was based on a basic difference in moral values or facts? As an example, use differences about the moral justifiability of capital punishment.

6. What is moral realism, and how does it differ from scientific realism? Is it similar in any way to scientific realism?

Selected Bibliography

Baghramian, Maria. *Relativism.* New York: Routledge, 2004.

Bambrough, Renford. *Moral Skepticism and Moral Knowledge.* New York: Routledge & Kegan Paul, 1979.

Benedict, Ruth. *Patterns of Culture.* New York: Pelican, 1946.

Billet, Bret L. *Cultural Relativism in the Face of the West: The Plight of Women and Children.* Basingstoke, England: Palgrave Macmillan, 2003.

Brink, David. *Moral Realism and the Foundation of Ethics.* New York: Cambridge University Press, 1989.

Fishkin, James. *Beyond Subjective Morality.* New Haven, CT: Yale University Press, 1984.

Hamlin, Cynthia Lins. *Cognitive Rationality and Critical Realism.* Hamden, CT: Routledge, 2001.

Harman, Gilbert, et al. *Moral Relativism and Moral Objectivity.* Malden, MA: Blackwell Publishers, 1995.

Herskovits, Melville. *Cultural Relativism.* New York: Random House, 1972.

Kluckhorn, Clyde. "Ethical Relativity: Sic et Non," *Journal of Philosophy* 52 (1955): 663–666.

Krausz, Michael (Ed.). *Relativism: Interpretation and Confrontation.* South Bend, IN: Notre Dame University Press, 1989.

Ladd, John. *Ethical Relativism.* Washington, DC: University Press of America, 2002.

Macklin, Ruth. *Against Relativism: Cultural Diversity and the Search for Ethical Universals in Medicine.* New York: Oxford University Press, 1999.

Moser, Paul K., and Thomas L. Carson (Eds.). *Moral Relativism.* New York: Oxford University Press, 2000.

Rachels, James. *Ethical Theory 1, The Question of Objectivity.* New York: Oxford University Press, 1998.

Streiffer, Robert. *Moral Relativism and Reasons for Acting.* New York: Routledge, 2003.

Summer, W. G. *Folkways.* Lexington, MA: Ginn, 1906.

Taylor, Paul W. "Four Types of Ethical Relativism," *Philosophical Review* 62 (1954): 500–516.

Timmons, Mark. *Morality Without Foundations, A Defense of Ethical Contextualism.* New York: Oxford University Press, 1998.

Villanueva, Enrique, et al. *Realism and Relativism.* Oxford, England: Blackwell, 2003.

Westermarck, Edward. *Ethical Relativity.* Atlantic Highlands, NJ: Humanities Press, 1960.

Williams, Bernard. *Moral Luck.* New York: Cambridge University Press, 1982.

Wong, David. *Moral Relativity.* Berkeley: University of California Press, 1984.

3

Egoism

In this chapter, we will give thought to the issues raised by the following dialogue. Because the issues concern *egoism* and its opposite, *altruism,* our speakers are Edna Egoist and Alan Altruist.

Edna: I think that people are basically selfish. Everyone primarily looks out for number one.

Alan: That's not so. At least some people sometimes act unselfishly. Our parents made sacrifices for us. Remember the story in the news not long ago about Wesley Autrey, a New York City construction worker who became known as the "subway hero"? While Autrey was waiting on a subway platform with his two young daughters, a young man next to them suffered a seizure and fell onto the tracks. As an incoming train approached, Autrey jumped onto the tracks and held the young man down while the train passed inches above them. That was anything but selfish. And there are some people who dedicate their life to service projects such as helping the poor or those in need of medical care.

Edna: But isn't it possible that the man who saved the other on the subway tracks did it without thinking? And don't those dedicated to helping others receive satisfaction from what they are doing?

Alan: I don't think that they help others because they receive satisfaction, though. And wouldn't it be disappointing if that were true? And wouldn't it be an awful world if everyone just looked out for themselves? For one thing, there would be no

cooperation. Conflicts and wars would be everywhere.

Edna: I don't agree. Even if people are basically selfish, we do live together and we would need some rules. Otherwise, individuals would have no way to plan and get what they want.

Alan: If you were completely self-centered, then you wouldn't be likely to have many friends.

Edna: I would want the satisfaction of having friends. I would help them when they were in need, because I would want help in return when I needed it. Isn't that what friends are for?

Alan: I don't think so. That's not true friendship. Also, I think what John Kennedy said is right. "Ask not what your country can do for you but what you can do for your country." We do want too much from others, including the government, without giving of ourselves. And that is not right.

Edna: But if people didn't take care of themselves first, then they would have nothing to give to others. I think people should think of themselves first.

Notice in this dialogue that Edna and Alan first argue about whether people are basically self-centered or selfish. Then they move to talk about the implications or consequences of this type of behavior. Finally, they differ about whether such behavior would be a good or a bad thing. Notice that Edna and Alan disagree about two distinctly different issues. One is whether people are basically selfish; the second is whether being selfish is good or bad. These two issues illustrate two different versions or meanings of egoism. One is *descriptive*. According to this version, egoism is a theory that describes what people are like. Simply put, this theory holds that people are basically self-centered or selfish. It is a view about how people behave or why they do what they do. It is often referred to as *psychological egoism*. The other version of egoism is *normative*. It is a theory about how people ought to behave. Thus, it is an ethical theory and is called *ethical egoism*. We will examine each theory in turn, first attempting to understand it and what it holds. We will then try to evaluate it, asking whether it is reasonable or true. The final sections—"The Moral Point of View" and "Why Be Moral?"—are more technical. One can understand the basic philosophical concerns about egoism apart from these treatments. However, the issues are interesting, and the treatments of them do summarize key ideas from contemporary debates about egoism.

Another type of moral theory has a long history in Western philosophy and is also exemplified by Thomas Hobbes. That theory has come to be called *contractarianism*. In some ways, it can be considered a form of egoism in that it stresses individual self-interested choice. According to this theory, the best social rules are those we would accept if we chose rationally. The context in which we choose is society, so each person must make his or her choices depending on what others will do and in cooperation with them.[1] To the extent that this rational choice is a form of self-interested choice, this tradition in ethics may also belong in a chapter discussion of egoism. In the interests of simplicity, however, we will omit further discussion of it here. John Rawls's theory of justice exemplifies aspects of this tradition, and thus some discussion of it can be found in the summary of his theory in Chapter 13.

PSYCHOLOGICAL EGOISM

What Is Psychological Egoism?

In general, psychological egoism is a theory about what people are like, but we can understand what it asserts in several ways. One way to understand

it is to say that people are basically selfish. This is what Edna says in the dialogue. The implication of this version is that people usually or always act for their own narrow and short-range self-interest. However, another formulation of this theory asserts that although people do act for their own self-interest, this self-interest is to be understood more broadly and as being more long-term. Thus, we might distinguish between acting selfishly and acting in our own self-interest.

On the broader view, many things are in a person's interest: good health, satisfaction in a career or work, prestige, self-respect, family, and friends. Moreover, if we really wanted to attain these things, we would need to avoid being shortsighted. For example, we would have to be self-disciplined in diet and lifestyle to be healthy. We would need to plan long-term for a career. And we would need to be concerned about others and not overbearing if we wanted to make and retain friends.

However, as some people have pointed out, we would not actually need to be concerned about others but only to appear to be concerned. Doing good to others, as Edna suggested, would be not for their sake but to enable one to call on those friends when they were needed. This would be helping a friend not for the friend's sake but for one's own sake.

Putting the matter in this way also raises another question about *how* to formulate this theory. Is psychological egoism a theory according to which people always act in their own best interest? Or does it hold that people are always motivated by the desire to attain their own best interest? The first version would be easily refuted; we notice that people do not always do what is best for them. They eat too much, choose the wrong careers, waste time, and so forth. This may be because they do not have sufficient knowledge to be good judges of what is in their best interest. It may be because of a phenomenon known as "weakness of will." For example, I may want to lose weight or get an A in a course but may not quite get myself to do what I have to do to achieve my goal. Philosophers have puzzled over how this can be so and how to explain it. It is a complex issue; to treat it adequately would take us beyond what we can do here.[2] On the other hand, it might well be true that people always do what they *think* is the best thing for them. This version of psychological egoism, which we will address next, asserts that human beings act for the sake of their own best interests. In this version, the idea is not that people sometimes or always act in their own interests, but that this is the only thing that ultimately does motivate people. If they sometimes act for others, it is only because they think that it is in their own best interests to do so. This is what Edna Egoist said in the dialogue about the subway hero.[3]

Is Psychological Egoism True?

Not long ago, a study was done in which people were asked whether they believed in or supported the jury system; that is, should people be proven guilty or not guilty by a group of peers? Most responded that they did. However, when asked whether they would serve on a jury if called, significantly fewer said they would.[4] Those who answered the two questions differently might have wanted justice for themselves but were not willing to give it to others. Or consider the story about Abraham Lincoln.[5] It was reported that one day as he was riding in a coach over a bridge he heard a mother pig squealing. Her piglets had slipped into the water and she could not get them out. Lincoln supposedly asked the coachman to stop, got out, and rescued the piglets. When his companion cited this as an example of unselfishness, Lincoln responded that it was not for the sake of the pigs that he acted as he did. Rather, it was because he would have no peace later when he recalled the incident if he did not do something about it now. In other words, although it seemed unselfish, his action was quite self-centered.

Is the tendency to be self-oriented something that is innate to all of us, perhaps part of our survival instinct? Or are these traits learned? Developmental psychologists tell us about how children develop egoistic and altruistic tendencies. Are female children, for example, expected to be altruistic and caring while male children are taught to be independent and self-motivated? In the dialogue above, you may have noticed that

these expectations have been deliberately turned around: Edna is the egoist and Alan the altruist. Although psychologists describe the incidence and development of these characteristics, philosophers speculate about how a person comes to be able to sympathize with another and take the other's point of view. These philosophical speculations and empirical descriptions attempt to tell us what the case is about: human development and motivation. Do they also make the case for or against psychological egoism?

How are we to evaluate the claims of psychological egoism? Note again that the view we will examine is a theory about human motivation. As such a theory, however, we will find it difficult, if not impossible, to prove. Suppose, for example, that Edna and Alan are trying to assess the motivations of particular people—say, their parents or the subway hero. How are they to know what motivates these people? They cannot just assume that their parents or the subway hero are acting for the sake of the satisfaction they receive from what they do. Nor can we ask them, for people themselves are not always the best judge of what motivates them. We commonly hear or say to ourselves, "I don't know why I did that!"

Moreover, suppose that their parents and the subway hero do, in fact, get satisfaction from helping others. This is not the same thing as acting for the purpose of getting that satisfaction. What psychological egoism needs to show is not that people do get satisfaction from what they do, but that achieving satisfaction is their aim. Now we can find at least some examples in our own actions to test this theory. Do we read the book to get satisfaction or to learn something? Do we pursue that career opportunity because of the satisfaction that we think it will bring or because of the nature of the opportunity? In addition, directly aiming at satisfaction may not be the best way to achieve it. We probably have a better chance of being happy if we do not aim at happiness itself but rather at the things that we enjoy doing.

Thus, we have seen that the most reasonable or common form of psychological egoism, a theory about human motivation, is especially difficult to prove. Even if it were shown that we *often* act for the sake of our own interest, this is not enough to prove that psychological egoism is true. According to this theory, we must show that people *always* act to promote their own interests. We need next to consider whether this has any relevance to the normative question of how we *ought* to act.

ETHICAL EGOISM

What Is Ethical Egoism?

Ethical egoism is a normative theory. It is a theory about what we *ought* to do, how we *ought* to act. As with psychological egoism, we can formulate the normative theory called ethical egoism in different ways. One version is *individual ethical egoism.* According to this version, I ought to look out only for my own interests. I ought to be concerned about others only to the extent that this also contributes to my own interests. In the dialogue, Edna first said only that she would do what was in her own best interest. Her final comment also implied that she believed that others also ought to do what is in their own best interests. According to this formulation of ethical egoism, sometimes called *universal ethical egoism,* everyone ought to look out for and seek only their own best interests. As in the individual form, in this second version people ought to help others only when and to the extent that it is in their own best interest to do so.

Is Ethical Egoism a Good Theory?

We can evaluate ethical egoism in several ways. We will consider four: its grounding in psychological egoism, its consistency or coherence, its derivation from economic theory, and its conformity to commonsense moral views.

Grounding in Psychological Egoism Let us consider first whether psychological egoism, if true, would provide a good basis for ethical egoism. If people were always motivated by their own interests, then would this be a good reason to hold that they ought to be so moved? On the one hand, it seems superfluous to tell people that they ought to do what they always do anyway or will do no matter what. One would think that at least sometimes one

of the functions of moral language is to try to motivate ourselves or others to do what we are not inclined to do. For example, I might tell myself that even though I could benefit by cheating on a test, it is wrong, and so I should not do it.[6]

On the other hand, the fact that we do behave in a certain way seems a poor reason for believing that we ought to do so. If people cheated or lied, we ask, would that in itself make these acts right? Thus, although it may at first seem reasonable to rely on a belief about people's basic selfishness to prove that people ought to look out for themselves alone, this seems far from convincing.

Consistency or Coherence Universal ethical egoism in particular is possibly inconsistent or incoherent. According to this version of ethical egoism, everyone ought to seek their own best interests. However, could anyone consistently support such a view? Wouldn't this mean that we would want our own best interests served and at the same time be willing to allow that others serve their interests—even to our own detriment? If food were scarce, then I would want enough for myself, and yet at the same time would have to say that I should not have it for myself when another needs it to survive. This view seems to have an internal inconsistency. (We will return to this problem in our discussion of Kant's moral theory in Chapter 5.) We might compare it to playing a game in which I can say that the other player ought to block my move, even though at the same time I hope that she or he does not do so. These arguments are complex and difficult to fully evaluate. Philosophers disagree about whether universal ethical egoism is inconsistent on the grounds that no one can will it as a universal practice.[7]

Derivation from Economic Theory One argument for ethical egoism is taken from economic theory—for example, that proposed by Adam Smith. He and other proponents of laissez-faire or government-hands-off capitalism believe that self-interest provides the best economic motivation. The idea is that when the profit motive or individual incentives are absent, people will either not work or not as well. If it is my land or my business, then I will be more likely to take care of it than if the profits go to others or the government. In addition, Smith believed that in a system in which each person looks out for his or her own economic interests, the general outcome will be best, as though an "invisible hand" were guiding things.[8]

Although this is not the place to go into an extended discussion of economic theory, it is enough to point out that not everyone agrees on the merits of laissez-faire capitalism. Much can be said for the competition that it supports, but it does raise questions about those who are unable to compete or unable to do so without help. Is care for these people a community responsibility? Recent community-oriented theories of social morality stress just this notion of responsibility and oppose laissez-faire capitalism's excessive emphasis on individual rights.[9] (Further discussion of capitalism can be found in Chapter 13.) In any case, a more basic question can be asked about the relevance of economics to morality. Even if an economic system worked well, would this prove that morality ought to be modeled on it? Is not the moral life broader than the economic life? For example, are all human relations economic relations?

Furthermore, the argument that everyone ought to seek his or her own best interest because this contributes to the general well-being is not ethical egoism at all. As we will come to see more clearly when we examine it, this is a form of utilitarianism. Thus, we can evaluate it in our discussion of utilitarianism in the next chapter.

Conformity to Commonsense Morality   Finally, is ethical egoism supported by commonsense morality? On the one hand, some elements of ethical egoism are contrary to commonsense morality. For example, doesn't it assume that anything is all right as long as it serves an individual's best interests? Torturing human beings or animals would be permitted so long as this served one's interests. When not useful to one's interests, traditional virtues of honesty, fidelity, and loyalty would have no value. Ethical egoists could argue on empirical or factual grounds that the torturing of others is never in one's best interests because this would make one less sensitive, and being sensitive is

generally useful to people. Also, they might argue that the development of traditional virtues is often in one's own best interest because these traits are valued by the society. For example, my possessing these traits may enable me to get what I want more readily. Whether this is a good enough reason to value these virtues or condemn torture is something you must judge for yourself.

On the other hand, it may well be that people ought to take better care of themselves. By having a high regard for ourselves, we increase our self-esteem. We then depend less on others and more on ourselves. We might also be stronger and happier. These are surely desirable traits. The altruist, moreover, might be too self-effacing. He might be said to lack a proper regard for himself. There is also some truth in the view that unless one takes care of oneself, one is not of as much use to others. This view implies not ethical egoism, but again a form of utilitarianism.

THE MORAL POINT OF VIEW

Finally, we will consider briefly two issues related to ethical egoism that have puzzled philosophers in recent times. One is whether one must take a particular point of view to view things morally and whether this is incompatible with egoism. The other, which is treated in the next section, is whether there are self-interested reasons to be moral.

Suppose that a person cares for no one but herself. Would you consider that person to be a *moral* person? This is not to ask whether she is a morally *good* person, but rather whether one can think of her as even operating in the moral realm, so to speak. In other words, the question concerns not whether the person's morality is a good one but whether she has any morals at all.

To take an example from W. D. Falk, suppose we want to know whether a person has been given a moral education.[10] Someone might answer that she had because she had been taught not to lie, to treat others kindly, not to drink to excess, and to work hard. When asked what reasons she had been given for behaving thus, suppose she responded that she was taught not to lie because others would not trust her if she did. She was taught to treat others well because then they would treat her well in return. She was taught to work hard because of the satisfaction this brought her or because she would be better able then to support herself. Would you consider her to have been given a moral education?

Falk thinks not. He suggests that she was given counsels of prudence, not morality. She was told what she probably should do to succeed in certain ways in life. She was taught the means that prudence would suggest she use to secure her own self-interest. According to Falk, only if she had been taught not to lie because it was wrong to do so, or because others had a right to know the truth, would she have been given a moral instruction. Only if she had been taught to treat others well because they deserved to be so treated, or that it would be wrong to do otherwise, would the counsel be a moral one. Similarly with working hard, if she had been told that she ought not to waste her talents or that she ought to contribute to society because it was the right thing to do, the teaching would have been a moral one. In summary, the education would not have been a moral one if it had been egoistically oriented. Do you agree?

Taking the moral point of view on this interpretation would then involve being able to see beyond ourselves and our own interests. It may also mean that we attempt to see things from another's point of view or to be impartial. Morality would then be thought of as providing rules for social living—ways, for example, of settling conflicts. The rules would apply equally to all, or one would have to give reasons why some persons would be treated differently than others. One reason might be that some persons had worked harder than others or their role demanded differential treatment.

In contrast, we do not think that we have to justify treating those close to us differently and more favorably than others. If we care more for our own children or our own friends than others, does this mean that we are not operating in the moral domain? Questions can be raised about the extent to which impartiality colors the moral domain or is required in order to be moral. Some feminists, for example, would rather define it in terms of

sympathy and caring. See Chapter 7 for further treatment of this issue.

WHY BE MORAL?

Let us assume that morality does involve being able at least sometimes to take the other's point of view and at some level to treat people equally or impartially. Why should anyone do that, especially when it is not in her or his best interest to do so? In other words, are there any reasons that we can give to show why one should be moral? One reason is that doing what one ought to do is just what being moral means. One should not ask why one ought to do what one ought to do! However, perhaps something more can be said.

Notice that this is a question about why I as an individual ought to be moral. This is not the same as asking why everyone ought to be moral. We could argue that it is generally better for people to have and follow moral rules. Without such rules, our social lives would be pretty wretched. As Alan Altruist noted in the dialogue, our life together would be one of constant conflict and wars. However, this does not answer the question concerning why I should be moral when it is not in my best interest to do so.

If you were trying to convince someone why he should be moral, how would you do it? You might appeal to his fear of reprisal if he did not generally follow moral rules. If he is not honest, then he will not be trusted. If he steals, he risks being punished. In *The Republic* by Plato, Glaucon tells the story of a shepherd named Gyges. Gyges comes into possession of a ring that he discovers makes him invisible when he turns it around on his finger. He proceeds to take advantage of his invisibility and take what he wants from others. Glaucon then asks whether we all would not do the same if we, like Gyges, could get away with it. He believes we would. But is he right? Is the only reason why people are just or do the right thing to avoid being punished for not doing so?

There are other more positive but still self-interested reasons you might offer someone to convince her that she ought to be moral. You might tell her that, as in Falk's moral education example, being virtuous is to one's own advantage. You might recall some of the advice from Benjamin Franklin's *Poor Richard's Almanac*.[11] "A stitch in time saves nine." "Observe all men, thyself most." "Spare and have is better than spend and crave." These are the self-interested counsels of a practical morality. Contemporary philosophers such as Philippa Foot also believe that most of the traditional virtues are in our own best interest.[12]

You might go even further in thinking about reasons to be moral. You might make the point that being moral is ennobling. Even when it involves sacrifice for a cause, being a moral person gives one a certain dignity, integrity, and self-respect. Only humans are capable of being moral, you might say, and human beings cannot flourish without being moral. You can give more thought to this question when you read about Kant's moral theory. For Kant, human dignity and worth is wholly bound up with being able to act for moral reasons.

Nevertheless, one can point to many examples in which people who break the moral rules seem to get away with it and fare better than those who keep them. "Nice guys [and gals?] finish last," baseball great Leo Durocher put it. If being moral seems too demanding, then some say this is too bad for morality. We ought to have a good life, even if it means sacrificing something of morality. In another view, if being moral involves sacrificing something of the personally fulfilling life and perhaps even "finishing last" sometimes, then this is what must be done. No one ever said being moral was going to be easy![13]

NOTES

1. See David Gauthier, *Morals by Agreement* (New York: Oxford University Press, 1986), and Peter Vallentyne (Ed.), *Contractarianism and Rational Choice*. New York: Cambridge University Press, 1991.

2. For a discussion of "weakness of will," see Gwynneth Matthews, "Moral Weakness," *Mind, 299* (July 1966): 405–419; Donald Davidson, "How Is Weakness of the Will Possible?" in *Moral Concepts,* Joel Feinberg (Ed.), 93–113 (New York: Oxford University Press, 1970).

3. A stronger version of psychological egoism asserts that people cannot do otherwise. According to this stronger version, people are such that they cannot do anything but act for the sake of their own interest. But how would we know this? We know how people do act, but how could we show that they cannot act otherwise? Perhaps we could appeal to certain views about human nature. We could argue that we always seek our own best interests because we are depraved by nature or perhaps by a religious "fall" such as the one described in the biblical book of Genesis.

4. Amitai Etzioni, a presentation at the University of San Francisco, December 1, 1992.

5. From the *Springfield Monitor* (ca. 1928), cited in Louis Pojman, *Ethics, 41* (Belmont, CA: Wadsworth, 1990).

6. However, we might by nature always act in our short-term interest. Morality might require, rather, that we act in our long-term interest. In this case, another problem arises. How could we be commanded by morality to do what we are not able to do? As we shall see in Chapter 5, according to Kant, "an ought implies a can."

7. We will return to this argument in looking at discussions on egoism by Kant. Other discussions of it can be found, for example, in James Sterba, "Justifying Morality: The Right and the Wrong Ways," *Synthese, 72* (1987): 45–69; and James Rachels, "Egoism and Moral Skepticism," in *A New Introduction to Philosophy,* Steven M. Cahn (Ed.) (New York: Harper & Row, 1971).

8. See Adam Smith, *The Wealth of Nations* (New York: Edwin Cannan, 1904).

9. See the communitarian views in Robert Bellah, *Habits of the Heart* (Berkeley: University of California Press, 1985), and Amitai Etzioni, *The Spirit of Community: Rights, Responsibilities, and the Communitarian Agenda* (New York: Crown, 1993).

10. W. D. Falk, "Morality, Self and Others," in *Morality and the Language of Conduct,* Hector-Neri Castaneda and George Nakhnikian (Eds.), 25–67 (Detroit: Wayne State University Press, 1963).

11. Benjamin Franklin, "Poor Richard's Almanac," in *American Philosophy: A Historical Anthology,* Barbara MacKinnon (Ed.), 46–47 (New York: State University of New York Press, 1985).

12. However, Foot has some problems fitting the virtue of justice into this generalization. Furthermore, she thinks of our best interest broadly—that

is, as a kind of human flourishing. More discussion of this view can be found in Chapter 6 on natural law theory.

13. See Thomas Nagel's discussion of these different possibilities of the relation between the good life and the moral life in "Living Right and Living Well," in *The View from Nowhere,* 189–207 (New York: Oxford University Press, 1986). Also see David Gauthier, "Morality and Advantage," *The Philosophical Review* (1967): 460–475.

REVIEW EXERCISES

1. Explain the basic difference between psychological egoism and ethical egoism.
2. Give two different formulations or versions of each.
3. To prove that the motivational version of psychological egoism is true, what must be shown?
4. How is psychological egoism supposed to provide support for an argument for ethical egoism? What is one problem for this argument?
5. Summarize the arguments regarding the consistency or inconsistency of ethical egoism.
6. In what sense does the argument for ethical egoism based on economics support not egoism but utilitarianism—in other words, the view that we ought to do what is in the best interest of all or the greatest number?
7. What is meant by taking the "moral point of view"?
8. How does the example of the "ring of Gyges" illustrate the question "Why be moral?"

Selected Bibliography

Baier, Kurt. *The Moral Point of View.* Ithaca, NY: Cornell University Press, 1958.

Bishop, Lloyd. *In Defense of Altruism: Inadequacies of Ayn Rand's Ethics and Psychological Egoism.* New Orleans: University Press of the South, 2001.

Campbell, Richmond. "A Short Refutation of Ethical Egoism," *Canadian Journal of Philosophy* 2 (1972): 249–254.

Feinberg, Joel. "Psychological Egoism" in *Reason and Responsibility.* Belmont, CA. Wadsworth, 1985.

Gauthier, David (Ed.). *Morality and Rational Self-Interest.* Englewood Cliffs, NJ: Prentice-Hall, 1970.

MacIntyre, Alasdair. "Egoism and Altruism" in Paul Edwards (Ed.), *The Encyclopedia of Philosophy,* vol. 2, 462–466. New York: Macmillan, 1967.

Milo, Ronald D. (Ed.). *Egoism and Altruism.* Belmont, CA: Wadsworth, 1973.

Nagel, Thomas. *The Possibility of Altruism.* Oxford, England: Clarendon, 1970.

Olson, Robert G. *The Morality of Self-Interest.* New York: Harcourt Brace Jovanovich, 1965.

Osterberg, Jan. *Self and Others: A Study of Ethical Egoism.* Dordrecht, Netherlands: Kluwer Academic Publishers, 1988.

Rand, Ayn. *The Virtue of Selfishness.* New York: New American Library, 1964.

Shaver, Robert William. *Rational Egoism.* New York: Cambridge University Press, 1998.

Van Ingen, John. *Why Be Moral? The Egoistic Challenge.* New York: Peter Lang Publishing, 1994.

4

Utilitarianism

In 2004, a filmmaker installed a camera on the Golden Gate Bridge in order to "capture people on film as they jumped to their deaths."[1] The cameras ran for almost all of 2004 and filmed nineteen people attempting to commit suicide. We don't know how many succeeded. In 2006, there were thirty-four attempts. This famous American bridge is known as "the world's number one suicide destination." Among those who jumped in 2007 were a fourteen-year-old girl and a sixteen-year-old boy.[2] The filmmaker claimed that his work was intended to help us understand the gravity of the situation. And the death is a horrible one: A human body falling from the bridge reaches a speed of 75 miles per hour in just four seconds before it hits the water, so bones crack and limbs are torn away. If people survive this ordeal, they still usually drown.[3] At the same time, some people have criticized the filmmaker's project as voyeuristic and say that it bears a horrible resemblance to a snuff film.

From 1937, when the bridge first opened, an estimated 1,300 people have leaped to their death.[4] One of the first to jump that year was a veteran of World War I. He said to a stranger he was passing, "This is as far as I go," and then jumped to his death.[5] Many of those who attempt suicide are depressed or mentally ill. Many people's lives might have been spared if it had not been relatively easy to jump from the bridge. For many years, Bay Area citizens and officials have debated whether to build a suicide barrier on the bridge.

Currently, the railing is only 4 feet high; some people say this is because the bridge's chief engineer was only 5 feet tall and he wanted to be able to see over the railing.[6] One proposed solution consisted of an 8-foot high barrier of metal bars placed along the current railing. There had been concerns about the effect of wind on a higher railing, but recent studies suggest that the higher railing would only need to be 12 percent to 24 percent solid.[7] People arguing against the barrier also have cited the cost, which is now estimated to be between $15 million and $25 million. Others doubt that it would have much effect on the incidence of suicide, claiming that people intent on killing themselves would find some other way to do so. Still others object to the barrier because of its negative aesthetic effect. People can now use a sidewalk on the bridge to cross it and thus easily and clearly take in the beautiful views as they stroll. After many years of debate, it seemed as if there was a real possibility that a barrier would be built. The Golden Gate Bridge District's directors finally agreed to language that would not require that the barrier "be totally effective," only that it "impede the ability of an individual to jump."

Should such a barrier be erected? In an earlier poll conducted by the *San Francisco Examiner*, 46 percent of respondents said there should be a barrier on the bridge, but 54 percent said there should not.[8] Typical of the reasons given by those voting for the barrier is the idea that it would save lives and "serve as a message that society cares, that we don't want you to kill yourself." Those voting against the barrier said that it would not prevent suicides anyway, and we should and cannot do everything possible to prevent people from hurting themselves. Another asked, "Why punish millions who want to enjoy a breathtakingly beautiful view as we walk or drive across the bridge?"[9]

Many people were horrified when the pictures of the abuse and humiliation of prisoners by American soldiers at Abu Ghraib prison in Iraq were made public. The prisoners were photographed naked, in embarrassing sexual positions, crawling on leashes, and being threatened by dogs. Questions were raised about whether higher-ups knew about the treatment, whether the soldiers involved were ordered to behave this way in order to "soften up" the prisoners for interrogation, or whether this was instead mere "entertainment" for the soldiers involved. Some of those soldiers were tried before military courts and sentenced to prison for their behavior.

Did this treatment constitute torture? And whether or not it did, would such tactics or torture ever be justified in order to obtain information that might prevent terrorist attacks? On the one hand, some assert that torture is never permissible because it violates the Geneva Conventions, which prohibit torture and partially define it as "any act by which severe pain or suffering, whether physical or mental, is intentionally inflicted on a person for such purposes as obtaining from him or a third person information or a confession."[8] On the other hand, suppose, for example, that torture could save many lives. Would it then be justified? A Pentagon study of "the ethics of troops on the front line" in Iraq found that 41 percent said that "torture should be allowed to save the life of a soldier or Marine" and about the same number said that it "should be allowed to gather important information from insurgents."[10] Does a good end justify otherwise objectionable means? What kind of moral reasoning would permit this? The theory treated in this chapter is meant to clarify this.

How should such matters as suicide barriers and torture be decided? One way is to compare the benefits and costs of each alternative. Whichever has the greater net benefit is the best alternative. This method of cost–benefit analysis is a contemporary version of the moral theory called "utilitarianism." We begin our study of moral theories with utilitarianism because in some ways it is the easiest to understand and the closest to common sense. Put simply, this moral theory asserts that we ought to produce the most happiness or pleasure that we can and reduce suffering and unhappiness.

HISTORICAL BACKGROUND

Jeremy Bentham and John Stuart Mill

The classical formulation of utilitarian moral theory is found in the writings of Jeremy Bentham (1748–1832) and John Stuart Mill (1806–1873). Jeremy Bentham was an English-born student of law and the leader of a radical movement for social and legal reform based on utilitarian principles. His primary published work was *Introduction to the Principles of Morals and Legislation* (1789). The title itself indicates his aim—namely, to take the same principles that provide the basis for morals as a guide for the formation and revision of law. He believed that there are not two sets of principles, one for personal morality and another for social morality.

James Mill, the father of John Stuart Mill, was an associate of Bentham's and a supporter of his views. John Stuart was the eldest of his nine children. He was educated in the classics and history at home. By the time he was twenty, he had read Bentham and had become a devoted follower of his philosophy. The basic ideas of utilitarian moral theory are summarized in his short work, *Utilitarianism,* in which he sought to dispel misconceptions that morality had nothing to do with usefulness or utility or that it was opposed to pleasure. According to one writer, John Stuart Mill "is generally held to be one of the most profound and effective spokesmen for the liberal view of man and society."[11] He was also a strong supporter of personal liberty, and in his pamphlet *On Liberty* he argued that the only reason for society to interfere in a person's life to force that person to behave in certain ways was to prevent him or her from doing harm to others. People might choose wrongly, but he believed that allowing bad choices was better than government coercion. Liberty to speak one's own opinion, he believed, would benefit all. However, it is not clear that utility is always served by promoting liberty. Nor is it clear what Mill would say in cases where liberty must be restricted to promote the general good. In his work *On the Subjection of Women,* Mill also emphasized the general good and criticized those social treatments of women that did not allow them to develop their talents and contribute to the good of society. Consistent with these views, he also supported the right of women to vote. Later in life he married his longtime companion and fellow liberal, Harriet Taylor. Mill also served in the British Parliament from 1865 to 1868.

The original utilitarians were democratic, progressive, empiricist, and optimistic. They were democratic in the sense that they believed that social policy ought to work for the good of all persons, not just the upper class. However, they also believed that when interests of various persons conflicted, the best choice was that which promoted the interests of the greater number. The utilitarians were progressive in that they questioned the status quo. They believed that if, for example, the contemporary punishment system was not working well, then it ought to be changed. Social programs should be judged by their usefulness in promoting what was deemed to be good. Observation would determine whether a project or practice promoted this good. Thus, utilitarianism is part of the empiricist tradition in philosophy, for we only know what is good by observation or by appeal to experience. Bentham and Mill were also optimists. They believed that human wisdom and science would improve the lot of humanity. Mill wrote in *Utilitarianism,* "All the grand sources of human suffering are in a great degree, many of them almost entirely, conquerable by human care and effort."[12]

In this chapter, you will learn about the basic principle of utilitarianism and how it is used to make moral judgments in individual cases. You will also learn something about different forms of utilitarianism. You can examine a few criticisms of the theory so as to judge for yourself whether it is

a reasonable theory. Again, you will have the substance of utilitarianism in these sections. More detail about the theory can be found in the sections on act and rule utilitarianism, on Mill's proof of the theory, and on contemporary versions of utilitarianism.

THE PRINCIPLE OF UTILITY

The basic moral principle of utilitarianism is called the *principle of utility* or the *greatest happiness principle.* This principle has several formulations in Bentham and Mill as well as in utilitarianism after them. Here are two simplified formulations, one correlated with each title:

The morally best (or better) alternative is that which produces the greatest (or greater) net utility, where utility is defined in terms of happiness or pleasure.

We ought to do that which produces the greatest amount of happiness or pleasure for the greatest number of people.

A Consequentialist Principle

First, utilitarianism is *teleological* in orientation. In other words, it stresses the end or goal of actions. Second, it is also a *consequentialist* moral theory. Consider the diagram used to classify moral theories given in Chapter 1.

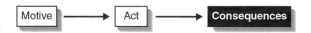

According to utilitarian moral theory, when we evaluate human acts or practices we consider neither the nature of the acts or practices nor the motive for which people do what they do. For example, building a suicide barrier on a bridge in itself is neither good nor bad. Nor is it sufficient that people supporting the building of such a barrier be well intentioned. As Mill put it, "He who saves a fellow creature from drowning does what is morally right, whether his motive be duty or the hope of being paid for his trouble."[13] It is the result of one's action—that a life is saved—that matters morally. According to utilitarianism, we ought to decide which action or practice is best by considering the likely or actual consequences of each alternative. If erecting a suicide barrier on the Golden Gate Bridge is likely to have overall better consequences than not doing so, then that is what should be done. If one version of the barrier will save more lives than another at lesser or equal cost, then that is preferable. If the status quo has a greater balance of good over bad, then that is best. Nevertheless, this is not so simple to understand or calculate. Thus, we will need to consider the theory and its method in more detail.

The Intrinsic Good: Pleasure or Happiness

It is not sufficient to say we ought to do that which has the best results or consequences because this in itself does not tell us which type of consequences are good. Any sort of consequences might be considered good—for example, power or fame or fortune. However, classical utilitarianism is a *pleasure* or *happiness* theory. It was not the first such theory to appear in the history of philosophy. Aristotle's ethics, as we shall see in Chapter 6, is a happiness theory although different from utilitarianism. Closer to utilitarianism is the classical theory that has come to be known as *hedonism* (from *hedon*, the Greek word for pleasure) or *Epicureanism* (named after Epicurus, 341 B.C.–270 B.C.). Epicurus held that the good life was the pleasant life. For him, this meant avoiding distress and desires for things beyond one's basic needs. Bodily pleasure and mental delight and peace were the goods to be sought in life.

Utilitarians also have believed that pleasure or happiness is the good to be produced. As Bentham put it, "Nature has placed mankind under the governance of two sovereign masters, *pain* and *pleasure*. It is for them alone to point out what we ought to do, as well as to determine what we shall do."[14] Things such as fame, fortune, education, and freedom may be good, but only to the extent that they produce pleasure or happiness. In philosophical terms, they are *instrumental* goods because they are useful for attaining the goals of happiness and pleasure. Happiness and pleasure are the only *intrinsic* goods—that is, the only things good in themselves.

In this explanation of utilitarianism, you may have noticed the seeming identification of pleasure and happiness. In classical utilitarianism, there is no difference between pleasure and happiness. Both terms refer to a kind of psychic state of satisfaction. However, there are different types of pleasure of which humans are capable. According to Mill, we experience a range of pleasures or satisfactions from the physical satisfaction of hunger to the personal satisfaction of a job well done. Aesthetic pleasures, such as the enjoyment of watching a beautiful sunset, are yet another type of pleasure. We also can experience intellectual pleasures such as the peculiar satisfaction of making sense out of something. We express this satisfaction in phrases such as "Ah, so that's it!" or "Now I see!" If this wider sense of pleasure is accepted, then it is easier to identify it with happiness.

We should consider the range of types of pleasure in our attempts to decide what the best action is. We also ought to consider other aspects of the pleasurable or happy experience. According to the greatest happiness or utility principle, we must measure, count, and compare the pleasurable experiences likely to be produced by various alternative actions in order to know which is best.

Calculating the Greatest Amount of Happiness

Utilitarianism is not an egoistic theory. As we noted in the previous chapter's presentation on egoism, those versions of egoism that said we ought to take care of ourselves because this works out better for all in the long run are actually versions of utilitarianism, not egoism. Some philosophers have called utilitarianism *universalistic* because it is the happiness or pleasure of all who are affected by an action or practice that is to be considered. We are not just to consider our own good, as in egoism, nor just the good of others, as in altruism. Sacrifice may be good, but not in itself. As Mill puts it, "A sacrifice which does not increase or tend to increase the sum total of happiness, [utilitarianism] considers as wasted."[15] Everyone affected by some action is to be counted equally. We ourselves hold no privileged place, so our own happiness counts no more than that of others. I may be required to do what displeases me but pleases others. Thus, in the following scenario, Act B is a better choice than Act A:

Act A makes me happy and two other people
  happy.
Act B makes me unhappy but five others happy.

In addition to counting each person equally, these five elements are used to calculate the greatest amount of happiness: the net amount of pleasure or happiness, its intensity, its duration, its fruitfulness, and the likelihood of any act to produce it.[16] Note also that Jeremy Bentham, as well as J. S. Mill, held that the pleasures of *any* sentient being should be counted (see also Chapter 16, "Animal Rights").

Pleasure Minus Pain Almost every alternative that we choose produces unhappiness or pain as well as happiness or pleasure for ourselves, if not for others. Pain is intrinsically bad and pleasure is intrinsically good. Something that produces pain may be accepted, but only if it causes more pleasure overall. For instance, if the painfulness of a punishment deters an unwanted behavior, then we ought to punish but no more than is necessary or useful. When an act produces both pleasure or happiness and pain or unhappiness, we can think of each moment of unhappiness as canceling out a moment of happiness, so that what is left to evaluate is the remaining or *net* happiness or unhappiness. We are also to think of pleasure and pain as coming in bits or moments. We can then calculate this net amount by adding and subtracting units of pleasure and displeasure. This is a device for calculating the greatest amount of happiness even if we cannot make mathematically exact calculations. The following simplified equation indicates how the net utility for two acts, A and B, might be determined. Think of the units as either happy persons or days of happiness:

Act A produces twelve units of happiness and six
  of unhappiness ($12 - 6 = 6$ units of happiness).
Act B produces ten units of happiness and one of
  unhappiness ($10 - 1 = 9$ units of happiness).

On this measure, Act B is preferable because it produces a greater net amount of happiness—namely, nine units compared with six for Act A.

Intensity Moments of happiness or pleasure are not all alike. Some are more intense than others. The thrill of some exciting adventure—say, running river rapids—may produce a more intense pleasure than the serenity we feel in view of one of nature's wonders. All else being equal, the more intense the pleasure, the better. All other factors being equal, if I have an apple to give away and am deciding which of two friends to give it to I ought to give it to the friend who will enjoy it most. In calculations involving intensity of pleasure, a scale is sometimes useful. For example, we could use a positive scale of 1 to 10 degrees, from the least pleasurable to the most pleasurable. In the following scenario, then, Act B is better (all other things being equal) than Act A, even though Act A gives pleasure to thirty more people; this result is because of the greater intensity of pleasure produced by Act B:

Act A gives forty people each mild pleasure
  ($40 \times 2 = 80$ degrees of pleasure).
Act B gives ten people each intense pleasure
  ($10 \times 10 = 100$ degrees of pleasure).[17]

Duration Intensity is not all that matters regarding pleasure. The more serene pleasure may last longer. This also must be factored in our calculation. The longer lasting the pleasure the better, all else being equal. Thus, in the following scenario, Act A is better than Act B because it gives more total days of pleasure or happiness. This is so even though it affects fewer people (a fact that raises questions about how the number of people counts in comparison to the total amount of happiness):

Act A gives three people each eight days of
  happiness
  ($3 \times 8 = 24$ days of happiness).
Act B gives six people each two days of happiness
  ($6 \times 2 = 12$ days of happiness).

Fruitfulness A more serene pleasure from contemplating nature may or may not be more fruitful than an exciting pleasure such as that from running rapids. The fruitfulness of experiencing pleasure depends on whether it makes us more capable of experiencing similar or other pleasures. For example, the relaxing event may make one person more capable of experiencing other pleasures of friendship or understanding, whereas the thrilling event may do the same for another. The fruitfulness depends not only on the immediate pleasure but also on the long-term results. Indulging in immediate pleasure may bring pain later on, as we know only too well! So also the pain today may be the only way to prevent more pain tomorrow. The dentist's work on our teeth may be painful today, but it makes us feel better in the long run by providing us with pain-free meals and undistracted, enjoyable meal conversations.

Likelihood If before acting we are attempting to decide between two available alternative actions, we must estimate the likely results of each before we compare their net utility. If we are considering whether to go out for some competition, for example, we should consider the chances of doing well. We might have greater hope of success trying something else. It may turn out that we ought to choose an act with lesser rather than greater beneficial results if the chances of it happening are better. It is not only the chances that would count but also the size of the prize. In the following equation, A is preferable to B. In this case, "A bird in the hand is worth two in the bush," as the old saying goes:

Act A has a 90 percent chance of giving eight
   people each five days of pleasure
(40 days $\times$ .90 = 36 days of pleasure).
Act B has a 40 percent chance of giving ten
   people each seven days of pleasure
(70 days $\times$ .40 = 28 days of pleasure).

QUANTITY AND QUALITY OF PLEASURE

Bentham and Mill are in agreement that the more pleasure or happiness, the better. However, there is one significant difference between them. According to Bentham, we ought to consider only the *quantity* of pleasure or happiness brought about by various acts: how much pleasure, to how many people, how intense it is, how long-lasting, how fruitful, and how likely the desired outcome will occur. Consider Bentham's own comment on this point: The "quantity of pleasure being equal, pushpin [a game] is as good as poetry."[18] The aesthetic or intellectual pleasure that one might derive from reading and understanding a poem is no better in itself than the simple pleasures gained from playing a mindless game (which we suppose pushpin to be).

Although Mill agreed with Bentham that the greater amount of pleasure and happiness the better, he believed that the *quality* of the pleasure should also count. In his autobiography, Mill describes his experience of a mental crisis in which he realized that he had not found sufficient place in his life for aesthetic experiences; he realized that this side of the human personality also needed developing and that these pleasures were significantly different from others. This experience and his thoughts about it may have led him to focus on the quality of pleasures. Some are intrinsically better than others, he believed. Intellectual pleasures, for example, are more valuable in themselves than purely sensual pleasures. Although he does not tell us how much more valuable they are (twice as valuable?), he clearly believed this ought to be factored into our calculation of the "greatest amount of happiness." Although I may not always be required to choose a book over food (for example, I may now need the food more than the book), the intellectual pleasures that might be derived from reading the book are of a higher quality than the pleasures gained from eating. Bentham, in contrast, would have asked how such pleasures can be more valuable except as they give us a greater amount of pleasure.

Mill attempts to prove or show that intellectual pleasures are better than sensual ones. We are to ask people who have experienced a range of pleasures whether they would prefer to live a life of a human, in spite of all its disappointments and pains, or the life of an animal, which is full of pleasures but only sensual pleasures. He believes that people generally would choose the former. They would prefer, as he puts it, "to be a human being dissatisfied than a pig satisfied; better to be Socrates dissatisfied than a fool satisfied."[19] Socrates, as you may know, was often frustrated in his attempt to know certain things. He did not know what was true beauty or justice. Because human beings have greater possibilities for knowledge and achievement, they also have greater potential for failure, pain, and frustration. The point of the argument is that the only reason we would prefer a life of fewer net pleasures (the dissatisfactions subtracted from the total satisfactions of human life) to a life of a greater total amount of pleasures (the life of the pig) is that we value something other than the *amount* of pleasures; we value the *kind* of pleasures as well.[20] When considering this argument, you might ask yourself two questions. First, would people generally prefer to be Socrates than the pig? Second, if Mill is correct on his factual assessment, then what does this fact prove? If people do want a certain type of life with certain pleasures, does this fact make it a better life and the pleasures better pleasures? For that matter, this argument may introduce another independent criterion for what is good and perhaps create a quite different type of moral theory than utilitarianism.

EVALUATING UTILITARIANISM

The following are just some of the many considerations raised by those who wish to determine whether utilitarianism is a valid moral theory.

Application of the Principle

One reaction to calculating the greatest amount of happiness that students often have is that this theory is too complex. When we consider all of the variables concerning pleasure and happiness that are to be counted when trying to estimate the "greatest amount of pleasure or happiness," the task of doing so looks extremely difficult. We must consider how many people will be affected by alternative actions, whether they will be pleased or pained by them, how pleased or pained they will be and for how long, and the likelihood that what we estimate will happen will, in fact, come

to be. In addition, if we want to follow Mill, rather than Bentham, we must consider whether the pleasures will be the more lowly sensual pleasures, the higher types of more intellectual pleasures, or something in between. However, in reality we may at any one time only have to consider a couple of these variables because only they may be relevant.

The point of this criticism is that no one can consider all of the variables that utilitarianism requires us to consider: the probable consequences of our action to all affected in terms of duration, intensity, fruitfulness, likelihood, and type or quality of pleasure.[21] However, a utilitarian could respond that, although given this complexity no one is a perfect judge, we do make better judgments the better we are able to consider these variables. No moral theory is simple in its application. A more difficult problem in how to apply the principle of utility comes from Mill's own statements of it. It may well be that in some cases, at least, one cannot both maximize happiness and make the greatest number of people happy. Thus, one choice may produce 200 units of happiness—but for just one person. The other alternative might produce 150 units of happiness, 50 for each of three people. If the maximization overall is taken as primary, then we should go with the first choice; if the number of people is to take precedence, then we should go with the second choice. The best reading of Mill, however, seems to give preference to the maximization overall. In that case, how the happiness was distributed (to one or three) would not in itself count. This is one problem some people have with this theory.

Utilitarianism and Personal Integrity

A more substantive criticism of utilitarianism concerns its universalist and maximizing nature: that we should always do that which maximizes overall happiness. For one thing, this theory seems to allow us to consider neither our own happiness in some privileged place nor the happiness of those closer to us when to do so does not maximize happiness. I can give no more weight to my own projects or my own children in determining what to do than other peoples' similar projects or others' children. For some philosophers, that I must treat all persons equally is contrary to common sense. Utilitarians might respond that we should probably give more attention to our own projects and our own children, but only because this is likely to have better results overall. We know better how to promote our own projects and have more motivation to do so. Thus, giving preference to ourselves will probably be more effective. The objection remains that not to give some preference to ourselves is an affront to our personal integrity.[22] The idea is that utilitarianism seems to imply that I am not important from my own point of view. However, a utilitarian might respond that it is important that people regard themselves as unique and give due consideration for their own interests because this will probably have better consequences for both the society and themselves.

Ends and Means

A second criticism concerns utilitarianism's consequentialist nature. You may have heard the phrase "The end justifies the means." People often refer to it with a certain amount of disdain. Utilitarianism, as a consequentialist moral theory, holds that it is the consequences or ends of our actions that determine whether particular means to them are justified. This seems to lead to conclusions that are contrary to commonsense morality. For example, wouldn't it justify punishing an innocent person, a "scapegoat," in order to prevent a great evil or promote a great good? Or could we not justify on utilitarian grounds the killing of some for the sake of the good of a greater number? Or could I not make an exception for myself from obeying a law, alleging that it is for some greater long-term good? Utilitarians might respond by noting that such actions or practices will probably do more harm than good, especially if we take a long-range view. In particular, they might point out that practices that allow the punishment of those known to be innocent are not likely to deter as well as those that punish only the guilty or proven guilty.

ACT AND RULE UTILITARIANISM

One criticism that is brought against utilitarianism described thus far is that it justifies any action just so long as it has better consequences than other available actions. Therefore, cheating, stealing, lying, and breaking promises may all seem to be justified, depending on whether they maximize happiness in some particular case. Whether as a response to this type of criticism or for other reasons, a slightly different version of utilitarianism has been developed in the decades since Mill. Some people find evidence for it in Mill's own writings.[23] This second version is usually called *rule utilitarianism,* and it is contrasted with *act utilitarianism,* or what we have so far described.

Both are forms of utilitarianism. They are alike in requiring us to produce the greatest amount of happiness or pleasure (in all of the senses described) for the greatest number of people. They differ in what they believe we ought to consider in estimating the consequences. Act utilitarianism states that we ought to consider the consequences of *each act separately.* Rule utilitarianism states that we ought to consider the consequences of the act performed as a *general practice.*[24]

Take the following example. Sue is considering whether to keep or break her promise to go out with Ken. She believes that if she breaks this promise in order to do something else with other friends, Ken will be unhappy, but she and the other friends will be happier. According to act utilitarianism, if the consequences of her breaking the promise are better than keeping it, then that is what she ought to do. She may use handy "rules of thumb" to help her determine whether keeping the promise or breaking it is more likely to result in the better consequences. Mill called these "direction points along the way" that one can use.[25] "Honesty is the best policy" is one such guide. It is still the consequences of the act under consideration that determine what Sue ought to do.

Act utilitarianism: Consider the consequences of some particular act such as keeping or breaking one's promise.

A rule utilitarian, on the other hand, would tell Sue to consider what the results would be if everyone broke promises or broke them in similar situations. The question "What if everyone did that?" is familiar to us.[26] She should ask what the results would be if this were a general practice or a general rule that people followed. It is likely that trust in promises would be weakened. This would be bad, she might think, because the consequences would be that if we could not trust one another to keep our promises, then we would generally be less capable of making plans and relating to one another, two sources of human happiness. So, even if there would be no breakdown in that trust from just this one case of breaking a promise, Sue should still probably keep her promise according to rule utilitarian thinking.

Rule utilitarianism: Consider the consequences of some practice or rule of behavior—for example, the practice of promise keeping or promise breaking.

Another way to consider the method of reasoning used by the rule utilitarian is the following: I should ask what would be the best practice. For example, regarding promises, what rule would have the better results when people followed that rule? Would it be the rule or practice "Never break a promise made"? At the other extreme end of the spectrum would be a practice of keeping promises only if the results of doing so would be better than breaking them. (This actually amounts to act utilitarian reasoning.) However, there might be a better rule yet such as "Always keep your promise unless to do so would have very serious harmful consequences." If this rule were followed, then people would generally have the benefits of being able to say, "I promise," and have people generally believe and trust them. The fact that the promise would not be kept in some limited circumstances would probably not do great harm to the practice of making promises.

Some philosophers go further and ask us to think about sets of rules. It is not only the practice of truthfulness but also of promise keeping and bravery and care for children that we must evaluate.

Moreover, we should think of these rules as forming a system in which there are rules for priority and stringency. These rules would tell us which practices were more important and how important they were compared to the others. We should then do what the best system of moral rules would dictate, where *best* is still defined in terms of the maximization of happiness.[27]

Which form of utilitarianism is better is a matter of dispute. Act utilitarians can claim that we ought to consider only what will or is likely to happen if we act in certain ways, not what *would* happen if we acted in certain ways but will not happen because we are not going to so act. Rule utilitarians can claim that acts are similar to one another and so can be thought of as practices. My lying in one case to get myself out of a difficulty is similar to others' lying in other cases to get themselves out of difficulties. Because we should make the same judgments about similar cases (for consistency's sake), we should judge this act by comparing it with the results of the actions of everyone in similar circumstances. We can thus evaluate the general practice of "lying to get oneself out of a difficulty." You be the judge of which reasoning is more persuasive.

"PROOF" OF THE THEORY

One of the best ways to evaluate a moral theory is to examine carefully the reasons that are given to support it. Being an empiricist theory, utilitarianism must draw its evidence from experience. This is what Mill does in his attempt to prove that the principle of utility is the correct moral principle. (Note, however, that Mill himself believes that the notion of "proof" is different for moral theory than perhaps for science.) His argument is as follows: Just as the only way in which we know that something is visible is its being seen, and the only way we can show that something is audible is if it can be heard, so also the only proof that we have that something is desirable is its being desired. Because we desire happiness, we thus know it is desirable or good. In addition, Mill holds that happiness is the only thing we desire for its own sake. All else we desire because we believe it will lead to happiness. Thus, happiness or pleasure is the only thing good in itself or the only intrinsic good. All other goods are instrumental goods; in other words, they are good in so far as they lead to happiness. For example, reading is not good in itself but only in so far as it brings us pleasure or understanding (which is either pleasurable in itself or leads to pleasure).

There are two main contentions here in this argument. One is that people's desiring something is a good basis for its being, or being thought to be, good. The other is that happiness in particular is the only thing desired for itself and thus it is the only intrinsic good. Critics have pointed out that Mill's analogy between what is visible, audible, and desirable does not hold up under analysis. In all three words, the suffix means "able to be," but in the case of *desirable,* Mill needs to prove not only that we can desire happiness (it is able to be desired) but also that it is *worth* being desired. Furthermore, just because we do desire something does not necessarily mean that we ought to desire it or that it is good. The moral philosopher David Hume put it succinctly: You cannot derive an "ought" from an "is."[28] However, Mill himself recognizes the difficulty of proving matters in ethics, and that the proofs here will be indirect rather than direct. On the second point, Mill adds a further comment to bolster his case about happiness, in particular. He asserts that this desire for happiness is universal and that we are so constructed that we can desire nothing except what appears to us to be or to bring happiness. You may want to consider whether these latter assertions are consistent with his empiricism. Does he know these things from experience? In addition, Mill may be simply pointing to what we already know rather than giving a proof of the principle. You can find out what people believe is good by noticing what they do desire. In this case, they desire to be happy or they desire what they think will bring them happiness.[29]

CONTEMPORARY VERSIONS

In this chapter, we have examined classical utilitarian moral theory. We have described its main characteristics and looked at some objections to it. You will have further opportunities to think about this theory when you see how it is applied to particular ethical issues in Part Two of this text.

There are also other forms of utilitarian or consequentialist moral theories that do not take happiness as the only intrinsic good. Instead they hold that knowledge, peace, freedom, education, beauty, or power were the goods to be maximized. Depending on what was on the list of intrinsic goods, different forms of utilitarianism or consequentialism could be developed. Details similar to those in the classical formulation would then need to be worked out. Since Mill's writings, other forms of utilitarianism also have been developed. Two of these forms are *preference utilitarianism* and *cost-benefit analysis.*

Preference Utilitarianism

Some philosophers of a more behaviorist orientation who are skeptical of being able to measure and compare human feelings of happiness or pleasure have turned instead to considerations of preference satisfaction. They have developed what has been called *preference utilitarianism.* According to this version, the action that is best is the one that satisfies the most preferences, either in themselves or according to their strength or their order of importance. Theories that attempt to do this can become quite complex. However, democracy is just such a system in which we count people's preferences. In voting, nevertheless, we do not take into consideration the strength of people's preferences or support or what they would choose in the second or third place, for example.

One method of identifying people's preferences is looking at what they say they want or prefer. People express their preferences in a variety of ways, such as through polls. In the Golden Gate Bridge suicide barrier poll mentioned earlier in this chapter, results showed that 54 percent of those polled opposed the barrier. The best choice, then, would be to satisfy the majority of preferences and not build the barrier. Critics, of course, may want to know how informed the choices were and whether the poll was scientific or valid. Another method of knowing what people want or value is *implied* from their behavior. If we want to know whether people appreciate the national parks, we ought to consider the numbers of people who visit them. If we want to know whether people prefer fancy sports cars or SUVs, we ask, "Which cars do they buy?"

Although making such calculations has practical problems, this form of utilitarianism also has more substantive difficulties. One of these difficulties is that any preference seems to count equally with any other, no matter if it is hurting or helping others. Some philosophers have attempted to get around this objection by considering only self-regarding preferences. Thus, our preferences for others, whether to benefit them or harm them, will not be considered. Do you think that this revision of preference utilitarianism satisfies this objection to it?

Cost–Benefit Analysis

A version of utilitarianism used widely today is *cost–benefit analysis.* One policy is better than another if it is the least costly compared with the benefits expected. Often the measure is money. Cost–benefit analysis is a measure of efficiency. One problem with this method of evaluation is that it is difficult, if not impossible, to put a dollar value on things such as freedom or a life—so-called intangibles. Nevertheless, there are many times in which we explicitly or implicitly do make such dollar assignments. Insurance and court settlements for loss of life or limb, and decisions about how much to pay to reduce risk to human life, as in safety regulations, are but two of these. According to one method of valuing human life, we ought to consider what people are willing to pay to reduce their risk of death by a certain amount. Or we can calculate what increase in compensation people would accept to do a job in which the risk to their lives is correspondingly increased. From these calculations, economists can figure a dollar amount that is equivalent to the value that people seem to place on their own lives.[30] (See Chapter 15 on environmental ethics for further discussion of this method.)

Now consider how this version might be used to determine whether to build a suicide-prevention barrier for the Golden Gate Bridge. We would have to estimate the number of lives likely to be saved by this barrier, and then give some monetary value to each life. Then we would have to estimate the likely negative consequences of building the barrier, such as the estimate of financial cost. In addition, we would have to determine the negative aesthetic effect, not only by counting the number of lost aesthetic experiences but also by calculating their value. Although we tend to think that putting a dollar value either on lives or on aesthetic experiences is not something we can or ought to do, that is what is done in many instances in policy. For example, although we could make our buildings and highways and bridges safer by spending more—consider the recent collapse of the bridge in Minneapolis—we seem implicitly to believe that we need not spend more than a certain amount.

Another example of the use of cost–benefit analysis was a debate over the U.S. federal budget deficit. One issue that arose in this debate was how to value the cost of social programs that benefit the poor or the elderly. Ought the value of such people be judged by their contributions to society or the number of years of life they are expected to live, or ought every life be valued equally? A further problem would be added if we considered the effect of this spending on future generations. For example, if the spending increased the federal deficit, then would this have a negative effect on future people? Are these people, who do not yet exist, also to be valued for the purposes of cost–benefit calculations?[31]

Utilitarianism is a highly influential moral theory that also has had significant influence on a wide variety of policy assessment methods. It can be quite useful for evaluating alternative health care systems, for example. Whichever system brings the most benefit to the most people with the least cost is the system that we probably ought to support. Although Mill was quite optimistic about the ability and willingness of people to increase human happiness and reduce suffering, there is no doubt that the ideal is a good one. Nevertheless, utilitarianism has difficulties, some of which we have discussed here. You will know better how to evaluate this theory when you can compare it with those treated in the following chapters.

NOTES

1. *San Francisco Chronicle,* Jan. 19, 2005, p. A1.
2. Yahoo News, Jan 18, 2007.
3. Kevin Caruso, "Golden Gate Bridge Suicides: Horrible Deaths that Are Preventable," February 22, 2007 (online at www.suicide.org).
4. Peter Fimrite, "Rule Change May Allow Suicide Barrier on Span," *San Francisco Chronicle,* April 22, 2005, pp. B1, B4.
5. Caruso, op. cit.
6. Fimrite, op. cit.
7. *San Francisco Chronicle,* Jan. 27, 2007, p. B1.
8. *San Francisco Examiner,* Feb. 2, 1993, p. A4.
9. Ibid.
10. Office of the United Nations High Commissioner for Human Rights. *Convention Against Torture and Other Cruel, Inhuman or Degrading Treatment or Punishment* (online at www.ohchr.org/english/law/cat.htm); *San Francisco Chronicle,* May 5, 2007, p. A5.
11. Sneewind in *The Encyclopedia of Philosophy,* Paul Edwards (Ed.), vol. 5 (New York: Macmillan, 1967): 314.
12. *Utilitarianism,* Oskar Priest (Ed.) (Indianapolis, IN: Bobbs-Merrill, 1957): 20.
13. Ibid., 24.
14. Jeremy Bentham, *An Introduction to the Principles of Morals and Legislation* (New York: Oxford University Press, 1789).
15. Priest, op. cit., 22.
16. These elements for calculation of the greatest amount of happiness are from Bentham's *Principles of Morals and Legislation,* op. cit.
17. You may have noticed some ambiguity in the formulation of the greatest happiness principle version just described and used so far in our explanation. In this example, Act A makes more people happy than Act B, but the overall amount of happiness when we consider degrees is greater in Act B. Thus, it is the greater amount of happiness that we have counted as more important than the greater number of people. One must choose whether we shall count the greatest amount of happiness or the greatest number of people; we cannot always have both.
18. Bentham, *Principles of Morals and Legislation,* op. cit.
19. Priest, op. cit., 14.
20. Note that this is an empiricist argument: It is based on an appeal to purported facts. People's actual preferences for intellectual pleasures (if true) is the only source we have for believing them to be more valuable.
21. It also requires us to have a common unit of measurement of pleasure. Elementary units called *hedons* have been suggested. We must think of pleasures of all kinds, then, as variations on one basic type. Obviously, this is problematic.
22. J. J. C. Smart and Bernard Williams, *Utilitarianism: For and Against* (New York: Cambridge University Press, 1973). Also see Samuel Scheffler, *The Rejection of Consequentialism* (New York: Oxford University Press, 1984). In *The Limits of Morality* (New York: Oxford University Press, 1989), Shelley Kagan distinguishes the universalist element of utilitarianism—its demand that I treat all equally—from the maximizing element—that I must bring about the most good possible. The first element makes utilitarianism too demanding, whereas the second allows us to do anything as long as it maximizes happiness overall.
23. One comment from *Utilitarianism* has a decidedly rule utilitarian ring: "In the case of abstinences indeed—of things which people forbear to do from moral considerations, though the consequences in the particular case might be beneficial—it would be unworthy of an intelligent agent not to be consciously aware that the action is of a class which, if practiced generally, would be generally injurious, and that this is the ground of the obligation to abstain from it" (p. 25). Other such examples can be found in the final chapter of Mill's work.
24. See, for example, the explanation of this difference in J. J. C. Smart, "Extreme and Restricted Utilitarianism," *Philosophical Quarterly,* IV (1956).
25. Ibid., 31.
26. Just how to formulate the "that," the practice or rule whose consequences we are to consider, is a significant problem for rule utilitarians—and one we will not develop here. Suffice it to note that it must have some degree of generality and not be something that applies just to us: "What if everyone named John Doe did that?" It would be more like, "What if everyone broke their promise to get themselves out of a difficulty?"
27. Richard Brandt, "Some Merits of One Form of Rule Utilitarianism," in *Morality and the Language of Conduct,* H. N. Castaneda and George Nakhnikian (Eds.) (Detroit: Wayne State University Press, 1970): 282–307.

28. David Hume, *Treatise on Human Nature* (London, 1739–1740).
29. This explanation is given by Mary Warnock in her introduction to the Fontana edition of Mill's *Utilitarianism*, 25–26.
30. See Barbara MacKinnon, "Pricing Human Life," *Science, Technology & Human Values, 11,* no. 2 (Spring 1986): 29–39.
31. This example was provided by one reviewer.

REVIEW EXERCISES

1. Give and explain the basic idea of the principle of utility or the greatest happiness principle.
2. What does it mean to speak of utilitarianism as a consequentialist moral theory? As a teleological moral theory?
3. What is the difference between intrinsic and instrumental good? Give examples of each.
4. Which of the following statements exemplify consequentialist reasonings? Can all of them be given consequentialist interpretations if expanded? Explain your answers.
   a. Honesty is the best policy.
   b. Sue has the right to know the truth.
   c. What good is going to come from giving money to a homeless person on the street?
   d. There is a symbolic value present in personally giving something to another person in need.
   e. It is only fair that you give him a chance to compete for the position.
   f. If I do not study for my ethics exam, it will hurt my GPA.
   g. If you are not honest with others, you cannot expect them to be honest with you.
5. Is utilitarianism a hedonist moral theory? Why or why not?
6. Using utilitarian calculation, which choice in each of the following pairs is better, X or Y?
   a. X makes four people happy and me unhappy. Y makes me and one other person happy and three people unhappy.
   b. X makes twenty people happy and five unhappy. Y makes ten people happy and no one unhappy.
   c. X will give five people each two hours of pleasure. Y will give three people each four hours of pleasure.
   d. X will make five people very happy and three people mildly unhappy. Y will make six people moderately happy and two people very unhappy.
7. What is Mill's argument for the difference in value between intellectual and sensual pleasures?
8. Which of the following is an example of act utilitarian reasoning and which rule utilitarian reasoning? Explain your answers.
   a. If I do not go to the meeting, then others will not go either. If that happens, then there would not be a quorum for the important vote, which would be bad. Thus, I ought to go to the meeting.
   b. If doctors generally lied to their patients about their diagnoses, then patients would lose trust in their doctors. Because that would be bad, I should tell this patient the truth.
   c. We ought to keep our promises because it is a valuable practice.
   d. If I cheat here, I will be more likely to cheat elsewhere. No one would trust me then. So I should not cheat on this test.

Selected Bibliography

Albee, Ernest. *A History of English Utilitarianism.* New York: Routledge, 2004.

Bailey, James W. *Utilitarianism, Institutions, and Justice.* New York: Oxford University Press, 1997.

Bentham, Jeremy. *Introduction to the Principles of Morals and Legislation* (1789), W. Harrison (Ed.). Oxford, UK: Hafner, 1948.

Brandt, Richard B. "In Search of a Credible Form of Rule-Utilitarianism," in H. N. Castaneda and George Nakhnikian (Eds.), *Morality and the Language of Conduct.* Detroit: Wayne State University Press, 1953.

Braybrooke, David. *Utilitarianism: Restorations; Repairs; Renovations.* Toronto: University of Toronto Press, 2004.

Cooper, Wesley E., Kai Nielsen, and Steven C. Patten (Eds.). "New Essays on John Stuart Mill and Utilitarianism," *Canadian Journal of Philosophy,* supplementary vol. 5 (1979).

Feinberg, Joel. "The Forms and Limits of Utilitarianism," *Philosophical Review* 76 (1967): 368–381.

Feldman, Fred. *Utilitarianism, Hedonism, and Desert.* New York: Cambridge, 1997.

Frey, R. G. (Ed.). *Utility and Rights.* Minneapolis: University of Minnesota Press, 1984.

Gorovitz, Samuel (Ed.). *Mill: Utilitarianism, with Critical Essays.* New York: Bobbs-Merrill, 1971.

Hare, Richard M. *Freedom and Reason.* New York: Oxford University Press, 1965.

Lyons, David. *Forms and Limits of Utilitarianism.* New York: Oxford University Press, 1965.

———. *Mill's Utilitarianism: Critical Essays.* New York: Rowman & Littlefield, 1997.

Mill, John Stuart. *On Liberty.* London: J. W. Parker, 1859.

———. *Utilitarianism.* London: Longmans, Green, 1863.

———. *Utilitarianism and On Liberty: Including 'Essay on Bentham' and Selections from the Writings of Jeremy Bentham and John Austin.* Malden, MA: Blackwell Publishers, 2002.

Rosen, F. *Classical Utilitarianism from Hume to Mill.* New York: Routledge, 2003.

Ryan, Alan. *Utilitarianism and Other Essays.* New York: Penguin, 1987.

Scheffler, Samuel (Ed.). *Consequentialism and Its Critics.* New York: Oxford University Press, 1988.

Scheffler, Samuel. *The Rejection of Consequentialism.* New York: Oxford University Press, 1982.

Sen, Amartya, and Bernard Williams (Eds.). *Utilitarianism and Beyond.* New York: Cambridge University Press, 1982.

Sheng, C. L. *Defense of Utilitarianism.* Lanham, MD: University Press of America, 2004.

Smart, J.J.C., and Bernard Williams. *Utilitarianism: For and Against.* New York: Cambridge University Press, 1973.

Smith, James M., and Ernest Sosa (Eds.). *Mill's Utilitarianism: Text and Criticism.* Belmont, CA: Wadsworth, 1969.

5

Kant's Moral Theory

Between 1932 and 1972, experiments were conducted in Tuskegee, Alabama, in which 390 poor and illiterate African American men who had syphilis were followed in order to determine the progress of the disease, whether it was always fatal, and how it was spread. The men were even denied penicillin treatment when it became available in the early 1940s. The study was ended in 1972 when it became public and people objected. The reasons were by now obvious: These men had not been treated with respect but had been used for the purpose of obtaining information. In the first place, they were not informed of the true purpose of the study.[1] They were used as guinea pigs in the same way those animals are used in experimentation. However, experimentation using human subjects through the years has led to important medical discoveries that benefited others. Moreover, it is necessary to test new techniques and drugs on actual human subjects before they become widely available. This is often done in controlled clinical trials, in which a control group is compared to the group receiving the treatment. Are these experiments morally unobjectionable? Ethicists distinguish therapeutic and nontherapeutic experimentation. In the case of therapeutic experimentation, the persons involved have some medical condition that the new therapy might help. They are informed and give their consent. In the case of nontherapeutic experimentation, the subjects are volunteers without the condition. The quality of the consent and the degree of risk compared to the potential benefit are also relevant.

According to utilitarian thinking, the Tuskegee experiment may well have been quite justifiable. If the psychological harm done to the participants was minimal and the study had no other negative effects, and if the knowledge gained about obedience to authority was valuable, then the study would be justified.[2] It would have done more good than harm, and that is the basis for judging it to be morally praiseworthy. However, since the post–World War II trials of Nazi war criminals held in Nuremberg, Germany, other standards for treatment of human research subjects have become widely accepted. One of the most basic principles of the Nuremberg Code is this: "The voluntary consent of the human subject is absolutely essential."[3] Consent must be informed and uncoerced. Implied in this principle is the belief that persons are autonomous, and this autonomy ought to be respected and protected even if this means that we cannot do certain types of research and cannot thereby find out valuable information. This view of the significance of personal autonomy, and that people ought not to be used as they possibly were in this experiment, is also a central tenet of the moral philosophy of Immanuel Kant, which we will now examine.

HISTORICAL BACKGROUND: IMMANUEL KANT

Immanuel Kant (1724–1804) was a German philosophy professor who taught at the University of Königsberg in what is now the city of Kaliningrad in the westernmost section of Russia. He was such a popular lecturer that university students who wanted a seat had to arrive at his classroom at six in the morning, one hour before Kant was due to begin his lecture![4] After many years of financial and professional insecurity, he finally was appointed to a chair in philosophy. The writings that followed made him renowned even in his own time. Kant is now regarded as a central figure in the history of modern philosophy. Modern philosophy itself is sometimes divided into pre-Kantian and post-Kantian periods. In fact, some people regard him as the greatest modern philosopher. Although he is renowned for his philosophy, he wrote on a variety of matters including science, geography, beauty, and war and peace. He was a firm believer in the ideas of the Enlightenment, especially reason and freedom, and he also was a supporter of the American Revolution.

Two of the main questions that Kant believed philosophy should address were: "What can I know? What ought I do?"[5] In answering the first question, he thought he was creating a new Copernican revolution. Just as the astronomer Copernicus had argued in 1543 that we should no longer consider the Earth as the center of the solar system with heavenly bodies revolving around it, Kant asserted that we should no longer think of the human knower as revolving around objects known. Knowledge, he believed, was not the passive perception of things just as they are. Rather, he argued, the very nature of human perception and understanding determines the basic character of the world as we experience it. Forms within the mind determine the spatial and temporal nature of our world and give experience its basic structure.

In his moral philosophy, Kant addressed the other question, "What ought I do?" His answers can be found for the most part in two works. One is the *Fundamental Principles* (or *Foundations*) *of the Metaphysics of Morals* (1785), which one commentator described as "one of the most important ethical treatises ever written."[6] The other is the *Critique of Practical Reason* (1788). You will be able to understand the basic elements of Kant's moral philosophy from the following sections on the basis of morality and the categorical imperative.

You should benefit in your own reflections on this theory from the section on evaluating Kant's moral theory. The final sections on perfect and imperfect duties and contemporary versions of Kantian moral theory add further detail to this basic treatment.

WHAT GIVES AN ACT MORAL WORTH?

One way to begin your examination of Kant's moral theory is to think about how he would answer the question, What gives an act *moral* worth? It is not the consequences of the act, according to Kant. Suppose, for example, that I try to do what is right by complimenting someone on her achievements. Through no fault of my own, my action ends up hurting that person because she misunderstands my efforts. According to Kant, because I intended and tried to do what I thought was right, I ought not to be blamed for things having turned out badly. The idea is that we generally ought not to be blamed or praised for what is not in our control. The consequences of our acts are not always in our control and things do not always turn out as we want. However, Kant believed that our motives are in our control. We are responsible for our motive to do good or bad, and thus it is for this that we are held morally accountable.

Kant also objected to basing morality on the consequences of our actions for another reason. To make morality a matter of producing certain states of affairs, such as happy experiences, puts matters backward, he might say. On such a view we could be thought of as having *use value*. We would be valued to the extent that we were instrumental in bringing about what itself was of greater value—namely, happy states or experiences. However, in Kant's view, we should not be used in this way for we are rational beings or *persons*. Persons have intrinsic value, according to Kant, not simply instrumental value. The belief that *people ought not to be used,* but ought to be regarded as having the highest intrinsic value, is central to Kant's ethics, as is the importance of *a motive to do what is right.* As we shall see in the next two sections, Kant uses this second idea to answer the question, What gives an act moral worth?

What Is the Right Motive?

Kant believed that an act has specifically moral worth only if it is done with a right intention or motive.[7] He referred to this as having a "good will." In his famous first lines of the first section of *Foundations,* Kant writes that only such a will is good unconditionally. Everything else needs a good will to make it good. Without a right intention, such things as intelligence, wit, and control of emotions can be bad and used for evil purposes.[8] Having a right intention is to do what is right (or what one believes to be right) just because it is right. In Kant's words, it is to act "out of duty," out of a concern and respect for the moral law. Kant was not a relativist. He believed that there was a right and a wrong thing to do, whether or not we knew or agreed about it. This was the moral law.

To explain his views on the importance of a right motive or intention, Kant provides the example of a shopkeeper who does the right thing, who charges the customers a fair price and charges the same to all. But what is her motive? Kant discusses three possible motives. (1) The shopkeeper's motive or reason for acting might be because it is a good business practice to charge the same to all. It is in her own best interest that she do this. Although not necessarily wrong, this motive is not praiseworthy. (2) The shopkeeper might charge a fair and equal price because she is sympathetic toward her customers and is naturally inclined to do them good. Kant said that this motive is also not the highest. We do not have high moral esteem or praise for people who simply do what they feel like doing, even if we believe they are doing the right thing. (3) However, if the shopkeeper did the right thing just because she believed it was right, then this act would have the highest motive. We do have a special respect, or even a moral reverence, for people who act out of a will to do the right thing, especially when this is at great cost to themselves. Only when an act is motivated by this concern for morality, or for the moral law as Kant would say, does it have moral worth.

Now we do not always *know* when our acts are motivated by self-interest, inclination, or pure respect for morality. Also, we often act from mixed motives. We are more certain that the motive is pure, however, when we do what is right even

when it is not in our best interest (when it costs us dearly) and when we do not feel like doing the right thing. In these cases, we can know that we are motivated by concern to do the right thing because the other two motives are missing. Moreover, this ability to act for moral reasons and resist the pushes and pulls of nature or natural inclination is one indication of and reason why Kant believes that it is persons that have a unique value and dignity. The person who says to himself, "I feel like being lazy (or mean or selfish), but I am going to try not to because it would not be right," is operating out of the motive of respect for morality itself. This ability to act for moral reasons or motives, Kant believes, is one part of what makes people possess particularly high and unique value.

What Is the Right Thing to Do?

For our action to have moral worth, according to Kant, we must not only act out of a right motivation but also do the right thing. Consider again the diagram that we used in the first chapter.

As noted earlier, Kant does not believe that morality is a function of producing good consequences. We may do what has good results, but if we do so for the wrong motive, then that act has no moral worth. However, it is not only the motive that counts for Kant. We must also do what is right. The act itself must be morally right. Both the act and the motive are morally relevant. In Kant's terms, we must not only act "out of duty" (have the right motive) but also "according to duty" or "as duty requires" (do what is right). How then are we to know what is the right thing to do? Once we know this, we can try to do it just because it is right.

To understand Kant's reasoning on this matter, we need to examine the difference between what he calls a *hypothetical imperative* and a *categorical imperative.* An imperative is simply a form of statement that tells us to do something, for example, "Stand up straight" and "Close the door" and also "You ought to close the door." Some, but only some, imperatives are moral imperatives. Other imperatives are hypothetical. For example, the statement "If I want to get there on time, I ought to leave early" does not embody a moral "ought" or imperative. What I ought to do in that case is a function of what I happen to want—to get there on time—and of the means necessary to achieve this—leave early. Moreover, I can avoid the obligation to leave early by changing my goals. I can decide that I do not need or want to get there on time. Then I need not leave early. These ends may be good or bad. Thus, the statement "If I want to harm someone, then I ought to use effective means" also expresses a hypothetical "ought." These "oughts" are avoidable, or, as Kant would say, contingent. They are contingent or dependent on what I happen to want or the desires I happen to have, such as to please others, to harm someone, to gain power, or to be punctual.

These "oughts" are also quite individualized. What I ought to do is contingent or dependent on my own individual goals or plans. These actions serve as means to whatever goals I happen to have. Other people ought to do different things than I because they have different goals and plans. For example, I ought to take introduction to sociology because I want to be a sociology major, while you ought to take a course on the philosophy of Kant because you have chosen to be a philosophy major. These are obligations only for those who have these goals or desires. Think of them in this form: "If (or because) I want X, then I ought to do Y." Whether I ought to do Y is totally contingent or dependent on my wanting X.

Moral obligation, on the other hand, is quite different in nature. Kant believed that we experience moral obligation as something quite demanding. If there is something I morally ought to do, I ought to do it no matter what—whether or not I want to, and whether or not it fulfills my desires and goals or is approved by my society. Moral obligation is not contingent on what I or anyone happens to want or approve. Moral "oughts" are thus, in Kant's terminology, unconditional or necessary. Moreover, whereas hypothetical "oughts" relate to goals we each have as individuals, moral "oughts" stem from the ways in which we are alike as persons, for only persons are subject to morality. This is because persons are rational beings and only persons can act from a reason or from principles. These "oughts" are thus not individualized but universal as they apply to all persons. Kant calls moral "oughts" categorical imperatives because they tell us what we ought to do no matter what, under all conditions, or categorically.

It is from the very nature of categorical or moral imperatives, their being unconditional and universally binding, that Kant derives his views about what it is that we ought to do. In fact, he calls the statement of his basic moral principle by which we determine what we ought and ought not to do simply the *categorical imperative.*

THE CATEGORICAL IMPERATIVE

The categorical imperative, Kant's basic moral principle, is comparable in importance for his moral philosophy to the principle of utility for utilitarians. It is Kant's test for right and wrong. Just as there are different ways to formulate the principle of utility, so also Kant had different formulations for his principle. Although at least four of them may be found in his writings, we will concentrate on just two and call them the first and second forms of the categorical imperative. The others, however, do add different elements to our understanding of his basic moral principle and will be mentioned briefly.

The First Form

Recall that moral obligation is categorical; that is, it is unconditional and applies to all persons as persons rather than to persons as individuals. It is in this sense universal. Moreover, because morality is not a matter of producing good consequences of any sort (be it happiness or knowledge or peace), the basic moral principle will be formal, without content. It will not include reference to any particular good. Knowing this, we are on the way to understanding the first form of the categorical imperative, which simply requires that we only do what we can accept or will that everyone do. Kant's own statement of it is basically the following:

Act only on that maxim that you can will as a universal law.

In other words, whatever I consider doing, it must be something that I can will or accept that all others do. To will something universally is similar to willing it as a law, for a law by its very nature has a degree of universality. By *maxim,* Kant means a description of the action that I will put to the test. This is put in the form of a rule or principle. For example, I might want to know whether "being late for class" or "giving all my money to the homeless" describe morally permissible actions. I need only formulate some maxim or rule and ask whether I could will that everyone follow that maxim. For example, I might ask whether I could will the maxim or general rule, "Whenever I have money to spare, I will give it to the homeless." However, this needs further clarification.[9]

How do I know what I can and cannot will as a universal practice? As a rational being, I can only will what is noncontradictory. What do we think of a person who says that it is both raining and not raining here now? It can be raining here and not there or now and not earlier. But it is either raining here or it is not. It cannot be both. So also we say that a person who wants to "have his cake and eat it, too" is not being rational. "Make up your mind," we say. "If you eat it, it is gone."

How I know if I can rationally, without contradiction, will something for all can best be explained by using one of Kant's own examples. He asks us to consider whether it is morally permissible for me to "make a lying or false promise in order to extricate myself from some difficulty." Thus, I would consider the maxim, "Whenever I am in some difficulty that I can get out of only by making a lying or false promise, I will do so." To know whether this would be morally acceptable, it must pass the test of the categorical imperative. If I were to use this test, I would ask whether I could will that sort of thing for all. I must ask whether I could will a general practice in which people who made promises—for example, to pay back some money—made the promises without intending to keep them. If people who generally made such promises did so falsely, then others would know this and would not believe the promises. Consider whether you would lend money to a person if she said she would pay you back but you knew she was

lying. The reasoning is thus: If I tried to will a general practice of false promise making, I would find that I could not do it because by willing that the promises could be false I would also will a situation in which it would be impossible to make a lying promise. No one could then make a promise, let alone a false promise, because no one would believe him or her. Part of being able to make a promise is to have it believed. This universal practice itself could not even exist. It is a self-destructive practice. If everyone made such lying promises, no one could!

Now consider the example at the beginning of this chapter: the experiment using people without their full knowing consent. Using Kant's categorical imperative to test this, one would see that if it were a general practice for researchers to lie to their subjects in order to get them into their experiments, they would not be able to get people to participate. They could not even lie because no one would believe them. The only way a particular researcher could lie would be if other researchers told the truth. Only then could she get her prospective subjects to believe her. But, on this interpretation of the case, this would be to make herself an exception to the universal rule. Because a universal practice in which researchers lied to their prospective subjects could not even exist, it is a morally impermissible action.[10]

The Second Form

The first form of Kant's categorical imperative requires universalizing one's contemplated action. In the second form, we are asked to consider what constitutes proper treatment of persons as persons. According to Kant, one key characteristic of persons is their ability to set their own goals. Persons are autonomous. They are literally self-ruled or at least capable of being self-ruled (from *auto,* meaning "self," and *nomos,* meaning "rule" or "law"). As persons, we choose our own life plans, what we want to be, our friends, our college courses, and so forth. We have our own reasons for doing so. We believe that although we are influenced in these choices and reasons by our situation and by others, we let ourselves be so influenced, and thus these choices are still our own choices.[11] In this way, persons are different from things. Things cannot choose what they wish to do. We decide how we shall use things. We impose our own goals on things, using the wood to build the house and the pen or computer to write our words and express our ideas. It is appropriate in this scheme of things to use things for our ends, but it is not appropriate to use persons as though they were things purely at our own disposal and without a will of their own. Kant's statement of this second form of the categorical imperative is as follows:

Always treat humanity, whether in your own person or that of another, never simply as a means but always at the same time as an end.

This formulation tells us several things. First, it tells us how we ought to treat ourselves as well as others for we are persons as they are. Second, it tells us to treat ourselves and others as ends rather than merely as means. Kant believes that we should treat persons as having intrinsic value and not just as having instrumental value. People are valuable in themselves, regardless of whether they are useful or loved or valued by others. However, this form also specifies that we should not simply use others or let ourselves be used. Although I may in some sense use someone for example, to paint my house—I may not simply use them. The goal of getting my house painted must also be the goal of the painter, who is also a person and not just an object to be used by me for my own ends. She must know what is involved in the project. I cannot lie to her to manipulate her into doing something to which she otherwise would not agree. And she must agree to paint the house voluntarily rather than be coerced into doing it. This is to treat the person as an end rather than as a means to my ends or goals.

We can also use this second form to evaluate the examples considered for the first form of the categorical imperative. The moral conclusions should be the same whether we use the first or second form. Kant believes that in lying to another—for example, saying that we will pay back the money when we have no intention of doing so—we would be attempting to get that other to do what we want but which she or he presumably does not want to

do—namely, just give us the money. This would violate the requirement not to use persons. So also in the experiment described at the beginning of this chapter, the researcher would be using deception to get people to "volunteer" for the study. One difficulty presented by this type of study, however, is that if the participants were to know the truth, it would undermine the study. Some people have argued that in such studies we can presume the voluntary consent of the subjects, judging that they would approve if they did know what was going on in the study. Do you think that presuming consent in this or similar cases would be sufficient?

We noted above that Kant had more than these two formulations of his categorical imperative. In another of these formulations, Kant relies on his views about nature as a system of everything that we experience because it is organized according to laws. Thus, he says that we ought always to ask whether some action we are contemplating could become a universal law of nature. The effect of this version is to stress the universality and rationality of morality, for nature necessarily operates according to coherent laws. Other formulations of the categorical imperative stress autonomy. We are to ask whether we could consider ourselves as the author of the moral practice that we are about to accept. We are both subject to the moral law and its author because it flows from our own nature as a rational being. Another formulation amplifies what we have here called the second form of the categorical imperative. This formulation points out that we are all alike as persons and together form a community of persons. He calls the community of rational persons a "kingdom of ends"—that is, a kingdom in which all persons are authors as well as subjects of the moral law. Thus, we ask whether the action we are contemplating would be fitting for and further or promote such a community. These formal actions of the categorical imperative involve other interesting elements of Kant's philosophy, but they also involve more than we can explore further here.

EVALUATING KANT'S MORAL THEORY

There is much that is appealing in Kant's moral philosophy, particularly its central aspects—fairness, consistency, and treating persons as autonomous and morally equal beings. They are also key elements of a particular tradition in morality, one that is quite different than that exemplified by utilitarianism with its emphasis on the maximization of happiness and the production of good consequences. To more fully evaluate Kant's theory, consider the following aspects of his thought.

The Nature of Moral Obligation

One of the bases on which Kant's moral philosophy rests is his view about the nature of moral obligation. He believes that moral obligation is real and strictly binding. According to Kant, this is how we generally think of moral obligation. If there is anything that we morally ought to do, then we simply ought to do it. Thus, this type of obligation is unlike that which flows from what we ought to do because of the particular goals that we each have as individuals. To evaluate this aspect of Kant's moral philosophy, you must ask yourself if this is also what you think about the nature of moral obligation. This is important for Kant's moral philosophy, because acting out of respect for the moral law is required for an action to have moral worth. Furthermore, being able to act out of such a regard for morality is also the source of human dignity, according to Kant.

The Application of the Categorical Imperative

Critics have pointed out problems with the universalizing form of the categorical imperative. For example, some have argued that when using the first form of the categorical imperative there are many things that I could will as universal practices that would hardly seem to be moral obligations. I could will that everyone write their name on the top of their test papers. If everyone did that, it would not prevent anyone from doing so. There would be no contradiction involved if this were a universal practice. Nevertheless, this would not mean that people have a moral obligation to write their names on their test papers. A Kantian might explain that to write your name on your test paper is an example of a hypothetical, not a categorical, imperative. I write my name on my paper because I want to be given credit for it. If I can will it as a universal practice, I then know it is a morally permissible action. If I cannot will it universally, then it is impermissible or wrong. Thus, the categorical imperative is actually a negative test—in other words, a test for what we should not do, more than a test for what we ought to do. Whether or not this is a satisfactory response, you should know that this is just one of several problems associated with Kant's universalizing test.

Note, too, that although both Kantians and rule utilitarians must universalize, how their reasoning proceeds from there is not identical. Rule utilitarians, on the one hand, require that we consider what the results would be if some act we are contemplating were to be a universal practice. Reasoning in this way, we ask what would be the results or consequences of some general practice, such as making false promises, or whether one practice would have better results than another. Although in some sense Kant's theory requires that we consider the possible consequences when universalizing some action, the determinant of the action's morality is not whether its practice has good or bad consequences, but whether there would be anything contradictory in willing the practice as a universal law. Because we are rational beings, we must not will contradictory things.

The second form of the categorical imperative also has problems of application. In the concrete, it is not always easy to determine whether one is using a person, for example, what is coercion and what is simply influence, or what is deception and what is not. When I try to talk a friend into doing something for me, how do I know whether I am simply providing input for the person's own decision making or whether I am crossing the line and becoming coercive? Moreover, if I do not tell the whole truth or withhold information from another, should this count as deception on my part? (See further discussion of this issue in Chapter 10 on sexual morality.) Although these are real problems for anyone who tries to apply Kant's views about deceit and coercion, they are not unique to his moral philosophy. Theories vary in the ease of their use or application, but, as Kant puts it, "Ease of use and apparent adequacy of a principle are not any sure proof of its correctness."[12] The fact that a theory has a certain amount of ambiguity should not necessarily disqualify it. Difficulty of application is a problem for most, if not all, reasonable moral philosophies.

Duty

Some of the language and terminology found in Kant's moral theory can sound harsh to modern ears. Duty, obligation, law, and universality may not be the moral terms most commonly heard today. Yet if one considers what Kant meant by *duty,* the idea may not be so strange to us. He did not mean any particular moral code or set of duties that is held by any society or group. Rather, duty is whatever is the right thing to do. However, Kant might respond that there is a streak of absolutism in his philosophy. Recall from Chapter 2 that *absolutism* is distinguished from objectivism and usually refers to a morality that consists in a set of exceptionless rules. Kant does, at times, seem to favor such rules. He provides examples in which it seems clear that he believes that it is always wrong to make a false promise or to lie deliberately. There is even one example in which Kant himself suggests that if a killer comes to the door asking for a friend of yours inside whom he intends to kill, you must tell the truth. But Kant's philosophy has only one exceptionless rule and that is given in the categorical imperative. We are never permitted to do what we cannot will as a universal law or what violates the requirement to treat persons as persons. Even with these tests in hand, it is not always clear just how they apply. Furthermore, they may not give adequate help in deciding what to do when they seem to give us contradictory duties, as in the example, both to tell the truth and preserve life. Kant believed that he was only setting basic principles of morality and establishing it on a firm basis. Nevertheless, it is reasonable to expect that a moral theory should go further.

Moral Equality and Impartiality

One positive feature of Kant's moral theory is its emphasis on the moral equality of all persons, which is implied in his view about the nature of moral obligation as universally binding. We should not make exceptions for ourselves but only do what we can will for all. Moral obligation and morality itself flow from our nature as persons as rational and autonomous. Morality is grounded in the ways in which we are alike as persons rather than the ways in which we are different as individuals. These views might provide a source for those who want to argue for moral equality and equal moral rights. (For other reflection on the nature of rights, refer to the discussion of it in Chapters 6 and 13.) Not to treat others as equal as a person is, in a way, disrespecting them. Not to be willing to make the same judgment for cases similar to one's own, or not to be willing to have the same rules apply to all, could be viewed as a form of hypocrisy. When we criticize these behaviors, we act in the spirit of Kant.[13]

Another feature of Kant's moral philosophy is its spirit of impartiality. For an action to be morally permissible, we should be able to will it for all. However, persons do differ in significant ways. Among these are differences in gender, race, age, and talents. In what way does morality require that all persons be treated equally and in what way does it perhaps require that different persons be treated differently? (Further discussion of this issue can be found in Chapter 12 on equality and discrimination.)[14]

Other people have wondered about Kant's stress on the nature of persons as rational beings. Some believe it is too male-oriented in its focus on reason rather than emotion. In Chapter 7, we will examine a type of morality that stresses the emotional and personal ties that we have to particular individuals. Kant might reply that we often have no control over how we feel and thus it should not be the key element of our moral lives. He might also point out that it is the common aspects of our existence as persons, and not the ways in which we are different and unique, that give us dignity and are the basis for the moral equality that we possess.

PERFECT AND IMPERFECT DUTIES

In his attempt to explain his views, Kant provides us with several examples. We have already considered one of these: making a false promise. His conclusion is that we should not make a false or lying promise, both because we could not consistently will it for all and because it violates our obligation to treat persons as persons and not to use them only for our own purposes. Kant calls such duties *perfect* or *necessary duties.* As the terms suggest, perfect duties are absolute. We can and should absolutely refrain from making false or lying promises. From the perspective of the first form of the categorical imperative, we have a perfect duty not to do those things that could not even exist and are inconceivable as universal practices. Using the second form of the categorical imperative, we have a perfect duty not to do what violates the requirement to treat persons as persons.

However, some duties are more flexible. Kant calls these duties *imperfect* or *meritorious duties.* Consider another example he provides us: egoism. Ethical egoism, you will recall, is the view that we may rightly seek only our own interest and help others only to the extent that this also benefits us. Is this a morally acceptable philosophy of life? Using the first form of Kant's categorical imperative to test the morality of this practice, we must ask whether we could will that everyone was an egoist. If I try to do this, I would need to will that I was an egoist as well as others, even in those situations when I needed others' help. In those situations, I must allow that they not help me when it is not in their own best interest. But being an egoist myself, I would also want them to help me. In effect, I would be willing contradictories: that they help me (I being an egoist) and that they not help me (they being egoists). Although a society of egoists could indeed exist, Kant admits, no rational person could will it, for a rational person does not will contradictories. We have an imperfect or meritorious duty, then, not to be egoists but to help people for their own good and not just for ours. However, just when to help others and how much is a matter of some choice. There is a certain flexibility here. One implication of this view is that there is no absolute duty to give one's whole life to helping others. We, too, are persons and thus have moral rights and also can at least sometimes act for our own interests.

The same conclusion regarding the wrongness of egoism results from the application of the second form of the categorical imperative. If I were an egoist and concerned only about myself, then no one could accuse me of using other people. I would simply leave them alone. According to Kant, such an attitude and practice would be inconsistent with the duty to treat others as persons. As persons, they also have interests and plans, and to recognize this I must at least sometimes and in some ways seek to promote their ends and goals. One implication of this distinction is in handling conflicts of duties. Perfect duties will take precedence over imperfect ones such that we cannot help some by violating the rights of others.

VARIATIONS ON KANTIAN MORAL THEORY

Just as there are contemporary versions of and developments within the utilitarian tradition, so also we can find many contemporary versions of Kantian moral philosophies. One is found in the moral philosophy of W. D. Ross (1877–1971), who also held that there are things that we ought and ought not do regardless of the consequences.[15] According to Ross, we not only have duties of beneficence, but also have duties to keep promises, pay our debts, and be good friends and parents and children. (Refer to the discussion of moral pluralism in Chapter 2.) Contrary to Kant, Ross believed that we can know through moral intuition in any instance what we ought to do. Sometimes we are faced with a conflict of moral duties. It seems intuitively that we ought to be both loyal and honest but we cannot be both. We have *prima facie* or conditional duties of loyalty and honesty. Ross is the source of this phrase, which is often used in ethical arguments. (See our use of it in Chapter 15.) In such cases, according to Ross, we have to consider which duty is the stronger—that is, which has the greater balance of rightness over wrongness. In choosing honesty in some situation, however, one does not negate or forget that one also has a duty to be loyal. Obvious problems arise for such a theory. For example, how does one go about determining the amount of rightness or wrongness involved in some action? Don't people have different intuitions about the rightness or wrongness? This is a problem for anyone who holds that intuition is the basis for morality.

One of the most noted contemporary versions of Kant's moral philosophy is found in the political philosophy of John Rawls. In *A Theory of Justice,* Rawls applies Kantian principles to issues of social justice. According to Rawls, justice is fairness.[16] To know what is fair, we must put ourselves imaginatively in the position of a group of free and equal rational beings who are choosing principles of justice for their society. In thinking of persons as free and equal rational beings in order to develop principles of justice, Rawls is securely in the Kantian tradition of moral philosophy. Kant has also stressed autonomy. It is this aspect of our nature that gives us our dignity as persons. Kant's categorical imperative also involved universalization. We must do only those things that we could will that everyone do. It is only a short move from these notions of autonomy and universalization to the Rawlsian requirement to choose those principles of justice that we could accept no matter whose position we were in. For details about the principles, see Chapter 13 on economic justice. Just as utilitarian moral theory is still being debated today and has many followers, so also Kantian types of philosophy continue to intrigue and interest moral thinkers. You will also be able to better evaluate this theory as you see aspects of it applied to issues in Part Two of this text.

NOTES

1. See http://en.wikipedia.org/wiki/Tuskegee_syphilis_study.
2. At least this might be true from an act utilitarian point of view. A rule utilitarian might want to know whether the results of the general practice of not fully informing research participants would be such that the good achieved would not be worth it.
3. From *The Trials of War Criminals Before the Nuremberg Military Tribunals Under Control Council Law,* No. 10, vol. 2 (Washington, DC: U.S. Government Printing Office, 1949): 181–182.
4. Reported by philosopher J. G. Hammann and noted in Roger Scruton's *Kant* (Oxford: Oxford University Press, 1982): 3–4.
5. Immanuel Kant, *Critique of Pure Reason,* Norman Kemp Smith (Trans.) (New York: St. Martin's, 1965): 635.
6. Lewis White Beck, introduction to his translation of Kant's *Foundations of the Metaphysics of Morals* (New York: Bobbs-Merrill, 1959): vii. The title is also sometimes translated as *Fundamental Principles of the Metaphysics of Morals.* For a readable interpretation of Kant's ethics, see Onora O'Neill's "A Simplified Account of Kant's Ethics," *Matters of Life and Death,* Tom Regan (Ed.) (New York: McGraw-Hill, 1986).
7. We will not distinguish here *motive* and *intention,* although the former usually signifies that out of which we act (a pusher) and the latter that for which we act (an aim).
8. Kant, *Foundations,* 9.
9. I thank Professor Joyce Mullan for suggestions regarding what Kant means by *maxim.*
10. In some ways, Kant's basic moral principle, the categorical imperative, is a principle of fairness. I cannot do what I am not able to will that everyone do. In the example, for me to make a lying promise, others must generally make truthful promises so that my lie will be believed. This would be to treat myself as an exception. But this is not fair. In some ways, the principle is similar to the so-called golden rule, which requires us only to do unto others what we would be willing for them to do unto us. However, it is not quite the same, for Kant's principle requires our not willing self-defeating or self-canceling, contradictory practices, whereas the golden rule requires that we appeal in the final analysis to what we would or would not like to have done to us.
11. Kant does treat the whole issue of determinism versus freedom, but it is difficult to follow; to attempt explaining it would involve us deeply in his metaphysics. Although it is a serious issue, we will assume for purposes of understanding Kant that sometimes, at least, human choice is free.
12. Kant, *Foundations,* 8.
13. I would like to thank one of this book's reviewers for this suggestion.
14. See also the criticism of Kantian theories of justice in the treatment of gender and justice in Susan Moller Okin, *Justice, Gender, and the Family* (New York: Basic Books, 1989): 3–22. See also Marilyn Friedman, "The Social Self and the Partiality Debates," in *Feminist Ethics,* Claudia Card (Ed.) (Lawrence: University of Kansas Press, 1991).

15. W. D. Ross, *The Right and the Good* (Oxford: Oxford University Press, 1930).

16. John Rawls, *A Theory of Justice* (Cambridge, MA: Harvard University Press, 1971).

REVIEW EXERCISES

1. Give one of Kant's reasons for opposing the locating of an action's moral worth in its consequences.
2. Does Kant mean by "a good will" or "good intention" wishing others well? Explain.
3. What does Kant mean by "acting out of duty"? How does the shopkeeper exemplify this?
4. What is the basic difference between a categorical and a hypothetical imperative? In the following examples, which are hypothetical and which are categorical imperatives? Explain your answers.
   a. If you want others to be honest with you, then you ought to be honest with them.
   b. Whether or not you want to pay your share, you ought to do so.
   c. Because everyone wants to be happy, we ought to consider everyone's interests equally.
   d. I ought not to cheat on this test if I do not want to get caught.
5. How does the character of moral obligation lead to Kant's basic moral principle, the categorical imperative?
6. Explain Kant's use of the first form of the categorical imperative to argue that it is wrong to make a false promise. (Note that you do not appeal to the bad consequences as the basis of judging it wrong.)
7. According to the second form of Kant's categorical imperative, would it be morally permissible for me to agree to be someone's slave? Explain.
8. What is the practical difference between a perfect and an imperfect duty?

Selected Bibliography

Acton, Harry. *Kant's Moral Philosophy.* New York: Macmillan, 1970.

Annas, George J., and Michael A. Grodin (Eds.). *The Nazi Doctors and the Nuremberg Code.* New York: Oxford University Press, 1992.

Aune, Bruce. *Kant's Theory of Morals.* Princeton, NJ: Princeton University Press, 1979.

Beck, Lewis White. *A Commentary on Kant's Critique of Practical Reason.* Chicago: University of Chicago Press, 1960.

Frierson, Patrick. *Freedom and Anthropology in Kant's Moral Philosophy.* New York: Cambridge University Press, 2003.

Gulyga, Arsenij. *Immanuel Kant: His Life and Thought.* Marijan Despalotovic (Trans.). Boston: Birkhauser, 1987.

Guyer, Paul. *The Cambridge Companion to Kant.* New York: Cambridge University Press, 1992.

Harrison, Jonathan. "Kant's Examples of the First Formulation of the Categorical Imperative," *Philosophical Quarterly* 7 (1957): 50–62.

Hill, Thomas E., Jr. "Kantian Constructivism in Ethics," *Ethics* 99 (1989).

Kant, Immanuel. *Critique of Practical Reason.* Lewis White Beck (Trans.). Indianapolis, IN: Bobbs-Merrill, 1956.

———. *Foundations of the Metaphysics of Morals.* J. H. J. Paton (Trans.). New York: Harper & Row, 1957.

Korner, Stephen. *Kant.* New Haven, CT: Yale University Press, 1982.

Korsgaard, Christine M. "Kant's Formula of Universal Law," *Pacific Philosophical Quarterly* 66 (1985): 24–47.

O'Neill, Onora. *Acting on Principle: An Essay on Kantian Ethics.* New York: Columbia University Press, 1975.

Paton, Herbert J. *The Categorical Imperative: A Study in Kant's Moral Philosophy.* Chicago: University of Chicago Press, 1948.

Robinson, Hoke (Ed.). *Selected Essays on Kant by Lewis White Beck.* Rochester, NY: University of Rochester Press, 2002.

Ross, Sir William David. *Kant's Ethical Theory.* New York: Oxford University Press, 1954.

Scruton, Roger. *Kant.* New York: Oxford University Press, 1982.

Stratton-Lake, Philip. *Kant, Duty, and Moral Worth.* New York: Routledge, 2004.

Sullivan, Roger J. *An Introduction to Kant's Ethics.* New York: Cambridge University Press, 1994.

Walker, Ralph C. *Kant.* New York: Methuen, 1982.

Wolff, Robert P. *The Autonomy of Reason: A Commentary on Kant's "Groundwork of the Metaphysics of Morals."* New York: Harper & Row, 1973.

6

Natural Law and Natural Rights

In 1776, Thomas Jefferson wrote in the Declaration of Independence, "We hold these truths to be self-evident, that all men are created equal, that they are endowed by their Creator with certain inalienable rights, that among these are life, liberty and the pursuit of happiness."[1] Jefferson had read the work of English philosopher John Locke, who had written in his *Second Treatise on Government* that all human beings were of the same species, born with the same basic capacities.[2] Thus, Locke argued, because all humans had the same basic nature, they should be treated equally.

Following the 2001 terrorist attack on the World Trade Center and the Pentagon, and with the U.S. invasion of Afghanistan, the question arose about what to do with people captured by the United States and considered to be terrorists. Since 2004, they have been transferred to Guantanamo Bay in Cuba, a U.S. naval base on the southeastern side of the island (the United States still held a lease to this land because of the 1903 Cuban-American Treaty). A prison was set up, and those who were thought to be members, supporters, or sympathizers of al Qaeda or the Taliban were transferred there. It was said that they were not part of any army of any state and thus not prisoners of war but "enemy combatants" and thus not covered by any of the protections of the Geneva Conventions. They also were not given the protections of U.S. laws, and they were denied such basic human rights as knowing the charges against them and being allowed to defend themselves in court.

As of 2007, many of the 500 or so detainees had been sent back to the countries of their origins. Some were finally allowed lawyers, although not of their own choice. U.S. courts had ruled that the detainees must be given trials, not in the United States, but in U.S. military courts. As of this time, more prisoners are scheduled for release and some 250 may be held indefinitely.[3] (Also see the discussion of torture in Chapter 4.) What is meant by "human rights"—and does every person possess such rights? This is one of the questions addressed in this chapter.

The Nuremberg trials were trials of Nazi war criminals held in Nuremberg, Germany, from 1945 to 1949. There were thirteen trials in all. In the first trial, Nazi leaders were found guilty of violating international law by starting an aggressive war. Nine of them, including Hermann Goering and Rudolf Hess, were sentenced to death. In other trials, defendants were accused of committing atrocities against civilians. Nazi doctors who had conducted medical experiments on those imprisoned in the death camps were among those tried. Their experiments maimed and killed many people, all of whom were unwilling subjects. For example, experiments for the German air force were conducted to determine how fast people would die in very thin air. Other experiments tested the effects of freezing water on the human body. The defense contended that the military personnel, judges, and doctors were only following orders. However, the prosecution argued successfully that even if the experimentation did not violate the defendants' own laws, they were still "crimes against humanity." The idea was that a law more basic than civil laws exists—a moral law—and these doctors and others should have known what this basic moral law required.

The idea that the basic moral law can be known by human reason and that we know what it requires by looking to human nature are two of the tenets of natural law theory. Some treatments of human rights also use human nature as a basis. According to this view, human rights are those things that we can validly claim because they are essential for functioning well as human beings. This chapter will present the essential elements of both of these theories.

NATURAL LAW THEORY

One of the first questions to ask concerns the kind of law that natural law is. After addressing this question, we will examine the origins of this theory. Then we will explain what the theory holds. Finally, we will suggest things to think about when evaluating the theory.

What Kind of Law Is Natural Law?

Let us consider first, then, what type of law that natural law is. The *natural law,* as this term is used in discussions of natural law theory, should not be confused with those other "laws of nature" that are the generalizations of natural science. The laws of natural science are descriptive laws. They tell us how scientists believe nature behaves. Gases, for example, expand with their containers and when heat is applied. Boyle's law about the behavior of gases does not tell gases how they *ought* to behave. In fact, if gases were found to behave differently from what we had so far observed, then the laws would be changed to match this new information. Simply put, scientific laws are descriptive generalizations of fact.

Moral laws, on the other hand, are prescriptive laws. They tell us how we *ought* to behave. The natural law is the moral law written into nature itself. What we ought to do, according to this theory, is determined by considering certain aspects of nature. In particular, we ought to examine our nature as human beings to see what is essential for us to function well as members of our species. We look to certain aspects of our nature to know what is our good and what we ought to do.

Civil law is also prescriptive. As the moral law, however, natural law is supposed to be more basic or higher than the laws of any particular society. Although laws of particular societies vary and change over time, the natural law is supposed to be universal and stable. In an ancient Greek tragedy by Sophocles, the protagonist Antigone disobeys the king and buries her brother. She did so because she believed that she must follow a higher law that required her to do this. In the story, she lost her life for obeying this law. In the Nuremberg trials, prosecutors had also argued that there was a higher law that all humans should recognize—one that takes precedence over state laws. People today sometimes appeal to this moral law in order to argue which civil laws ought to be instituted or changed.[4]

HISTORICAL ORIGINS: ARISTOTLE

The tradition of natural law ethics is a long one. Although one may find examples of the view that certain actions are right or wrong because they are suited to or go against human nature before Aristotle wrote about them, he is the first to develop a complex ethical philosophy based on this view.

Aristotle was born in 384 B.C. in Stagira in northern Greece. His father was a physician for King Philip of Macedonia. Around age seventeen, he went to study at Plato's Academy in Athens. Historians of philosophy have traced the influence of Plato's philosophy on Aristotle, but they have also noted significant differences between the two philosophers. Putting one difference somewhat simply, Plato's philosophy stresses the reality of the general and abstract, this reality being his famous forms or ideas that exist apart from the things that imitate them or in which they participate. Aristotle was more interested in the individual and the concrete manifestations of the forms. After Plato's death, Aristotle traveled for several years and then for two or three years was the tutor to Alexander, the young son of King Philip, who later became known as Alexander the Great. In 335 B.C., Aristotle returned to Athens and organized his own school called the Lyceum.

There he taught and wrote almost until his death thirteen years later in 322 B.C.[5] Aristotle is known not only for his moral theory but also for writings in logic, biology, physics, metaphysics, art, and politics. The basic notions of his moral theory can be found in his *Nicomachean Ethics,* named for his son Nicomachus.[6]

Nature, Human Nature, and the Human Good

Aristotle was a close observer of nature. In fact, in his writings he mentions some 500 different kinds of animals.[7] He noticed that seeds of the same sort always grew to the same mature form. He opened developing eggs of various species and noticed that these organisms manifested a pattern in their development even before birth. Tadpoles, he might have said, always follow the same path and become frogs, not turtles. So also with other living things. Acorns always become oak trees, not elms. He concluded that there was an order in nature. It was as if natural beings such as plants and animals had a principle of order within them that directed them toward their goal—their mature final form. This view can be called a *teleological* view from the Greek word for goal, *telos,* because of its emphasis on a goal embedded in natural things. It was from this that Aristotle developed his notion of the good.

According to Aristotle, "the good is that at which all things aim."[8] We are to look at the purpose or end or goal of some activity or being to see what is its good. Thus, the good of the shipbuilder is to build ships. The good of the lyre player is to play well. Aristotle asks whether there is anything that is the good of the human being—not as shipbuilder or lyre player, but simply as human. To answer this question, we must first think about what it is to be human. According to Aristotle, natural beings come in kinds or species. From their species flow their essential characteristics and certain key tendencies or capacities. A squirrel, for example, is a kind of animal that is, first of all, a living being, an animal. It develops from a young form to a mature form. It is a mammal and has other characteristics of mammals. It is bushy-tailed, can run along telephone wires, and gathers and stores nuts for its food. From the characteristics that define a squirrel, we

also can know what a *good* squirrel is. A good specimen of a squirrel is one that is effective, successful, and functions well. It follows the pattern of development and growth it has by nature. It does, in fact, have a bushy tail and good balance, and it knows how to find and store its food. It would be a bad example of a squirrel or a poor one that had no balance, couldn't find its food, or had no fur and was sickly. It would have been better for the squirrel if its inherent natural tendencies to grow and develop and live as a healthy squirrel had been realized.

According to the natural law tradition from Aristotle on, human beings are also thought to be natural beings with a specific human nature. They have certain specific characteristics and abilities that they share as humans. Unlike squirrels and acorns, human beings can choose to do what is their good or act against it. Just what is their good? Aristotle recognized that a good eye is a healthy eye that sees well. A good horse is a well-functioning horse, one that is healthy and able to run and do what horses do. What about human beings? Was there something comparable for the human being as human? Was there some good for humans as humans?

Just as we can tell what the good squirrel is from its own characteristics and abilities as a squirrel, according to natural law theory, the same should be true for the human being. For human beings to function well or flourish, they should perfect their human capacities. If they do this, they will be functioning well as human beings. They will also be happy, for a being is happy to the extent that it is functioning well. Aristotle believed that the ultimate good of humans is happiness, blessedness, or prosperity: eudaimonia. But in what does happiness consist? To know what happiness is, we need to know what is the function of the human being.

Human beings have much in common with lower forms of beings. We are living, for example, just as plants are. Thus, we take in material from outside us for nourishment, and we grow from an immature to a mature form. We have senses of sight and hearing and so forth as do the higher animals. But is there anything unique to humans? Aristotle believed that it was our "rational element" that was peculiar to us. The good for humans, then, should consist in their functioning in a way consistent with and guided by this rational element. Our rational element has two different functions: One is to know, and the other is to guide choice and action. We must develop our ability to know the world and the truth. We must also choose wisely. In doing this, we will be functioning well specifically as humans. Yet what is it to choose wisely? In partial answer to this, Aristotle develops ideas about prudential choice and suggests that we choose as a prudent person would choose.

One of the most well known interpreters of Aristotle's philosophy was Thomas Aquinas (1224–1274). Aquinas was a Dominican friar who taught at the University of Paris. He was also a theologian who held that the natural law was part of the divine law or plan for the universe. The record of much of what he taught can be found in his work the *Summa Theologica*.[9] Following Aristotle, Aquinas held that the moral good consists in following the innate tendencies of our nature. We are by nature biological beings. Because we tend by nature to grow and mature, we ought to preserve our being and our health by avoiding undue risks and doing what will make us healthy. Furthermore, like sentient animals, we can know our world through physical sense capacities. We ought to use our senses of touch, taste, hearing, and sight; we ought to develop and make use of these senses for appreciating those aspects of existence that they reveal to us. We ought not to do, or do deliberately, what injures these senses. Like many animals we reproduce our kind not asexually but sexually and heterosexually. This is what nature means for us to do, according to this version of natural law theory. (See further discussion of this issue in Chapter 10 on sexual morality.)

Unique to persons are the specific capacities of knowing and choosing freely. Thus, we ought to treat ourselves and others as beings capable of understanding and free choice. Those things that help us pursue the truth, such as education and freedom of public expression, are good. Those things that hinder pursuit of the truth are bad. Deceit and lack of access to the sources of knowledge are morally objectionable simply because they prevent

us from fulfilling our innate natural drive or orientation to know the way things are.[10] Moreover, whatever enhances our ability to choose freely is good. A certain amount of self-discipline, options from which to choose, and reflection on what we ought to choose are among the things that enhance freedom. To coerce people and to limit their possibilities of choosing freely are examples of what is inherently bad or wrong. We also ought to find ways to live well together, for this is a theory according to which "no man—or woman—is an island." We are social creatures by nature. Thus, the essence of natural law theory is that we ought to further the inherent ends of human nature and not do what frustrates human fulfillment or flourishing.

Evaluating Natural Law Theory

Natural law theory has many appealing characteristics. Among them are its belief in the objectivity of moral values and the notion of the good as human flourishing. Various criticisms of the theory have also been advanced, including the following two.

First, according to natural law theory, we are to determine what we ought to do from deciphering the moral law as it is written into nature—specifically, human nature. One problem that natural law theory must address concerns our ability to read nature. The moral law is supposedly knowable by natural human reason. However, throughout the history of philosophy various thinkers have read nature differently. Even Aristotle, for example, thought that slavery could be justified in that it was in accord with nature.[11] Today people argue against slavery on just such natural law grounds. Philosopher Thomas Hobbes defended the absolutist rule of despots and John Locke criticized it, both doing so on natural law grounds. Moreover, traditional natural law theory has picked out highly positive traits: the desire to know the truth, to choose the good, and to develop as healthy mature beings. Not all views of the essential characteristics of human nature have been so positive, however. Some philosophers have depicted human nature as deceitful, evil, and uncontrolled. This is why Hobbes argued that we need a strong government. Without it, he wrote, life in a state of nature would be "nasty, brutish, and short."[12]

Moreover, if nature is taken in the broader sense—meaning *all* of nature—and if a natural law as a moral law were based on this, then the general approach might even cover such theories as Social Darwinism. This view holds that because the most fit organisms in nature are the ones that survive, so also the most fit should endure in human society and the weaker ought to perish. When combined with a belief in capitalism, this led to notions such as that it was only right and according to nature that wealthy industrialists at the end of the nineteenth century were rich and powerful. It also implied that the poor were so by the designs of nature and we ought not interfere with this situation.

A second question raised for natural law theory is the following. Can the way things are by nature provide the basis for knowing how they ought to be? On the face of it, this may not seem right. Just because something exists in a certain way does not necessarily mean that it is good. Floods, famine, and disease all exist, but that does not make them good. According to David Hume, as noted in our discussion of Mill's proof of the principle of utility in Chapter 4, you cannot derive an "ought" from an "is."[13] Evaluations cannot simply be derived from factual matters. Other moral philosophers have agreed. When we know something to be a fact, that things exist in a certain way, it still remains an open question whether it is good. However, the natural law assumes that nature is teleological, that it has a certain directedness. In Aristotle's terms, it moves toward its natural goal, its final purpose. Yet from the time of the scientific revolution of the seventeenth century, such final purposes have become suspect. One could not always observe nature's directedness, and it came to be associated with the notion of nonobservable spirits directing things from within. If natural law theory does depend on there being purposes in nature, it must be able to explain how this can be so.

Consider one possible explanation of the source of whatever purposes there might be in nature. Christian philosophers from Augustine on believed that nature manifested God's plan for the universe. For Aristotle, however, the universe was eternal; it always existed and was not created by God. His concept of God was that of a most perfect being

toward which the universe was in some way directed. According to Aristotle, there is an order in nature, but it did not come from the mind of God. For Augustine and Thomas Aquinas, however, the reason why nature had the order that it did was because God, so to speak, had put it there. Because the universe was created after a divine plan, nature not only was intelligible but also existed for a purpose that was built into it. Some natural law theorists follow Thomas Aquinas on this, whereas others either follow Aristotle or abstain from judgments about the source of the order (telos) in nature. But can we conceive of an order in nature without an orderer? This depends on what we mean by order in nature. If it is taken in the sense of a plan, then this implies that it has an author. However, natural beings may simply develop in certain ways as if they were directed there by some plan—but there is no plan. This may just be our way of reading or speaking about nature.[14]

Evolutionary theory also may present a challenge to natural law theory. If the way that things have come to be is the result of many chance variations, then how can this resulting form be other than arbitrary? Theists often interpret evolution itself as part of a divine plan. There is no necessary conflict between belief in God and evolution. Chance, then, would not mean without direction. Even a nontheist such as mid–nineteenth century American philosopher Chauncey Wright had an explanation of Darwin's assertion that chance evolutionary variations accounted for the fact that some species were better suited to survive than others. Wright said that "chance" did not mean "uncaused"; it meant only that the causes were unknown to us.[15]

Natural Rights

A second theory according to which moral requirements may be grounded in human nature is the theory of natural rights. John Locke provided a good example that Jefferson used in the Declaration of Independence, as noted at the beginning of this chapter. Certain things are essential for us if we are to function well as persons. Among these are life itself and then also liberty and the ability to pursue those things that bring happiness. These are said to be rights not because they are granted by some state but because of the fact that they are important for us as human beings or persons. They are thus moral rights first, though they may also need the enforcement power of the law.

There is a long tradition of natural rights in Western philosophy. For example, we find a variant of the natural rights tradition in the writings of the first- and second-century A.D. Stoics. Their key moral principle was to "follow nature." For them, this meant that we should follow reason rather than human emotion. They also believed that there were laws to which all people were subject no matter what their local customs or conventions. Early Roman jurists believed that a common element existed in the codes of various peoples: a *jus gentium*. For example, the jurist Grotius held that the moral law was determined by right reason. These views can be considered variations on natural law theory because of their reliance on human nature and human reason to ground a basic moral law that is common to all peoples.[16]

Throughout the eighteenth century, political philosophers often referred to the laws of nature in discussions of natural rights. For example, Voltaire wrote that morality had a universal source. It was the "natural law . . . which nature teaches all men" what we should do.[17] The Declaration of Independence was influenced by the writings of jurists and philosophers who believed that a moral law was built into nature. Thus, in the first section it asserts that the colonists were called on "to assume among the powers of the earth, the separate and equal station, to which the laws of nature and of nature's God entitle them."[18]

Today various international codes of human rights, such as the United Nations' Declaration of Human Rights and the Geneva Convention's principles for the conduct of war, contain elements of a natural rights tradition. These attempt to specify rights that all people have simply as a virtue of their being human beings, regardless of their country of origin, race, or religion.

Evaluating Natural Rights Theory

One problem for a natural rights theory is that not everyone agrees on what human nature requires or which human natural rights are central. In the

1948 U.N. Declaration of Human Rights, the list of rights includes welfare rights and rights to food, clothing, shelter, and basic security. Just what kinds of things can we validly claim as human rights? Freedom of speech? Freedom of assembly? Housing? Clean air? Friends? Work? Income? Many of these are listed in various documents that nations have signed that provide lists of human rights. However, more is needed than lists. A rationale for what is to be included in those lists of human rights is called for. This is also something that a natural rights theory should provide. Some contemporary philosophers argue that the basic rights that society ought to protect are not welfare rights such as rights to food, clothing, and shelter, but liberty rights such as the right not to be interfered with in our daily lives.[19] (See further discussion of negative and positive rights in Chapter 13, the section on socialism.) How are such differences to be settled? Moreover, women historically have not been given equal rights with men. In the United States, for example, they were not all granted the right to vote until 1920 on grounds that they were by nature not fully rational or that they were closer in nature to animals than males! The women of Kuwait only gained the right to vote in 2005. How is it possible that there could be such different views of what are our rights if morality is supposed to be knowable by natural human reason?

A second challenge for a natural rights theory concerns what it must prove to justify its holdings. First, it must show that human nature as it is ought to be furthered and that certain things ought to be granted to us in order to further our nature. These things we then speak of as rights. Basic to this demonstration would be to show why human beings are so valuable that what is essential for their full function can be claimed as a right. For example, do human beings have a value higher than other beings and, if so, why? Is a reference to something beyond this world—a creator God, for example—necessary to give value to humans or is there something about their nature itself that is the reason why they have such a high value? Second, a natural rights theorist has the job of detailing just what things are essential for the good functioning of human nature.

Finally, not all discussions of human rights have been of the sort described here. For example, Norman Daniels claims that the reason why people have a right to basic health care is because of the demands of justice; that is, justice demands that there be equal opportunity to life's goods, and whether people have equal opportunity depends, among other things, on their health.[20] Another example is found in the writings of Walter Lippmann, a political commentator more than half a century ago. He held a rather utilitarian view that we ought to agree that there are certain rights because these provide the basis for a democratic society, and it is the society that works best. It is not that we can prove that such rights as freedom of speech or assembly exist, we simply accept them for pragmatic reasons because they provide the basis for democracy.[21]

The notion of rights can be and has been discussed in many different contexts. Among those treated in this book are issues of animal rights (Chapter 16), economic rights (Chapter 13), fetal and women's rights (Chapter 9), equal rights and discrimination (Chapter 12), and war crimes and universal human rights (Chapter 18).

NOTES

1. Thomas Jefferson, "The Declaration of Independence," in *Basic Writings of Thomas Jefferson,* Philip S. Foner (Ed.) (New York: Wiley, 1944): 551.
2. John Locke, *Two Treatises of Government* (London, 1690), Peter Laslett (Ed.) (Cambridge: Cambridge University Press, 1960).
3. http://en.wikipedia.org/wiki/Guantanamo_Bay_detention_camp.
4. This is the basic idea behind the theory of civil disobedience as outlined and practiced by Henry David Thoreau, Mahatma Gandhi, and Martin Luther King, Jr. When Thoreau was imprisoned for not paying taxes that he thought were used for unjust purposes, he wrote his famous essay, "Civil Disobedience." In it he writes, "Must the citizen ever for a moment, or in the least degree, resign his conscience to the legislator? Why has every man a conscience, then? I think that we should be men first, and subjects afterward. It is not desirable to cultivate a respect for the law, so much as for the right." Henry David Thoreau,
"Civil Disobedience," in *Miscellanies* (Boston: Houghton Mifflin, 1983): 136–137.
5. W. T. Jones, *A History of Western Philosophy: The Classical Mind,* 2nd ed. (New York: Harcourt, Brace, & World, 1969): 214–216.
6. This was asserted by the neo-Platonist Porphyry (ca. A.D. 232). However, others believe that the work got its name because it was edited by Nicomachus. See Alasdair MacIntyre, *After Virtue* (Notre Dame, IN: Notre Dame University Press, 1984): 147.
7. W. T. Jones, op. cit., p. 233.
8. *The Nicomachean Ethics.*
9. Thomas Aquinas, "Summa Theologica," in *Basic Writings of Saint Thomas Aquinas,* Anton Pegis (Ed.) (New York: Random House, 1948).
10. This is obviously an incomplete presentation of the moral philosophy of Thomas Aquinas. We should at least note that he was as much a theologian as a philosopher, if not more so. True and complete happiness, he believed, would be achieved only in knowledge or contemplation of God.
11. Aristotle, *Politics,* Chap. V, VI.
12. Thomas Hobbes, *Leviathan,* Michael Oakeshott (Ed.) (New York: Oxford University Press, 1962).
13. David Hume, *Treatise on Human Nature* (London, 1739–1740).
14. Such a view can be found in Kant's work *The Critique of Judgment.*
15. See Chauncey Wright, "Evolution by Natural Selection," *The North American Review* (July 1872): 6–7.
16. See Roscoe Pound, *Jurisprudence* (St. Paul, MN: West, 1959).
17. Voltaire, *Ouvres,* XXV, 39; XI, 443.
18. Thomas Jefferson, *Declaration of Independence.*
19. On negative or liberty rights see, for example, the work of Robert Nozick, *State, Anarchy and Utopia* (New York: Basic Books, 1974). See further discussion on welfare and liberty rights in Chapter 13, "Economic Justice."
20. Norman Daniels, "Health-Care Needs and Distributive Justice," *Philosophy and Public Affairs, 10, 2* (Spring 1981): 146–179.
21. The term *pragmatic* concerns what "works." Thus, to accept something on pragmatic grounds means to accept it because it works for us in some way. For Walter Lippmann's views, see *Essays in the Public Philosophy* (Boston: Little, Brown, 1955).

REVIEW EXERCISES

1. Give a basic definition of natural law theory.
2. What is the difference between the scientific laws of nature and the natural law?
3. In what way is natural law theory teleological?
4. What specific natural or human species capacities are singled out by natural law theorists? How do these determine what we ought to do, according to the theory?

5. What is the difference between Aristotle and Aquinas on the theistic basis of natural law?
6. Explain one area of concern or criticism of natural law theory.
7. Describe the basis of rights according to natural rights theorists.
8. Give examples of a natural rights tradition.
9. Explain one of the things that a natural rights theorist must show to prove that we can ground rights in human nature.

Selected Bibliography

Natural Law

Ackrill, J. L. *Aristotle's Ethics.* New York: Humanities Press, 1980.

Aquinas, St. Thomas. *Summa Theologica,* I–II, QQ. 90–108.

Aristotle. *The Nicomachean Ethics.* J. E. C. Welldon (Trans.), 1897. New York: Prometheus Books, 1987.

———. *Aristotle's Eudemian Ethics.* Oxford, England: Clarendon, 1982.

Cooper, John M. *Reason and the Human Good in Aristotle.* Cambridge, MA: Harvard University Press, 1975.

Engberg-Pedersen, Troels. *Aristotle's Theory of Moral Insight.* Oxford, England: Clarendon, 1983.

George, Robert P. (Ed.). *Natural Law Theory: Contemporary Essays.* Oxford: Clarendon, 1992.

Haakonssen, Knud. *Natural Law and Moral Philosophy.* New York: Cambridge University Press, 1996.

Kraut, Richard. *Aristotle on the Human Good.* Princeton, NJ: Princeton University Press, 1991.

Nelson, Daniel Mark. *The Priority of Prudence: Virtue and Natural Law in Thomas Aquinas and the Implications for Modern Ethics.* Pittsburgh: Pennsylvania State University Press, 1992.

Rorty, Amelie (Ed.). *Essays on Aristotle's Ethics.* Berkeley: University of California Press, 1980.

Sherman, Nancy (Ed.). *Aristotle's Ethics, Critical Essays.* New York: Rowman and Littlefield, 1999.

Stump, Eleanore. *Aquinas.* New York: Routledge, 2003.

Urmson, J. O. *Aristotle's Ethics.* Oxford, England: Clarendon, 1988.

Williams, B. A. O. "Aristotle on the Good," *Philosophical Quarterly 12* (1962): 289–296.

Natural Rights

Brownlie, Ian (Ed.). *Basic Documents on Human Rights.* Oxford: Clarendon, 1971.

Cicero. *De Republica.* Bk. III, xxii, 33. New York: Putnam's, 1928.

Feinberg, Joel. *Rights, Justice and the Bounds of Liberty.* Princeton, NJ: Princeton University Press, 1980.

Finnis, John. *Natural Law and Natural Rights.* New York: Oxford University Press, 1980.

Hannum, Hurst (Ed.). *Guide to International Human Rights Practice.* Philadelphia: University of Pennsylvania Press, 1984.

Harris, Ian. *The Mind of John Locke.* New York: Cambridge University Press, 1994.

Locke, John. *Second Treatise on Civil Government.* Peter Laslett (Ed.). Cambridge, England: Cambridge University Press, 1960.

Lowe, E. J. *Locke.* New York: Routledge, 2005.

Luytgaarden, Eric van de. *Introduction to the Theory of Human Rights.* Utrecht: Utrecht University, 1993.

Machan, Tibor R. *Individuals and Their Rights.* LaSalle, IL: Open Court, 1989.

Nino, Carlos Santiago. *The Ethics of Human Rights.* New York: Oxford University Press, 1991.

Selby, David. *Human Rights.* New York: Cambridge University Press, 1987.

Shue, Henry. *Basic Rights.* Princeton, NJ: Princeton University Press, 1980.

Simmons, A. John. *The Lockean Theory of Rights.* Princeton, NJ: Princeton University Press, 1994.

Thomson, Judith. *Rights, Restitution and Risk.* William Parent (Ed.). Cambridge, MA: Harvard University Press, 1990.

Wellman, Carl. *Real Rights.* New York: Oxford University Press, 1995.

7

Virtue Ethics

Many of us are familiar with at least some aspects of the biblical story of Abraham. In various versions, it is part of the heritage of three major religions: Christianity, Judaism, and Islam. According to one part of the story, to test Abraham's faith and obedience, God tells him to sacrifice his son, Isaac. Crushed by the order but dedicated to his God, Abraham brings Isaac to Mount Moriah. Just as Abraham is about to plunge his knife into Isaac, God stays his hand. Whatever you think about the story, and whether you think Abraham should have been willing to sacrifice his son, this story may be taken as an example of a person's being able to do something extremely difficult because of certain virtues or strengths he had.

When I have treated the topic of virtue in ethics classes, I have often begun by asking students about people whom they admire. Most often they name mothers, fathers, sisters, or brothers. At other times they name people in the public eye: athletes, inventors, artists. I then try to bring out the reasons, asking about the traits that are the basis for their admiration. The list of traits is instructive. It often includes perseverance, loving nature, generosity, independence, and standing up to others. These are among the traits of character traditionally known as *virtues*.

VIRTUES AND EVERYDAY LIFE

The theories that we have treated so far in this text are concerned with how we determine what is the right thing to do. In this chapter, we will examine a rather different approach to morality. It is focused on virtue or virtues. Rather than help us determine what we ought to *do,* virtue ethics asks how we ought to *be.* It is concerned with those traits of character that make one a good person. We can all think of persons whom we admire, and we can sometimes tell why we admire or look up to them. When we do so, we often say that they are generous, kind, patient, persevering, or loyal, for example. When these traits are unusually well developed, these persons may be regarded as heroes (such as the person who rescued someone on the tracks of the New York subway as described in Chapter 3) or even as saints. People can also exhibit bad character traits. For example, they can be tactless, careless, boorish, stingy, vindictive, disloyal, lazy, or egotistical. An ethics focused on virtue encourages us to develop the good traits and get rid of the bad ones.

The ethical issues that are treated in the second half of this text are generally controversial social issues: the death penalty, abortion, and terrorism, for example. Virtue ethics seems more personal. It involves not so much asking which side of some social issue one should support as what kind of person one wants to be. It is everyday life and how one lives it that matters: How to treat one's relatives, friends, or co-workers; how honest one should be; what is fair in various situations; or what should one teach one's children by both word and example.

In this chapter, we will ask basic questions about what virtue is, whether there are different kinds or classes of virtues, and whether a virtue ethics presents an adequate account of morality.

WHAT IS VIRTUE?

Let us begin by examining the very notion of virtue. Although we probably do not use the term *virtuous* as commonly today as in times past, we still understand the essence of its meaning. A virtuous person is a morally good person, and virtues are good traits. Loyalty is a virtue, and so is honesty. The opposite of virtue is vice. Stinginess is a vice. A moral philosophy that concentrates on the notion of virtue is called a *virtue ethics*. For virtue ethics, the moral life is about developing good *character*. The moral life is about determining what are the ideals for human life and trying to embody these ideals in one's own life. The virtues are then ways in which we embody these ideals. If we consider honesty to be such an ideal, for example, then we ought to try to become honest persons.

As noted in the previous chapter, Aristotle was one of the earliest writers to ground morality in nature, and specifically human nature. His ethics or moral theory also stressed the notion of virtue. For Aristotle, virtue was an excellence of some sort. Our word *virtue* originally came from the Latin *vir* and referred to strength or manliness.[1] In Aristotle's ethics, the term used for what we translate as virtue was *arete*. It referred to excellences of various types.

According to Aristotle, there are two basic types of excellence or virtues: intellectual virtues and moral virtues. Intellectual virtues are excellences of mind, such as the ability to understand and reason and judge well. Aristotle said that these traits are learned from teachers. Moral virtues, on the other hand, dispose us to act well. These virtues are learned not by being taught but by repetition. For instance, by practicing courage or honesty, we become more courageous and honest. Just as repetition in playing a musical instrument makes playing easier, so also repeated acts of

honesty make it easier to be honest. The person who has the virtue of honesty finds it easier to be honest than the person who does not have the virtue. It has become habitual or second nature to him or her. The same thing applies to the opposite of virtue—namely, vice. The person who lies and lies again finds that lying is easier and telling the truth more difficult. One can have bad moral habits (vices) as well as good ones (virtues). Just like other bad habits, bad moral habits are difficult to change or break. Aristotle's list of virtues includes courage, temperance, justice, pride, and magnanimity.

However, Aristotle is probably most well known for his position that virtue is a mean between extremes. Thus, the virtue of courage is to be understood as a mean or middle between the two extremes of deficiency and excess. Too little courage is cowardice, and too much is foolhardiness. We should have neither too much fear when facing danger or challenges, which makes us unable to act; nor too little fear, which makes us throw all caution to the wind, as we say. Courage is having just the right amount of fear, depending on what is appropriate for us as individuals and for the circumstances we face. So, also, the other virtues are means between extremes. Consider the examples from Aristotle's list on the following page, and see if you could add any.

Our own list today might be both similar to and differ from this. For example, we might include loyalty and honesty in our list. If loyalty is a virtue, then is it also a middle between two extremes? Can there be such a thing as too little or too much loyalty? What about honesty? Too much honesty might be seen as undisciplined openness, and too little as deceitfulness. Would the right amount of honesty be forthrightness? Not all virtues may be rightly thought of as means between extremes. We could exemplify Aristotle's view of virtue as a mean with the childhood story of Goldilocks. When she entered the bears' house, she ate the porridge that was not too hot and not too cold, but "just right"![2] For example, if justice is a virtue, then could there be such a thing as being too just or too little just?

	Deficit (Too Little)	Virtue (the Mean)	Excess (Too Much)
Fear	Cowardice	Courage	Foolhardiness
Giving	Illiberality	Liberality	Prodigality
Self-Regard	Humility	Pride	Vanity
Pleasures	[No Name Given]	Temperance	Profligacy

Various contemporary moral philosophers have also stressed the importance of virtue.[3] Philippa Foot, for example, has developed a type of neonaturalistic virtue ethics. She believes that the virtues are "in some general way, beneficial. Human beings do not get on well without them."[4] According to Foot, it is both ourselves and our community that benefit from our having certain virtues, just as having certain vices harms both ourselves and our communities. Think of courage, temperance, and wisdom, for example, and ask yourself how persons having these virtues might benefit others as well as themselves. Some virtues such as charity, however, seem to benefit mostly others. She also wonders how we should determine which beneficial traits are to be thought of as moral virtues and which are not. Wit or powers of concentration benefit us, but we would probably not consider them to be *moral* virtues. Foot also asks whether the virtue is in the intention or the action. Think of generosity. Does the person who intends to be generous but cannot seem to do what helps others really possess the virtue of generosity? Or rather is it the person who actually does help who has the virtue? She believes that possessing the virtue of generosity must be more than simply having a naturally outgoing personality. It is something we choose to develop and work at. Furthermore, following Aristotle, Foot also agrees that the virtues are corrective.[5] They help us be and do things that are difficult for us. Courage, for example, helps us overcome natural fear. Temperance helps us control our desires. People differ in their natural inclinations and thus would also differ in what virtues would be most helpful for them to develop. This is just one example of how the notion of virtue continues to be discussed by moral philosophers.

MASCULINE AND FEMININE VIRTUES

Not long ago, a moral question about the following hypothetical situation was posed to two eleven-year-old children, Jake and Amy.[6] A man's wife was extremely ill and in danger of dying. A certain drug might save her life, but the man could not afford it, in part because the druggist had set an unreasonably high price for it. The question was whether the man should steal the drug. Jake answered by trying to figure out the relative value of the woman's life and the druggist's right to his property. He concluded that the man should steal the drug because he calculated that the woman's life was worth more. Amy was not so sure. She wondered what would happen to both the man and his wife if he stole the drug. "If he stole the drug, he might save his wife then, but if he did, he might have to go to jail, and then his wife might get sicker again." She said that if the husband and wife talked about this they might be able to think of some other way out of the dilemma.

One interesting thing about this case is the very different ways in which the two children tried to determine the right thing to do in this situation. The boy used a rational calculation in which he weighed and compared values from a neutral standpoint. The girl spoke about the possible effects of the proposed action on the two individuals and their relationship. Her method did not give the kind of definitive answer apparent in the boy's method. Perhaps the difference in their moral reasoning was the result of their sex or their gender.[7]

Another example also seems to show a gender difference in moral reasoning. In explaining how they would respond to a moral dilemma about maintaining one's moral principles in the light of peer or family pressure, two teens responded quite differently. The case was one in which the religious views of the teens differed from their parents. The male said that he had a right to his own opinions, although he respected his parents' views. The female said that she was concerned about how her parents would react to her views. "I understand their fear of my new religious ideas." However, she added, "they really ought to listen to me and try to understand my beliefs."[8] Although their conclusions were similar, their reasoning was not. They seemed to have two decidedly different orientations or perspectives. The male spoke in terms of an individual's right to his own opinions, while the female talked of the need for the particular people involved to talk and to come to understand one another. These two cases raise questions about whether a gender difference actually exists in the way people reason about moral matters.

Debate about sex or gender differences in moral perspectives and moral reasoning has been sparked by the work of psychologist Carol Gilligan.[9] She interviewed both male and female subjects about various moral dilemmas and found that the women she interviewed had a different view than the men of what was morally required of them. They used a different moral language to explain themselves, and their reasoning involved a different moral logic. They talked in terms of hurting and benefiting others, and they reasoned that they ought to do that which helped the people involved in a particular case at hand. She concluded that males and females had different kinds of ethics. Since then, other philosophers have noted a variety of qualities that characterize male and female ethics. The debate that has followed has focused on whether there is a specifically feminine morality— that is, an ethics of caring or care. First, we will examine the supposed characteristics of feminine morality. Then we will summarize various explanations that have been given for it. Finally, we will suggest some things to consider in evaluating the theory that a feminine ethics of care does indeed exist.

Several contrasting pairs of terms are associated with or can be used to describe the two types of ethical perspective. These are listed in the table.

The various characteristics or notions in this list may need explanation. First, consider the supposed typical *female moral perspective.* The context for women's moral decision making is said to be one of *relatedness.* Women think about particular people and their relations and how they will be affected by some action. Women's morality is highly personal. They are partial to their particular loved ones and think that one's moral responsibility is first of all to these persons. It is the private and personal natural relations of family and friends that are the model for other relations. Women stress the concrete experiences of this or that event and are concerned about the real harm that might befall a particular person or persons. The primary moral obligation is to prevent harm and to help people. Women are able to empathize with others and are concerned about how they might feel if certain things were to happen to them. They believe that moral problems can be solved by talking about them and by trying to understand the perspectives of others. Caring and compassion are key virtues. The primary moral obligation is not to turn away from those in need. Nel Noddings's work *Caring: A Feminine Approach to Ethics and Moral Education* provides a good example and further description of the ethics of care.[10]

The supposed typical *male moral perspective* contrasts with a feminine ethics of care. Supposedly, men take more universal and more impartial standpoints in reasoning about what is morally good and bad. Men are more inclined to talk in terms of fairness and justice and rights. They ask about the

Female Ethical Perspective	Male Ethical Perspective
Personal	Impersonal
Partial	Impartial
Private	Public
Natural	Contractual
Feeling	Reason
Compassionate	Fair
Concrete	Universal
Responsibility	Rights
Relationship	Individual
Solidarity	Autonomy

overall effects of some action and whether the good effects, when all are considered, outweigh the bad. It is as though they think moral decisions ought to be made impersonally or from some unbiased and detached point of view. The moral realm would then in many ways be similar to the public domain of law and contract. The law must not be biased and must treat everyone equally. Moral thinking, in this view, involves a type of universalism, recognizing the equal moral worth of all as persons both in themselves and before the law. People ought to keep their promises because this is the just thing to do and helps create a reliable social order. Morality is a matter of doing one's duty, of keeping one's agreements, and respecting another person's rights. Impartiality and respectfulness are key virtues. The primary obligation is not to act unfairly.

If there are these two very different moral perspectives, there may also be said to be two different types of virtues paralleling them. One would be those habits or ways of being that involve caring and orientation to the particular. The other would be those habits or ways of being that involve concern for rights and justice and equal treatment of all. But whether these virtues come in groups and whether they are particularly associated with females and males are further questions. It may well be that the most human of persons exhibit traits from both sets. If these virtues are described in a positive way—say, caring and not subservience—then would they not be traits that all should strive to possess? These traits might be simply different aspects of the human personality rather than the male or female personality. They would then be human virtues and human perspectives rather than male or female virtues and perspectives. In this view, an ethics of fidelity and care and sympathy would be just as important for human flourishing as an ethics of duty and justice and acting on principle. Although there would be certain moral virtues that all persons should develop, other psychological traits could also vary according to temperament and choice. Individuals would be free to choose to manifest, according to their own personality, any combination of characteristics. Manifestation of some of each set of characteristics and virtues

would make one androgynous (from the term *androgyny*); in other words, one manifests both stereotypical masculine and stereotypical feminine traits.[11]

EVALUATING VIRTUE ETHICS

One question that has been raised for virtue ethics concerns how we determine which traits are virtues. Are there any universally valuable traits, for example? Wherever friendship exists, loyalty would seem necessary, although the form it might take would vary according to time and place. So also would honesty seem necessary for human relations wherever they exist. We might think that Aristotle's own list of virtues reflected what were considered civic virtues of his day. Our lists today might more reflect aspects of our own times. Contemporary moral philosopher Alasdair MacIntyre believes that virtues depend at least partly on the practices that constitute a culture or society. A warlike society will value heroic virtues, whereas a peaceful and prosperous society might think of generosity as a particularly important virtue.[12] However, these must be virtues specific to human beings as humans, for otherwise one could not speak of "human excellences." But this is just the problem. What is it to live a full human life? Can one specify this apart from what it is to live such a life in a particular society or as a particular person? This problem is related to the issue regarding stereotypical masculine and feminine virtues noted above. The problem here is not only how we know what excellences are human excellences but also whether there are any such traits that are ideal for all persons.

Another problem about virtue is raised by Philippa Foot. Who manifests the virtue of courage most—the person "who wants to run away but does not or the one who does not even want to run away"? One reason why this question is difficult to answer is that we generally believe that we ought to be rewarded for our moral efforts and thus the person who wants to run away but does not seems the more courageous. On the other hand, if one has the virtue of courage, it is supposed to make it easier to be brave. Part of her own answer to this dilemma has to do with the distinction between those fears for which we are in some way responsible and those that we cannot help. Thus, the person who feels like running away because he or she has contributed by their choices to being fearsome is not the more virtuous person.

We can also ask whether virtue ethics is really a distinct type of ethics. Consider the other theories we have treated: utilitarianism and Kantianism. The concept of virtue is not foreign to Mill or Kant. However, for both of them it is secondary. Their moral theories tell us how we ought to decide what to *do*. Doing the right thing—and with Kant, for the right reason—is primary. However, if the development of certain habits of action or tendencies to act in a certain way will enable us to do good more easily, then they would surely be recognized by these philosophers as good. Utilitarians would encourage the development of those virtues that would be conducive to the maximization of happiness. If temperance in eating and drinking will help us avoid the suffering that can come from illness and drunkenness, then this virtue ought to be encouraged and developed in the young. So also with other virtues. According to a Kantian, it would be well to develop in ourselves and others habits that would make it more likely that we would be fair and treat people as ends rather than simply as means.

In virtue ethics, however, the primary goal is to be a good person. Now, some people argue that *being* good is only a function of being more inclined to *do* good. For every virtue, there is a corresponding good to be achieved or done. The just person acts justly and does what increases justice, for example. Is virtue then simply one aspect of these otherwise action-oriented moral philosophies? Perhaps so. However, virtue ethics still has a different emphasis. It is an ethics whose goal is to determine what is essential to be a well-functioning or flourishing human being or person. It stresses the ideal for humans or persons. As an ethics of ideals or excellences, it is an optimistic and positive type of ethics. One problem that it may face is what to say about those of us who do not meet the ideal. If we fall short of the ideal, does

this make us bad? As with all moral theories, many questions concerning virtue remain to engage and puzzle us.

NOTES

1. Milton Gonsalves, *Fagothy's Right and Reason*, 9th ed. (Columbus, OH: Merrill, 1989): 201.
2. I thank reviewer Robert P. Tucker of Florida Southern College for this example.
3. See, for example, the collection of articles in Christina Hoff Sommers, *Vice and Virtue in Everyday Life* (New York: Harcourt Brace Jovanovich, 1985).
4. Philippa Foot, *Virtues and Vices* (Oxford, England: Oxford University Press, 2002).
5. Ibid.
6. This is a summary of a question that was posed by researchers for Lawrence Kohlberg. In Carol Gilligan, *In a Different Voice* (Cambridge, MA: Harvard University Press, 1982): 28, 173.
7. We use the term *sex* to refer to the biological male or female. The term *gender* includes psychological feminine and masculine traits as well as social roles that are assigned to the two sexes.
8. From Carol Gilligan, "Moral Orientation and Moral Development," in *Women and Moral Theory*, Eva Kittay and Diana Meyers (Eds.) (Totowa, NJ: Rowman & Littlefield, 1987): 23.
9. Ibid. Also see Gilligan, "Concepts of the Self and of Morality," *Harvard Educational Review* (Nov. 1977): 481–517.
10. Nel Noddings, *Caring: A Feminine Approach to Ethics and Moral Education* (Berkeley: University of California Press, 1984).
11. See Joyce Treblicot, "Two Forms of Androgynism," *Journal of Social Philosophy VIII*, no. 1 (Jan. 1977): 4–8.
12. Alasdair MacIntyre, "The Virtue in Heroic Societies" and "The Virtues at Athens," in *After Virtue* (Notre Dame, IN: Notre Dame University Press, 1984), 121–145.

REVIEW EXERCISES

1. What is the basic difference between a virtue ethics and other types of ethics we have studied?
2. According to Aristotle, what is the difference between intellectual and moral virtues?

3. In what sense are virtues habits?
4. Give a list of some traits that have been thought to be virtues, according to Aristotle and other virtue theorists.
5. According to Aristotle, how is virtue a mean between extremes? Give some examples.
6. How do the two examples given of male and female reasoning exemplify the various supposed characteristics of female and male ethical perspectives?
7. Contrast stereotypical feminine and masculine virtues.
8. What is androgyny?
9. Explain the problem of whether virtues are human perfections or excellences or socially valuable traits.
10. Explain the problem raised by Philippa Foot as to who most exemplifies the virtue of, say, courage: the person who finds it difficult to be courageous or easy.

Selected Bibliography

Allard-Nelson, Susan K. *An Aristotelian Approach to Ethical Theory—The Norms of Virtue.* Lewiston, NY: Edwin Mellen Press, 2004.

Aquinas, St. Thomas. *Treatise on the Virtues.* John A. Oesterle (Trans.). Notre Dame, IN: Notre Dame University Press, 1984.

Baron, Marcia. "Varieties of Ethics of Virtue," *American Philosophical Quarterly* 22 (1985): 47–53.

Bishop, Sharon, and Marjorie Weinzweig. *Philosophy and Women.* Belmont, CA: Wadsworth, 1993.

Card, Claudia (Ed.). *Feminist Ethics.* Lawrence: University of Kansas Press, 1991.

Crisp, Roger (Ed.) *Virtue Ethics.* New York: Oxford University Press, 1997.

Darwall, Stephen L. (Ed.). *Virtue Ethics.* Malden, MA: Blackwell Publishers, 2002.

Foot, Philippa. *Virtues and Vices.* London: Blackwell, 1978.

Geach, Peter. *The Virtues.* Cambridge: Cambridge University Press, 1977.

Hardie, W. F. R. *Aristotle's Ethical Theory.* Oxford, England: Clarendon, 1968.

hooks, bell. *Feminist Theory: From Margin to Center.* Boston: South End, 1984.

Hursthouse, Rosalind. *On Virtue Ethics.* New York: Oxford University Press, 2002.

Kruschwitz, Robert B., and Robert C. Roberts (Eds.). *The Virtues: Contemporary Ethics and Moral Character.* Belmont, CA: Wadsworth, 1987.

Machan, Tibor R. *Generosity: Virtue in the Civil Society.* Washington, DC: Cato Institute, 1998.

MacIntyre, Alasdair. *After Virtue.* Notre Dame, IN: Notre Dame University Press, 1981.

Mahowald, Mary B. *Connected Lives: Human Nature and an Ethics of Care.* New York: Rowman & Littlefield, 2004.

Noddings, Nel. *Caring: A Feminine Approach to Ethics and Moral Education.* Berkeley: University of California Press, 1984.

Sherman, Nancy (Ed.). *Aristotle's Ethics: Critical Essays.* New York: Rowman & Littlefield, 1999.

———. *The Fabric of Character: Aristotle's Theory of Virtue.* Oxford, England: Clarendon, 1989.

———. *Making a Necessity of Virtue: Aristotle and Kant on Virtue.* New York: Cambridge University Press, 1997.

Slote, Michael. *Goods and Virtues.* Oxford, England: Clarendon, 1983.

———. *From Morality to Virtue.* New York: Oxford University Press, 1992.

Statman, Daniel. *Virtue Ethics: A Critical Reader.* Washington, DC: Georgetown University Press, 1997.

Swanton, Christine. *Virtue Ethics: A Pluralistic View.* New York: Oxford University Press, 2003.

Taylor, Richard. *Virtue Ethics: An Introduction.* Amherst, NY: Prometheus Books, 2001.

Tessitore, Aristide. *Reading Aristotle's Ethics: Virtue, Rhetoric, and Political Philosophy.* Albany: State University of New York Press, 1996.

Uehling, Theodore, Jr., Peter French, and Howard K. Wettstein (Eds.). *Ethical Theory, Character and Virtue.* South Bend, IN: University of Notre Dame Press, 1988.

Wallace, James. *Virtues and Vices.* Ithaca, NY: Cornell University Press, 1978.

Part Two

Ethical Issues

8

Euthanasia

On June 8, 2002, Carol Carr entered the nursing home room where her two sons, forty-two-year-old Michael and forty-one-year-old Andy, lay in bed. She took out a handgun and shot both of them in the head and killed them. Afterward, she went into the waiting room of the Sunbridge Care and Rehabilitation Center and waited for the police. When they arrived, she said "I did it, I shot them, . . . I want you to kill me."[1] Both sons had Huntington's disease. The boy's father had the disease and died from it in 1995. Her sons were both in its later stages. They needed total care and could no longer communicate. Carol had dedicated herself to their care until she could no longer manage to do so and placed them in the nursing home.

Huntington's disease is a genetic disorder that is passed from parent to child. It is named after doctor George Huntington, who in 1972 wrote a paper describing the disease. It is sometimes called Huntington's *chorea,* the latter term coming from a Greek term meaning "dancelike" for the involuntary movements that are among the disease's symptoms. If one parent has the disease, a child has a 50:50 chance of having the gene for the disease and eventually developing it. The disease usually does not begin to be symptomatic until the person is between thirty and fifty years old. It becomes progressively worse until it ends in death usually twenty or so years later. The disease affects cognitive abilities and causes confusion and memory loss. It also causes emotional and behavioral characteristics such as depression, mood swings, and anxiety as well as motor problems that lead to difficulties in coordination and involuntary movements. Eventually, the person is unable to communicate and dies from choking, infection, or pneumonia. There is no cure for the disease, although some symptoms may now be alleviated with medication. The gene that causes the disease was discovered in 1993, and research is now proceeding to determine if a cure can be found. People who have a family history of the disease may or may not want to get the genetic test to see if they have the gene.[2]

Carol Carr faced charges of felony murder. However, a plea bargain was reached, and she agreed to plead guilty to charges of assisted suicide. She was given a five-year sentence. She was released in 2004 after serving approximately one-third of her sentence.

In another case, this time in Italy, anesthesiologist Mario Ricci administered a sedative to Piergiogio Welby and disconnected his respirator on which Welby had depended for many years because of his advanced case of muscular dystrophy. *Muscular dystrophy* is the name given to a group of genetic diseases that involves "progressive weakness and degeneration of the skeletal or voluntary muscles which control movement." There is no cure, but physical therapy can be of help in some cases. Some persons live long lives, while others die at a younger age.[3] Mr. Welby had a serious case of the disease and had been bedridden for some time. He himself had requested that the doctor allow him to die. Italian law did not permit someone to assist a suicide, and thus Dr. Ricci was prosecuted after he acted on Mr. Welby's request. However, these charges were later dropped after a committee of doctors reviewed the case and agreed that he should not be prosecuted.[4]

Cases such as these can be heartrending. Cases of conflict about right-to-die decisions within families are especially difficult and all too common. In one case, a family had to decide whether a woman who was in a coma but needed the amputation of almost all of her hands and feet should undergo that surgery. Some family members insisted she would not want to live like that. Doctors even disagreed on the extent of the amputation needed and even her chances of survival. In this case, her prognosis worsened, the physicians did not do the surgery, and she died.[5] In another case, the family of a man who suffered severe brain damage from an auto accident had to decide whether to remove him from life support. He had no written instructions but was reported to have said, "If I can't fish, I want to die." In this case, time changed things as he regained some mental function.[6] Sometimes, family and physician disagreements can be resolved by a mediation process similar to those used in business and divorce.[7]

Euthanasia has been a controversial topic for decades. It involves issues of patient rights, life and death, the proper function of doctors, the ethics of suicide, and the overlap between law and morality. This chapter will address each of these issues. However, we begin with an issue that sometimes confuses discussions of euthanasia—namely, the issue of brain death.

BRAIN DEATH, COMA, AND PERSISTENT VEGETATIVE STATE

Years ago, an article in *The New York Times* reported on the case of a judge who was presiding over a disputed medical situation. The dispute concerned whether a woman's respirator could be disconnected. The judge was reported to have said, "This lady is dead, and has been dead, and they are keeping her alive artificially."[8] Did the judge believe that the woman was alive or dead?

She could not be both. He said that she was dead but also that she was being kept alive by machines. If the woman was really dead, then machines may have been keeping some of her body functions going but could not have been keeping her alive. Perhaps the judge meant that, given her condition, she should be allowed to die. If so, then he should not have said she was dead. I note this item to make the point that people, even judges, confuse questions about whether someone is dead or ought to be considered dead with other questions about whether it is permissible to do things that might hasten death.

It is important to distinguish these two questions. Not doing so has practical consequences. For example, the judge's comment seems to imply that the only reason why the woman's respirator or other machine could be disconnected was because she was dead. However, we need not believe an individual to be dead in order to think it justifiable to disconnect her from a respirator and let her die. In fact, only if someone is not dead can we then sensibly ask whether we may let him die. It seems useful here to think briefly about *how* we do determine whether someone is dead so as to distinguish this issue from other questions that are properly euthanasia questions. Similar confusion and questions exist today.

Throughout history, people have used various means to determine whether someone is dead, and those means were a function of what they believed to be essential aspects of life. For example, if spirit was thought of as essential and was equated with a kind of thin air or breath, then the presence or absence of this life breath would indicate whether a person was living. When heart function was regarded as the key element of life, and the heart was thought to be like a furnace, then people would feel the body to see if it was warm in order to know whether the person was still living. Even today, with our better understanding of the function of the heart, other organs, and organ systems, we have great difficulty with this issue. One reason for this is that we now can use various machines to perform certain body functions such as respiration (oxygenation of the blood) and blood circulation. Sometimes, this is a temporary measure such as during a surgery. However, in other cases, the person may have lost significant brain function. In this latter sort of case, it is important to know whether the person is to be considered alive or dead.

Being able to give precise conditions and tests for determining whether or when an individual is dead was particularly problematic just three decades ago. It was problematic not only because of the arrival of new medical technologies, but also because surgeons had just begun doing human heart transplants. One could not take a heart for transplant from someone who was considered living, only from someone who had been declared dead. Was an individual whose heart function was being artificially maintained but who had no brain function considered living or dead? We still wonder about this today. In one odd case, a man accused of murder pleaded guilty to a lesser charge of assault and battery, claiming that even though the victim had lost all brain function his heart was still beating after the assault. The defendant argued that it was the doctor at Stanford Medical Center who removed the heart for transplant who had killed this individual![9]

In 1968, an ad hoc committee of the Harvard Medical School was set up to establish criteria for determining when someone is dead. This committee determined that someone should be considered dead if she or he has permanently lost all detectable brain function. This meant that if there was some nonconscious brain function, for example, or if the condition was temporary, then the individual would not be considered dead. Thus, various tests of reflexes and responsiveness were required to determine whether an individual had sustained a permanent and total loss of all brain function.[10] This condition is now known as *whole brain death* and is the primary criterion used for the legal determination of death. This is true even when other secondary criteria or tests such as loss of pulse are used, for it is assumed that lack of blood circulation for more than five to ten minutes results in brain cell death.

Whole brain death is distinguished from other conditions such as *persistent vegetative state (PVS)*. In PVS, the individual has lost all cerebral cortex

function but has retained some good brain stem function. Many nonconscious functions that are based in that area of the brain—respiratory and heart rate, facial reflexes and muscle control, and gag reflex and swallowing abilities—continue. Yet the individual in a permanent or persistent vegetative state has lost all conscious function. One reason for this condition is that the rate of oxygen use by the cerebral cortex is much higher than that of the brain stem, so these cells die much more quickly if deprived of oxygen for some time. The result is that the individual in this state will never regain consciousness but can often breathe naturally and needs no artificial aid to maintain circulation. Such an individual does not feel pain because he or she cannot interpret it as such. Because the gag reflex is good, individuals in this condition can clear their airways and thus may live for many years. They go through wake and sleep cycles in which they have their eyes open and then closed. This was the case with Terri Schiavo, who became such a contentious political issue in 2005. She was a twenty-six-year-old woman who simply collapsed one morning. Her husband called 911, and the emergency personnel who arrived shortly resuscitated her. However, her brain had been deprived of oxygen for some time and she remained in a coma for the next fifteen years. She was in a persistent vegetative state as described here. At that point, her husband wanted to remove her from the feeding tube on which she depended, but her parents objected. Her husband prevailed in court, her feeding tube was removed, and she died. An autopsy later revealed that her brain had shrunk to half its normal size and thus she had not been conscious or aware. To some people, she seemed to follow their motions and to respond to their voices. However, we know from her autopsy as well as earlier brain scans that she had no conscious function and that these were autonomic or reflexive responses. Nevertheless, this is a disconcerting aspect of PVS. Patients in this state are unconscious but "awake." In contrast, someone who is not totally brain dead but who is in a coma is unconscious but "asleep." His or her brain stem functions poorly, and thus this person does not live as long as someone in a persistent vegetative state.[11] If we use whole brain death criteria to determine whether someone is dead, then neither a person in a persistent vegetative state nor a person in a coma is dead. In these cases, euthanasia questions about whether to let them die can be raised. On the other hand, if someone is dead by whole brain death criteria, then disconnecting equipment is not any form of euthanasia. We cannot let someone die who is already dead.

MEANING AND TYPES OF EUTHANASIA

The term *euthanasia* has Greek roots and literally means "good death." Although the term itself implies that there can be a good death, in itself it does not tell us when or under what conditions death is good. Is a good death one that comes suddenly or after some time to think about and prepare for it? Is it one that takes place at home and in familiar surroundings or one that occurs in a medical facility? Is it one that we know is coming and over which we have control or one that comes on us without notice? We usually think of life as a good, so the more of it the better. But we also know that in some conditions life is difficult and that some people have judged it too painful to continue.

Active and Passive Euthanasia

If you were approached by a pollster who asked whether you supported euthanasia, you would do well first to ask what she meant and to what kind of euthanasia she was referring. It is important to distinguish what is called *passive euthanasia* from what is labeled *active euthanasia.*

Passive euthanasia refers to withholding or withdrawing certain treatment and letting a patient die. It is now a common practice and is not prohibited by law. In recent years, many doctors, as many as 96 percent, have withdrawn or withheld life-prolonging treatment for their patients. Most of the time this is done at the request of the patient or the patient's family. However, in some cases, doctors have done this unilaterally either without consulting patients or their families or even against their wishes.[12] The reasons given in either case were generally that such treatment would not extend the patient's life for long or that the patient's life would not be worth lengthening

such as when they were not expected to regain consciousness.

The landmark cases of Karen Quinlan in 1975 and Nancy Cruzan in 1990 brought this type of practice to public attention.[13] In Ms. Quinlan's case, the issue was whether a respirator that was keeping her alive could be disconnected. For some still unknown reason (some say it was a combination of barbiturates and alcohol), she had gone into a coma. When doctors assured them that she would not recover, her parents sought permission to retain legal guardianship (since by then she was twenty-one years old) and have her respirator disconnected. After several court hearings and final approval by the supreme court of the state of New Jersey, the Quinlans were finally permitted to disconnect her respirator. Although they expected she would die shortly after her respirator was removed, she continued to live in this comatose state for ten more years. One basic reason given by this court for its opinion in this case was that Karen did not lose her right of privacy by becoming incompetent and that she could thus refuse unwanted and useless interventions by others to keep her alive. None of the various state interests or social concerns that might override this right were found to be relevant in her case.

Nancy Cruzan was twenty-five years old at the time of her accident in 1983. It left her in a permanent vegetative state until her death eight years later. In her case, the issue brought to the courts was whether a feeding tube that was providing her with food and water could be withdrawn. This case eventually reached the U.S. Supreme Court, which ruled that such lifesaving procedures could be withdrawn or withheld, but only if there was "clear and convincing evidence" that Nancy would have wanted that herself. Eventually, such evidence was brought forward. By that time, those who were protesting her case had withdrawn, and her feeding tube was removed and she was allowed to die.

Active euthanasia is using certain death-causing means to bring about or cause the death of a person. In the past, it used to be called "mercy killing." Drugs are the most common means. Rather than letting a person die, these means are used actually to kill the person. This is generally regarded as much more problematic and is generally legally prohibited.

On November 28, 2000, the lower house of the Dutch parliament approved the legalization of (active) euthanasia by a vote of 104 to 40; the upper house followed on April 10, 2001, by a vote of 46 to 28.[14] The process involved injecting "a sedative and a muscle relaxant."[15] For decades, the country had informally accepted the practice, and since 1993 rules have allowed doctors to carry out the procedure without fear of prosecution. The Netherlands has had a historical tradition of tolerance going back centuries, as evidenced by its provision of refuge for Jews, Catholics, and such controversial philosophers as Descartes and Spinoza.[16] The new law allowed physicians to medically end a patient's life if the following conditions were met:

1. The patient's request must be voluntary and clearly understood and repeatedly voiced.
2. The patient must be faced with unbearable and continuing suffering (although he or she need not be terminally ill, and the suffering need not be physical or physical only).
3. The patient must believe that no reasonable alternative is acceptable.
4. The doctor must consult with at least one other independent physician who also has examined the patient.
5. Physicians and not others must provide medically acceptable means to bring about the patient's death.
6. Children ages 12 to 16 who request it must also have parental consent, although not from age 16 onward.
7. Physicians were not to suggest this possibility to patients.
8. Euthanasia cases must be officially reported to authorities.[17]

It is difficult to get reliable statistics on how this practice has proceeded over the years when these guidelines were accepted but did not have the full force of law. However, it seems that not all of them have been fully complied with. For example, in 25 percent of the cases reported by physicians, not *current* suffering but fear of *future* suffering was the reason given for the requests.[18] The Dutch courts have said that if means to relieve suffering are available, even though the patient refuses them, this is not grounds for euthanasia; in 17 percent of cases, it was administered anyway. There have been difficulties in getting physicians to consult with other physicians who are independent and who actually will come to see the patient. In 2001, approximately 54 percent of euthanasia and assisted suicide deaths were not reported to the coroner as required by the guidelines; however, by 2005 the number of reported cases had risen to 80 percent.[19]

Approximately 8,400 people there each year ask for either euthanasia or physician-assisted suicide. Out of this number, there were approximately 2,300 actual cases of euthanasia and 100 of physician-assisted suicide. "In 2005, 1.7 percent of all deaths in the Netherlands were the result of euthanasia and 0.1 percent were the result of physician-assisted suicide." This is down from 2.6 percent and 0.2 percent, respectively, in 2001. The decrease is thought to result from changing demographics and better pain control.[20]

It is difficult to know whether there are still cases of involuntary euthanasia—that is, doctors actively killing their patients without the patients' knowledge or consent. In 1990, a reported 1,040 people (an average of three per day) died from involuntary euthanasia. A 1997 study published in the British medical journal *The Lancet* reported that some 8 percent of all infants who die in the Netherlands are euthanized—approximately eighty per year.[21] In Holland, it is also the case that health care is a universal right, whereas it is not in the United States. This may also be problematic in the United States in cases where physicians with HMOs are given bonuses for keeping costs down. Thus, in Holland, there is less reason for people to request euthanasia because they do not have access to adequate health care. Another interesting fact is that the suicide rate in Holland has decreased since euthanasia has been available. Among people older than fifty, the numbers of suicide in the last two decades fell by one-third.

In October 2001, the Belgian senate voted by a ratio of 2 to 1 to allow doctors to provide assistance in dying to patients who request it. This law became effective on January 1, 2002. It differs somewhat from the Dutch law by allowing advance directives (see the later discussion of this) and by promoting "the development of palliative care."[22] The Australian government had passed a similar measure but withdrew it when it was thought too open to abuse. With its own past history of Nazis gassing some 100,000 people who were deemed physically or mentally handicapped, Germany has criticized the Dutch approval as the dangerous breaching of a dike.[23] Still, 80 percent of Dutch citizens support the law as the best way to allow people to control their own lives.

Other arguments for and against euthanasia follow. It is sufficient here to give this as an example of what is called *active euthanasia,* which is distinguishable from *passive euthanasia.* These two ways of facing death may then be judged separately.

Passive euthanasia: Stopping (or not starting) some treatment, which allows the person to die. The person's condition causes his or her death.

Active euthanasia: Doing something such as administering a lethal drug or using other means that cause the person's death.

Physician-Assisted Suicide

Every year, some 30,000 people commit suicide in the United States, approximately 1.2 percent of all deaths. It is estimated that there are twenty-five nonfatal attempts for every actual suicide.[24] For every woman who completes a suicide attempt, four men do. Fifty-seven percent of suicides are by firearm; "suicide rates were increased four to ten times in adolescents if there was a gun in their household."[25] In the United States, every two hours or so one young person between ages fifteen and twenty-four commits suicide. Suicide is the second leading cause of death for college students after accidents. "A 1999 survey reported that 20 percent of high school students seriously contemplated suicide during the previous year."[26] On the other hand, the elderly attempt suicide less often than younger people but they succeed more often.

This issue is related to that of euthanasia because one form—physician-assisted suicide—is a form of suicide. In these cases, the physician does not actually inject a patient with a death-causing drug as in active euthanasia, but rather provides patients with drugs that they will take themselves. It is thus basically a form of suicide, with the doctor providing the means to carry it out. Just as questions can be raised about whether suicide is ever morally acceptable, so also can questions be raised about whether it is morally permissible for physicians (or others for that matter) to help someone commit suicide. What is also different about doctor-assisted suicide is that it involves doctors. It thus jumps the barrier that prevents doctors from actually doing something that will cause the death of a person. In some ways, it looks like active euthanasia. In passive euthanasia, the doctor refrains from trying to do what saves or prolongs life, but in active euthanasia the doctor acts to bring about the death by some cause or means. However, the causation by the doctor here is not immediate or direct, but takes place through the action of the patient.

What moral difference there might or might not be between these forms of euthanasia we will consider later in this chapter. It is interesting here, however, to recount a little of the recent history of the practice of physician-assisted suicide. The most well-known advocate and practitioner has been retired pathologist Jack Kevorkian. His activities in assisting suicides have been much publicized. For several years, he helped people who went to him to die by providing them with the means to kill themselves. His first method was a "suicide machine" that consisted of a metal pole to which bottles of three solutions were attached. First, a simple saline solution flowed through an intravenous needle that had been inserted into the person's vein. The patient then flipped a switch that started a flow of an anesthetic, thiopental, that caused the person to become unconscious. After sixty seconds, a solution of potassium chloride followed, causing death within minutes by heart seizure. In a later version of the machine, carbon monoxide was used. When a person pushed a control switch, carbon monoxide flowed through a tube to a bag placed over his or her head.[27] For eight years from 1990, he assisted more than 100 suicides (he claimed the number was 130), almost all of them in Michigan. To prevent these incidents from taking place in their state, Michigan legislators passed a law in 1993 against assisting a suicide. However, the law was struck down in the courts. Kevorkian was brought to trial in three separate cases, but the juries found him not guilty in each case. However, in November 1998, he himself administered a lethal injection to a fifty-two-year-old man who was suffering from Lou Gehrig's disease. He also provided the news media with a videotape of the injection and death. It was aired on CBS's *60 Minutes* on November 22, 1998. This was no longer a case of suicide and, after a brief trial, on April 13, 1999, he was convicted of second-degree murder and sentenced to serve a 10- to 25-year prison term in a Michigan prison. He is terminally ill with hepatitis C and was paroled for that reason on June 1, 2007.[28]

Many families of people he has helped to die speak highly of Dr. Kevorkian. In the videotapes that he made before each death, the individuals who died were seen pleading to be allowed to die. His critics have a different view, however. They say that at least some of the people who wanted to die might not have done so if they had been helped—if their pain were adequately treated, for example. Some of the people were not terminally ill. One was in the early stages of Alzheimer's disease, and another had multiple sclerosis. The primary physician of another who claimed to have multiple sclerosis said the patient showed no evidence of this or any other disease; the patient had a history of depression, however. Another "patient" was determined by the medical examiner to have no trace of an earlier diagnosed cancer.[29] In one case, a woman had what has come to be called "chronic fatigue syndrome" and a history of abuse by her husband. Kevorkian's "patients" have been predominantly women who may have been worried about the impact of their disease on others as much as the difficulty of the disease itself or its prospects for them. In fact, three times as many women as men attempt suicide, though men succeed more often than do women.[30] Some critics suggest that their attempts are more of a cry for help. Death may also appear different to women. "If it is given a human face by a soothing physician/assister there is all the more reason why the super-altruistic

woman with a life spent serving others would want to put down her burdens, and succumb."[31]

Although the American Medical Association continues to oppose doctor-assisted suicide, federal appeals courts covering the states of Washington and New York have upheld the practice as constitutionally protected, one on grounds of privacy, and the other on the assertion that physician-assisted suicide was the same as turning off a respirator.[32] In one analysis, the reason for the difference between the court and physicians may be that "members of the legal profession have a higher opinion of their colleagues in medicine than the doctors do of themselves. Or perhaps physicians simply have a better understanding of the pressures of contemporary medical practice than do judges."[33] Bills that have sought to legalize doctor-assisted suicide have been rejected in some twenty states. In 1990, backers of a proposed California proposition sought to legalize active euthanasia for those with terminal illnesses who request it either at the time of illness or earlier through an advance directive; the backers failed to obtain the necessary signatures for a ballot measure. In Washington State in 1991, a similar ballot measure also failed. In 1997, the U.S. Supreme Court upheld court rulings regarding laws in New York and Washington State that made assisted suicide illegal. The Court based its findings on the conclusion that there was no constitutional "right to die." However, it said that individual states could make laws either permitting or prohibiting it.

Thirty-five states have laws explicitly making it a crime to assist a suicide; in nine others, it is against common law. North Carolina, Utah, and Wyoming have no laws criminalizing assisted suicide. Nine states criminalize assisted suicide through common law. Three states have abolished the common law of crimes and do not have statutes criminalizing assisted suicide. Ohio's supreme court has ruled that it is not a crime. In 1997, the Supreme Court stated that there is no constitutional right to die with the help of a physician and "upheld state laws banning assisted suicide."[34]

Oregon voters narrowly approved the state's Death with Dignity Act in 1994 but reaffirmed it with a larger margin in 1997. When this law was challenged by the Bush administration in 2001, a federal appeals court judge ruled that the U.S. attorney general "did not have legal authority to decide that doctors acting in compliance with Oregon's law were in violation of the federal Controlled Substances Act."[35] A subsequent appeal of this ruling was rejected in the state's favor by the U.S. Supreme Court in 2006.[36] Under Oregon's law, two doctors must examine a patient and conclude that he or she is of sound mind and has less than six months to live. A third doctor must also certify this. The patient must submit a written request and then a second oral request. Two days later, the patient is given a strong barbiturate: secobarbital or pentobarbital capsules. The patient must be able to take the drugs on his or her own. In the nine years between the time the practice was legalized and implemented in Oregon and the end of 2006, 292 terminally ill patients who requested the medication had used it to end their lives. Not all those who asked for prescriptions received them. According to one survey, 22 percent of physicians reported that they had refused to give prescriptions. Moreover, not all who received prescriptions used them. The number per year ranged from twenty-one patients out of forty-four (47.7 percent) to twenty-seven out of thirty-three (81.8 percent). In some of these cases, the patients died from natural causes. The primary reason patients cited for wanting to kill themselves was not pain or financial problems but the importance of autonomy and personal control.

Pain Medication That Causes Death

One type of action may be confused with active euthanasia but ought to be distinguished from it: giving pain medication to gravely ill and dying patients. Physicians are often hesitant to prescribe sufficient pain medication to such patients because they fear that the medication will actually cause their deaths. They fear that this would be considered comparable to mercy killing (or active euthanasia), which is legally impermissible. Some philosophers believe that the *principle of double effect* may be of some help here.[37] According to this principle, it is one thing to intend and do something bad as a means to an end, and it is another to do something morally permissible for

the purpose of achieving some good while knowing that it also may have a bad secondary effect.

The following diagram may be used to help understand the essence of this principle. It shows a morally permissible act with two effects: one intended main effect and one unintended side effect.

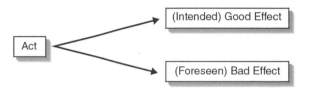

According to the principle of double effect, it may be morally permissible to administer a drug with the intention of relieving pain (a good effect) even though we know or foresee that our action also may have a bad effect (weakening the person and risking his death). Certain conditions must be met, however, for this to be permissible. *First,* the act must be morally permissible. One cannot do what is wrong to bring about a good end. *Second,* the person who acts must intend to bring about the good end rather than the harmful result. *Third,* the good results must outweigh the bad ones.

The idea behind the double effect principle is that there is a moral difference between intending to kill someone and intending to relieve pain. There is a moral difference between intending that someone die by *means of* one's actions (giving a drug overdose) and foreseeing that they will die *because of* one's actions (giving medication to relieve pain). Doing the latter is not, strictly speaking, active euthanasia. Active euthanasia would be the intentional giving of a drug with the purpose of bringing about a person's death. The difference is seen in the case of the dentist who foresees that she might pain her patient and the dentist who seeks to produce pain in her patient. The principle of double effect, nevertheless, continues to be the object of debate.[38]

In actual practice, it may be difficult to know what is going on—whether, for example, a person intends to use a prescribed drug just to relieve pain or actually bring about death. People may also have mixed or hidden motives for their actions. Yet it would seem helpful to use this principle so that doctors are permitted to give their patients sufficient pain medication without fear of being prosecuted for homicide. The fact that they might cause addiction in their patients is another reason why some doctors hesitate to give narcotics for pain relief. This seems hardly a reasonable objection, especially if the patient is dying! This principle may also help those who want patients to have good pain relief but are morally opposed to active euthanasia.

It is also interesting to note advances in the treatment of pain. For example, at a San Francisco meeting of members of the American Society of Anesthesiologists in October 2000, various new advances were described. For example, physicians described "pouches of anesthetics and narcotics that can be planted near the spine to give out steady bits of painkillers and muscle relaxants."[39] They also noted that "pacemaker-like devices" could be implanted near nerves to make buzzing sensations that would "drown out pain messages." One of the difficulties of some morphine-type pain medications is that they negatively affect consciousness. According to doctors at this meeting, one new drug being developed is "a highly diluted form of an exotic snail poison that blocks pain without being addictive or altering mental function."[40] New developments here may make it possible to treat pain without causing death, thereby keeping this issue separate from that of active euthanasia.

Ordinary and Extraordinary Measures

Philosophers have sometimes labeled those measures that are ineffective or excessively burdensome as *extraordinary*. They are often called *heroic* in the medical setting in the sense that using such measures is above and beyond what is required. A person's hospital medical chart might have the phrase "no heroics" on it, indicating that no such measures are to be used. There are other cases in which what is refused would actually be effective for curing or ameliorating a life-threatening condition. And yet decisions are made not to use these measures and to let the person die. These measures are called *ordinary*—not because they are common but because they promise reasonable

hope of benefit. With ordinary measures, the chances that the treatment will help are good, and the expected results are also good. One difficulty with determining whether a treatment would be considered ordinary or extraordinary is making an objective evaluation of the benefit and burden. It would be easier to do this if there were such a thing as a range for a normal life. Any measure that would not restore a life to that norm could then be considered extraordinary. However, if we were to set this standard very high, using it might also wrongly imply that the lives of disabled persons are of little or no benefit to them.

What would be considered an ordinary measure in the case of one person may be considered extraordinary in the case of another; a measure may effectively treat one person's condition, but another person will die shortly even if the measure were used (a blood transfusion, for example). Furthermore, the terminology can be misleading because many of the things that used to be experimental and risky are now common and quite beneficial. Drugs such as antibiotics and technologies such as respirators, which were once experimental and of questionable benefit, are now more effective and less expensive. In many cases, they would now be considered ordinary, whereas they once could have been considered extraordinary. It is their proven benefit in a time period and for particular individuals that makes them ordinary in our sense of the term, however, and not their commonness.

The basic difference between ordinary and extraordinary measures of life support, then, is as follows:

Ordinary measures: Measures or treatments with reasonable hope of benefit, or the benefits outweigh the burdens to the patient.

Extraordinary measures: Measures or treatments with no reasonable hope of benefit, or the burdens outweigh the benefits to the patient.

One question that arises in relation to the Terri Schiavo case, as well as others, is how to view in this regard the withholding or withdrawing of artificial nutrition. It is instructive to know that though the family was Catholic; there has been a tradition in Catholic theology that provides the basis for much of the understanding of the distinctions between ordinary and extraordinary measures. Although the definitions are made in the context of making moral judgments about euthanasia, which we will discuss below, the key to the difference is whether that which is withheld or withdrawn offers "a reasonable hope of benefit" or not.[41] Although guidelines assert that "a person may forgo extraordinary or disproportionate means of preserving life . . . there should be a presumption in favor of providing nutrition and hydration to all patients, including patients who require medically assisted nutrition and hydration, as long as this is of sufficient benefit to outweigh the burdens involved to the patient."[42] In other words, in some cases this form of medical intervention would be deemed of insufficient benefit to a patient—for example, if it did not promise to return him or her to a conscious state.

Voluntary and Nonvoluntary Euthanasia

Before we move on to consider arguments regarding the morality of euthanasia, one more distinction needs to be made between what can be called *voluntary* and *nonvoluntary* euthanasia. In many cases, it is the person whose life is at issue who makes the decision about what is to be done. This is voluntary euthanasia. In other cases, people other than the one whose life is at issue decide what is to be done. These are cases of nonvoluntary euthanasia.[43] Nonvoluntary simply means not *through* the will of the individual. It does not mean *against* their will. Sometimes, others must make the decision because the person or patient is incapable of doing so. This is true of infants and small children and a person who is in a coma or permanent vegetative state. This is also true of people who are only minimally competent, as in cases of senility or certain psychiatric disorders. Deciding who is sufficiently competent to make decisions for themselves is clear in many but not all cases. What should we say, for example, of the mental competence of the eighty-year-old man who refuses an effective surgery that would save his life and at the same time says he does not want to die? Is such a person being rational?

In some cases, when a patient is not able to express his or her wishes, we can attempt to imagine what the person would want. We can rely, for example, on past personality or statements the person has made. Perhaps the person commented to friends or relatives as to what he or she would want if such and such a situation occurred.

In other cases, a person might have left a written expression of his or her wishes in the form of a *living will.* The living will may specify that one does not want extraordinary measures used to prolong life if one is dying and unable to communicate. However, it leaves it up to the physician—who may be a stranger—to determine what is extraordinary. A better directive is called a *durable power of attorney.* In this case, you appoint someone close to you who knows what you want under certain conditions if you are dying and unable to communicate this. This person need not be a lawyer but will be your legal representative to make medical decisions for you in the event that you are incapacitated. The form for durable power of attorney also provides for individualized expressions in writing about what you would want done or not done under certain conditions. The person you appoint will also be the only one to give permission for *do not resuscitate (DNR)* orders, or orders not to resuscitate under certain conditions. You should also have one or two alternates. Whether such orders are to be given is often a problem, especially if the physician believes that resuscitating will be futile or even make the patient worse off and some family members do not want to give up.[44] At the very least, these directives have moral force. They also have legal force in those states that have recognized them.[45] However, even then these directives are often not followed by physicians, especially if the patient is a woman. These measures can, if enforced or strengthened, give people some added control over what happens to them in their last days. To further ensure this, in December 1991 the Patient Self-Determination Act passed by the U.S. Congress went into effect. This act requires that health care institutions that participate in the Medicare and Medicaid programs have written policies for providing individuals in their care with information

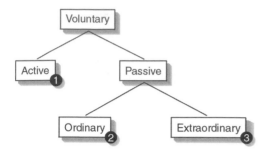

about and access to advance directives such as living wills.

Again, the difference between voluntary and nonvoluntary cases can be specified as follows:

Voluntary euthanasia: The person whose life is at issue knowingly and freely decides what shall be done.

Nonvoluntary euthanasia: Persons other than the one whose life is at issue decide what shall be done.

Combining the Types of Euthanasia

We have noted the differences between various types of euthanasia: voluntary and nonvoluntary, active and passive, and (if passive) the withholding of ordinary and extraordinary measures. Combining the types of euthanasia gives six forms, as illustrated above.

There are three types of voluntary euthanasia.

1. Voluntary active euthanasia: The person who is dying says, "Give me the fatal dose."
2. Voluntary passive euthanasia, withholding ordinary measures: The person says, "Don't use lifesaving or life-prolonging medical measures even though the likely results of using them would be good and the costs or burdens minimal, because I want to die."
3. Voluntary passive euthanasia, withholding extraordinary measures: The person says, "Don't use those medical measures because the chances of benefit in terms of lifesaving or life extension would be small, the burdens too great, or both."

Likewise, there are three types of nonvoluntary euthanasia.

4. Nonvoluntary active euthanasia: Others decide to give the person the fatal drug overdose.
5. Nonvoluntary passive euthanasia, withholding ordinary measures: Others decide not to use lifesaving or life-prolonging medical measures even though the likely results of using them would be good and the costs or burdens minimal.
6. Nonvoluntary passive euthanasia, withholding extraordinary measures: Others decide not to use those medical measures because the chances of benefit—saving or extending life—are small, the burdens are too great, or both.

So far, we have attempted only to classify types of euthanasia. Our purpose has been to describe the various possible types so that we will then be better able to make appropriate distinctions in our moral judgments about these cases.

MORALITY AND THE LAW

Before we consider the moral arguments about euthanasia, we should first distinguish moral judgments from assertions about what the law should or should not be on this matter. Although we may sometimes have moral reasons for what we say the law should or should not do, *the two areas are distinct*. There are many things that are moral matters that ought not to be legislated or made subject to law and legal punishment. *Not everything that is immoral ought to be illegal.* For example, lying, while arguably a moral issue, is only sometimes subject to the law. In our thinking about euthanasia, it would be well to keep this distinction in mind.

On the one hand, in some cases we might say that a person acted badly, though understandably, in giving up too easily on life. Yet we also may believe that the law should not force some action here if the person knows what he or she is doing, and the person's action does not seriously harm others. On the other hand, a person's request to end his or her life might be reasonable given his circumstances, but there might also be social reasons why the law should not permit it. These reasons might be related to the possible harmful effects of some practice on other persons or on the practice of medicine. *Just because some action (for example, euthanasia) might be morally permissible does not necessarily mean that it ought to be legally permissible.*

MAKING MORAL JUDGMENTS ABOUT EUTHANASIA

One way to get a handle on what to think about the morality of euthanasia is to look at its various types. We can then ask ourselves whether euthanasia of a certain type is morally justifiable. One way to help us answer these questions is to use the distinction made in our chapters on moral theory between *consequentialist* theories (such as utilitarianism) and *nonconsequentialist* theories (such as Kant's moral theory or natural law theory). If you think that it is the consequences rather than the nature of actions themselves that matter morally, then you can focus on those considerations. If you think that we should judge whether some action is right or wrong in itself for some reason, then you can focus on those considerations and reasons.

The Moral Significance of Voluntariness

Today, an individual's rights over his or her own life are highly valued. And yet the commonsense moral view is that there are limits to this right. It is limited, for example, when it conflicts with the interests or rights of others. Under what conditions and for what reasons should a person's own wishes prevail in euthanasia matters? How important is voluntary consent?

Consequentialist Considerations From your study of utilitarianism, you know that one major method of deciding moral right and wrong appeals to the consequences of our actions (act utilitarianism) or

practices (rule utilitarianism). From this perspective, voluntariness matters morally only to the extent that it affects human happiness and welfare. Respecting people's own choices about how they will die surely would have some beneficial consequences. For example, when people know that they will be allowed to make decisions about their own lives and not be forced into things against their will, then they may gain a certain peace of mind. Thus, many of the persons who have used Oregon's assisted suicide law reported that they did so because they did not want to be dependent and felt better being in control over their lives. Moreover, knowing themselves better than others knew them, they also may be the ones best able to make good decisions in situations that primarily affect them. These are good consequentialist reasons to respect a person's wishes in euthanasia cases. But it is not just the person who is dying who will be affected by the decision. Thus, it also can be argued that the effects on others—on their feelings, for example—are also relevant to the moral decision making.

However, individual decisions are not always wise and do not always work for the greatest benefit of the person making them or for others. For example, critics of euthanasia worry that people who are ill or disabled would refuse certain lifesaving treatment because they lack or do not know about services, support, and money that are available to them. More than a decade ago, the Nevada supreme court ruled that people must receive information about care alternatives before they may refuse lifesaving treatment.[46] On consequentialist grounds, we should do what, in fact, is most likely to bring about the greatest happiness, not only to ourselves but also to all those affected by our actions. It does not in itself matter who makes the judgment. But it does matter insofar as one person rather than another is more likely to make a better judgment, one that would have better consequences overall, including consequences to the individual.

Moreover, from the perspective of rule utilitarian thinking, we ought to consider which policy would maximize happiness. (It is here that morality comes closer to concerns about what the law should be.) Would a policy that universally follows individual requests about dying be most likely to maximize happiness? Or would a policy that gives no special weight to individual desires, but which directs us to do whatever some panel decides, be more likely to have the best outcome? Or would some moderate policy be best, such as one that gives special but not absolute weight to what a person wants? An example of such a policy might be one in which the burden of proof not to do what a person wishes is placed on those who would refuse it. In other words, they must show some serious reason not to go along with what the person wanted.

Nonconsequentialist Considerations To appeal to the value of personal autonomy in euthanasia decisions is to appeal to a nonconsequentialist reason or moral norm. The idea is that autonomy is a good in itself and therefore carries heavy moral weight. We like to think of ourselves, at least ideally, as masters of our own fate. A world of robots would probably be a lesser world than one populated by people who make their own decisions, even when those decisions are unwise. In fact, according to Kant, only in such a world is morality itself possible. His famous phrase, "an ought implies a can," indicates that if and only if we can or are *free* to act in certain ways can we be *commanded* to do so. According to a Kantian deontological position, persons are unique in being able to choose freely, and this ought to be respected.

However, in many euthanasia cases a person's mental competence and thus autonomy is compromised by fear and lack of understanding. Illness also makes a person more subject to undue influence or coercion. There is also a high correlation between suicide and depression. According to a 1998 study, it is not pain that makes one in ten terminally ill patients in the United States seriously consider suicide, it is depression and dependence on others.[47] "The most seriously depressed patients were twice as likely to have considered suicide as all terminally ill patients."[48] How, in such instances, do we know what the person really wants? Perhaps he or she primarily wants to talk to someone. These are practical problems that arise when

attempting to respect autonomy. In addition, the issue raises theoretical problems. *Autonomy* literally means self-rule. But how often are we fully clear about who we are and what we want to be? Is the self whose decisions are to be respected the current self or one's ideal or authentic self? These issues of selfhood and personal identity are crucial to euthanasia arguments that focus on autonomy and personal decision making. It is also the case that they take us beyond ethics itself into philosophical notions of the self and freedom as well as into empirical psychology.

Note also here that although we have concentrated on pointing out the kinds of things that would be morally relevant from both consequentialist and nonconsequentialist points of view, the issues also may be analyzed from the perspective of an ethics of care. One would suppose that from this perspective both matters that relate to benefits and harms and those that relate to a person's autonomy would be relevant.

Active Versus Passive Euthanasia

The distinction between active and passive euthanasia is a conceptual distinction, a matter of classification. Giving a patient a lethal drug to end her life is classified as active euthanasia. Stopping or not starting some life-lengthening treatment, knowing that a patient will die, is classified as passive euthanasia. For example, either not starting a respirator or disconnecting it is generally considered passive euthanasia because it is a matter of not providing life-prolonging aid for the person. In this case, the person's illness or weakness is the cause of his death if he dies. This does not mean that it is either justified or unjustified.

Let us pose the *moral* question about active and passive euthanasia like this: Is there any moral difference between them? This prompts the following questions: Is active euthanasia more morally problematic than passive euthanasia? Or are they on a moral par such that if passive euthanasia is morally permissible in some case, then so is active euthanasia? Is physician-assisted suicide (in which a physician only provides the means of death to the person) any more or less problematic than cases in which the physician actually administers the drug or uses other means to bring about death?

Consequentialist Concerns Again, if we take the perspective of the consequentialist or act utilitarian, for example, we should only be concerned about our actions in terms of their consequences. The means by which the results come about do not matter in themselves. They matter only if they make a difference in the result. Generally, then, if a person's death is the *best outcome* in a difficult situation, it would not matter whether it came about through the administration of a lethal drug dose or from the discontinuance of some lifesaving treatment. Now, if one or the other means did make a difference in a person's experience (as when a person is relieved or pained more by one method than another), then this would count in favor of or against that method.

If we take the perspective of a rule utilitarian, we would be concerned about the consequences of this or that practice or policy. We would want to know which of the various alternative practices or policies would have the best results overall. Which would be the best policy: one that allowed those who were involved to choose active euthanasia, one that required active euthanasia in certain cases, one that permitted it only in rare cases, or one that prohibited it and attached legal penalties to it? Which policy would make more people happy and fewer people unhappy? One that prohibited active euthanasia would frustrate those who wished to use it, but it would prevent some abuses that might follow if it were permitted. Essential to this perspective are predictions about how a policy would work. Some people are concerned in particular about the effects of physician participation in the practice of euthanasia. It may have the positive results of being under the control of a profession known for its ethical concerns. Or it may have negative effects such as the lessening of patient trust in physicians. The disability advocacy group called Not Dead Yet has voiced its concerns about physician-assisted suicide and the plight of the disabled. Its members wonder whether people would be more inclined to think their lives were not worth living and

whether there would be pressure on them to commit suicide.[49]

Even those who support physician-assisted suicide and in some cases actual active euthanasia worry about whether these practices would be open to abuse. The argument that there would be abuse has been given various names, depending on the particular metaphor of choice: the "domino effect," "slippery slope," "wedge," or "camel's nose" argument. The idea is that if we permit active euthanasia in a few reasonable cases, then we would slide and approve it in more and more cases until we were approving it in cases that were clearly unreasonable. In other words, if we permit euthanasia when a person is soon dying, in unrelievable pain, and has requested that his life be ended, then we will permit it when a person is not dying or has not requested to be killed. Evidence from the Netherlands cited above may or may not apply in the United States or elsewhere, but the questions to ask are: Would we slide down the slope? Is there something about us that would cause us to slide? Would we be so weak of mind that we could not see the difference between these cases? Would we be weak of will, not wanting to care for people whose care is costly and burdensome? This is an empirical and predictive matter. To know the force of the argument, we would need to show evidence for one or the other positions about the likelihood of sliding.[50]

Nonconsequentialist Concerns Many arguments and concerns about active and passive euthanasia are not based on appeals to good or bad results or consequences. Arguments about the right to die or to make one's own decisions about dying are nonconsequentialist arguments. On the one hand, some people argue that respecting personal autonomy is so important that it should override any concerns about bad results. Thus, we might conclude that people ought to be allowed to end their lives when they choose as an expression of their autonomy, and that this choice should be respected regardless of the consequences to others or even mistakes about their own cases.

On the other hand, some people believe that there is a significant moral difference between killing another person or themselves and letting a person die. Killing people except in self-defense is morally wrong, according to this view. Just why it is thought wrong is another matter. Some people rely on reasons like those purported by natural law, citing the innate drive toward living as a good in itself, however compromised—a good that should not be suppressed. Kant used reasoning similar to this. He argued that using the concern for life that usually promotes it to make a case for ending life was inherently contradictory and a violation of the categorical imperative.[51] Some people use religious reasons such as the belief that life-and-death decisions are for God and not ourselves to make. Some people use reasons that rely on concerns about the gravity of ending a life directly and intentionally, that in doing so we ally ourselves with what is at best a necessary evil.

We each need to consider what role consequentialist and nonconsequentialist reasons play in our own views about the morality of active and passive euthanasia. If consequentialist arguments have primacy, then one's argument for or against active euthanasia will depend on empirical judgments about the predicted consequences. If nonconsequentialist reasons have primacy, then these reasons must be evaluated. Are the nonconsequentialist reasons about autonomy, for example, stronger than the nonconsequentialist arguments about the morality of killing? This text does not intend to answer these questions for the student, but it does assume that a good start can be made in answering them if one is able to know whether an argument is based on consequentialist or nonconsequentialist considerations.

Ordinary Versus Extraordinary Measures

There is considerable disagreement about the usefulness of the distinction between ordinary and extraordinary measures of life support. People disagree first of all about the definitions of the terms.[52] If the terms are defined primarily in terms of commonness and uncommonness, then surely it is difficult to see that this should make a moral difference. It would amount to saying that we ought to use those things that we commonly use and not use those we usually do not use. However, if the terms are defined in relation to benefit and burden, then they are by their nature morally relevant because these are value terms. The primary difficulty with using this distinction is that it is difficult to measure and compare benefits and burdens (as noted earlier). For instance, should financial cost to a family or society be part of the calculation? One danger with including the effect on others in the calculation, and not just the benefits and burdens to the patient herself, is that we might be inclined to say that some people should die because the burdens of caring for them are just too great.

If we could determine what are ordinary and extraordinary measures in a particular case, we would be on the way to deciding whether there is at least some good reason to provide the measures. If we judge them ordinary, then they probably ought to be provided. If we judge them extraordinary, then they probably need not be provided.

INFANT EUTHANASIA

Today, at least half of all live-born infants weighing less than 1,000 grams (2.2 pounds) survive, compared with less than 10 percent just twenty-five years ago. Survival rates for those who are born with congenital defects also have shown marked improvements.[53] However, some seriously ill newborns do not fare well. Some have low birth weight or severe defects and cannot survive for long, while others have serious impairments. Thus, improvements in medicine that have enabled us to save the lives of newborns also have given us new life-and-death decisions to make.

Every few years, a case of disputed life-and-death decisions regarding an infant seems to appear in the news. They are called Baby Doe cases to protect the families' privacy. Those that have drawn the most criticism are cases like the one in which an infant born with Down's syndrome was left untreated and died. Down's syndrome (also called trisomy 21) is a genetic anomaly that causes mental retardation and sometimes physical problems as well. In this case, the child had a repairable but life-threatening blockage between the stomach and the small intestines. The parents refused permission for surgery to repair the problem, and the doctors followed their wishes and let the infant die. Critics of this case protested that this surgery was simple and effective, and the infant, although retarded, could lead a generally happy life.

Not to treat in such cases has been interpreted as not using what would be considered ordinary means of life support—*ordinary* because the benefits to the patient would outweigh any burdens. Such cases have been criticized for their "buck-passing"—that is, shifting responsibility for the death to nature, as though in this situation but not elsewhere in medicine we should "let nature take its course."[54] Because the infant is not able to express his wishes, these will always be cases of nonvoluntary euthanasia. Although strong arguments can be made for treatment in such cases, in other cases knowing what is best is not so simple. Recently, a hospital in the Netherlands has proposed guidelines that allow for active euthanasia of some ill newborns. So far, the practice has officially been limited to those parents who themselves knowingly and freely requested it. The proposal, known as the Gronigen Protocol, allows doctors to "actively end the life of newborns deemed to be in similar pain (as adults) from incurable disease or extreme deformities."[55] The type of cases under consideration are of infants with a hopeless prognosis, as well as those with extremely poor quality of life. This latter designation specifically includes "severe cases of spina bifida," a birth defect in which the spinal column does not fully close in development; the most serious cases result in death or, if treated, may leave the person with "muscle weakness or paralysis below the area of the spine where the incomplete closure (or cleft) occurs, loss of sensation below the cleft, and loss of bowel and bladder control."[56] In some cases, spinal fluid builds up and can cause learning problems. In cases such as this, it is not clear whether medical assistance is in the infant's best interest. However, people have survived spina bifida and been able to enjoy life and contribute to their communities.[57] Moreover, some cases raise again the issue of determining when an individual is dead. In cases in Florida and California, for example, parents of a

newborn with anencephaly, or no upper brain, wanted their child declared brain dead so that its organs could be used for transplant. However, such infants are not brain dead according to statutes in these states.

Two different types of moral questions can be raised about such cases. One is the question, *who* would be the best to decide whether to provide or deny certain treatments? The other is, what are the *reasons* to provide or deny care? Some people insist that the primary decision makers should be the parents because they not only are most likely to have the infant's best interests at heart, but also will be the ones to provide care for the child. Needless to say, we can imagine situations in which the parents would not be the most objective judges. They might be fearful, disappointed at the child's birth, or simply disagree about what is best to do. A presidential commission that was established to review medical ethical problems concluded that parents ought to make decisions for their seriously ill newborns, except in cases of decision-making incapacity, an unresolvable difference between them, or a choice that is clearly not in the infant's best interests. According to this commission, if a treatment is futile it is not advised. However, in other cases, the infant's best interests are said to be primary.

> Permanent handicaps justify a decision not to provide life-sustaining treatment only when they are so severe that continued existence would not be a net benefit to the infant. Though inevitably somewhat subjective and imprecise in actual application, the concept of "benefit" excludes honoring idiosyncratic views that might be allowed if a person were deciding about his or her own treatment. Rather, net benefit is absent only if the burdens imposed on the patient by the disability or its treatment would lead a competent decision maker to choose to forgo the treatment. As in all surrogate decision making, the surrogate is obligated to try to evaluate benefits and burdens from the infant's own perspective.[58]

A society has an interest in protecting and providing for its children and thus is obligated to intervene in cases of parental neglect or abuse.

However, just what constitutes neglect or abuse and what is reasonable parental decision making is far from clear. In addition, there are practical legal difficulties involved in treatment decisions for children. What would be the best policy regarding ill newborns? Should the federal government require state child-abuse agencies to monitor treatment of newborns and withhold funds if states do not comply? Critics of such a policy believe that this would be an unwarranted state interference in legitimate medical decision making. Obviously, more than medical decisions about diagnosis and prognosis are involved in such cases. These are judgments about what is best to do—these are value or moral judgments. Finding the best balance between the need to protect children and support parents in difficult and painful decision making remains a continuing problem.

NOTES

1. *The New York Times,* Jan. 30, 2003, p. A16.
2. Huntington's Disease Society of America: www.hdsa.org
3. http://pediatrics.about.com/cs/conditions/a/msp_md.htm.
4. www.medscape.com; www.italymag.co.uk/2007/news-from-italy/lifestyle/euchanasia-case-against-doctor-shelved.
5. Pam Belluck, "As a Life Ebbs, the Ultimate Family Quarrel," *The New York Times,* Nov. 27, 2004, pp. A1, A22.
6. Ibid.
7. John Schwartz, "At Life's End, Hospital Finds Junction of Ethics and Medicine," *The New York Times,* July 4, 2005, p. A13.
8. *The New York Times,* Dec. 5, 1976.
9. The case occurred in Oakland, California. The jury in the case found the defendant guilty even though California did not then have a "brain death" statute. See the *San Francisco Examiner* for May 1972.
10. Ad Hoc Committee of the Harvard Medical School to Examine the Definition of Brain Death, "A Definition of Irreversible Coma," *Journal of the American Medical Association, 205* (1968): 377.
11. Two types of cases are to be distinguished from both persistent vegetative state and coma. One is called *locked-in syndrome* in which a person may be conscious but unable to respond. The other is

dementia, or senility, in which the content of consciousness is impaired, as in Alzheimer's disease. Neither the person in a persistent vegetative state or coma nor the person with locked-in syndrome or dementia is considered dead by whole brain death criteria. We may say the person's life has a diminished value, but he or she is not legally dead. However, some people argue that because the ability to think is what makes us persons, when someone loses this ability, as in the case of PVS, we ought to consider the person dead. Newborns with little or no upper brain or brain function also then and for the same reason can be considered dead. However, these are living, breathing beings, and it would be difficult to think of them as dead in the sense that we would bury them as they are. Rather than declare them dead, as some people have argued, others believe that it would be more practical and reasonable to judge these cases in terms of the kind of life they are living and to ask whether it would be morally permissible to bring about their deaths or allow them to die.

12. *San Francisco Chronicle,* Feb. 2, 1995, p. A4.
13. See *In re Quinlan,* 70 N.J. 10, 335 A. 2d 647 (1976); and *Cruzan* v. *Director, Missouri Department of Health,* United States Supreme Court, 110 S. Ct. 2841 (1990).
14. Raphael Cohen-Almagor, "Why the Netherlands?" *Journal of Law, Medicine & Ethics, 30,* no.1 (Spring 2002): 95–116.
15. Yahoo News, Nov. 30, 2004.
16. Herbert Hendin, "The Dutch Experience," *Issues in Law & Medicine, 17,* no. 3 (Spring 2002): 223–247.
17. *The New York Times,* Nov. 29, 2000, p. A3.
18. Ibid.
19. http://law.jrank.org/pages/1100/Euthanasia-Assisted-Suicide-Euthanasia-in-Netherlands.html; http://news.yahoo.com/s/hsn/20070510.
20. http://news.yahoo.com/s/hsn/20070510.
21. Ibid.; www.internationaltaskforce.org/fctholl. htm.
22. Richard H. Nicholson, "Death Is the Remedy?" *Hastings Center Report, 32,* no. 1 (Jan–Feb. 2002): 9.
23. *The New York Times,* April 12, 2001, p. A6.
24. Ronald W. Maris, "Suicide," *The Lancet, 360,* no. 9329 (July 27, 2002): 319.
25. Ibid.
26. *The Christian Century, 119,* no. 6 (March 13, 2002): 5.
27. *The New York Times,* Dec. 4, 1990, describes the first publicized case in which Dr. Kevorkian's "suicide machine" was used, and the other two

cases can be found, for example, in the *San Francisco Chronicle*, Oct. 29, 1991.

28. *The New York Times,* April 14, 1999.

29. Stephanie Gutmann, "Death and the Maiden," *The New Republic* (June 24, 1996): 20–28.

30. Ibid.

31. Ibid.

32. *The New York Times,* July 15, 1996, p. A11. For a good analysis of these two court opinions, see "What Right to Die?" by Jeffrey Rosen in *The New Republic* (July 24, 1996): 28–31.

33. Ibid.

34. www.euthanasia.com/bystate.html; www.washingtonpost.com/wp-srv/national/longterm/supcourt/1996-97/assist96.htm.

35. Steve Perlstein, "Ruling Upholding Oregon Assisted Suicide Law Gets Mixed Reviews," *Family Practice News, 32,* no. 10 (May 15, 2002): 31.

36. *The New York Times,* Feb. 18, 1999, p. A1. See also *Oregon's Death with Dignity Act Annual Report 1999,* Oregon Health Division, Oregon Department of Human Resources (www.ohd.hr.state.or.us/cdpe/chs/pas/ar-tbl 1.htm), http://egov.oregon.gov/DHS/ph/pas/docs/prescriptionhistory.pdf, and www.boston.com/news/nation/articles/2006/01/18/doctor_assisted_suicide_gains_ground/.

37. This principle was developed by the theologians of Salmance, in particular by John of St. Thomas in *De Bonitate et Malitia Actuum Humanorum.* See Antony Kenny, "The History of Intention in Ethics" in *Anatomy of the Soul* (London: Basil Blackwell, 1973): 140ff.

38. See, for example, Warren S. Quinn, "Actions, Intentions, and Consequences: The Doctrine of Double Effect," *Philosophy and Public Affairs, 18,* no. 4 (Fall 1989): 334–351.

39. *San Francisco Chronicle,* Oct. 15, 2000, p. D3.

40. Ibid.

41. Directives 56 and 57 of the *Ethical and Religious Directives for Catholic Health Care Services,* approved by the U.S. bishops in 1995 and approved by the Vatican. See James Keenan, S. J., "A 400-year-old Logic," in *Boston College Magazine,* Spring 2005, pp. 41–42.

42. Ibid.

43. Some writers on this topic also list *involuntary* as a third type of euthanasia. Because it is a conceptual distinction rather than a moral one that is at issue here, I believe that the two-type classification system is preferable.

44. *The New York Times,* Oct. 10, 2006, pp. D1, D6.

45. However, what is requested in these documents may or may not be followed, depending on the circumstances and on what is requested. Medical staff may decide not to stop lifesaving treatments for a person who is not otherwise dying, even if she has stated this in writing. Staff members also may decide not to do certain things that they consider not medically appropriate or not legally permissible, even though these things have been requested in writing.

46. Reported in *Medical Ethics Advisor, 7,* no. 4 (April 1991): 50–54.

47. *San Francisco Chronicle,* July 1, 1998, p. A5.

48. Ibid.

49. Debra Saunders, "Better Choice: Death with Longevity," *San Francisco Chronicle,* March 16, 1999, p. A19.

50. In an interesting version of this consequentialist argument, Susan Wolff writes that we ought to maintain a sharp dividing line between active and passive euthanasia, which allows a wide range of permissible cases of passive euthanasia but prohibits active euthanasia. The reason she gives is that if we do not have such a line and attempt to allow active euthanasia even in only a limited number of cases, then this will cause concern about the whole area of euthanasia and in the end work to limit acceptance of passive euthanasia as well. To retain freedom for passive euthanasia, she argues, we need to maintain the prohibition against active euthanasia. Again, this is an argument that relies on predictions of what would be likely to occur, and we would need some reason to believe that this would be so. From a presentation at a conference on "The Ethics and Economics of Death," the University of California at San Francisco Medical Center, November 1989.

51. Immanuel Kant, *Foundations of the Metaphysics of Morals,* second section, number 422.

52. Comments about the history of the distinction and the debate over its usefulness can be found in *The President's Commission Report,* "Deciding to Forgo Life Sustaining Treatment" (March 1983): 82–89.

53. Ibid.

54. From a comment made by a reviewer of this text, Robert P. Tucker of Florida Southern College, who has had hospital experience in this regard.

55. Toby Sterling, "Netherlands Hospital Euthanizes Babies," Yahoo News, Nov. 30, 2004.

56. Spina bifida fact sheet: www.nichcy.org/ubs/factshe/fs12txt.htm.
57. John Schwartz, "When Torment Is Baby's Destiny, Euthanasia Is Defended," *The New York Times,* March 10, 2005, p. A3.
58. *The President's Commission Report,* op. cit. For a perspective from a handicapped person, see "Unspeakable Conversations" by Harriet McBryde Johnson, *New York Times Magazine,* Feb. 16, 2003. I thank Jennifer MacKinnon for this reference.

REVIEW EXERCISES

1. What is the difference between "whole brain death" and "persistent vegetative state"?
2. If a person has whole brain death, then what kind of euthanasia is possible? Explain.
3. What is the difference between active and passive euthanasia? Is physician-assisted suicide more like active or passive euthanasia? How so?
4. Where do advance directives such as living wills and durable powers of attorney fit into the distinction between voluntary and nonvoluntary euthanasia?
5. What is the difference between ordinary and extraordinary measures of life support? If some measure of life support were rather common and inexpensive, would this necessarily make it an ordinary means of life support? Explain.
6. Label the following as examples of voluntary or nonvoluntary *and* active or passive euthanasia; if passive, are the measures described more likely to be considered ordinary or extraordinary measures of life support?
   a. A person who is dying asks to be given a fatal drug dose to bring about his death.
   b. A dying patient asks that no more chemotherapy be administered because it is doing nothing but prolonging her death, which is inevitable in a short time anyway.
   c. Parents of a newborn whose condition involves moderate retardation refuse permission for a simple surgery that would repair a physical anomaly inconsistent with continued life, and they let the infant die.
   d. A husband gives his wife a lethal overdose of her pain medicine because he does not want to see her suffer anymore.
   e. Doctors decide not to try to start artificial feeding mechanisms for their patient because they believe that it will be futile—that is, ineffective given the condition of their patient.
7. List the consequentialist concerns that could be given in arguing about whether the actions proposed in three of the scenarios in Question 6 are justified.
8. What nonconsequentialist concerns could be given in arguing about these same three scenarios?

DISCUSSION CASES

1. Respirator Removal. Jim was an active person. He was a lawyer by profession. When he was forty-four years old, a routine physical revealed that he had a tumor on his right lung. After surgery to remove that lung, he returned to a normal life. However, four years later, a cancerous tumor was found in his other lung. He knew he had only months to live. Then came the last hospitalization. He was on a respirator. It was extremely uncomfortable for him, and he was frustrated by not being able to talk because of the tubes. After some thought, he decided that he did not want to live out his last few weeks like this and asked to have the respirator removed. Because he was no longer able to breathe on his own, he knew this meant he would die shortly after it was removed.

Did Jim or the doctors who removed the respirator and then watched Jim die as a result do anything wrong? Why or why not? Would there be any difference between this case and that of a person such as Terri Schiavo, who was in a persistent vegetative state, was not able to express her current wishes, and had left no written request? Would there be a difference in cases such as hers between removing a respirator (which she was not using) and removing a feeding tube? How would you tell whether either one would be considered an ordinary or extraordinary means of life support? Would it matter which one it would be labeled?

2. Pill Overdose. Mary Jones had a severe case of cerebral palsy. She now had spent twenty-eight years of life trying to cope with the varying disabilities it caused. She could get around somewhat in her motorized wheelchair. An aide fed her and took care of her small apartment. She had gone to junior college and earned a degree in sociology. She also had a mechanism whereby she could type on a computer. However, she had lately become weary with life. She saw no improvement ahead and wanted to die. She had been receiving pain pills from her doctor. Now she asked for several weeks' worth of prescriptions so that she would not have to return for more so often. Her doctor suspected that she might be suicidal.

Should Mary Jones's doctor continue giving her the pills? Why or why not? Would she be assisting in Mary's suicide if she did? Does Mary Jones have a right to end her life if she chooses? Why or why not? Should her physician actually be able to administer some death-causing drug and not just provide the pills? Why or why not?

3. Teen Euthanasia. Thirteen-year-old Samantha is in the last stages of cancer. She says she doesn't want any further treatment because she thinks that it is not going to make her well. Her parents want the doctors to try a new experimental therapy for which there is some hope. If they cannot convince Samantha to undergo this experimental procedure, should the doctors sedate Samantha and go ahead with it anyway or should they do what she asks and let her die? Do you think that they should be allowed to end her life with a fatal dose of a drug if that is what she wishes, even though her parents object and they are still her legal guardians?

4. Baby John Doe. Sarah and Mike's baby boy was born with a defect called *spina bifida,* which consists of an opening in the spine. In his case, it was of the more severe kind in which the spinal cord also protruded through the hole. The opening was moderately high in the spine, and thus they were told that his neurological control below that level would be affected. He would have no bowel and bladder control and would not be able to walk unassisted. The cerebral spinal fluid had already started to back up into the cavity surrounding his brain, and his head was swelling. Doctors advised that they could have a shunt put in place to drain this fluid from the brain and prevent pressure on the brain. They could also have the spinal opening repaired. If they did not do so, however, the baby would probably die from the infection that would develop. Sarah and Mike are afraid of raising such a child and think that he also would have an extremely difficult life. In a few cases, however, children with this anomaly who do not have the surgery do not die, and then they are worse off than if the operation were done.

What should Sarah and Mike do? Why?

Selected Bibliography

Baird, Robert, and Stuart E. Rosenbaum (Eds.). *Euthanasia: The Moral Issues.* Buffalo, NY: Prometheus, 1989.

Battin, M. Pabst. *The Least Worst Death.* New York: Oxford University Press, 1994.

Beauchamp, Tom L., and Robert M. Veatch (Eds.). *Ethical Issues in Death and Dying.* Upper Saddle River, NJ: Prentice Hall, 1995.

———. *Intending Death: The Ethics of Assisted Suicide and Euthanasia.* Upper Saddle River, NJ: Prentice Hall, 1995.

Behnke, John A., and Sissela Bok. *The Dilemmas of Euthanasia.* New York: Doubleday Anchor, 1975.

Biggar, Nigel. *Aiming to Kill: The Ethics of Suicide and Euthanasia.* Cleveland, OH: Pilgrim Press, 2004.

Burleigh, Michael. *Death and Deliverance: "Euthanasia" in Germany 1900–1945.* New York: Cambridge University Press, 1995.

Cantor, Norman I. *Advance Directives and the Pursuit of Death with Dignity.* Bloomington: Indiana University Press, 1993.

Cohen-Almagor, Raphael. *Euthanasia in the Netherlands: The Policy and Practice of Mercy Killing.* New York: Kluwer Academic Publishers, 2004.

Dudley, William (Ed.). *Euthanasia.* Farmington Hills, MI: Gale Group, 2002.

Dworkin, Gerald, R. G. Frey, and Sissela Bok. *Euthanasia and Physician-Assisted Suicide (For and Against).* New York: Cambridge University Press, 1998.

Gentles, In (Ed.). *Euthanasia and Assisted Suicide: The Current Debate.* Don Mills, Ontario, Can: Stoddart Publishing, 1995.

Griffiths, John, Alex Bood, and Heleen Weyers. *Euthanasia and Law in the Netherlands.* Ann Arbor: University of Michigan Press, 1998.

Griffiths, John, et al. *Euthanasia and Law in the Netherlands.* Amsterdam: Amsterdam University Press, 1998.

Griffiths, John, et. al. *Euthanasia and the Law in Europe: With Special Reference to the Netherlands and Belgium.* Oxford, UK: Hart Publishing Limited, 2007.

Grisez, Germain, and Joseph M. Boyle, Jr. *Life and Death with Liberty and Justice: A Contribution to the*

Euthanasia Debate. South Bend, IN: University of Notre Dame Press, 1979.

Hamel, Ronald P. et. al. *Artificial Nutrition and Hydration and the Permanently Unconscious Patient: The Catholic Debate.* Washington, D.C.: Georgetown University Press, 2007.

Harris, Nancy. *The Ethics of Euthanasia.* Farmington Hills, MI: The Gale Group, 2004.

Huxtable, Richard. *Euthanasia, Ethics and the Law.* London: Taylor & Francis Group, 2007.

Jamison, Stephen. *Assisted Suicide: A Decision-Making Guide for Health Professionals.* San Francisco: Jossey-Bass Publishers, 1997.

Keown, John (Ed.). *Euthanasia Examined: Ethical, Clinical and Legal Perspectives.* New York: Cambridge University Press, 1996.

————, **and Daniel Callahan.** *Euthanasia Examined: Ethical, Clinical and Legal Perspectives.* New York: Cambridge University Press, 1997.

Kohl, Marvin (Ed.). *Beneficent Euthanasia.* Buffalo, NY: Prometheus, 1975.

Lynn, Joanne (Ed.). *By No Extraordinary Means: The Choice to Forgo Life-Sustaining Food and Water.* Bloomington: Indiana University Press, 1986.

Maguire, Daniel C. *Death by Choice.* New York: Doubleday, 1974.

Manning, Michael. *Euthanasia and Physician-Assisted Suicide: Killing or Caring.* Mahwah, NJ: Paulist Press, 1998.

McLean, Sheila. *Assisted Dying.* London: Taylor & Francis Group, 2007.

Mitchell, John B. *Understanding Assisted Suicide: The Nine Issues.* Ann Arbor: University of Michigan Press, 2007.

Moreno, Jonathan D. (Ed.). *Arguing Euthanasia: The Controversy over Mercy Killing, Assisted Suicide and the "Right to Die."* New York: Simon & Schuster, 1995.

Morgan, Robert, and Derrick Morgan (Eds.). *Death Rites: Law and Ethics at the End of Life.* New York: Routledge, 1994.

Prado, C. G., and S. J. Taylor. *Assisted Suicide: Theory and Practice in Elective Death.* Amherst, NY: Prometheus, 1999.

President's Commission for the Study of Ethical Problems in Medicine and Biomedical and Behavioral Research. *Deciding to Forgo Life-Sustaining Treatment.* New York: Concern for Dying, 1983.

Scherer, Jennifer M., and Rita James Simon. *Euthanasia and the Right to Die: A Comparative View.* Lanham, MD: Rowman & Littlefield, 1999.

Scherer, Jennifer M., et al. *Euthanasia and the Right to Die: A Comparative View.* Lanham, MD: Rowman & Littlefield, 1999.

Steinbock, Bonnie (Ed.). *Killing and Letting Die.* Englewood Cliffs, NJ: Prentice-Hall, 1980.

————, **and Alastair Norcross (Eds.).** *Killing and Letting Die.* New York: Fordham University Press, 1994.

Walton, Douglas N. *On Defining Death: An Analytic Study of the Concept of Death in Philosophy and Medical Ethics.* Montreal: McGill-Queen, 1979.

Weir, Robert F. *Selective Nontreatment of Handicapped Newborns: Moral Dilemmas in Neonatal Medicine.* New York: Oxford University Press, 1984.

Yount, Lisa. *Euthanasia.* Farmington Hills, MI: Gale Group, 2001.

9

Abortion

Imagine the case of a single young woman who believes she is pregnant but does not want to be a young single mother. Then she sees a billboard with the words "Pregnant and Scared" followed by a telephone number. She calls the number thinking that she can get information about how to obtain an abortion. The person answering the phone says that she can help and invites her to visit the Pregnancy Support Center. When the young woman arrives, she finds out that it is not at all what she expected. Rather than direct her to where she can obtain an abortion, a counselor offers her a free ultrasound test. When it reveals that the woman, is in fact, pregnant, the counselor hands her some hand-knit baby booties and says, "Congratulations, you are a mother." She is also shown little tiny rubber fetuses, about as big as a thumb. She also may be told that there is a "higher incidence of breast cancer, infertility, and depression and suicide in those who have had abortions."

Such clinics or centers are set up for the purpose of talking women out of having an abortion and encouraging them to give birth. They are most often associated with Christian charities. One group says that it has approximately 2,300 such centers around the country. Critics such as Planned Parenthood and prochoice groups argue that these centers take advantage of women at an emotionally difficult moment. They also point out that mistaken factual information is being given, such as the increased cancer and other risks from abortion. In fact, the National Cancer Institute in a 2003 study found no increased risk of breast cancer. Other studies note that "fewer than 0.3% of patients experience a complication serious enough to require hospitalization." Abortion, rather, is said to be "one of the most common surgical procedures" and especially in the first trimester is "extremely safe."[1]

Those who do provide abortion services are often harassed. In March 1993, a doctor who performed abortions was shot and killed by an antiabortion protester. More than five years later, in October 1998, Dr. Barnett Slepian was shot to death in his home by someone with a high-powered rifle. Like six other clinic workers before him, Dr. Slepian was killed for performing abortions. On July 18, 2005, Eric Rudolph was sentenced to life in prison in Alabama for placing a bomb at a women's health care clinic that also performed abortions. This bomb killed an off-duty police officer and seriously injured and blinded the director of nursing at the clinic. Rudolph was also responsible for bombs placed at another abortion clinic, a gay club, and the 1996 Olympics, crimes for which he had yet to be sentenced. At his latest sentencing, he continued to insist that he was justified in what he did. Some in the prolife movement, however, disagree with the tactics of more militant antiabortion individuals and groups. They believe that these tactics and the murders of physicians have hurt their cause. They preach nonviolence and urge respect for all persons, including the unborn.[2] In 2003, the only abortion provider in a small North Carolina town had her center's windows blown out by a shotgun, an event that caused the doctor to put a fence around the building and install cameras, alarms, and a security guard. At one point, flyers designed like wanted posters with her picture on them were circulated around the town. The director met with members of a local church where one of those responsible attended, and this helped.[3]

In 1994, the U.S. Supreme Court upheld a Florida statute that required a thirty-six-foot buffer zone around abortion clinics; the zone had been established to protect patients who were entering the clinics from antiabortion demonstrators and undue noise. Although the Court ruled that protesters could not enter this buffer zone, it overturned elements of the statute restricting them from displaying signs and talking to people beyond this thirty-six-foot zone.[4] Still, we continue to see such scenes as described in the opening on the evening news and described in newspapers. Why? Abortion is an issue about which people have extremely strong opinions. Expressions of their opinions are often highly emotionally charged. Among the probable reasons why it is such a volatile issue is that it is a matter of life and death and involves beliefs about the very meaning of life itself. It is also a gender issue and touches our beliefs about the most intimate and powerful aspects of our lives as women and men and as mothers and fathers. Sometimes, people's views are based on religious beliefs, but this is not always or necessarily the case.

To complicate matters further, people do not always notice that there is a difference between asking about the morality of abortion and asking what the law ought or ought not to be in its regard. In addition, the language that is used in the debate over abortion often influences the debate. What is meant by *prolife?* Do not both those who oppose and those who condone abortion act in support of life? What is meant by *prochoice?* The position supporting a woman's right to choose abortion is the usual meaning of *prochoice.* The terms *proabortion* and *antichoice* have significantly different overtones than the terms generally used. This shows the importance of language in how an ethical debate is couched. In this chapter, we try to avoid labels and analyze the issues and arguments

in such a way as to help us focus more clearly on the alternative views and the reasons that support them.

What we say about the morality of abortion will depend on several issues. Some are strictly ethical matters and involve basic ethical perspectives, such as the nature and basis of moral rights. Others are factual matters, such as what happens at different stages of fetal development and what the likely consequences are of certain actions given particular social conditions. Others still are conceptual matters, such as the meaning of *abortion* or *a person* or *a human being.* We begin our analysis with certain factual matters about the stages of fetal development and contemporary methods of abortion.

STAGES OF FETAL DEVELOPMENT

When considering stages of fetal development, the label given to the developing fetus at particular stages is not likely to be relevant to any ethical argument because these are just names given for purposes of identification and communication; in fact, they are terms that are used throughout the biological sciences and pertain to most if not all vertebrates. The newly fertilized egg is called a *zygote,* which simply means "joining together." When the ball of cells reaches the uterus seven to ten days after fertilization, it is called a *blastocyst*—a *blastula* is a fluid-filled cavity surrounded by a single layer of cells. From the second to eighth week of gestation, the developing organism is called an *embryo,* as is any animal at this early stage of primitive tissue and organ development. From then until birth, it is called a *fetus,* which means "young unborn." We will simplify things and use the term *fetus* throughout development, but use of this term does not imply anything about its value or status. We can single out the following stages of fetal development (times are approximate).

■ Day 1: Fertilization—An ovum, or egg (23 chromosomes), is penetrated by sperm (23 chromosomes), and one cell is formed that contains 46 chromosomes.
■ Days 2–3: The fertilized ovum passes through the fallopian tube as cell division increases.

- Days 7–10: The blastocyst reaches the uterus; it has now become a "ball of cells."
- Week 2: The developing embryo becomes embedded in the uterine wall.
- Weeks 2–8: Organ systems such as the brain, spinal cord, heart, and digestive tube and certain structural features such as arm and leg buds begin and then continue to develop.
- Weeks 12–16: "Quickening" occurs, and the mother can feel the fetus's movements; the fetus is approximately $5\frac{1}{2}$ inches long.
- Weeks 20–24: So-called brain waves become detectable as the human cortex begins to form. Nevertheless they are not of the kind that is present much later in fetal development as the structure of the brain develops. Otherwise, electrical activity detected earlier is more like that detected in plants or other organs or skin.[5]
- Weeks 20–28: The process of "viability" takes place, and the fetus is able to live apart from its mother, depending on size (2+ pounds) and lung development.
- Week 40: Birth.

All changes during fetal development occur gradually. Even conception takes some time as the sperm penetrates the egg and together they come to form one cell. Any of these stages may or may not be morally relevant as we shall consider shortly.

METHODS OF ABORTION

From perhaps their earliest times, human beings have discovered and known various methods of abortion. The Hippocratic Oath of the fourth century B.C. mentions it. When we speak of abortion, we mean induced abortion. This is to be distinguished from spontaneous abortion or what we generally call "miscarriage." Among current methods of inducing abortion are the following.

- **Morning-after pill:** This chemical compound, which the U.S. Food and Drug Administration refers to as Plan B, prevents the blastocyst from embedding in the uterine wall (the intrauterine device—IUD—and some contraceptive pills operate in a similar way, causing the fertilized egg to be expelled by making the uterine wall inhospitable). Since August 2006, this pill has been available over the counter for customers eighteen years of age and older.
- **RU486 (mifepristone):** This drug was developed in France and induces uterine contractions and expulsion of the embryo. It must be used within seven weeks of a missed menstrual period.[6]
- **Uterine or vacuum aspiration:** In this procedure, the cervix (the opening of the uterus) is dilated, and the uterine contents are removed by suction tube.
- **Dilation and curettage (D&C):** This procedure also dilates the cervix so that the uterus can be scraped with a spoon-shaped curette. This method is similar to the vacuum method except that it is performed somewhat later and requires that the fetus be dismembered and then removed.
- **Saline solution:** A solution of salt and water is used to replace amniotic fluid and thus effect a miscarriage.
- **Prostaglandin drugs:** These pharmaceuticals induce early labor.
- **Hysterotomy:** This uncommon procedure is similar to a cesarean section but is used for later term abortions.
- **Dilation and extraction (D&X) or Intact D&E or "Partial birth abortion":** In this uncommon second- and third-trimester procedure, forceps are used to deliver the torso of the fetus, its skull is punctured and the cranial contents suctioned out, and then delivery is completed.

In 2003, 1.29 million abortions were performed in the United States, down from a high of 1.61 million in 1990.[7] Each year, two out of every 100 women aged 15–44 have an abortion. Forty-eight percent of them have had at least one previous abortion. Fifty-two percent of those having abortions are under 25 years of age, and 33 percent are between the ages of 20 and 24. "Black women are almost four times as likely as white women to have an abortion, and Hispanic women are 2.5 times as likely."[8] One cause of this higher rate is likely to be the cuts for family planning funding over the last ten years, resulting in, among other things, reduced contraceptive use, especially among poor women.[9]

The rate of abortions for women living below the federal poverty line is more than four times that of women with incomes 300 percent above that level. In terms of claimed religious affiliation, 43 percent were Protestant and 27 percent were Catholic. A 2004 study reported that among the reasons that women cite for choosing an abortion are that:

- it would dramatically change their lives, their ability to continue with school or work, or their ability to care for others (74 percent);
- they could not afford children (73 percent);
- they were finished having children (38 percent); or
- they did not want to become single mothers (48 percent).

Few cited health problems of either fetus or mother (12 percent).[10] Around the world, abortions are legal in fifty-four countries (61 percent of the world's population) and illegal in ninety-seven countries (39 percent of the world's population). Seventy-eight percent of all abortions are obtained in developing countries, and 22 percent occur in developed countries.[11] "There are approximately 46 million abortions conducted each year" around the world; "20 million of them [are] obtained illegally."[12]

In China, abortion has resulted in a demographic phenomenon. Because of Chinese parents' preferences for boys (who can care for their parents in their old age) and government fines for those who have more than one or two children, the ratio of boys to girls in some sections of China today is now 144 to 100. With the availability of ultrasound scanners since the 1990s, many potential parents choose to terminate pregnancy if the child is to be a girl. This is less so in larger cities where women have a higher status.[13]

ABORTION AND THE LAW

Much of the contemporary debate about abortion is concerned with whether the law ought to permit abortion and, if so, what if any legal regulations ought to be placed on it. The relationship between morality and the law is often ignored in these debates. Sometimes, it is assumed that if abortion is immoral, it ought to be illegal just for that reason, or if it is morally permissible, it therefore ought to be legally permissible. As noted in the previous chapter on euthanasia, this equivalence between morality and the law is questionable. We can think of actions that are possibly immoral but that we would not want to be legally prohibited. For example, I may wrongly waste my talents, but I would not want the law to force me to develop and use them. However, many of our laws, such as civil rights laws, are grounded in moral reasons. What one believes the law should and should not do is bound up with an entire philosophy of law. Because this is an ethics text, we will not be able to explore this here. (Some treatment of this issue can be found in the following chapter's discussion of the legal regulation of pornography.) What we can do is note and be aware of the recent legislation about abortion. We can also note, as we summarize here, that some of the reasons given for these laws do nevertheless involve appeals to rights and other moral values.

Abortion has not always been condemned, even by churches now opposed to it.[14] Nor has it always been illegal, even in the United States. In fact, according to U.S. Supreme Court Justice Blackmun, writing in 1973, "At the time of the adoption of our Constitution, and throughout the major portion of the 19th century, abortion was viewed with less disfavor than under most American statutes currently in effect."[15] In the first half of the twentieth century, most states passed laws regulating or making abortion illegal, except in certain cases such as a pregnancy resulting from rape or incest or when the pregnant woman's life or health was threatened. However, women continued to have abortions illegally and under dangerous conditions. In the early 1970s, a pregnant woman from Texas, who was given the fictitious name Jane Roe, appealed the denial of a legal abortion. This case finally made its way to the U.S. Supreme Court, which ruled in its 1973 decision known as *Roe* v. *Wade.* In this decision, the Court stated that no state may prohibit abortion before the time of fetal viability and a fundamental "right to privacy" was grounded in the Constitution, chiefly in the liberty and due process clauses of the Fourteenth Amendment. The term *privacy* here does not refer to matters that must be kept secret or to what goes on in one's own home, but to a basic liberty, a freedom from restraint in decisions about how to live and enjoy one's life.[16] However, the Court noted that the state did have some interest in protecting what it called the "potential life" of the fetus as well as an interest in maternal health. (Note that the phrase *potential life* is not especially illuminating, because most people do not deny that the fetus is actually alive.) In the case of maternal health, this interest becomes "compelling" (1) from the end of the first trimester (or third month) of pregnancy on, and (2) in the case of the fetus's "potential life," beginning with viability. The right to privacy was said not to be absolute but limited when these compelling state or social interests were at stake. The decision divided pregnancy into three trimesters and ruled that

1. from the end of the first trimester on, states could make laws to ensure the medical safety of the abortion procedures;
2. before the time of viability, about the end of the second trimester (the sixth month), the abortion decision should be left up to the pregnant woman and her doctor; and
3. from the time of viability on, states could prohibit abortion except in those cases in which the continued pregnancy would endanger the life or health of the pregnant woman.[17]

Since *Roe* v. *Wade,* the U.S. Supreme Court has handed down several other abortion-related decisions. These have restricted Medicaid funding to cases in which the woman's life was at risk or the pregnancy resulted from rape or incest (*Harris* v. *McRae,* 1980), or they have put other restrictions on the timing of an abortion and on its procedure. In *Akron* v. *Center for Reproductive Health* (1983), a state law that required a twenty-four-hour waiting period and notification of risks was held to be unconstitutional,[18] and in *Webster* v. *Reproductive Health Services* (1989), a ban on the use of public facilities and employees for performing abortion and a test to determine fetal viability were also found to be constitutional. However, in a 1992 opinion concerning a Pennsylvania case, *Planned Parenthood* v. *Casey,* the Court again found some state restrictions to be permissible while also

affirming the basic decision in *Roe* v. *Wade.* Noting that there had been no significant factual or legal changes or developments since the 1973 decision, and that it was important that the Court not change significant opinions on which people had come to depend, the 1992 decision again supported the legal right to privacy and abortion. It commented on the relationship of abortion to the situation of equal opportunity for women. It also reiterated the state's interest in protecting life and argued that states could make regulations for such things as waiting periods to support this interest. However, it argued that these restrictions should not place an *undue burden* on women in the exercise of their constitutional right to privacy. This means that state laws may not create "substantial obstacles" for women who wish abortions.[19] The Supreme Court has ruled that "minors must have an alternative, such as the ability to seek a court order authorizing the procedure."[20] Some states have attempted to restrict abortion in various ways. On April 18, 2007, the Supreme Court by a vote of five to four upheld the law banning so called partial birth abortion passed by Congress in 2003. It held that this law was not unconstitutional, and did not impose "an undue burden on women's exercise of their right to end a pregnancy."[21] The reasoning of the majority opinion said that there were alternatives to this procedure, and that the law enacted by Congress reflected the government's "legitimate, substantial interest in preserving and promoting fetal life." It allowed exceptions to protect a woman's life but not her health. However, critics assert that this procedure is sometimes necessary to protect a woman's health because it is "often the safest to use late in the pregnancy because it minimizes the chances of injury to the uterus." It was deemed appropriate for certain cases by the American College of Obstetricians and Gynecologists, the dissenting opinion noted. This ruling resulted in part from the recent appointment of two conservative justices and the retirement of Justice Sandra Day O'Connor.[22]

Also controversial are state laws that require underage daughters to obtain parental or state permission to have legal abortions. One issue here is whether abortion should follow the rule for surgeries in general, needing permission from a legal guardian, or whether it is uniquely personal and thus a matter for private decision even by those under ages eighteen or twenty-one.

Also problematic are certain so-called feticide laws that more than half the U.S. states now have. These are laws that make it a crime to cause harm to a fetus. Thus, someone who attacks a pregnant woman and kills the fetus that she wanted to carry to term can be found guilty of murder or manslaughter. States differ in how they classify the crime, whether as "feticide" or under general manslaughter or murder laws. It may seem contradictory that the woman can end her fetus's life through abortion but a third party who kills the fetus she wanted may be guilty of murder. Some have said that the difference is between one who exercises a "reproductive choice" and another person who does not. Further questions are raised by states who want to protect fetal life from harmful actions of the pregnant woman such as ingesting drugs. She could be punished if her fetus is born harmed but not if she aborts the fetus. Should a state be able to prevent her from continuing drug use during pregnancy?

Although these Supreme Court decisions have not been unanimous, they seem to be attempts to balance concerns for the various moral values involved in abortion. In doing so, however, these decisions have made neither side in the abortion debate particularly happy. On the one hand, they stressed the values of privacy, liberty, and equal opportunity; on the other hand, they concluded that some recognition ought to be given to the origins of human life. Because these are moral values reflected in the law, some of the issues about the morality of abortion will be relevant to what we think the law should or should not do here. In what follows, however, we will concentrate on the question of the morality of abortion.[23]

ABORTION: THE MORAL QUESTION

Although the position that abortion ought to be a private matter and not a matter of law is debatable, it is much more difficult to make an argument that abortion is not a moral matter. After all, abortion involves issues of rights, happiness, and well-being, as well as the value of human life. If these things are morally relevant, then abortion is a moral matter. This is not to say that it is good or bad, simply that it is morally important.

What one says about abortion also may have relevance for what to think about fetal research. For example, promising studies have shown that tissue from aborted fetuses might be used to relieve the symptoms of some persons with Parkinson's disease, an incurable degenerative neurological condition.[24] And recent developments in cloning technology have shown possibilities for taking stem cells from the embryo at the blastocyst stage and programming them to produce organs such as kidneys for transplant.[25]

Rather than outlining so-called conservative, liberal, and moderate views on abortion, let us approach the issue somewhat differently. Then we can take a new look at it and not get caught up in labels. Suppose we consider two types of arguments both for and against abortion: arguments for which the moral status of the fetus is irrelevant and arguments for which it is relevant. We may suppose that all arguments regarding abortion hinge on this issue, but this is not the case. "Moral status of the fetus" is meant to cover questions about whether the fetus is a human being or whether it is a person, and whether the fetus has any value or any rights, including a right to life. We look first at arguments that do not concern themselves with the fetus's moral status. As you examine the arguments, you may find that one or another seems more valid or reasonable to you.

ARGUMENTS THAT DO NOT DEPEND ON THE MORAL STATUS OF THE FETUS

First, we will consider arguments for which the moral status of the fetus is irrelevant. These arguments are based on utilitarian reasoning and issues of persons' rights.

Utilitarian Reasoning

Many arguments that focus on something other than the moral status of the fetus are consequentialist in nature and broadly utilitarian. Arguments for abortion often cite the bad consequences that may result from a continued pregnancy—for example, the loss of a job or other opportunities for the pregnant woman, the suffering of the future child, the burden of caring for the child under particular circumstances, and so on. Some arguments against abortion also cite the loss of happiness and the future contributions of the being who is aborted.

According to act utilitarian reasoning, each case or action stands on its own, so to speak. Its own consequences determine whether it is good or bad, better or worse than other alternatives. Act utilitarians believe that the people making the abortion decision must consider the likely consequences of the alternative actions—in other words, having or not having an abortion (as well as such considerations as where and when). Among the kinds of consequences to consider are health risks and benefits, positive or negative mental or psychological consequences, and financial and social aspects of the alternative choices. For example, a pregnant woman should consider questions such as these: What would be the effect on her of having the child versus ending the pregnancy? What are the consequences to any others affected? Would the child, if born, be likely to have a happy or unhappy life, and how would one determine this? How would an abortion or the child's birth affect her family, other children, the father, the grandparents, and so on?

Notice that the issue of whether the fetus (in the sense we are using it here) is a person or a human being is not among the things to consider when arguing from this type of consequentialist perspective. Abortion at a later stage of pregnancy might have different effects on people than at an earlier stage, and it might also have different effects on the fetus in terms of whether it might experience pain. It is the effects on the mother, child, and others that matter in utilitarian thinking, not the moral status of the fetus (what kind of value it has) or its ontological status (i.e., what kind of being we say it is; see note 29) at that stage of development.[26] Also notice that on utilitarian or consequentialist grounds, abortion sometimes would be permissible (the morally right thing to do) and sometimes not: It would depend on the consequences of the various sorts noted earlier. Moral judgments about

abortion will be better or worse, according to this view, depending on the adequacy of the prediction of consequences.

Critics of utilitarian reasoning generally object to its seeming disregard of rights. They may point out that if we do not take the right to life seriously, then utilitarian reasoning may condone the taking of any life if the overall consequences of doing so are good! Thus, some critics might argue that the moral status of the fetus, such as whether it is the kind of being that has a right to life, is quite relevant to moral decisions about abortion. Others would insist that we address the matter of the rights of the pregnant woman (or others) and the problem of conflicts of rights.

Some Rights Arguments

Some arguments about abortion *do* consider the rights of persons but still maintain that the moral status of the fetus is irrelevant. It is irrelevant in the sense that whether or not we think of the fetus as a person with full moral rights is not crucial for decisions about the morality of abortion. An article on abortion by Judith Jarvis Thomson makes such an argument. She does assume for the purpose of argument that the fetus is a person from early on in pregnancy. But her conclusion is that abortion is still justified, even if the fetus is a person with a right to life (and she assumes it is also permissible if the fetus is not a person).[27] This is why the argument does not turn on what we say about the moral status of the fetus.

The question she poses is whether the pregnant woman has an obligation to sustain the life of the fetus through providing it with the means of life. To have us think about this, she asks us to consider an imaginary scenario. Suppose, she says, that you wake up one morning and find yourself attached through various medical tubings to a famous violinist. You find out that during the night you have been kidnapped and hooked up to this violinist. The violinist has severe kidney problems, and the only way that his life can be saved is through being hooked up to another person so that the other person's kidneys will do the job of purifying his blood for some period of time until his own kidneys have recovered. The question Thomson poses is this: Would you be morally permitted or justified in "unplugging" the violinist, even though to do so would result in his death? Thomson argues that you would be justified, in particular, because you had not consented to save the violinist. The point of this example applies most obviously to cases of rape. However, Thomson means it to apply more widely, and she uses other analogies to help make her point. One would only have a responsibility to save the violinist (or nurture the fetus) if one had agreed to do so. The consent that Thomson has in mind is a deliberate and planned choice. She argues that although it would be generous of you to save the life of the violinist (or the fetus), you are not obligated to do so. Her point is that no one has a right to use your body, even to save his own life, unless you give him that right. Such views are consistent with a position that stresses that women are persons and have a right to bodily integrity as do other people, and that as people they ought not to be used against their will for whatever purposes by others, even noble purposes such as the nurturing of children. Critics of this argument point out that it may apply at most to cases of rape, for in some other cases one might be said to implicitly consent to a pregnancy if one did what one knew might result in it. One response to this is that we do not always consider a person to have consented to chance consequences of their actions.

The persons' rights and utilitarian arguments are examples of arguments about abortion that do not depend on what we say about the moral status of the fetus, but other arguments hold this issue to be crucial. Some arguments for the moral permissibility of abortion as well as some against it rely in crucial ways on what is said about the fetus. We next consider some of these arguments.

ARGUMENTS THAT DEPEND ON THE MORAL STATUS OF THE FETUS

Not all arguments depend on what we say about the fetus as we have just seen, but some abortion arguments turn on what is said about the moral status of the fetus. They ask such questions as: Is it a human being? A person? Alive? Let us for the moment focus not on these terms and what they might mean, but on the more general issue—that is, let us focus on the question of what kind of

value or moral status the developing fetus has. Does it have a different status in various stages of development? If so, when does the status change, and why? (Further issues would include how to weigh its value or rights in comparison to other values or the rights of others.) I suggest that we examine a first approach and call it "Method I" and distinguish it from a broader approach that I will call "Method II." Briefly put, Method I focuses on the characteristics of the fetus and asks when it has what should be considered so significant that it is a person or has a new moral status from that point on. Method II asks a more general question. It asks us to think about what kind of beings of any sort, human or nonhuman, have some special moral status and possibly also rights such as a right to life. In this way it is also related to issues of animal rights (see Chapter 15).

Method I

In using this method, we focus on fetal development and ask three things about possibly significant stages: (1) *What* is present? (2) *When* is this present (at what stage)? and (3) *Why* is this significant—in other words, why does this give this being special moral status, if it does? By "special moral status" we might mean various things. Among the most important would be whether the status were such that the fetus would be thought to have something like a right to life. If this were the case, then abortion would become morally problematic.[28]

Suppose we try Method I on various stages in fetal development and see what the arguments would look like. In each case, let us consider the arguments for the position and then some criticisms of these arguments.

Conception or Fertilization Fertilization, or when sperm penetrate the ovum, is the time at which many opponents of abortion say that the fetus has full moral status. The reason usually given is that this is when the fetus has the full genetic makeup from the combining of sperm and egg. In times past, people held that the egg provided the entire substance and the sperm only gave it a charge or impetus to grow, or that the sperm was "the little man" and only needed a place to grow and obtain nourishment, which the egg provided! We now know about the contribution of both sperm and ovum to the zygote. The argument for taking this stage as the morally significant one supposes an ontological argument something like this:[29] If we say that the resulting being that is born is a human being or person, and if there is no significant change in its development from its initial form, then it is the same being all the way through the development period. Otherwise, we would be implying that different beings are succeeding one another during this process.

Critics of this position may point out that, although fetal development is continuous, the bare genetic basis present at conception is not enough to constitute a person at that point. In this early stage, the cells are *totipotent* and can become skin cells or heart cells or many other types of cells.[30] There is no structure or differentiation at this point, nothing that resembles a person in this initial form. There is not even an individual there. Consider, for example, what happens in the case of identical twinning. Before implantation, identical twins are formed by the splitting of cells in the early embryo. Each resulting twin has the same genetic makeup. Now what are we to think of the original embryo? Suppose conception is the time when we are supposed to have an individual being. We will call him John. The twins that develop and later are born are Jim and Joe. What happened to John, if there was a John? Jim and Joe are two new individuals, genetically alike as twins, but also two different people. Is there a little of John in each of them? Or does the fact that there are two individuals after twinning mean that there was not any individual there before that time—that John never existed? Those who support conception as the crucial time at which we have a being with full moral status and rights must explain how there can be an individual at conception, at least in the case of identical twinning.

Detectable Brain Waves Another possibility for when a fetus might attain new moral status is that point at which brain waves begin to be detectable. The idea is reasonable given that the human brain is the locus of consciousness, language, and communication, and it is what makes us crucially dif-

ferent from other animals. Moreover, we now use the *cessation* of brain function as the determinant of death. Why should we not use the *beginning* of brain function as the beginning of an individual's life? We can detect brain activity between the sixth and eighth weeks of fetal development, which makes that point the significant time for this view.

Critics of this argument point out that brain activity develops gradually and we can single out no one time during its development as unique. However, this may be only a practical problem. We might be satisfied with an approximation rather than a determinate time. Other questions about the type of brain function also might be raised. At six to eight weeks, the brain is quite simple; only much later do those parts develop that are the basis of conscious function. At earlier stages, the brain is arguably not that different from other animal brains in structure or function.

Quickening Usually, the pregnant woman can feel the fetus kick or move in approximately the fourth month of fetal development. This is what is meant by *quickening*. In former times, people may have thought there was no fetal movement before this time, and this would then be a more persuasive reason to consider this stage as crucial. Still, we could think of the movement present at this time as self-initiated movement because it now stems from a new level of brain development. This would make a better reason for considering this the beginning of the being's new life because it would now be moving about on its own.

Critics will raise the same issue for this point as for brain development—namely, that there is no dramatic break in development of the ability of the fetus to move. Moreover, they might also point out that other animals and even plants move on their own, and this does not give them special moral status or a right to life. Furthermore, those who argue for animal rights usually do so because of their sentience, their ability to feel pleasure and pain, and not their ability to move.

Viability Viability is approximately the fifth month in fetal development, at which time the fetus is capable of existing apart from the pregnant woman or mother. All its organs and organ systems are sufficiently developed that it can function on its own. The last system to be functionally complete is the respiratory system. During previous stages of fetal development, the fetus "breathes" amniotic fluid. Before twenty-three or twenty-four weeks of gestation, "capillaries have not yet moved close enough to the air sacs to carry gases to and from the lung."[31] A lubricant, surfactant, can be administered to "help the lungs expand and take in air," but even then the chance of survival is slim. One practical problem with using viability as a criterion is its variability. When *Roe* v. *Wade* took effect, viability was considered to be approximately twenty-six weeks; the estimation has since been shortened by a couple of weeks. At twenty-three or twenty-four weeks, the "micropremie" weighs slightly less than a pound. Its prematurity is also a function of this weight and the mother's socioeconomic status; if she's poor, then the chances are that her nutrition is poor. Prematurity also varies by sex and race: Girls are approximately one week ahead of boys in development, and blacks are approximately one week ahead of whites.[32]

Why is the stage of viability singled out as the stage at which the fetus may take on a new moral status? Some answer that it is the capacity for *independent* existence that is the basis for the new status. However, if it were delivered at this time and left on its own, no infant would be able to survive. Perhaps the notion of *separate* existence is what is intended. The idea would be that the fetus is more clearly distinct from the mother before birth at this point. Or perhaps the notion of *completeness* is what is intended. Although the fetus is not fully formed at viability because much development takes place after birth, the argument might be that the viable fetus is sufficiently complete, enabling us to think of it as a new being.

Critics of viability can point again to the gradual nature of development and the seeming arbitrariness of picking out one stage of completeness as crucially different from the others. They also can point out that the viable fetus would still be dependent on others even if it were delivered at the point of viability. In addition, they can question the whole notion of making moral status a function of independence. We are all dependent on one another, and those who are more independent—just because of viability—have no greater value than those who are more dependent. Even someone dependent on machines is not for this reason less human, they might argue. Furthermore, the viable unborn fetus is still, in fact, dependent on the mother and does not have an existence separate from her. Birth, on these terms, would be a better time to pick than viability, they might argue, if it is separateness and independence that are crucial.

Each point in fetal development may provide a reasonable basis for concluding something about the moral status of the fetus. However, as we can clearly see, none are problem-free. In any case, the whole idea of grounding moral status and rights on the possession of certain characteristics also may be called into question. We might be able to get some help in thinking about this problem by looking at a second method.

Method II

If what we say about the fetus is crucial to a position about the morality of abortion, then we may do well to compare what we say here to what we say about beings other than human fetuses. Why, for example, do we believe that people generally have rights? Are we significantly different from other animals such that we have unique moral status simply because we are *human beings*? Or is the crucial determinant of special moral status or worth the ability to reason or think or imagine or dream? If so, then if there are other intelligent beings in the universe, would they have the same moral status as we do, even if they were not members of our species? Or suppose further that we consider cases in which human beings do not have the capacity for thought and reasoning and communication. Think, for example, of a newborn with anencephaly—that is, without a developed upper brain and thus no chance of consciousness or thought. In fact, such an infant does not usually live for long. But it is a human being biologically and not a member of some other species. Or take the case at the other end of life in which a person is in a permanent vegetative state. There is no doubt that the person is still human in the biological sense, but does this person lack human rights because he or she lacks some mental qualities that are the basis for rights? Finally, perhaps it is not actual ability to think or communicate but the potential for the development of these characteristics that grounds special moral worth and rights. A normal fetus would have this potentiality whereas a two-year-old dog would not. Of course, this depends on the level or type of thinking that is seen to be crucial, because dogs do have some type of mental capacity and some ability to communicate.

Taking each suggestion and giving it a name, we might have something like the following positions.[33] Each gives an answer to this question: What kind of beings have special moral status, which may include something like a right to life?[34]

Being Human According to one point of view, it is being a human being that counts—being a member of the human species. Now, using this criterion, we can note that human fetuses are members of the human species and conclude that they have equal moral status with all other human beings. The argument for this position might include something about the moral advance we make when we recognize that all humans have equal moral worth. This has not always been the case, such as when children or women were considered more as property than as human beings with equal and full moral status as humans, or when African American slaves were each considered to be three-fifths of a person. Nevertheless, questions can be raised about why only members of the human species are included here. If some other species of being were sufficiently like us in the relevant respects, then should they not be considered to have the same worth as members of our own species? In considering this possibility, we may be better able to decide whether it is membership in a species or something else that grounds moral worth.

Being Like Human Beings Suppose that moral status (or personhood) depends on being a member of any species whose members have certain significant characteristics like human beings. But what characteristics are significant enough to ground high moral value and status, including rights? For example, consider the abilities to communicate, reason, and plan. Depending on how high a level of communicating, reasoning, and planning is required, perhaps other animals would qualify for the high moral status envisioned. Some chimpanzees and gorillas, for instance, can learn to communicate through sign language, according to some scientists. If there are beings elsewhere in the universe who are members of a different species but who can communicate, reason, and plan, then according to this criterion they too would have the same moral worth as humans. If a lower level of ability were used, then members of other animal species would also qualify.

These first two criteria are alike in that it is membership in a species that is the determinant of one's moral status. If any humans have this status, then they all do. If chimpanzees have this status, or Martians, then all members of their species also have this status. It does not matter what the individual member of the species is like or what individual capacities she or he possesses. On the other hand, perhaps it is not of what species you are a member but what individual characteristics you have that forms the basis of the special moral status we are concerned with here. If this were the case, then there would be at least three other possible positions about the basis of moral status. These are as follows.

Potentiality *Potentiality* literally means "power." According to this criterion, all beings that have the power to develop certain key characteristics have full moral worth. Thus, if a particular fetus had the potential for developing the requisite mental capacities, then this fetus would have full moral status. However, any fetus or other human being that does not have this potential (anencephalic infants or those in a permanent vegetative state, for example) does not have this status.

Yet how important is potential—and what, in fact, is it? Suppose that one had the potential to become a famous star or hold political office. Would one then have the same respect and rights due the actual star, say, or the legislator? Consider a fictitious story.[35] Suppose that we have a kitten that will grow into a mature cat if left alone. We also have a serum that if injected into the kitten will make it grow into a human being. After the injection, first the fur changes, then the tail goes, and so forth. Now if we ask whether the kitten had the potential to be a human being before the injection, we probably would say no, or that it had potential in only the weakest sense. But what would we say about the potential of the kitten to be a human being after it was injected? Only then, critics of the potentiality criterion might argue, would the potential for being a human being or person be relevant to treating the injected kitten differently than an ordinary kitten. In any case, the notion of potentiality may be morally significant, but supporters of this view must be able to address the issues raised by these criticisms.

Actuality At the other end of the spectrum is the view according to which simple "potentiality" for developing certain characteristics counts for nothing (or at least does not give one the kind of moral status about which we are concerned). Only the actual possession of the requisite characteristics is sufficient for full moral status. Again, it makes a significant difference to one's position here whether the characteristics are high-level or low-level. For example, if a rather high level of reasoning is required before an individual has the requisite moral status, then newborns probably would not be included, as well as many others.[36] According to this view, although the fetus, newborn infant, and extremely young child are human beings biologically, they are not yet persons or beings with the requisite moral status. They are not yet members of the moral community. There may be good reasons to treat them well and with respect, but it is not because they are persons with rights.

Evolving Value Finally, let us consider a position that is intermediate between the last two positions. Its underlying idea is that potential counts—but not as much as actual possession of the significant characteristics. Furthermore, as the potential is gradually developed, the moral status of the being also grows. This position also could be described in terms of competing interests and claims. The stronger the claim, the more it should prevail. If this is my book, then I have a stronger claim over it than you who would like to have the book.

In applying this criterion to fetal development, the conclusion would be that the early term fetus has less moral value or moral status than the late-term fetus. Less of a claim or interest on the part of others is needed to override its claim to consideration. Moderately serious interests of the pregnant woman or of society could override the interests or claims of the early term fetus, but it would take more serious interests to override the claims of the late-term fetus. In the end, according to this view, when potentiality is sufficiently actualized, the fetus or infant has as much right as any other person. Although some people may view the evolving value position as a reasonable moral one, it would be more difficult to use it in a legal context in which claims and interests would need to be publicly weighed and compared.

We might note a variant view held by some feminists. Most feminists support a woman's legal right to abortion, but they are not all happy with the rationale for it provided in *Roe* v. *Wade*.[37] For example, some worry that the "right to privacy" could be interpreted in ways that are detrimental to women. If this right is taken to imply that everything done in the privacy of one's home is out of the law's reach, then this would include some abuse of women and children.[38] Some feminists also have misgivings about the implications of some abortion supporters' views of the moral status of the fetus. Like the last of the five positions in Method II, they argue that the fetus is surely human. It is both part and not part of the pregnant woman, but a separate being. Abortion is morally problematic, in some of these views, because the loss of an early form of human life is, in fact, loss of part of the mother's own life. However, this is not to imply that these views grant the fetus full moral status and rights. These critics do not necessarily conclude that abortion is morally impermissible.

These positions, as well as those summarized in Method I, focus on what to say about the status of the fetus. If the fetus does not have the requisite moral status, then abortion is probably morally permissible. If it does have that status, then abortion is morally problematic. If the fetus is said to have a somewhat in-between status, then the conclusion about abortion would be mixed. Again, these are positions that put the whole weight of the moral judgment about abortion on what status the fetus does or does not have. As the utilitarian and persons' rights arguments exemplified, however, there are other considerations about what counts in thinking about the morality of abortion. Finally, remember that unless you believe that everything that is immoral ought to be illegal, then even if abortion were in some case thought to be immoral, one would need to give further reasons about the purpose of law to conclude that it also ought to be illegal. So also if you believe that the only reason why something ought to be illegal is if it is immoral, then if abortion is morally permissible you should conclude that it ought to be legally permissible. From this point of view, there would be no other relevant legal considerations. Both views are problematic.

NOTES

1. *Time,* Feb. 26, 2007, p. 28.
2. Based on a report in *The New York Times,* March 7, 1993, p. B3, and March 11, 1993, p. A1. Also see Jennifer Gonnerma, "The Terrorist Campaign Against Abortion," Nov. 3–9, 1998 (www.villagevoice.com/features/9845/abortion.shtml)
3. *Time,* Feb. 26, 2007, p. 30.
4. *Madsen v. Women's Health Ctr., Inc., U.S.* (June 30, 1994).
5. Thanks to Charles Cardwell for calling this to my attention.
6. The drug has been used by 200,000 European women and the U.S. Food and Drug Administration (FDA) has determined that it is safe and effective. The FDA also noted that "safe" does not mean risk-free. The drug's administration requires a two-stage procedure. Patients first take 600 milligrams of mifepristone and then return two days later for 200 micrograms of misoprostol, which triggers contractions 95 percent of the time. In the remaining 5 percent of cases, a surgical abortion is recommended. See *The New York Times,* July 20, 1996, pp. A1, A11. Once this method became available, there was expectation that it would become a method of choice. However, because of the greater time and expense, surgical abortions have not been replaced by this method.
7. *Time,* Feb. 26, 2007, p. 26.
8. See www.abortiontv.com/Misc/AbortionStatistics .htm.
9. *The New York Times,* May 5, 2006, p. A19.
10. *Time,* Feb. 26, 2007., p. 27.
11. www.abortiontv.com/Misc/AbortionStatistics.htm.
12. www.womensissues.about.com/cs/abortionstats/ a/aaabortionstats.htm.
13. Stanley K. Henshaw, Sushelela Singh, and Taylor Haas, "Recent Trends in Abortion Rates Worldwide," *Family Planning Perspectives, 25,* no. 1 (March 1999). Also see *The New York Times,* June 21, 2002.
14. In fact, abortion also has not always been condemned or treated as equivalent to the killing of a human being by one of its strongest opponents—the Roman Catholic Church. Following the teachings of Thomas Aquinas, the Church held until perhaps the fifteenth and sixteenth centuries that the fetus was not human until sometime after conception when the matter was suitable for the reception of a human soul. See John Noonan, *The Morality of Abortion* (Cambridge, MA: Harvard University Press, 1970). 18ff
15. Associate Justice Harry A. Blackmun, majority opinion in *Roe v. Wade,* United States Supreme Court, 410 U.S. 113 (1973).
16. See comments about this interpretation in Ronald Dworkin, "Feminists and Abortion," *New York Review of Books, XL,* no. 11 (June 10, 1993): 27–29.
17. Blackmun, *Roe v. Wade.*
18. Thanks to Alan Preti of Montgomery County Community College for calling this aspect of the ruling to my attention.
19. See http://members.aol.com'_ht_a/abtrbng/ overview.htm?mtbrand=Aol_US.
20. http://www.guttmacher.org/pubs/fb_induced_ abortion.html.
21. *The New York Times,* April 18, 2007.
22. Ibid.
23. Further thoughts on the relation between morality and the law can be found in Chapter 11 and its discussion of pornography and the law.
24. For more information, check www.nytimes.com/ library/national/science/042299sci-parkinsons.
25. See Shirley J. Wright, "Human Embryonic Stem-Cell Research: Science and Ethics," *American Scientist, 87* (July–August, 1999): 352–361.
26. Recall that rule utilitarian reasoning about abortion would be somewhat different. A rule

utilitarian must consider which practice regarding abortion would be best. Whatever she judged to be the best practice, she should follow. She should mentally survey various possible practices or rules. Would the rule "No one should have an abortion" be likely to maximize happiness? Would the rule "No one should have an abortion unless the pregnancy threatens the mother's health or well-being" have better consequences overall? What about a rule that says "Persons who are in situations *x, y,* or *z* should have abortions"? How would too easy access to abortion affect our regard for the very young? How would the practice of abortion when the fetus has certain abnormalities affect our treatment of the physically or mentally disabled in general? How would a restrictive abortion policy affect women's ability to participate as equal human beings, enjoying jobs and other opportunities? Whichever practice or rule is likely to have the better net results—that is, more good consequences and fewer bad ones—is the best practice.

27. Judith Jarvis Thomson, "A Defense of Abortion," *Philosophy and Public Affairs, 1,* no. 1 (Fall 1971): 47–66.
28. Note that if the fetus had no right to life, then this would not automatically make abortion problem-free. See the comments in the last paragraph under "Method II."

29. An *ontological* argument is one that has to do with the nature and identity of beings; *ontos* means "being."
30. This issue has recently arisen with developments in stem cell research and cloning.
31. Sheryl Gay Stolberg, "Definition of Fetal Viability Is Focus of Debate in Senate," *The New York Times,* May 15, 1997, p. A13.
32. Ibid.
33. This is based on notes of mine whose source I could not find.
34. Compare this discussion with similar discussions in Chapters 15 and 16 on the environment and animal rights. In particular, note the possible distinction between having moral value and having rights.
35. This is taken from Michael Tooley's "Abortion and Infanticide," *Philosophy and Public Affairs, 2,* no. 1 (1972): 37–65.
36. This is the position of Mary Ann Warren in "On the Moral and Legal Status of Abortion," *The Monist, 57,* no. 1 (January 1973): 43–61.
37. See the summary of these views in Dworkin, "Feminists and Abortion," op. cit.
38. Note that this was not the interpretation of the "right to privacy" given earlier in this chapter. As based in the liberty clause of the Fourteenth Amendment, it was noted that it was a liberty right, the right or power to make one's own decisions about personal matters.

REVIEW EXERCISES

1. Outline the various stages of fetal development.
2. Explain the conclusions of *Roe* v. *Wade* and *Planned Parenthood* v. *Casey.*
3. Give a utilitarian argument for abortion. Give one against abortion. Are these act or rule utilitarian arguments? Explain.
4. Describe how Thomson uses the violinist analogy to make an argument about the moral permissibility of abortion.
5. Use Method I to make one argument for and one against abortion.
6. Which of the following positions under Method II does each statement exemplify?

a. Because this fetus has all the potential to develop the abilities of a person, it has all the rights of a person.
b. Only when a being can think and communicate does it have full moral status. Because a fetus does not have these abilities, it has neither moral rights nor claims.
c. If it is a human being, then it has full moral status and rights.
d. Its ability to feel pain gives a being full moral status. The fetus has this beginning in the fifth or sixth month, and so abortion is not morally justifiable beyond that stage.
e. Early term fetuses do not have as much moral significance as later-term fetuses because their potential is not as well developed as later.

DISCUSSION CASES

1. Abortion for Sex Selection. The sex of a child can now be determined before birth. In the waiting room of a local women's clinic, June has started a conversation with another woman, Ann. She finds out that each is there for an amniocentesis to determine the sex of her fetus. June reveals that she wants to know the sex because her husband and his family really want a boy. Because they plan to have only one child, they plan to end this pregnancy if it is a girl and try again. Ann tells her that her reason is different. She is a genetic carrier of a particular kind of muscular dystrophy. Duchenne muscular dystrophy is a sex-linked disease that is inherited through the mother. Only males develop the disease, and each male child has a 50 percent chance of having it. The disease causes muscle weakness and often some mental retardation. It causes death through respiratory failure, usually in early adulthood. Ann does not want to risk having such a child, and this abnormality cannot yet be determined through prenatal testing. Thus, if the prenatal diagnosis reveals that her fetus is male, she plans to end this pregnancy.

What do you think of the use of prenatal diagnosis and abortion for purposes of sex selection in these or in other cases?

2. Father's Consent to Abortion. Jim and Sue had been planning to have a child for two years. Finally, she became pregnant. However, their marriage had been a rough one, and by the time she was in her third month of pregnancy they had decided to divorce. At that point, both parents were ambivalent about the pregnancy. They had both wanted the child, but now things were different. Sue finally decided that she did not want to raise a child alone and did not want to raise Jim's child. She wanted to get on with her life. However, Jim had long wanted a child, and he realized that the developing fetus was partly his own because he had provided half of its genetic makeup. He did not want Sue to end the pregnancy. He wanted to keep and raise the child. The case was currently being heard by the court.

Although the primary decision is a legal one, do you think that Jim had any moral rights in this case or should the decision be strictly Sue's? Why or why not?

3. Parental Consent to Abortion. Judy is a high school sophomore and fifteen years old. She recently became sexually active with her boyfriend. She does not want to tell him that she is now pregnant and she does not feel that she can talk to her parents. They have been quite strict with her and would condemn her recent behavior. They also oppose abortion. Judy would like simply to end this pregnancy and start over with her life. However, minors in her state must get parental consent for an abortion; it is a medical procedure, and parents must consent to other medical procedures for their children.

What should Judy do? Do you agree that states should require parental consent for abortion for their minor children? Why or why not?

4. Pregnant Woman Detained. In 1995, a woman who was pregnant and refused to discontinue her use of cocaine was reported by her obstetrician to child-abuse authorities, who obtained an order from the juvenile court to take custody of the unborn child. Obviously, this involved detaining the mother. The case was settled after the child was born. If the fetus was regarded as a child who was being abused, then would it be reasonable in your view to detain the mother? Would it also be reasonable for a pregnant woman to be able to use a car pool lane by counting her fetus as a second person in the car? (Reported by Tamar Lewin, "Detention of Pregnant Woman for Drug Use Is Struck Down," *The New York Times,* April 23, 1997, p. A10.)

YOU MAKE THE DECISION

Apply the theories and issues discussed in this chapter by accessing this animated simulation on the Ethics Resource Center.

Use the passkey that accompanies your book to gain access. If you do not have a passkey, visit cengage brain.com to purchase instant access to additional study material.

In other words, she should have the right to an abortion. Do you agree? Why or why not?

Ethics Module 09 : Abortion   ◄◄ ▶ ▶▶   MUTE 🔇

© Cengage Learning

Selected Bibliography

Arkes, Hadley. *Natural Rights and the Right to Choose.* New York: Cambridge University Press, 2004.

Baird, Robert M., et al. *The Ethics of Abortion: Pro-Life vs. Pro-Choice.* Amherst, NY: Prometheus Books, 2004.

Beckwith, Francis J. *Defending Pro-Life: A Philosophical and Constitutional Case.* New York: Cambridge University Press, 2007.

Bender, Karen, et. al. *Choice: True Stories of Birth, Contraception, Infertility, Adoption, Single Parenthood, and Abortion.* San Francisco, CA: MacAdam/Cage Publishing, 2007.

Callahan, Daniel. *Abortion: Law, Choice, and Morality.* New York: Macmillan, 1970.

Cline, David P. *Creating Choice: A Community Responds to the Need for Abortion and Birth Control, 1961–1973.* New York: Palgrave Macmillan, 2007.

Colker, Ruth. *Abortion and Dialogue: Pro-Choice, Pro-Life, and American Law.* Bloomington: Indiana University Press, 1992.

Durrett, Deanne. *The Abortion Conflict: A Pro/Con Issue.* Berkeley Heights, NJ: Enslow Publishers, 2000.

Feinberg, Joel (Ed.). *The Problem of Abortion,* 2d ed. Belmont, CA: Wadsworth, 1984.

Garfield, Jay L., and Patricia Hennessy. *Abortion: Moral and Legal Perspectives.* Amherst: University of Massachusetts Press, 1985.

Graber, Mark A. *Rethinking Abortion: Equal Choice, the Constitution, and Reproductive Politics.* Princeton, NJ: Princeton University Press, 1996.

Hadley, Janet. *Abortion: Between Freedom and Necessity.* Philadelphia: Temple University Press, 1997.

Kamm, F. M. *Creation and Abortion: A Study in Moral and Legal Philosophy.* New York: Oxford University Press, 1992.

Kirk, Peggy. *You Aren't Alone: The Voices of Abortion.* Grass Valley, CA: Blue Dolphin Publishing, 2003.

Luker, Kristin. *Abortion and the Politics of Motherhood.* Berkeley: University of California Press, 1984.

Martin, Tracie. *Interests in Abortion: A New Perspective on Foetal Potential and the Abortion Debate.* Aldershot, NH: Ashgate Publishing, 2000.

McDonnell, Kathleen. *Not an Easy Choice: Re-Examining Abortion.* Toronto: Second Story Press, 2003.

Naden, Corinne J. *Abortion.* Tarrytown, NY: Marshall Cavendish Books, Limited, 2007.

Nicholson, Susan. *Abortion and the Roman Catholic Church.* Knoxville, TN: Religious Ethics, 1978.

Noonan, John T., Jr. (Ed.). *The Morality of Abortion. Legal and Historical Perspectives.* Cambridge, MA: Harvard University Press, 1970.

Ojeda, Auriana. *Should Abortion Rights Be Restricted?* Farmington Hills, MI: Gale Group, 2002.

Overall, Christine. *Ethics and Human Reproduction: A Feminist Analysis.* Boston: Allen & Unwin, 1988.

Perkins, Robert (Ed.). *Abortion: Pro and Con.* Cambridge, MA: Schenkman, 1974.

Podell, Janet (Ed.). *Abortion.* New York: H. W. Wilson, 1990.

Pojman, Louis P., and Francis Beckwith (Eds.). *The Abortion Controversy: 25 Years After Roe v. Wade.* Belmont, CA: Wadsworth, 1998.

Reiman, Jeffrey H. *Abortion and the Ways We Value Human Life.* Lanham, MD: Rowman & Littlefield, 1999.

Sanger, Alexander. *Beyond Choice: Reproductive Freedom in the 21st Century.* New York: Public Affairs, 2004.

Shapiro, Ian. *Abortion: The Supreme Court Decisions.* Indianapolis: Hackett, 1995.

Shrage, Laurie. *Abortion and Social Responsibility: Depolarizing the Debate.* New York: Oxford University Press, 2003.

Steinbock, Bonnie. *Life Before Birth: The Moral and Legal Status of Embryos and Fetuses.* New York: Oxford University Press, 1992.

Summer, L. W. *Abortion and Moral Theory.* Princeton, NJ: Princeton University Press, 1981.

Tietze, Christopher. *Induced Abortion: A World Review.* New York: Population Council, 1981.

Tooley, Michael. *Abortion and Infanticide.* New York: Oxford University Press, 1983.

Williams, Mary E. *Abortion.* Farmington Hills, MI: Gale Group, 2002.

10

Sexual Morality

In a comprehensive study of data from fifty-nine nations on sexual behavior done by *The Lancet,* a British medical journal, many myths are dispelled. Although the study was conducted by asking people to self-report, and thus is subject to some error, it was thought to be basically reliable. The survey found that sexual behavior is not starting earlier than a decade ago. It found that the first sexual experience for both men and women was in the late teens, "from 15 to 19 years old—with generally younger ages for women than for men, especially in developing countries."[1] Whereas the first sexual experiences of men and women in Britain was sixteen and one-half and seventeen and one-half, respectively, in Indonesia it was twenty-four and one-half and eighteen and one-half. People in industrialized countries had higher numbers of multiple partners than those in countries with higher rates for the human immunodeficiency virus (HIV) and acquired immune deficiency syndrome (AIDS). And there was some variation in this as men and women in Western countries had equal numbers of sexual partners, whereas men in Cameroon and Kenya "had multiple partners while women had only one."[2] The study also found that married people had more sex than did singles. Among the reasons teenagers cited for not having had sex were having made a conscious decision to wait and worry about sexually transmitted diseases (STDs) and pregnancy.[3]

Moreover, a recent study that explored teens' postsex emotions found that many first-time experiences resulted in guilt or feeling manipulated, with girls more often reporting this than boys. Of the teens who had engaged in oral sex, 41 percent "said they felt bad about themselves later" and "nearly 20 percent felt guilty, and 25 percent felt used, while the figures were 42 percent and 38 percent for sexual intercourse.[4] Even though teenagers in the United States are not more sexually active than those in other Western countries, they have the highest birthrate. They are also more likely to become pregnant. "American girls are four times as likely as German girls to become pregnant, almost five times as likely as French girls to have a baby, and more than seven times as likely as Dutch girls to have an abortion.[5] Researchers believe this is because, contrary to other countries, "we don't educate about birth control in sex education classes, we don't discuss it at home, we don't give teens good access to it, and we don't advertise it in our media."[6] Some people believe that doing so would increase the rate of pregnancy, but studies have found that it does not. Furthermore, "abstinence-only" sex education that does not also include information about contraception has not led to decreased sexual activity, but it has increased the incidence of STDs. Although the birthrates for U.S. teens have been declining in the past decade, it still is the case that those who do give birth are more likely not to finish high school and to end up on welfare.[7]

The incidence of cohabitation, or living with one's partner before marriage, has also increased dramatically in recent years, nearly tripling between 1990 and 2000.[8] This compares to 70 percent in England and 50 to 80 percent in other Western countries.[9] With the rise in the practice of cohabitation comes the fact that people marry later, and those who marry after age twenty-five are less likely to divorce than those who marry in their teens. It is often assumed that cohabiting couples who marry are more likely to divorce than those who did not live together before they married, and there is some evidence for this.[10] However, this may also be because of the type of people who do this, being more liberal and less religious, for example. If they are engaged or committed or their relationship is based on love, then they are no less likely to later divorce.[11]

Still, people may actually be more conservative sexually than they are depicted in the media. Some 70 percent of Americans report having had only one sexual partner in the previous year, and 80 percent said they have never had an extramarital affair.[12] Several groups that promote sexual abstinence before marriage have formed. According to members of these groups, "having sex before achieving a level of intimacy is a hindrance to building a quality relationship."[13] Many people believe there should be no sex without love. However, there continues to be a gender difference concerning the importance of love to sex. More adolescent females than males think affection should be a precursor to sexual intimacy.[14]

Almost everywhere in the world, different sexual standards apply to men and to women. In some Arab countries, men and women may not even socialize together in public. A particularly extreme example of sexual practice is that of female genital mutilation or so-called female circumcision. Although many countries have outlawed it, the practice persists in more than twenty-eight African countries and several countries in Asia and the Middle East as well as some immigrant communities in the West. It is estimated that 135 million women and girls have been subjected to this practice, with 2 million girls every year, or 6,000 each day.[15] In rural Ethiopia, up to 90 percent of girls still undergo this practice. The practice involves degrees of severity, from excision of the skin surrounding the clitoris to removal of all or part of the clitoris and some of the surrounding tissues to stitching the labia together so that only a small opening remains. Among the cultural and parental reasons given for these practices are to enable families to exercise control over reproduction, to keep women virgins until marriage, and to reduce or eliminate female sexual pleasure.[16] The procedure is usually done without even a local anesthetic and often with unclean and crude instruments. Often a reverse cutting is necessary later in marriage before intercourse can take place, which can be quite painful. It also causes problems in childbirth.[17] In fact, this procedure raises "by more than 50 percent the likelihood that the woman or her baby will die."[18] The more extensive forms of cutting resulted in higher rates of maternal and infant death during childbirth" and "even many years later." The incidence is thought actually to be higher because the study on which these figures were based were for women who delivered in hospitals where many women, especially in Africa, deliver their babies at home.[19]

The 1996 U.S. federal Criminalization of Female Genital Mutilation Act prohibited this practice for women under eighteen years of age. Human rights groups have lobbied internationally for an end to this practice, which in some countries is "routinely forced on girls as young as four or five years old, and . . . sustained through social coercion."[20] In Africa, between 60 percent and 90 percent of all women and girls in these countries undergo the procedure, even in countries where it is illegal. Muslim critics argue that there is no basis for this practice in the Koran; in fact, they note that this holy book commands parents to protect their children from harm and regards people's anatomy as part of God's creation.[21]

Elsewhere in the world, many people believe that women as well as men have a right to benefit from sexual pleasure. Pharmaceutical companies in particular recognize this attitude and have been investing in research into drugs to improve sexual response and function in both women and men. Some of these pharmaceuticals, such as Viagra, are vasodilators that increase blood flow in the genitals. Testosterone pills and patches increase libido, particularly in males, but they may have negative side effects.[22]

Sexual behavior and moral judgments about it also should be influenced by considering related health risks, which include various STDs and HIV. The U.S. Centers for Disease Control and Prevention estimates that "19 million STD infections occur annually, almost half of them among youth ages 15–24."[23] This includes chlamydia, gonorrhea, and syphilis but not the less reportable viral infections such as human papillomavirus and herpes. Current figures show that the rate of HIV infection in the United States has remained approximately the same since the early 1990s, approximately 40,000 new cases each year. This is down from 150,000 new cases per year in the late 1980s.[24] "More than 830,000 cases of AIDS have been reported in the United States since 1981" when it was first diagnosed. Nearly a million people in the United States now have the AIDS virus, and approximately one-quarter of these do not know it.[24] The World Health Organization estimates that approximately 40 million people around the world are living with AIDS or HIV. The mortality rate from AIDS is declining, but it is still high. In 2006, 2.9 million people died of AIDS-related illnesses. Thirty-two percent of the people infected with HIV live in sub-Saharan Africa, and thirty-four percent of AIDS related deaths occur there. In some African countries, as many as one-quarter of the people are infected with HIV. Approximately 8.6 million people in Asia are HIV-positive.[25] Even China, the most populous nation on the planet, has begun to recognize its own problem. It is estimated that between 430,000 and 1.5 million people are infected with HIV in China.[26]

Also relevant to moral judgments about sex is the issue of rape. Reliable statistics on the incidence of rape are difficult to establish. One reason is underreporting. Another reason is the incidence of acquaintance rape. This form of sexual assault is particularly prevalent among college students. "Eighty percent of all rapes are believed to be acquaintance rapes."[27] Among the factors that accompany acquaintance rape are "consumption of alcohol . . . private date locations . . . and misinterpretation of sexual intent."[28] Contributing to the uncertainty regarding the incidence of all types of rape is the way the statistics are determined. For example, surveys from random phone interviews give different numbers from the cases reported to police. One such survey in the United States, for example, showed the number of rapes in 1999 to be 141,070 but 92,440 in 2000.[29] Rape is not just a moral issue, but also a matter of law. So also is sex trafficking. It is estimated that around the world perhaps "two million women and children are sold into the sex trade every year."[30] The women who are trafficked are often from poor backgrounds and are lured with the promise of jobs and better lives. However, when they arrive they find out that this is not the case. Often they have no way to get away or out of the control of those who have lured them. Sex tourism is also a problem. In this case, very young girls are sometimes sold by their parents to a pimp who keeps them as prisoners for the exploitation of tourists, who are often from the West. Governments and nongovernmental organizations are working to prevent these practices and to punish those who are responsible.

Returning to the issue of morality itself, perhaps too much is made of the morality of sexual behavior, often as if it is the only moral issue. What are we to make of the various views and practices of sexual behavior? When we hear expressions such as "Doesn't he have any morals?" or "She has loose morals," the speakers most probably are referring to the person's sexual morals. But many other moral issues are arguably more important than sexual behavior.

Some of you might even be inclined to say that one's sexual behavior is not a moral matter at all. Is it not a private matter and too personal and individual to be a moral matter? To hold that it is not a moral matter, however, would seem to imply that our sexual lives are morally insignificant. Or it might imply that something has to be public or universal in order to have moral significance. However, most of us would not want to hold that personal matters *cannot* be moral matters. Furthermore, consider that sexual behavior lends itself to valuable experiences—those of personal relations, pleasure, fruitfulness and descendants, and self-esteem and enhancement. It also involves unusual opportunities for cruelty, deceit, unfairness, and selfishness. Because these are moral matters, sexual behavior must itself have moral significance.

CONCEPTUAL PROBLEMS: WHAT IS AND IS NOT SEXUAL

To discuss sexual morality, we might benefit from preliminary thinking about the subject of our discussion. Just what are we talking about when we speak of sexual pleasure, sexual desire, or sexual activity? Consider the meaning of the qualifier *sexual.* Suppose we said that behavior is sexual when it involves "pleasurable bodily contact with another." Will this do? This definition is quite broad. It includes passionate caresses and kisses as well as sexual intercourse. But it would not include activity that does not involve another individual such as masturbation or looking at sexually stimulating pictures. It would also not include erotic dancing or phone sex, because these activities do not involve physical contact with another. So the definition seems to be too narrow.

However, this definition is also too broad. It covers too much. Not all kisses or caresses are sexual, even though they are physical and can be pleasurable. And the contact sport of football is supposedly pleasurable for those who play it, but presumably not in a sexual way. It seems reasonable to think of sexual pleasure as pleasure that involves our so-called erogenous zones—those areas of the body that are sexually sensitive. Thus, only after a certain stage of biological development do we become capable of sexual passions or feelings. Could we then say that sexuality is necessarily bodily in nature? To answer this question, try the following thought experiment. Suppose we did not have bodies—in other words, suppose we were ghosts or spirits of some sort. Would we then be sexual beings? Could we experience sexual desire, for example? If we did, it would surely be different from that which we now experience. Moreover, it is not just that our own bodily existence seems required for us to experience sexual desire, but sexual desire for another would seem most properly to be for the embodied other. It cannot be simply the body of another that is desirable—or

dead bodies generally would be sexually stimulating. It is an *embodied* person who is the normal object of sexual desire. This is not to say that bodily touching is necessary, as is clear from the fact that dancing can be sexy and phone sex can be heated. Finally, if the body is so important for sexuality, we also can wonder whether there are any significant differences between male and female sexuality in addition to, and based on, genital and reproductive differences.

Let us also note one more conceptual puzzle. Many people refer to sexual intercourse as "making love." Some people argue that sexual intercourse should be accompanied by or be an expression of love, while others do not believe that this is necessary. Probably we would do best to consult the poets about the meaning of love. Briefly consider what you would regard as the difference between being in love (or falling in love) and loving someone. To "be in love" seems to suggest passivity. Similarly, to "fall in love" seems to be something that happens to a person. Supposedly, one has little control over one's feelings and even some thoughts in such a state. One cannot get the other person out of one's mind. One is, so to speak, "head over heels in love" or "madly in love"; one has "fallen passionately in love." Yet compare these notions to those of loving someone. To love someone is to be actively directed to that person's good. We want the best for him or her. In his essay on friendship in *The Nicomachean Ethics,* Aristotle wrote that true friendship is different from that which is based on the usefulness of the friend or the pleasure one obtains from being with the friend. The true friend cares about his friend for the friend's own sake. According to Aristotle, "Those who wish well to their friends for their sake are most truly friends."[31] This kind of friendship is less common, he believed, though more lasting. For Aristotle and the Greeks of his time, true friendship was more or less reserved for men. One contribution an ethics of care makes to this discussion is the importance to all of friendship and loving care. Moreover, we need not be in love with someone to love them. We can love our friends, or parents, or children, and yet we are not in love with them. So when considering what sex has to do with love, we would do well to consider the kind of love that is intended. We might also do well to ponder what happens when sexual feelings are joined with friendship.

RELEVANT FACTUAL MATTERS

In addition to conceptual clarification, certain factual matters may also be relevant to what we say about matters of sexual morality. For example, would it not be morally significant to know the effects of celibacy or of restraining sexual urges? It is well known that Freud thought that if we repressed our sexual desires we would either become neurotic or artists! Art, he argues, provides an emotional expressive outlet for repressed sexual feelings. Freudian theory about both sexual repression and the basis of art still has supporters—Camille Paglia, for example.[32] It also has not gone unchallenged. Knowing what the likely effects would be, both psychologically and physically, of sexual promiscuity might also be useful for thinking about sexual morality. Does separating sex and bodily pleasure from other aspects of oneself as a complete person have any effect on one's ability to have a more holistic and more fulfilling sexual experience? Furthermore, factual matters such as the likelihood of contracting a disease such as AIDS would be important for what we say about the moral character of some sexual encounters. Our conclusions about many factual or empirical matters would seem to influence greatly what we say about sexual morality—that is, the morality of sex, just like the morality of other human activities, is at least sometimes determined by the benefits and harms that result from it.

SEXUAL MORALITY AND ETHICAL THEORIES

Factual matters may be relevant only if we are judging the morality of actions on the basis of their consequences. If instead we adopt a nonconsequentialist moral theory such as Kant's, then our concerns will not be about the consequences of sexual behavior but about whether we are enhancing or using people, for example, or being fair or unfair. If we adopt a natural law position, our concerns will again be significantly different, or at least based on different reasons. We will want to know

whether certain sexual behavior fits or is befitting human nature.

In fact, the moral theory that we hold will even determine how we pose the moral question about sex. For example, if we are guided by a consequentialist moral theory such as utilitarianism, then we will be likely to pose the moral question in terms of good or bad, better or worse sexual behavior. If we are governed by Kantian principles, then our questions will more likely be in terms of right or wrong, justifiable or unjustifiable sexual behavior. And if we judge from a natural law basis, then we will want to know whether a particular sexual behavior is natural or unnatural, proper or improper, or even perverted. Let us consider each of these three ways of posing moral questions about sexual matters and see some of the probable considerations appropriate to each type of reasoning.

Consequentialist or Utilitarian Considerations

If we were to take a consequentialist point of view—say, that of an act utilitarian—we would judge our actions or make our decisions about how to behave sexually one at a time. In each case, we would consider our alternatives and their likely consequences for all who would be affected by them. In each case, we would consider who would benefit or suffer as well as the type of benefit or suffering. In sexual relations, we would probably want to consider physical, psychological, and social consequences. Considerations such as these are necessary for arguments that are consequentialist in nature. According to this perspective, the sexual practice or relation that has better consequences than other possibilities is the preferred one. Any practice in which the bad consequences outweigh the good consequences would be morally problematic.

Among the negative consequences to be avoided are physical harms, including sexually transmitted diseases such as syphilis, gonorrhea, and HIV, which causes AIDS. Psychic sufferings are no less real. There is the embarrassment caused by an unwanted sexual advance and the trauma of forced sex. Also to be considered are possible feelings of disappointment and foolishness for having false expectations or of being deceived or used. Pregnancy, although regarded in some circumstances as a good or a benefit, may in other circumstances be unwanted and involve significant suffering. Some people might include as a negative consequence the effects on the family of certain sexual practices. In consequentialist reasoning, all of the consequences count, and short-term benefit or pleasure may be outweighed by long-term suffering or pain. However, the pain caused to one person also can be outweighed by the pleasure given to another or others, and this is a major problem for this type of moral theory.

Many positive consequences or benefits also may come from sexual relations or activity. First of all, there is sexual pleasure itself. Furthermore, we may benefit both physically and psychologically from having this outlet for sexual urges and desires. It is relaxing. It enables us to appreciate other sensual things, and to be more passionate and perhaps even more compassionate. It may enhance our perceptions of the world. Colors can be brighter and individual differences more noticeable. For many people, intimate sexual relations supposedly improve personal relations by breaking down barriers. However, one would think that this is likely to be so only where a good relationship already exists between the involved persons.

What about sex in the context of marriage and children? Because children are people too, any possible effects on them of sexual activity also must play a role in consequentialist considerations. The availability of contraception now makes it easier to control these consequences, so offspring that result from sexual relations are presumably (but not necessarily) more likely to be wanted and well cared for. Abortion and its consequences also may play a role in determining whether a particular sexual relation is good from this perspective.

Finally, consequentialist thinking has room for judging not only what is good and bad, or better and worse, but also what is worst and best. This perspective is entirely open to talking about better and worse sex or the best and worst. On utilitarian grounds, the most pleasurable and most productive of overall happiness is the best. If one cannot have the ideal best, however, then one should choose the best that is available, provided that this choice does not negatively affect one's ability to have the best or cause problems in other aspects of one's life. It is consistent with a consequentialist perspective to judge sexual behavior not in terms of what we must avoid to do right but in terms of what we should hope and aim for as the best. Nevertheless, in classical utilitarianism, the ideal is always to be thought of in terms of happiness or pleasure.

Nonconsequentialist or Kantian Considerations

Nonconsequentialist moral theories, such as that of Kant, would direct us to judge sexual actions as well as other actions quite differently than consequentialist theories. Although the golden rule is not strictly the same thing as the categorical imperative, there are similarities between these two moral principles. According to both, as a person in a sexual relation, I should only do what would seem acceptable no matter whose shoes I were in or from whose perspective I judged. In the case of a couple, each person should consider what the sexual relation would look like from the other's point of view, and each should only proceed if a contemplated action or relation is also acceptable from that other viewpoint.

This looks like a position regarding sexual relations according to which anything is permissible sexually as long as it is agreed to by the participants. In some versions of Kantianism, this would probably be so. The primary concern would then be whether the agreement was real. For example, we would want to know whether the participants were fully informed and aware of what was involved. Lying would certainly be morally objectionable. So also would other forms of deceit and refusal to inform. Not telling someone that one was married or that one had a communicable disease could also be forms of objectionable deceit, in particular when this information, if known, would make a difference to the other person's willingness to participate.

In addition, the relation would have to be freely entered into. Any form of coercion would be morally objectionable on Kantian grounds. This is one of the strongest reasons for prohibiting sex with children—namely, that they cannot fully consent to it. They have neither the experience nor understanding of it, and they are not independent enough to resist pressure or coercion. As with deceit, what counts as coercion is not always easy to say, both in general and in any concrete case. Certainly, physically forcing a person to engage in sexual intercourse against his or her will is coercion. We call it rape. However, some forms of "persuasion" may also be coercive. Threats to do what is harmful are coercive. For example, threatening to demote an employee or deny him promotion if he does not engage in a sexual relation, when he deserves the former but not the latter, can be coercive. But more subtle forms of coercion also exist, including implied threats to withhold one's affection from the other or to break off a relationship. Perhaps even some offers or bribes are coercive, especially when what is promised is not only desirable but also something that one does not have and cannot get along without. Saying "I know that you are starving, and I will feed you if you have sex with me" is surely coercive.

Naturalness Considerations

Some naturalistic moral theories described in Chapter 6 hold that morality is grounded in human nature. That is good which furthers human nature or is fitting for it, and that is bad or morally objectionable which frustrates or violates or is inconsistent with human nature. How would such a theory be used to make moral judgments about sexual behavior? Obviously, the key is the description of human nature.

In any use of human nature as a basis for determining what is good, a key issue will be describing that nature. To see how crucial this is, suppose that we examine a version of natural law theory that stresses the biological aspects of human nature. How would this require us to think about sexual morality? It would probably require us to note that an essential aspect of human nature is the orientation of the genital and reproductive system toward reproducing young. The very nature of heterosexual sexual intercourse (unless changed by accident or human intervention by sterilization or contraception) is to release male sperm into a female vagina and uterus. The sperm naturally tend to seek and penetrate an egg, fertilizing it, and forming with the egg the beginning of a fetus, which develops naturally into a young member of the species. On this version of natural law theory, that which interferes with or seeks deliberately to frustrate this natural purpose of sexual intercourse as oriented toward reproduction would be morally objectionable. Thus, contraception, masturbation, and homosexual sexual relations would be contrary to nature. Further arguments would be needed to show that sexual relations should take place only in marriage. These arguments would possibly have to do with the relation of sex and commitment, with the biological relation of the child to the parents, and with the necessary or best setting for the raising of children.

We could also envision other natural law–like arguments about sexual morality that are based on somewhat different notions of human nature. For example, we could argue that the natural purpose of sexual relations is pleasure, because nature has so constructed the nerve components of the genital system. Furthermore, the intimacy and naturally uniting aspect of sexual intercourse may provide a basis for arguing that this is its natural tendency—to unite people, to express their unity, or to bring them closer together.

To believe that there is such a thing as sexual behavior that is consistent with human nature—or *natural*—also implies that there can be sexual behavior that is inconsistent with human nature or unnatural. Sometimes the term *perverted* has been used synonymously with *unnatural*. Thus, in the context of a discussion or analysis of natural law views about sexual morality, we also can consider the question of whether there is such a thing as sexual perversion. This is not to say that notions of sexual perversion are limited to natural law theory, however. *Perversion* literally means turned against or away from something—usually away from some norm. Perverted sexual behavior would then be sexual behavior that departs from some norm for such behavior. "That's not normal," we say. By *norm* here we mean not just the usual type of behavior, for this depends on what in fact people do. Rather, by *norm* or *normal* we mean what coincides with a moral standard. If most human beings in a particular famine-ridden society died before age thirty-five, then we could still say that this was abnormal because it was not the norm for human survival in most other societies.[33]

To consider whether there is a natural type of sexual behavior or desire, we might compare it with another appetite—namely, the appetite of hunger, whose natural object we might say is food. If a person were to eat pictures of food instead of food, this would generally be considered abnormal. Would we also say that a person who was satisfied with pictures of a sexually attractive person and used them as a substitute for a real person was in some sense abnormal or acting abnormally? This depends on whether there is such a thing as a normal sex drive and what its natural object would be. People have used the notion of normal sex drive and desire to say that things such as shoe fetishism (being sexually excited by shoes) and desire for sex with animals or dead bodies are abnormal. One suggestion is that sexual desire in its normal form is for another individual and not just for the other but for the other's mutual and embodied response.

These notions of perverted versus normal sexual desire and behavior can belong in some loose way to a tradition that considers human nature as a moral norm. Like the utilitarian and Kantian moral traditions, natural law theory has its own way of judging sexual and other types of behavior. These three ways of judging sexual behavior are not necessarily incompatible with one another, however. We might find that some forms of sexual behavior are not only ill-fit for human nature but also involve using another as a thing rather than treating her or him as a person, and that they also have bad consequences. Or we may find that what is most fitting for human nature is also what has the best consequences and treats persons with the respect that is due them. The more difficult cases will be those in which no harm comes to persons from a sexual relation, but they have nevertheless been used, or cases in which

knowing consent is present but it is for activities that seem ill-fit for human nature or do not promise happiness, pleasure, or other benefits.

HOMOSEXUALITY

When making moral judgments about homosexuality, the same considerations can be used as for sexual morality generally: conseqentialist and nonconsequentialist considerations, and naturalness. Some issues are conceptual, such as what is meant by *homosexual* as opposed to *heterosexual* and *bisexual*. Also, some issues are empirical or factual—for example, whether homosexuality is a fixed orientation or a chosen lifestyle, when sexual orientation becomes evident in a person's life, and what happens to the children of gays and lesbians. Arguments for and against homosexuality often depend on these conceptual and empirical issues.

From a consequentialist point of view, there is nothing in the nature of sex itself that requires that it be heterosexual or occur only between married individuals or for reproductive purposes. In some cases, where the consequences would be better, sex should be reserved for a married relation. It would depend on the individual persons. If particular individuals find sex fulfilling only in the context of a long-term or married relationship and where it is part of a desire to have children together, then this is what would be best for them. But this is not always the case, for people vary in how they are affected by different experiences. The social context and rules of a society may well make a difference. This may be especially true for homosexuality. Social acceptability or stigma will make a difference in whether people can be happy doing what they do. But it is happiness or pleasure and unhappiness or displeasure alone, from a classical consequentialist point of view, that determines the morality. In homosexual as well as in heterosexual relations, questions about whether monogamy is the best practice will be raised. Gay men and lesbian women, for example, have been known to disagree on this issue. Likewise, when they have disagreed on whether disclosing one's sexual orientation is a good thing, the debate has often turned on a disagreement about the likely consequences of such action.

Nonconsequentialist considerations also may apply here. For example, as in other sexual relations, considerations of honesty or dishonesty and free choice or coercion are relevant. One of the most common nonconsequentialist arguments against homosexual sex is that it is unnatural, that it goes against nature. According to traditional natural law theory, although we differ individually in many ways, people share a common human nature. I may have individual inclinations—or things may be natural to me that are not natural to you, simply because of our differing talents, psychic traits, and other unique characteristics. Natural law theory tells us that certain things are right or wrong not because they further or frustrate our individual inclinations, but because they promote or work against our species' inclinations and aspects of our common human nature. When appealing to a traditional type of natural law theory to make judgments about homosexual behavior, we need to determine whether this is consistent with common human nature rather than individual natures. The argument that gay men or lesbian women find relating sexually to members of their own sex "natural" to them as individuals may or may not work as part of a natural law argument that supports that behavior. However, if one had a broader view of sexuality in its passionate, emotional, and social aspects, then one could make a reasonable natural law–type of argument that these are also aspects of a common human sexuality that is manifested in several ways, including homosexual sex. Historically, natural law arguments have not gone this way. But this is not to say that such an argument could not be reasonably put forth.

Recent legal issues concerning gay and lesbian rights also have highlighted issues of sexual morality. In May 1996, for example, the U.S. Supreme Court struck down a Colorado law that banned legal protection for homosexuals.[34] Supporters of the ban argued that the people of Colorado had a right to do what they could to preserve what they saw as traditional moral values. Those who sought to overturn the ban saw it as a matter of protection from discrimination and equal rights for all. The issue of legal recognition of same-sex marriage and "civil unions" have also been the subject of heated debate recently. It may be helpful to put this issue in a larger context. For example, African Americans in the United States were not allowed to marry until after the Civil War, and mixed race couples could not do so everywhere in the United States until a Supreme Court decision in 1967. Since 2001, same-sex couples have been allowed to marry in Holland and since 2003 in Belgium and Ontario, Canada. Marriage is now even more widely available in Canada. Since June 2005, even Spain allows marriage licenses to same-sex couples. At this time, only Massachusetts permits same sex marriage in the United States. Elsewhere, state courts have held that "marriage is between a man and a woman." It is not clear on what this is based in all cases. In some it was written into a state's constitution or other state legislation such as "defense of marriage" acts. In others, it may well be tradition or religion-based.

More widely available are so-called civil unions or domestic partnerships that grant many of the same legal benefits as married couples have. On May 10, 2007, Oregon became the latest U.S. state to pass such legislation.[35]

Laws that address issues of rights, whether in this area or others, are often grounded in questions of morality. Nevertheless, morality is a distinct realm, and we may ask whether certain actions or practices are morally good or bad apart from whether they ought to be regulated by law. So, in the realm of sexual matters, we can ask about the morality of certain actions or practices. Questions about sexual morality are obviously quite personal. Nevertheless, because this is one of the major drives and aspects of a fulfilling human life, it is important to think about what may be best and worst, and what may be right and wrong in these matters.

NOTES

1. *San Francisco Chronicle,* Nov. 1, 2006, p. A12.
2. Ibid.
3. See www.msnbc.com/id/6839072/.
4. *San Francisco Chronicle,* Feb. 15, 2007, pp. B1, B5.
5. Nicholas D. Kristof, "Bush's Sex Scandal," *The New York Times,* Feb. 16, 2005, p. A27.
6. See www.coolnurse.com/teen_pregnancy_rates.htm.
7. Ibid.

8. Dennie Hughes, "Is It So Wrong to Live Together?" *USA Weekend,* Jan. 16–18, 2004, p. 12.
9. See www.members.aol.com/cohabiting/facts.htm.
10. David Whitman, "Was It Good for Us?" *U.S. News & World Report, 122,* 19 (May 19, 1997): 56.
11. Hughes, op. cit.
12. E. D. Widmer, J. Treas, and R. Newcomb, "Attitudes Toward Nonmarital Sex in 24 Countries," *Journal of Sex Research, 35* (1998); 349–358.
13. "Insight on the News," *Washington Times,* May 20, 1996, p. 48.
14. Ronald Jay Werner-Wilson, "Gender Differences in Adolescent Sexual Attitudes," *Adolescence, 33* (Fall 1998): 519.
15. See www.amnesty.org/ailib/intcam/femgen/fgm1.htm.
16. James Ciment, "Senegal Outlaws Female Genital Mutilation," *British Medical Journal, 3* (Feb. 6, 1999): 348; and Joel E. Frader et al., "Female Genital Mutilation," *Pediatrics, 102* (July 1998): 153.
17. Ibid.
18. *The New York Times,* June 2, 2006, p. A10.
19. Ibid.
20. Xiaorong Li, "Tolerating the Intolerable: The Case of Female Genital Mutilation," *Philosophy and Public Policy Quarterly, 21,* 1 (Winter 2001): 4.
21. Ibid., p. 6.
22. Judith Newman, "Passion Pills," *Discover, 20* (Sept. 1999): 66.
23. See www.cdc.gov/std/stats/trends2005.htm.
24. www.immuncentral.com/diseases/aids.cfm.
25. www.kaisernetwork.org/daily_reports/rep_index.cfm?DR_ID=4119226. See http:en.wikipedia.org/wiki/HIV/AIDS_in_China
27. See www.ume.maine.edu/~healthed/rape/incidence.html.
28. See http://psy.ucsd.edu/~hflowe/acrpe.htm.
29. See www.equityfeminism.com/discussion/fullthread$msgnum=38711.
30. http://archives.cnn.com/2001/WORLD/europe/03/08/women.trafficking/index.html.
31. Aristotle, *The Nicomachean Ethics,* Book VIII, Chap. 4.
32. Camille Paglia, *Sex, Art, and American Culture* (New York: Vintage Books, 1992).
33. There are obvious problems here with determining the norm because longevity is a function of nutrition and exercise as well as genetics. We also might be inclined to consider norms for sexual behavior as partly a function of the setting or cultural conditions.
34. *San Francisco Chronicle,* May 21, 1996, pp. A1, A13.
35. www.religioustolerance.org/hom_marr.htm.

REVIEW EXERCISES

1. Distinguish "conceptual" from "factual" matters with regard to sexual morality. What is the difference between them?
2. What are some factual matters that would be relevant for consequentialist arguments regarding sexual behavior?
3. According to a Kantian type of morality, we ought to treat persons as persons. Deceit and coercion violate this requirement. In this view, what kinds of things regarding sexual morality would be morally objectionable?
4. How would a natural law theory be used to judge sexual behavior? Explain.
5. What is meant by the term *perversion?* How would this notion be used to determine whether there was something called "sexual perversion"?

DISCUSSION CASES

1. Date Rape? The students at a local university had heard much about date rape, what it was, what could lead to it, and that it was morally wrong and legally a crime. However, they were not always so clear about what counted as true consent to a sexual relation or experience. John insisted that unless the other person clearly said "No," consent should be implied. Amy said it was not so easy as that. Sometimes the issue comes up too quickly for a person to realize what is happening. The person has voluntarily gone along up to a certain point but may be ambiguous about proceeding further. Bill insisted that he would want a clear expression of a positive desire to go on for him to consider there to be a real consent. He also said that guys also could be ambiguous and sometimes not actually want to get involved sexually but be talked into it against their will by their partners.

What do you think is required for true consent to a sexual involvement?

2. Defining Marriage. Several localities in recent years have been grappling with the issue of whether to broaden the definition of marriage as a union between a man and a woman. The issue is whether the state should recognize a commitment between members of the same sex. Those who argue for this broadening say that same-sex couples can be just as committed to one another as heterosexuals and they thus should have whatever rights marriage bestows on them. Those who argue against this cite religious or natural law–like sources and reasons. They say this would open up the definition of marriage also to include more than two people—polygamy. How would you go about deciding whether to vote for such an ordinance? Although this involves more than issues of sexual morality, it may depend partly on what you say on this issue.

YOU MAKE THE DECISION

Apply the theories and issues discussed in this chapter by accessing this animated simulation on the Ethics Resource Center.

Use the passkey that accompanies your book to gain access. If you do not have a passkey, visit cengage brain.com to purchase instant access to additional study material.

Which of the following is closest to your main reason for declining to officiate?

Ethics Module 10 : Gay Marriage   ◀◀ ▶ ▶▶   MUTE 🔇

Selected Bibliography

Atkinson, Ronald. *Sexual Morality.* New York: Harcourt Brace & World, 1965.

Baker, Robert, and Frederick Elliston (Eds.). *Philosophy and Sex.* Buffalo, NY: Prometheus Books, 1984.

Barry, Kathleen. *The Prostitution of Sexuality.* New York: New York University Press, 1996.

Batchelor, Edward (Ed.). *Homosexuality and Ethics.* New York: Pilgrim Press, 1980.

Bertocci, Peter A. *Sex, Love, and the Person.* New York: Sheed & Ward, 1967.

Hunter, J. F. M. *Thinking About Sex and Love.* Toronto: Macmillan, 1980.

Hyde, Janet Shibley, et al. *Understanding Human Sexuality.* Whitby, Ontario, Canada: McGraw-Hill Ryerson, Limited, 2003.

King, Bruce M. *Human Sexuality Today.* Don Mills, Ontario, Canada: Pearson Education Canada, 2004.

Kosnik, Anthony, et al. *Human Sexuality: New Directions in American Catholic Thought.* New York: Paulist Press, 1977.

Levesque, Roger J. R. *Sexual Abuse of Children: A Human Rights Perspective.* Bloomington: Indiana University Press, 1999.

Lickona, Tom, et al. *Sex, Love and You: Making the Right Decision.* Notre Dame, IN: Ave Maria Press, 2003.

Monti, Joseph. *Arguing About Sex: The Rhetoric of Christian Sexual Morality.* Albany. State University of New York Press, 1995.

Nussbaum, Martha. *Sex and Social Justice.* New York: Oxford University Press, 1999.

————, **and David Eslund.** *Sex, Preference, and Family.* New York: Oxford University Press, 1998.

Paglia, Camille. *Sex, Art, and American Culture.* New York: Vintage, 1992.

Posner, Richard. *Sex and Reason.* Cambridge: Harvard University Press, 1992.

Regners, Mark. *Forbidden Fruit: Sex and Religion in the Lives of American Teenagers.* New York: Oxford University Press, 2007.

Soble, Alan (Ed.). *The Philosophy of Sex.* Totowa, NJ: Littlefield, Adams, 1980.

Stewart, Robert (Ed.). *Philosophical Perspectives on Sex and Love.* New York: Oxford University Press, 1995.

Taylor, Richard. *Having Love Affairs.* Buffalo, NY: Prometheus, 1982.

Tong, Rosemarie. *Women, Sex, and the Law.* Totowa, NJ: Rowman & Allanheld, 1984.

Vanoy, Russell. *Sex Without Love.* Buffalo, NY: Prometheus, 1980.

Verene, D. P. *Sexual Love and Western Morality.* Belmont, CA: Wadsworth, 1995.

Watkins, Christine. *Teen Sex.* Farmington Hills, MI: Gale Group, 2005.

Wertheimer, Alan. *Consent to Sexual Relations.* New York: Cambridge University Press, 2003.

Whiteley, C. H., and W. N. Whiteley. *Sex and Morals.* New York: Basic Books, 1967.

11

Pornography

Those who do such counting now estimate that Americans spend almost $12 billion per year on "adult entertainment."[1] This includes movies, video and DVD sales and rentals, and adult magazines. Approximately 11,000 X-rated video titles are produced annually in the United States.[2] Companies making money from this market include the General Motors subsidiary DirecTV, Time Warner, Comcast (with its pay-per-view services), and major hotel chains such as Marriott, Hilton, and Westin.[3] In recent years with the rise of the Internet, the portion of profits from various media has changed. Thousands of new adult Web sites are established each month, approximately 260 each day.[4] Recently, "video-capable wireless devices" such as some cell phones allow people to access and download pornography from the Internet or view pornographic video clips. American cellular carriers are anxious about this, especially if there are no blocking devices that prevent children from accessing such sites. However, when they see how lucrative these devices might be, they may lose their hesitancy. Already people in Europe and Asia "spend tens of millions of dollars a year on phone-based pornography."[5]

The porn industry, however, is less glamorous than it lets on. It is an insular world with people who like to flaunt society's rules. Although there is fast money to be made, the women who find the industry initially enticing often only perform in one video before quitting. Frequently, their experiences are painful, embarrassing, and humiliating. They are also usually not protected from sexually transmitted diseases.

Child pornography is also on the increase. Although illegal in the United States and many other countries, it can still be found, especially on the Internet. It is estimated that 7 percent of the pornography market is child pornography. One group that works against the sexual abuse of children says that it "receives over 60,000 reports of suspect child pornography annually" and sends these to the National Center for Missing and Exploited Children, the FBI, or states' attorneys general offices.[6] Some experts believe that child pornography is such an essential aspect of pedophile psychology and behavior that it becomes compulsive. Child molesters "almost always collect child pornography or child erotica." The children are often needy and seduced by an adult whom they view as a caring father figure who gives them gifts. Sometimes these pedophiles justify their actions as the result of their own abusive treatment as children. "The typical child molester will abuse more than 360 victims over the course of his lifetime."[7]

Before we start this brief discussion of pornography and the law, we might usefully examine some problems we have in defining the subject matter. The term *pornography* itself comes from the classical Greek roots *porno* for "prostitute" and *graphy* for "to write." This may be a strange association. However, some scholars have pointed out that in much pornography women are treated as sexual servants or servicers in ways that are similar to the function of prostitutes. Pornography can be of many kinds, including writings, pictures, photographs, three-dimensional art forms, vocalizations (songs, phone conversations), live-person presentations, and even computerized games.

But what is—and is not—pornography? Is it all in the mind of the perceiver? Is one person's pornography another person's art? In fact, legal definitions of pornography have usually tried to distinguish pornography from art. Suppose that we define pornography as "sexually explicit material that has as its primary purpose the stimulation of sexual excitement or interest." Compare this definition with one that says that pornography is "verbal or pictorial explicit representations of sexual behavior that . . . have as a distinguishing characteristic the degrading and demeaning portrayal of the role and status of the human female . . . as a mere sexual object to be exploited and manipulated sexually."[8] The first definition is morally neutral: It does not imply that pornography is good or bad. It could be called a *descriptive* definition. It is also quite broad and would include both violent and nonviolent pornography. The second definition is not morally neutral, and it applies only to some types of such material. The question of the moral value of this pornography is no longer totally open. Definitions of this type are *normative* or *value-laden* definitions. Still another definition is the legal one. It defines pornography as "obscenity." As such, it defines a type of pornography that is morally suspect and legally not protected as is other free speech. In fact, this term is used instead of pornography in the legal definition modeled after a 1954 version of the American Law Institute. In 1973, the U.S. Supreme Court in *Miller* v. *California* included this definition and defined obscenity as depictions or works that were "patently offensive" to local "community standards," that appeal to "prurient interests," and that taken as a whole lack "serious literary, artistic, political or scientific value."[9] This latter aspect is known as the *LAPS test.* In any case, whether we define pornography as degrading and immoral or in a more morally neutral way, the question of whether there should be laws regulating pornography remains unanswered.

Because pornography is sexually explicit material, it may be judged morally by the same criteria that are used to judge sexual behavior in general, as was done in the previous chapter. For example, one may ask about the consequences of pornographic production and use in terms of how much they do or do not contribute to happiness and pleasure to individuals and society. One would want to consider the possible coercion that it may involve. In the case of adults, this is controversial; in the case of children, however, there is no question that coercion would be involved. Nor is there question about the harm that is done to the children. According to some experts, pornography not only involves child molestation but also is permanent material that "increases the harm to the child when it is circulated (and) . . . contributes to the demand of child pornography that requires more children to be exploited."[10] One may also use naturalness criteria to evaluate pornography. For example, one may consider the public nature of pornography and ask whether sex is not by nature an intimate experience and thus ought to be private.

However, much of the debate concerns whether the law ought to regulate pornography in any way and why or why not. The issue can be phrased in various ways, but one has to do with human liberty or freedom and the extent to which pornography can be rightly limited by law and legal force.

LIBERTY-LIMITING PRINCIPLES

To decide whether the law should regulate pornography, we need to have some idea about what sort of things we think the law should and should not regulate and why. This is to raise, if only briefly, certain issues in the philosophy of law or jurisprudence.[11] Let us rephrase the question somewhat before proceeding. We will assume a basic principle of liberty: that people ought to be able to do what they choose unless there is some reason to restrict their behavior by force of law. In other words, we are not asking whether the behavior is morally praiseworthy, but whether people should be free to act or should be prevented by law from doing so, whatever the moral character of the act.[12]

To think about this question in general and in relation to the issue of pornography, consider some possible options or positions. These can be called *liberty-limiting principles* because they are principles or norms for determining when the law may rightly restrict our liberty and for what reasons.[13] One might support one or more of these principles.

The Harm Principle

According to the *harm principle,* the law may rightly restrict a person from doing what he wants in order to prevent him from harming others. To J. S. Mill, this is the primary reason why we may legitimately restrict people's behavior by legal force.

Essential to the nature as well as the application of Mill's principle is the notion of *harm.* The paradigm notion of harm is *physical* harm. To cut off someone's arm or leg or damage her body in such a way that she dies is clearly to harm her. However, unless one views human beings as only physical beings, we must accept that we can be harmed in other ways as well, some of which clearly also have physical repercussions and some not obviously so. Thus, to threaten someone or otherwise harass them so that they seriously fear for their lives is to harm them psychologically. Damage also can be done to persons' reputations and their livelihoods. People can be harmed in subtle ways by the creation of a certain climate or ambience, a notion that is used in legal definitions of sexual harassment in the workplace. Moreover, some harms are more serious than others. Causing another to have a temporary rash is not as serious as causing her to have a life-threatening disease.

In applying this principle, we would have to decide when a harm is serious enough that the society ought to prevent individuals by force of law from causing that type of harm to others.[14] Moreover, the law would need to determine, among other things, what counts as causing a harm, how proximate the cause is, and who can be said to play a role in causing the harm. In addition, the harm principle may be formulated in such a way that liberty is thought to be so important that only strict proof of harm to others would be sufficient to justify restricting people from doing what they choose to do.

How would this liberty-limiting principle be applied in the case of pornography? One application would be to determine whether its making harms anyone or whether the viewing or reading of pornographic materials leads those doing so to harm others. For example, we would need to know whether viewing violent pornographic films leads people to engage in sexually violent acts. Obviously, violent pornography is sexually stimulating to some people. But does it take the place of real violence, or does it lead to it? There are anecdotal reports and some studies that suggest pornography leads to specific acts. In one study, women reported that they were asked or forced by their mates to imitate sex acts that were depicted in pornography. One researcher who interviewed 114 convicted rapists "concluded that the scenes depicted in violent porn are repeated in rapists' accounts of their crimes." This included one who told his female victim, "You love being beaten. . . . You know you love it, tell me you love it. . . . I seen it all in the movies."[15] If this were true of the effects of certain violent types of pornography, then according to the harm principle there could be grounds for prohibiting it.

One critical issue here is the type and degree of "proof" required. For example, it has been reported that "young men shown sexually violent films and then asked to judge a simulated rape trial are less likely to vote for conviction than those who haven't seen the films." And "surveys of male college students who briefly watch porn report that thirty percent of the women they know would enjoy aggressively forced sex."[16] Does this prove that such pornography has an effect on people's attitudes about what is acceptable, or does it also show that this will lead people to act in certain harmful ways? If convicted rapists have had significantly more contact with pornographic materials than nonrapists, then would this be sufficient to show that the pornography caused or was a contributing factor to the rapes? There could be an association between the two without one being the cause of the other. In the study of logic, you can learn about a fallacy labeled *post hoc, ergo propter hoc.* Roughly translated, it means "after something, therefore because of something." This is regarded as a fallacy; just because one thing follows another (or is associated with it) does not mean that it was caused by it.

For instance, Tuesday follows Monday but is not caused by it. But it also doesn't mean that there is no causal connection between frequently associated events. Even if there were a correlation between violent pornography and sexual violence, the cause might be some other thing that led to both the desire for violent pornography and the committing of sexual violence. On the other hand, if the other thing is the cause and the violence is the symptom, then it is not necessarily the case that we would attack the cause and not the symptom. Moreover, sexual violence is not the only possible harm that pornography can do. This is further discussed in the section on feminist views of pornography.

Finally, a society must provide a way of balancing interests or settling conflicts between people. Thus, in applying the harm principle, we ought to consider whether restricting a behavior to protect the interests of some will negatively affect the interests of others. It then would require us to compare the value of the interests and the cost of restrictions. For example, sexuality is a significant and important aspect of human experience, and some people may be helped in this part of their lives by writings and pictures that depict sexual behavior. Furthermore, some people argue that in trying to define and restrict pornography the society risks impinging on valued free speech rights. For example, the late U.S. Supreme Court Justice William Brennan argued that, in principle, it is impossible to define pornography in such a way that it does not include legitimate free speech. In restricting pornography, he argued, we also would be restricting free speech.[17] For example, sexual expression in the form of pictures or print of various sorts might be seen as a form of sexual speech protected by the U.S. Constitution. Yet we do restrict speech in many cases, including that which incites to riot and defamatory and fraudulent speech. We also may need to determine the value of free speech. Is it the expression itself that is good, or is it valued for the sake of other goods such as knowledge or political power? The idea would be that allowing free speech enhances our ability to improve understanding by sharing opinions, and we ensure more democratic political

participation. If these are the purposes of free speech, and if some sexual expression does not serve but hinders these goals, then according to the harm principle there could be grounds for prohibiting or restricting it. As one person puts it, "Pornographers are free riders on the liberties of everyone else."[18] Whether this is so is up to you to judge. In surveys, most people say that the government should at least protect children from access and exposure to pornography and to dangerous people on the Internet. Thus, there is some general support for filtering software and systems. In fact, child pornography is not legally protected as free speech by the First Amendment to the Constitution. Nor is certain other activity protected as free speech. For example, some people believe in some restriction on and censoring of bomb-making information on the Internet and sites that support political terrorism. However, one can question whether this can even be done in such a way that there are no creeping phenomena in which other rightfully protected free speech and information is also restricted. Because the definition of pornography is problematic and because of the possible creeping phenomena, legal efforts by local communities to restrict pornography have been difficult and often fail.

The Social Harm Principle

A second version of the harm principle, called the *social harm principle,* is sometimes confused with or not distinguished from the harm principle itself. The idea involved in this second liberty-limiting principle is that the law may prevent people from doing what they wish or choose to do when their action causes harm to society itself.

For example, if a society is a theocracy, then anything that will seriously erode the rule of religious leaders is a threat to that kind of society. If a society is a democracy, then anything that seriously erodes public participation in political decision making is a threat to that society. The powerful role of lobbyists and money in the political process can be challenged in this regard. If a society is a free-market society, then anything that seriously erodes market competition is a threat to it. Antitrust laws might be seen as an example of the application of the social harm principle. (However, such laws also might be grounded in the harm principle.) In any society, anything that seriously threatens its ability to defend itself would also threaten its continued existence.

One need not believe that the social structure is a good one to use this principle. In fact, in some cases, we could argue that the society in its current form should not endure, and threats to its continuation in that form are justified. Nevertheless, it is useful to distinguish the social harm principle from the harm principle, which tells us what the law may prevent us from doing to individuals, even many individuals. Thus, emitting harmful pollution from my factory may be regulated by society under the harm principle, for in regulating or preventing this pollution the factory owner is prevented from harming individuals, though not necessarily the society itself.

How would this principle apply to the issue of the legal regulation of pornography? As one person puts it, "Society has the right to protect itself from the disorder and oral disintegration that result from individuals unduly pursuing their sexual self-interest. . . . [T]he government has the right, therefore to limit such forms of expression."[19] According to some theorists, pornography can be seen as a threat to society. One argument states that certain types of pornography weaken the ties of love and sex and thus also the family structure. If strong families are essential to a society, then pornography could be regulated for the good of the society itself.[20] But is this connection empirically substantiated? And are "strong families" of a particular sort essential to society? We would need to answer these questions to justify restricting pornography on the basis of this principle. If the society is essentially an egalitarian one, then one might argue that some types of pornography threaten its continued existence because those forms reinforce views of women as subservient. (See the following section on feminist concerns.) Furthermore, as with all liberty-limiting principles, one would need to decide first whether the principle is valid for restricting people's liberty. Only if one believes that the principle is valid would one go on to ask if a behavior is such a threat to an essential aspect of society that it can be rightly restricted by law. This would be true for the case of pornography as well as for other acts and practices.

The Offense Principle

The *offense principle* holds that society may restrict people's choice to do what they want in order to prevent them from offending others. This principle may be considered a separate principle or a version of the harm principle. Here the harm is presumably a psychic one. According to those who support this principle, just as with the harm principle, only sufficiently offensive harms would be restricted. For example, we might consider that a public square display of nude corpses is sufficiently offensive to restrict this behavior. Not only the seriousness of the offense would have to be determined, but also how widely offensive it was. Anything we do might offend someone. What is needed is some degree of universality for the offense to be restricted. Moreover, some people have argued that if this principle were to be used, then it also would have to involve another element—avoidability. Only those actions that would be unavoidable by people who would be offended by them could be restricted. Those that people could easily avoid would not be.

How would this principle be applied to pornography? First, instead of labeling certain explicit sexual material as pornographic, *obscenity* is the term that is often used. Obscenity, however, has been as difficult to define as pornography. Among the phrases defining it, as noted earlier, is "patently offensive."[21] Pornography offends some people's sensibilities. The question we then ask is whether pornography may be legally restricted on the grounds that it is offensive to some or to most people. We might want to consider whether it is offensive to a major part of a population or to some local community. Thus, also offensiveness, or serious offense, to women or to a specific racial group might be a sufficient basis for restriction. This relies on the criterion of universality.

As to the other criterion, avoidability, if live sex shows and materials were limited to a particular section of a city, for example, then the offense principle could not be used to justify banning them because this section could be avoided by people who would be offended. However, if there were displays in the public square or supermarket that people could not avoid, and should not have to avoid, then the offensive displays might be rightly restricted on this principle. However, as with the other principles, there remains the first and most basic question about whether the principle is a good one or not. Ought people be restricted in doing what offends others in certain ways? If you answer "No," then you need not go on to consider the details mentioned here. However, if you believe that some offenses are serious enough to warrant social restriction, then details related to avoidability and universality and degree of offense would have to be determined. This principle becomes especially problematic with the rise of "adult" home entertainment, whether Internet or video. Here it is not on Main Street where some people may be disturbed by it, but rather out of the public eye.

Legal Paternalism

According to the principle of *legal paternalism,* people's liberty also may be restricted to prevent them from doing harmful things to themselves. Granted that the kind and degree of harm would again have to be specified, the distinctive element in this principle is its application to the individual. For instance, should the law be able to tell me that I must wear a seatbelt when riding in a car or a helmet when riding a motorcycle? There may be nonpaternalistic reasons behind some of the existing legislation in this area. If you are injured in an accident, it not only harms you, but also possibly others, for they may have to pay for your medical care. Yet there may also be paternalistic reasons for such restraints. "We want to prevent you from harming yourself," say proponents of this type of law.

Just how or whether this principle might justify restriction on pornography is a tough question. The argument would have to be something like the following. Pornography is not good for you, and thus we can restrict your access to it. Whether pornography harms its users, and what kind of harm it might do, are matters open to question and argument. For example, does pornography infantilize people because they substitute it for real-life sexual relations, or does it help people with practical sexual function or understanding their own sexual desires? If people are forced to participate in pornographic activities and this participation is harmful to them, then the harm principle would come into play and be used to prevent those who would forcefully harm others.

Note that all of these principles are directed to adult behavior and restrictions on it. There are obviously further reasons to restrict the behavior of children, including paternalistic restrictions on their freedom for their own good. The more problematic case is that of restricting the behavior of adults— behavior that is either harmless or not likely to harm anyone but themselves. To establish whether the principle of legal paternalism is a good principle, one would need to determine the role society ought to play in relation to individual citizens. Does or should society function as a kind of father (or mother) and look out to see that its "children" are not making foolish or unduly risky choices? Even if this principle were not accepted as valid, there would still be reasons for social intervention to inform people about the results of their choices. Thus, laws that require truth in labeling and advertising would still be fitting, for they would be covered by the harm principle. This would restrict advertisers and sellers from harming users and buyers.

Legal Moralism

The final liberty-limiting principle is *legal moralism.* The idea is that the law may rightly act to prevent people from doing what is immoral just because it is immoral. It is easy to confuse this principle with the harm principle. We can agree that harming others may be immoral. But we need not focus on the immorality of harming them in order to say that the law can restrict this behavior because it falls under the harm principle. Thus, legal moralism usually applies to supposedly harmless immoralities or to so-called victimless crimes.

The principle of legal moralism involves a quite different notion of the purpose of law. It may view the state as a moral being in itself or as having a moral purpose. For example, the Puritans came to the New World with one overriding purpose: to establish a new society that would be a moral example for all other nations to follow. Since that time, however, the relation between morality or religion and the state has been weakened in the United States. Laws that promote the separation of church and state exemplify this trend. Nevertheless, many elements of the original idea are present in our society: from the "In God We Trust" phrase written on our money to the prayers that begin or end various public services. (However, there is some controversy about some of this, as demonstrated recently when the Ten Commandments were displayed in public buildings.)

The application of this principle to the issue of pornography is basically as follows. If certain sorts of pornography are thought to be morally degrading or show an improper regard for sex, then on these grounds alone pornography can be restricted by law. Just whose view of what is morally right and wrong ought to be used will be a problem for the application of this principle. Those who support the principle also will want to consider the seriousness of the wrong and not make all wrong actions subject to legal sanction. But, as in the case of the other principles, the first question to ask is whether the principle itself is a good one. We would ask whether the immoral character of an action would be a good reason to restrict it by law and by the force of legal punishment.

Although this treatment of the liberty-limiting principles has taken place in the context of a discussion of pornography, the principles obviously apply more widely. Whether there should be legal restrictions on drug use, regulations for tobacco smoking, or laws regarding euthanasia and abortion are only a few of the matters that may depend on what we say about the relation of law and morality. You could now return to the chapters on euthanasia and abortion and ask about the particular liberty-limiting principles that might apply. Although thinking about the relation of the law and morality in terms of these principles is not the only way to pursue the issue, it is one approach that can help clarify our thinking.

FEMINISM AND PORNOGRAPHY

For more than three decades, many feminists have spoken out and written against pornography. Some feminists argue that certain forms of pornography, those that are simply erotica, are not objectionable. However, much of contemporary pornography, these feminists believe, is much more problematic. They believe that pornography that involves women often includes a degrading portrayal of women as subordinate and as wanting to be raped, bound, and bruised.[22] Music videos and album covers and lyrics provide examples of this today. It is not just the portrayal of degrading or abusive sex that feminists find objectionable, but that the portrayal is set in a context in which the harmful results of degrading women are not shown as well. What they also find objectionable are portrayals with "implicit, if not explicit, approval and recommendation of sexual behavior that is immoral, i.e. that physically or psychologically violates the personhood of one of the participants."[23] A few incidents of this might be ignored, but if this type of pornographic material is widespread and mass-produced, these feminists argue, then it can create a climate of support for attitudes that harm women. These attitudes can prevent women from occupying positions of equality and may contribute to the lack of adequate social response to the abuse of women.

According to Andrea Dworkin, "Pornography creates attitudes that keep women second class citizens. . . . Porn teaches men that what they see reflects our natural attitudes."[24] She and lawyer Catharine MacKinnon wrote ordinances that define the harms of pornography as civil rights violations—in particular, as forms of sex discrimination. Written at the request of local governments and passed by legislatures or by citizens in referenda, the ordinances recognize that pornography violates women's civil rights and grants women equal citizenship by providing them with means of redressing such violation. On their analysis, making the harms of pornography actionable by its victims would promote equality of the sexes in part because pornography "eroticizes hierarchy. . . . It makes dominance and submission into sex."[25]

One issue here is whether such laws are violations of free speech. In 1984, legal restrictions on pornography as a violation of civil rights were found to be unconstitutional by a federal court in Indianapolis.[26] However, we may still ask which interest takes precedence—the civil rights of women or the free speech rights of others? For example, is the harm to women well documented and so serious that some restriction of free speech is justifiable? Or is this really a violation of a right to freedom of speech? The answer to these questions will at least partly depend on what we say about the purpose and value of free speech. Is self-expression a good in itself, or is the freedom to speak out a good because it promotes the free exchange of ideas or political freedoms? If it is the latter, then it will be more difficult to believe that pornography ought to come under legal protection as free speech. Rather, it would be judged in terms of the ends it promotes. If these ends include the undermining of the equality and dignity of women, then it would be even more difficult to make a case for its protection. However, as others have noted, the connection between pornography of various sorts and harms to women is a difficult one to make. That is another reason why this issue will continue to be a matter of debate among people who care about these important values.

NOTES

1. www.dailynews.com/ci_6059391.
2. www.beliefnct.com/story/120/story 12060 1.html; http://sfgate.com/cgi-bin/article.cgi?f=/c/a/2004/02/13/BUGEN4VSS11.DTL.
3. Ibid.
4. www.techcrunch.com/2007/05/12/internet-pornography-stqats/.
5. www.iht.com/articles/2005/09/16/business/porn.php; http.usatoday.com/tech/products/services/2005 12 12-pornography-cellphones_x.htm.
6. Association of Sites Advocating Child Protection; www.asacp.org/index.php.
7. Ibid.
8. Helen Longino, "Pornography, Oppression, and Freedom: A Closer Look," in *Take Back the Night: Women on Pornography* (New York: William Morrow, 1980).
9. U.S. Supreme Court. 413 U.S. 15, 24. This was based on the 1954 Model Penal Code of the American Law Institute.
10. See www.adultweblaw.com/laws/childporn.htm.
11. This distinction has been partially based on the works of Joel Feinberg in his volumes *Harm to Others* (1984), *Offence to Others* (1985), *Harm to Self* (1986), and *Harmless Wrongdoing* (1988). Recall

that we had raised similar questions about the distinction between moral questions about euthanasia and abortion and questions about what the law should or should not do, and we suggested strongly that these are two different types of question and need two different types of reasoning.
12. Note that this is not the only way to pose the question about the relation of law and morality. We might, for example, also want to know the more general purpose of a nation-state: Is it, for example, simply to keep order and prevent people from impinging on others' rights, or does it have a more positive purpose such as to "promote the general welfare"? We discuss this issue further in Chapter 13, "Economic Justice."
13. The names and ordering of these principles in writings on the subject vary. However, this is generally the type of division that is discussed. See, for example, Joel Feinberg, *Social Philosophy* (Englewood Cliffs, NJ: Prentice Hall, 1973): 28–45.
14. The prevention can be through physical detention or through threat of punishment for nonconformity with the law. The issue of deterrent threats will be considered in Chapter 14 on legal punishment and the death penalty.
15. Study by Diana Scully, reported in *Newsweek* (March 18, 1985): 65.
16. Ibid., 62, studies by Edward Donnerstein.
17. See, for example, the minority opinion of Justice William Brennan in *Paris Adult Theatre I* v. *Slaton*, U.S. Supreme Court, 413 U.S. 49 (1973).
18. Alan Wolfe, "Dirt and Democracy: Feminists, Liberals and the War on Pornography," *The New Republic, 202,* no. 8 (Feb. 19, 1990): 27–31.
19. Susan Wendell as reported by McKenzie Davis in "Pornographic Censorship on the Internet," www.cohums.ohio-state.edu/english/People/Hogsette.1/g1Porn.htm.
20. From the majority opinion in *Paris Adult Theatre I* v. *Slaton*.
21. *Roth* v. *United States* (1954) and *Miller* v. *California* (1973).
22. This is not to ignore pornography that involves homosexuals or children. There are obvious objections to using children.
23. Longino, "Pornography," op. cit.
24. *Newsweek* (March 18, 1985): 60.
25. Catharine MacKinnon, *Feminism Unmodified* (Cambridge, MA: Harvard University Press, 1987).
26. *American Booksellers* v. *Hudnut*, 598 F. Supp. 1316, 1334 (S.D. Ind. 1984).

REVIEW EXERCISES

1. Distinguish normative from descriptive definitions of pornography.
2. Label each statement below regarding the legal regulation of pornography as an example of one of the types of "liberty-limiting principles."
   a. It is important to any society that its citizens be self-disciplined. One area of self-discipline is sexual behavior. Thus, a society in its own interest may make legal regulations regarding sexual matters, including pornography.
   b. Only if pornography can be proven to lead people to commit sexual assaults on others can it rightly be restricted by law.
   c. Pornography manifests sexual immaturity, and a society should not encourage such immaturity in its members and thus may limit pornography.
   d. Pornography depicts improper and degrading sex acts and thus should be legally banned.
   e. Just as we prevent people from walking nude in public places because it upsets people, so pornography should not be allowed in public places.
3. To which types of pornography do some feminists object and why?

DISCUSSION CASES

1. Pornographic Lyrics. One of the latest hot hits on the ABC label has been described as pornographic by certain women's groups. It uses explicit sexual language. It uses crude language to describe women's genitalia. It also suggests that it is all right to abuse women sexually and that they like to be treated this way. The women's groups want the album banned as pornography that harms women. The music company is protesting that this is a free country and this is simply free speech. You might not like it and it may be tasteless, they argue, but consumers who find it so do not have to buy it.

Do you agree with the record company or the women's groups? Why?

2. Porn Star. Jim had been dating Penelope for a couple months before he found out that she has been acting in pornographic films. He did not feel good about this, thinking that his relationship, including sexual intimacies, had been compromised. She explained to him that this was just her job and that she liked the pay, the nudity did not bother her, and the sex did not mean anything to her. He did not like the idea of her being seen by others in such films and decided this relationship was not for him. What do you think about his decision? About hers?

3. Class Argument. Sue's class has been debating the moral issue of pornography. Some of her classmates argued that pornography degrades women and thus is morally objectionable. Others said that it was a personal matter and that if some people didn't like it, they shouldn't look at it and shouldn't object. Others argued that sex is personal and should only be part of a loving relationship and for the most part by people who were married. Some even agreed with this last view but said that for the law to prohibit it goes too far and threatens other freedoms that we value. Which view do you agree with and why?

YOU MAKE THE DECISION

Apply the theories and issues discussed in this chapter by accessing this animated simulation on the Ethics Resource Center.

Use the passkey that accompanies your book to gain access. If you do not have a passkey, visit cengage brain.com to purchase instant access to additional study material.

Do you ask the guys to cancel their subscription?

Ethics Module 11 : Pornography

Selected Bibliography

Akdeniz, Yaman. *Internet Child Pornography and the Law's Response: National and International.* Aldershot, NH: Ashgate Publishing, 2008.

Assiter, Alison. *Pornography, Feminism and Individualism.* Cambridge, MA: Unwin Hyman, 1990.

Berger, Fred R. *Freedom of Expression.* Belmont, CA: Wadsworth, 1980.

Burstyn, Varda (Ed.). *Women Against Censorship.* Vancouver, BC: Douglas & McIntyre, 1985.

Carr, Indira. *Pornography and the Internet.* Aldershot, NH: Ashgate Publishing, 2009.

Chancer, Lynn S. *Reconcilable Differences: Confronting Beauty, Pornography, and the Future of Feminism.* Berkeley: University of California Press, 1998.

Copp, David, and Susan Wendell. *Pornography and Censorship.* Buffalo, NY: Prometheus, 1983.

Cornell, Drucilla. *Feminism and Pornography.* New York: Oxford University Press, 2000.

Cothran, Helen. *Pornography.* Farmington Hills, MI: Gale Group, 2001.

Devlin, Patrick. *The Enforcement of Morals.* New York: Oxford University Press, 1965.

Dworkin, Ronald M. (Ed.). *The Philosophy of Law.* New York: Oxford University Press, 1977.

Dwyer, Susan. *The Problem of Pornography.* Belmont, CA: Wadsworth, 1999.

Feinberg, Joel. *Offense to Others.* New York: Oxford University Press, 1985.

Gruen, Lori, and George B. Panichas (Eds.). *Sex, Morality, and the Law.* New York: Routledge, 1996.

Hixson, Richard F. *Pornography and the Justices: The Supreme Court and the Intractable Obscenity Problem.* Carbondale, IL: Southern Illinois University Press, 1996.

Kendall, Christopher N. *Gay Male Pornography: An Issue of Sex Discrimination.* Vancouver: University of British Columbia Press, 2004.

Lederer, Laura (Ed.). *Take Back the Night: Women on Pornography.* New York: Morrow, 1980.

Mackey, Thomas C. *Pornography on Trial: A Sourcebook with Cases, Laws, and Documents.* Cambridge, MA: Hackett Publishing, 2008.

MacKinnon, Catharine. *Feminism Unmodified.* Cambridge, MA: Harvard University Press, 1987.

———**, and Andrea Dworkin (Eds.).** *In Harm's Way: The Pornography Civil Rights Hearings.* Cambridge, MA: Harvard University Press, 1998.

Mason-Grant, Joan. *Pornography Embodied: From Speech to Sexual Practice.* New York: Rowman & Littlefield, 2004.

Paul, Pamela. *Pornified: How Pornography Is Transforming Our Lives, Our Relationships and Our Families.* New York: Henry Holt and Company, 2006.

Procida, Richard, et al. *Global Perspectives on Social Issues: Pornography.* Lanham, MA: Lexington Books, 2003.

Procida, Richard, and Rita James Simon. *Approaches to Pornography: A Comparative Assessment.* Lanham, MD: Lexington Books (Rowman & Littlefield), 2002.

Saarenmaa, Laura. *Pornification: Sex and Sexuality in Media Culture.* Oxford, UK: Berg Publishers, 2007.

Soble, Alan. *Pornography, Sex and Feminism.* Amherst, NY: Prometheus Books, 2001.

Strossen, Nadine. *Defending Pornography.* New York: New York University Press, 2000.

Taylor, Maxell, et al. *Child Pornography: An Internet Crime.* Philadelphia: Brunner-Routledge, 2003.

U.S. Department of Justice. *Attorney General's Commission on Pornography.* Final Report, July 1986.

12

Equality and Discrimination

In November 2006, six imams (Muslim religious leaders) returning from an Islamic conference boarded a US Airways flight in Minneapolis. Several other passengers complained that the imams' behavior was suspicious. They had knelt and prayed loudly at the boarding gate and had chanted "Allahu Akbar," a phrase that many Americans associate with Muslim terrorists, and they were complaining about U.S. foreign policy. When they got on the plane, they sat in different places throughout the plane, and a couple of them asked for seat belt extenders with heavy buckles on the ends, even though these passengers didn't seem to need the extenders. Security personnel were called, and they asked the six imams to leave the plane. When they refused, the police were called, and they were handcuffed and taken off the plane. After hours of questioning, they were allowed to take another flight to their destination of Phoenix.[1]

After they returned home, the imams complained to US Airways and the Muslim American Society. They complained that they had been humiliated and were the victims of religious or racial discrimination, or both. They noted that they had round-trip tickets and had carry-on luggage. They said that they had prayed at the boarding gate because that was the time of the day when prayers were supposed to be given. In March 2007, they filed a lawsuit against US Airways, the airport, and the passengers who had complained.[2]

Now some of the details of what happened have been disputed. But if this account is basically correct, would you say that this was in fact unjust discrimination? Or did the airline act reasonably given the post-9/11 concerns about airline security?

Racial profiling has also been raising questions about discrimination in other areas. What exactly is it? "Racial profiling is any police or private security practice in which a person is treated as a suspect because of his or her race, ethnicity, nationality or religion." This could be drug searches or stopping drivers on the highway. There are cases, for example, of drivers allegedly being stopped simply because they were African Americans—the supposed crime of "driving while black." In 1992 in Orlando, Florida, for example, 5 percent of the drivers were black or Hispanic, but they accounted for 70 to 80 percent of those who were stopped and searched.[3] In 2006, Dallas police pulled over more than 267,000 motorists. The number of black motorists stopped (36 percent) was disproportionate to their numbers in the local population (26 percent).[4] More recent numbers are hard to come by, and negative publicity over this type of incident may have lessened its occurrence. Other racial profiling concerns relate to drug-enforcement practices. Operation Pipeline of the federal Drug Enforcement Administration also has used racial profiles in its work. Recently, 95 percent of those who were stopped for suspicion of being drug couriers were minorities.[5]

Whether a policy counts as racial profiling and whether it always implies racial bias and discrimination is a matter of some debate. For example, when decisions to stop motorists are made primarily or solely on the basis of race, this is surely discriminatory. However, in other cases in which race is just one of many factors in selecting targets of investigation, the question of discrimination is not so clear. This is the difference between "hard" and "soft" profiling. In the former case, race is the only factor that is used to single out someone, whereas in the latter it is just one of many factors. An example of the latter is "questioning or detaining a person because of the confluence of a variety of factors—age (young), dress (hooded sweatshirt, baggy pants, etc.), time (late evening), geography (the person is walking through the 'wrong' neighborhood)—that include race (black)."[6] Or consider the New Jersey highway patrolman who pulls over a black driver who is speeding in a Nissan Pathfinder because the police have intelligence that Jamaican drug rings favor this car as a means for their marijuana trade in the Northeast.[7] Is this an example of unjust discrimination or a reasonable procedure?

A clearer form of discrimination is that of *hate crime*. During a speech in Paris on July 17, 2005, to mark the sixty-third anniversary of the roundup of French Jews in World War II, the French prime minister spoke against anti-Semitism and hate crimes committed in its name.[8] In the weeks after the attacks on the London subway trains and buses in July 2005, there were several attacks on mosques. They were attacked in a case of misguided retaliation for the suicide bombings by men of Pakistani background.[9] In the summer of 2005, a group devoted to stopping hate crimes in Eugene, Oregon, reported that it had recently seen an increase in such incidents. Volunteers from the group handed out fliers with the words "Hate Free Zone" written large. The fliers informed people what to do if they witnessed any hate crimes taking place. As a result, there were reports of racist, anti-Semitic, and antigay activity by local Nazi skinheads in the area.[10]

It is difficult to get overall good numbers on the incidence of hate crimes. However, if anecdotal reports are indicative, the number seems to be increasing. For example, according to authorities, there has been a significant jump of 32 percent in the number of antigay hate crimes in the city of New York in 2005.[11] Moreover, there were 514

hate crimes reported for L.A. County in 2006. Overall in California for 2006, 1,306 hate crimes were reported. Sixty-four percent of these were for race, ethnicity, or national origin; 15.7 percent by antireligion motives; 18.8 percent for sexual orientation; 0.2 percent for antidisability reasons; and 0.6 percent for antigender motives.[12] Just as there are more severe penalties for killing a police officer than a layperson, so some people argue that there ought to be more severe penalties for crimes motivated by hatred. Critics respond that to do this is to punish people for the views they hold, and that no matter how objectionable these might be, such a designation would constitute a violation of free speech.

Discrimination in the application of *criminal laws* also has not been completely overcome. Some social critics cite this as one reason for the high incidence of AIDS among minorities. In 1992, for example, 30 percent of those who were diagnosed with AIDS were blacks, who formed only 12 percent of the population; Latinos were 17 percent of AIDS cases but only 9 percent of the population. Thus, Latinos and blacks together accounted for 46 percent of AIDS cases. In 1996, blacks and Latinos represented 66 percent of infected youths. Although the causes for such numbers may be many, not the least of which is the combination of historic patterns of discrimination and current patterns of drug use and promiscuity, some critics believe that it is also the product of racial bias in the war against drugs. For example, it may well be that "fear of arrest compels injection drug users to rely on syringes borrowed at the moment of injection," and "persistent police harassment has promoted the spread of underground shooting galleries." Also as a result, male drug users expose "women and their offspring who live in those neighborhoods to a much higher risk of infection from unprotected sex."[13]

Education has been the great equalizer and the hope of the less fortunate. However, here also problems remain. The dropout rate for African American college students is higher than for white students. "Compared to white students, African Americans are 20 percent less likely to complete college within a six-year period." The causes are many, but prominent to many observers are the stress and feelings of not belonging and the disincentives that follow from racial discrimination.[14] Officers at some of the nation's elite colleges have pointed out that few students who come from poor families attend their schools. Financial aid is insufficient to adequately increase their numbers. In 1995, of students entering the top nineteen schools, only "3.1 percent . . . were from lower-income families." Fewer of these students are fast-tracked at school from early on. For example, "wealthy students are six times more likely to take the SAT and score at least 1200 as students from poor homes."[15] And at the University of Michigan, there were more students entering the freshman class whose parents make more than $200,000 a year than those who make "less than the national median of about $53,000."[16]

Racial stereotypes also have been thought to be the cause of continuing discriminatory attitudes. Although news media have done much better in recent years in weeding out racial stereotypes, a 1997 survey found that many national news magazines and television shows continued to "show blacks in stories about poverty 62 percent to 65 percent of the time, yet only 29 percent of poor Americans are black."[17]

If we look at *employment statistics,* we also find problems. In 1985, "50 percent of all black men were chronically unemployed." In 2004, black men earned only 74.5 percent and Hispanic men only 63.2 percent of what white men earned. The income of all women compared to men has improved over the years, but in 2004 they still only earned 77 percent of what men earned. Furthermore, the wage gap "cuts across a wide spectrum of occupations. The Bureau of Labor Statistics reported that in 2005 female physicians and surgeons earned 60.9% of the median weekly wages of male physicians, and women in sales occupations earned just 63.4% of men's wages in equivalent positions."[18] A look at the professions also gives us reason to be concerned. The American Bar Association (ABA) is concerned that too few lawyers are members of ethnic minority groups. "Our Society is increasingly racially and ethnically diverse, but our profession is not," the ABA's head said in 1999. Although 30 percent of U.S. Americans are members of racial or ethnic minorities, they constitute less than 10 percent of lawyers.[19]

Asian Americans also face problems of misunderstanding and prejudice even though their academic achievements have been phenomenal. However, figures for median income for Asian Americans, especially more recent immigrants, are often deceiving, particularly when family income is the focus, because three to five household workers may be contributing to that income.

Forty-three million Americans have one or more physical or mental disabilities. Although great efforts have been made to remove barriers and ensure that positions are open to such people, they still are disadvantaged in many areas.[20] Stereotypes and prejudice remain. Older workers are also often the victims of discrimination, subjected to arbitrary age limits in employment, where age alone rather than judgments of individual job performance are used to dismiss someone.[21] It also has been reported that 85 percent of Americans surveyed "favor equal treatment in the workplace for homosexuals and heterosexuals." As a result, by 1996, 313 companies, thirty-six cities, twelve counties, and four states had extended health benefits to gay partners of their employees. And in early 2000, the Vermont legislature passed a law recognizing "civil unions" between gay and lesbian couples, giving them many of the benefits provided by law to married heterosexual couples.[22]

Gender discrimination also continues to be a problem. For example, males continue to dominate the fields of science and engineering. One causal cultural factor is that "more girls are not steered into math and science at an early age" and specific attitudes and behaviors seem to be reinforced early in girls' lives. For several years, Barbie dolls, for example, were programmed to say, "Math class is tough." The line was discontinued in 1992 after the doll maker received complaints. It's not surprising that many girls believe that it is not cool to be smarter than boys. There continue to be fewer women in mathematics and science and engineering than in other fields. However, some progress is evidently being made. A 2004 report of the National Center for Education Statistics points out that from kindergarten through twelfth grade, "math and computer usage gender gaps have disappeared (though) a small science proficiency gap remains. . . . Males were more likely to take AP exams in science and calculus but in terms of performance, there were no significant differences between girls' and boys' proficiency in mathematics."[23]

Progress is also being made by women in wages. Women now earn on average 80 percent of what men do, which is a significant increase from the 62 percent of twenty-five years ago.[24] However, the cause may be problematic: During recent recessionary times, men were laid off their jobs, while women who were cheaper to hire retained theirs, thus raising the average rate. Moreover, more women were employed in recession-proof fields such as health care and education. More positive was the fact that women were reaching higher educational levels and thus obtaining higher-paying jobs.[25]

Still, sexual harassment incidents negatively affect women's status and functioning in the workplace. Between 1992 and 1996, 67,751 sexual harassment complaints were filed with the Equal Employment Opportunity Commission. Some 143,842 were filed between 1997 and 2006. Between 41 percent and 48 percent of these were found to have no reasonable cause, and between 5 percent and 10 percent were determined to have reasonable cause. Between 11 percent and 15 percent of the complaints were filed by males.[26] These incidents are also a problem in education. Recently, the U.S. Supreme Court ruled that school districts can be held financially liable for sexual harassment of students by other students if school administrators knew about the harassment and were "deliberately indifferent" to it. Even men who sexually harass other men can be sued for harassment.[27]

Discrimination is an international problem. For example, many European countries do not have effective antidiscrimination laws. Although their governments claim that workers have freedom of movement, such movement is affected by discrimination. For example, "in Germany, the driving force behind the European Union, racist violence rose by 25 percent in 1997, and the authorities recorded 11,720 offences by far-right groups."[28] Cases of anti-Semitism have also been on the rise

in recent years. In many countries, women and men do not have equal rights. In Afghanistan, for example, the ruling Islamic fundamentalist Taliban group had banned women from working except in nursing, and girls older than eight could not attend formal schools. Migrant workers in the United States and Europe and other parts of the world continue to face discrimination. In Singapore, for example, "most working women are limited to low-paying jobs in both periphery and core industries"—partly, it is said, to protect male economic success![29]

Numerous examples of sex discrimination continue to be documented internationally. A recent meeting of women's groups to review the progress of women's rights since the 1995 Beijing meeting focused on "honor killings," dowry deaths, female infanticide, and acid attacks. Even in countries where such killing is illegal, families who murder their daughters because they have brought shame to them often are not prosecuted. According to recent studies by UNICEF, in 1997 India reported "more than 6,000 dowry deaths" and an equal number of bride burnings. "The women died because they did not bring what in-laws considered satisfactory dowries or, sometimes, because the grooms were not happy with brides chosen by their families."[30] Bangladesh also reported that in 1998 more than 200 women were disfigured in assaults, often by acid and most often by men or boys whom the women had rejected.[31] The U.N. Population Fund has estimated that some 5,000 females are killed each year by honor killings. These are cases in which sometimes even suspected sexual misbehavior of a female family member is thought to dishonor the family; the suspicion or the fact becomes grounds for their murder. These cases are typically in Middle East countries or those with majority Muslim populations. However, "many Islamic leaders and scholars condemn the practice and deny that it is based on religious doctrine." They contend that it is rather a "pre-Islamic, tribal custom stemming from the patriarchal and patrilineal society's interest in keeping strict control over familial power structures."[32] Another tragic example of gender discrimination is found in the AIDS epidemic in sub-Saharan Africa. Women there are three times more likely than men of the same age to be infected. Because women are dependent economically on men, they often "marry older men who have been sexually active for decades."[33]

Patterns of gender difference also exist in domestic violence and homicide statistics. For example, "on average, more than three women are murdered by their husbands or boyfriends in this country every day."[34]

Statistics on forced prostitution also exemplify discriminatory treatment of women. "Activists estimate that 2 million women and children are sent across borders into some form of prostitution each year, and the State Department believes that approximately 50,000 could be in the United States."[35]

Clearly, the ideal of equal treatment and equal respect for all people regardless of race, sex, national origin, age, sexual orientation, and ethnicity has not been fully realized. However, it is not clear just what is required of us and why. After a brief look at some of the civil rights movement's history, particularly in the United States, we will examine key ethical issues: What is discrimination? What is wrong with it and why? A second section deals with the related issue of affirmative action.

CIVIL RIGHTS LAWS: A BRIEF HISTORY

We like to think that civil rights laws enacted in the United States and other Western countries have lessened racial injustice and promoted equal treatment for all citizens. Consider, for example, the following highlights of U.S. civil rights–related legislation.

- **1868** The Fourteenth Amendment to the Constitution, the equal protection clause, declared that no state may "deny to any person within its jurisdiction the equal protection of the law." This followed the Thirteenth Amendment in 1865, which prohibited slavery.
- **1920** The Nineteenth Amendment to the Constitution gave women the right to vote. This followed efforts and demonstrations by the suffragettes and the enactment of state laws that gave this right to women. (This is also fifty years after blacks were given the right to vote.)

- **1954** The U.S. Supreme Court's ruling in *Brown* v. *Board of Education* overturned the "separate but equal" schooling decision of the Court's 1896 *Plessy* v. *Ferguson* ruling.
- **1959** Vice President Richard M. Nixon ordered preferential treatment for qualified blacks in jobs with government contractors. In an executive order in 1961, President John F. Kennedy called for affirmative action in government hiring; and in 1965, President Lyndon B. Johnson issued enforcement procedures such as goals and timetables for hiring women and underrepresented minorities.
- **1963** The Equal Pay Act required equal pay for substantially equal work by companies that were engaged in production for commerce.
- **1964** The Civil Rights Act, Title VII, prohibited discrimination in employment by private employers, employment agencies, and unions with fifteen or more employees. It prohibited the sex segregation of jobs and required that there be a *bona fide occupational qualification (BFOQ)* to allow preferences for specific group members for certain jobs—for instance, for wet nurses and clothing models.
- **1978** The U.S. Supreme Court ruling *Bakke* v. *U.C. Davis Medical School* forbade the use of racial quotas in school admissions but allowed some consideration of race in admissions decisions. This decision was challenged by the 1995 decision *Adarand* v. *Pena*. According to this 5–4 decision, *any* race-conscious federal program must serve a "compelling state interest" and must be "narrowly tailored" to achieve its goal. However, in 2003, a less rigid standard for acceptance of a race conscious program was appealed to by the U.S. Supreme Court in its decision regarding the affirmative action practices of the University of Michigan. In *Grutter* v. *Bollinger,* a 5-to-4 decision, the Court upheld the university's law school policy, which considers an applicant's race as one factor among others such as test scores, talent, and grade-point averages in admissions. The Court rejected the undergraduate school's more mechanical practice of giving set extra points for race. It also gave added support to earlier rulings that there was a "compelling state interest" in

racial diversity in education.[36] In another case, the 1979 *Weber* v. *Kaiser Aluminum* decision, the Court permitted a company to remedy its past discriminatory practices by using race as a criterion for admission to special training programs. These programs were aimed at ensuring that a percentage of black persons equal to that in the local labor force would be moved up to managerial positions in the company.

■ **1991** The congressional Civil Rights Act required that businesses that use employment practices with a discriminatory impact (even if unintentional) must show that the practices are business necessities; otherwise, the business must reform its practices to eliminate this impact.[37] Quotas were forbidden except when required by court order for rectifying wrongful past or present discrimination. Sexual harassment was also noted as a form of discrimination. Although cases of sexual harassment began to appear in court in the late 1970s, the concept is still being defined by the courts. Two forms of this harassment are generally recognized: One promises employment rewards for sexual favors, and the other creates a "hostile work environment."

These are just a few of the highlights of the last 150 years of civil rights laws as enacted by various government bodies and persons. They have played a major role in the way we carry out our common social and economic life. We might also cite other laws and court decisions that concern housing, lending, and the busing of school students, as well as laws that have been designed to prevent discrimination on the basis of not only race and sex but also religion, age, disability, and sexual orientation.[38] Many of these laws rely on and are based on legal precedent. But they also are grounded in moral notions such as equality and justice and fairness. In this chapter, we will examine some of the moral notions and arguments that play a role in discussions about what a just society should be like.

RACISM AND SEXISM

Some time ago, I came across an article titled "What's Wrong with Racism?" It is an intriguing title. To answer the question, we ought first to ask,

what is racism? Race, as a biological classification of humans, is based on a selection of common characteristics. Among these have been appearances, blood groups, geographic location, and gene frequency. Depending on which of these are the focus, anthropologists have classified the human species into anywhere from six to eighty races. One traditional division is into the following groups: "Caucasians, black Africans, Mongoloids, South Asian aborigines, Native Americans, Oceanians, and Australian Aborigines."[39] If we focus on genetic variation, then we find that only 8 to 10 percent of the differences between human individuals are associated with differences in race, whereas 85 percent accounts for individual differences and 15 percent for differences in local populations. Differences in skin color are not solely genetic and so-called racial differences change over time with mobility and intermixing. For example, "differences between frequencies of West Africans and American blacks show that 20% to 25% of the genes of urban black Americans have come from European and American Indian ancestors. . . ."[40]

On the other hand, race has sometimes been thought also to involve cultural differences, either real or imagined. Examples include preferences for certain foods, dress, or music; religious affiliation; and certain psychological or even ethical traits. It is these supposed differences that have influenced racist views—as much as, or possibly more than, biological and geographical differences. Still, certain constructions of race are of some interest. For example, if people want to be or think of themselves as belonging to a particular racial or ethnic group, should this count in how they are classified? For example, a white person who wants to fit in with black friends may adopt certain mannerisms and preferences of the group. Does that make this person black? Or perhaps a black person undergoes surgeries and medical procedures that make him look white. Does this make him white, or is he still black even though he no longer has that coloration?

A more controversial recent effort has been to investigate the genetic basis of race. Although most of us have mixed ancestry, genetic variations have been noted. In particular, they incline us to different disease susceptibilities. These scientific studies aim to "catalogue and compare the genetics of people with African, Asian, and European ancestry."[41] The particular effort is known as the International Haplotype Project and is financed by organizations and governments from Japan, the United Kingdom, Canada, China, Nigeria, and the United States. The Human Genome Project (see Chapter 17) completed in 2000 found that "humans as a species are 99.9 percent genetically identical." However, according to researchers now, this 0.1 percent difference is significant and made up of genetic variations that may include racial differences. The purpose of the project is to ultimately find out why certain groups suffer differential rates of high blood pressure and heart attacks by finding, for example, the genetic variants or mutations that may be involved in these diseases. In so doing, the hope is that drugs and treatment can be tailor-made for people in these groups. The populations studied are 270 people from Yoruba in Ibadan, Nigeria; Japanese in Tokyo; Han Chinese in Beijing; and Utah residents with ancestry from northern and western Europe.[42]

Obviously, if other traits are included, such as athletic ability or intelligence, then the project becomes more controversial and could be used for racist purposes. However, simply to note certain genetic or phenotypic variations by race is not itself racism. First of all, racism involves making race a significant factor about the person—more important, say, than height or strength. Race becomes a key identifying factor. It sets people of one race apart from people of other races, making us think of "us" and "them" on the basis of this classification.

History has long provided examples of such insider–outsider phenomena. Sometimes, it is a matter of blood and kin that determines the border. Sometimes, it is religious beliefs. Those with different religions may have been tolerated in some cases but not given equal rights. Muslims tolerated Christians and Jews in the Middle East, and Muslims were tolerated in Christian Europe. With the rise of democracies around the world, however, tolerance was no longer enough. People demanded equality.[43] Racism involves not only making distinctions and grouping people but also denigration. It involves believing that all persons

of a certain race are inferior to persons of other races in some way. Does this necessarily make racism wrong?

In the abstract, it would seem that believing that someone is shorter than another or less strong is not necessarily objectionable, especially if the belief is true. However, what we presume makes racism wrong is that it involves making false judgments about people. It also involves value judgments about their worth as people. A similar definition could be given of sexism—namely, having false beliefs about people because of their sex or devaluing them because of this. It also involves power and oppression, for those groups that are devalued by racism are also likely to be treated accordingly.

Furthermore, racism and sexism are not the same as prejudice. Prejudice is making judgments or forming beliefs before knowing the truth about something or someone. These prejudgments might accidentally be correct beliefs. However, the negative connotation of the term *prejudice* indicates that these beliefs or judgments are formed without adequate information and are also mistaken. Moreover, prejudice in this context also may be a matter of judging an individual on the basis of judgments about the characteristics of a group to which he or she belongs. They are supposedly false generalizations. Thus, if I think that all people of a certain race or sex like to drink warm beer because I have seen some of that group do so, then I am making a false generalization—one without adequate basis in the facts. Racism or sexism, although different from prejudice, may follow from prejudiced beliefs.

Knowing what racism is, we can then answer the question, what is wrong with it? We believe racism, like sexism, is wrong because it is unjust or unfair. It is also wrong because it is harmful to people. The racist or sexist treats people of a particular race or sex differently and less well simply because of their race or sex.

Yet we still have not gotten to the root of what is wrong with racism or sexism. Suppose that our views about members of a group are not based on prejudice but on an objective factual assessment about the group. For example, if men differ from women in significant ways—and surely they do—then is this not a sufficient reason to treat them differently? A moral principle can be used to help us think about this issue: the *principle of equality*. The general idea embodied in this principle is that we should treat equals equally and unequals unequally. In analyzing this principle, we will be able to clarify what is meant by discrimination, and whether or why it is morally objectionable. We also will be able to consider what is meant by affirmative action or reverse discrimination, and analyze the arguments for and against them.

THE PRINCIPLE OF EQUALITY

The principle of equality can be formulated in various ways. Consider the following formulation:

It is unjust to treat people differently in ways that deny to some of them significant social benefits unless we can show that there is a difference between them that is relevant to the differential treatment.

To understand the meaning of this principle, we will focus on its emphasized parts.

Justice

First, we notice that the principle is a principle of *justice*. It tells us that certain actions or practices that treat people unequally are unjust, and others presumably just. To understand this principle fully, we would need to explore further the concept of justice. Here we do so only briefly. (Further treatment of the nature of justice occurs in Chapter 13.) Consider, for instance, our symbols of justice. Outside the U.S. Supreme Court building in Washington, D.C., is a statue of a woman. She is blindfolded and holds a scale in one hand. The idea of the blindfold is that justice is blind—in other words, it is not biased. It does not favor one person over another on the basis of irrelevant characteristics. The same laws are supposed to apply to all. The scale indicates that justice may involve not strict equality but proportionality. It requires that treatment of persons be according to what is due them on some grounds. Therefore, it requires that there be valid reasons for differential treatment.

Social Benefits and Harms

We are not required to justify treating people differently from others in every case. For example, I may give personal favors to my friends or family and not to others without having to give a reason. However, sometimes social policy effectively treats people differently in ways that penalize or harm some and benefit others. This harm can be obvious or it can be subtle. In addition, there is a difference between primary racism or sexism and secondary racism or sexism.[44] In primary racism or sexism, a person is singled out and directly penalized simply because he or she is a member of a particular race or sex—as when denied school admissions or promotions just because of this characteristic. In secondary racism or sexism, criteria for benefit or harm are used that do not directly apply to members of particular groups and only indirectly affect them. Thus, the policy "last hired, first fired" is likely to have such an effect. Such policies may be allowed in the workplace or other social settings, policies that may seem harmless but actually have a harmful effect on certain groups. What we now label "sexual harassment" is an example of harmful discriminatory practices. This aspect of the principle of equality, then, directs us to consider the ways in which social benefits and penalties or harms sometimes occur for reasons that are not justified.

Proof

The principle states that we must show or prove that certain differences exist that justify treating people differently in socially significant ways. The principle can be stronger or weaker depending on the kind of proof of differences required by it. It is not acceptable to treat people differently on the basis of differences that we only think or suspect exist. Scientific studies of sex differences, for example, must be provided to show that certain sex differences actually exist.

Real Differences

The principle of equality requires that we show or prove that actual differences exist between the people that we would treat differently. Many sex differences are obvious, and others that are not obvious have been confirmed by empirical studies—such as differences in metabolic rate, strength and size, hearing acuity, shoulder structure, and disease susceptibility. However, it is unlikely that these differences would be relevant for any differential social treatment. Those that would be relevant are differences such as type of intellectual ability, aggressiveness, or nurturing capacity.

We might look to scientific studies of sex differences to help us determine whether any such possibly relevant sex differences exist. Women have been found to do better on tests that measure verbal speed and men to do better on being able to imagine what an object would look like if it were rotated in three-dimensional space. Recent discoveries have shown that men and women use different parts of their brains to do the same tasks. For example, to recognize whether nonsense words rhyme, men used a tiny area in the front left side of the brain, whereas women used a comparable section of the right side.[45] Whether this difference has a wider significance for different types of intelligence is a matter of some debate. So also are the studies of aggressiveness. Testosterone has been shown to increase size and strength, but whether it also makes males more aggressive than females is disputed. This is not only because of the difficulties we have in tracing physical causation, but also because of our uncertainty about just what we mean by aggressiveness.

However, most studies that examine supposed male and female differences also look at males and females after they have been socialized. Thus, it is not surprising that they do find differences. Suppose that a study found that little girls play with dolls and make block enclosures while little boys prefer trucks and use the blocks to build imaginary adventure settings. Would this necessarily mean that some innate difference causes this? If there were such differences and if they were innate, then this may be relevant to how we would structure education and some other aspects of society. We might prefer women for the job of nurse or early child-care provider, for example. We might provide women, but not men, with paid child-care leave.[46]

However, if we cannot prove that these or any such characteristics come from nature rather than by nurture, then we are left with the following type of problem. For many years, society thought that females had lesser mathematical abilities than males. Thus, in our educational practices we have not expected females to have these abilities, and teachers have tended to treat their male and female mathematics students differently. For instance, in a 1987 study, female students in the fourth through seventh grades who ranked high in mathematics were found to be "less likely to be assigned to high-ability groups by their teachers than were males with comparable scores."[47] Suppose that at a later point we tested people on mathematical ability and found a difference between the male and female scores. Would that mean we could justly prefer one group over the other for positions and jobs that required this skill? It would seem that if we wanted the jobs done well, we should do this. But suppose also that these jobs were the highest-paying and had the greatest esteem and power connected with them. Socialization has contributed to people's being more or less well qualified for valued positions like these in society. We should consider whether our social institutions perpetuate socially induced disadvantages. Using the principle of equality, we could rightly criticize such a system of reward for socially developed skills as unfair because it causes certain traits in people and then penalizes them for having those traits!

Relevant Differences

The principle of equality requires more than showing that real differences exist between people, not just socially learned differences, before we are justified in treating them differently. It also requires that the differences be relevant. This is the idea embodied in the BFOQ of the 1964 Civil Rights Act mentioned earlier. For example, if it could be shown that women were by nature better at bricklaying than men, then this would be a "real" difference between them. Although we might then be justified in preferring women for the job of bricklayer, we would not be justified in using this difference to prefer women for the job of airline pilot. On the other hand, if men and women think differently and if certain jobs required these particular thinking skills, then according to the principle of equality we may well prefer those with these skills for the jobs.

The relevance of a talent or characteristic or skill to a job is not an easy matter to determine. For example, is upper body strength an essential skill for the job of firefighter or police officer? Try debating this one with a friend. In answering this question, it would be useful to determine what kinds of things firefighters usually have to do, what their equipment is like, and so forth. Similarly, with the job of police officer we might ask how much physical strength is required and how important are other physical or psychological skills or traits. And is being an African American, Asian American, or female an essential qualification for a position as university teacher of courses in black studies, Asian studies, or women's studies? It may not be an essential qualification, but some people argue that this does help qualify a person because she or he is more likely to understand the issues and problems with which the course deals. Nevertheless, this view has not gone unchallenged.

In addition to determining what characteristics or skills are relevant to a particular position, we must be able to assess adequately whether particular persons possess these characteristics or skills. Designing tests to assess this presents a difficulty. Prejudice may play a role in such assessments. For instance, how do we know whether someone works well with people or has sufficient knowledge of the issues that ought to be treated in a women's studies course? This raises another issue. Should or must we always test or judge people as individuals, or is it ever permissible to judge an individual as a member of a particular group? The principle of equality seems better designed for evaluating differential group treatment than differential treatment of individuals. This is just one issue that can be raised to challenge the principle of equality.

Challenges to the Principle

The first problem that this principle faces stems from the fact that those group differences that are both real and relevant to some differential treatment are often, if not always, average differences. In other words, a characteristic may be typical of a group of people, but it may not belong to every member of the group. Consider height. Men are typically taller than women. Nevertheless, some women are taller than some men. Even if women were typically more nurturing than men, it would still be likely or at least possible that some men would be more nurturing than some women. Thus, it would seem that we ought to consider what characteristics an individual has rather than what is typical of the group to which he or she belongs. This would only seem to be fair or just. What, then, of the principle of equality as an adequate or usable principle of justice? It would seem to require us to do unfair things—specifically, to treat people as members of a group rather than as individuals.

Are we ever justified in treating someone differently because of her membership in a group and because of that group's typical characteristics— even if that person does not possess them? We do this in some cases, and presumably think it is not unjust. Consider our treatment of people as members of an age group, say, for purposes of driving or voting. We have rules that require that a person must be at least fifteen years old to obtain a driver's permit or license. But is it not true that some individuals who are fourteen would be better drivers than some individuals who are eighteen? Yet we judge them on the basis of a group characteristic rather than their individual abilities. Similarly, in the United States, we require that people be eighteen years of age before they can vote. However, some people who are less than eighteen would be more intelligent voters than some who are older than eighteen. Is it not unjust to treat persons differently simply because of their age group rather than on the basis of their own individual characteristics and abilities?

Consider possibilities for determining when treating people as members of a group is unfair or wrong and when it is justified. Take our two examples. If an individual is well qualified to drive but is not yet fifteen or sixteen, then she has only to wait one year. This causes no great harm to her. Nor is any judgment made about her natural abilities. Even those fifteen and older have to take a test on which they are judged as individuals and not just as members of a group. Furthermore, suppose that we tried to judge people as individuals for the purposes of voting. We would need to develop a test of "intelligent voting ability." Can you imagine what political and social dynamite this testing would be? The cost to our democracy of instituting such a policy would be too great, whereas the cost to the individual to be judged as a member of an age group and wait a couple years to vote is minimal. Thus, this practice does not seem unduly unfair.

However, if real and relevant sex differences existed, and if we treated all members of one sex alike on the basis of some characteristic that was typical of their group rather than on the basis of their characteristics as individuals, then this would involve both significant costs and significant unfairness. It would be of great social cost to society not to consider applicants or candidates because of their sex; these individuals might otherwise make great contributions to society. In addition, those who are denied consideration could rightly complain that it was unfair to deny them a chance at a position for which they qualified, something that would also affect them their whole lives. Thus, we could argue that the ideal of the principle of equality is generally valid but would need to be supplemented by such considerations concerning when judging a person as a member of a group would be permissible.

The second challenge to the principle of equality, or to its application, can be found in the debates over *preferential treatment* programs. Could not those people who support these programs claim that past discrimination was, in fact, a relevant difference between groups of people and that we would thus be justified in treating people differently on this basis? Preferential treatments would be designed to benefit those who are members of groups that have been discriminated against in the past. We will look shortly at the various forms of affirmative action and the arguments for and against them. It is useful here, however, to note the way in which the principle of equality might be used to justify some of these programs. The claim would be that being a member of a group was a sufficient reason to treat someone in a special way. Would we need to show that every member of that group was in some way harmed or

affected by past discrimination? Some individual members of particular groups would not obviously have been harmed by past discrimination. However, we should also be aware of the subtle ways in which group or community membership affects a person and the subtle ways in which she might thus be harmed. On the other hand, the attempt to use the principle of equality to justify preferential treatment of members of certain groups would contradict the aspect of the principle of equality that requires that the differences that justify differential treatment be real—in other words, caused by nature rather than by nurture—as well as significant.

The third problem users of the principle of equality must address concerns the equality–inequality dilemma. We can exemplify this by using sex or gender differences, but it also could be applied to cultural differences. Women have sought equality with men in the workplace, in education, and in public life generally. At the same time, they remain the primary child-care providers, which places them at an inevitable disadvantage in terms of advancement in many professions and so forth. Some feminists have argued that the liberal notion of equality can be detrimental to women.[48] Rather than think of women as similar to men, or use only a formal notion of equality devoid of content, some feminists argue for a more concrete notion of a person.[49] Thus, differences between males and females in such areas as parental responsibilities would be relevant to the justness of requirements for professional advancement.

Issues of multiculturalism also could be raised here. Sometimes, a person identifies him- or herself more by ethnic background than by race. "Whereas race is used for socially marking groups based on physical differences, ethnicity allows for a broader range of affiliation, based for example on shared language, shared place of origin, or shared religion."[50] We live in a complex society in which there are many forms of cultural expression and heritage. To what extent should this cultural heritage be acknowledged and encouraged? Sometimes, respect for cultural practices would lead to the condoning of gender inequality and discrimination.[51] Problems about multiculturalism also arise, for example, in education and its content and in debates about how to present history to young children and what to include in literary canons. Obviously, this is an area that raises many issues for heated debate. However, keep in mind that there probably ought to be some balance between equal treatment under the law and basic civility toward all on the one hand, and acknowledging our differences and respecting the contributions that we all make because of the ways in which we differ on the other hand.

AFFIRMATIVE ACTION AND PREFERENTIAL TREATMENT

Recently, demographics has led to an unusual problem in college and university enrollment figures. Women now earn approximately 56 percent of bachelor's degrees compared to 43 percent thirty years ago.[52] To remedy this problem, some college admissions officers are thinking about instituting programs that would increase undergraduate male enrollments. In effect, these programs would be affirmative action programs that would benefit males. However, when the figures are examined more closely, one finds that the numbers are partially affected by the larger proportion of minority and older women enrollees. For example, African American undergraduates of traditional age are 63 percent female and only 37 percent male. Moreover, the entering class numbers, 51 percent women and 49 percent men, are different than the graduating numbers. This is partly because male college freshmen spend more time exercising, watching TV, or partying than studying. Nevertheless, it is an interesting problem for affirmative action, reversing the usual issues.[53]

As mentioned earlier in the summary of civil rights legislation, the use of the term *affirmative action* and the policy itself originated more than three decades ago. Disputes about the justification of these practices continue, however. The first thing to note about affirmative action is that it comes in many forms. The idea suggested by the term is that to remedy certain injustices we need to do more than follow the negative requirement "Don't discriminate" or "Stop discriminating." The basic argument given for doing something more is

usually that the other way will not or has not worked. Psychological reasons may be cited, for example, that discrimination and prejudice are so ingrained in people that they cannot help discriminating and do not even recognize when they are being discriminatory or prejudiced. According to one writer, it is as though we were transported to a land of giants where everything was made for folks their size. They just couldn't see why anyone else had difficulties, assuming that we were just inferior or incompetent.[54] Social and political reasons also can be given, for example, that the discrimination is institutionalized. Many rules and practices have a built-in discriminatory impact, such as the discriminatory result of the seniority system. It's like a top that just keeps on spinning, even when we take our hand away.[55] The only way to change things, the argument goes, is to do something more positive.

But what are we to do? There are many possibilities. One is to make a greater positive effort to find qualified persons. Thus, in hiring, a company might place ads in minority newspapers. In college admissions, counselors might be sent to schools with heavy student populations of underrepresented minority groups, or invite the students to campus, or give them special invitations to apply. Once the pool is enlarged, then all in the pool would be judged by the same criteria, and no special preferences would be given on the basis of race or sex.

Other versions of affirmative action involve what have come to be known as *preferences*. Preference or some special favoring or a plus factor could be given to minority group members or women who were equally well qualified with the other finalists to give them some edge. Preference also may be given for minority group members or women who were somewhat less well qualified than other applicants. In either case, it is clear that determining equality of qualification is in itself a problem. One reason for this is that applicants for a position that has several qualifications are usually stronger on some qualifications and weaker on others. Another is the difficulty of deciding just what qualifications are necessary or important for some position. Although those people who support and oppose preferences seem to imply that determining this is easy, it is not at all that simple.

Other forms of affirmative action also exist. For example, companies or institutions may establish goals and quotas to be achieved for increasing minority or female representation. *Goals* are usually thought of as ideals that we aim for but that we are not absolutely required to reach. Goals can be formulated in terms of percentages or numbers. As of now, for example, U.S. federal contractors and all institutions with fifty or more employees and who receive federal funds of $50,000 or more must adopt affirmative action plans. These plans have sometimes involved setting goals for increasing the number of underrepresented minority members and women so that it might more closely reflect their percentage in the local labor pool. Companies might have specific recruiting plans for reaching their goals. These plans could, but would not necessarily, involve preferential treatments. *Quotas,* in contrast, are usually fixed percentages or numbers that a company intends to actually reach. Thus, a university or professional school might set aside a fixed number of slots for its incoming first-year class for certain minority group members (note the Bakke and Weber cases mentioned earlier). The institution would fill these positions even if this meant admitting people with lesser overall scores or points in the assessment system.

In summary, the following types of affirmative action can be specified:

1. Enlarging the pool of applicants, then hiring on the basis of competence.
2. Giving preferences among equally qualified applicants.
3. Giving preferences for less-qualified applicants.
4. Setting goals or ideal numbers for which to aim; they need not involve preferences.
5. Setting quotas or fixed numbers to actually attain; these usually do involve preferences.

The next question, then, to ask ourselves is, are these practices good or bad, justified or unjustified? All of them, or some of them, or none of them? In any discussion of affirmative action, it is important to specify what kind of practice one favors or opposes. Let us examine the arguments for and against the various types of affirmative action in terms of the reasons given to support them. These again can be easily divided into consequentialist and nonconsequentialist types of arguments.

Consequentialist Considerations

Arguments both for and against various affirmative action programs have relied on consequentialist considerations for their justification. These considerations are broadly utilitarian in nature. The question is whether such programs do more good than harm or more harm than good. Those people who argue in favor of these programs urge the following sorts of considerations: These programs benefit us all. We live in a multiracial society and benefit from mutual respect and harmony. We all bring diverse backgrounds to our employment and educational institutions, and we all benefit from the contributions of people who have a variety of diverse perspectives. Our law schools should have representation from all of the people who need adequate representation in society. We need to break the vicious circle of discrimination, disadvantage, and inequality. Past discrimination has put women and some minority group members at a continuing disadvantage. Unless something is done, they will never be able to compete on an equal basis or have an equal chance or equal opportunity.

Family plays a crucial role in what chances a child has.[56] To put it simply, low family income leads to poorer education for children, which leads to lower-paying jobs, which leads to low family income, and so on and so on. Affirmative action is one way to break the vicious circle of disadvantage. Children need role models to look up to. They need to know that certain types of achievement and participation are possible for them. Otherwise, they will not have hope and not work to be what they can become. Without affirmative action programs, supporters argue, things are not likely to change. Discrimination is so entrenched that drastic measures are needed to overcome it. The statistics show that while some progress has been made, a great gap continues in the major indicators of success between members of certain minority groups and women and others in the society. And the programs have shown some success. In their 1998 work, *The Shape of the River,* the former presidents of Princeton and Harvard, William G. Bowen and Derek Bok, showed that race-sensitive policies in college admissions have worked.[57] Students admitted under these programs have graduated at good rates and "were just as likely as their white classmates to earn advanced degrees in law, business, or medicine."[58]

Legal challenges to preferential treatment continue to raise problems for affirmative action. In its 1996 decision in *Hopwood* v. *Texas,* a three-judge panel of the U.S. Court of Appeals for the Fifth Circuit struck down an affirmative action program at the University of Texas law school. This program had accepted lower scores on the Law School Admission Test (LSAT) for black and Mexican American applicants. In a parallel development, Proposition 209 in California outlawed racial preferences in the public sector, and in 1995 the board of regents of the University of California (UC) system voted to ban race considerations in admissions. As a result, the number of black applicants who gained admittance to the UC system dropped 18 percent between the fall of 1997 and the fall of 1998. The number of African Americans admitted to the University of Texas at Austin law school declined 37.6 percent.[59] In 2003, the U.S. Supreme Court ruled in two related cases that the affirmative action program at the law school at the University of Michigan used race as one factor to create a more diverse student body in admissions was constitutional. It also found that the undergraduate program that gave explicit numbers of points to minority members was unconstitutional as a form of quotas outlawed by the 1978 Bakke case.[60]

Those who argue against affirmative action on consequentialist grounds believe that the programs do not work or do more harm than good. They cite statistics to show that these programs have benefited middle-class African Americans, for example, but not the lower class. "The most disadvantaged black people are not in a position to benefit from preferential admission."[61] Unless affirmative action admissions programs are accompanied by other aid, both financial and tutorial, they are

often useless or wasted. Some critics point out that lawsuits filed under the 1964 Civil Rights Act have done more than affirmative action to increase the percentage of blacks in various white-collar positions.[62] There is also the likelihood of stigma attached to those who have been admitted or hired through affirmative action programs. This can be debilitating to those who are chosen on this basis. Black neoconservatives, for example, argue that quotas and racially weighted tests "have psychologically handicapped blacks by making them dependent on racial-preference programs rather than their own hard work."[63] Those who oppose affirmative action programs also cite the increased racial tension that they believe results from these programs: in effect, a white male backlash against women and members of minority groups. Recently, some of the same writers who support affirmative action for underrepresented minority groups and women have also made a case for giving special attention to economically disadvantaged students in college and university admissions.[64] They point out that elite universities have only a miniscule percentage of admissions from lower-income families. It also is in the interest not only of fairness (see the following nonconsequentialist arguments) but also of increasing class diversity.

The key to evaluating these consequentialist arguments both for and against affirmative action is to examine the validity of their assessments and predictions. What, in fact, have affirmative action programs for college admissions achieved? Have they achieved little because they benefit those who least need it and might have succeeded without them, or have they actually brought more disadvantaged students into the system and into better and higher-paying jobs, thus helping break the vicious circle? Have other affirmative action programs increased racial harmony by increasing diversity in the workforce and in various communities, or have they only led to increasing racial tensions? These are difficult matters to assess. Here is another place where ethical judgments depend on empirical information drawn from the various sciences or other disciplines. The consequentialist argument for affirmative action programs will succeed if it can be shown that there is no better way to achieve the goods the programs are designed to achieve and that the good done by these affirmative action programs, or at least some of them, outweighs any harm they cause, including some racial tension and misplaced awards. The consequentialist argument against affirmative action programs will succeed if it can be shown that there are better ways to achieve the same good ends or that the harm they create outweighs the good they help achieve.

Nonconsequentialist Considerations

However, not all arguments about affirmative action programs are based on appeals to consequences. Some arguments appeal to considerations of justice. For instance, some people argue for affirmative action programs on the grounds that they provide justice, a way of making compensation for past wrongs done to members of certain groups. People have been harmed and wronged by past discrimination, and we now need to make up for that by benefiting them, by giving them preferential treatment. However, it is difficult to know how preferential treatment can right a past wrong. We may think of it as undoing the past harm done. Then we find that it is often difficult to undo the harm. How does one really prevent or erase results such as the loss of self-esteem and confidence in the minority child who asks, "Mom, am I as good as the white kid?" or in the little girl who says, "I can't do that; I'm a girl"?[65] This interpretation of making compensation then becomes a matter of producing good consequences or eliminating bad ones. It is a matter of trying to change the results of past wrongs. Thus, if making compensation is to be a nonconsequentialist reason, then it must involve a different sense of righting a wrong, a sense of justice being done in itself whether or not it makes any difference in the outcome.

Some people also argue against affirmative action on grounds of its injustice. They appeal to the principle of equality, arguing that race and sex are irrelevant characteristics. Just as it was wrong in the past to use these characteristics to deny people equal chances, so it is also wrong in the present, even if it is used this time to give them preferences. Race and sex are not differences that should count in treating people differently to deny benefits to some and grant them to others. Preferences for some also mean denial to others. For this reason, preferential treatment programs have sometimes been labeled *reverse discrimination*. Moreover, opponents of affirmative action criticize the use of compensatory justice arguments. In a valid use of the principles of compensatory justice, they might argue, those and only those wronged should be compensated, and those and only those responsible for the wrong should be made to pay. But some programs of affirmative action have actually compensated people regardless of whether they themselves have been harmed by past discriminatory practices. They have also required that some people pay who have not been responsible for the past discrimination. Those who lose out in affirmative action programs, they argue, may not have ever been guilty of discrimination or may not have wronged anyone.

The arguments for affirmative action based on considerations of justice will succeed only if those people who make them also can make a case for the justice of the programs, that they do in fact compensate those who have been wronged, even if they have been affected by discrimination in ways that are not immediately obvious, and it is not unjust if other people have to pay. Supporters may cite the fact that those who lose out are not badly harmed—they have other opportunities and are not demeaned by their loss. Though they have not intentionally wronged anyone, they have likely benefited from past discrimination.

The arguments against affirmative action based on considerations of justice will succeed only if they can respond to these claims and make the principle of equality work for their case. They may cite the matter of consistency in applying the principle, for example. But if they rely primarily on the harms done by continuing to use race or sex as a characteristic that grounds differential treatment, then they will be appealing to a consequentialist consideration and must be judged on that basis. To answer this question, the more basic issues of the moral status of considerations of justice would need to be addressed. Justice is treated further in Chapter 13.

NOTES

1. www.msnbc.msn.com/id/15824096/; http://en
   .wikipedia.org/wiki/Flying_Imams_controversy.
2. http://www.militantislammonitor.org/article/id/
   2576
3. David Cole and John Marcello, "Symposium:
   Insight on the News," *Washington Times,* July 19,
   1999, p. 24.
4. www.racialprofilinganalysis.neu.edu/; www
   .dallasnews.com/sharedcontent/dws/news/
   localnews/stories/DN-profiling_21met.ART
   .State. Edition1.20897ec.html; www.aclu.org/
   racialjustice/racialprofiling/index.html.
5. Cole and Marcello, op. cit., 24 (fn). It is interesting
   to note that "in the early 1970s it primarily was
   white U.S. citizens who controlled cocaine smug-
   gling" into the United States, but in the 1980s
   Nigerian heroin smugglers "carried the drugs
   themselves, and then they started recruiting
   young white females" (ibid.).
6. Randall Kennedy, "Suspect Policy," *New Republic*
   (Sept. 13 and 20, 1999): 35.
7. Heather MacDonald, "The Myth of Racial
   Profiling," *City Journal, 11,* no. 2 (Spring 2001).
   Found at www.city-journal.org/html/11_2_the-
   myth.html.
8. Associated Press; *CBS World News,* July 17, 2005.
9. "More Hate Crimes, Attacks on Mosques,"
   International Indian Express Web, online, July 12,
   2005.
10. Jodi Unruh, "Hate Crimes," KVAL-13 News, July 14,
    2005 (online at www.kval.com).
11. Lucy Yang, "Hate Crimes Against Gays Up,"
    WABC News, New York, June 19, 2005.
12. Naush Boghossian and Lisa M. Sodders, "School
    Hate Crimes Spike," June 2005 (online at www
    .dailynews.com); L.A. County Commission on
    Human Relations, "2006 Hate Crime Report" (http://
    lahumanrelations.org/hatecrime/hatecrimereport
    .htm); and the California Attorney General's Report
    2006 (http://lahumanrelations.org/hatecrime/
    hatecrimereport.htm).
13. Cathy Lisa Schneider, "Racism, Drug Policy, and
    AIDS," *Political Science Quarterly, 113,* no. 3 (Fall
    1998): 427.
14. Alberto F. Cabrera, "Campus Racial Climate and
    the Adjustment of Students to College," *Journal
    of Higher Education, 70* (March–April 1999):
    134.
15. *San Francisco Chronicle,* April 17, 2004, p. A5.
16. *The New York Times,* April 22, 2004, p. A22.
17. "Media Portrays Most Poor People as Black," *Jet,
    92* (Sept. 8, 1997): 25.
18. www.infoplease.com/ipa/A0763170.html.
19. "Bar Association Chief Assails Racial Disparity,"
    The New York Times, Aug. 11, 1999, p. A17. Also see
    http://www.abanet.org/minorities/publications/
    milesummary.html
20. Legal Information Institute, "US Code Collection"
    (found at www4.law.cornell.edu/uscode/42/
    12101.html).
21. See www4.law.cornell.edu/uscode/29/621.html.
22. James Brooke, "Denver Breaks New Ground on
    Gay Rights," *The New York Times,* Sept. 18, 1996.
23. "Women in Engineering: A Review of the 2004
    Literature." Available from the Society of Women
    Engineers (www.swe.org).
24. Louis Uchitelle, "Gaining Ground on the Wage
    Front," *The New York Times,* Dec. 31, 2004,
    pp. C1–C2.
25. Ibid.
26. Anne Fisher, "After All This Time, Why Don't
    People Know What Sexual Harassment Means?"
    Fortune, 137, no. 1 (Jan. 12, 1998): 156. Also see
    www.eeoc.gov/stats/harass.html and www
    .eeoc.gov/stats/harass-a.html.
27. "Harassed or Hazed; Why the Supreme Court Rules
    that Men Can Sue Men for Sexual Harassment,"
    Time, 151, no. 10 (March 16, 1998): 55.
28. Hans Kudnani, "Europe's Colour-Blind Prejudice,"
    New Statesman, 127, no. 4390 (June 19, 1998): 18.
29. William Keng Mun Lee, "Gender Inequality and
    Discrimination in Singapore," *Journal of Contem-
    porary Asia, 28* (Oct. 1998): 484.
30. Barbara Crosette, "UNICEF Opens a Global Drive
    on Violence Against Women," *The New York Times,*
    March 9, 2000, p. A6.
31. Ibid.
32. Nikki Katz, "Honor Killings—What You Need to
    Know About Honor Killings," Nov. 4, 2003
    (online at www.womensissues.about.com/cs/
    honorkillings/a/honorkillings.htm).
33. "The Feminization of AIDS," *The New York Times,*
    Dec. 13, 2004, p. A28; www.iwhc.org/resources/
    soroptimist041504.cfm.
34. Erica Goode, "When Women Find Love Is Fatal,"
    The New York Times, Feb. 15, 2000, pp. D1, D6.
    Also see www.endabuse.org/resources/facts.
35. Hanna Rosin and Steven Mufson, "Feminists Join
    Forces with Right Wing: 'Prostitution' Definition
    Rejected," *San Francisco Examiner,* Jan. 16, 2000,
    p. A8.

36. Linda Greenhouse, "University of Michigan Ruling Endorses the Value of Campus Diversity," *The New York Times,* June 24, 2003, pp. A1, A25.

37. This aspect of the bill confirmed the "disparate impact" notion of the 1971 U.S. Supreme Court ruling in *Griggs* v. *Duke Power Company,* which required companies to revise their business practices that perpetuated past discrimination. This was weakened by the Court's 1989 ruling in *Wards Cove Packing Co.* v. *Antonio,* which, among other things, put the burden of proof on the employee to show that the company did not have a good reason for some discriminatory business practice.

38. We also could cite legislation aimed against discrimination on the basis of age and the disabled: for example, the Age Discrimination Act (1967) and the Americans with Disabilities Act (1991).

39. R. C. Lewontin, "Race: Temporary Views on Human Variation," *Encyclopedia Americana* (online at http://ea.grolier.com). Also see R. C. Lewontin, *Human Diversity* (New York: W. H. Freeman, 1982).

40. Ibid.

41. Carolyn Abraham, "Race," *The Globe and Mail,* June 18, 2005, pp. F1, F8.

42. See www.hapmap.org.

43. Bernard Lewis, "The Historical Roots of Racism," *The American Scholar, 67,* no. 1 (Winter 1998): 17A.

44. See Mary Ann Warren, "Secondary Sexism and Quota Hiring," *Philosophy and Public Affairs, 6,* no. 3 (Spring 1977): 240–261.

45. Gina Kolata, "Men and Women Use Brain Differently, Study Discovers," *The New York Times,* Feb. 16, 1995, p. A8.

46. In this regard, the 1993 federal Family and Medical Leave Act allows both men and women to take unpaid leave to take care of a sick child or other close relative without losing their jobs or medical insurance.

47. M. T. Hallinan and A. B. Sorensen, *Sociological Education, 60,* no. 63 (1987), as reported in *Science, 237* (July 24, 1987): 350.

48. *The New York Times,* Feb. 16, 1995, pp. A1, A8.

49. Iris Marion Young, "Polity and Group Difference: A Critique of the Ideal of Universal Citizenship," in *Feminism and Political Theory,* Sunstein Cass (Ed.) (Chicago: University of Chicago Press, 1990).

Cited in an unpublished manuscript by Jennifer MacKinnon, "Rights and Responsibilities: A Reevaluation of Parental Leave and Child Care in the United States," Spring 1993.

50. Alaka Wali, "Multiculturalism: An Anthropological Perspective," *Report from the Institute for Philosophy and Public Policy,* Spring/Summer 1992, 6–8.

51. Susan Moller Okin, *Is Multiculturalism Bad for Women?* Joshua Cohen, Matthew Howard, and Martha C. Nussbaum (Eds.) (Princeton, NJ: Princeton University Press, 2000).

52. "Should the Lack of Males in College Be a Cause for Concern?" *On Campus,* Dec. 2000–Jan. 2001, p. 4.

53. Ibid.

54. Robert K. Fullinwider, "Affirmative Action and Fairness," *Report from the Institute for Philosophy and Public Policy, 11,* no. 1 (Winter 1991): 10–13.

55. Ibid.

56. See James Fishkin, *Justice, Equal Opportunity and the Family* (New Haven, CT: Yale University Press, 1983), for documentation and analysis.

57. William G. Bowen and Derek Curtis Bok, *The Shape of the River: Long-Term Consequences of Considering Race in College and University Admissions* (Princeton, NJ: Princeton University Press, 1998).

58. David R. Corgen, "A Study in Black and White: Why Race-Sensitive College Admissions Policies Work," *U.S. News & World Report, 125,* no. 14 (Oct. 12, 1998): 84.

59. William H. Gray III, "In the Best Interest of America, Affirmative Action in Higher Education Is a Must," *The Black Collegian, 29,* no. 2 (Feb. 1999): 144.

60. www.npr.org/news/specials/michigan/; www.wsws.org/articles/2003/jun2003/affi-j25.shtml.

61. Stephen Carter, *Reflections of an Affirmative Action Baby* (New York: Basic Books, 1991).

62. Professor Jonathan Leonard, cited in the *San Francisco Examiner,* Sept. 29, 1991.

63. *Time* (May 27, 1991): 23.

64. Amy Argetsinger, "Princeton's Former President Challenges 'Bastions of Privilege'" *San Francisco Chronicle,* April 17, 2004, p. A5.

65. A parent's report.

REVIEW EXERCISES

1. In the history of affirmative action and civil rights legislation:
   a. When were the terms *preferential treatment* and *affirmative action* first used?
   b. What is the difference between the Equal Pay Act and Title VII of the 1964 Civil Rights Act?
   c. Has the U.S. Supreme Court ever forbidden the use of racial quotas? Approved them?
2. What is meant by *racism? sexism?* Are there any other similar "ism"s?
3. Explain the five different elements of the principle of equality as it was given here.

4. What is the difference between individual, group, and average differences? How are these an issue in the application of the principle of equality?
5. What is "affirmative action," and why does it have this name? Give five different types of affirmative action. Which of them involve or may involve giving preferential treatment?
6. Summarize the consequentialist arguments for and against affirmative action.
7. Summarize the nonconsequentialist arguments for and against affirmative action.

DISCUSSION CASES

1. Preferences in Hiring. XYZ University has an opening in its philosophy department. Currently, the full-time faculty in this department is all-male. The department has received 200 applications for this position. It has been advised by the dean that because half the student body is female, the department should seek a woman to fill this position. The school is also under affirmative action guidelines because it receives federal funding for some of its programs. The faculty members have agreed to consider seriously the several applications from females that they have received. The qualifications for the position, the field of specialization, have been advertised. But there are several other ways in which the position is open. The list has been narrowed to the ten top candidates, two of whom are women. All ten are well qualified in their own ways. The department is split on what to do. Some members believe that because all ten are well qualified, they should choose one of the two women. The other members believe that the most qualified of the final group do not include the two women.

What do you think the department should do? Why?

2. Campus Diversity. During the last couple of decades, colleges and universities have tried to increase their numbers of minority students by various forms of affirmative action. At Campus X, this has led to no small amount of dissension. Some students complain that the policy of accepting students with lower SAT and other scores just because of their race or minority status is unfair. Others believe that the diversity that results from such policies is good for everyone because we should learn to live together and a university campus should be a place to do this. Still, there is some question even among members of this group as to how well the integration is working. Furthermore, a different type of problem has recently surfaced. Because Asian Americans were represented in numbers greater than their percentage of the population, some universities were restricting the percentage they would accept even when their scores were higher than others they did accept. Also, in some cases where affirmative action has been eliminated, the number of minority members accepted into certain medical and law schools has plummeted, and many people find this alarming.

Do you think that diversity ought to be a goal of campus admissions? Or do you believe that only academic qualifications ought to count? Why?

3. Racial Profiling. The U.S. Border Patrol has been accused of using racial profiling in its decisions about whom to select for questioning in border regions. People who "look Mexican" have been stopped and questioned under suspicion of being illegal immigrants. Border Patrol agents say that this is justified because a high percentage of Latinos in border areas are in the United States illegally. Latinos who are U.S. citizens say that they are repeatedly stopped just because of their race and appearance, and they resent this. Do you believe that using race in such decisions is a justifiable law-enforcement tactic or is it unjust discrimination? Is the use of race as one element in deciding whom to stop or question ever justified? What if there are sociological data to show that a high percentage of people of some racial or ethnic group account for an unusually high percentage of those who are responsible for a certain type of crime? How do we weigh the costs of such profiling to social harmony and to those individuals wrongly accused?

YOU MAKE THE DECISION

Apply the theories and issues discussed in this chapter by accessing this animated simulation on the Ethics Resource Center.

Use the passkey that accompanies your book to gain access. If you do not have a passkey, visit cengage brain.com to purchase instant access to additional study material.

Gender   Race

You and a few others in your school's health sciences department are asked by the hiring committee to give your opinion on the final two candidates for a position in the nursing faculty.

Ethics Module 12 : Equality and Discrimination   ◀◀ ▶ ▶▶   UNMUTE ◀

© Cengage Learning

Selected Bibliography

Appiah, Anthony K., and Amy Gutmann (Eds.). *Color Conscious: The Political Morality of Race.* Princeton, NJ: Princeton University Press, 1996.

Arthur, John. *Race, Equality, and the Burdens of History.* New York: Cambridge University Press, 2007.

Arthur, John, and Amy Shapiro (Eds.). *Color Class Identity: The New Politics of Race.* New York: Westview Press, 1996.

Baez, Benjamin. *Affirmative Action, Hate Speech, and Tenure: Narratives about Race, Law, and the Academy.* New York: Routledge, 2001.

Beckwith, Francis J., and Todd E. Jones. *Affirmative Action: Social Justice or Reverse Discrimination.* New York: Prometheus Books, 1997.

Bell, Linda A., and David Blumenfeld (Eds.). *Overcoming Racism and Sexism.* Lanham, MD: Rowman & Littlefield, 1995.

Bergmann, Barbara R. *In Defense of Affirmative Action.* New York: Basic Books, 1996.

Bittker, Boris. *The Case for Black Reparations.* New York: Random House, 1973.

Bowen, William G., and Derek Curtis Bok. *The Shape of the River: Long-Term Consequences of Considering Race in College and University Admissions.* Princeton, NJ: Princeton University Press, 1998.

Bravo, Ellen, and Ellen Casedy. *The 9 to 5 Guide to Combating Sexual Harassment.* New York: Wiley, 1992.

Bulmer, Martin, et al. *Researching Race and Racism.* New York: Routledge, 2004.

Butler, Judith. *Undoing Gender.* New York: Routledge, 2004.

Cahn, Steven M. *Affirmative Action and the University: A Philosophical Inquiry.* Philadelphia: Temple University Press, 1995.

————. *The Affirmative Action Debates.* New York: Routledge, 2002.

————. **(Ed.).** *Affirmative Action Debate.* New York: Routledge, 2002.

Cohen, Marshall, Thomas Nagel, and Thomas Scanlon (Eds.). *Equality and Preferential Treatment.* Princeton, NJ: Princeton University Press, 1976.

Curry, George E., and Cornel West (Eds.). *The Affirmative Action Debate.* Reading, MA: Addison, 1996.

Delgado, Richard. *Critical Race Theory: The Cutting Edge.* Philadelphia: Temple University Press, 1995.

Faludi, Susan. *Backlash: The Undeclared War Against American Women.* New York: Crown, 1991.

Ferguson, Ann. *Sexual Democracy: Women, Oppression, and Revolution.* Boulder, CO: Westview, 1991.

Fishkin, James. *Justice, Equal Opportunity and the Family.* New Haven, CT: Yale University Press, 1983.

Francis, Leslie Pickering. *Sexual Harassment in Academe.* Lanham, MD: Rowman & Littlefield, 1996.

Friedman, Marilyn, and Jan Narveson. *Political Correctness: For and Against.* Lanham, MD: Rowman & Littlefield, 1994.

Fullinwider, Robert. *The Reverse Discrimination Controversy.* Totowa, NJ: Rowman & Littlefield, 1980.

Garry, Ann, and Marilyn Pearsall (Eds.). *Women, Knowledge, and Reality: Explorations in Feminist Philosophy.* Boston: Unwin Hyman, 1989.

Gerstmann, Evan. *The Constitutional Underclass: Gays, Lesbians, and the Failure of Class-Based Equal Protection.* Chicago: University of Chicago Press, 1999.

Goldberg, Steven. *The Inevitability of Patriarchy.* New York: William Morrow, 1973.

Goldman, Alan. *Justice and Reverse Discrimination.* Princeton, NJ: Princeton University Press, 1979.

Haney-Lopez, Ian. *Racism on Trial: The Chicano Fight for Justice.* Cambridge, MA: Harvard University Press, 2004.

Harding, Sandra (Ed.). *The "Racial" Economy of Science.* Bloomington: Indiana University Press, 1993.

hooks, bell. *Ain't I a Woman? Black Women and Feminism.* Boston: South End, 1981.

Jaggar, Alison. *Feminist Politics and Human Nature.* Sussex, NJ: Rowman & Littlefield, 1983.

Jolovich, S. *Gender of Justice.* Hampshire, UK: Taylor & Francis Group, 2008.

King, Richard C. *Sport and Race.* Oxford, UK: Berg Publishers, 2008.

Koppleman, Andrew. *Antidiscrimination Law and Social Equality.* New Haven, CT: Yale University Press, 1998.

Kymlicka, Will. *Multicultural Citizenship: A Liberal Theory of Minority Rights.* New York: Oxford University Press, 1995.

Levine, Michael P. *Racism in Mind.* Ithaca, NY: Cornell University Press, 2004.

Maccoby, E., and C. Jacklin. *The Psychology of Sex Differences.* Palo Alto, CA: Stanford University Press, 1974.

Macklem, Timothy. *Beyond Comparison: Sex and Discrimination.* New York: Cambridge University Press, 2003.

Miller, Diane Helene. *Freedom to Differ: The Shaping of the Gay and Lesbian Struggle for Civil Rights.* New York: New York University Press, 1998.

Mills, Charles W. *Blackness Visible: Essays on Philosophy and Race.* Ithaca, NY: Cornell University Press, 1998.

Mohanram, Radhika. *Black Body: Women, Colonialism, and Space.* St. Paul: University of Minnesota Press, 1999.

Mooney Cotter, Anne-Marie. *Just a Number: An International Legal Perspective on Age Discrimination.* Aldershot, NH: Ashgate Publishing, 2008.

Mosley, Albert G., and Nicholas Capaldi. *Affirmative Action: Social Justice or Unfair Preference?* Lanham, MD: Rowman & Littlefield, 1996.

Mostern, Kenneth. *Autobiography and Black Identity Politics: Racialization in Twentieth-Century America.* New York: Cambridge University Press, 1999.

Murray, Charles. *Losing Ground.* New York: Basic Books, 1984.

Nava, Michael, and Robert Dawidoff. *Created Equal: Why Gay Rights Matter to America.* New York: St. Martin's Press, 1995.

Plunkett, Jeff. *Is Racism a Serious Problem?* Farmington Hills, MI: Gale Group, 2005.

Rae, Douglas. *Equalities.* Cambridge, MA: Harvard University Press, 1981.

Rakowski, Eric. *Equal Justice.* New York: Oxford University Press, 1991.

Remick, H. *Comparable Worth and Wage Discrimination.* Philadelphia: Temple University Press, 1985.

Rosenfield, Michael. *Affirmative Action and Justice: A Philosophical and Constitutional Inquiry.* New Haven, CT: Yale University Press, 1993.

Rubio, Philip. *A History of Affirmative Action, 1619–2000.* Jackson: University Press of Mississippi, 2001.

Shiell, Timothy C. *Campus Hate Speech on Trial.* Lawrence: University Press of Kansas, 1998.

Sowell, Thomas. *The Economics and Politics of Race: An International Perspective.* New York: William Morrow, 1983.

Squires, Judith. *Politics of Gender Equality.* NY: Palgrave Macmillan, 2007.

Sterba, James P. *Justice: Alternative Political Perspectives,* 2d ed. Belmont, CA: Wadsworth, 1992.

Taylor, Charles. *Multiculturalism: Examining the Politics of Recognition.* Princeton, NJ: Princeton University Press, 1994.

Texler Segal, Marcia, et al. *Gender, Race, and Class: Central Issues in a Changing Landscape.* Oxfordshire, UK: Scion Publishing, 2001.

Thernstrom, Stephan, and Abigail Thernstrom. *America in Black and White: One Nation, Indivisible.* New York: Simon & Schuster, 1999.

Thomson, Faye, Faye J. Crosby, Sharon D. Herzberger, and Rita J. Simon (Eds.). *Affirmative Action: The Pros and Cons of Policy and Practice.* Lanham, MD: Rowman & Littlefield, 2001.

Veatch, Robert M. *The Foundations of Justice: Why the Retarded and the Rest of Us Have Claims to Equality.* New York: Oxford University Press, 1986.

Williams, Kadifa. *"Race," Racism and Criminal Justice: Virtual Criminality and Marginalized Groups.* Aldershot, NH: Ashgate Publishing, 2008.

Williams, Mary E. *Racism.* Farmington Hills, MI: Gale Group, 2004.

Wolfson, Nicholas. *Hate Speech, Sex Speech, Free Speech.* New York: Praeger, 1997.

Young, Iris Marion. *Justice and the Politics of Difference.* Princeton, NJ: Princeton University Press, 1990.

Zack, Naomi. *Thinking About Race.* Belmont, CA: Wadsworth, 1998.

13

Economic Justice

Perhaps you have heard something like the following dialogue. It might be carried on between a student majoring in business and another majoring in philosophy. Here we will call them Betty Business Major and Phil Philosophy Major.

Betty: I think that people have a right to make and keep as much money as they can as long as they do not infringe on others' rights. Thus, we should not be taxing the rich to give to the poor.

Phil: Is it fair that some people are born with a silver spoon in their mouths and others are not? The poor often have not had a chance to get ahead. Society owes them that much. They are people just like everyone else.

Betty: But how could we guarantee that they will not waste what we give them? In any case, it is just not right to take the money of those who have worked hard for it and redistribute it. They deserve to keep it.

Phil: Why do they deserve to keep what they have earned? If they are in the position that they are in because of the good education and good example provided by their parents, how do they themselves deserve what they can get with that?

Betty: In any case, if we take what such people have earned, whether they deserve it or not, they will have no incentive to work. Profits are what make the economy of a nation grow.

Phil: And why is that so? Does this imply that the only reason people work is for their own self-interest? That sounds like good old capitalism to me, as your idol Adam Smith would have it. But is a capitalistic system a just economic system?

Betty: Justice does not seem to me to require that everyone have equal amounts of wealth. If justice is fairness, as some of your philosophers say, it is only fair and therefore just that people get out of the system what they put into it. And, besides, there are other values. We value freedom, too, don't we? People ought to be free to work and keep what they earn.

At least we can agree on one thing, that something ought to be done about the latest corporate scandals. There is too much corporate greed and corruption. If there is not sufficient transparency in corporate business practices, then investors will not be able to make wise decisions and inefficiency will taint and harm the system.

Phil: It is also unfair for corporate executives to greedily take more than their honest share of a company's profits. It is the little guy and gal who are saving for their kids' college education or retirement that get hurt the most from such schemes.

The issues touched on in this conversation belong to a group of issues that fall under the topic of what has been called *economic justice*. There are others as well. For example, do people have a right to a job and good wages? Is welfare aid to the poor a matter of charity or justice? Is an economic system that requires a pool of unemployed workers a just system? Is it fair to tax the rich more heavily than the middle class?

INCOME INEQUALITY

In 2007, Alan Greenspan, the former chair of the board of governors of the Federal Reserve, noted: "Income inequality is where the capitalist system is most vulnerable. You can't have the capitalist system if an increasing number of people think it is unjust."[1]

The gap between the rich and poor in the United States, for example, has been widening for some time. In recent years, the gap has been the widest since our government began to keep records on it in 1947. In 2005, "the top one percent of households received 21.8 percent of all pre-tax income." This counted capital gains as well as income. Moreover, "between 1979 and 2005, the top five percent of American families saw their real incomes increase 81 percent" while "over the same period, the lowest-income fifth saw their real incomes decline 1 percent." In 2005, "All of the income gains in 2005 went to the top 10 percent of households, while the bottom 90 percent of households saw income declines." And in another startling matter, "the richest one percent of U.S. households now owns 34.3 percent of the nation's private wealth, more than the combined wealth of the bottom 90 percent."[2]

The income of all women compared to men has improved over the years, but in 2004 it was still only 77 percent of what men earned. Furthermore, the wage gap "cuts across a wide spectrum of occupations. The Bureau of Labor Statistics reported that in 2005 female physicians and surgeons earned 60.9% of the median weekly wages of male physicians, and women in sales occupations earned just 63.4% of men's wages in equivalent positions."[3] This income gap is partly because more women leave work to care for children and elderly parents, and they are more likely to work part-time. However, when they work at jobs with similar skills, women who have never had children earn close to 98 percent of what men do.[4]

Race is also a factor in income. In 2004, for example, black men earned only 74.5 percent and Hispanic men only 63.2 percent of what white men earned.

The income gap narrows somewhat when taxes and welfare income are factored in. The gap partly results from an influx of immigrants who have, on average, lower levels of education than native-born Americans.[5] More recently, with the slowing of the economy and fewer jobs, the gap between rich and poor will probably continue or widen.

Most people find such inequality unsettling. This is particularly true when they compare the huge salaries and bonuses of top corporate executives to the incomes of ordinary workers. In 1894, the income of industrialist John D. Rockefeller was $1.25 million. This was some 7,000 times the average national income. In 2004, "the average CEO of a major company received $9.84 million in total compensation. This was an increase of 12 percent over the previous year. Compare this with the average pay of nonsupervisory workers of $27,485, an increase of 2.2 percent over the previous year."[6] And in 2006, James Simon, a hedge-fund manager, made $1.7 billion. This was more than 38,000 times the average national income for that year.[7] In 1980, corporate executives of large companies earned forty-five times more than nonsupervisory workers, but by 2000 the pay of the executives was 458 times that of ordinary workers.[8] Such great differences seem neither fair nor just.

Health Care

In one important area, income inequities are matched by inequities in health care. One's savings can be wiped out with a major health problem when a family has no health insurance. Those facing the greatest risk are workers not covered by their employers (59.5 percent receive their health insurance coverage through an employer) and not over age sixty-five (and thus eligible for the federal Medicare program, which covers hospital costs through part A and doctor's expenses through part B, which charges a premium based on one's income). In 2005, 46.6 million people in the United States (15.9 percent of the population) were without health care insurance for at least part of that year. Certain of the very poorest citizens are eligible for Medicaid, a program run partly by the states.[9]

Although genes and lifestyle certainly play their roles in a person's health, poverty does so as well. Strangely perhaps, but poor people are more likely to be obese than those who are economically better off. If you have little to spend on food and want to get the most calories for your dollar, you will find these foods in the center section of your local supermarket. Notice that the healthy fruits and vegetables and the meat sections are located on the periphery. In the center of the store are processed foods that have little nutritional value, such as cookies, chips, and sodas. Orange juice and carrots may be better for you, but they cost more.[10]

Justice, Charity, and Efficiency

It is important to distinguish justice from certain other moral notions. For example, justice is not the same as charity. It is one thing to say that a community, like a family, will help its poorer members when they are in need out of concern for their welfare. But is helping people in need ever a matter of justice? If we say that it is, then we imply that it is not morally optional. We can think of *justice* here as the giving of what is rightly due, and *charity* as what is above and beyond the requirements of justice. Furthermore, justice is not the only relevant moral issue in economic matters. *Efficiency* and *liberty* are also moral values that play a role in discussions on ethics and economics. When we say that a particular economic system is efficient, we generally mean that it produces a maximum amount of desired goods and services, or the most value for the least cost. Thus, some people say that a free-market economy is a good economic system because it is the most efficient type of system, the one best able to create wealth. But it is quite another question to ask whether such a system is also a *just* system. Nevertheless, efficiency is important, and so too is freedom or liberty. If we could have the most just and perhaps even the most efficient economic system in the world, then would it be worth it if we were not also free to make our own decisions about many things, including how to earn a living and what to do with our money?

In this chapter, we will be discussing what is generally termed *distributive justice*. Distributive justice has to do with how goods are allocated among persons—for example, who and how many people have what percentage of the goods or wealth in a society. Thus, suppose that in some society 5 percent of the people possessed 90 percent of the wealth, and the other 95 percent of the people possessed the other 10 percent of the wealth. Asking whether this arrangement would be just is raising a question of distributive justice. Now how would we go about answering this question? It does seem that this particular distribution of wealth is quite unbalanced. But must a distribution be equal for it to be just? To answer this question, we can examine two quite different ways of approaching distributive justice. One is what we can call a *process view*, and the other is an *end state view*.

PROCESS DISTRIBUTIVE JUSTICE

According to some philosophers, any economic distribution (or any system that allows a particular economic distribution) is just if the process by which it comes about is itself just. Some call this *procedural justice*. For example, if the wealthiest 5 percent of the people got their 90 percent of the wealth fairly—they competed for jobs, they were honest, they did not take what was not theirs— then what they earned would be rightly theirs. In contrast, if the wealthy obtained their wealth through force or fraud, then their having such wealth would be unfair because they took it unfairly. But there would be nothing unfair or unjust about the uneven distribution in itself. We might suspect that because talent is more evenly distributed, there is something suspicious about this uneven distribution of wealth. We might suspect that coercion or unjust taking or unfair competition or dishonesty was involved. Now some people are wealthy because of good luck and fortune, and others are poor because of bad economic luck. However, in this view, those who keep money that through luck or good fortune falls to them from the sky, so to speak, are not being unjust in keeping it even when others are poor.

END STATE DISTRIBUTIVE JUSTICE

Other philosophers believe that the process by which people attain wealth is not the only consideration relevant to determining the justice of an economic distribution. They believe that we also should look at the way things turn out, the end state, or the resulting distribution of wealth in a society, and ask about its fairness. Suppose that the lucky people possessed the 95 percent of the wealth through inheritance, for example. Would it be fair for them to have so much wealth when others in the society were extremely poor? How would we usually judge whether such an arrangement was fair? We would look to see if there is some good reason why the wealthy are wealthy. Did they work hard for it? Did they make important social contributions? These might be nonarbitrary or good reasons for the wealthy to possess their wealth rightly or justly. However, if they are wealthy while others are poor because they, unlike the others, were born of a certain favored race or sex or eye color or height, then we might be inclined to say that it is not fair for them to have more. What reasons, then, justify differences in wealth?

Several different views exist on this issue. Radical egalitarians deny that there is any good reason why some people should possess greater wealth than others. Their reasons for this view vary. They might stress that human beings are essentially alike as human and that this is more important than any differentiating factors about them, including their talents and what they do with them. They might use religious or semireligious reasons such as that the Earth is given to all of us equally, and thus we all have an equal right to the goods derived from it. Even egalitarians, however, must decide what it is that they believe should be equal. Should there be equality of wealth and income or equality of satisfaction or welfare, for example? These are not the same. Some people have little wealth or income but nevertheless are quite satisfied, while others who have great wealth or income are quite dissatisfied. Some have champagne tastes, and others are satisfied with beer!

On the other hand, at least some basic differences between people should make a difference in what distribution of goods is thought to be just. For example, some people simply have different needs than others. People are not identical physically, and some of us need more food and different kinds of health care than others. Karl Marx's "To each according to his need" captures something of this variant of egalitarianism.[11] Nevertheless, why only this particular differentiating factor— need— should justify differences in wealth is puzzling. In fact, we generally would tend to pick out others as well—differences in merit, achievement, effort, or contribution.

Suppose, for example, that Jim uses his talent and education and produces a new electronic device that allows people to transfer their thoughts to a computer directly. This device would alleviate the need to type or write the thoughts—at least, initially. Surely, people would value this device, and Jim would probably make a great deal of money from his invention. Would not Jim have a right to or *merit* this money? Would it not be fair that he had this money and others who did not come up with such a device had less? It would seem so. But let us think about why we might say so. Is it because Jim had an innate or *native talent* that others did not have? Then through no fault of their own, those without the talent would have less. Jim would have had nothing to do with his having been born with this talent and thus becoming wealthy.

Perhaps it is because Jim not only had the talent but also used it. He put a great deal of *effort* into it. He studied electronics and brain anatomy for many years, and spent years working on the invention in his garage. His own effort, time, and study were his own contribution. Would this be a good reason to say that he deserved the wealth that he earned from it? This might seem reasonable, if we did not also know that his particular education and his motivation also might have been in some ways gifts of his circumstance and family upbringing. Furthermore, effort alone would not be a good reason for monetary reward, or else John, who took three weeks to make a pair of shoes, should be paid more than Jeff, who did them up in three hours. This would be similar to the student who asks for a higher grade because of all the effort and time he spent on study for the course, when the result was actually more consistent with the lower grade.

Finally, perhaps Jim should have the rewards of his invention because of the nature of his *contribution,* because of the product he made and its value to people. Again, this argument seems at first reasonable, and yet there are also fairness problems here. Suppose that he had produced this invention before there were computers. The invention would be wonderful but not valued by people because they could not use it. Or suppose that others at the same time produced similar inventions. Then this happenstance would also lessen the value of the product and its monetary reward. He could rightly say that it was unfair that he did not reap a great reward from his invention just because he happened to be born at the wrong time or finished his invention a little late. This may be just bad luck. But is it also unfair? Furthermore, it is often difficult to know how to value particular contributions to a jointly produced product or result. How do we measure and compare the value of the contributions of the person with the idea, the money, the risk takers, and so forth so that we can know what portion of the profits are rightly due them? Marxists are well known for their claim that the people who own the factories or have put up the money for a venture profit from the workers' labor unfairly or out of proportion to their own contribution.

It may not be possible to give a nonproblematic basis for judging when an unequal distribution of wealth in a society is fair by appealing to considerations of merit, achievement, effort, or contribution. However, perhaps some combination of process and end state views and some combination of factors as grounds for distribution can be found. At least this discussion will provide a basis for critically evaluating simple solutions.

EQUAL OPPORTUNITY

Another viewpoint on economic justice does not fit easily under the category of process or end state views. In this view, the key to whether an unequal distribution of wealth in a society is just is whether people have a fair chance to attain those positions of greater income or wealth—that is, equality of wealth is not required, only equal opportunity to

attain it. The notion of equal opportunity is symbolized by the Statue of Liberty in New York Harbor. It sits on Liberty Island, where historically new immigrants to the United States were processed. The statue symbolizes the idea of hope—namely, that in this country all people have a chance to make a good life for themselves provided they work hard. But just what is involved in the notion of equal opportunity, and is it a realizable goal or ideal? Literally, it involves both opportunities and some sort of equality of chances to attain them. An opportunity is a chance to attain some benefit or goods. People have equal chances to attain these goods first of all when there are no barriers to prevent them from attaining them. Opportunities can still be said to be equal if barriers exist as long as they affect everyone equally. Clearly, if racism or prejudice prevents some people from having the same chances as others to attain valued goals or positions in a society, then there is not equal opportunity for those who are its victims. For example, if women have twice the family responsibilities as men, then will they have effective equal opportunity to compete professionally?

According to James Fishkin, if there is equal opportunity in my society, "I should not be able to enter a hospital ward of healthy newborn babies and, on the basis of class, race, sex, or other arbitrary native characteristics, predict the eventual positions in society of those children."[12] However, knowing what we do about families and education and the real-life prospects of children, we know how difficult this ideal would be to realize. In reality, children do not start life with equal chances. Advantaged families give many educational, motivational, and experiential advantages to their children that children of disadvantaged families do not have, and this makes their opportunities effectively unequal. Schooling greatly affects equal opportunity, and money spent for a school—teachers, facilities, and books—can make a big difference in the kind of education provided. However, funding per pupil on schooling in this country varies considerably according to locale. Some states spend more per student on the average than others: For example, for the 2004 school year, New Jersey spent $12,981 per pupil and New York $12,930 per pupil, while Mississippi spent $6,237, Oklahoma $6,176, and Idaho $6,028.[13]

One version of equal opportunity is a starting-gate theory. It assumes that if people had equal starts, then they would have equal chances. Bernard Williams provides an example.[14] In his imaginary society, a class of skillful warriors has for generations held all of the highest positions and passed them on to their offspring. At some point, the warriors decide to let all people compete for membership in their class. The children of the warrior class are much stronger and better nourished than other children who, not surprisingly, fail to gain entrance to the warrior class. Would these children have had effective equality of opportunity to gain entrance to the warrior class and its benefits? Even if the competition was formally fair, the outside children were handicapped and had no real chance of winning. But how could initial starting points then be equalized? Perhaps by providing special aids or help to the other children to prepare them for the competition. Applying this example to our real-world situation would mean that a society should give special aid to the children of disadvantaged families if it wants to ensure equal opportunity. According to James Fishkin, however, to do this effectively would require serious infringements on family autonomy. For it would mean not only helping disadvantaged children but also preventing wealthier parents from giving special advantages to their children. Moreover, people have different natural talents and abilities, and those who have abilities that are more socially valued will likely have greater opportunities. Does this mean, then, that the idea of equal opportunity is unrealizable? It may mean that our efforts to increase equality of opportunity must be balanced with the pursuit of other values such as family autonomy and efficiency.

Still, some philosophers have other questions about the ideal of equal opportunity. Some point out that the whole emphasis on equality is misplaced and distracts us from what is really important. Rather than focus on the fact that some have more than others, according to Harry Frankfurt, it would be better to focus on whether people have enough. We care not that one billionaire makes a few million more than another, but it is important that people have what they need so they can do what they want to in life. All too often, this is not the case. Frankfurt calls his position the "doctrine of sufficiency."[15]

Although the doctrine of equal opportunity is appealing because it implies equal rewards for equal performance and doors open to all, still other people object to the notion of meritocracy on which it is based. According to John Schaar, it is based on notions of natural if not social aristocracy.[16] Those of us who do not have the natural talent of an Einstein, a Lance Armstrong, a Roger Federer, or a Tiger Woods, given that we value such talent, will not have the same chances to succeed and prosper as those of us without such talents. We can enter the race, but we delude ourselves if we think that we have a real chance to win it. Schaar believes that stress on equal opportunity thus contributes to the gap between rich and poor. He also argues that equal opportunity threatens the very notion of equality and democracy and human solidarity. It is based on the notion of a marketplace in which we, as atomic individuals, compete against our fellows. As such, it threatens human solidarity. It does so even more if it is accompanied by a tendency to think that those who win are in some way more valuable as persons.[17] There is also something essential to notions of justice that people should not be penalized for something for which they are not responsible. Thus, it would seem unjust or unfair for those who, through no fault of their own, cannot compete or cannot compete well in the market, to suffer—for example, the physically or mentally ill, or the physically or mentally handicapped.[18]

POLITICAL AND ECONOMIC THEORIES

Within discussions of economic justice, people often make use of certain terms and refer to certain theories. Key among them are *libertarianism, capitalism, socialism, modern liberalism,* and *communitarianism.* To more fully understand the central issues of economic justice, it would be helpful to take a closer look at these terms and theories. They do not divide along the same lines, but we can nevertheless discuss them together. In fact, some of the theories—capitalism and socialism, for example—can be differentiated from one another not only by basic definitions but also by the different emphases they place on the values of liberty, efficiency, and justice. They also are differentiated by how they favor or disfavor process or end state views of distributive justice. These values and these views of distributive justice will become clearer if we examine these theories briefly.

Libertarianism

Libertarianism is a political theory about both the importance of liberty in human life and the role of government. (See the discussion of negative rights below in the comparison between libertarianism and socialism.) Although a political party goes under this name and draws on the theory of libertarianism, we will examine the theory itself. Libertarians believe that we are free when we are not constrained or restrained by other people. Sometimes, this type of liberty is referred to as a basic right to noninterference. Thus, if you stand in the doorway and block my exit, you are violating my liberty to go where I wish. However, if I fall and break my leg and am unable to exit the door, then my liberty rights are violated by no one. The doorway is open and unblocked, and I am free to go out. I cannot go out simply because of my injury.

According to libertarianism, government has but a minimal function: an administrative function. It should provide an orderly place where people can go about their business. It does have an obligation to ensure that people's liberty rights are not violated, that people do not block freeways (if not doorways), and so forth. However, it has no obligation to see that my broken leg is repaired so that I can walk where I please. In particular, it has no business taking money from you to pay for my leg repair or any other good that I might like to have or even need. This may be a matter of charity or something that charities should address, but it is not a matter of social justice or obligation.

Libertarians would be more likely to support a process view of distributive justice than an end state view. Any economic arrangement would be just so long as it resulted from a fair process of competition, and so long as people did not take what is not theirs or get their wealth by fraudulent or coercive means. Libertarians do not believe, however, that governments should be concerned with end state considerations. They should not try to even out any imbalance between rich and poor that might result from a fair process. They should not be involved in any redistribution of wealth. Libertarianism is a theory about the importance of liberty, of rights to noninterference by others, and of the proper role of government. Libertarians also have generally supported capitalist free-market economies, so brief comments about this type of economic system and its supporting values are appropriate here.

For example Robert Nozick argues that people ought to be free to exchange or transfer to others what they have not acquired unjustly, so long as they do so in ways that are not wrong. In this he also differs from the end state views described here that he refers to as "patterned" or "current time-slice principles of justice." Following other libertarians, he thinks of taxation of earnings to achieve even good ends as "on a par with forced labor." You can reflect further on these views as you study this selection.

Capitalism

Capitalism is an economic system in which individuals or business corporations (not the government, or community, or state) own and control much or most of the country's capital. Capital is the wealth or raw materials, factories, and so forth that are used to produce more wealth. Capitalism is also usually associated with a free-enterprise system, an economic system that allows people freedom to set prices and determine production, and to make their own choices about how to earn and spend their incomes. Sometimes, this is also referred to as a *market economy* in which people are motivated by profit and engage in competition, and in which value is a function of supply and demand.

Certain philosophical values and beliefs also undergird this system. Among these can be a libertarian philosophy that stresses the importance of liberty and limited government. Certain beliefs about the nature of human motivation also are implicit—for example, that people are motivated by self-interest. Some people argue that capitalism and a free-market economy constitute the best economic system because it is the most efficient one, producing greater wealth for more people than any other system. People produce more and better, they say, when something is in it for them or their families, or when what they are working for is their own. Moreover, we will usually make only what people want, and we know what people want by what they are willing to buy. So people make their mousetraps and their mind-reading computers, and we reward them for giving us what we want by buying their products. Exemplifying this outlook is the view of economist Milton Friedman that the purpose of a business is to maximize profits, "to use its resources and engage in activities designed to increase its profits. . . ."[19] It is a further point, however, to assert that people have a right in justice to the fruits of their labors. Although libertarian and other supporters of capitalism will stress process views of justice, when end state criteria for distributive justice are given, they most often are *meritocratic criteria*—people are judged to deserve what they merit or earn.

Socialism

Socialism is an economic system, a political movement, and a social theory. It holds that government should own and control most of a nation's resources. According to this theory, there should be public ownership of land, factories, and other means of production. Socialists criticize capitalism because of its necessary unemployment and poverty, unpredictable business cycles, and inevitable conflicts between workers and owners of the means of production. Rather than allow the few to profit often at the expense of the many, socialism holds that government should engage in planning and adjust production to the needs of all of the people. Justice is stressed over efficiency, but central planning is thought to contribute to efficiency as well as justice. Socialism generally is concerned with end state justice and is egalitarian in orientation, allowing only for obvious differences among people in terms of their different needs. It holds that it is not only external constraints that limit people's liberty. True liberty or freedom also requires freedom from other internal constraints. Among those constraints are the lack of

the satisfaction of basic needs, poor education, and poor health care. These needs must be addressed by government. As with all labels, they simplify. Thus, there are also different kinds or levels of socialism. Some are highly centralized and rely on a command economy. At the other end are versions that stress the need for government to cushion the economy in times of slump, for example, by manipulating interest rates and monetary policy.

One key distinction between a libertarian and a socialist conception of justice is that the former recognizes only *negative rights* and the latter stresses *positive rights*.[20] Negative rights are rights not to be harmed in some way. Because libertarians take liberty as a primary value, they stress the negative right of people not to have their liberty restricted by others. These are rights of noninterference. In the economic area, they support economic liberties that create wealth, and they believe that people should be able to dispose of their wealth as they choose. For the libertarian, government's role is to protect negative rights, not positive rights. Contrary to this view, socialists believe that government should not only protect people's negative rights not to be interfered with but also attend to their positive rights to be given basic necessities. Consequently, a right to life must not only involve a right not to be killed but also a right to what is necessary to live— namely, food, clothing, and shelter. Positive rights to be helped or benefited are sometimes called "welfare rights." Those who favor such a concept of rights may ask what a right to life would amount to if one did not have the means to live. Positive economic rights would be rights to basic economic subsistence. Those who favor positive rights would allow for a variety of ways to provide for this from outright grants to incentives of various sorts.

None of these three systems is problem-free. Socialism, at least in recent times, often has not lived up to the ideals of its supporters. Central planning systems have failed as societies become more complex and participate in international economic systems. Socialist societies have tended in some cases to become authoritarian, because it is difficult to get voluntary consent to centrally decided plans for production and other policies.

Basic necessities may be provided for all, but their quality has often turned out to be low.

Capitalism and a free-market economy also are open to moral criticism. Many people, through no fault of their own, cannot or do not compete well and fall through the cracks. Unemployment is a natural part of the system, but it is also debilitating. Of what use is the liberty to vote or travel if one cannot take advantage of this freedom? Where, some people ask, is the concern for the basic equality of persons or the common good?

Libertarianism has been criticized for failing to notice that society provides the means by which individuals seek their own good—for example, by means of transportation and communication. It fails to notice that state action is needed to protect liberty rights and rights to security, property, and litigation. It must at least admit social welfare in terms of publicly funded compulsory primary education.[21] It also may be criticized for ignoring the effects of individuals' initial life circumstance on their equal chances to compete fairly for society's goods.

Let us consider whether a mixed form of political and economic system might be better. We shall call it "modern liberalism," even though the term *liberalism* has meant many things to many people. One reason for using this name is that it is the one given to the views of one philosopher who exemplified it and whose philosophy we shall also treat here: John Rawls.

Modern Liberalism

Modern liberalism follows in the footsteps of the classical liberalism of John Stuart Mill, John Locke, and Adam Smith with their stress on liberty rights. However, it also stresses the primacy of justice. Suppose we were to attempt to combine the positive elements of libertarianism, capitalism, and socialism. What would we pull from each? Liberty, or the ability to be free from unjust constraint by others, the primary value stressed by libertarianism, would be one value to preserve. However, we may want to support a fuller notion of liberty that also recognizes the power of internal constraints. We also might want to recognize both positive and negative rights and hold that government ought to play some role in supporting the former as well as

the latter. Stress on this combination of elements characterizes modern liberalism.

In writing the American Declaration of Independence, Thomas Jefferson had prepared initial drafts. In one of these, when writing about the purpose of government and the inalienable rights to life, liberty, and happiness, he wrote, "in order to *secure these ends* governments are instituted among men." In the final draft, the phrase is "in order to secure these rights governments are instituted among men."[22] In some ways, these two versions of the purpose of government, according to Jefferson, parallel the two versions of determining when a distribution of wealth is just—the end state view and a stress on positive rights ("to secure these ends"), and the process view and a focus on negative rights of noninterference ("to secure these rights"). Whichever we believe to be more important will determine what view we have of the role of government in securing economic justice.

We would want our economic system to be efficient as well as just. Thus, our system would probably allow capitalist incentives and inequalities of wealth. However, if we value positive rights, then we also would be concerned about the least advantaged members of the society. Companies and corporations would be regarded as guests in society, because they benefit from the society as well as contribute to it. They could be thought to owe something in return to the community—as a matter of justice and not just as something in their own best interest. It is also true that the economic productivity and efficiency of a society depend on human development and communication and transportation systems. Public investment in education, health, roads, technology, and research and development pay off for companies in the long run.[23]

John Rawls's Theory of Justice

Among the most discussed works on justice of the last two decades is John Rawls's 1971 book, *A Theory of Justice.*[24] In summarizing the basic ideas in this book, we can review elements of the theories discussed earlier.

According to Rawls, justice is the first virtue of social institutions as truth is of scientific systems. It is most important for scientific systems to be true or well supported. They may be elegant or interesting or in line with our other beliefs, but that is not the primary requirement for their acceptance. Something similar would be the case for social and economic institutions. We would want them to be efficient, but it would be even more important that they be just. But what is justice, and how do we know whether an economic system is just? Rawls sought to develop a set of principles or guidelines that we could apply to our institutions, enabling us to judge whether they are just or unjust. But how could we derive, or where could we find, valid principles of justice?

Rawls used an imaginary device called the *original position.* He said that if we could imagine people in some initial fair situation and determine what they would accept as principles of justice, then these principles would be valid ones. In other words, we would first have our imaginary people so situated or described that they could choose fairly. We then would ask what they would be likely to accept. To make their choice situation fair, we would have to eliminate all bias from their choosing. Suppose that we were those people in the imaginary original position. If I knew that I was a college professor and was setting up principles to govern my society, then I would be likely to set them up so that college professors would do very well. If I knew that I had a particular talent for music or sports, for example, I might be likely to bias the principles in favor of people with these talents, and so on. To eliminate such bias, then, the people in the original position must not be able to know biasing things about themselves. They must not know their age, sex, race, talents, and so on. They must, as he says, choose from behind what he calls a "veil of ignorance."

If people could choose under such conditions, then what principles of justice would they choose? We need not think of these people as selfless. They want what all people want of the basic goods of life. And as persons, their liberty is especially important to them. If they also chose rationally, rather than out of spite or envy, then what would they choose? Rawls believes that they would choose two principles; the first has to do with their political liberties, and the second concerns economic arrangements. Although he varies the wording of the principles, according to a more developed version they are as follows:

1. Each person is to have an equal right to the most extensive total system of equal basic liberties compatible with a similar system of liberty for all.
2. Social and economic inequalities are to be arranged so that they are
   a. to the greatest benefit of the least advantaged . . . , and
   b. attached to offices and positions open to all under conditions of fair equality of opportunity.[25]

Rawls believes that if people were considering an imaginary society in which to live and for which they were choosing principles of justice, and if they did not know who they would be in the society, they would require that there be *equality of liberties*—that is, they would not be willing to be the people who had less freedom than others. They would want as much say about matters in their society that affect them as any other people. This is because of the importance of liberty to all people as people. When it comes to wealth, however, Rawls believes that these people would *accept unequal wealth* provided certain conditions were met. They would be willing that some would be richer and some would be not so rich provided that the not so rich are better off than they otherwise would be if all had equal amounts of wealth.

You can test yourself to see if your choices coincide with Rawls's belief about people accepting unequal wealth. The table shows the number of

Wealth Levels	Society A	Society B	Society C
High income	100,000	700	100
Medium income	700	400	100
Low income	50	200	100

people at three different wealth levels (high, medium, and low) in three societies. If you had to choose, to which society would you want to belong?

If you chose Society A, then you are a risk taker. According to Rawls, you do not know what your chances are of being in any of the three positions in the society. You do not know whether your chances of being in the highest group are near zero or whether your chances of being in the lowest group are very good. Your best bet when you do not know what your chances are, and you do want the goods that these numbers represent, is to choose Society B: No matter what position you are in, you will do better than any position in Society C. And because you do not know what your chances are of being in the lowest group, even if you were in the lowest position in Society B, you would be better off than in the lowest position in either A or C. This is a *maximin* strategy: In choosing under uncertainty, you choose that option with the best worst or minimum position.

Now what is the relevance of this to his second principle of justice and Rawls's method of deriving it? It is this. When the people in the original position choose, they do not know who they are, and so they will not bias the outcome in their favor. They do not know in what position they will be in the society for which they are developing principles. Thus, they will look out for the bottom position in that society. They will think to themselves that if they were in that lowest position in their society, then they would accept that some people are more wealthy than they, provided that they themselves also were thereby better off. Thus, the first part of the second principle of justice, which addresses the improvement of the least advantaged, is formulated as it is.

Another reason why Rawls believes there must be some special concern in justice to provide for the least advantaged is what he calls the "redress of nature." Nature, so to speak, is arbitrary in doling out initial starting points in life. Some people start off quite well, and others are less fortunate. Justice opposes arbitrariness. If inequalities are to be just, then there must be some good reason for them. But there seemingly is no good reason that some are born wealthy and some poor. If some are born into unfortunate circumstances, it

is through no fault of their own but merely because of the arbitrariness of the circumstances of their birth. Justice requires that something be done about this. Thus, again justice requires some special concern about the lot of the least advantaged, and this is part of the requirement for a just society that has inequality of wealth.

The second part of the second principle is an equal opportunity principle. For the institutions in a society that allow inequality of income and wealth to be just, that society must provide equal opportunity for those with the interest and talent to attain the positions to which the greater wealth is attached. As noted in our earlier discussion about equal opportunity, there remain problems with the justness of reward on the basis of talent itself, if naturally endowed talent is arbitrary. However, to do otherwise and require equal opportunity for all no matter what their talents would violate the demands of efficiency and most probably would not be something that people in the original position would accept.

In a more recent work, *Political Liberalism,* Rawls points out that his two principles of justice would not necessarily be those chosen by any persons whatsoever. They are, rather, the principles most likely to be accepted by people who are brought up in the traditions and institutions of a modern democratic society.[26] Modern democratic societies are pluralistic—that is, their people will have many different and irreconcilable sets of moral and religious beliefs. How, then, would they ever agree on substantive matters of justice? Consider what goes on during presidential elections in the United States. People have and manifest extremely strong and diverse political and moral beliefs, yet as members of a modern democratic society they will also share certain political values. One is that for a political system to be legitimate it must have rules that determine a system of fair cooperation for mutual advantage by members who are regarded as free and equal persons. This conception is modeled by the original position, which gives us the two principles of justice: The first specifies that people have equal political liberties, and the second lays down conditions for unequal distribution of wealth—namely, principles of equal opportunity and the improvement of the least advantaged. A free-market system must be limited by the concerns of justice, which is the primary virtue of social institutions.[27]

Communitarianism

The liberalism described above is based on the notion of free and equal persons who agree to certain things. It is also premised on the fact that in modern societies people have sharply different moral and religious views—that is, an irremediable pluralism. Thus, the only way that they can agree is by thinking of themselves as persons who want whatever persons want and who do not bias the rules of society in their own favor. Some recent writers object to what they believe are the universalist and atomistic conceptions of such theories. Rather, they believe, people are by nature social and naturally tend to belong to communities. Rather than focusing on individuals or the community of all members of the human race, they stress the importance of belonging to families, cities, nations, religious communities, neighborhood associations, political parties, and groups supporting particular causes. Their views on what justice requires are then influenced by the views of the groups to which they belong. It is a matter of tradition and culture. (See the bibliographic selections on communitarianism at the end of this chapter.)

One problem with these views, voiced even by those supporting them, is that we can think of societies with views of justice that we believe are just wrong: those supporting slavery, for example, or condoning forced marriages. Both sides of this issue have modified their view. Liberals, such as Rawls, have more recently attempted to make more room for social consensus, and communitarians have attempted to find ways to avoid a seeming ethical relativism according to which whatever society approves is right.

NOTES

1. www.demos.org/inequality/; www.demos.org/inequality/news.cfm#344E2A72-3FF4-6C82-559A685517836D04.
2. www.demos.org/inequality/numbers.cfm.
3. www.infoplease.com/ipa/A0763170.html.
4. "The Wage Gap Myth," National Center for Policy Analysis, April 12, 2002 (at www.ncpa.org/pub/ba/ba392).
5. Michael J. Mandel, "The Rich Get Richer, and That's O.K.," *Business Week,* no. 3796 (Aug. 26, 2002): 88.
6. See "2004 Trends in CEO Pay"; www.aflcio.org/corporateamerica/paywatch/pay/.
7. Paul Krugman, *The New York Times,* April 27, 2007.
8. Paul Krugman, "Crony Capitalism, U.S.A.," *The Great Unraveling: Losing Our Way in the New Century* (New York: Norton, 2003): 108.
9. http://en.wikipedia.org/wiki/Health_care_in_the_United_States.
10. *New York Times Magazine,* April 22, 2007, pp. 15–18.
11. We associate the saying "From each according to his ability, to each according to his need" with Karl Marx, but it actually originated with the "early French socialists of the Utopian school, and was officially adopted by German socialists in the Gotha Program of 1875." Nicholas Rescher, *Distributive Justice* (Indianapolis, IN: Bobbs-Merrill, 1966): 73–83.
12. James Fishkin, *Justice, Equal Opportunity, and the Family* (New Haven, CT: Yale University Press, 1983): 4.
13. "National Spending Per Student Rises to $8,287." *Report of the U.S. Census Bureau,* April 3, 2006 (www.census.gov/Press-Release/www/releases/archives/economic surveys/006685.html).
14. Bernard Williams, "The Idea of Equality," in *Philosophy, Politics and Society* (second series), Peter Laslett and W. G. Runciman (Eds.) (Oxford: Basil Blackwell, 1962): 110–131.
15. Harry Frankfurt, "Equality as a Moral Ideal," *Ethics, 98* (1987): 21–43.
16. John H. Schaar, "Equality of Opportunity, and Beyond," in *NOMO SIX: Equality,* J. Chapman and R. Pennock (Eds.) (New York: Atherton Press, 1967).
17. Ibid.
18. See Thomas Nagel, "Justice," in *What Does It All Mean: A Very Short Introduction to Philosophy* (New York: Oxford University Press, 1987): 76–86.
19. Milton Friedman, *Capitalism and Freedom* (Chicago: University of Chicago Press, 1982): 133.
20. This distinction has been stressed by Philippa Foot in her article, "Killing and Letting Die," in *Abortion: Moral and Legal Perspectives,* Jay Garfield (Ed.) (Amherst: University of Massachusetts Press,

1984): 178–185. This distinction is the subject of some debate among recent moral philosophers.

21. Stephen Holmes, "Welfare and the Liberal Conscience," *Report from the Institute for Philosophy and Public Policy, 15,* no. 1 (Winter 1995): 1–6.

22. Morton White, *The Philosophy of the American Revolution* (New York: Oxford University Press, 1978): 161.

23. Robert B. Reich, "The Other Surplus Option," *The New York Times,* July 11, 1999, p. A23.

24. John Rawls, *A Theory of Justice* (Cambridge, MA: Harvard University Press, 1971).

25. Ibid., 302.

26. John Rawls, *Political Liberalism* (New York: Columbia University Press, 1993). This work is a collection of some of Rawls's essays and lectures over the preceding two decades, together with an overview introduction and several new essays.

27. John Rawls, "The Primacy of the Right over the Good," in *Political Liberalism.*

REVIEW EXERCISES

1. What is the difference between a *process view* of distributive justice and an *end state view?*

2. Discuss the meaning and problems associated with using the end state view criteria of merit, achievement, effort, and contribution.

3. What is the literal meaning of "equal opportunity"? What criterion does Fishkin use for judging whether it exists? What is Bernard Williams' "starting-gate theory" of equal opportunity?

4. Describe some problems raised by philosophers Frankfurt and Schaar regarding equal opportunity.

5. Explain the libertarian position on liberty and the role of government.

6. What are the basic differences between capitalism and socialism as social and economic theories?

7. What is Rawls's "original position," and what role does it play in his derivation of principles of justice?

8. What is Rawls's *maximin* principle, and how is it related to his second principle of justice?

9. How does communitarianism differ from liberalism?

DISCUSSION CASES

1. The Homeless. Joe was laid off two years ago at the auto repair company where he had worked for fifteen years. For the first year he tried to get another job. He read the want ads and left applications at local employment agencies. After that, he gave up. He had little savings and soon had no money for rent. He has been homeless now for a year. He will not live in the shelters because they are crowded, noisy, and unsafe. As time goes by, he has less and less chance of getting back to where he was before. When he can, he drinks to forget the past and escape from the present. Other people he meets on the streets are mentally retarded or psychologically disturbed. He realizes that the city offers some things to try to help people like him, but there is little money and the numbers of homeless people seem to be growing.

Does society have any responsibility to do anything for people like Joe? Why or why not?

2. Rights to Keep What One Earns. Gene and his co-workers have been talking over lunch about how their taxes have continued to rise. Some complain that the harder they work, the less they are making. Others are upset because their taxes are going to pay for things that they do not believe the government should support with our tax dollars—the arts, for example. "Why should we support museums or the opera when we don't ever go to them?" they argue. These should be matters for charity. They also complain that they work hard but that their income is being used to take care of others who could work but do not.

Are they right? Why?

3. Class Debate on Equal Opportunity. The topic for class debate one day was "equal opportunity." First, students were asked what they thought it meant. What would you say? How important do you think it is and why? A second question concerned whether there was equal opportunity in society today and, if there were areas where changes needed to be made to enhance equal opportunity, what would they be? What do you think?

YOU MAKE THE DECISION

Apply the theories and issues discussed in this chapter by accessing this animated simulation on the Ethics Resource Center.

Use the passkey that accompanies your book to gain access. If you do not have a passkey, visit cengage brain.com to purchase instant access to additional study material.

Smitty's laissez-faire policy? Or Carla's redistributive plan?

Ethics Module 13 : Economic Justice

© Cengage Learning

Selected Bibliography

Ackerman, Bruce A. *Social Justice in the Liberal State.* New Haven, CT: Yale University Press, 1980.

————. *The Future of Liberal Revolution.* New Haven, CT: Yale University Press, 1992.

Arthur, John, and William Shaw (Eds.). *Justice and Economic Distribution,* 2nd ed. Englewood Cliffs, NJ: Prentice Hall, 1991.

Bell, Daniel. *Communitarianism and Its Critics.* New York: Oxford University Press, 1993.

Bowie, Norman (Ed.). *Equal Opportunity.* Boulder, CO: Westview, 1988.

Boylan, Michael. *A Just Society.* New York: Rowman & Littlefield, 2004.

Cauthen, Kenneth. *The Passion for Equality.* Totowa, NJ: Rowman & Littlefield, 1987.

Christodoulidis, Emilos A. *Communitarianism and Citizenship.* Aldershot, NH: Ashgate Publishing, 1998.

Daniels, Norman. *Reading Rawls.* New York: Basic Books, 1976.

Delaney, D. F. (Ed.). *The Liberalism-Communitarianism Debate.* Lanham, MD: Rowman & Littlefield, 1994.

Etzioni, Amitai. *Political Unification Revisited: On Building Supranational Communities.* Lanham, MD: Lexington Books, Rowman & Littlefield, 2001.

Fishkin, James S. *The Dialogue of Justice.* New Haven, CT: Yale University Press, 1992.

————. *Justice, Equal Opportunity, and the Family.* New Haven, CT: Yale University Press, 1983.

Fleischacker, Samuel. *A Short History of Distributive Justice.* Cambridge, MA: Harvard University Press, 2004.

Frankel Paul, Ellen, et al. *Equal Opportunity.* London: Basil Blackwell, 1987.

Friedman, Milton. *Capitalism and Freedom.* Chicago: University of Chicago Press, 1962.

Gutmann, Amy. *Democracy and Disagreement.* Cambridge, MA: Harvard University Press, 1998.

————. *Liberal Equality.* Cambridge, UK: Cambridge University Press, 1980.

Hardin, Garrett. *Promethean Ethics.* Seattle: University of Washington Press, 1980.

Harrington, Michael. *Socialism Past and Future.* New York: Arcade, 1989.

Haslett, David W. *Capitalism with Morality.* New York: Oxford University Press, 1994.

Held, Virginia (Ed.). *Property, Profits, and Economic Justice.* Belmont, CA: Wadsworth, 1980.

Hendrickson, Mark W. (Ed.). *The Morality of Capitalism.* Irving-on-Hudson, NY: Foundation for Economic Education, 1997.

Kelly, P. J. *Rethinking Distributive Justice.* Malden, MA: Blackwell Publishing, 2003.

Kennedy, Paul. *Preparing for the 21st Century.* New York: Random House, 1993.

Khatchadourian, Haig. *Community and Communitarianism.* New York: Peter Lang Publishing, 1999.

Le Blanc, Paul. *Black Liberation and the American Dream: The Struggle for Racial and Economic Justice.* Amherst, NY: Prometheus Books, 2008.

MacKinnon, Catharine. *Toward a Feminist Theory of the State.* Cambridge, MA: Harvard University Press, 1989.

Narveson, Jan. *The Libertarian Idea.* Philadelphia: Temple University Press, 1989.

Nielsen, Kai. *Equality and Liberty: A Defense of Radical Egalitarianism.* Totowa, NJ: Rowman & Littlefield, 1984.

Nozick, Robert. *Anarchy, State, and Utopia.* New York: Basic Books, 1974.

Okin, Susan Moller. *Gender and Justice.* New York: Basic Books, 1982.

Paul, Jeffrey, and Ellen Frankel Paul (Eds.). *Economic Rights.* New York: Cambridge University Press, 1993.

Rae, Douglas, et al. *Equalities.* Cambridge, MA: Harvard University Press, 1981.

Rakowski, Eric. *Equal Justice.* New York: Oxford University Press, 1991.

Regan, Tom (Ed.). *Just Business: New Introductory Essays in Business Ethics.* Philadelphia: Temple University Press, 1983.

Sterba, James P. *How to Make People Just.* Lanham, MD: Rowman & Littlefield, 1988.

————. *Justice: Alternative Political Perspectives,* 2d ed. Belmont, CA: Wadsworth, 1992.

Tam, Henry. *Communitarianism: A New Agenda for Politics and Citizenship.* New York: New York University Press, 1998.

Thompson, Michael. *The Politics of Inequality: A Political History of the Idea of Economic Inequality in America.* New York: Columbia University Press, 2007.

Veatch, Robert M. *The Foundations of Justice: Why the Retarded and the Rest of Us Have Claims to Equality.* New York: Oxford University Press, 1986.

Walzer, Michael. *The Spheres of Justice.* New York: Basic Books, 1983.

Young, Iris Marion. *Justice and the Politics of Difference.* Princeton, NJ: Princeton University Press, 1990.

Zucker, Ross. *Democratic Distributive Justice.* New York: Cambridge University Press, 2003.

14

Legal Punishment

You may remember the recent case of Jessica Lundsford. On February 23, 2005, she disappeared from her home in Homosassa, Florida. John Couey, a convicted sex offender, was staying with his half-sister in a trailer home nearby. He abducted Jessica during the night and took her to his bedroom where he sexually assaulted her. Three days later, he tied her wrists, put her in a garbage bag, and buried her alive near the house, where she suffocated to death. Couey had a long criminal history; because of this, he became a prime suspect. Within a month, he was arrested and then confessed. Police found Jessica's body in a shallow grave. Couey was tried and found guilty of kidnapping and first-degree murder on March 7, 2007. The jury recommended that he receive the death penalty. Under Florida law, his sentence is automatically under appeal to the state's supreme court.[1]

The father of thirteen-year-old Dwayne had been locked up in a maximum security prison since Dwayne was five years old. Not long ago, because she thought a father's voice would help her control Dwayne, his mother brought Dwayne and their two other children to visit their father. Dwayne appeared not to care, but after their meeting he sobbed in the car all the way home. The point is that imprisonment affects not only the one imprisoned, but others as well, including children and families. The number of children alone with fathers in prison in 2007 had risen to 2.1 million.

As of May 2006, 2.2 million people were living in U.S. prisons and jails, which was one person for every 136 people in the country. This is the highest rate of incarceration in the world, nearly five times the historic norm and seven times higher than the rates of most Western European countries. In 2006, the United States added almost 1,100 people per week to this population.[2]

The reasons cited for the increase are mandatory sentences for drug crimes, an increase in the number of so-called three-strikes and truth-in-sentencing laws that lessen the number of prisoners released early.[3] As noted, the United States has the highest rate of incarceration of any country in the world, with the next highest rates in Britain, China, France, Japan, and Nigeria.[4] Approximately "40 percent of all felony probationers are rearrested for fresh felonies within three years of being placed under community supervision."[5]

In 2006, the annual cost to incarcerate an inmate was between $24,000 and $40,000. When multiplied by the 2.2 million inmates, the annual cost overall is staggering. In California alone, the operating budget for the state prison system is more than $10 billion, and the state plans to "spend $7.4 billion to build 40,000 new prison beds" because its prisons are now so overcrowded. Within five years of 2007, "the prison budget will overtake spending on the state's public universities."[6]

In 2004, almost 60 percent of prisoners were racial or ethnic minorities, some 40 percent black, 35 percent white, 19 percent Hispanic, and 2 percent other.[7] That is also 12.6 percent of all black men ages twenty-five to twenty-nine and

3.6 percent of Hispanic men and 1.7 percent of white men of those same ages.[8] "Black men in their early thirties are imprisoned at seven times the rate of whites in the same age group." All high school dropouts are at greater risk for being in prison, but "by the time they reach their mid-thirties, a full 60 percent of black high school dropouts are now prisoners or ex-cons." Related to the racial disparities of incarceration are political effects. For example, given that many states disallow even ex-felons to vote and that a high percentage of blacks vote Democratic, many Republicans would not have been elected to Congress. In fact, if even ex-felons had been able to vote in the 2000 election in Florida and using conservative figures on voting, Al Gore would have carried the state by 30,000 votes and thus the electoral college to become president.[9]

Although many prisoners are incarcerated for having committed violent crimes, more than half are there for nonviolent crimes, many of these for drug-related offenses (although violent crimes can also be the result of attempts to get drug money.) Moreover, it is estimated that some 16 percent of the prison population has some mental illness.

In fact, a report by a Ford Foundation commission, *Confronting Confinement* (June 2006), noted that "America's prisons are dangerously overcrowded, unnecessarily violent, excessively reliant on physical segregation, breeding grounds of infections disease, lacking in meaningful programs for inmates and staffed by underpaid and undertrained guards in a culture that promotes abuse." One of those accused of abuse at Abu Ghraib prison in Iraq had been a prison guard.[10] When these inmates return to society, they bring the results of such prison conditions with them.

In 2005, 128 people were sentenced to death in the United States, the lowest number since the death penalty was reinstated in 1976 (see below). This compares to 138 in 2004, 153 in 2003, 167 in 2002, 162 in 2001, and 232 in 2000.[11]

By mid-2007, there had been 1,076 executions since 1976. As of September 4, there had been thirty-six executions in 2007, twenty-three in Texas alone. All of these were by lethal injection. Of this number, eleven were white, five black, and three Latino. Twelve states do not have the death penalty, with another five having carried out no executions in the past thirty years, and several more having executed no more than three people.[12]

Between 1977 and 2006, there were 368 executions in Texas, eighty in Oklahoma, 66 in Missouri, 96 in Virginia, and 60 in Florida. The last electrocution took place in Virginia in July 2006, the last death by gas chamber in 1999 in Arizona, the last death by firing squad in 1996 in Utah, and the last death by hanging in 1996 in Delaware. Five states account for more than two-thirds of executions since 1977.

Throughout the world, 91 percent of executions were in China, Iran, Iraq, Sudan, Pakistan, and the United States. The number of executions estimated to have occurred in China in recent years varies widely between 1,000 and 8,000 annually.[13]

From 1976, when the U.S. Supreme Court reinstated the death penalty, until August 13, 1999, 560 people had been executed.[14] By 1968, a majority of people in the country had come to oppose the death penalty. Not long after this, in 1972, the U.S. Supreme Court revoked it, ruling that the penalty had become too "arbitrary and capricious" and thus violated the federal Constitution's ban on cruel and unusual punishment.[15] By 1976, however, the country's mood had again begun to change, and states had established less arbitrary sentencing guidelines. That year, the high court reinstated the death penalty in *Gregg* v. *Georgia,* arguing that it did not violate the Eighth Amendment's ban on cruel and unusual punishment and thus could be constitutionally applied for convicted murderers. Public support for the death penalty has varied in the decades since. It peaked in the mid-1980s, with as many as 83 percent of Americans supporting it. However, there remain great differences in who receives the death penalty, and it depends often on where one committed the crime and the makeup of the jury. In May 2006, a Gallup poll found that although support for the death penalty was approximately 65 percent, when people were allowed to choose life without parole or the death penalty for those convicted of crimes, that number fell to 47 percent.[16] The main public concern seems to be the risk of executing innocent people, primarily because of "revelations of withheld evidence, mistaken eyewitness identification, questionable forensic practices, prosecutorial misconduct and simple error."[17] Defendants have had poorly trained and poorly paid lawyers—and even lawyers who dozed during their trials. "In the last three years, 24 death row inmates in 14 states have been given new trials or freed altogether, often on the basis of DNA evidence."[18]

By May 1, 2007, 201 people had been found to be innocent as a result of DNA testing. They were released after spending a combined 2,500 years in prison for crimes they did not commit.[19] Some of those released were the result of the work of the Innocence Project, which was started by two attorneys, Barry Scheck and Peter Neufeld. On February 3, 1997, the American Bar Association, the largest and most influential organization of lawyers in the United States, voted for a moratorium on executions until greater fairness in the process could be ensured, especially in the quality of representation that defendants receive.[20]

In three Illinois cases, a Northwestern University journalism teacher and his class reviewed the cases and proved the inmates' innocence. These were three of thirteen people in Illinois who had been scheduled to be executed but had recently been found to be innocent and released. One inmate had been scheduled for execution in just forty-eight hours. On January 31, 2000, the governor of Illinois, George Ryan, ordered that all executions in his state be halted. "Until I can be sure with moral certainty that no innocent man or woman is facing a lethal injection," he said, "no one will meet that fate."[21] Because of these concerns and a review of the cases, on January 11, 2003, Ryan, in one of his last acts as governor, pardoned four inmates and commuted the death sentences of the remaining 167 (163 men and four women).

There also is some evidence of racial bias in death penalty sentencing. Taking Florida as one example, although 12.5 percent of the population is black, 35 percent of those on death row are black. Actually, it is as much the race of the victim as of the defendant that seems to play a key role in sentencing. A Florida commission recently concluded that "people who kill whites are three to four times more likely to receive the death sentence than people who kill blacks." Of the forty-four executions since 1980, whereas half of the victims were black, only five of the defendants were executed for killing blacks.[22]

Moreover, the makeup of the jury is also important. "More than 20% of black defendants who have been executed were convicted by all-white juries." Although there are now more whites on death row than blacks, blacks have a higher rate similar to their presence in the prison population: "80 percent of completed capital cases involve white victims even though nationally only 50 percent of murder victims are white."[23]

Other issues related to the death penalty have recently gained public attention: for example, whether mentally retarded persons or juveniles should be executed. In June 2002, the U.S. Supreme Court ruled that mentally retarded defendants should not be subject to the death penalty. This same court had ruled in 1989 that execution of the retarded was not unconstitutional. However, the majority of justices now stated that because of "evolving standards of decency," they were reversing themselves. This could affect approximately 200 inmates currently on death rows in various states. Obviously, one practical problem that will be faced in such cases is just how to determine when someone is retarded and what degree of mental retardation should count. In March 2005, the U.S. Supreme Court, in a 5-to-4 vote, ruled that it was cruel and unusual punishment, forbidden by the Constitution, to execute those who were under age 18 when they committed their crimes.[24] The Court had ruled the other way just fifteen years earlier. The key vote was that of Associate Justice Anthony Kennedy, who wrote that he changed his position because of the changing social standards of what counts as cruel and unusual punishment. Adolescents are thought to "lack mature judgment and a full appreciation of the consequences of their actions."[25] The United States had been the only remaining country that executed juveniles.

The cost for a sentence of life in prison is now estimated to be approximately $800,000 per person, but the cost of a death penalty case is between $2 million and $5 million.[26] In North Carolina, for example, an execution can cost as much as $2.16 million more than the cost of life in prison. In California, it costs $90 million more than life in prison. In Texas, the cost of an appeal of a death sentence is more than $2 million, whereas life in prison would be around $750,000.[27] In 1985, after several years of trying, the Kansas legislature passed a death penalty bill. However, when legislators figured out that it would probably cost the state $10 million in the first year and $50 million by 1990, they repealed the law. Those who protested the death penalty argued that the long appeals process results from strong moral opposition to state-sanctioned killing. Indeed, moral sentiments on this issue are strong on both sides.

To know what to think about cases like this and the various crime statistics, we need to examine some of the reasons that have been given for the practice of legal punishment itself. Only then can we appreciate the nature and strength of the arguments for and against the death penalty.

THE NATURE OF LEGAL PUNISHMENT

The most visible form of legal criminal punishment is imprisonment. However, we also punish with fines, forced work, and corporal punishment, which includes death. What we want to examine here is not *any* sort of punishment, only legal punishment. Eight-year-old Jimmy's parents can punish him with no TV for a week for a failing grade, and I can punish myself for a momentary caloric indulgence. Legal punishment is like parental and self-punishment in that it is designed to "hurt." If something is gladly accepted or enjoyed, then it is not really punishment.

However, legal punishment is distinct in several ways from other forms of punishment. Legal punishment must follow legal rules of some sort. It is authorized by a legal authority and follows a set of rules that establish who is to be punished, how, and by how much. Lynching is not legal punishment. Furthermore, "Every dog gets his first bite," as the old saying goes. You must first commit the crime or be suspected of it. Whatever we say about the justification of detaining people before they commit (or we think they will commit) a crime, it is not punishment. Punishment of any sort presumes someone has done something to merit the penalty. In the

case of legal punishment, it is a penalty for doing what the law forbids. Law, by its very nature, must have some sanction, some threat attached to breaking it, or else it loses its force. Without such force, it may be a request, but it is not law.

Thus, we can say that legal punishment is the state's infliction of harm or pain on those who break the law according to a set of legally established rules. But is such a practice justified? What gives a society the right to inflict the pain of punishment on any of its members? In asking this, we are asking a moral and not just a legal question. Is legal punishment of some sort morally justifiable? If so, why?

THE DETERRENCE ARGUMENT

One answer to the question of whether legal punishment is morally justifiable is, "Yes, if (and only if) the punishment could be fashioned to prevent or deter crime." The general idea involved in this first rationale for legal punishment is related to both the *nature of law* and *its purpose.* For a law to be a law and not just a request, sanctions must be attached to it. It must have force behind it. Moreover, as we have seen from the discussion in Chapter 11, law has many possible purposes. One purpose is to prevent people from harming others. Our laws presumably are directed to achieving some good. Having penalties as sanctions attached to breaking these laws helps to ensure that the good intended by the laws will be achieved. Of course, not all laws are good laws. However, the idea is that we want not only to have good laws but also to have them enforced in ways that make them effective.

Legal punishment, according to this reasoning, is for the purpose of *preventing* people from breaking the law, *deterring* them from doing so, or both. As such this is a forward-looking consequentialist rationale. Broadly interpreted, the deterrence argument involves these two mechanisms. We can prevent crime by detaining would-be or actual criminals—that is, by simply holding them somewhere so that they cannot do social damage. We also can prevent crime by means such as increased street lighting, more police officers, and stricter handgun laws. We can deter crime by holding out a punishment as a threat to persuade those who contemplate breaking the law not to do so. If a punishment works as a deterrent, then it works in a particular way—through the would-be law-breaker's thinking and decision-making processes. One considers the possibility of being punished for doing some contemplated action and concludes that the gain achieved from the act is not worth the price to be paid—namely, the punishment. Then one acts accordingly.

Problematic Aspects

If deterrence works in this way, then we also can notice that it is not likely to work in some cases. It is not likely to deter crimes of passion, in which people are overcome, if you will, by strong emotions. Not only are they not in the mood to calculate the risks versus the benefits, but also they are unlikely to stop themselves from continuing to act as they will. Punishment as a threat is also not likely to work in cases where people do calculate the risks and the benefits and think the benefits are greater than the risks. These would be cases in which the risks of being caught and punished are perceived as small and the reward or benefit is great. The benefit could be financial or the reward of group or gang respect. It also might be the reward of having done what one believed to be right, as in acts of civil disobedience or in support of any cause whether actually good or bad. Although punishment does not deter in some cases, in others presumably people will be motivated by the threat of punishment. A system of legal punishment will be worthwhile if it works for the greater majority, even if not for all, and if there are no bad consequences that outweigh the good ones.

The issue of cost and benefit also helps make another point about the deterrence rationale for legal punishment: Punishment, in this view, is *externally related* to lawbreaking. In other words, it is not essential. If something else works better than punishment, then that other means ought to be used either as a substitution for punishment or in addition to it. Some people argue that punishment itself does not work, but combined with rehabilitation, job training, or psychological counseling, punishment might be effective. However, if a punishment system is not working, then, in this view, it is not morally justifiable, for the whole idea

is not to punish for punishment's sake but to achieve the goal of law enforcement. On utilitarian grounds, pain is never good in itself. Thus, if punishment involves suffering, it must be justified. The suffering must be outweighed by the good to be achieved by it.

The deterrence argument has a more serious problem: Some people morally object to using this rationale as the sole grounds for legal punishment. For example, if the whole purpose is to enforce the law, and a particular form of punishment will actually work and work better than other measures to achieve the desired deterrent effect, then it would seem that we ought to use it. Suppose that a community has a particularly vexing problem with graffiti. To clean it up is costing the community scarce resources that could be better spent elsewhere. To get rid of the problem, suppose the community decides to institute a program whereby it would randomly pick up members of particular gangs believed to be responsible for the graffiti and punish these individuals with floggings in the public square. Or suppose that cutting off their hands would work better! We would surely have serious moral objections to this program. One objection would be that these particular individuals may not themselves have been responsible for the defacing. They were just picked at random because of suspicion. Another would be that the punishment seems all out of proportion to the offense. However, in itself (or in principle), on deterrence grounds there would be nothing essentially wrong with this program of law enforcement. It would not be necessary that the individual herself be guilty or that the punishment fit the crime. What would be crucial to determine is whether this punishment worked or worked better than alternative forms.

There is another version of the deterrence argument, and it has to do with how deterrence is supposed to work. According to this view, legal punishment is part of a system of social moral education. A society has a particular set of values. One way in which it can instill these values in its members from their youth is to establish punishments for those who undermine them. If private property is valued, then society should punish those who damage or take others' property. These punishments would then become a deterrent in the sense that they had helped individuals internalize social values, giving them internal prohibitions against violating those values. Key to evaluating this view is to determine whether punishment does work in this fashion. What does punishment teach the young and the rest of us? Does it help us internalize values, and does it motivate us? The way the system is administered also can send a message—and in some cases, it might be the wrong message. For example, if legal punishment is not applied fairly, then the lesson that some might learn may not be the one we would desire.

THE RETRIBUTIVIST ARGUMENT

The second primary rationale for legal punishment is retribution. On the retributivist view, legal punishment is justified as a means of making those who are responsible for a crime or harm pay for it. As such it is a backward-looking argument because it is based on past actions. We can understand the idea embodied in this rationale in several ways. It is an argument that uses the concept of justice. Thus, a proponent might say that because someone caused a great deal of pain or harm to another, it is only just or fair that he suffer similarly or proportionately to the harm or pain he caused the other person. Or we might say that she deserves to suffer because she made her victim suffer. The punishment is only just or a fair recompense. In this view, punishment is *internally related* to the wrongful conduct. One cannot, as in the case of the deterrence argument, say that if something else works better than punishment, then that is what ought to be done. Here the punishing itself is essential for justice to be done.

Let us examine this reasoning a bit further. It is based on a somewhat abstract notion of justice. We punish to right a wrong or restore some original state, or we reset the scales of justice. However, in many cases we cannot really undo the suffering of the victim by making the perpetrator suffer. One can pay back the money or return the property to its original state before it was damaged. But even in these cases, there are other harms that cannot be undone, such as the victim's lost sense of privacy or security. Thus, the erasing, undoing, or

righting of the wrong is of some other abstract or metaphysical type. It is difficult to explain, but supporters of this rationale for punishment believe that we do have some intuitive sense of what we mean when we say "justice was done."

According to the retributivist view, payment must be made in some way that is equivalent to the crime or harm done. Writers distinguish two senses of equivalency: an *egalitarian* sense and a *proportional* sense. With egalitarian equivalency, one is required to pay back something identical or almost identical to what was taken. If you make someone suffer two days, then you should suffer two days. However, it would also mean that if you caused someone's arm to be amputated, then your arm should also be cut off. Thus, this version is often given the label *lex talionis.* Translated literally, it means the "law of the talon," of the bird of prey's claw. We also call it the "law of the jungle" or taking "an eye for an eye."

Proportional equivalency holds that what is required in return is not something more or less identical to the harm done or pain caused, but something proportional. In this version, we can think of harms or wrongs as matters of degree—namely, of bad, worse, and worst. Punishments are also scaled from the minimal to the most severe. In this view, punishment must be proportional to the degree of the seriousness of the crime.

Obviously, there are serious problems, both practical and moral, with the *lex talionis* version of the retributivist view. In some cases—for example, in the case of multiple murders—it is not possible to deliver something in like kind, for one cannot kill the murderer more than once. We would presumably also have some moral problems with torturing the torturer or raping the rapist. If one objects to this version of the retributivist view, then one would not necessarily have to object to the proportional version, however.

We also should notice that the retributivist justification of legal punishment does respond to two major problems that the deterrence argument has—that is, it is essential from this point of view that the payment or punishment be just. For it to be just, it must fit both the perpetrator and the crime. First, it must fit the perpetrator in the following ways. Only those who are responsible for a crime should be punished, and only to the degree that they are responsible. It would be important from this perspective that guilt be proved, and that we not single out likely suspects or representatives of a group to make examples of them or use them to intimidate other group members, as in our graffiti example. It also would be important that the punishment fit the person in terms of the degree of his responsibility. This requirement would address the concerns that we have about accomplices to a crime and also about the mental state of the criminal. Diminished mental capacity, mitigating circumstances, and duress, which lessen a person's responsibility, are significant elements of our criminal punishment system.

Second, it is essential in the retributivist view that the punishment fit the crime. Defacing property is not a major wrong or harm and thus should not be punished with amputation of the perpetrator's hand, however well that might work to deter the graffiti artists. This view then requires that we do have a sense of what is more or less serious among crimes and also among punishments so that they can be well matched.

It is because the punishment should fit the crime that many people have problems with the three-strikes laws that several states have passed. These laws provide for life imprisonment for anyone who has a criminal record with two previous convictions for serious crimes and is then found guilty of a third felony. As of the end of 2004, there were "almost 43,000 inmates serving time in prison under the three strikes law" in California, which is about 26 percent of the total number of prisoners.[28] What has happened, however, is that the third "strike" in some instances has been petty theft. A life sentence looks quite out of proportion to such infractions. On the other side is the consequentialist argument that points out that people who have a history of law-breaking are removed from society and prevented from continuing in such behavior.

Problematic Aspects

Just as in the case of the deterrence argument, the retributivist argument regarding legal punishment has problems. We have already referred to one: that

punishing the perpetrator does not concretely undo the wrong done to the victim. If there is undoing, then it is only in some abstract or perhaps metaphysical sense. Those people who defend this argument would have to explain in what sense the balance is restored or the wrong righted by punishment. However, the retributivist would not have any problem with those who point out that a particular form of punishment does not work. According to a retributivist, this is not the primary reason to punish. Someone should be punished as a way of making satisfaction or restitution even if it does the perpetrator or others no good.

A more common objection to the retributivist view is that it amounts to a condoning of revenge. To know whether or not this were true, we would have to clarify what we mean by *revenge*. Suppose we mean that particular people—say, a victim or her family—will get a sense of satisfaction in seeing the wrongdoer punished. But the retributivist view is arguably based on a different sense of justice. According to this view, justice is done when a perpetrator is punished whether or not people feel good about it. However, some may question whether any type of justice exists that is not a matter of providing emotional satisfaction to victims or others who are enraged by a wrong done to them.

Finally, we can wonder whether the retributivist view provides a good basis for a system of legal punishment. Is the primary purpose of such a system to see that justice is done? Do we not have a system of legal punishment to ensure social order and safety? If so, then it would seem that the deterrence argument is the best reason for having any system of legal punishment. One solution to this problem about which justification is better to use for legal punishment is to use both.[29] In designing this system, we can retain consequentialist and thus deterrence and prevention reasons for having a legal punishment system, and consider first what works to deter and prevent crimes. However, we then can bring in our retributivist concerns to determine who is punished (only those who are guilty and only to the extent that they are guilty) and how much (the punishment fitting the crime). In fashioning the punishment system, however, there may be times when we need to determine which rationale takes precedence. For example, in setting requirements for conviction of guilt, we may need to know how bad it is to punish an innocent person. We may decide to give precedence to the retributivist rationale and then make the requirements for conviction of guilt very strenuous, requiring unanimous jury verdicts and guilt beyond a reasonable doubt. In so doing, we also let some guilty people go free and thus run the risk of lessening the deterrent effect of the punishment system. Or we may decide to give precedence to the deterrence rationale. We thus may weaken the requirements for conviction so that we may catch and punish more guilty people. In doing so, however, we run the risk of also punishing more innocent persons.

PUNISHMENT AND RESPONSIBILITY

A key element of our legal punishment system and practice is the supposed tie between punishment and responsibility. Responsibility is essential for punishment from the retributivist point of view. The retributivist believes it is unjust to punish those who are not responsible for a crime. This also can be supported on deterrence grounds: It probably would work better to punish only those who are responsible, otherwise who would have respect for or obey the law if we could be punished whether or not we obeyed it? Responsibility is essential from the retributivist point of view, but only possibly important from the deterrence point of view.

Thus, our legal punishment system contains defenses that are grounded in the requirement that a person be responsible to be punished. For example, the defense of duress can be viewed this way. If a person were forced to commit a crime, either physically forced or under threat to life, then we would probably say that that person was not responsible. The person may have committed the crime, but that is not enough. We do not have a system of strict liability in which the only issue is whether or not you actually did or caused something.

One of the most problematic defenses in our criminal justice system may well be the insanity defense. It involves a plea and a finding of "not guilty by reason of insanity" or something similar

such as "mental defect." This defense has a long history going back at least into the nineteenth century in England with the *M'Naughton Rule* (1843). According to this rule, people are not responsible for their actions if they did not know what they were doing or did not know that it was wrong. This is often referred to as the "right from wrong test." Since that time, other attempts also have been made to list the conditions under which people should not be held responsible for their actions. One example is the "irresistible impulse test." The idea underlying this test for insanity is that sometimes persons are not able to control their conduct and thus act through no fault of their own. Of course, if a person does what he knows will put him in a condition in which he will not be able to control himself and then he unlawfully harms others, then he is held responsible. Thus, the person who drinks and then drives and harms another is held legally liable. However, the person who has some biochemical imbalance that prevents her from controlling her conduct would not be in the same position. In some cases, the insanity defense has been defined in medical terms when the behavior is said to be the result of mental disease. Thus, the *Durham Rule* defines insanity as the "product of mental disease or defect," some sort of abnormal mental condition that affects mental and emotional processes and impairs behavior controls. In our current criminal justice system, mental competence is one requirement for criminal liability. It is called the *mens rea,* or mental element.

Common criticisms of the insanity defense concern our ability to determine whether someone is mentally insane or incompetent. Can't someone feign this? How do psychiatrists or other experts really know whether a person knows what she is doing? However, if we could diagnose these conditions, then a more basic question would still remain—namely, would the conditions diminish or take away responsibility? If so, then would punishment be appropriate? In the extreme case in which a person has a serious brain condition that prevents normal mental function, we assume that this would excuse him from full responsibility. He may, however, be dangerous, and this may be another reason to detain as well as treat him.

Some people have criticized the entire notion of mental illness, especially as it is used in criminal proceedings. They are concerned about the results of a finding such as "not guilty by reason of insanity." For example, it may result in indeterminate sentences for minor crimes, because one must remain in custody in a criminal mental institution until sane. Others find the whole idea wrongheaded and dangerous. For example, one longtime critic of the penal system, Thomas Szasz, held that we have sometimes used this diagnosis of mental illness to categorize and stigmatize people who are simply different.[30] He found this diagnosis often to be a dangerous form of social control.

Some of us also tend to look at some heinous crime and say that "no sane person could have done that!" Or we say that a certain crime was "sick." We use the horror of the crime, its serious wrongness, to conclude that the person committing it must be mentally diseased. One problem with this conclusion is that it implies that the person is not responsible. Are we then implying that no one who does evil things is responsible for what they do? If so, then perhaps they should not be punished. The connection between punishment and responsibility is not only central to our system of legal punishment but also an important element of a morality of legal punishment. In fact, if all acts were determined, in other words they were caused by external or internal influences, and no one of us was responsible for what we do (in the sense that we could have done otherwise), then it would seem that punishment as such (at least in the retributive sense of giving someone what was due them) would never seem to be appropriate.

THE DEATH PENALTY

We now return to a discussion of the death penalty. Throughout history, people have been executed for various, and often political, reasons. Lethal injection, which was first used in Texas in 1982, has been the preferred method more recently. The same two arguments regarding legal punishment—deterrence and retribution—generally are used in arguments about the death penalty. We will return now to these rationales and see what

considerations would be relevant to arguments for and against the death penalty.

On Deterrence Grounds

Is the death penalty a deterrent? Does it prevent people from committing certain capital crimes? Consider first the issue of prevention. One would think that at least there is certainty here. If you execute someone, then that person will not commit any future crime—including murders—because he will be dead. However, on a stricter interpretation of the term *prevent,* this may not necessarily be so.[31] Suppose that we meant that by preventing X from doing Y, we stop X from doing what she would have done—namely, Y. Next, we ask whether by executing a convicted murderer we prevent that person from committing any further murders. The answer is, "Maybe." If that person would have committed another murder, then we do prevent him from doing so. If that person would not have committed another murder, then we would not have prevented him from doing so. In general, by executing all convicted murders we would, strictly speaking, have prevented some of them (those who would have killed again) but not others (those who would not have killed again) from doing so. How many? It is difficult to tell. Those who support the death penalty will insist that it will have been worth it, no matter how small the number of murders being prevented, because the people executed are convicted murderers anyway. The last point must mean that their lives are not worth that much!

What about the deterrence argument for the death penalty? If having the death penalty deters would-be murderers from committing their crimes, then it will have been worth it, according to this rationale. Granted, it would not deter those who kill out of passion or those murders committed by risk takers, but it would deter others. This argument depends on showing that the death penalty is an effective deterrent. There are two kinds of resources to use to make this case. One is to appeal to our own intuitions about the value of our lives—that we would not do what would result in our own death. Threats of being executed would deter us, and thus we think they also would deter others. More likely, however, reasons other than fear of the death penalty restrain most of us from killing others.

The other resource for making the case for the death penalty's deterrent effect is to use empirical studies to make comparisons. For example, we could compare two jurisdictions, say, two states: One has the death penalty, and one does not. If we find that in the state with the death penalty there are fewer murders than in the state without the death penalty, can we assume that the death penalty has made the difference and is thus a deterrent? Not necessarily. Perhaps it was something else about the state with the death penalty that accounted for the lesser incidence of murder. For example, the lower homicide rate could be the result of good economic conditions or a culture that has strong families or religious institutions. Something similar could be true of the state with a higher incidence of homicide. The cause in this case could be factory closings or other poor economic conditions. So, also, if there were a change in one jurisdiction from no death penalty to death penalty (or the opposite), and the statistics regarding homicides also changed, then we might conclude that the causal factor was the change in the death penalty status. But again this is not necessarily so. For example, the murder rate in Canada actually declined after that country abolished the death penalty in 1976.[32] Other studies found no correlation between having or instituting or abolishing the death penalty and the rate of homicide.[33] For example, statistics show that states without the death penalty and with similar demographic profiles do not differ in homicide rates from states with the death penalty. Moreover, homicide rates in states that instituted the death penalty have not declined more than in states that did not. For example, "Massachusetts and Rhode Island, with no death penalty, had homicide rates of 3.7 per 100,000 and 4.2 per 100,000, respectively, from 1977 to 1997, while Connecticut, a death penalty state, had a rate of 4.9 per 100,000."[34] And homicide rates in states with the death penalty have been found to be higher than states without it. The murder rate in states with the death penalty is consistently higher than in the twelve states without the death

penalty: in recent years, between 37 percent and 46 percent higher.[35]

To make a good argument for the death penalty on deterrence grounds, a proponent would have to show that it works in this fashion. In addition, the proponent may have to show that the death penalty works better than other alternatives—for example, life in prison without the possibility of parole. If we do not know for sure, then we can ask what are our options. If we have the death penalty and it does not provide an effective deterrent, then we will have executed people for no good purpose. If we do not have the death penalty and it would have been an effective deterrent, then we risk the lives of innocent victims who otherwise would have been saved. Because this is the worse alternative, some argue, we ought to retain the death penalty.[36] Because the deterrence argument broadly construed is a consequentialist argument, using it also should require thinking more generally of costs and benefits. Here the cost of execution could be compared to the cost of life imprisonment.

On Retributivist Grounds

As we have already noted, according to the retributivist argument for legal punishment, we ought to punish people in order to make them pay for the wrong or harm they have done. Those who argue for the death penalty on retributivist grounds must show that it is a fitting punishment and the only or most fitting punishment for certain crimes and criminals. This is not necessarily an argument based on revenge—that the punishment of the wrongdoer gives others satisfaction. It appeals rather to a sense of justice and an abstract righting of wrongs done. Again, there are two different versions of the retributive principle: egalitarian (or *lex talionis*) and proportional. The egalitarian version says that the punishment should equal the crime. An argument for the death penalty would attempt to show that the only fitting punishment for someone who takes a life is that her own life be taken in return. In this view, the value of a life is not equivalent to anything else, thus even life in prison is not sufficient payment for taking a life, though it would also seem that the only crime deserving of the death penalty would be murder. Note that homicide is not the only crime for which we have assigned the death penalty. We have also done so for treason and rape. Moreover, only some types of murder are thought by proponents of the death penalty to deserve this form of punishment. And as noted in the critique of the *lex talionis* view above, strict equality of punishment would be not only impractical in some cases but also morally problematic.

Perhaps a more acceptable argument could be made on grounds of proportionality. In this view, death is the only fitting punishment for certain crimes. Certain crimes are worse than all others, and these should receive the worst or most severe punishment. Surely, some say, death is a worse punishment than life in prison. However, some people argue that spending one's life in prison is worse. This form of the retributivist principle would not require that the worst crimes receive the worst possible punishment. It only requires that, of the range of acceptable punishments, the worst crimes receive the top punishment on the list. Death by prolonged torture might be the worst punishment, but we probably would not put that at the top of our list. So, also, death could but need not be included on that list.

Using the retributivist rationale, one would need to determine the most serious crimes. Can these be specified and a good reason given as to why they are the worst crimes? Multiple murders would be worse than single ones, presumably. Murder with torture or of certain people also might be found to be among the worst crimes. What about treason? What about huge monetary swindles? What about violation of laws against weapons sales to certain foreign governments? We rate degrees of murder, distinguishing murder in the first degree from murder in the second degree. The first is worse because the person not only deliberately intended to kill the victim but also did so out of malice. These are distinguished from manslaughter, which is killing also, both its voluntary and involuntary forms. The idea supposedly is that the kind of personal and moral involvement makes a difference: The more the person planned with intention and deliberateness, the more truly the person owned the act. The more malicious crime is also thought to be worse. Critics of the death penalty sometimes argue that such

rational distinctions are perhaps impossible to make in practice. However, unless it is impossible in principle or by its very nature, supporters could continue to try to refine the current distinctions.

Other Concerns

Not all arguments for and against the death penalty come easily or neatly under the headings of deterrence or retributivist arguments. Some, for example, appeal to the uniqueness of the action by which society deliberately takes the life of a human being. People die all the time. But for some individuals or for the state's representatives deliberately to end the experience and thoughts and feelings of a living human being is the gravest of actions, they argue. As mentioned previously, most Western nations no longer have a death penalty. Some have given it up because they believe it to be uncivilized, brutalizing, degrading, barbarous, and dehumanizing. The one put to death, depending on the form of execution, gasps for air, strains, and shakes uncontrollably. The eyes bulge, the blood vessels expand, and sometimes more than one try is needed to complete the job. In June 1999, for example, 344-pound Allen Lee Davis was executed in Florida's new electric chair. It replaced "Old Sparky," a chair built in 1923 that had ended the lives of 225 convicted murderers. The execution caused blood to appear on Davis's face and shirt. Some believed that this showed that he had suffered. Others said it was simply a nosebleed.[37] On January 7, 2000, the Florida legislature voted to use lethal injections instead of the electric chair in future executions.[38]

Just as the electric chair was thought to be more humane (painless and swift) when Thomas Edison invented it in 1888, so now death by lethal injection is to take the place of electrocution and other less humane methods. Three chemicals are used in this procedure and are injected intravenously. First, an ultrashort-acting barbiturate, usually sodium thiopental, is given. This causes the inmate to become unconscious. Next, a muscle relaxant, either pancuronium bromide or a similar drug, is given to cause paralysis of the muscles, including those responsible for breathing. Finally, potassium chloride, which causes cardiac arrest, is given. If all goes as expected, the inmate falls asleep and does not experience any pain as death takes place. The entire process can take as short as ten minutes or much longer. Some of the delay is caused by the difficulty the technicians sometimes have in finding an acceptable vein to use. There have been cases of drug users, for example, whose veins were not in good condition or who had to help the technician find a good vein. It is important that it be a vein rather than an artery used because the chemicals go straight to the heart. It is also possible that the person does not remain unconscious or is partially conscious and does experience pain or the feeling of suffocating, but because of the inability to move caused by the second chemical cannot communicate this. Technicians can be more or less capable of giving the drugs correctly and in sufficient amount, though difficult cases seem to be occurring less frequently. Doctors would be more capable but are prohibited by their code of ethics from taking part in executions in this way.[39] There have been thirty-eight botched cases recorded since 1976. In the last few years, half a dozen states have suspended using lethal injection because of concerns about these cases.[40] Clearly, both opponents and supporters of the death penalty may have ammunition for their position in the description of the process of lethal injection as a more humane method of execution.

Other opponents of the death penalty appeal to religious reasons, declaring the wrongness of "playing God." Only God can take a life, they argue. Another argument appeals to the inalienable right to life possessed by all human beings. Critics of this argument assert that those who deliberately kill other human beings forfeit their own right to life. Consider, further, whether a condemned prisoner should have the right to choose his own means of execution. Not long ago, a convicted murderer in Oregon asked to be hanged![41] Do some forms of execution (the guillotine, for example) violate the Eighth Amendment's ban on cruel and unusual punishment? Should executions become public or videotaped for purposes of information and instruction? When we ask questions such as these, our views on the death penalty and our reasons for supporting or opposing it will be put to the test, which is probably not a bad thing.

Also relevant to a discussion of the morality of legal punishment and the death penalty is the matter of rehabilitation. From a consequentialist perspective, if special programs in prison would help reduce the rate of recidivism or repeat offenders and also help convicted persons lead productive lives when released, then they would be morally recommended. From a nonconsequentialist perspective, there might also be grounds for stressing such programs. One might want to consider whether persons ought to be given a second chance in light of the fact that, given certain circumstances, they might not have been fully responsible for their crimes. On the other hand, those who argue from a consequentialist perspective might in some cases point out that in certain kinds of cases—say, with sexual predators—there is not much likelihood of reform. Or from a nonconsequentialist perspective, some might argue that given the severity of certain crimes, persons deserve the strictest and most severe punishment, not a second chance. As you can see from the discussions in this chapter, matters of legal punishment and the death penalty in particular are complex. Hopefully, the distinctions made in this chapter will help readers make more informed decisions about this subject.

NOTES

1. http://en.wikipedia.org/wiki/Jessica Lunsford.
2. www.breitbart.com/article.php?id=D8HODD7G0&show_article=1.
3. Associated Press, "Nation's Inmate Population Increased 2.3 Percent Last Year," *The New York Times,* April 25, 2005, p. A14.
4. Siobhan McDonough, "U.S. Prison Population Soars in 2003, ''04," April 25, 2005 (at www.news.yahoo.com).
5. John J. Dilulio Jr. and Joseph P. Tierney, "An Easy Ride for Felons on Probation," *The New York Times,* Aug. 29, 2000, p. A27.
6. *San Francisco Chronicle,* May 21, 2007, p. A1; www.uscourts.gov/newsroom/incarcerationcosts. html.
7. Fox Butterfield, "Despite Drop in Crime, An Increase in Inmates," *The New York Times,* Nov. 8, 2004, p. A14. Figures are for 2003.
8. *The New York Times,* April 15, 2005, p. A14.
9. *New York Review of Books,* April 12, 2007, pp. 33, 36.
10. Ibid., p. 34.

11. See www.deathpenaltyinfo.org.
12. Ibid.
13. Ibid.
14. Thomas Strickler, "Death Watch," *National Catholic Reporter, 35,* no. 36 (Aug. 13, 1999): 6.
15. U.S. Supreme Court, *Furman* v. *Georgia,* 1972.
16. www.deathpenaltyinfo.org.
17. Mike Farrell, "Death Penalty Thrives in Climate of Fear," *San Francisco Chronicle,* Feb. 24, 2002, p. D3.
18. Raymond Bonner, "Still on Death Row, Despite Mounting Doubts," *The New York Times,* July 8, 2002, p. A15.
19. www.innocenceproject.org.
20. Ibid.
21. Margaret Carlson, "Death, Be Not Proud," *Time* (Feb. 21, 2000): 38.
22. Sara Rimer, "Florida Lawmakers Reject Electric Chair," *The New York Times,* Jan. 7, 2000, p. A14.
23. www.deathpenaltyinfo.org.
24. See, for example, Claudia Wallis, "Too Young to Die," *Time,* March 14, 2005, p. 40.
25. Ibid.
26. Caroline Moorehead, "Tinkering with Death," *World Press Review, 42,* no. 7 (July 1995): 38–39.
27. www.mindspring.com/~phporter/econ.html.
28. http://www.lao.ca.gov/2005/3_Strikes/3_strikes_102005.htm.
29. See Richard Brandt, *Ethical Theory* (Englewood Cliffs, NJ: Prentice Hall, 1959).
30. Thomas Szasz, *The Myth of Mental Illness* (New York: Harper & Row, 1961).
31. See Hugh Bedau, "Capital Punishment and Retributive Justice," in *Matters of Life and Death,* Tom Regan (Ed.) (New York: Random House, 1980): 148–182.
32. It dropped from 3.09 people per 100,000 residents in 1975 to 2.74 per 100,000 in 1983. "Amnesty International and the Death Penalty," Amnesty International USA, *Newsletter* (Spring 1987).
33. See H. Bedau, *The Death Penalty in America* (Chicago: Aldine, 1967), in particular Chapter 6, "The Question of Deterrence."
34. Ford Fessenden, "Deadly Statistics: A Survey of Crime and Punishment," *The New York Times,* Sept. 22, 2000, p. A19.
35. www.deathpenaltyinfo.org; www.truthinjustice.org/922death.htm.
36. See Ernest van den Haag, "Deterrence and Uncertainty," *Journal of Criminal Law, Criminology and Police Science, 60,* no. 2 (1969): 141–147.
37. "Uproar over Bloody Electrocution," *San Francisco Chronicle,* July 9, 1999, p. A7; "An Execution Causes Bleeding," *The New York Times,* July 8, 1999, p. A10.
38. *The New York Times,* Jan. 7, 2000, p. A14.
39. See Adam Liptak, "Critics Say Execution Drug May Hide Suffering," *The New York Times,* Oct. 7, 2003, pp. A1, A18.
40. *The New York Times,* April 24, 2007, p. A17; www.deathpenaltyinfo.org.
41. I thank one of my reviewers, Wendy Lee-Lampshire of Bloomsburg University, for sharing this fact and calling this problem to my attention.

REVIEW EXERCISES

1. What essential characteristics of legal punishment distinguish it from other types of punishment?
2. What is the difference between the mechanisms of deterrence and prevention? Given their meanings, does the death penalty prevent murders? Deter would-be killers? How?
3. If legal punishment works as a deterrent, then how does it work? For whom would it work? For whom would it not likely work?
4. Summarize the positive aspects of the deterrence view regarding the justification of legal punishment.
5. Explain two moral problems with the deterrence view, using an example comparable to the graffiti example in the text.
6. How does the retributivist view differ from the deterrence view?
7. What is the *lex talionis* version of this view? How does it differ from the proportional view?
8. Discuss the arguments for and against the identification of retributivism with revenge.
9. Why is the notion of responsibility critical to the retributivist view of legal punishment? How does the defense of insanity fit in here?
10. Discuss the use of deterrence arguments for the death penalty. Also summarize opponents' criticisms of these arguments.
11. Discuss the use of retributivist arguments for the death penalty. Summarize also opponents' criticisms of these arguments.

DISCUSSION CASES

1. Imprisonment Numbers. According to figures given in the first part of this chapter, there are currently more than 2 million people in U.S. prisons and jails. This is approximately one person for every 138 residents. These figures are striking. Why do you think the imprisonment rate in this country is so high? Do you think this is an acceptable rate? Why or why not? If not, what do you think should be done about it?

2. Doctors and Execution. When a person is executed, it is the practice that a physician certify that the person executed is dead and when he or she has died. A state medical association has recently objected to the participation of doctors in executions. They assert that doctors take an oath to preserve life and should not be accessories to the taking of life. The state insisted that the doctors certifying death do not participate in the execution.

Should doctors be present at and certify the death of persons executed by the state? Why or why not?

3. Death Penalty Cases. Suppose that you were a member of a congressional or other committee that had as its mandate determining the type of crime that could be considered to be punishable by death. What kinds of cases, if any, would you put on the list? Sexual assault and killing of a minor? Planned killing of a batterer by his (or her) spouse? Persons convicted of war crimes? Mob leaders or others who give an order to kill but who do not carry it out themselves? Killing of a police officer or public figure? Multiple murderers? Others?

Why would you pick out just those crimes on your list as appropriately punished by death or as the worst crimes?

YOU MAKE THE DECISION

Apply the theories and issues discussed in this chapter by accessing this animated simulation on the Ethics Resource Center.

Use the passkey that accompanies your book to gain access. If you do not have a passkey, visit cengage brain.com to purchase instant access to additional study material.

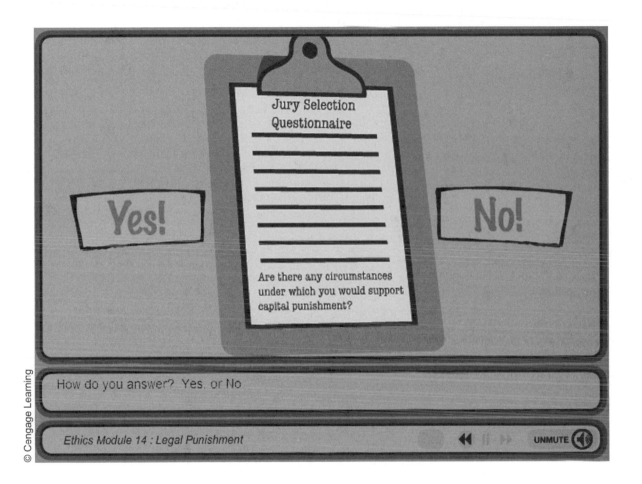

Jury Selection
Questionnaire

Are there any circumstances under which you would support capital punishment?

Yes!

No!

How do you answer? Yes, or No

Ethics Module 14 : Legal Punishment   ◀◀ ❚❚ ▶▶   UNMUTE 🔊

© Cengage Learning

Selected Bibliography

Adenaes, Johannes. *Punishment and Deterrence.* Ann Arbor: University of Michigan Press, 1974.

Bagaic, Mirko. *Punishment and Sentencing: A Rational Approach.* London: Cavendish Publishing, 2001.

Baird, Robert M., and Stuart E. Rosenbaum (Eds.). *The Philosophy of Punishment.* Buffalo, NY: Prometheus, 1988.

Bedau, Hugo Adam. *The Death Penalty in America.* New York: Oxford University Press, 1982.

————. *Death Is Different: Studies in the Morality, Law, and Politics of Capital Punishment.* Boston: Northeastern University Press, 1987.

———— **(Ed.).** *The Death Penalty in America: Current Controversies.* New York: Oxford University Press, 1998.

Berns, Walter. *For Capital Punishment.* New York: Basic Books, 1979.

Black, Charles L., Jr. *Capital Punishment: The Inevitability of Caprice and Mistake,* 2nd ed. New York: Norton, 1981.

Costanzo, Mark. *Just Revenge: Costs and Consequences of the Death Penalty.* New York: St. Martins Press, 1997.

Coyne, Randall, and Lyn Entzeroth. *Capital Punishment and the Judicial Process.* Durham, NC: Carolina Academic Press, 2001.

Currie, Elliott. *Crime and Punishment in America.* New York: Henry Holt & Co., 1998.

Duff, Anthony (Ed.). *A Reader on Punishment.* New York: Oxford University Press, 1995.

Elliott, Carl. *The Rules of Insanity: Moral Responsibility and the Mentally Ill Offender.* Albany: State University of New York Press, 1996.

Elster, Jean Alicia. *The Death Penalty.* Farmington Hills, MI: Gale Group, 2004.

Gisanick, Nick. *The Ethics of Capital Punishment.* Farmington Hills, MI: Gale Group, 2005.

Gottfried, Ted. *The Death Penalty: Justice or Legalized Murder?* Minneapolis: Twenty-First Century Books, 2004.

Hart, H. L. A. *Punishment and Responsibility.* New York: Oxford University Press, 1968.

Hood, Roger. *The Death Penalty: A Worldwide Perspective.* New York: Oxford University Press, 2007.

Jones, Delores J. *Race, Crime and Punishment.* Broomall, PA: Chelsea House, 2000.

Marzilli, Alan. *Capital Punishment.* Langhorne, PA: Chelsea House, 2003.

Montague, Phillip. *Punishment as Societal-Defense.* Lanham, MD: Rowman & Littlefield, 1995.

Murphy, Jeffrie G. *Punishment and Rehabilitation,* 2nd ed. Belmont, CA: Wadsworth, 1985.

Nathanson, Stephen. *An Eye for an Eye: The Morality of Punishing by Death.* Totowa, NJ: Rowman & Littlefield, 1987.

O'Shea, Kathleen. *Women and the Death Penalty in the United States, 1900–1998.* New York: Praeger, 1999.

Pojman, Louis P., and Jeffrey Reiman. *The Death Penalty: For and Against.* Lanham, MD: Rowman & Littlefield, 1998.

Prejean, Helen. *The Death of Innocents: An Eyewitness Account of Wrongful Executions.* Mississauga, Ontario: Random House of Canada, 2004.

Roman, Espejo. *Does Capital Punishment Deter Crime?* Farmington Hills, MI: Gale Group, 2002.

Rothchild, Jonathan, et al. *Doing Justice to Mercy: Religion, Law, and Criminal Justice.* Charlottesville: University Press of Virginia, 2007.

Schabas, William. *The Abolition of the Death Penalty in International Law.* New York: Cambridge University Press, 1997.

Simon, Rita J. *A Comparative Analysis of Capital Punishment: Statutes, Policies, Frequencies and Public Attitudes the World Over.* Lanham, MD: Lexington Books, Rowman & Littlefield, 2002.

Sorell, Tom. *Moral Theory and Capital Punishment.* Oxford: Blackwell, 1988.

Stearman, Kaye. *The Death Penalty.* New York: Rosen Publishing Group, 2007.

Stefoff, Rebecca. *Furman v. Georgia: Debating the Death Penalty.* Tarrytown, NY: Marshall Cavendish Books, 2007.

Todd, Allan. *Crime, Punishment and Protest.* New York: Cambridge University Press, 2002.

Van Den Haag, Ernest, and John P. Conrad. *The Death Penalty: A Debate.* New York: Plenum, 1983.

Walker, Nigel. *Why Punish?* New York: Oxford University Press, 1991.

15

Environmental Ethics

In January 2007, 50 feet of Roger Middleton's sugar-beet farm fell into the North Sea. Middleton, who lives on the southeastern coast of England, has also lost 23 acres of potato field to the sea. In this and other sections of the world, coastal erosion is occurring in ways never before experienced. This process has greatly accelerated in recent years and is said to be one effect of global climate change produced by global warming.[1]

The Arctic ice cap is melting and may be gone by 2020, if not earlier. Since the 1970s, the melting has increased dramatically. Unlike Antarctica, the Arctic ice is only 10 feet thick, and there is no land underneath. This white ice reflects the sun, but as it melts, the dark blue water of the ocean absorbs the solar rays, warming the nearby air in a feedback effect. Moreover, the ice that covers Greenland, the biggest landmass of the Arctic region, has also been melting at an alarming rate and slipping into the sea. "It is shedding 11 cubic miles of ice per year." If this Arctic melting and similar melting and breaking of sections of the Antarctic ice shelves continues, one result will be a serious rise in the height of ocean waters around the world. Although scientists can't predict how much the ocean waters will rise, it could be as much as 20 feet, and low-lying coastal areas will be underwater. This may produce hundreds of millions of environmental refugees. In his slide show, which was made into the award-winning movie *An Inconvenient Truth,* and in the book of the same name, former Vice President Al Gore shows what would happen

to Florida, San Francisco Bay, Amsterdam, and Beijing, among other cities around the world. For example, "In Calcutta and Bangladesh, 60 million people would be displaced." A similar estimate is given by the May 4, 2007, report of the U.N.-sponsored Intergovernmental Panel on Climate Change that was meeting in Brussels. The panel is made up of scientists and government officials from more than one hundred countries.[2]

Other likely effects of the melting of the Arctic ice include changes in the patterns of ocean currents that have been stable for the last 10,000 years. The Gulf Stream, for example, pulls warm water north from near the equator and into the north Atlantic where some of it evaporates; as the water evaporates, the ocean becomes saltier and heavier and sinks, cooling and starting a return southern path and then eastward around the globe. This will create unpredictable weather changes.[3]

Unusual weather patterns also include increasing numbers of and strengths of hurricanes and tornados. Think, for example, of the 2004 hurricanes Katrina and Rita in the Gulf of Mexico and the flooding and destruction of vast sections of New Orleans. In 2005, there were twenty-seven hurricanes and tropical storms. The World Meteorological Organization ran out of letters of the alphabet with which to name them all.

We can see from just these few examples, and others later in this chapter, how our environment affects us and how changes such as global warming can have dramatic and disastrous effects.

But just what is meant by the term *environment* and how ought we to morally evaluate our actions and why?

THE ENVIRONMENT

Being clear about the terms we use in an ethical debate is one of the first things that can help us. We can start with the meaning of the term *environment.* It comes from *environs,* which means "in circuit" or "turning around in" in Old French.[4] From this comes the common meaning of environment as surroundings; note its spatial meaning as an area. However, we also have come to use the term to refer to what goes on in that space and to all of the climate and other factors that act on living organisms or individuals that inhabit the space. "The environment is what Nature becomes when we view it as a life-support system and as a collection of materials."[5] We can think of the system in a mechanistic fashion—that is, as a collection of materials with various physical and chemical interactions. Or we can think of it in a more organic way, giving attention to the many ways in which the individuals are interdependent in their very nature. From the latter viewpoint, we cannot even think of an individual as an isolated atomic thing, because its environment is a very part of itself. From this point of view, the environment stands in relation to the beings within it—not externally, but internally.

VALUE

You may have seen signs urging us to "Save the Earth." Although we literally cannot kill the planet, we can make it better or worse for us.[6] Most people realize the important effects that their environment has on them. Those things that produce benefit are good or of positive value, and those that cause harm are bad or of negative value. Most of the time it is a mixture of both. Growth is generally good, and poison is bad. But where does this goodness and badness, or positive or negative value, come from? Is it there in the poison or in growth? This is a considerably difficult metaphysical and moral problem. (Refer to the discussion of moral realism in Chapter 2.) Does a thing have value in the same sense that it has hair or weight? This does not seem to be so, because a thing's value does not seem to be something it possesses. When we value something, we have a positive response toward it. However, it may not quite be as some philosophers have said, that things have value only in so far as we do happen to respond positively to them—that is, prefer or desire them. Rather, we want to know whether we *should* value them or value them highly. Is there something about the things that we value, some attributes that they have, for example, that are the legitimate basis for our valuing them? Although we will not go further into a discussion of the nature and basis of value here, we can be aware of the problems involved in trying to give an account of it. We also should be aware that the notion of value and its basis plays a key role in discussions of environmental ethics, as we shall see.

One distinction about value plays a particularly significant role in environmental ethics: that between intrinsic and instrumental value. Things have *intrinsic value* or worth (sometimes referred to as *inherent* value) when they have value or worth in themselves for some reason. Pleasure, as we saw earlier in Chapter 4, is supposed to be intrinsically valuable: We value it for its own sake and not for what we can get or do with it. Something has *instrumental value* if it is valued because of its usefulness for some other purpose and for someone. Some environmentalists believe that trees, for example, have only instrumental and not intrinsic value. They think that trees are valuable because of their usefulness to us. Other environmentalists believe that plants and ecosystems have value in themselves in some sense, as we shall note later in this chapter.

Another term sometimes used in discussions in environmental ethics is *prima facie* value, which literally means "at first glance" or "at first sight." Something has prima facie value if it has the kind of value that can be overcome by other interests or values. For example, we might say that economic interests of one group are to be given weight and thus have prima facie value, but they may be overridden by stronger interests of another group or by greater values such as human health.

These considerations about the nature and kinds of value play a key role in judging ethical matters that relate to the environment. This is exemplified by two quite different perspectives in environmental ethics. One is *anthropocentrism,* and the other *ecocentrism* or *biocentrism.* We will consider each in turn here.

ANTHROPOCENTRISM

As you may know, the terms *anthropocentrism* and *anthropocentric* refer to a human-centered perspective. A perspective is anthropocentric if it holds that humans alone have *intrinsic worth* or value. According to this perspective, those things are good that promote the interests of human beings. Thus, for example, some people believe that animals are valuable simply in so far as they promote the interests of humans or are useful to us in one or more of a variety of ways. (More discussion of this is found in the following chapter on animal rights.) For example, animals provide emotional, aesthetic, nutritional, clothing, entertainment, and medical benefits for us. Those people who hold an anthropocentric view also may believe that it is bad to cause animals needless pain, but if this is necessary to ensure some important human good, then it is justified. Another example is the substance taxol, a synthesized chemical from the bark of the Pacific yew tree that has been found to be promising in the treatment of ovarian and breast cancers. Estuaries, grasslands, and ancient forests also purify our air and clean our water. Nature provides us with our food and shelter and clothing.

According to an anthropocentric perspective, the environment or nature has no value in itself. Its value is measured by how it affects human beings. Wilderness areas are instrumentally valuable to us as sources of recreation and relaxation and for providing some of our physical needs such as lumber for building. Sometimes, anthropocentric values conflict. For instance, we cannot both preserve the trees for their beauty or historical interest and yet also use them for lumber. Therefore, we need to think about the relative value of aesthetic experiences and historical appreciation as compared with cheaper housing and lumbering jobs. What is the value, for example, of being able to reflect on our history and our ancestors? Consider some 2,000-year-old trees. Touching one of these giants today is in some way touching the beginning of the common era. We can think of all of the great moments and events of history that have occurred in the life of this tree and thus appreciate the reality of the events and their connection with us. How would the value of this experience compare with other values? Cost–benefit analyses present one method for making such comparisons.

Cost–Benefit Analysis

Because many environmental issues involve diverse values and competing interests, we can use a technique known as *cost–benefit analysis* to help us think about what is best to do. (Refer to the discussion of this in Chapter 4.) If we have a choice between various actions or policies, then we need to assess and compare the various harms or costs and benefits that each entails in order to know which is the better policy. Using this method, we should choose the alternative that has the greater net balance of benefits over harms or costs. It is basically a utilitarian form of reasoning. If we clean up the smoke stacks, then emissions are reduced and acid rain and global warming are curtailed—important *benefits*. However, this also creates costs for the companies, their employees, and those who buy their products or use their services. We want to know whether the benefits will be worth those costs. We also need to assess the relative costs and benefits of other alternatives.

Involved in such analyses are two distinct elements. One is an *assessment*—that is, a determination or description of these factual matters as far as they can be known. What exactly are the likely effects of doing this or that? The other is *evaluation*, the establishment of relative values. In cost–benefit evaluations, the *value* is generally a function of the usefulness to, or effect on, humans. The usual use of cost–benefit analysis is in the overall context of anthropocentrism. Some things we find more useful or valuable to us than others. In addition, if we have a fixed amount of money or resources to expend on some environmental project, then we know that this money or these resources will not be available for work elsewhere or to buy other things. Thus, every expenditure will have a certain *opportunity cost.* In being willing to pay for the environmental project, we will have some sense of its importance in comparison with other things that we will not then be able to do or have. However, if we value something else just as much or more than a slight increase in cleaner air or water, for example, then we will not be willing to pay for the cleaner air or water.

In making such evaluations, we may know what monetary costs will be added to a particular forest product such as lumber if certain cutting were to be curtailed. However, we are less sure about how we should value the 2,000-year-old tree. How do we measure the historical appreciation or the aesthetic value of the tree or the animals that live in the tree? How do we measure the recreational value of the wilderness? What is beauty or a life worth? The value of these "intangibles" is difficult to measure because measuring implies that we use a standard measure of value. Only if we have such a standard can we compare, say, the value of a breathtaking view to that of a dam about to be built on the site. However, we do sometimes use monetary valuations, even of such intangibles as human lives or life years. For example, in insurance and other contexts, people attempt to give some measure of the value of a life.[7] Doing so is sometimes necessary, but it is obviously also problematic. (See Chapter 17 for further discussion of calculating the value of a life.)

Human Environmental Impact

Taking an anthropocentric instrumentalist point of view of the environment also means thinking about the various ways in which the environment affects us. Consider, for example, just the following four environmental problems: global warming, ozone depletion, waste disposal and pollution, and wilderness preservation.

Global Warming The great majority of scientists now agree that our modern industrial society has created a potentially deadly phenomenon known as the *greenhouse effect*. The phenomenon is caused by the burning of fossil fuels by many modern industries. The resulting gases—carbon dioxide, methane, fluorocarbons, nitrous oxide, among others—are released into the atmosphere.

Automobile exhaust contributes as well. When "we burn fossil fuels (oil, natural gas, and coal) in our homes, cars, factories, and power plants . . . we release CO_2 into the atmosphere." There these gases combine with water vapor and prevent the sun's infrared rays from radiating back into space. The trapped solar radiation thus contributes to increased air temperature. In this way, the gases function much as do the glass panes of a greenhouse. They will remain in the atmosphere for thirty to one hundred years, and their buildup will continue to increase over time. Deforestation also contributes to the warming because less carbon dioxide can be absorbed when vegetation has been removed.

Carbon dioxide accounts for 80 percent of greenhouse gas emissions. "Sixty percent of the methane currently in the atmosphere is produced by humans; it comes from landfills, livestock farming, fossil-fuel burning, wastewater treatment, and other industry." As of the beginning of 2007, the United States produced more greenhouse gases than any other country—30 percent—compared to 27.7 percent for all of Europe and 2.5 percent and 3.8 percent, respectively, for Africa and Central and South America. The annual amount of carbon emissions per person is higher in the United States—5.5 tons per person—compared to approximately 2.5 per person for Japan and Europe, respectively. In fact, with only 20 percent of the world's population, developed countries account for 60 percent of all carbon emissions. However, as it continues to grow its economy, China is catching up to the United States. In fact, by July 2007, China surpassed the United States in greenhouse gas emissions. The country is currently building one new coal-fired power plant per day, enough annually to "light all of Britain." Globally, overall emissions have risen approximately 70 percent since 1970 and are expected to rise another 90 percent by 2030 unless we take measures to reduce them.[8]

Although climate changes have occurred throughout the Earth's history, they have usually been gradual. However, this has not always been the case. Sixty-five million years ago, the dinosaurs are thought to have been wiped out by a dramatic and rapid change in climate caused by a giant meteorite that hit the Earth close to the Yucatan peninsula. The meteorite apparently put so much dust into the air "that sunlight was greatly reduced, temperatures plummeted, many plants didn't grow, and the food chain collapsed."[9] Within the time span of human existence, climate changes have occurred over several generations, allowing people to adapt. If these changes occur rapidly, however, such adaptation becomes more difficult. Food supplies, for example, could be severely stressed.[10] The reduced land fertility will also pose a threat to international security. If crop yields decrease and water shortages increase, those peoples and nations that are affected may resort to violence over the shortage of land and water sources. "More than two billion people already live in regions facing a scarcity of water" and soon "the amount of water needed for a rapidly growing population will double." Alternately, these people may migrate to urban slums and make such places even worse than they already are.[11]

How do we know that present day global warming is not just a part of a natural pattern? Scientists have determined that recent temperatures and the amount of carbon dioxide in the atmosphere increases are dramatically greater than anything in the past. Scientists have drilled deep into the ice and brought up cylinders of ice, ice cores, that have markings like that of tree rings. They can read the age of the sections and analyze the chemicals and air bubbles in them to determine the average temperature of each year and the carbon dioxide content. Samples as old as 600,000 years have been obtained, and from these samples scientists know that the temperature and greenhouse gases have increased dramatically in the past decades. From this they can also predict how these will continue to rise unless the emissions are controlled.[12]

Scientists still disagree, however, on how much the Earth will warm, how fast, and how different regions will be affected. Still, evidence is now accumulating for the acceleration of this effect in receding glaciers and in the spreading of plants and forests farther north and to higher altitudes. Some European butterfly species have moved their habitats from 20 to 150 miles north of their previous ranges, and British birds are laying their eggs earlier in the spring. More evidence of global warming has included the nearly complete melting of the glacier on Mount Kilimanjaro in central Africa, thawing of Arctic permafrost, increasing rain in some areas, and increasing drought in others. Again, Al Gore's book and movie provide dramatic pictures of the changes that are taking place elsewhere among the world's glaciers. Glacier National Park has now lost almost all of its glaciers and should probably be renamed. Similar scenes are shown for Perito Moreno Glacier in Patagonia, Argentina; the Columbia Glacier in Prince William Sound in Alaska; and glaciers in Peru, Switzerland, and Italy, among others around the world.[13]

Some people benefit from, but more are harmed by the phenomenon of global warming. However, those who are most responsible for the warming are the least likely to be harmed, and people in developing countries are most likely to be harmed. Moreover, the cost to future generations would also have to be considered.[14] How much we would be willing to pay to prevent the various possible negative effects on us will depend on how bad we consider these effects to be. Those who calculate the costs and benefits involved in this area also must be able to factor in the uncertainties that are involved.

What can be done about global warming? And is it too late? Scientists generally believe that we still have a little time; according to Jim Hansen at NASA, "we have until 2015 to reverse the flow of carbon into the atmosphere before we cross a threshold and create a different planet."[15]

Among the means of reducing greenhouse gases are better mileage standards for cars and better public transportation. Other methods include alternative sources of power such as wind, solar, and nuclear. Germany, for example, adds 2,000 windmills each year and now has almost 20,000. France generates three-quarters of its electricity by nuclear plants. And there are also alternative biofuels such as biodiesel from vegetable oil and gas with an ethanol additive derived from corn or sugar cane or cellulose. However, people are hesitant to invest in biorefineries until they are more certain that so-called flex-fuel vehicles will be available.[16]

Other people suggest the implementation of a carbon tax that would charge "anyone who burns fossil fuels for the problems that ensue." This tax could be used, for example, to reimburse home-owners for solar cells or energy-efficient appliances and research for ways to capture carbon dioxide. A small tax could yield some $50 billion for such purposes. Al Gore even proposes that such a tax be used in place of payroll taxes for Social Security and Medicare that is paid by both employers and employees.[17]

Ozone Depletion A second environmental problem about which we have been concerned for some time is *ozone depletion*. In the past twenty years, scientists have detected holes or breaks in the layer of ozone at the upper reaches of the stratosphere. This layer of ozone protects us from the damaging effects of excessive ultraviolet radiation from the sun, which can cause skin cancer and cataracts. The ozone layer holes are caused by chlorine-bearing pollutants such as the chlorofluorocarbons used in fire extinguishers and as refrigerants, cleaning agents, and spray propellants. Carbon dioxide, which causes the greenhouse effect and global warming, also has been found to contribute to ozone depletion.[18] Currently, the largest known hole is above Antarctica, where the ozone levels have declined by one-third in recent years. However, there are suspicions that it has migrated over Australia and led to increased biological abnormalities there. On certain days, Australian school children have been advised to stay inside. "Between 1996 and 2001, the ozone hole over the Antarctic reached more than 9 million square miles . . . roughly three times the size of the United States." Nearly all of the ozone over Antarctica has been destroyed, with the highest level of depletion occurring in October, the Antarctic spring. Lately, scientists have observed that the ozone hole has dwindled and even split into two sections, a phenomenon now puzzling scientists.[19] Scientists also had been predicting openings over areas in the northern hemisphere, where they have recently found a 9 percent to 14 percent decline in ozone

levels.[20] The effects are widespread. For example, fish in waters around Great Britain "are suffering sunburn and blisters caused by the thinning ozone layer," and such effects literally threaten the existence of some fish species.[21]

From a cost–benefit perspective, we need to ask whether the cost to us to decrease or eliminate the causes of ozone depletion is worth the savings in lives. Here again we come up against the issue of how to value human life. The greater its value, the more surely we ought to stop using these chemicals, and the harder we ought to work to find alternatives.

Waste Disposal and Pollution A third area of environmental impact on us is *waste disposal and pollution*. No one wants the city dump located next to them, yet the tons of garbage that we produce each year must be put somewhere. Industrial waste is washed into our rivers and lakes and blown into our air. It is estimated that one person per hour dies prematurely in California because of air pollution.[22]

Currently, the United States "has almost 9,000 curbside pickup programs for garbage and recyclables." However there is still more trash going into dumps and landfills because we are consuming more and throwing away more. Americans produce 236 million tons of garbage in a year. Only about 30 percent of this is recycled or composted. Packaging makes up about a third of an average city's trash. Recycled bottles and cans can be turned into reusable metal and glass as well as roads, bike parts, and carpets.[23] In fact, recycling one aluminum can saves enough electricity to run a TV for three hours.[24]

So-called e-waste is also becoming a major problem. This includes outdated cell phones, computers, TVs, and printers. Approximately 50 million tons of this waste is discarded globally per year. Such items contain huge amounts of toxins, "including beryllium in computer motherboards, cadmium in semiconductors, chromium in floppy disks, lead in batteries and computer monitors, and mercury in alkaline batteries and fluorescent lamps." One good sign of progress in dealing with the problem is that environmental groups have persuaded several technology companies, including "Hewlett-Packard, Dell, LG Electronics, Samsung, Sony, Sony Ericsson and Nokia to eliminate most hazardous materials from their products." This is also a particular problem in developing countries such as India. It is estimated that the United States sends approximately 75 percent to 80 percent of its older e-machines to India and China because their recycling costs are less than here.[25]

Recycling, in fact, is tackling a wide variety of problems related to waste disposal and pollution. For example, "a team of chemical engineers has taken the first step to turning plant wastes"—or other forms of biomass such as decaying plant and animal matter—"into Earth-friendly hydrogen fuel that one day could keep the lights burning and engines running without depleting diminishing reservoirs of precious natural resources."[26] Recycling programs aim to reduce the amount of aluminum, glass, paper, and plastics that we throw away each year. Again, we need to determine the economic value of health and life to determine what we ought to pay to eliminate or lessen the risks from these sources.

Wilderness Preservation A fourth environmental issue that concerns us is *wilderness preservation.* The United States now has 671 federally designated wilderness areas, but these are being encroached on by mining, mineral leasing, and road building, among other enterprises.[27] The National Forest Service has responsibility for almost 200 million acres of land and the management of more than 150 national forests. Of the 385 units in the U.S. National Park system, among the ten most endangered are Big Bend National Park, Everglades National Park, Glacier National Park, and the Great Smoky Mountains National Park. Almost 10 million people visit this last park annually. Unfortunately, it is currently "enveloped in polluted air and still lacking the operating funds needed to protect it."[28]

Recovering natural gas, oil, and other forms of energy from roadless areas in national forests is a hotly argued topic. On one side of the argument are those who say such efforts will reduce U.S. reliance on foreign energy resources. On the other side are those who argue that such resource extractions would make a minimal contribution, meeting U.S. oil and gas needs for only fifteen days and nine to eleven weeks, respectively.[29]

Forests and wilderness areas are valuable for many reasons. One-fourth of today's medicines, for example, had their origins in rain forests. Forests provide habitats for wildlife, including threatened species. They provide us with leisure and relaxation and with many possibilities for recreational opportunities such as white-water rafting, boating, fishing, hiking, and skiing. They also provide aesthetic and religious experiences and simple communing with the wider world of nature.

International Environmental Conventions Because of widespread concerns about these environmental issues, many meetings and conventions have been held over the past two decades. One example is an Earth Summit, the U.N. Conference on Environment and Development, which was held in Rio de Janeiro, Brazil, in 1992. Its two themes symbolized the interrelation between environmental issues and sustainable development. Some 2,400 representatives from nongovernmental organizations and 17,000 people overall attended the summit. At its conclusion, the conference issued a general *Report of the United Nations Conference on Environment and Development,* Agenda 21, the Rio Declaration, the Framework Convention on Climate Change, a Convention on Biological Diversity, and a Statement of Forest Principles. The Framework on Climate Change, for example, went into force in March 1994 and had as its primary objective "stabilization of greenhouse gas concentrations in the atmosphere." The United States, along with many other nations, signed this agreement. The Kyoto Protocol is the principal update to this agreement. It was negotiated in Kyoto, Japan, in 1997. Although the United States helped develop this agreement, Congress refused to pass it and President George W. Bush pulled out of the agreement when he took office in 2001, holding that it was flawed and would hurt the U.S. economy. It was ratified eventually by 141 other nations, including Russia, and took effect on February 16, 2005. Key provisions included mandatory restrictions on greenhouse gas emissions to "at least 5 percent below levels measured in 1990" by the year 2012.[30] The protocol also allowed the thirty-five industrialized countries that were covered by it to "earn credits toward their treaty targets by investing in emissions cleanups outside their borders," a so-called cap-and-trade system.[31] Developing countries such as India and China were exempt from the controls so as to give them a better chance to catch up economically with the more developed nations. Although the United States alone among industrialized nations has refused to sign this accord, it accounts for some 36 percent of greenhouse gas emissions; still, U.S. businesses that are international in scope will be subject to the protocol's requirements. Moreover, the United States has made known that it would be willing to return to the elements in the original 1994 agreement as a basis for continuing discussions.

Kyoto was chosen for the signing of the treaty in 1997 because of Japan's deep cultural conservation roots with "its disapproval of waste and excess." However, today many Japanese youth are Americanizing and showing preferences for big gas-guzzling cars and high levels of consumption. The Kyoto Protocol has not quite worked as hoped because countries have not met their goals. Even though the United States never ratified the treaty, many U.S. cities have nonetheless adopted it. Developing countries were not covered, although China, for example, has now become an emissions titan. Under the treaty, the United States was supposed to reduce its emissions 7 percent below 1990 levels by 2012. But by 2004, U.S. emission levels were already 16 percent higher. In 2004, Greece's emissions were 19 percent higher than their target, and Spain is not even close to its target. Only Great Britain and Sweden will likely reach their targets by 2012.[32]

In 2002, another world summit on sustainable development was held in Johannesburg, South Africa. One of the promising developments at this summit was the publication of various joint efforts between nongovernmental organizations concerned about the environment and private industry. For example, Greenpeace has joined forces with British Petroleum to improve environmental aspects of oil drilling, and the World Wildlife Fund has teamed up with the World Bank and Amazon River basin nations to protect that valuable environment.[33]

What is the extent of our obligation to preserve these forests and wilderness areas, especially in light of the fact that the preservation often has a negative effect on other human interests such as the ability of many people to make a living?

ECOCENTRISM

According to the anthropocentric perspective, environmental concerns ought to be directed to the betterment of people, who alone have intrinsic value. In contrast with this view is one that is generally called an *ecocentric* (or *biocentric*) perspective. It holds that it is not just humans that have intrinsic worth or value. There are variations within this perspective, with some theorists holding that individual life forms have such intrinsic worth and others stressing that it is whole systems or ecosystems that have such value. The ethical questions then become matters of determining what is in the best interests of these life forms or what furthers or contributes to, or is a satisfactory fit with, some ecosystem.

Ecocentrists are critical of anthropocentrists. Why, they ask, do only humans have intrinsic value and everything else only use value? Some fault the Judeo-Christian tradition for this view. In particular, they single out the biblical mandate to "subdue" the Earth and "have dominion over the fish of the sea and over the birds of the air and every living thing that moves upon the Earth" as being responsible for this instrumentalist view of nature and other living things.[34] Others argue that anthropocentrism is reductionistic. All of nature, according to this view, is reduced to the level of "thinghood." The seventeenth-century French philosopher René Descartes is sometimes cited as a source of this reductionist point of view because of his belief that the essential element of humanity is the ability to think ("I think, therefore I am," etc.) and his belief that animals are mere machines.[35] Evolutionary accounts also depict humans at the pinnacle of evolution or the highest or last link in some great chain of being. We can ask ourselves whether we place too high a value on human beings and their powers of reason and intelligence. "Knowledge is power" is a modern notion. One source of this view was *The New Organon* by the early modern philosopher Francis Bacon.[36] Ecocentrists criticize the view that we ought to seek to understand nature so that we can have power over it because it implies that our primary relation to nature is one of domination.

Ecocentrists hold that we ought rather to regard nature with admiration and respect, because of their view that nature and natural beings have intrinsic value. Let us return to our example of the 2,000-year-old trees. You may have seen or viewed pictures of trees large enough for tunnels to be cut through which cars can be driven. In the 1880s, such a tunnel was cut through one such tree, a giant sequoia, near Wawona on the south end of what is now Yosemite National Park. Tourists enjoyed driving through the tunnel. However, some people claimed that this was a mutilation of and an insult to this majestic tree. They claimed that the tree itself had a kind of integrity, intrinsic value, and dignity that should not be invaded lightly. Another way to put it would be to say that the tree itself had moral standing.[37] What we do to the tree itself matters morally, they insisted.

On what account could trees be thought to have this kind of moral standing? All organisms, it might be argued, are self-maintaining systems:

They grow and are irritable in response to stimuli. They reproduce. . . . They resist dying. They post a careful if also semipermeable boundary between themselves and the rest of nature; they assimilate environmental materials to their own needs. They gain and maintain internal order against the disordering tendencies of external nature. They keep winding up, recomposing themselves, while inanimate things run down, erode, and decompose.[38]

Because they are organized systems or integrated living wholes, they are thought to have intrinsic value and even moral standing. The value may be only *prima facie,* but nevertheless they have their own value in themselves and are not just to be valued in terms of their usefulness to people. According to this perspective, the giant sequoias of Wawona should not just be thought of in terms of their tourist value. There are things that can be good and bad for the trees themselves. The tunnel in the Wawona tree, for example, eventually weakened the tree, and it fell over in a snowstorm in 1968. Although trees are not *moral agents* who act responsibly for reasons, according to this general view they can still be thought of as moral patients. A *moral patient* is any being for which what we do to it matters in itself. A moral patient is any being toward whom we can have *direct duties* rather than simply *indirect duties.* We ought to behave in a certain way toward the tree for its sake and not just indirectly for the sake of how it will eventually affect us. There are things that are in the best interests of trees, even if they take no conscious interest in them. (See further discussion of this in the treatment of "rights" in the following chapter.)

In addition to those ecocentrists who argue that all life forms have intrinsic value are others who stress the value of ecosystems. An *ecosystem* is a whole of interacting and interdependent parts within a circumscribed locale. "Ecosystems are a continuum of variation, a patchy mosaic with fuzzy edges. Some interactions are persistent, others occasional."[39] They are loosely structured wholes. The boundary changes and some members come and go. Sometimes there is competition within the whole. Sometimes there is symbiosis. The need to survive pushes various creatures to be creative in their struggle for an adaptive fit. There is a unity to the whole, but it is loose and decentralized. Why is this unity to be thought of as having value in itself? One answer is provided by Aldo Leopold. In the 1940s, he wrote in his famous essay "The Land Ethic" that we should think about the land as "a fountain of energy flowing through a circuit of soils, plants, and animals."[40] Look at any section of life on our planet and you will find a system of life, intricately interwoven and interdependent elements that function as a whole. It forms a *biotic pyramid* with myriad smaller organisms at the bottom and gradually fewer and more complex organisms at the top. Plants depend on the Earth, insects depend on the plants, and other animals depend on the insects. Leopold did not think it amiss to speak about the whole system as being healthy and unhealthy. If the soil is washed away or abnormally flooded, then the whole system suffers or is sick. In this system, individual organisms feed off one another. Some elements come and others go. It is the whole that continues. Leopold also believed that a particular type of ethics follows from this view of nature—a biocentric or ecocentric ethics. He believed that "a thing is right when it tends to preserve the integrity, stability, and beauty of the biotic community. It is wrong when it tends to do otherwise."[41] The system has a certain *integrity* because it is a unity of interdependent elements that combine to make a whole with a unique character. It has a certain *stability,* not in that it does not change, but that it changes only gradually. Finally, it has a particular *beauty.* Here beauty is a matter of harmony, well-ordered form, or unity in diversity.[42] When envisioned on a larger scale, the entire Earth system may then be regarded as one system with a certain integrity, stability, and beauty. Morality becomes a matter of preserving this system or doing only what befits it.

The kind of regard for nature that is manifest in biocentric views is not limited to contemporary philosophers. *Native American* views on nature provide a fertile source of biocentric thinking. For example, Eagle Man, an Oglala Sioux writer, speaks of the unity of all living things. All come from tiny seeds and so all are brothers and sisters. The seeds come from Mother Earth and depend on her for sustenance. We owe her respect for she comes from the "Great Spirit Above."[43] Also certain forms of *romanticism* have long regarded nature in a different way than that found in dominant Western perspectives. Such were the views of transcendentalists Ralph Waldo Emerson and Henry Thoreau. *Transcendentalism* was a movement of romantic idealism that arose in the United States in the mid-nineteenth century. Rather than regarding nature as foreign or alien, Emerson and Thoreau thought of it as a friend or kindred spirit. In fact, nature for them symbolized spirit. Thus, a rock is a sign of endurance and a snake of cunning. The rock and the snake can symbolize spirit because nature itself is full of spirit. As a result of this viewpoint, Thoreau went to Walden Pond to live life to its fullest and commune with nature. He wanted to know its moods and all its phenomena. Although he and Emerson read the lessons of nature, they also read their Eastern texts. Some have characterized aspects of their nature theory as *idealism,* the view that all is ideas or spirit; or as *pantheism,* the doctrine that holds that all is God.

John Muir, the prophet of Yosemite and founder of the Sierra Club, once urged Emerson to spend more time with him. He wrote to Emerson:

> I invite you to join me in a month's worship with Nature in the high temples of the great Sierra Crown beyond our holy Yosemite. It will cost you nothing save the time and very little of that for you will be mostly in eternity. . . . In the name of a hundred cascades that barbarous visitors never see . . . in the name of all the rocks and of this whole spiritual atmosphere.[44]

Such romantic idealistic views provide a stark contrast to anthropocentric views of a reductionist type. However, they also raise many questions. For example, we can ask the transcendentalist how nature can be spirit or god in more than a metaphorical sense. And we can ask followers of Aldo Leopold the following question: Why is the way things are or have become good? Nature can be cruel, at least from the point of view of certain animals and even from our own viewpoint as we suffer the damaging results of typhoons or volcanic eruptions. And, more abstractly, on what basis can we argue that whatever exists is good?

DEEP ECOLOGY

Another variation within ecocentrism is the deep ecology movement. Members of this movement wish to distinguish themselves from establishment environmentalism, which they call "shallow ecology" and which is basically anthropomorphic. The term *deep ecology* was first used by Arne Naess, a Norwegian philosopher and environmentalist.[45] Deep ecologists take a holistic view of nature and believe that we should look more deeply to find the *root causes* of environmental degradation. The idea is that our environmental problems are deeply rooted in the Western psyche, and radical changes of viewpoint are necessary if we are to solve them. Western *reductionism, individualism,* and *consumerism* are said to be the causes of our environmental problems. The solution is to rethink and reformulate certain metaphysical beliefs about whether all reality is reducible to atoms in motion. It is also to rethink what it is to be an individual. Are individual beings as so many separate independent beings? Or are they interrelated parts of a whole? According to those who hold this perspective, solving our environmental problems also requires a change in our views about what is a good quality of life. The good life, they assert, is not one that stresses the possession of things and the search for satisfaction of wants and desires.

In addition to describing the radical changes in our basic outlook on life that we need to make, the deep ecologist platform also holds that any intrusion into nature to change it requires justification. If we intervene to change nature, then we must show that a vital need of ours is at stake.[46] We should not intervene lightly not only because we are not sure of the results of our action, which will be possibly far-reaching and harmful, but also because nature *as it is* is regarded as good and right and well balanced. This platform also includes the belief that the flourishing of nonhuman life requires a "substantial decrease in the human population."[47] In a more recent collection of writings on deep ecology, George Sessions argues that the Earth's wild ecosystems have intrinsic value and a right to exist on their own, as well as instrumental value for our own well being. He argues that "humanity must drastically scale down its industrial activities on Earth, change its consumption lifestyles, stabilize" and "reduce the size of the human population by humane means."[48] The members of the deep ecology movement have been quite politically active. Their creed contains the belief that people are responsible for the Earth. Beliefs such as this often provide a basis for the tactics of groups such as Earth First! Its tactics have included various forms of "ecosabotage"—for example, spiking trees to prevent logging and cutting power lines.[49]

Both the tactics and the views that underlie them have been criticized. The tactics have been labeled by some as "ecoterrorism."[50] The view that all incursions into nature can be justified only by our vital needs seems to run counter to our intuitions, for the implication is that we must not build the golf course or the house patio because these would change the Earth and vegetation, and the need to play golf or sit on a patio are hardly vital. Others might have difficulty with the implication that nature and other natural things have as much value as people and thus people's interests should not take precedence over the good of nature. The view that nature itself has a "good of its own" or that the whole system has value in itself is also problematic for many people. However, at the least, deep ecologists have provided a valuable service by calling our attention to the possible deep philosophical roots and causes of some of our environmental problems.

ECOFEMINISM

A new variant of ecological ethics put forth some twenty years ago by some feminists is called *ecofeminism* or *ecological feminism*.[51] It may be seen as part of a broader movement that locates the source of environmental problems not in metaphysical or worldviews, as deep ecologists do, but in social practices. *Social ecology*, as this wider movement is called, holds that we should look to particular social patterns and structures to discover what is wrong with our relationship to the environment. Ecofeminists believe that the problem lies in a male-centered view of nature—that is, one of human domination over nature. According to Karen Warren, ecofeminism is "the position that there are important connections . . . between the domination of women and the domination of nature, an understanding of which is crucial to both feminism and environmental ethics."[52] Note here that deep ecologists and ecofeminists do not generally get along well with one another. The deep ecologists criticize ecofeminists for concentrating insufficiently on the environment, and ecofeminists accuse deep ecologists of the very male-centered view that they believe is the source of our environmental problems.[53] However, a variety of ecofeminist views are espoused by diverse groups of feminists.[54]

One version acknowledges the ways in which women differ from men and rejoices in it. This view is espoused by those who hold that because of their female experience or nature women tend to value relationships and the concrete individual. They stress caring and emotion, and they seek to replace conflict and assertion of rights with cooperation and community. These are traits that can and should carry over into our relationship to nature, they believe. Rather than use nature in an instrumentalist fashion, they urge, we should cooperate with nature. We should manifest a caring and benevolent regard for nature just as for other human beings. One version of this view would have us think of nature itself as in some way divine. Rather than think of God as a distant creator who transcends nature, these religiously oriented ecofeminists think of God as a being within nature. Some also refer to this god as Mother Nature or Gaia, after the name of the Greek goddess.[55]

Another version of ecofeminism rejects the dualism that its adherents find in the above position. They hold that this position promotes the devaluing and domination of both women and nature. Rather than divide reality into contrasting elements—the active and passive, the rational and emotional, the dominant and subservient—they encourage us to recognize the diversity within nature and among people. They would similarly support a variety of ways of relating to nature. Thus, they believe that even though science that proceeds from a male orientation of control over nature has made advances and continues to do so, its very orientation misses important aspects of nature. If instead we also have a feeling for nature and a listening attitude, then we might be able better to know what actually is there. They also believe that we humans should see ourselves as part of the community of nature, not as distinct nonnatural beings functioning in a world that is thought to be alien to us.

It is sometimes difficult to know just what, in particular, are the practical upshots of ecocentrism, ecological feminism, and deep ecology. Yet the following sentiment is indicative of a view that might make a difference: "In behalf of the tiny beings that are yet to arrive on Earth, but whose genes are here now, let's try a little CPR for the Earth—conservation, protection and restoration. And a little tender loving care for the only bit of the universe we know to be blessed with life."[56]

As noted above, some anthropocentrists contend that they also believe in a wise use of nature, one that does not destroy the very nature that we value and on which we depend. On the other hand, it may well be that if we care for and about nature, then our treatment of it will be better in some important ways.

SUSTAINABLE DEVELOPMENT

The preservation of the environment is also a global issue. Although many problems are specific to certain areas of the world, others are shared in common. When we think of the developing world, for example, we find that attention to the environment is not the first concern. Many people who work for the development of poor nations even view the environmentalist movement as an example of Western elitism.[57] For example, only such environmental elitists, they suggest, can afford to preserve unchanged an environment or wilderness that the poor need to use and change in order to survive. Yet others see the two concerns, development and environment, as closely intertwined and capable of moving forward together. What is needed, they say, is not development that ignores environmental concerns, but "sustainable development." For example, James Gustave Speth, president of World Resources Institute, writes, "It is . . . clear that development and economic reforms will have no lasting success unless they are suffused with concern for ecological stability and wise management of resources."[58] The idea is that if the forests in an area are depleted or the land is ruined by unwise or short-sighted overuse, then the people living there will not have what they need to continue to develop; that is, development will not be sustainable. We can learn about the disastrous consequences of environmental degradation and unsustainable development from "collapsed" or failed societies such as that on Easter Island and the Maya in the Yucatan.[59] However, poverty also causes environmental problems as people destroy forests for fuel, for example. Pricing policies as well as weak agrarian reforms and mismanagement and intergroup conflict are among the other factors that contribute to "the vicious downward spiral of poverty and environmental degradation. The poor have been exploited, shifted, and marginalized to the extent that they often have no choice but to participate in the denigration of resources, with full knowledge that they are mortgaging their own future."[60] Sustainable development also is connected with issues of biodiversity. For example, the introduction of technological advances into developing nations can reduce the variety of plants that local cultures independently manage for their own development. External and centralized control of what is planted and of the seeds used may sometimes work against rather than for development.[61] On a positive note, Jessica Tuchman Mathews suggests that we can have development without environmental destruction, but we need to "change the means of production, developing technologies that will enable us to meet human needs without destroying the [E]arth."[62]

NOTES

1. Elizabeth Rosenthal, "As the Climate Changes, Bits of England's Coast Crumble," *The New York Times,* May 4, 2007, p. A4.
2. Al Gore, *An Inconvenient Truth* (New York: Rodale, 2006): 194–209; Andrew Revkin, "Climate Panel Reaches Consensus on the Need to Reduce Harmful Emissions," *The New York Times,* May 4, 2007, p. A6; Tim Appenzeller, "The Big Thaw," *National Geographic,* June 2007.
3. Gore, op. cit., pp. 148–151.
4. Ernest Weekley, *An Etymological Dictionary of Modern English* (New York: Dover, 1967): 516, 518.
5. Mark Sagoff, "Population, Nature, and the Environment," *Report from the Institute for Philosophy and Public Policy, 13,* no. 4 (Fall 1993): 10.
6. "How to Save the Earth," *Time Magazine,* Special Report (Aug. 26, 2002): A1–A62.
7. Safety regulation needs to make use of such monetary equivalencies, for how else do we decide how safe is safe enough? There is no such thing as perfect safety, for that would mean no risk. Thus, we end up judging that we ought to pay so much to make things just so much safer but no more. The implication is that the increased life years or value of the lives to be saved by stricter regulation is of so much but no more than this much value. See Barbara MacKinnon, "Pricing Human Life," *Science, Technology and Human Values* (Spring 1986): 29–39.
8. Andrew C. Revkin, "Climate Panel Reaches Consensus on the Need to Reduce Harmful Emissions," *The New York Times,* May 4, 2007, p. A4; Jane Kay, "Report Predicts Climate Calamity," *The New York Times,* May 9, 2007, pp. C1, C5; David Perlman, "Increase in Carbon Emissions Seen Tripling Since '90s," *San Francisco Chronicle,* May 22, 2007, p. A3; Gore, op. cit., p. 253; Robert Collier, "Warming Strikes a Note in China," *San Francisco Chronicle,* July 8, 2007, p. A4.
9. See www.unfccc.int/essential_background/items/2877.php.
10. Kendrick Taylor, "Rapid Climate Change," *American Scientist, 87* (July–Aug. 1999): 320–327.
11. Thomas Homer-Dixon, "Terror in the Weather Forecast," *The New York Times,* April 24, 2007, p. A25; Celia W. Dugger, "Need for Water Could Double in 50 Years, U.N. Study Finds," *The New York Times,* Aug. 22, 2006, p. A12; Jane Kay, "Report Predicts Climate Calamity," *San Francisco Chronicle,* May 7, 2007, p. A1.
12. Gore, op. cit., pp. 60–67.
13. Ibid., pp. 42–59; Appenzeller, p. 60.
14. Bob Herbert, "Rising Tides," *The New York Times,* Feb. 22, 2001, p. A29.
15. Bill McKibben, "How Close to Catastrophe?" *The New York Review of Books,* Nov. 16, 2006, pp. 23–25.
16. Jim Suhr, "Ethanol Enjoying a Booming Renaissance," *San Francisco Chronicle,* May 6, 2007, p. D4; Bill McKibben, "How Close to Catastrophe?" *The New York Review of Books,* Nov. 16, 2006, pp. 23–25.
17. Michael Riordan, "Time for a Carbon Tax?" *San Francisco Chronicle,* March 23, 2007, p. B11.
18. Taylor, "Rapid Climate Change," *Science* (Nov. 24, 1992): B8.
19. By September 2002, the hole seemed to have shrunk to approximately 6 million square miles. Richard Stenger, "Antarctic Ozone Hole Splits in Two," *CNN Report,* Oct. 1, 2002 (see www.cnn.com/2002/TECH/space/09/30/ozone.holes/).
20. *Science* (April 23, 1993): 490–491.
21. "Study: Fish Suffer Ozone Hole Sunburn," *San Francisco Sunday Examiner and Chronicle,* Nov. 12, 2000, p. A20.
22. *Cal Pirg, 13,* no. 2 (Summer 1997): 1.
23. *Sierra Club Magazine,* Nov.–Dec. 2005, pp. 42–47.
24. The History Channel, *Modern Marvels,* April 25, 2007.
25. Anuj Chopra, "Developing Countries Are Awash in E-Waste," *San Francisco Chronicle,* March 30, 2007, pp. A1, A19.

26. "Chemists Try to Turn Plant Waste to Fuel," *Chemical Online,* Aug. 28, 2002 (www.chemicalonline.com/content/news/article.asp/).

27. Joseph R. des Jardins, *Environmental Ethics* (Belmont, CA: Wadsworth, 1993): 48.

28. "Ten Most Endangered," National Parks Conservation Association (www.npca.org/across_the_nation/ten_most_endangered/).

29. Pete Morton, Chris Weller, and Janice Thomson, "Energy and Western Wildlands, A GIS Analysis of Economically Recoverable Oil and Gas," *Newsroom, The Wilderness Society Special Report* (www.wilderness.org/newsroom/report_energy 101402.htm).

30. Larry Rohter and Andrew C. Revkin, "Cheers, and Concern, for New Climate Pact," *The New York Times,* Dec. 13, 2004, p. A6.

31. Ibid.

32. Joe Nation, "Coordinate Carbon Trading Markets," *San Francisco Chronicle,* March 23, 2007, p. B11; Robert Collier, "Japan Hot and Cold on Warming," *San Francisco Chronicle,* April 16, 2006, pp. A1, A8.

33. Andrew C. Revkin, "Small World After All: At Summit, Ecologists and Corporations Unite in Opposition to Global Warming," *The New York Times,* Sept. 5, 2002, p. A8.

34. Genesis 1: 26–29. Others will cite St. Francis of Assisi as an example of the Christian with a respectful regard for nature.

35. René Descartes, *Meditations on First Philosophy.* However, it might be pointed out that for Descartes this was not so much a metaphysical point as an epistemological one; that is, he was concerned with finding some sure starting point for knowledge and found at least that he was sure that he was thinking even when he was doubting the existence of everything else.

36. Francis Bacon, *Novum Organum,* Thomas Fowler (Ed.) (Oxford, 1889).

37. See Christopher Stone, *Do Trees Have Standing? Toward Legal Rights for Natural Objects* (Los Altos, CA: William Kaufmann, 1974).

38. Holmes Rolston III, *Environmental Ethics: Duties to and Values in the Natural World* (Philadelphia: Temple University Press, 1988): 97.

39. Ibid., 169.

40. Aldo Leopold, "The Land Ethic," in *Sand County Almanac* (New York: Oxford University Press, 1949).

41. Ibid., 262.

42. See John Hospers, *Understanding the Arts* (Englewood Cliffs, NJ: Prentice Hall, 1982).

43. Eagle Man, "We are All Related," from Ed McGaa, *Mother Earth Spirituality: Native American Paths to Healing Ourselves and Our World* (San Francisco: Harper & Row, 1990): 203–209.

44. Quoted in the *San Francisco Examiner,* May 1, 1988, p. E5.

45. Arne Naess, *Ecology, Community, and Lifestyle,* David Rothenberg (Trans.) (Cambridge, UK: Cambridge University Press, 1989).

46. Paul Taylor, *Respect for Nature* (Princeton, NJ: Princeton University Press, 1986).

47. Naess, *Ecology, Community, and Lifestyle,* op. cit.

48. George Sessions (Ed.), *Deep Ecology for the 21st Century: Readings on the Philosophy and Practice of the New Environmentalism* (Boston: Shambhala Publications, 1995), xxi.

49. On the tactics of ecosabotage, see Bill Devall, *Simple in Means, Rich in Ends: Practicing Deep Ecology* (Layton, UT: Gibbs Smith, 1988).

50. See Michael Martin, "Ecosabotage and Civil Disobedience," *Environmental Ethics, 12* (Winter 1990): 291–310.

51. According to Joseph des Jardins, the term *ecofeminism* was first used by Françoise d'Eaubonne in 1974 in her work *Le Feminisme ou la Mort* (Paris: Pierre Horay, 1974). See des Jardins, *Environmental Ethics,* op. cit., 249.

52. Karen J. Warren, "The Power and Promise of Ecological Feminism," *Environmental Ethics, 9* (Spring 1987): 3–20.

53. I thank an anonymous reviewer for this point.

54. See the distinctions made by Allison Jaggar between liberal (egalitarian) feminism, Marxist feminism, socialist feminism, and radical feminism. *Feminist Politics and Human Nature* (Totowa, NJ: Rowman & Allanheld, 1983).

55. See Carol Christ, *Laughter of Aphrodite: Reflections on a Journey to the Goddess* (San Francisco: Harper & Row, 1987).

56. David R. Brower, "Step Up the Battle on Earth's Behalf," *San Francisco Chronicle,* Aug. 18, 1993, p. A15.

57. See Ramachandra Guha, "Radical American Environmentalism and Wilderness Preservation: A Third World Critique," in *Environmental Ethics, 11* (Spring 1989): 71–83.

58. James Gustave Speth, "Resources and Security: Perspectives from the Global 2000 Report," *World Future Society Bulletin* (1981): 1–4.

59. Jared Diamond, *Collapse* (New York: Viking Press, 2005).

60. R. Paul Shaw, World Bank official, as quoted in Mark Sagoff, "Population, Nature, and the Environment," *Report from the Institute for Philosophy and Public Policy, 13,* no. 4 (Fall 1993): 8.

61. See Vandana Shiva, "Biotechnological Development and the Conservation of Biodiversity," in *Biopolitics: A Feminist and Ecological Reader on Biotechnology,* Vandana Shiva and Ingunn Moser (Eds.) (London: Zed Books, 1995): 193–213.

62. As quoted in Sagoff, "Population," 9; from Jessica Tuchman Mathews, "Redefining Security," *Foreign Affairs* (Spring 1989).

REVIEW EXERCISES

1. What is meant by the term *environment?*
2. Why is the notion of *value* problematic?
3. What are the differences among intrinsic, instrumental, and prima facie values? Give an example of each.
4. What is anthropocentrism? How is it different from ecocentrism?
5. How do cost–benefit analyses function in environmental arguments? Give an example of an environmental problem today and how a cost–benefit analysis would be used to analyze it.
6. Describe two different types of ecocentrism.
7. What is Aldo Leopold's basic principle for determining what is right and wrong in environmental matters?
8. What is deep ecology? According to this view, what are the root causes of our environmental problems?
9. Summarize the different ecofeminist views described in this chapter.
10. What is "sustainable development" and why do developmentalists support it?

DISCUSSION CASES

1. The Greenhouse Effect. People disagree about the greenhouse effect. A minority believes that no actual warming trend has or will occur because of the release of greenhouse gases into the atmosphere. Others point out that there have been periods of warming and cooling throughout the Earth's history. Several bills are pending before the U.S. Congress that will restrict the amount of greenhouse gases that may be released into the atmosphere. Such legislation, if passed, would affect car manufacturers, coal-burning manufacturing plants, and the makers of aerosol sprays, cleaning solvents, and refrigerators.

As a member of Congress, would you vote for or against the bills? Why?

2. Preserving the Trees. XYZ Timber Company has been logging forests in the Pacific Northwest for decades. It has done moderately well in replanting where trees have been cut, but it has been cutting in areas where some trees are hundreds of years old. Now the company plans to build roads into a similar area of the forest and cut down similar groups of trees. An environmental group, "Trees First," is determined to prevent this. Its members have blocked the roads that have been put in by the timber company and also engaged in the practice known as *tree spiking.* In this practice, iron spikes are driven into trees to discourage the use of power saws. Loggers are outraged, because this makes cutting in such areas extremely dangerous. When their saws hit these spikes, they become uncontrollable, and loggers have been seriously injured. Forest rangers have been marking trees found to be spiked and noted that some spikes are in so far that they are not visible. They will be grown over and thus present a hidden danger for years to come. People from Trees First insist that this is the only way to prevent the shortsighted destruction of the forests.

Who is right? Why?

3. Asphalt Yard. Bill Homeowner has grown weary of keeping the vegetation on his property under control. Thus, he decides to simply pave over the whole of it.

Even if Bill had a legal right to do this to his property, would there be anything ethically objectionable about it? Why or why not?

4. Sustainable Development. What would you say to the people of the Amazon River basin region who burn the forest so that they can have land to farm to make a living for themselves and their families? The burning and the deforestation have negative worldwide effects. The people point out that North Americans already have destroyed much of their own forests and become prosperous, so is it fair that we now criticize them? We even may be contributing to the loss of the rain forest because we buy mahogany furniture that comes from trees grown there. What should be done?

YOU MAKE THE DECISION

Apply the theories and issues discussed in this chapter by accessing this animated simulation on the Ethics Resource Center.

Use the passkey that accompanies your book to gain access. If you do not have a passkey, visit cengage brain.com to purchase instant access to additional study material.

So who gets the land? Sylvia, or Bill?

Ethics Module 15 : Environmental Ethics

Selected Bibliography

Armstrong, Susan J., and Richard G. Botzler (Eds.). *Environmental Ethics.* New York: McGraw-Hill, 1993.

Attfield, Robin, and Andrew Belsey (Eds.). *Philosophy and the Natural Environment.* New York: Cambridge University Press, 1994.

Benson, John. *Environmental Ethics: An Introduction with Readings.* New York: Routledge, 2000.

Bigwood, Carol. *Earth Muse.* Philadelphia: Temple University Press, 1993.

Bookchin, Murray. *The Philosophy of Social Ecology.* Montreal: Black Rose Books, 1990.

Botzler, Richard G., and Susan L. Armstrong. *Environmental Ethics: Divergence and Convergence.* New York: McGraw-Hill, 1997.

Boylan, Michael. *Environmental Ethics.* Upper Saddle River, NJ: Prentice Hall, 2000.

Callicott, J. Baird. *Beyond the Land Ethic: More Essays in Environmental Philosophy.* Albany: State University of New York Press, 1999.

———. *In Defense of the Land Ethic.* Albany: State University of New York Press, 1989.

———. *Encyclopedia of Environmental Ethics and Philosophy.* Hampshire, UK: Routledge, 2008.

———, **and Clare Palmer.** *Environmental Philosophy.* New York: Routledge, 2004.

Clayton, Patti H., and Charles Mason. *Connection on the Ice: Environmental Ethics in Theory and Practice.* Philadelphia: Temple University Press, 1998.

Deane-Drummond, Celia. *The Ethics of Nature.* Malden, MA: Blackwell Publishing, 2004.

DesJardins, Joseph R. *Environmental Ethics: An Introduction to Environmental Philosophy.* Belmont, CA: Wadsworth, 2000.

Devall, Bill. *Simple in Means, Rich in Ends: Practicing Deep Ecology.* Layton, UT: Gibbs Smith, 1988.

Diamond, Irene, and Gloria Feman Orenstein (Eds.). *Reweaving the World.* San Francisco: Sierra Club Books, 1990.

Flader, Susan L. *Thinking Like a Mountain: Aldo Leopold and the Evolution of an Ecological Attitude toward Deer, Wolves, and Forests.* Madison: University of Wisconsin Press, 1994.

Gaard, Greta Claire. *Ecological Politics: Ecofeminists and the Greens.* Philadelphia: Temple University Press, 1998.

Goldstein, Robert J. *Ecology and Environmental Ethics: Green Wood in the Bundle of Sticks.* Aldershot, NH: Ashgate Publishing, 2004.

———. *Environmental Ethics and Law.* Aldershot, NH: Ashgate Publishing, 2004.

Gore, Albert. *Earth in the Balance.* New York: Houghton Mifflin, 1992.

———. *An Inconvenient Truth.* New York: Rodale, 2006.

Gottlieb, Roger S. *The Ecological Community: Environmental Challenges for Philosophy, Politics, and Morality.* New York: Routledge, 1997.

Gruen, Lori, and Dale Jamieson (Eds.). *Reflecting on Nature: Readings in Environmental Philosophy.* New York: Oxford University Press, 1994.

Heyd, Thomas. *Encountering Nature.* Aldershot, NH: Ashgate Publishing, 2007.

Jenkins, Willis. *Ecologies of Grace: Environmental Ethics and Christian Theology.* New York: Oxford University Press, 2007.

Leopold, Aldo. *Sand County Almanac.* New York: Oxford University Press, 1949.

Light, Andrew, Eric Katz, and Erick Kata (Eds.). *Environmental Pragmatism.* New York; Routledge, 1998.

Light, Andrew, and Holmes Rolston (Eds.). *Environmental Ethics.* New York: Blackwell, 2002.

List, Peter (Ed.). *Environmental Ethics and Forestry: A Reader.* Philadelphia: Temple University Press, 2000.

Lovelock, James. *Gaia: A New Look at Life on Earth.* New York: Oxford University Press, 1981.

Marshall, Peter. *Nature's Web: Rethinking Our Place on Earth.* New York: Paragon House, 1995.

Merchant, Carolyn. *The Death of Nature: Women, Ecology, and the Scientific Revolution.* New York: Harper & Row, 1980.

Morito, Bruce. *Thinking Ecologically: Environmental Thought, Values and Policy.* Black Point, Nova Scotia: Fernwood Publishing, 2004.

Naess, Arne. *Ecology, Community, and Lifestyle,* David Rothenberg (Trans.). Cambridge, UK: Cambridge University Press, 1989.

O'Neill, John, R. Kerry Turner, and Ian Bateman (Eds.). *Environmental Ethics and Philosophy.* Boulder, CO: Edward Elgar Publishing, 2002.

Pojman, Louis P. *Global Environmental Ethics.* Mountain View, CA: Mayfield, 1999.

———. *Environmental Ethics: Readings in Theory and Application.* Belmont, CA: Wadsworth, 2000.

Rasmussen, Larry L. *Earth Community, Earth Ethics.* Maryknoll, NY: Orbis Books, 1998.

Rolston, Holmes, III. *Environmental Ethics: Duties to and Values in the Natural World.* Philadelphia: Temple University Press, 1988.

Sagoff, Mark. *The Economy of the Earth: Philosophy, Law, and the Environment.* Cambridge, UK: Cambridge University Press, 2007.

Sandler, Ronald L. *Character and Environment: A Virtue-Oriented Approach to Environmental Ethics.* New York: Columbia University Press, 2008.

Schmidtz, David, and Elizabeth Willott (Eds.). *Environmental Ethics: What Really Matters, What Really Works.* New York: Oxford University Press, 2001.

Schoch, Robert M. *Environmental Ethics: A Case Studies Approach.* Boston, MA: Jones & Bartlett Publishers, 2007.

Sessions, George (Ed.). *Deep Ecology for the 21st Century.* Boston: Shambhala Publications, 1995.

Shiva, Vandana, and Maria Miles. *Ecofeminism.* Atlantic Highlands, NJ: Zed Books, 1993.

Shrader-Frechette, K. S. *Taking Action, Saving Lives: Our Duties to Protect Environmental and Public Health.* New York: Oxford University Press, 2007.

Sikora, R. I., and Brian Barry (Eds.). *Obligations to Future Generations.* Philadelphia: Temple University Press, 1978.

Stenmark, Mikael. *Environmental Ethics and Policy-Making.* Aldershot, NH: Ashgate Publishing, 2002.

Sterba, James P. (Ed.). *Earth Ethics: Environmental Ethics, Animal Rights, and Practical Applications.* Upper Saddle River, NJ: Prentice Hall, 1995.

Stone, Christopher. *Do Trees Have Standing? Toward Legal Rights for Natural Objects.* Los Altos, CA: William Kaufmann, 1974.

Sutton, Philip W. *Nature, Environment and Society.* New York: Palgrave Macmillan, 2004.

Taylor, Paul. *Respect for Nature.* Princeton, NJ: Princeton University Press, 1986.

Thoreau, Henry David. "Maine Woods," in *The Writings of Henry David Thoreau.* Boston: Houghton Mifflin, 1894–95.

Tucker, Mary Evelyn. *Confucianism and Ecology: The Interrelation of Heaven, Earth, and Humans.* Cambridge: Harvard University Press, 1998.

VanDeVeer, Donald, and Christine Pierce. *People, Penguins, and Plastic Trees.* Belmont, CA: Wadsworth, 1986.

———. *The Environmental Ethics and Policy Book: Philosophy, Ecology and Economics.* Belmont, CA: Wadsworth, 2002.

Warren, Karen. *Ecological Feminism.* Boulder, CO: Westview, 1994.

Wenz, Peter S. *Environmental Ethics Today.* New York: Oxford University Press, 2000.

Westra, Laura, and Patricia N. Werhane (Eds.). *The Business of Consumption: Environmental Ethics and the Global Economy.* Lanham, MD: Rowman & Littlefield, 1998.

16

Animal Rights

In May 2007, two humpback whales, a mother and her calf, were stranded up the Sacramento River in fresh water. They were migrating from Mexico to Alaska when they made a wrong turn and swam under the Golden Gate Bridge, into San Francisco Bay, and then up the Sacramento River to the Sacramento delta, some 90 miles from the Pacific Ocean. They caused quite a spectacle as sightseers lined the banks of the river to catch a glimpse of them. They were given the names of Delta, after the delta, and Dawn. After two weeks hanging around the port of Sacramento, they suddenly turned around and swam south some 20 miles. Then they hesitated to swim under a bridge over the river. The Coast Guard had tried several means to encourage them to continue back to the ocean, including banging on underwater pipes, herding them with boats, playing killer whale sounds, and using a fire hose to create bubbles in the water. Still nothing seemed to be working. Thousands of people had sent e-mails and made phone calls to government agencies with suggestions of their own on how to get the whales to move on. Among their suggestions were using trained dolphins and dumping some of their favorite fish food downstream. People were becoming worried about these creatures because they had signs of injuries on their skin. Fortunately, the whales soon swam back into the Pacific Ocean.[1]

Why do people care about these creatures? And should they be spending so much time and effort when there are so many other needs of people to be served?

Every year, millions of Americans go hunting. Sometimes they are successful and sometimes not. However, part of their pleasure comes from just the uncertainty and skills involved. Recently, a new type of hunt has arisen, a hunt that is "rigged." For profit, companies have established areas and procedures in which animals are confined in certain ways and hunters have a much better chance of a kill or trophy. These companies obtain their animals from exotic animal auctions— for example, "zebras, camels, ostriches, kangaroos, and lion cubs."[2] Many hunters and hunters' groups as well as animal lovers have denounced these practices, which are, however, supported by the National Rifle Association. Critics believe that these practices are not only bad sport, but cruel. "Only 13 states have passed laws to ban canned hunts involving mammals."[3]

In 1921, an Ontario doctor and his assistant severed the connection between the pancreases and digestive systems of dogs in order to find the substance that controlled diabetes. In so doing, they isolated insulin and thus opened the possibility for treating the millions of people who have that disease.[4] Today, laboratory researchers are using leopard frogs to test the pain-killing capacity of morphine, codeine, and Demerol. Japanese medaka fish are being used as a model to determine the cancer-causing properties of substances that are released into rivers and lakes. And research using the giant Israeli scorpion is determining whether a protein in its venom can help the

24,000 Americans who die each year from tumors called *gliomas*.[5]

The number of animals used in research and experimentation each year varies according to the source of the information and the category. However, there is fairly good agreement that the number of animals used in the United States recently was approximately 1.5 million. This does not count rats and mice, which account for 90 percent to 95 percent of all animals used.[6] This would imply that some 15 million animals in total are used in animal experiments each year in the United States. Worldwide, the estimate is between 60 million and 70 million are used each year.[7] The number peaked in 1970 and has decreased ever since because of "higher standards of animal welfare, scientific advances and stricter controls."[8] Still, in 2002, according to one accounting, 77,091 cats, 96,061 primates, 77,906 dogs, 304,039 guinea pigs, 312,630 rabbits, and 193,115 hamsters were used for research and experimentation in the United States alone.[9] All of these examples raise a basic question: Are we justified in using nonhuman animals for research that may help us humans or is this wrongful and cruel treatment of other sentient beings?

U.S. laws that protect animals include the Marine Mammal Protection Act of 1972, which "establishes a moratorium on the taking and importation of marine mammals, including parts and products." The Department of the Interior is charged with enforcing the management and protection of sea otters, walruses, polar bears, dugong, and manatees.[10] The 1973 Endangered Species Act protects animals whose continued existence is threatened and whom the secretaries of the interior or commerce place on a list of endangered species.

International efforts to protect animal species are also under way. For example, international conferences such as the U.N. Convention on International Trade in Endangered Species, held in November 2002, in Santiago, Chile, try to address the problem. Among the issues that were to be decided at this particular conference were whether certain African nations should be allowed to sell ivory from their stockpiles. The United States, however, would continue to prohibit imports of ivory because elephants are protected in this country by not only the Endangered Species Act but also the African Elephant Conservation Act.[11]

Although we would like to do things to help our fellow humans, we also care about the proper treatment of animals. However, we are less sure about what this requires of us and why. We are uncertain because we are often unclear about our ultimate reasons for what we think we can rightly do to animals. We relate to and depend on our nonhuman counterparts in many ways. They are pets and provide some of us with companionship and comfort. Many people enjoy watching them in our zoos and circuses. Others find sport in the racing of animals or in the display of riding skills. Animals are used for work, for example, in herding sheep and cattle. Some people find pleasure and others economic interest or necessity in the hunting and trapping of animals. Animals are sources of food (such as meat, fish, milk, eggs, and cheese) and clothing (leather, fur, and wool). Animals are used in experiments to test not only the safety and effectiveness of medical drugs and devices but also the possible side effects of cosmetics. They provide us with medicinal aids such as hormones, blood-clotting factors, and treatments for diseases such as diabetes. "In fact, about forty percent of all prescriptions written today are composed from the natural compounds of different species."[12] Threats to the health of animal species can also warn us about possible dangers to human health. Nonhuman animals are also of obvious commercial benefit—as jobs and income come from fishing and tourism, for example. Recently, ecotourism, in which people travel to learn and appreciate and photograph animals in their natural habitats, has become quite popular. Animals are also sources of wonderment because of their variety, beauty, and strength. However, nonhuman animals are also sentient creatures. They can feel pleasure and pain just as we do and can at times seem almost human in their perceptions of and reactions to us. Thus, we can rightly ask whether we are justified in treating them in all of the ways we do.

SENTIENCE

According to some philosophers, sentience is the key to the ethical status of animals. In thinking about that status, some philosophers look to the utilitarian Jeremy Bentham, who wrote that to know the ethical status of animals, we need not ask if they can speak, but only whether or not they can suffer.[13] Besides feeling pleasure and pain, many higher animals probably also experience other types of emotions such as fear and anger. Unlike the philosopher Descartes, we do not think that animals are machines devoid of an inner sense or consciousness. Because of their sentience, we have laws that protect animals from cruelty. What counts as cruelty, however, will be disputed. Whether caging certain animals, for example, is cruel is a matter about which many people will disagree.

People also disagree about the reasons why we ought not to be cruel to animals. Some believe that a major reason is the effects on those who are cruel. If one is cruel to a sentient animal, then will he or she not more likely be cruel to people as well? The effects on the character of the person who is cruel to animals also will be negative. Moreover, those who witness cruelty to animals may be affected by it. They will themselves feel bad at seeing an animal suffer.

However, unless one believes that only human suffering can be bad, then the reason most people would tend to give for the injunction to not to be cruel to animals is because the suffering of the animals is bad for them. Whether or not something is cruel to an animal might be determined by the extent of the pain it experiences as when we speak of cruelty in terms of causing "unnecessary" pain. Not all pain is bad, even for us. It often tells us of some health problem that can be fixed. The badness of suffering also may be only *prima facie* bad. (See the discussion of this in the previous chapter.) The suffering may be worth it—that is, overcome by the good end to be achieved by it. Doing difficult things is sometimes painful, but we think it is sometimes worth the pain. In these cases, we experience not only the pain but also the benefit. In the case of animals, however, they would experience the pain of, say, an experiment performed on them while we would reap the benefit. Is this is ever justified? This is a central question for those who are concerned with our treatment of animals. Although we address the issue of animal experimentation below, it is well to consider in the first place whether and why the paining of animals is in itself a bad thing. We will also have to acknowledge that animals have different capacities to feel pain. Those with more developed and complex nervous systems and brains will likely have more capacity to feel pain as well as pleasure of various sorts.

One further comment on the issue of animal pain and pleasure is the following. In the wild, it is a fact of life that animals feed on and cause pain to one another. Predation prevails. Carnivores kill for food. The fawn is eaten by the cougar. Natural processes such as floods, fires, droughts, and volcanic eruptions also contribute to animal suffering and death. If animal suffering is important, then are we ethically obligated to lessen it in cases where we could do so? For example, in 1986 the Hubbard Glacier in Alaska began to move, and in a few weeks it had sealed off a particular fjord. Porpoises and harbor seals were trapped inside by the closure. Some people wanted to rescue the animals, while others held that this was a natural event that should be allowed to run its course.[14]

We tend to think that we are generally more bound not to *cause pain* or harm than we are to relieve it. In special cases, admittedly, there may seem to be no difference where we are bound by some duty or relation to *relieve pain* or prevent the harm. A lifeguard may have an obligation to rescue a drowning swimmer that the ordinary bystander does not. A parent has more obligation to prevent harm to his or her child than a stranger does. In the case of nonhuman animals, would we say the same? Do we also feel constrained to prevent the pain and death to animals in the wild? In general, it would seem that although we may choose to do so out of sympathy, we may not be obligated to do so. At least the obligation to *prevent the harm* seems lesser in stringency than the obligation not to *cause* a similar harm. If there is this moral difference between preventing and causing harm, then we could not argue that because we can allow the animals in the wild to die or suffer pain from natural processes, we thus also may cause a similar pain or harm to them. However, we also may be inclined to think that just because nature is cruel does not give us the right to be so.

ANIMAL RIGHTS

It is one thing to say that the suffering of a nonhuman animal, just as the suffering of us humans, is a *bad* thing in itself. It is another to say that we or the nonhuman animals have a *right* not to be caused to suffer or feel pain. To know what to say about the question of animal rights, we need to think a little about what a right is or what it means to have a right. A *right* (as opposed to something being right instead of wrong) is generally defined as a strong and *legitimate claim* that can be made by a claimant against someone. Thus, if I claim a right to freedom of speech, I am asserting my legitimate claim against anyone who would prevent me from speaking out. (See the further discussion of negative and positive rights in Chapter 13.) A person can claim a right to have or be given something (a positive right) as well as not to be prevented from doing something (a negative type). I can claim the bicycle because it is mine. This would also mean that others have a duty not to take the bicycle from me. So also, if I have a right to health care, others may have a duty to provide it. Sometimes, it is a contractual or other relation that is the reason why someone has a right to something. Thus, persons may come to have a right to care from a hospital because of a contractual relation they just have established, while a young child has a right to care from her parents because of the natural or legal relationship. We claim some of the rights as *legal rights,* because they are claims that the law recognizes and enforces. However, we also hold that there are *moral rights*—in other words, things we can rightly claim even if the law does not give its support to the claim. (Recall the discussion of natural rights in Chapter 6.)

Just who can legitimately claim a moral right to something, and on what grounds? One might think that to be the kind of being who can have rights, one must *be able to claim them.* If this were so, then the cat who is left money in a will would not have a right to it. But then neither would the infant who inherits the money. We think we speak correctly when we say that the infant has a right to care from its parents even if the infant does not recognize this right and cannot claim it. *Future generations* do not even exist, and yet some

believe that they have at least contingent rights (rights if they come to exist) that we not leave them a garbage-heap world depleted of natural resources.[15] Or one might think that only *moral agents* have rights. According to this view, only if one is a full member of the moral community with duties and responsibilities does one have rights. On the other hand, it is not unreasonable to think that this is too stringent a requirement. Perhaps it is sufficient for one to be a *moral patient* in order to be the type of being who can have rights. In other words, if one is the kind of being to whom what we do matters morally in itself, then one is the kind of being who can have rights. If this is the case and if (as we considered in the previous chapter) some trees can be thought to be moral patients, then they also would be rightly said to have rights. If this does not seem to be correct, then what other reasons should be given for why a being might have rights?

We could argue that it is just because they can feel pain that sentient beings have a *right not to suffer,* or at least suffer needlessly. This would mean that others have a *duty* with regard to this claim. However, we may have duties not to cause pain needlessly to animals even if they had no right not to be treated in ways that cause them pain. We have many duties to do or not do this or that which are not directly a matter of respecting anyone's rights. For example, I may have a duty not to destroy a famous building—but not because the building has a *right to exist.* Thus, from the fact that we have duties to animals, for example, not to make them suffer needlessly, we cannot necessarily conclude that they have rights. If we want to argue for this view, then we would need to make a clearer connection between duties and rights or to show why some particular duties also imply rights. Not all duties are a function of rights, as I might have a duty to develop my talents even though no one has a right that I do so. However, having a right seems to entail that someone has a duty to protect that right.

Some philosophers have pointed to the fact that animals have *interests* as a basis for asserting that they have rights. Having an interest in something is to have a consciousness of that thing and to want it. A being who has such a capacity is thus a being who can have rights, according to this position. Thus, Joel Feinberg says that it is because nonhuman animals have "conscious wishes, desires, and hopes; . . . urges and impulses," they are the kind of beings who can have rights.[16] It is these psychological capacities that give these animals the status that makes them capable of having rights to certain treatment, according to this view. Tom Regan argues that the reason nonhuman animals have rights just as we do is because they are what he calls the "subject of a life."[17] The idea is similar to Feinberg's in that it is the fact that animals have an inner life, which includes conscious desires and wants, that is the basis for their status as rights possessors. Nonhuman animals differ among themselves in their capacity to have these various psychic experiences, and it probably parallels the development and complexity of their nervous system. A dog may be able to experience fear, but most probably the flea on its ear does not. This difference would be a problem for these writers only in practice where we would have to determine the character of a particular animal's inner life. The more serious challenge for them is to support the view itself that these inner psychic states are the basis for animal rights.

Peter Singer has made one of the stronger cases for the view that animals' interests are the basis for their having rights and rights that are equal to those of humans. Animals may have different interests than we do, but that does not mean that their interests are to be taken more lightly. According to Singer, not to respect the interests of animals is *speciesism*.[18] This is, he believes, an objectionable attitude similar to racism or sexism— objectionable because it treats animals badly simply because they are members of a different species and gives preference to members of our own species simply because we are human beings. But on what grounds is this objectionable? According to Singer, having interests is connected to the ability to feel pleasure and pain, because the pleasure is derived from the satisfaction of an interest. Animals are different from plants in this regard. Plants have things that are *in their interest* even though they do not *have interests*. Because the interests of animals are similar to ours, they ought

to be given equal weight, according to Singer. This does not mean that they have a right to whatever we have a right to. It would make no sense to say that a pig or horse has a right to vote, because it has no interest in voting. However, according to Singer, it would make sense to say that they had a right not to suffer or not to suffer needlessly or not to be used for no good purpose.

Others argue that animals need not be treated as equal to humans and that their interests ought not to be given equal weight with ours. It is because of the difference in species' *abilities* and *potentialities* that animals are a lesser form of being, according to this view. This does not mean, however, that their interests ought to be disregarded. It may mean that peripheral interests of human being should not override more serious interests of animals. It is one thing to say that animals may be used if necessary for experiments that will save the lives of human beings and quite another to say that they may be harmed for the testing of cosmetics or clothing that is not important for human life. Whether this would provide a sufficient basis for vegetarianism would then depend on the importance of animal protein, for example, and whether animals could be raised humanely for food.

We have considered various reasons that have been given for why we ought to treat animals in certain ways and not others. One is their sentience. They can feel pleasure and pain. If pain is bad, then we ought not to cause it unless some greater good or duty pushes us to do so. Using this alone as a basis for treatment of animals would not show that we should never use animals for food or clothing or even as subjects of experimentation. In fact, some people have pointed out that by growing animals for food and clothing, we produce animals that otherwise would never have been born to have a sentient life and feel pleasures. Unless the processes involve a greater amount of pain than pleasure, they argue, we have done them a favor by our animal farming practices.

ANIMAL EXPERIMENTATION

The same reasoning might be given for using animals in experimentation. If we actually grow certain animals to provide subjects for experimental laboratories, then they will have been given a life and experiences that they otherwise would not have had. However, there are several "ifs" in this scenario. One is whether the raising or use of the animals does, in fact, involve a great deal of pain—such that it would be better for them if they had not been born.

The practice of using nonhuman animals for research or experimental purposes has a history going back some 2,000 years. In the third century b.c. in Alexandria, Egypt, animals were used to study bodily functions.[19] Aristotle cut open animals to learn about their structure and development. The Roman physician Galen used certain animals to show that veins do not carry air but blood. And in 1622, William Harvey used animals to exhibit the circulation of the blood. Animals were used in 1846 to show the effects of anesthesia and in 1878 to demonstrate the relationship between bacteria and disease.[20] In the twentieth century, research with animals made many advances in medicine possible, from cures for infectious diseases and the development of immunization techniques and antibiotics to the development of surgical procedures. For example, in the development of a vaccine for polio, hundreds of primates were sacrificed. As a result of these experiments, polio is now almost eradicated. In 1952, there were 58,000 cases of this crippling disease in the United States, and in 1984 just four. There are now few if any reported cases.[21] AIDS researchers are now using monkeys to test vaccines against HIV. Recently, "researchers at the University of Massachusetts Medical School have taken immature cells from the spinal cords of adult rats, induced them to grow and then implanted them in the gap of the severed spinal cords of paralyzed rats."[22] The rats soon were able to move, stand, and walk. This research has given hope to the 300,000 to 500,000 people in the United States and more around the world who suffer from spinal-cord damage. It is part of a growing field of tissue engineering in which scientists grow living tissue to use for replacement parts for the human body.

Other promising research creates transgenic animals to use as drug-producing machines. For example, scientists have spliced human genes into the DNA of goats, sheep, and pigs. These mammals then secrete therapeutic proteins in their milk. Among these therapeutics are those designed to treat hemophilia and cystic fibrosis.[23]

Opposition to these practices dates from at least the nineteenth century and the antivivisectionists who campaigned against all use of animals in experimentation. Currently, the animal rights movement has gained prominence and strength. In 1876, the British Parliament passed the first animal welfare act, the Cruelty to Animals Act. This was followed in the United States in 1966 by the Animal Welfare Act. In a 1976 amendment, however, Congress exempted rats, mice, birds, horses, and farm animals probably because of problems with enforcement and funding.[24] It is estimated that this could cost laboratories from $80 million to $280 million annually to implement.[25] In 2000, the U.S. agriculture department responded to a lawsuit brought by an animal rights group by agreeing to include rats, mice, and birds in the list of animals protected by this act. However, in an appropriations bill for 2002 passed by Congress and signed by the president, the designation of animals to be protected by this act would not be changed.[26] The law now applies only to warm-blooded animals, restricting it to cats, dogs, monkeys, hamsters, rabbits, and guinea pigs. In the past few years, 23 million rats, mice, and birds were used annually in U.S. labs. They accounted for 85 percent to 95 percent of all laboratory experimental animals: for example, so-called knockout mice, in which one or more genes are removed to determine what the mice cannot do without those genes. The act requires certain physical and psychological treatments of laboratory animals, including temperature, ventilation, and space requirements. Dogs are required to be properly exercised, and primates cannot be caused undue psychological stress—for example, humans are not allowed to stare at them because primates see this as challenge behavior. "Monkeys are caged, but they have televisions and can be seen enjoying episodes of 'Star Trek.'"[27]

Various institutions have adopted their own "institutional animal care and use committees." Johns Hopkins University, for example, now has its own Center for Alternatives to Animal Testing. The work of the Humane Society is well known, as is that of the Society for the Prevention of Cruelty to Animals and People for the Ethical Treatment of Animals (PETA). Some groups pursue their goals aggressively, conducting "animal rescues." For example, in 1989, the Animal Liberation Front released more than 1,200 laboratory animals (some of which had been infected with *Cryptosporidium,* a bacterium that could harm infants and people with weak immune systems). In 1987, an animal research lab being constructed at the University of California at Davis was burned, causing $3 million in damages.[28]

One issue in all of this is whether the use of animals was ever really *necessary* to effect the medical advances we have made. Animal rights activists argue that other sources of information can be used, including population studies or epidemiology, monitoring of human patients and development of databases, noninvasive medical imaging devices, autopsies, tissue and cell cultures, in vitro tests, and mathematical models.[29] Activists also argue that the use of animals as experimental subjects sometimes actually delayed the use of effective treatment. One example cited in this regard is the development of penicillin for bacterial infection. When Alexander Fleming used it on infected rabbits, it proved ineffective and thus he put it aside for a decade, not knowing that rabbits excrete penicillin in their urine.[30] It is also true that not only do nonhuman animals vary in their response to particular drugs, but also individual humans do. What works on some individuals does not work on others because of a variety of possible factors, including genetic predisposition. Activists argue that those who hold that we can use animals in experimentation are inconsistent because they want to say both that animals are different from humans and so can be used and at the same time that they are sufficiently like humans so what is learned in the research will apply to us.

Others answer this criticism by pointing out that mice, although quite different from humans, make very good models for the study of human genes simply because we share many genes with them.[31] Furthermore, they contend, cell and computer studies are insufficient. If we went directly from these cell or computer studies to use in humans, we would put humans at risk. This was the case in the use of the drug thalidomide in the 1950s, a case in which insufficient animal studies resulted in the deformation of many children who were born to women who used this drug to lessen nausea during pregnancy.

Whether using animals was necessary for various medical advances or whether other kinds of studies could have been substituted is an empirical matter. We need to turn to the history of medicine to help us determine this. However, most probably some animal research is redundant or other methods could serve just as well. For example, we should probably rely more on human epidemiological studies such as the Framingham heart study in which 5,000 adults were followed over fifty years and much was learned about the effect of cholesterol, diet, and exercise on heart health.[32]

A second concern about the use of nonhuman animals involves the extent to which *pain* is inflicted on these experimental subjects. "In 1984, the Department of Agriculture reported that 61% of research animals were not subjected to painful procedures and another 31% received anesthesia or pain-relieving drugs."[33] The rest did experience pain, but this was sometimes a necessary part of the experiment, such as in pain studies whose purpose is to find better ways to relieve pain in humans. Those who oppose animal research cite their own examples of cruelty to animal subjects. It is not just physical pain to which they point, but, for example, the psychological pain of being caged as in the case of primates. Because of their concern and political action, government restrictions and guidelines for animal research have been strengthened.[34]

There are three positions on the use of nonhuman animals in research. One opposes all use of animals. At the other end of the spectrum is the position that nonhuman animals have no rights or moral standing and thus can be used as we choose. In the middle is the belief that animals have some moral status and thus limits and restrictions should be placed on conducting research with these creatures. We already have discussed the problems regarding the basis for attributing moral status or rights to nonhuman animals, a matter that is crucial to determining what we want to say about animal experimentation. However, it is also useful to consider some of the other arguments used in this debate.

Even those who support animal rights sometimes agree that the uses of animals in experimentation can be ethically supported if they "serve important and worthwhile purposes."[35] They may be justified if they do, in fact, help us develop significant medical advances if the information cannot be obtained in any other way, and if the experiments are conducted with as little discomfort for the animals as possible. What we would want to say about other less vital purposes for using animals is still open. The use of nonhuman animals for food, entertainment, clothing, and the other purposes listed at the beginning of this chapter will probably need to be considered, each on its own terms. However, whatever we want to say about these practices, we will need to be as clear as we can about the other matters discussed in this chapter, matters about the nature and basis of moral standing and moral rights.

ENDANGERED SPECIES

According to a report of the World Conservation Union, in 2004 the number of animal species facing extinction was 15,589. This included "one in three amphibians and almost half of all freshwater turtles . . . on top of the one in eight birds and one in four mammals . . . in jeopardy."[36] In the United States alone in 2005, 389 species of animals were either endangered or threatened.[37] As of 2007, it was estimated that one out of every six mammals in Europe was threatened with extinction. More than one-third of U.S. fish species are currently in trouble.[38]

On the other hand, there has been some good news. After many years of efforts at conservation, "the mountain gorillas in Eastern Africa are showing a slow but steady comeback," according to the World Wildlife Fund (WWF), the global conservation organization.[39]

Some of the successes come from the fact that there are more than 3,500 protected areas in the world, including wildlife refuges and reserves. These areas include parks and other reserves. This is approximately 2 million square miles, or 3 percent of our total land area.[40]

Destruction of animal habitat may be the most potent threat to animal species. Although animals can often adapt to gradual changes in their environment, rapid change often makes such adjustment impossible. Many human activities cause such rapid change. Another cause is the introduction of non-native species into an environment, thus upsetting a delicate ecological balance. Overexploitation is also a source of extinction—for example, whaling and overfishing.[41] According to the WWF, dolphins and porpoises rank high on the list of endangered species that need immediate action.[42] One of the main remediable causes is *bycatch,* or accidental entrapment in fishing nets intended to catch other fish. The nets are gillnets, which because they are difficult for dolphins and porpoises to see, trap them underwater, and prevent them from reaching the surface to breathe. "This is the greatest threat globally to whales, dolphins, and porpoises. In 2003, researchers estimated that more than 300,000 (of these) cetaceans are killed in fishing gear each year in the world's oceans."[43] Especially affected are "harbor porpoises in the Black Sea . . . Atlantic humpback dolphins off the coast of West Africa, and franciscana dolphins in South America."[44] Worldwide, more than 1,000 animal species are now considered to be endangered.[45] The *Global 2000 Report* asserts that within a few decades we will lose up to 20 percent of the species that now exist if nothing is done to change the current trend.[46] Other people contest these figures and projections. For example, they claim that these estimates are extreme and far exceed any known loss of species.[47] They also point out that species have been lost naturally without human intervention. However, throughout evolution the species that have been lost have been replaced at a higher rate than they have disappeared and thus we have the wondrous diversity that we now see. The rate of replacement now may not be able to keep up because of the accelerated time scale of loss.

Although we do need to get our facts straight about the loss of species, we also need to ask ourselves why the loss of species matters. In the first place, we should distinguish the position that holds that *individual animals* have rights or a particular moral status from that position which holds that it is *animal species* that we ought to protect, not individual animals. We generally believe that we have good *anthropocentric reasons* for preserving animal as well as plant species. We have aesthetic interests in the variety of different life forms. Bird watchers know the thrill of being able to observe some rare species. The unusual and the variety itself are objects of wonder. We also have nutritional and health interests in preserving species. They may now seem useless, but we do not know what unknown future threat may lead us to find in them the food or medicine we need. Loss of species leaves us genetically poorer and vulnerable. We also have educational interests in preserving species. They tell us about ourselves, our history, and how our systems work or could work. "Destroying species is like tearing pages out of an unread book, written in a language humans hardly know how to read, about the place where they live."[48] If we destroy the mouse lemur, for example, we destroy the modern animal that is closest to the primates from which our own human line evolved.[49] From other species we can learn about the evolution of the senses of sight and hearing.

However, when we ask whether animal species have moral standing or intrinsic value or even rights, we run into matters that are puzzling. An animal species is not an individual. It is a collection and in itself cannot have the kind of interests or desires that may be the basis for the rights or moral standing of individual animals. Thus, according to philosopher Nicholas Rescher, "moral obligation is . . . always interest-oriented. But only individuals can be said to have interests; one only has moral obligations to particular individuals or particular groups thereof."[50] If we can have duties to a group of individuals and a species is a group, then we may have duties to species. Still this does not imply that the species has rights.

However, some people challenge the notion of a *species* as the *group* of the individuals that make it up. Consider just what we might mean by a "species." Is it not a *concept* constructed by us as a way of grouping and comparing organisms? Darwin had written, "I look at the term species, as one arbitrarily given for the sake of convenience to a set of individuals closely resembling each other."[51] If a species is but a term or *class* or *category,* then it does not actually exist. If it does not exist, then how could it be said to have rights? However, consider the following possibility suggested by Holmes Rolston. "A species is a living historical form (Latin *species*), propagated in individual organisms, that flows dynamically over generations."[52] As such, species are units of evolution that exist in time and space. According to Rolston, "a species is a coherent, ongoing form of life expressed in organisms, encoded in gene flow, and shaped by the environment."[53] If we think of species in this way, it may be intelligible to speak of our having duties to an animal species. What it would amount to is our respecting "dynamic life forms preserved in historical lines, vital informational processes that persist generically over millions of years, overleaping short-lived individuals."[54] Our duties then would be to a dynamic continuum, a living environmental process, a "lifeline." According to this view, species are like stories and thus, "To kill a species is to shut down a unique story."[55] Or, finally, as Rolston writes, "A duty to a species is more like being responsible to a cause than to a person. It is commitment to an *idea* (Greek, *idea,* 'form,' sometimes a synonym for the Latin *species*)." Although his explanation of the nature of species and his arguments for the view that we have duties to them are often metaphorical ("story," "lifeline"), his reasoning is nevertheless intriguing. It also raises real metaphysical questions about the reality status of an idea. At the least, he gives us cause to rethink the view that only individuals are the kinds of beings toward whom we can have duties, and even possibly also the kinds of beings who can have rights.

Those who support animal rights as the rights of individual animals to certain treatment do not always agree in concrete cases with those who believe that it is species that ought to be protected and not individual animals. Suppose, for example, that a certain population of deer is threatened because its numbers have outstripped the food supply and the deer are starving to death. In some such cases, wildlife officials have sought to thin herds by selective killing or limited hunting. It is thought to be for the sake of the herd that some are killed. Animal rights activists are generally horrified at this policy and argue that ways should be found to save all of the deer. Those who seek to protect species of animals might not object if the practice of thinning will, in fact, serve that goal. We can see that these two groups might be at odds with one another.[56]

In this chapter, we have raised many questions about the moral status of animals. The discussion of rights and duties and their grounding may seem abstract, but they do form a basis for thinking about and deciding for ourselves what we think are our obligations to and regarding nonhuman animals.

NOTES

1. Glen Martin and Marisa Lagos, "Latest Whale Rescue Tactic: Underwater Bubble Streams," *San Francisco Chronicle,* May 25, 2007, p. B4; Glen Martin and Tom Chorneau, "Hundreds Offer Ideas for Helping Lost Whales," *San Francisco Chronicle,* May 26, 2007, pp. A1, A9.
2. Wayne Pacelle, "Stacking the Hunt," *The New York Times,* Dec. 9, 2003, p. A29.
3. Ibid.
4. John F. Lauerman, "Animal Research," *Harvard Magazine* (Jan.–Feb. 1999): 49–57.
5. Ulysses Torassa, "Research Doctors Get Clues from Animals," *San Francisco Chronicle,* Jan. 24, 1999, p. A4.
6. www.all-creatures.org.
7. www.hsus.org.
8. www.rds-online.org.uk.
9. www.all-creatures.org.
10. www.endangeredspecie.com/protect.htm.
11. www.fingaz.co/zw/fingaz/2002/November/November7/3070.shtml.
12. www.endangeredspecie.com/Why_Save_.htm.
13. Jeremy Bentham, *Introduction to the Principles of Morals and Legislation* (1789), Chapter 17.
14. Reported by Holmes Rolston III in *Environmental Ethics: Duties to and Values in the Natural World* (Philadelphia: Temple University Press, 1988): 50.
15. Joel Feinberg, "The Rights of Animals and Unborn Generations," in *Animal Rights and Human Obligations,* Tom Regan and Peter Singer (Eds.) (Englewood Cliffs, NJ: Prentice Hall, 1976): 190–196.
16. Ibid.
17. Tom Regan, *The Case for Animal Rights* (Berkeley: University of California Press, 1983).
18. Peter Singer, *Animal Liberation: A New Ethic for Our Treatment of Animals* (New York: Random House, 1975). Singer was not the first to use the term *speciesism.* Ryder also used it in his work *Victims of Science* (London: Davis-Poynter, 1975).
19. Jerod M. Loeb, William R. Hendee, Steven J. Smith, and M. Roy Schwarz, "Human vs. Animal Rights: In Defense of Animal Research," *Journal of the American Medical Association, 262,* no. 19 (Nov. 17, 1989): 2716–2720.
20. Ibid.
21. Ibid.; see also www.who.int/immunization_monitoring/en/globalsummary/timeseries/tsincidencepol.htm.
22. Holcomb B. Noble, "Rat Studies Raise Hope of Conquering Paralysis," *The New York Times,* Jan. 25, 2000, p. D7.
23. Tom Abate, "Biotech Firms Transforming Animals into Drug-Producing Machines," *San Francisco Chronicle,* Jan. 25, 2000, p. B1.
24. Lauerman, "Animal Research." op. cit., 51.
25. www.biomedcentral.com/news/20010716/03/.
26. www.avma.org/onlnews/javma/feb02/s021502n/asp.
27. Nicholas Wade, "Lab Rats, Mice Gain Federal Protection," *San Francisco Chronicle,* Oct. 15, 2000.
28. Lauerman, "Animal Research." op. cit.
29. www.mrmcmed.org/crit3.html.
30. See Americans for Medical Advancement (www.curedisease.com/FAQ.html).
31. Lauerman, "Animal Research." op. cit.
32. Ibid.
33. This is a continuation of the estimate for 1980, as given by Peter Singer in "Animals and the Value of Life," in *Matters of Life and Death: New Introductory Essays in Moral Philosophy,* 2nd ed., T. Regan (Ed.) (New York: Random House, 1980, 1986): 339.
34. See, for example, the U.S. National Institutes of Health's *Guide for the Care and Use of Laboratory Animals,* rev. ed. (1985).
35. Singer, "Animals and the Value of Life," 374.
36. www.iucn.org.
37. www.ecos.fws.gov/tess_public/TessStatReport.
38. www.iucn.org/; www.endangeredspecie.com/Interesting_Facts.htm.
39. www.worldwildlife.org/news.
40. www.endangeredspecie.com/Interesting_Facts.htm.
41. www.endangeredspecie.com/causes_of_endangerment.htm.
42. www.worldwildlife.org/news.

43. Ibid.

44. Ibid.

45. www.endangeredspecie.com/Interesting_Facts.htm.

46. Council on Environmental Quality and the Department of State, *The Global 2000 Report to the President* (Washington, DC: U.S. Government Printing Office, 1980): 1, 37; 2, 327–333.

47. See, for example, Julian L. Simon and Aaron Wildavsky, "Facts, Not Species, Are Periled," *The New York Times,* May 13, 1993, p. A15.

48. Rolston, *Environmental Ethics,* op. cit. 129.

49. Ibid.

50. Nicholas Rescher, "Why Save Endangered Species?" in *Unpopular Essays on Technological Progress* (Pittsburgh: University of Pittsburgh Press, 1980): 83. A similar point is made by Tom Regan, *The Case for Animal Rights* (Berkeley: University of California Press, 1983): 359, and Joel Feinberg, "Rights of Animals and Unborn Generations," op. cit., 55–56.

51. Charles Darwin, *The Origin of Species* (Baltimore, MD: Penguin, 1968): 108.

52. Holmes Rolston III, op. cit., 135.

53. Ibid., 136.

54. Ibid., 137.

55. Ibid., 145.

56. In fact, one supporter of animal rights has referred to holistic views of the value of animals as "environmental fascism." Tom Regan, *The Case for Animal Rights* (Berkeley: University of California Press, 1983): 361–362.

REVIEW EXERCISES

1. List ten different ways in which we use nonhuman animals.

2. How is *cruelty* defined in terms of sentience?

3. How can the distinction between causing and allowing harm or pain be used to criticize the view that we can cause pain to animals because this is part of nature—that is, something that happens in the wild?

4. What is the meaning of the term *rights?*

5. For a being to be the kind of thing that can have rights, is it necessary that it be able to claim them? That it be a moral agent? Why or why not?

6. What do those who use the fact that animals have interests as a basis for their having rights mean by this?

7. Describe the issues involved in the debate over whether nonhuman animals' interests ought to be treated equally with those of humans.

8. List some anthropocentric reasons for preserving animal species.

9. What problems does the meaning of a "species" raise for deciding whether animal species have moral standing of some sort?

10. What reasons do supporters give for using nonhuman animals in experimental research? What reasons for opposing it do their opponents give? In particular, discuss the issues of pain and necessity.

DISCUSSION CASES

1. Animal Experimentation. Consider the experiments mentioned in this chapter in which nonhuman animals are used: dogs in early insulin discovery, frogs for testing pain relievers, fish for determining cancer-causing substances in lakes and rivers, monkeys for finding a vaccine for HIV, and various animals to show that veins do not carry air but blood, to test the effects of anesthesia, and to find a vaccine for polio. What do you think of using animals for experiments such as these? Do you agree with those who say that other methods should always be used even if we would then have to do without some life-enhancing or lifesaving knowledge or therapies? Would you distinguish between larger animals and mice and rats and fish? What are your primary reasons for believing as you do?

2. People Versus the Gorilla. Of the approximately 250 remaining mountain gorillas, some 150 are located in the 30,000-acre Parc des Volcans in the small African country of Rwanda. Rwanda has the highest population density in Africa. Most people live on small farms. To this population, the park represents survival land for farming. Eliminating the park could support 36,000 people on subsistence farms.

Should the park be maintained as a way to preserve the gorillas or should it be given to the people for their survival? Why?

3. What Is a Panther Worth? The Florida panther is an endangered species. Not long ago, one of these animals was hit by a car and seriously injured. He was taken to the state university veterinary medical school where steel plates were inserted in both legs, his right foot was rebuilt, and he had other expensive treatment. The Florida legislature was considering a proposal to spend $27 million to build forty bridges that would allow the panther to move about without the threat of other car injuries and death. Those who support the measure point out that the Florida panther is unique and can survive only in swamp land near the Everglades.

Should the state spend this amount of money to save the Florida panther from extinction? Why or why not?

YOU MAKE THE DECISION

Apply the theories and issues discussed in this chapter by accessing this animated simulation on the Ethics Resource Center.

Use the passkey that accompanies your book to gain access. If you do not have a passkey, visit cengage brain.com to purchase instant access to additional study material.

© Cengage Learning

Selected Bibliography

Armstrong, Susan, and Richard G. Botzler. *Animal Ethics Reader.* New York: Routledge, 2003.

Baird, Robert M., and Stuart E. Rosenbaum (Eds.). *Animal Experimentation: The Moral Issues.* New York: Prometheus, 1991.

Bekoff, Marc, et al. *Why Animals Matter: A Biologist's Case for the Compassionate, Respectful, and Humane Treatment of Animals.* Boston: Shambhala Publications, 2007.

Bostock, Stephen C. *Zoos and Animal Rights.* New York: Routledge, 1993.

Campbell, Tom. *Rights: A Critical Introduction.* New York: Routledge, 2005.

Christiansen, Stine, et al. *Animal Ethics in Veterinary and Animal Science.* Boston: Blackwell Publishing, 2008.

Clark, Stephen R. L. *Animals and Their Moral Standing.* New York: Routledge, 1997.

DeGrazia, David. *Taking Animals Seriously: Mental Life and Moral Status.* New York: Cambridge University Press, 1996.

————. *Animal Rights: A Very Short Introduction.* New York: Oxford University Press, 2002.

Fox, Michael Allan. *The Case for Animal Experimentation.* Berkeley: University of California Press, 1986.

Fraser, David. *Understanding Animal Welfare.* Boston: Blackwell Publishing, 2008.

Frey, R. G. *Interests and Rights: The Case Against Animals.* Oxford, UK: Clarendon, 1980.

Garner, Robert (Ed.). *Animal Rights: The Changing Debate.* New York: New York University Press, 1997.

Guerrini, Anita. *Animal and Human Experimentation. An Introductory History.* Baltimore: Johns Hopkins University Press, 2004.

Guither, Harold. *Animal Rights: History and Scope of a Radical Social Movement.* Carbondale, IL: Southern Illinois University Press, 1998.

Langley, Andrew. *What Do You Think? Should We Eat Animals?* Chicago: Heinemann Library, 2008.

Leahy, Michael P. *Against Liberation: Putting Animals in Perspective.* New York: Routledge, 1994.

Li, Hon-Lam, et al. *New Essays in Applied Ethics: Animal Rights, Personhood, and the Ethics of Killing.* New York: Palgrave Macmillan, 2007.

Luke, Brian. *Brutal: Manhood and the Exploitation of Animals.* Champaign: University of Illinois Press, 2007.

Machan, Tibor R. *Putting Humans First: Why We Are Nature's Favorite.* New York: Rowman & Littlefield, 2004.

Mason, Jim, and Peter Singer. *Animal Factories.* New York: Crown, 1980.

Midgley, Mary. *Animals and Why They Matter.* Athens: University of Georgia Press, 1998.

Nibert, David. *Animal Rights/Human Rights: Entanglements of Oppression and Liberation.* Lanham, MD: Rowman & Littlefield, 2002.

Norton, Bryan C. (Ed.). *Preservation of Species.* Princeton, NJ: Princeton University Press, 1986.

Orlans, F. Barbara. *In the Name of Science: Issues in Responsible Animal Experimentation.* New York: Oxford University Press, 1993.

Palmer, Clare. *Animal Rights.* Aldershot, NH: Ashgate Publishing, 2008.

Paul, Ellen Frankel. *Why Animal Experimentation Matters: The Use of Animals in Medical Research.* Somerset, NJ: Transaction Publishers, 2000.

Regan, Tom. *Animal Rights, Human Wrongs.* New York: Rowman & Littlefield, 2003.

————. *The Case for Animal Rights.* Berkeley: University of California Press, 1983.

———— **(Ed.).** *Earthbound: New Introductory Essays in Environmental Ethics.* New York: Random House, 1984.

————. *Empty Cages: Facing the Challenge of Animal Rights.* New York: Rowman & Littlefield, 2004.

————, **and Peter Singer (Eds.).** *Animal Rights and Human Obligations,* 2nd ed. Englewood Cliffs, NJ: Prentice-Hall, 1989.

Rollin, Bernard E. *The Frankenstein Syndrome: Ethical and Social Issues in the Genetic Engineering of Animals.* New York: Cambridge University Press, 1995.

————. *The Unheeded Cry: Animal Consciousness, Animal Pain, and Science.* New York: Oxford University Press, 1989.

Rowls, Mark, and Mark Rowlands. *Animal Rights: A Philosophical Defense.* New York: St. Martins Press, 2000.

Ryder, R. *Victims of Science.* London: Davis-Poynter, 1975.

Singer, Peter. *Animal Liberation,* 2nd ed. New York: New York Review of Books, 1990.

————. **(Ed.).** *In Defense of Animals.* Malden, MA: Blackwell, 2005.

Smith, Jane A., and Boyd, Kenneth M. (Eds.). *Lives in the Balance: The Ethics of Using Animals in Biomedical Research.* New York: Oxford University Press, 1991.

Sperlinger, David (Ed.). *Animals in Research: New Perspectives in Animal Experimentation.* New York: Wiley, 1981.

17

Stem Cell Research, Cloning, and Genetic Engineering

Genetics has come a long way since the Austrian monk Gregor Mendel's experiments with peas in the 1860s demonstrated that certain "hereditary factors" underlay the transmission of traits. Progress has accelerated since 1953, when biologists James Watson and Francis Crick determined the molecular structure of DNA, the basis of genetic information. The Human Genome Project, which mapped the entire human genome and was completed in 2000, promises even more wondrous things to come.

However, these scientific advances and their possibilities for human use have also been accompanied by serious ethical questions. This chapter will examine several of these as they relate to five central areas: stem cell research, human cloning, genetic engineering, genetically modified plants and animals, and genetic screening.

STEM CELL RESEARCH

Recently, several public figures have made public appeals for the funding of stem cell research with its potential for treating or curing certain serious diseases. For example, Mary Tyler Moore, who has type I (insulin-dependent) diabetes and chairs the Juvenile Diabetes Foundation, brought children with this condition to testify in hearings before Congress. These children are not able to produce enough insulin to change nutrients into the energy needed for life; they must monitor their blood sugar and be injected with the needed amount of manufactured human insulin every day. Nancy and Ron Reagan also support stem cell research and have spoken publicly about their hopes that this research can lead to cures for Alzheimer's disease, which afflicted the late President Ronald Reagan and currently 4.5 million other Americans. Actor Michael J. Fox has also promoted this research as a possible cure for the Parkinson's disease with which he is afflicted. Before he died, *Superman* star Christopher Reeve also lobbied for this research as a possible treatment for spinal cord injuries such as his.

Stem cell research is part of the field of *regenerative medicine*. The hope of its supporters is that efforts here can lead to the production of new cells, tissues, and organs that can be used to treat disease or injury. Certain stem cell therapies have been around for some time. One example is the transplantation of the stem cells present in bone marrow to treat certain forms of leukemia. Another more recent example is the extraction from cadavers of certain parts of the human pancreas for an experimental treatment of diabetes.[1]

What are stem cells and how are they supposed to play a role in such efforts? Stem cells are found in the early embryo and in other parts of the human body that are not yet, or not yet fully, differentiated. In other words, they have not yet developed into specific skin, muscle, or other types of body cells and tissues. Embryonic stem (ES) cells are the fifty to one hundred cells that make up the inner mass of cells of the *blastocyst* (the rest form the outer shell that becomes the *placenta*) that exists in the first week of embryonic development. These cells are undifferentiated for a short period of time—approximately five to seven days after fertilization. They can be removed and placed in a culture where they will continue to divide. They are the cells from which all of the body's organs develop and thus are called *pluripotent.* However, once removed in this manner, they can no longer develop into a fetus.

In the case of these embryonic stem cells, researchers hope to be able to learn how to control the process of their differentiation so as to be able to provoke them to become, for example, the insulin-producing beta cells of the pancreas (thus effecting the cure of diabetes) or neurons for the treatment of spinal cord injuries. Stem cells themselves cannot be directly implanted into the pancreas, however, because they can cause cancerous tumors to develop. Thus, it is necessary first to direct them into becoming the specialized cells that are needed.

On April 2, 2007, medical researchers from Britain reported that they had "grown human heart valve tissue from stem cells." If this is true, the replacement tissue generated could be used for heart disease patients within a few years.[2]

There are many practical problems with this process, among which are developing more efficient ways to obtain these cells, determining how to get them directed into such specialization, and controlling this process. Some researchers have pointed out that in the case of some diseases such as Lou Gehrig's disease and other autoimmune diseases, replacing the damaged cells may not help the patient because it is "the cellular environment" that is the problem, and the newly added cells could be damaged as well. The source of the problem with the environment would need first to be addressed.[3]

Just as problematic are the ethical problems that are raised by ES cell research. Among the central ethical issues is the moral status of the early embryo. Those who believe that a human being exists from the time of conception also hold that the blastocyst, although a ball of cells smaller than a grain of sand, has full moral status. As such, they believe it wrong to use these embryos, even to save another life. (See Chapter 9 on abortion for the arguments regarding the moral status of the embryo.) Supporters, however, point out that leftover embryos now stored in fertility clinics (approximately half a million are now frozen in the United States) could be used because they are often otherwise destroyed, and using them could do some good.

Legal and Ethical Issues

Legislative bodies around the world are grappling with the questions regarding the legal regulation or prohibition of stem cell research. In the United States since 2001—by presidential directive of George Bush—only those ES cell lines that were already established can be used for research that is funded by the federal government. At that time, it was thought that some sixty or so viable cell lines would be available. However, as of mid-2005, only fifteen to twenty of these cell lines existed, and these had been largely contaminated with, for example, the mouse feeder cells on which they had been cultured. Worldwide at this time, fewer than 150 lines have been created. In the United States, there currently are no laws prohibiting such research. However, it must be done through private or state funding. Such is California's Institute of Regenerative Medicine, for which voters approved $3 billion in funds for startup work. As of March 2007, this institute had decided to fund several groups after an extensive peer review process.[4] Scientists are concerned that the United States may lose its leadership role in this science to other countries. On April 11, 2007, the U.S. Senate passed the Human Cloning Ban and Stem Cell Research Protection Act of 2007; the House of Representatives then passed the bill by a wide margin. As the title indicates, although the ban on cloning human beings continues, the act holds that the federal government should provide funds for stem cell research. The Senate vote was sixty-three to thirty-four, with three more senators abstaining but in support. Nevertheless, the vote in favor was one vote short of that required to override an expected presidential veto. In June 2007, George W. Bush vetoed the bill as he had done the previous year.[5]

To overcome certain ethical concerns about the moral status of the early embryo, some people have suggested that adult stem cells be used. These exist in bone marrow and purportedly in other parts of the body such as the brain, skin, fat, and muscle.[6] The use of these cells seems to work in some cases. For example, "German doctors reported having repaired a large gap in a young girl's skull using a combination of bone graft and stem cells derived from her own fatty tissue."[7] Adult stem cells have also been used to treat heart failure patients, either by forming new heart muscle cells or by stimulating their production.[8] These adult stem cells may be part of the body's natural "repair mechanism."[9] However, at most, adult stem cells can be used to produce or spur the development of only a limited number of types of related tissues. They are *multipotent* rather than pluripotent. Moreover, they do not seem to be as vigorous as the ES cells. Recently, researchers have found evidence that stem cells might be present and obtainable from amniotic fluid. It would be a plentiful source and not as problematic as those obtained from embryos. Again, however, although they have elements in common with embryonic stem cells, it is not clear yet whether these amniotic stem cells would have the same potency as those taken from embryos.[10]

Another line of research is inspired by the newt, a small amphibian. If it loses a limb, the newt can regenerate a new one. The idea would be to see if certain already differentiated body cells could be reprogrammed in such a way that they could be *de*-differentiated—in other words, they might be brought back to a state closer to that of ES cells. Even further, this type of research might lead to a better understanding of the body's "innate capacity for regeneration" such as in wound healing.[11]

Because there is no federal funding in the United States for this type of research, there are also no ethical guidelines. To supply these, the National Academy of Sciences (NAS) has recently proposed a set of such recommendations for voluntary use by researchers. This set is modeled on the type of self-regulation that scientists proposed for recombinant DNA research in 1975, guidelines later adopted by the National Institutes of Health (NIH). These guidelines are particularly relevant for stem cell research in which the tissues and organs that might be developed would need to be tested first in animals. This may lead to the creation of *chimeras,* animals with some human cells or organs. This research is for medical purposes, not to produce the centaur and mermaids of mythology. In fact, doctors are already using pig heart valves that have some human cells to treat heart patients. While recommending that such testing be allowed, the NAS also recommended that (1) chimeraic animals not be allowed to mate because, if the cells invaded the sperm and eggs, this could lead to a human being conceived; (2) human stem cells not be allowed to become part or all of an animal's brain and not be injected into other primates; (3) the embryo should not be allowed to develop for more than fourteen days; and (4) women who donate eggs not be paid in order to avoid financial inducement.[12]

Recently, a task force of the International Society for Stem Cell Research published its own guidelines for embryonic stem cell research. They were developed by ethicists and scientists and legal experts from fourteen countries. They are much like those of the NAS in the United States but do allow some research on chimeraic animals— those that could carry human gametes—but only if it passes the review of an oversight committee. They also sought to justify the fourteen-day limit for embryo development, arguing that it is not until this point with the development of a "primitive streak" that the embryo "has begun to initiate organogenesis."[13]

HUMAN CLONING

A separate but possibly related issue is human cloning. There are basically two kinds of human cloning: therapeutic and reproductive. These should be treated separately.

Therapeutic Cloning

Therapeutic cloning is the use of cloning for medical purposes. It is possible to use this type of cloning in conjunction with stem cell therapy. The reason is that even if it were possible to direct embryonic stem cells to make tissue needed to treat a disease or injury, this tissue would be subject to immunological rejection by a patient's body. In this type of cloning, the nucleus of a somatic or bodily cell of a person, such as a skin cell, is inserted into an unfertilized egg that has had its own nucleus removed. The egg would then be stimulated and develop into an embryo. The stem cells in this blastocyst would be genetically identical to the person whose skin cell it was. The tissue would not then be rejected as foreign.

What is the current state of human therapeutic cloning? Recently, researchers from Korea's Seoul National University announced that they had produced stem cell lines from cloned human embryos. However, upon further investigation, it was found that the researchers had faked their data, and that they had not actually cloned human embryos.[14] In 2005, Dr. Ian Wilmut, the Scotland scientist who cloned Dolly, received a grant from the British government to "study how nerve cells go awry to cause motor neuron diseases."[15] Great Britain has allowed research cloning since 2001.

The ethical issues raised by this type of cloning mirror those of stem cell research and therapy as discussed above. However, additional ethical questions and concerns are raised by reproductive cloning.

Reproductive Cloning

A clone can be thought of as an individual or as a group of individuals who are genetically identical. Identical twins are such clones. Since the birth of Dolly the sheep at the Roslin Institute near Edinburgh, Scotland, in March 1996, people have wondered whether it also would be possible to produce humans by cloning. Dolly was a clone, a genetic "copy," of a six-year-old ewe. She was created by inserting the nucleus of a cell from the udder of this ewe into a sheep egg from which the nucleus had been removed. After being stimulated to grow, the egg was implanted into the uterus of another sheep from which Dolly was born. Because Dolly was a mammal like us, people concluded that it might be possible to clone human

beings as well. Moreover, Dolly was produced from a body or somatic cell of an adult sheep with already determined characteristics. Because the cells of an adult are already differentiated—that is, they have taken on specialized roles—scientists had previously assumed that cloning from such cells would not be possible. Now, it seemed, producing an identical, although younger, twin of an already existing human being might be possible.

The type of cloning described above is called *somatic cell nuclear transfer* (SCNT) because it transfers the nucleus of a somatic or bodily cell into an egg whose own nucleus has been removed. Cloning can also be done through a *fission* process, or cutting of an early embryo. Through this method it may be possible to make identical human twins or triplets from one embryo.

The potential for human cloning can be surmised from the progress of animal cloning. In just the past two decades, many higher mammals have been produced through cloning, including cows, sheep, goats, mice, pigs, rabbits, and a cat named "CC" for "carbon copy" or "copy cat." CC was produced in a project funded by an Arizona millionaire, John Sperling, who wanted to clone his pet dog, Missy, who had died. The company he and his team of scientists established, Genetic Savings and Clone, was based in Sausalito, California, and Texas A&M University at College Station, Texas.[16] In 2004, it was charging $50,000 for a cloned cat and $295 to $1,395 to store genetic material from a cat. Two kittens, Tabouli and Baba Ganoush, who were cloned from the same female Bengal tiger cat, were displayed at the annual cat show at Madison Square Garden in October 2004. According to the owners, the kittens have personality similarities as well as differences. In late 2004, the company also expected to deliver five more cloned kittens.[17] Cloned animals have themselves produced offspring in the natural way. Dolly had six seemingly normal lambs. Several generations of mice have also been produced through SCNT. Clones have been derived not only from udder cells but also from cells from embryos and fetuses, as well as from mice tails and cumulus cells.

On February 25, 2005, a cloned foal stallion of a prize race horse was born in Cremona, Italy.

The owners reported that the foal would be used primarily for breeding and, as of 2007, he appeared to be well and ready for that purpose.[18] In 2006, Genetic Savings and Clone closed its doors, going out of business. The owners found after all that their enterprise was not commercially viable.[19]

However, animal cloning has not always been efficient or safe. In the case of Dolly, for example, 277 eggs were used but only one lamb was produced. Moreover, cloned animals also have exhibited various abnormalities. In one study, all twelve cloned mice died between one and two years of age. Six of the cloned mice had pneumonia, four had serious liver damage, and one had leukemia and lung cancer. Dolly may have had arthritis, although this has been disputed. Some theorists suggest that this may be because she was cloned from the cell of an already aged adult sheep. In February 2003, Dolly was euthanized because she had developed an infectious and terminal lung disease.

In terms of human reproduction, cloning would be directed to the development of a new human being who would be the identical twin of the person whose cell was used in the process. On the one hand, reproductive cloning may be thought of as one of several reproductive technologies that have been developed in recent decades. Among these are artificial insemination, in vitro fertilization with its resulting "test-tube babies," donated and frozen embryos and eggs, and the use of surrogate mothers.

Although these other methods of reproduction have been widely accepted, there is almost universal objection to reproductive cloning, even among those countries that allow and support stem cell research or therapeutic cloning. Some countries, such as the United Kingdom, have laws prohibiting reproductive cloning while still actively supporting therapeutic cloning. Japan, China, Singapore, and South Korea have similar laws. However, Germany, Austria, France, and the Netherlands have banned both types of cloning. Countries in South America, the Middle East, and Africa also have a diversity of regulation. In the United States, bills to regulate or prohibit human cloning have been proposed, but none has yet passed both houses of Congress. One reason is the failure to agree on whether to make a distinction between the two types of cloning. Ethical questions are central to reproductive cloning, and thus our focus here is on that form.

Ethical Issues

Although much of the reaction to cloning humans has been the product of both hype and fear, serious ethical questions also have been raised. One of the most serious concerns is that cloning might lead to harm to a child produced in this way, just as it has in some cases of animal cloning. For this reason alone, caution is advised. Some people have pointed out, though, that fertility clinics have had broad experience in growing human embryos, and thus cloning humans might be less risky than cloning animals. However, objections are also based on other considerations.

One ethical objection to human cloning is that it would amount to "playing God." The idea is that only God can and should create a human life. This role is specifically reserved to God, so we take on a role we should not play when we try to do it ourselves. Those who hold this view might use religious reasons and sources to support it. Although this looks like a religious position, it is not necessarily so. For example, it might mean that the coming to be of a new person is a *creation,* not a making or production. A creation is the bringing into being of a human being, a mysterious thing and something that we should regard with awe. When we take on the role of producing a human being, as in cloning, we become makers or manipulators of a product that we control and over which we take power. Another version of this objection stresses the significance of nature and the natural. In producing a human being through cloning, we go against human nature. In humans, as in all higher animals, reproduction is sexual, not asexual. Cloning, however, is asexual reproduction. Leon Kass is one of the strongest proponents of this view. He alleges that in cloning someone, we would wrongly seek to escape the bounds and dictates of our sexual nature. According to another criticism of the "playing God" concept, attempting to clone a human being demonstrates *hubris* in that we think we are wise enough to know what we are doing when we are not. When we deal with human beings, we should be particularly careful. Above all, we should avoid doing what unknowingly may turn out to be seriously harmful for the individuals produced as well as for future generations.

Those who defend human cloning respond to this sort of objection by asking how this is any different from other ways we interfere with or change nature—in medicine, for example. Others argue that God gave us brains to use, and we honor God in using them especially for the benefit of humans and society. Critics also point out that in using technology to assist reproduction, we do not necessarily lose our awe in the face of the coming into being of a unique new being, albeit it happens with our help.

A second objection to the very idea of cloning a human being is that the person cloned would not be a *unique individual.* He or she would be the genetic copy of the person from whom the somatic cell was transferred. He or she would be the equivalent of an identical twin of this person, although years younger. Moreover, because our dignity and worth are attached to our uniqueness as individuals, cloned individuals would lose the something that is the basis of the special value we believe persons to have. Critics point out the difficulties that clones would have in maintaining their individuality—similar to the difficulties that identical twins have. Sometimes they are dressed alike, and often they are expected to act alike. The implication is that they do not have the freedom or ability to develop their own individual personalities. This objection is sometimes expressed as the view that a cloned human being would not have a soul, that he or she would be a hollow shell of a person. The idea is that if we take on the role of producing a human being through cloning, then we prevent God from placing a soul in that person.

One response to this objection points out how different the cloned individual would be from the original individual. Identical twins are more like each other than a clone would be to the one cloned. This is because they shared the same nuclear environment as well as the same uterus. Clones would have different mitochondria, the genes in the

cytoplasm surrounding the renucleated cell that play a role in development. Clones would develop in different uteruses and be raised in different circumstances and environments. Studies of plants and animals give dramatic evidence of how great a difference the environment makes. The genotype does not fully determine the phenotype—that is, the genes' actual physical manifestations. CC, the cloned cat mentioned above, does not quite look like its mother, Rainbow, a calico tricolored female. They have different coat patterns because genes are not the only things that control coat color. Just one year later, the visual difference was even more clear. CC also has a different personality. "Rainbow is reserved. CC is curious and playful. Rainbow is chunky. CC is sleek."[20] Although genes do matter, and thus there would be similarities between the clone and the one cloned, they would not be identical. On the matter of soul, critics wonder why could God not give each person, identical twin or clone, an individual soul because any living human being, cloned or not, would be a distinct being and so would have a human psyche or soul.

A third objection to human cloning is that any person has a *right to an open future* but that a cloned human being would not. He or she would be expected to be like the originating person and thus would not be free to develop as he or she chose. The person of whom someone was a clone would be there as the model of what he or she would be expected to be. Even if people tried not to have such expectations for the one cloned, they would be hard pressed not to do so. Critics of this argument may admit that there might be some inclination to have certain expectations for the clone, but, they argue, this undue influence is a possibility in the case of all parents and children, and one not limited to clones. Parents decide on what schools to send their children to and what sports or activities they will promote. The temptation or inclination may be there to unduly influence their children, but it is incumbent on parents to control it.

Related to the previous objection is one that holds that cloned children or persons would tend to be *exploited.* If one looks at many of the reasons given for cloning a person, the objection goes, they tend to be cases in which the cloning is for the sake of others. For example, the cloned child could be a donor for someone else. We might make clones who are of a certain sort that could be used for doing menial work or fighting wars. We might want to clone certain valued individuals, stars of the screen or athletics. In all of these cases, the clones would neither be valued for their own selves nor respected as unique persons. They would be valued for what they can bring to others. Kant is cited as the source of the moral principle that persons ought not simply be used but ought to be treated as ends in themselves.

Critics could agree with Kant but still disagree that a cloned human being would be any more likely than anyone else to be used by others for their own purposes only. Just because a child was conceived to provide bone marrow for a sick sibling would not prevent her from also being loved for her own sake. Furthermore, the idea that we would allow anyone to clone a whole group of individuals and imprison them while training them to be workers or soldiers is not living in the present world in which there are rightly legal protections against such treatment of children or other individuals. So, also, critics may contend, the possibility that some group might take over society and create a "brave new world" in which children were produced only through cloning is far-fetched and nothing more than fiction.

Some people believe that if human cloning were a reality, then it would only add to the *confusion within families* that is already generated by the use of other reproductive technologies. When donated eggs and surrogate mothers are used, the genetic parents are different from the gestational parents and the rearing parents, and conflicts have arisen regarding who the "real" parents are. Cloning, objectors contend, would be even more of a problem. It would add to this confusion the blurring of lines between generations. The mother's child could be her twin or a twin of her own mother or father. What would happen to the traditional relationships with the members of the other side of the family, grandparents, aunts, and uncles? Or what will be the relationship of the husband to the child who is the twin of the mother or the wife to the child who is the twin of her husband?

Critics of these arguments respond that, although there is a traditional type of family that, in fact, varies from culture to culture, today there are also many different kinds of nontraditional families. Among these are single-parent households, adopted families, blended families, and lesbian and gay families. It is not the type of family that makes for a good loving household, the argument goes, but the amount of love and care that exists in one.

A final objection to human cloning goes something as follows: Sometimes we have a *gut reaction* to something we regard as abhorrent. This objection is sometimes called the "yuck" objection. We are offended by the very thought of it. We cannot always give reasons for this reaction, yet we instinctively know that what we abhor is wrong. Many people seem to react to human cloning in this way. The idea of someone making a copy of themselves or many copies of a famous star is simply bizarre, revolting, and repulsive, and these emotional reactions let us know that there is something quite wrong with it, even if we cannot explain fully what it is.

Any adequate response to this argument would entail an analysis of how ethical reasoning works when it works well. Emotional reactions or moral intuitions may indeed play a role in moral reasoning. However, most philosophers would agree that adequate moral reasoning should not rely on intuition or emotion alone. Reflections about why one might rightly have such gut reactions are in order. People have been known to have negative gut reactions to things that, in fact, are no longer regarded as wrong—interracial marriage, for example. It is incumbent on those who assert that something is wrong, most philosophers believe, that they provide rational argument and well-supported reasons to justify these beliefs and emotional reactions.

Ethical objections to human cloning (whether reproductive or therapeutic) and stem cell research also often revolve around the treatment of embryos. Some of the same arguments regarding abortion are raised regarding these practices. One novel idea is to mix together embryos from fertility clinics. In some cases, the mixture would contain both male and female embryos. They would have virtually no chance of developing into a human being, and yet they would still produce stem cells. Thus, destroying them might not be objectionable.[21] It may also be possible to produce sources of stem cells from a human egg alone through parthenogenesis. Eggs do not halve their genetic total until late in their maturation cycle. Before that, they have a full set of genes. If they could be activated before this time and stimulated to grow, there might not be the same objection to using eggs as there has been to using early embryos made from combining sperm and egg.[22] The move to prohibit destroying new embryos but permit the use of already existing stem cell lines has proved to be problematic because these have been found to be limited in number and poor in quality.[23]

These concerns about the protection of embryos have also moved legislators to create laws restricting or prohibiting their use in research as in therapeutic or reproductive cloning. For example, since 1978, no federal funds have been allowed for use in human embryo research, and since 1996 Congress has attached a rider to the NIH budget that would prohibit funding any research that involves the destruction of embryos. Producing embryos from which to derive stem cells would involve their destruction. No such restrictions have been placed on research using private funding, and thus several nongovernment labs have been proceeding with such work. In early 1999, the legal counsel of the Department of Health and Human Services ruled that it is within the legal guidelines to fund human stem cell research if the cells are obtained from private funds. Most recently, the members of the National Bioethics Advisory Commission—fifteen geneticists, ethicists, and others appointed by President Clinton in 1996—voted against making such a distinction between producing and deriving the cells and simply using them. One suggestion is to use germline cells of fetuses that are already dead as a result of legal abortion. However, these cells may not be identical to stem cells derived from embryos, and deriving stem cells from this source is difficult. The National Bioethics Advisory Commission's charter expired in 2001. In its place was established the President's Council on Bioethics. This commission reported its conclusions

on human cloning in July 2002. It recommended a four-year moratorium on all types of human cloning. (See the note earlier in this chapter concerning the congressional bill banning human cloning.) The commission recommended that if no action is taken by Congress at the end of this period, the moratorium would lapse. As of May 2002, six states had banned cloning in one form or another, but only Michigan has banned cloning for research. California has reversed an earlier moratorium. In September 2002, the state's governor signed into law a bill that "explicitly allows research on stem cells from fetal and embryonic tissue."[24] The state also plans to fund such research. Some critics assert that it would be difficult to ban one type of cloning without the other. For example, if reproductive cloning were prohibited but research or therapeutic cloning were allowed, then how would one know whether cloned embryos were being used in fertility clinics? It would be impossible to distinguish them from ordinary ones. Furthermore, if there were no federal funds provided for research cloning, then there also would be no oversight. We would not know what was going on behind closed doors. Scientists also point out how essential federal research funds have been for new developments. Just how the public will continue to respond to these possibilities remains to be seen. However, we can and do generally believe it appropriate to regulate scientific research and industrial applications in other areas, and we may well consider such regulations appropriate for human cloning also. For example, regulations regarding consent, the protection of experimental subjects and children, and the delineation of family responsibilities are just some of the matters that may be appropriately regulated. Other ethical issues are raised by the use of *surrogate mothers* and *prenatal embryo transfer* and are related to social matters such as the nature of parentage and to concerns about the dangers of commercialization and the buying and selling of babies.[25]

GENETIC ENGINEERING

Developments in modern genetics also have presented us with new ethical problems. The Human Genome Project, an effort to map the entire human genome, was completed in the summer of 2000 and its results first published in early 2001. The map was expected to contain 100,000 genes, but scientists now believe that only 20,000 human genes exist. Humans have roughly the same number of genes as other animals, but scientists found that "we have only 300 unique genes in the human (genome) that are not in the mouse," for example.[26] However, although humans have approximately the same number of genes as a spotted green puffer fish, it is surmised that human capacity comes from "a small set of regulatory genes that control the activity of all the other genes." These would be different in the puffer fish.[27]

Two entities had competed in this race to map the entire human genome. One was a public consortium of university centers in the United States, Great Britain, and Japan. It made its findings publicly available. It used the genome from a mosaic of different individuals. The other research was done by Celera Genomics, a private company run by Dr. Craig Venter. It used a "shotgun" strategy. Its genetic source material came from Venter and four others. Celera also proposed to make its results available to the public after they have been analyzed—that is, to tell where the genes lay in the entire DNA sequence. Later the company expects to charge a fee to use its analyzed database. On September 4, 2007, Dr. Venter published his entire genetic sequence.[28]

The next efforts have been to determine what role the various elements, including the genes, play. In this effort, one focus has been on individual differences. The human genome, "a string of 3 billion chemical letters that spell out every inherited trait," is almost identical in all humans: 99.99 percent. But some differences, so-called genetic misspellings that are referred to as *single nucleotide polymorphisms* (SNPs or "snips"), can be used to identify genetic diseases. The SNPs give base variations that contribute to individual differences in appearance and health, among other things. Scientists will look for differences, for example, by taking DNA samples of 500 people with diabetes and a similar number from people without the disease and then look for DNA patterns.[29] The SNPs also influence how people react differently to medications. Some people can eat high-calorie and high-fat foods and

still not put on weight while others are just the opposite. Some have high risks of heart disease, whereas others do not. With genetic discoveries based on the Human Genome Project and more recent efforts, one hope is that diets will be able to be tailored to individual human genetic makeups. This opens new fields of personalized medicine and nutrition known as *pharmacogenomics* and *nutrigenomics*.[30] However, these fields are in their infancy and the science behind them is just emerging, so people are cautioned not to expect that they can plunk down $200 for an individual scan that will detail their personal genetics.

Still, much work is now being done in this area. For example, on October 30, 2002, "a $100 million project to develop a new kind of map of the human genome was announced." The group behind the effort is an international consortium of government representatives from Japan, China, and Canada, and the Wellcome Trust of London. The U.S. NIH is investing $39 million in the project. The "goal is to hasten discovery of the variant genes thought to underlie common human diseases like diabetes, asthma and cancer."[31] Scientists will use the Human Genome Project map as a master reference and compare individual genomes to it. They then expect to locate the genes that cause various diseases. Some diseases are caused by single genes, such as that producing cystic fibrosis, but others are thought to be caused by several genes acting together. Other genes might be discovered that relate to certain beneficial human traits. For example, some scientists are working on locating what they call a "skinny gene." Using mice from whom a single gene has been removed, scientists at Deltagen, a company in Redwood City, California, have been able to produce mice that remained slim no matter how much they were fed.[32] According to geneticist David Botstein, the impact of the Human Genome Project on medicine "should exceed that 100 years ago of X-rays, which gave doctors their first view inside the intact, living body."[33] Currently, "gene therapies are being developed that would block myostatin in humans," something directed to the treatment of muscular dystrophy and frailty in older persons. Myostatin curbs the growth of muscles. However, this also has wider applications.

For example, a breed of cattle called Belgian Blue has been developed that has huge muscles and very little fat.[34] This may also cause concern about its use by athletes, who could pump up without much effort. Moreover, "gene therapy leaves no trace in the blood or urine," which would make drug testing of athletes, which is already problematic, even more difficult. Other gene therapies, including so-called gene doping, have been and are being developed that could cause the human body to produce more red blood cells. Persons with this natural abnormality have been exceptional athletes, including a gold medalist in cross-country skiing.[35]

Ethical Issues

Before new developments in genetics can be transformed into practical benefits, studies using human subjects often must be done. Since the Nuremberg trials and the resulting code for ethical experimentation, informed consent has been a requirement for the conduct of research that involves human subjects. Consider a study designed to determine the possible benefits of an experimental treatment for Parkinson's disease.[36] This frightening disease afflicts 1.5 million people in the United States as well as many others around the world. Its sufferers first experience weakness and then slurred speech, uncontrollable tremors, and eventually death. The cause of the disease is not entirely known and there is no cure yet. What is known is that the disease works by destroying a small section of the brain, the substantia nigra, which controls movement. One new hope for treatment of Parkinson's disease uses the transplanted brain cells from aborted six-to eight-week-old fetuses.[37] Are the patients in this trial and others that involve genetic engineering likely to be able to give the requisite kind of informed consent to guarantee that the experiment is ethically acceptable? Consider the actual case. The potential participants already have experienced some symptoms of the disease. Here is a treatment that promises to help them. They are informed that the study is a randomized clinical trial and that if they agree to participate they may or may not get the experimental treatment. If they are randomized to the control group rather than the treatment group, then they will go through the same

procedure including having holes drilled in their skull and tubes passed into their brain, but they will not actually be receiving anything that will benefit them. In fact, like those in the treatment group, they will be subject to the usual risk of brain damage and stroke that accompanies the procedure.

What kind of thought procedure would such persons be likely to undergo in the process of deciding whether to participate in this trial? Is informed and free consent likely? Would they really be informed of the various details of the procedure? Would they really understand their chances of being in the treatment group? Would they be influenced, if not coerced, into joining the study because of the nature of their disease and great need? Would they also have to be willing to undergo this risky procedure solely for the sake of the knowledge that might be gained from the study and not for their own immediate benefit? In other words, would they have to be willing to be used as guinea pigs? It is possible that the conditions of genuine informed and free consent would be met. However, it is also likely that these conditions could not be met, because the patients either would not understand what was involved or would be coerced into participation.

As in the testing of many new medical therapies, modern scientific methodology demands that studies be controlled and randomized; otherwise, the information derived could be unreliable. However, to do this particular study we seem required to violate one demand for an ethical experiment that uses human subjects—namely, that the participants' consent be informed and uncoerced. What we have here is an example of one of the many ethical dilemmas that we face today because we live in a world in which modern science and technology are pervasive. We use knowledge gained by science to help us, but we are also subject to the demands of science. Modern technologies provide us with many goods and opportunities, yet in giving us more choices they also present us with more difficult ethical decisions. The decisions have no easy answers. Another ethical question that scientists sometimes face is whether one should let ethical concerns determine whether to carry on some research.

One example of this was the Tuskegee syphilis study in Chapter 5 when we introduced Kant's moral theory. Is knowing always a good and thus should the science that helps us know what is the case always be pursued? Those who analyze the ethics of research using human subjects continue to debate the issues surrounding the informed consent requirement. In the end, this requires that people not be used or that they not be used for goals and purposes to which they do not consent or make their own. You may recognize this as a requirement of Kant's moral philosophy and can refer to the discussion of its basis in Chapter 5. In this chapter, we will suggest ways to analyze a few other problems that modern science and technology now present us.

The possibility of gene therapy also presents us with new ethical problems. If it were possible to use these methods to activate, replace, or change malfunctioning genes, then this would be of great benefit for the many people who suffer from genetic diseases. Using genetic techniques to provide human blood-clotting factor for hemophiliacs, manufactured human insulin for diabetics, human growth hormone for those who need it, and better pain relievers for everyone is surely desirable and ethically defensible. However, use of the technology also raises ethical concerns. Among these questions are those related to the risks that exist for those who undergo experimental genetic therapies. We also should be concerned about the access to these procedures, so that it is not just those who are already well off who benefit from them. The biotechnology industry continues to grow. Should information and products of great medical benefit be able to be kept secret and patented by their developers? For example, the company Myriad Genetics recently announced that it had found a gene linked with breast cancer. The company also has attempted to patent the gene.[38] In another example, a newly developed technique allows the alteration of genes in sperm that would affect not the individual himself but his offspring and thus alter human lineage.[39] It is one thing to do this in the interest of preventing genetic disease in one's offspring, but it is quite another to add new genetically based capabilities to one's children or to the human race.

Although these are still somewhat remote possibilities, they give us cause for some concern, not the least of which is whether we are wise enough to do more good than harm by these methods. Two of the National Bioethics Advisory Commission's major topics of discussion are the rights of human research subjects and the use of genetic information. You can continue to follow news accounts of the new reproductive and genetic technologies as well as the reports of committees such as the President's Council on Bioethics. As you do, you should be more aware of the variety of ethical issues that they involve or address. The issues are complex, but the first step in responding to them is to recognize them.

GENETICALLY MODIFIED PLANTS AND ANIMALS

You may have seen or otherwise been made aware of protests against genetically modified food, sometimes called "Frankenfoods." The title most probably comes from the story of Dr. Frankenstein, who creates a monster that could not be controlled. Critics fear the same for food that has been genetically modified or tampered with. What are they talking about? These are crops that have been genetically modified to include desired traits such as drought tolerance or lowered freezing level. Although some of these traits could be established through traditional breeding methods, some could not. Genetic mechanisms both speed up the process and give more control over it.

Recently, the National Academy of Sciences has determined and reported that "genetically engineered crops do not pose health risks that cannot also arise from crops created by other techniques, including conventional breeding."[40] It is not the method of production that should be of concern, the NAS argues, but the resulting product. There is much that the general public does not understand about so-called genetically modified food.

Strictly speaking, genetic engineering involves inserting a specific gene from one organism into another—and the function of the gene is known. On the other hand, "nearly every food we eat has been genetically modified" in the broader sense in that plants have been cross-bred for centuries.[41]

Cross-breeding "involves the mixing of thousands of genes, most unknown."[42] In some cases, mutations are now caused by "bombarding seeds with chemicals or radiation" and seeing what comes of it. For example, lettuce, beans, and grapefruit have been so modified.[43]

Over the last few years, U.S. farms have gradually increased the amount of crops that have been genetically engineered. In 2002, one-third of the corn grown in the United States was genetically engineered. Farmers now grow "more than 79 million acres of genetically engineered corn and soybeans, the nation's two most widely planted commodities."[44] Of the cotton crop, 71 percent is also gene-altered. "Nearly two-thirds of the products on American supermarket shelves are estimated to contain genetically altered crops."[45] These crops are easier and cheaper to grow and can provide more food from less land. They need fewer chemicals in the way of insect repellants, herbicides, and fertilizers because they are "engineered to be toxic to insect pests or to be resistant to a popular weed killer."[46] For example, the insertion of *Bacillus thuringiensis (Bt)* genes into corn enables it to resist the corn borer. Environmentally damaging herbicides can then be reduced. New strains of rice may also help solve the world famine problem. So-called golden rice can also help lessen vitamin A deficiency in poor countries because it contains greater amounts of the vitamin than other rice strains. Vitamin A deficiency causes blindness and other infections in much of the world's poorest children. "Edible vaccines in tomatoes and potatoes" would make them more easily available to people than injectable ones.[47] Moreover, genetically modified foods can also lead to "more healthful foods, a cleaner environment, and a worldwide ability to produce more food on less land—using less water, fewer chemicals, and less money."[48] This is especially important for areas in the world— for example, some African countries—where famine and malnutrition are serious problems. For example, opposition to genetically modified food has led to Uganda prohibiting efforts to develop a fungus-resistant banana, even though this fungus has seriously damaged its banana crop, one of its most important.[49]

At the same time, protests have grown, especially in Europe and Japan, but also in the United States. Some of the criticism is probably based on ungrounded fears. On the other hand, some hazards may be real. Herbicide-resistant crops may help create "superweeds." Neighboring crops may be contaminated with foreign genes. New forms of insects that are resistant to the inbred herbicides may develop. Crop antibiotic resistance may transfer to humans.[50] However, earlier worries about negative effects on monarch butterflies seem to have been alleviated.[51] It is possible to reduce some of these risks, for example, by creating sterile plants—that is, plants that do not produce pollen, which could be a means of contamination. So far, many of the cited possible risks have not materialized, but this does not prove they do not exist.

Ethical Issues

Much of the debate about genetically modified food and crops has been a matter of comparing benefits and risks. As described in Chapter 4, cost–benefit analysis first involves estimating risks and benefits— an empirical matter—and then a comparative evaluation in which one tries to determine the various values to show whether the positive values outweigh the negative consequences. Longer and healthier lives for more people weigh on the positive side, and risks to both weigh on the negative side. There is also the problem of how to count speculative and unknown risks and who should prove what. If we are risk-averse and come down on the side of conservatism, then we may avoid unknown risks but also eliminate possible benefits, including that of saving lives.

A different ethical issue that concerns some people is the whole idea of interfering with nature. Are there not natural species of plants as well as animals that we should respect and not manipulate? One problem with this line of criticism is that it is difficult to distinguish good forms of manipulating nature from unacceptable ones. Those who object on these grounds may point out that cross-species transfers are what is objectionable. One problem with this objection is that similar transfers have occurred in nature—that is, if some essential elements of evolutionary theory are true.

Genetically modified animals may present some of the same ethical problems, for there are benefits and risks to be compared and also transfers among species. Some of the benefits from genetic modifications can be seen in animals such as goats, rabbits, and cows, which may be modified to include pharmaceuticals in their milk. PPL Therapeutics in the United Kingdom, for example, has been "experimenting with transgenic sheep's milk to produce protein drugs for cystic fibrosis and hemophilia."[52] Other species may be modified to produce more meat or meat with less fat or to have better resistance to disease. Still, in other cases, these practices promote economic efficiency. Genetically modified animals may also benefit us in other ways. For example, pigs have been created with human genes. The reason for this is that pig organs are similar to human organs and, if modified with human genes, may be transplanted into humans without immune rejection. This is called *xenotransplantation.* Cloned animals also present a kind of case of genetically modified animal. In the process of cloning, genes may be inserted or removed. One company has cloned five pigs—Millie, Christa, Alexis, Carrel, and Dotcom—with human genes as a prelude to use for transplants.[53]

Genetically modified animals are used in research. (See, for example, the knockout mice example from the previous chapter.) But they also might provide "better yields of meat, eggs, and milk."[54] Still, they may also pose risks. For example, some critics worry that farm-raised and genetically altered salmon, if released into the wild, might harm other species of fish.[55] There is uneasiness, too, about combining elements of different species because it transgresses natural boundaries. The same responses to these ethical problems here can be given as in the case of plants, however. In addition, the yuck objection is sometimes raised here also. For example, just the thought of having a pig heart or lung within one's own body might provoke this reaction in some people. The same response regarding the objection to human cloning noted earlier in this chapter may also be given here. Among the ethical issues that apply to animals but not plants is their ethical or humane treatment. This may involve not only the engineering of them but also their suffering and death—as in the case of pigs whose organs would be transplanted or mice who would be given a human cancer. (See the previous chapter on animal rights for more on this problem.)

GENETIC SCREENING

Advances in genetics have also made possible a new type of screening procedure. Insurers and prospective employers may now or soon have access to individual genetic information and be able to use that information to their own advantage—but not to the advantage of the person being screened. Although the procedures may be new, the ethical issues are similar to those raised by other types of screening, including drug screening.

If you are on the job in your office, should your employer be able to monitor your behavior with cameras, microphones, and access to your computer and other files? It may well be in the best interest of your employer to make sure that you are using your time well for the benefit of the company. However, you may want and expect a certain amount of privacy, even at work. Privacy is also at risk on the Internet. Many people are very concerned about giving out personal information over the World Wide Web and want to be assured that they will have control over how it is used.[56]

"In a typical five-day stay at a teaching hospital, as many as 150 people—from nursing staff to X-ray technicians to billing clerks—have legitimate access to a single patient's records."[57] Sixteen states do not now have any guarantees regarding the privacy of medical records.[58] Increasingly, more of the things that we used to take as guaranteed areas of privacy are no longer so. Thus, we need to consider whether this should be the case. We think that people generally have a right to privacy, but we are less sure what this means and what kinds of practices would violate privacy. Suppose, for example, that a technology existed that could read a person's mind and the condition of various parts of her body, could hear and see what goes on in one's home—his bedroom or bathroom—and could record all of these in a data bank that would be accessible to a variety of interested parties. What, if anything, would be wrong with this?[59] One of the things that we find problematic about others having access to this knowledge is that others would have access to matters that we would not want anyone else to know. According to Thomas Scanlon, this is what the right to privacy is—a right "to be free from certain intrusions."[60] Some things, we say, are just nobody else's business.

The Value of Privacy

If this definition of privacy seems reasonable, then we can ask why we would not want certain intrusions like those in the hypothetical example. Many reasons have been suggested, and you may sympathize with some more than others. Four are provided here. The first concerns the kinds of feelings that one would have about certain things being known or observed—one's thoughts, bathroom behavior, or sexual fantasies, for example. It may well be that one should not feel emotions like shame or unease at such things being known. Perhaps we have these feelings simply as a result of social expectation. Nevertheless, many of us do have these *negative feelings*.

A second reason why we might want certain things kept to ourselves is our desire to control information about us and to let it be known only to those to whom we choose to reveal it. Such control is part of our ability to own our own lives. We speak of it as a form of *autonomy* or self-rule. In fact, the loss of control over some of these more personal aspects of our lives is a threat to our very *selfhood*, some say. For example, in his study of what he calls "total institutions" such as prisons and mental hospitals, Erving Goffman described the way that depriving a person of privacy is a way of *mortifying* (literally killing) the self.[61] Having a zone of privacy around us that we control helps us define ourselves and mark us off from others and our environment. This reason for the value of privacy is related to both the third and fourth reasons.

Third, privacy helps in the formation and continuation of *personal relations*. We are more intimate with friends than with strangers, and even more so with lovers than with mere acquaintances. Those things about ourselves that we confide in with those closest to us are an essential part of those relationships. According to Charles Fried, "privacy is the necessary context for relationships which we would hardly be human if we had to do without—the relationships of love, friendship, and trust."[62] Sexual intimacies are thus appropriate in the context of a loving relationship because they are privacy sharings that also help to establish and further that relationship.

Fourth, we want to keep certain things private because of the risk that the knowledge might be used against us to cause us harm. *Screening* procedures in particular come to mind here. Drug screening, HIV testing, or genetic disease scans all make information available to others that could result in social detriment. For example, we could be harmed in our employment or our ability to obtain insurance. The problem of *data banks* is also at issue here. Our medical records, records of psychiatric sessions, histories of employment, and so forth could be used legitimately by certain people. However, they also may be misused by those who have no business having access to them. In a particularly problematic recent case, the managed care company that was paying for the psychological counseling of one patient asked to inspect his confidential files. The psychologist was concerned. "The audit occurred, they rifled through my files," he said, and "made copies and went. But it changed things. He (the patient) became more concerned about what he was saying. . . . A few visits later he stopped coming."[63] Another case is also illustrative of the harm that can be caused by the invasion of privacy. In 1992, someone obtained a copy of the hospital records of a person running for Congress and sent them anonymously to the press. *The New York Post* published the material, including notes about this person's attempt to kill herself with sleeping pills and vodka. In spite of this, the woman won the election; still, she sued the hospital for invasion of privacy.[64]

Screening and Conflicts of Interest

It is with this fourth reason in particular that the matter of possible *conflict of interest* arises. An employer may have a legitimate interest in having a drug-free workplace, for example. It is an economic interest, for one's employees may not be able to do an effective job if they have drug-use problems. Passengers on public transportation may also have a legitimate interest in seeing that those who build and operate the bus, train, or plane are able to function well and safely. Airline passengers may have an interest in having other passengers and their bags scanned to prevent dangerous materials from being carried on board. It is not clear in whose interest is the drug screening of athletes. In professional athletics, it may be the economic interests of the owners, and in collegiate athletics and nonprofessional competitions such as the Olympics it may be for the sake of the fairness of the competition as well as the health of the athletes themselves.

In cases of conflicts of interest generally, and in the cases given here, we want to know on which side the interest is stronger. In the case of *drug testing* of airline pilots, the safety of the passengers seems clearly to outweigh any interest the pilots might have in retaining their privacy. In the case of employee drug use, it is not so clear that employers' economic interests outweigh the employees' privacy interests. In these cases, one might well argue that unless there is observable evidence of inefficiency, drug testing should not be done, especially mandatory random drug testing. In the case of *genetic screening* by life or health insurance providers, the answer also seems less clear. If a person has a genetic defect that will cause a disease that will affect his life expectancy, is his interest in keeping this information secret more important than the financial interests of the insurer knowing that information? A person's ability to obtain life insurance will affect payments to others on his or her death. In the case of health insurance coverage where not socially mandated or funded, the weight might well be balanced in favor of the person because having access to health care plays such a major role in a person's health. In fact, some state legislatures are now moving to prevent health insurers from penalizing individuals who are "genetically predisposed to certain diseases."[65] In arguing for these laws, supporters insisted that they were designed to prevent "genetic discrimination." The phrase is apt in the sense that it seeks to prevent people from being singled out and penalized for things that are not in their power to control—their genes.

In the case of *AIDS screening,* consequentialist arguments might make the most sense. We would thus ask whether mandatory testing would really produce more harm than good or more good than harm overall. Would mandatory screening lead fewer people to come forth voluntarily? What of the mandatory screening of physicians, dentists, and their patients? Some people argue that "mandatory testing of health workers for the AIDS virus . . . would be costly, disruptive, a violation of doctors' right to privacy, and the ruination of some careers."[66] The well-known case of a Florida dentist infecting a patient who later died caused quite a bit of alarm. However, in one study of patients of a surgeon who died of AIDS, 1,652 of his total of 1,896 patients were found and only one, an intravenous drug user, had AIDS.[67] The risk also goes the other way, with patients infecting health care workers. In 1990, the U.S. Centers for Disease Control and Prevention reported that 5,819 of the 153,000 reported cases of AIDS, or 4 percent, involved health care workers. This included 637 physicians, 42 surgeons, 156 dentists and hygienists, and 1,199 nurses.[68] It is not known whether any of these had other risk factors, but it does raise serious concern for health care workers.

In the case of airport *security screening,* a "backscatter" machine has been developed that can see through a person's clothing—that is, down to the skin—so that security personnel can determine better than with metal detectors whether a person is carrying a concealed item that could pose a danger to others.[69] Will people mind this invasion of their privacy? They appear almost nude to the screeners. Or would the somewhat better detection achieved by this method not be worth the kind of invasion of privacy that is involved?

This as well as other screening procedures can be evaluated in several ways. However, one of the most reasonable is to compare the interests of the various parties involved in order to determine whether the interest in privacy on the part of the ones screened is stronger or more important morally than the interests of those who wish or need the information produced by the screening. Whether the privacy interest is stronger will depend on why privacy is important. You can determine this by considering some of the reasons why privacy is valuable as given above.

With every new scientific advance and development come new ethical problems, for there are new questions about what we ought and ought not to do. The areas treated in this chapter that are based on scientific advances in genetics are no different. As new genetic information comes along, still new ethical questions will need to be addressed. However, from the suggestions given for thinking ethically about the problems addressed here, hopefully a basis has been provided for future discussions as well.

NOTES

1. *Scientific American* (July 2005): A6–A27.
2. "British Researchers Grow Heart Tissue from Stem Cells," Agence France Presse, Yahoo News, April 2, 2007; "British Team Grows Human Heart Valve from Stem Cells," *The Guardian,* April 2, 2007 (at http://www.guardian.co.uk/medicine/story/0,2 048062,00.html).
3. Carl T. Hall, "Stem Cell Research Opens New Doors," *San Francisco Chronicle,* April 16, 2007, pp. A1, A9.
4. Carl T. Hall, "Stem Cell Grants Come with Dash of Criticism," *San Francisco Chronicle,* March 31, 2007, pp. B1–B2.
5. http://en.wikipedia.org/wiki/Stem cell controversy.
6. *Scientific American,* op. cit., pp. A12–A13.
7. Ibid., p. A13.
8. *The Johns Hopkins Medical Letter* (Nov. 2003), pp. 1, 2, 7.
9. *The New York Times,* Aug. 24, 2004, p. D1.
10. Carl T. Hall, "Amniotic Fluid a Promising Stem Cell Source, *San Francisco Chronicle,* Jan. 8, 2007, pp. A1, A6.
11. *Scientific American,* op. cit., p. A14.
12. *The New York Times,* April 27, 2005, pp. A1, A16.
13. George Q. Daley et al., "The ISSCR Guidelines for Human Embryonic Stem Cell Research," *Science,* vol. 315, February 2, 2007, pp. 603–604.
14. *The New York Times,* May 12, 2006, p. A12.
15. *The New York Times,* Feb. 9, 2005, p. A8.
16. Jason Thompson, "Here, Kitty, Kitty, Kitty, Kitty, Kitty!" *San Francisco Chronicle,* Feb. 24, 2002, p. D6. The project had a Web site (www .missyplicity.com).
17. *The New York Times,* Oct. 8, 2004, p. A24.
18. Yahoo News, April 14, 2005; www.cryozootech .com/index.php?m=the_horses&d=pieraz_st_ en&l=en.
19. Peter Fimrite, "Pet-Cloning Business Closes—Not 'Commercially Viable.'" *San Francisco Chronicle,* Oct. 11, 2006, p. B9.
20. "Copied Cat Hardly Resembles Original," CNN. com, Jan. 21, 2003. It is also interesting to note that CC has since given birth to normal, healthy kittens that were naturally fathered; see http://en .wikipedia.org/wiki/CC_%28cat%29.
21. Gina Kolata, "Hybrid Embryo Mixture May Offer New Source of Stem Cells for Study," *The New York Times,* June 5, 2002, p. D3.
22. Jose B. Cibel et al., "The First Human Cloned Embryo," *Scientific American* (Jan. 2002): 44–51.
23. Gina Kolata, "Researchers Say Embryos in Labs Aren't Available," *The New York Times,* Aug. 26, 2002, p. A1; Marjorie Miller, "New Breed of Cloned Pigs—Organs Wanted for Humans," *San Francisco Chronicle,* March 15, 2000, p. A3.
24. "California Law Permits Stem Cell Research," *The New York Times,* Sept. 23, 2002, p. A18.
25. The procedure known as *embryo transfer* involves flushing the embryo out of the uterus and implanting it in the uterus of another female. Sometimes this is done when a woman is able to carry a fetus but not able to conceive because of damaged or missing ovaries. A man can provide the sperm for artificial insemination of a surrogate. The procedure then transfers the fetus to her uterus, and she undergoes a normal pregnancy and birth.
26. Tom Abate, "Genome Discovery Shocks Scientists," *San Francisco Chronicle,* Feb. 11, 2001, p. A1.
27. *The New York Times,* Oct. 21, 2004, p. A23.
28. http://en.wikipedia.org/wiki/Human_Genome_ Project#Whose_genome_was_sequenced.3F.
29. Tom Abate, "Proofreading the Human Genome," *San Francisco Chronicle,* Oct. 7, 2002, p. E1; Nicholas Wade, "Gene-Mappers Take New Aim at Diseases," *The New York Times,* Oct. 30, 2002, p. A21.
30. Andrew Pollack, "New Era of Consumer Genetics Raises Hope and Concerns," *The New York Times,* Oct. 1, 2002, p. D5.
31. Wade, "Gene-Mappers."
32. "Decoding the Mouse," *San Francisco Chronicle,* Feb. 24, 2002, p. G2.
33. Nicholas Wade, "On Road to Human Genome, a Milestone in the Fruit Fly," *The New York Times,* March 24, 2000, p. A19.

34. To see a photo of the Belgian Blues go to www .ansi.okstate.edu/breeds/cattle/belgianblue.

35. *The New York Times,* Aug. 25, 2004, p. A23.

36. See Barbara MacKinnon, "How Important Is Consent for Controlled Clinical Trials?" *Cambridge Quarterly of Healthcare Ethics, 5,* no. 2 (Spring 1996): 221–227.

37. We will bracket the issue of using aborted fetuses in research for the purpose of focusing on the other aspects of this study.

38. Reported in *The New York Times,* May 21, 1996.

39. *The New York Times,* Nov. 22, 1994, p. A1.

40. *The New York Times,* July 28, 2004, p. A13.

41. *The New York Times,* Jan. 11, 2005, p. D7.

42. *The New York Times,* July 28, 2004, p. A13.

43. *The New York Times,* Jan. 11, 2005, p. D7.

44. Philip Brasher, "Plowing Ahead with Biotech Crops," *San Francisco Chronicle,* March 30, 2002, p. A4.

45. Carey Goldberg, "1,500 March in Boston to Protest Biotech Food," *The New York Times,* March 27, 2000, p. A14.

46. Brasher, op cit.

47. See www.csa.com/hottopics/gmfood/oview.html.

48. *The New York Times,* Jan. 1, 2005, p. D7.

49. Ibid.

50. See www.genewatch.org.

51. Jon Entine, "Starbucks Protest—Coffee, Tea or rbST?" *San Francisco Chronicle,* Feb. 24, 2002, p. D2.

52. Tom Abate, "Biotech Firms Transforming Animals into Drug-Producing Machines," *San Francisco Chronicle,* Jan. 17, 2000, p. B1.

53. Gina Kolata, "Company Says It Cloned Pig in Effort to Aid Transplants," *The New York Times,* March 15, 2000, p. A21; and Marjorie Miller, "New Breed of Cloned Pigs—Organs Wanted for Humans," *San Francisco Chronicle,* March 15, 2000, p. A3.

54. www.ornl.gov/sci/techresources/Human_ Genome/elsi/gmfood.shtml.

55. See www.greennature.com.

56. "Privacy in the Online World," *The New York Times,* March 23, 2000, p. A12.

57. "Who's Looking at Your Files?" *Time* (May 6, 1996): 60–62.

58. Ibid.

59. This is modeled after a "thought experiment" by Richard Wasserstrom in "Privacy," *Today's Moral Problems,* 2d ed. (New York: Macmillan, 1979): 392–408.

60. Thomas Scanlon, "Thomson on Privacy," in *Philosophy and Public Affairs, 4,* no. 4 (Summer 1975): 295–333. This volume also contains other essays on privacy, including one by Judith Jarvis Thomson on which this article comments. W. A. Parent offers another definition of privacy as "the condition of not having undocumented personal knowledge about one possessed by others." W. A. Parent, "Privacy, Morality, and the Law," *Philosophy and Public Affairs, 12,* no. 4 (Fall 1983): 269–288.

61. Erving Goffman, *Asylums* (Garden City, NY: Anchor Books, 1961).

62. Charles Fried, *An Anatomy of Values: Problems of Personal and Social Choice* (Cambridge, MA: Harvard University Press, 1970): 142.

63. "Questions of Privacy Roil Arena of Psycho-therapy," *The New York Times,* May 22, 1996, p. A1.

64. "Who's Looking at Your Files?" op. cit.

65. "Bill in New Jersey Would Limit Use of Genetic Tests by Insurers," *The New York Times,* June 18, 1996, p. A1.

66. *The New York Times,* Dec. 27, 1990, pp. A1, A15.

67. Ibid.

68. Ibid.

69. www.usatoday.com/travel/news/2005-05-15- airport-xray-bottomstrip_x.htm; http://en.wikipedia .org/wiki/Backscatter_X-ray.

REVIEW EXERCISES

1. What is cloning through somatic cell nuclear transfer?

2. What has been accomplished with animal cloning through this technique?

3. How might stem cells play a role in human cloning in the future?

4. Summarize the arguments for and against human cloning based on the idea that it would be "playing God."

5. Summarize the arguments that are based on possible threats that cloning might pose to individuality.

6. What is meant by a "right to an open future"? What might human cloning have to do with it?

7. Summarize the arguments regarding human cloning related to exploitation, confusion of families, and the so-called yuck factor.

8. What is the Human Genome Project and what did it produce?

9. What are the primary ethical concerns related to experimental genetic therapies?

10. What ethical issues have been raised regarding the production and use of genetically modified plants and crops?

11. What ethical concerns do people raise about genetically modified animals?

12. Discuss the value of privacy and how it relates to genetic and other types of screening.

DISCUSSION CASES

1. Human Cloning. Suppose this technique for producing children were perfected. If you were to choose to have children, would you consider using this technique? What if there was a chance that you otherwise might pass on a genetic disease? Would there be any circumstance in which you would consider human cloning?

2. Food Labeling. Jane belongs to a group that is concerned about genetically altered food. The group is pushing to have information about genetic modifications in foods and ingredients listed on the labels along with nutritional information so those who object to such modifications can make informed choices about what to buy for themselves and their families. The food industry believes that this would be costly to do and raise the price of these products for all, including those who do not object. The industry wonders what else might logically also be required to be on labels, where the food was produced, what pesticides were used, and so forth. Do you agree with Jane's group? Why or why not?

3. Genetic Screening. Suppose you are living twenty-five years from now. Suppose that among the advancements in genetics is the ability to screen individuals for particular genetically caused or influenced disorders and conditions. Would you want to have such information? What kinds of information would you want to access? Would there be any information that you would not want to know? How much would you be willing to pay for such a screen? Do you think society should pay for anyone's screening? Why or why not?

YOU MAKE THE DECISION

Apply the theories and issues discussed in this chapter by accessing this animated simulation on the Ethics Resource Center.

Use the passkey that accompanies your book to gain access. If you do not have a passkey, visit cengage brain.com to purchase instant access to additional study material.

So, do you create your own Mini-Me to save your sister? Yes or No?

Module 17 - Stem Cell Research, Cloning, and Genetic Engineering   ◀◀ ❚❚ ▶▶   MUTE 🔊

© Cengage Learning

Selected Bibliography

Ackerman, Terrence F., and Arthur W. Nienhuis (Eds.). *Ethics of Cancer Genetics and Gene Therapy.* New York: Humana Press, 2001.

Almond, Brenda, and Michael Parker (Eds.). *Ethical Issues in the New Genetics: Are Genes Us?* Aldershot, NH: Ashgate Publishing, 2003.

Alpern, Kenneth D. (Ed.). *The Ethics of Reproductive Technology.* New York: Oxford University Press, 1992.

Andrews, Lori B. *The Clone Age: Adventures in the New World of Reproductive Technology.* New York: Henry Holt & Co., 1999.

———. *Future Perfect: Confronting Decisions about Genetics.* New York: Columbia University, 2002.

Appleyard, Bryan. *Brave New Worlds: Staying Human in the Genetic Future.* New York: Viking Press, 1998.

Baldi, Pierre. *The Shattered Self: The End of Natural Evolution.* Cambridge, MA: MIT Press, 2002.

Bayertz, Kurt. *GenEthics: Technological Intervention in Human Reproduction as a Philosophical Problem.* New York: Cambridge University Press, 1994.

Brandeis, Louis D., and Charles Warren. "The Right to Privacy." *Harvard Law Review IV* (Dec. 15, 1890): 193–220.

Brannigan, Michael. *Ethical Issues in Human Cloning.* New York: Seven Bridges Press, 2000.

Buchanan, Allen, Dan Brock, Norman Daniels, and Daniel Wikler. *From Chance to Choice: Genetics and Justice.* New York: Cambridge University Press, 2001.

Burfoot, Annette (Ed.). *Encyclopedia of Reproductive Technologies.* Boulder, CO: Westview Press, 1999.

Callahan, Joan C. (Ed.). *Reproduction, Ethics, and the Law.* Bloomington: Indiana University Press, 1996.

———. *Reproduction, Ethics and the Law: Feminist Perspectives.* Bloomington: Indiana University Press, 1995.

Catudal, Jacques N. *Privacy and Rights to the Visual: The Internet Debate.* Lanham, MD: Rowman & Littlefield, 1999.

Chadwick, Ruth F. *The Ethics of Genetic Screening.* New York: Kluwer Academic Publishers, 1999.

Committee on Science. *Scientific and Medical Aspects of Human Reproductive Cloning.* Washington, DC: National Academy Press, 2002.

Cook, Robin. *Acceptable Risk.* Berkeley, CA: Berkeley Publishing Group, 1996.

Coors, Marilyn E. *The Matrix: Charting an Ethics of Inheritable Genetic Modification.* Lanham, MD: Rowman & Littlefield, 2002.

Decew, Judith Wagner. *In Pursuit of Privacy: Law, Ethics and the Rise of Technology.* Ithaca, NY: Cornell University Press, 1997.

Dorman, Peter. *Markets and Mortality: Economics, Dangerous Work, and the Value of Human Life.* New York: Cambridge University Press, 1996.

Drlica, Karl. *Double-Edged Sword: The Promises and Risks of the Genetic Revolution.* Reading, MA: Addison-Wesley, 1994.

Dudley, William. *The Ethics of Human Cloning.* Farmington Hills, MI: Gale Group, 2001.

Etzioni, Amitai. *The Limits of Privacy.* New York: Basic Books, 1999.

Fischhoff, Baruch, Stephen L. Derby, and Sarah Lichtenstein. *Acceptable Risk.* New York: Cambridge University Press, 1984.

Flaherty, David. *Protecting Privacy in Surveillance Societies.* Chapel Hill: University of North Carolina Press, 1989.

Gehring, Verna V. *Genetic Prospects, Essays on Biotechnology, Ethics, and Public Policy.* New York: Rowman & Littlefield, 2003.

Gelehrter, Thomas D., Francis Collins, and David Ginsburg. *Principles of Medical Genetics.* Baltimore: Lippincott, Williams & Wilkins, 1998.

Gerdes, Louise I. *Genetic Engineering: Opposing Viewpoints.* Farmington Hills, MI: Gale Group, 2005.

Hartoum, Valerie. *Cultural Conceptions: On Reproductive Technologies and the Remaking of Life.* St. Paul: University of Minnesota Press, 1997.

Hull, Richard T. (Ed.). *Ethical Issues in the New Reproductive Technologies.* Belmont, CA: Wadsworth, 1990.

Humber, James M., et al. *Human Cloning.* Totowa, NJ: Humana Press, 2004.

Inness, Julie. *Privacy, Intimacy, and Isolation.* New York: Oxford University Press, 1992.

Kass, Leon R. *Human Cloning and Human Dignity: An Ethical Inquiry.* Collingdale, PA: Diane Publishing, 2002.

Kolata, Gina Bari. *Clone: The Road to Dolly and the Path Ahead.* New York: William Morrow, 1999.

Krimsky, Sheldon, and Peter Shorett, (Eds.). *Rights and Liberties in the Biotech Age, Why We Need a Genetic Bill of Rights.* New York: Rowman & Littlefield, 2005.

Lauritzen, Paul (Ed.). *Cloning and the Future of Human Embryo Research.* New York: Oxford University Press, 2001.

MacKinnon, Barbara (Ed.). *Human Cloning: Science, Ethics and Public Policy.* Champaign: University of Illinois Press, 2002.

Maginnis, Tobin. *Security, Ethics and Privacy.* New York: Wiley & Sons, 2000.

McCuen, Gary E. (Ed.). *Cloning: Science and Society.* Hudson, WI: Gem Publications, 1998.

McGee, Glenn (Ed.). *The Human Cloning Debate.* Berkeley, CA: Berkeley Hills Books, 2002.

McLean, Sheila A. M. (Ed.). *The Genome Project and Gene Therapy.* Aldershot, NH: Ashgate, 2002.

Mehlman, Maxwell, and Jeffrey R. Botkin. *Access to the Genome: The Challenge to Equality.* Georgetown, MD: Georgetown University Press, 1998.

Miah, Andy. *Genetically Modified Athletes: Biomedical Ethics, Gene Doping and Sport.* New York: Routledge, 2004.

Nussbaum, Martha, and Cass R. Sunstein (Eds.). *Clones and Clones: Facts and Fantasies About Human Cloning.* New York: W. W. Norton, 1998.

Paul, Diane B. *Controlling Human Heredity, 1865 to the Present.* Atlantic Highlands, NJ: Humanities Press, 1995.

Pence, Gregory E. *Cloning After Dolly Who's Still Afraid.* New York: Rowman & Littlefield, 2005.

————— (Ed.). *The Ethics of Food: A Reader for the 21st Century.* Lanham, MD: Rowman & Littlefield, 2002.

Peters, Ted. *Playing God? Genetic Determinism and Human Freedom.* New York: Routledge, 2002.

Rantala, M. L, and Arthur Milgram (Eds.). *Cloning: For and Against.* LaSalle, IL: Open Court, 1999.

Rasko, John, and Rachel Ankeny (Eds.). *Explaining the Ethics of Germ-Line Gene Therapy.* New York: Cambridge University Press, 2004.

Robertson, John. *Children of Choice: Freedom and the New Reproductive Technologies.* Princeton, NJ: Princeton University Press, 1994.

Rothstein, Mark A. (Ed.). *Genetic Secrets: Protecting Privacy and Confidentiality in the Genetic Era.* New Haven, CT: Yale University Press, 1997.

Ruse, Michael. *Cloning: Responsible Science or Technomadness?* Amherst, NY: Prometheus Books, 2004.

Schoeman, Ferdinand David. *Privacy and Social Freedom.* New York: Cambridge University Press, 1992.

Shiva, Vandana, and Ingunn Moser (Eds.). *Biopolitics: A Feminist and Ecological Reader on Biotechnology.* Atlantic Highlands, NJ: Zed Books, 1995.

Siedler, Maurya. *The Ethics of Genetic Engineering.* Farmington Hills, MI: Gale Group, 2004.

Smith, George Patrick. *Bioethics and the Law: Medical, Socio-Legal and Philosophical Directions for a Brave New World.* Lanham, MD: University Press of America, 1993.

Stanworth, Michelle (Ed.). *Reproductive Technologies: Gender, Motherhood and Medicine.* Minneapolis: University of Minnesota Press, 1987.

Steinberg, Deborah Lynn. *Bodies in Glass: Genetics, Eugenics, Embryo Ethics.* New York: St. Martins Press, 1997.

Sulston, John, and Georgina Ferry. *The Common Thread: A Story of Science, Politics, Ethics and the Human Genome.* Washington, DC: National Academy Press, 2002.

Suzuki, David T. *Genethics: The Clash Between the New Genetics and Human Values.* Cambridge, MA: Harvard University Press, 1989.

Thomson, Judith Jarvis. "The Right to Privacy." *Philosophy and Public Affairs 4,* no. 4 (Summer 1975): 295–333.

Ticehurst, Flo, et al. *Living with the Genome: Ethical and Social Aspects of Human Genetics.* New York: Palgrave Macmillan, 2007.

Van Dyck, Jose. *Manufacturing Babies and Public Consent: Debating the New Reproductive Technologies.* New York: New York University Press, 1995.

Wachs, Raymond. *Personal Information: Privacy and the Law.* Oxford, UK: Clarendon, 1989.

Wilmut, Ian, Arthur Kaplan, and Glenn McGee (Eds.). *The Human Cloning Debate.* Berkeley, CA: Berkeley Hills Books, 2000.

Wilmut, Ian, et al. *After Dolly: The Uses and Misuses of Human Cloning.* London: Little, Brown Book Group Limited, 2007.

Yount, Lisa. *The Ethics of Genetic Engineering.* Farmington Hills, MI: Gale Group, 2001.

18

Violence, Terrorism, and War

On the morning of April 16, 2007, student Cho Seung-Hui entered Norris Hall at Virginia Tech in Blacksburg, Virginia, bolted the doors shut from the inside, and proceeded to go first to a German classroom where he slowly and deliberately shot the instructor and then as many students as he thought still alive. Next he proceeded to a French class where he did the same. Finally, he entered an engineering class and again shot the teacher and students. In all, he killed thirty people before turning the gun on himself as police were closing in. Earlier in the day, he had killed two more students in a dormitory. Cho was a loner who would rarely respond to the initiatives of others. One of his teachers was worried about his behavior and some of his violent writings. He was a troubled young man who was angry and felt marginalized as it became clear from videos sent to NBC News that he made of himself before the shootings. He was going to make people pay for the perceived slights he felt. He had been recommended for psychiatric care after being judged to be a danger to himself or others. It is not clear whether he was treated. However, since he had not been committed, he was able to legally purchase two guns in Virginia in the months before the killing spree. He had seemingly been preparing for this rampage for months or longer. He was unlike some other serial killers who seem to enjoy the killings that take place over many years. Such school killings are, in fact, rare, although shocking. "Mass killings are less than one-quarter of 1% of U.S. homicides."[1]

Among the questions we ask about these various forms and examples of violence is, why? What was behind these events and actions? What can be done to decrease or prevent such violence? There are also moral questions that can be addressed. Put simply, is violence, or terrorism, or war ever justified? If so, why and under what conditions? If not, why not? This chapter is meant to address these questions.

VIOLENCE

Worldwide, violence claims the lives of between one and two million people each year. According to a recent report by the World Health Organization, 14 percent of all deaths for American males in 2001 resulted from violence, and 7 percent for females. Men were responsible for more than three-quarters of all homicides, with males aged fifteen to twenty-nine having the highest rates.[2]

According to the lobbying group Handgun Control, "more Americans were killed with guns in the 18-year period between 1979 and 1997 (651,697) than were killed in battle in all wars since 1775 (650,858)."[3] An American dies from a gunshot wound every eighteen minutes. Of the 60,000 Americans to die from guns between 1998 and 2000, 1,500 died accidentally, 15,000 committed suicide, and 11,000 were murdered.[4] Although exact numbers are difficult to come by, one can assume that this number remains much the same. Arguments about the contribution of gun availability to violent gun deaths often depend on empirical claims that are difficult to verify. Supporters of gun ownership most often appeal to particular interpretations of the Second Amendment to the U.S. Constitution and its stipulations about the "right to bear arms." Critics of such claims point out that this had to do with the need at the time for an armed militia as an internal protective force and that the same conditions no longer apply.

Violence is generally thought of as the use of physical force to cause injury to another or others. Physical assaults, shooting, and bombing are examples. However, we would not say that someone who pushed another out of the way of an oncoming car had been violent or acted violently. This is because violence also implies infringement of another in some way. It also has the sense of something intense or extreme. A small injury to another may not be considered an act of violence. Whether some sports—for example, football—can be considered violent games is something to think about.

Those who study the issue seek to understand the incidence and causes of violence. Violence has also been found to be correlated with income, and the majority of violent deaths are recorded in poor countries. In the United States, there is also more violent crime in low-income neighborhoods. Homicide rates have been correlated with economic downturns as well. Also, children and young adults who commit violent crimes are often found to have been subject to violence in their homes growing up.

On the other hand, studies have also shown that violence may be linked to violence in the media. According to some social scientists, movies today may provoke and play a causal role in violence, and many believe that the rash of school shootings as well as other random attacks can be linked to children and young people watching violent acts in movies and TV shows. This is particularly true, they claim, for children, who are more vulnerable to such influence and are less able to distinguish fiction from reality. No one study proves this conclusively, but hundreds of studies show a high probability of this connection.[5] One study showed that "children who watched more violence behaved more aggressively the next year than those who watched less violence on television, and more aggressively than would have been expected based

on how they had behaved the previous year."[6] Even after the killings at Virginia Tech, Canadian-based Lions Gate Studios released *Hostel: Part II*—about the torture killing of college students—less than two months later. Another movie example is *Scream,* which "opens with a scene in which a teenage girl is forced to watch her jock boyfriend tortured and then disemboweled by two fellow students . . . the killers stab and torture the girl, then cut her throat and hang her body from a tree so that Mom can discover it when she drives up."[7] Characters joke about the murders. They take it as great fun. In *Natural Born Killers,* killing is also treated as a way to have a great time. *Pulp Fiction, Seven,* and *The Basketball Diaries* (and you may be able to think of others) also involve random killing in grotesque ways, with whimpering and pleading victims, some of them high school classmates. These movies make big money for their producers—whether Disney, Miramax, or Time-Warner, for example—because today's teens to whom they appeal make up a large segment of the movie audience. Prime-time TV network shows "now average up to five violent acts per hour," and "the typical American boy or girl . . . will observe a stunning 40,000 dramatizations of killing by age 18."[8]

Just as many people are concerned about violence in movies, they also wonder about the effects of violent video games. For example, the two teen killers at Columbine High School in 1999 were addicted to the game *Doom.* In a video they made themselves, the two even compared *Doom*'s shotguns with their own.[9] Whether this game actually influenced their killing spree is controversial. Some research shows a low correlation between such game violence and aggressive behavior. The violence is too unreal, some researchers suggest. Others believe that it could be one factor in many that influence such behavior, especially if the violence is intense and realistic. The Entertainment Software Rating Board gives ratings to video and computer games from "Suitable for Children" to "For Adults Only." Among the terms used to describe the content is "intense violence," which is defined as "graphic and realistic-looking depictions of physical conflict. May involve extreme and/or realistic blood, gore, weapons, and depictions of human injury or death."[10] Such games could function as a release, provide simple fantasy experiences, or be incitements to commit certain aggressive acts.

Among the ethical questions related to these matters are the nature of the responsibility of corporations such as those that benefit financially from violent TV, movies, and video games. Even if there are no legal limits on graphic violence, is there not some moral responsibility to limit gratuitous depictions, especially knowing the good probability of some negative effects? Another moral question concerns freedom of speech. One of the points of free speech proponents is that being able to air different views does make a difference in what people believe and do. If this is so, then one cannot simultaneously support free speech and use this as a basis to be free to make whatever movies one wants, claiming that they do not affect people's behavior.

We can use the same ethical theories and perspectives to evaluate violence that we have used for other issues in this text. For example, consequentialists such as utilitarians would want to weigh the harms caused in the violence with the supposed good, in at least some cases, to be produced by that violence. For example, one may be justified in killing an intruder who is threatening your life. However, killing any number of innocent people for your own profit would not be justified. Nonconsequentialists such as Kant would want to evaluate the violence from a perspective of using persons or doing something that involves something irrational, such as saying that my killing is permissible but others in similar situations are not. We can also see how violence would be judged by looking at two particular kinds of violence: terrorism and war.

TERRORISM

Although there had been both warnings of terrorist attacks on Americans and American interests and some incidents in the preceding decade, nothing compared with the September 11, 2001, attacks on the twin towers of the World Trade Center in New York and the Pentagon in Washington, D.C., in which some 3,000 people were killed. There have been further threats of more attacks. People worry about attacks on water supplies, transportation systems, computer systems, and fuel depots. Individual suicide attacks in Israel have targeted civilians in shopping malls and buses. The number of terrorist attacks sharply increased from 2005 to 2006. One-half of the 20,000 terrorist-caused fatalities worldwide were in Iraq. In 2005, terrorists in Iraq killed 8,262 people in 3,468 attacks, and in 2006 the number climbed to 13,340 from 6,600. attacks.[11] Terrorists use weapons and materials such as explosives that are widely available. They do not need complicated or high-tech mechanisms to cause serious damage and widespread fear. Terrorists can be domestic or international. If international, they can be state-sponsored or members of loosely affiliated groups.

Before considering the ethical questions concerning whether terrorism or terrorist attacks are ever morally justified and why or why not, we should first clarify for ourselves what is meant by *terrorism.* After this, we can also understand it better by considering particular kinds of terrorism.

There are many different definitions of terrorism. The term's first known use was during the French Revolution for those who, like Maximilien Robespierre, used violence *on behalf of* a state. Only later was the term used to categorize violence *against* a state. The U.S. Department of State uses the following definition: "The term 'terrorism' means premeditated, politically motivated violence perpetrated against noncombatant targets by subnational groups or clandestine agents, usually intended to influence an audience." The U.S. Department of Defense defines terrorism as "the calculated use of violence or the threat of violence to inculcate fear; intended to coerce or to intimidate governments or societies in the pursuit of goals that are generally political, religious, or ideological."[12] By combining these definitions, we see that terrorism is, first of all, a particular kind of violence with particular aims and goals. The more immediate goal is to create fear. This is why civilians simply going about their daily routines are targeted at random. The more distant goals vary. In some cases, terrorists may use such violence to achieve some political goal such as independence. In Iraq, for example, it may be to cause the Americans and their allies to leave. Web sites used by terrorist groups also speak of wanting to rid the Arab world of Western infidels. They may see their way of life and values as threatened. They may feel that they are serving the will of God. According to Thomas Friedman, one reason why so many young Sunni Muslim men are willing to blow themselves up is that, although they believe that Islam is a superior monotheistic religion, "its decision to ban the reform and reinterpretation of Islam since the [twelfth] century has choked the spirit of innovation out of Muslim lands" and left them less economically developed and less powerful. One way to assert their worth is to fight Western decadence and the presence of foreigners in their land by becoming suicide bombers.[13] Most suicide bombers are young and thus probably more idealistic and easily influenced and manipulated. Furthermore, they seem to lack any ability to empathize with the innocent victims of their attacks. Many of the hundreds of Web sites devoted to some of these causes include graphic videos of beheadings and bombings to the accompaniment of spirited music, often giving the violence a religious blessing. It has also been determined that those behind these sites use them to contact users they think may be possible recruits.[14]

It has also been suggested that fundamentalist preaching and religious schools such as the madrassas play a key role in recruiting young people to the cause. However, those who have investigated the background of known terrorists find that most of them are at least middle class and most often well educated. Of the seventy-five terrorists behind recent attacks, 53 percent had "either attended college or had received a college degree . . . [whereas] only 52 percent of Americans have been to college."[15] Some terrorists are more rational in their goals than others in having sufficient historical and political sense to know what will and will not work. In other cases, it seems that there is no realistic calculation of what the results of terrorist actions are likely to be.

What moves other terrorists, according to this analysis, are certain aspects of their personalities. Some are unhappy with their life prospects. They find meaning in belonging to and being accepted by their group. They find it difficult to see things from the perspective of their victims or to think of them as real individuals. They think they themselves cannot be wrong. They demonize others and thus help make them acceptable targets.

A third motivating factor for some terrorists is said to be certain cultural beliefs that are difficult for others to appreciate. Willingness to be a martyr for the cause and regarding their actions as divinely sanctioned are two such culturally influenced traits. Some see outsiders as threatening to their way of life and values. They feel they have no other way to influence the state of affairs than to resort to terrorism.[16]

Another analysis of al Qaeda in particular likens its motives to those of leftist Western groups over the years. It sees this group not simply as a product of Islamic fundamentalism but also as having a "global revolutionary, anti-Western perspective that echoed the anti-imperialism of the older Arab and European new left and even today's anti-globalization movement."[17] The solution, according to this analyst, is to integrate these folks into Western society and to help remove social and economic obstacles to such integration.

Ethical Issues

We should first of all grant that some uses of the term *terrorism* are evaluative in nature. In other words, as with the term *pornography* discussed in an earlier chapter, one uses the term if one wants to say that something is bad. In any case, if we want to be able to make moral assessments of terrorism, and if we do not want to settle its moral status before we start our evaluation, then we should narrow and stabilize the definition so that we will know what we are about to judge.

What kind of ethical justification could be given in support of terrorism? The reasoning that supports terrorism is most often basically consequentialist and utilitarian. The end is thought to justify these means. If one supported this type of reasoning, then one would want to know whether, in fact, the benefits or good of the end or cause was such that it outweighed the harm and suffering caused by the means. One also could do empirical studies to see if these means when used actually have produced the desired effects. Did the Oklahoma City bombing lessen the power of such federal agencies as the FBI or the Department of Treasury's Bureau of Alcohol, Tobacco, Firearms, and Explosives? Did the Unabomber stop the progress of technology? Did the bombing of American embassies weaken the position of the United States in the world? Did the September 11 attacks bring down the U.S. government or change its international behavior?

One also might question the very notion that violence can achieve a peaceable good end. Does not violence instead beget violence, some ask? Similar questions are asked by pacifists (see below). Or one can question the consequentialist nature of this type of reasoning. Are there not other ethical imperatives to consider? One long-standing element of international law and the just war theory (discussed below) is the inviolability of civilians or noncombatants. Sometimes, the reasoning behind this has been to avoid the inefficient use of power and resources and concentrate force on subduing the opposite military power rather than unarmed nonmilitary personnel. At other times, a nonconsequentialist element becomes part of the ethical arguments. Although self-defense of some sort might be a basis for using violence against another, those who are not attacking but are simply going about the business of life cannot be used by others no matter how good the latter's cause. Thus the Geneva Conventions, including the fourth (adopted on August 12, 1949—almost sixty years ago), enunciated principles to protect civilian populations from the worst effects of war. For example, they hold that civilians not be the direct objects of attack. Where the attack of civilians has occurred, the offenders often are accused of "war crimes" and sometimes subject to international arrest and prosecution (see the discussion below).

Another ethical issue that arises in discussions of terrorism has to do with the means used to combat it. A much debated means is the U.S.A. Patriot Act. The full title of this act is "Uniting and Strengthening America by Providing Appropriate Tools Required to Intercept and Obstruct Terrorism Act of 2001." It was introduced less than a week after the September 11 attacks, hastily considered by Congress, and signed into law by President George W. Bush on October 26, 2001. The purpose was to strengthen the country's defenses against terrorism. It amended several laws in a way that expanded and strengthened the government's surveillance and investigative powers by increasing its ability to "monitor private communications and access personal information."[18] For example, although the government was previously required to show probable cause of the commission of a crime in order to obtain a court order for such surveillance, this is no longer the case in many instances. For example, it is now easier for the government to obtain "roving wiretaps" when suspects switch phone numbers. A suspect's business, medical, educational, and library records may be accessed. Critics worry about the effect the act may have on civil liberties and privacy rights. The ethical issue may be formulated in terms of a balancing act: How important are the provisions of the act, what risk does it curtail, and how important are the privacy and liberty rights that might be compromised? The same issue arose earlier in this text in relation to genetic screening, and one can consider the ethical arguments by reviewing that section.

Another means used is video surveillance. For example, London has an extensive system of video surveillance—closed-circuit television (CCTV)—on its subways and throughout much of the city, which seems to have led to the identification of the bombers involved in the July 7, 2005, attacks. San Francisco has CCTV cameras installed on all of its subway station platforms. In New York City, the placement and use of cameras is sporadic. Only in some cases in the United States are the videos recorded and stored. However, new electronic surveillance technology has made it easier to store and retrieve such images, which are also much more clear and detailed.[19] The ethical issue here is also one of balancing whether the increase in safety provided by these systems is also worth the reduction in privacy.

PACIFISM

Pacifism is the view that the use of force, including lethal force, is morally objectionable. It is the opposite of militarism, or the view that the use of force, especially military force, is noble and just. In his essay "The Moral Equivalent of War," American pragmatist philosopher William James knew that fighting a war required the virtues of heroism, self-sacrifice, and loyalty.[20] Yet he called for a substitute for war, something that could develop those same virtues without the destruction of armed conflict. He envisioned something like today's California Conservation Corps, in which groups of people work to clear brush and clean up the environment. Not all pacifists oppose the use of all types of force. After all, there are nonphysical means of exerting force. One can think of there being degrees of pacifism—that is, in terms of the degree and type of force thought acceptable. Some pacifists also support the use of physical and even lethal physical force when it is necessary, such as to defend oneself. The question, then, is whether such lethal means are ever justified to defend others or a nation.

The reasons given in support of pacifism vary. Some people believe that nonviolent means to achieve some good end are preferable to violent means because they work better. You will recognize this consequentialist form of reasoning. Violence does more harm than good, they argue, because it can only beget violence. How can we determine whether or not this is true? We can look to see if historical examples support the generalization. We also can inquire whether this may result from something in human nature—that we are prone to violence and easily imitate the violent behavior of others, for example. Our judgments will then depend on adequate factual assessments. However, nonconsequentialist reasons are also given in support of pacifism—for example, that to kill another is wrong in itself. The reasons for this must be presented, and any exceptions to the rule must be discussed. Pacifists must address the criticism that it seems inconsistent to hold that life is of the highest value and yet not be willing to use force to defend it.

Intermediate between the more extreme versions of some forms of pacifism and militarism is a range of positions according to which the use of force, including military force, is sometimes justified. The problem is to circumscribe when it is and is not morally permissible to use force—even lethal force. Some people who have been long known for their opposition to war, for example, have relented when faced with situations such as those in Somalia, Bosnia, and Kosovo. "Moral isolation is simply not a defensible position for those opposed to war," according to longtime pacifist William Sloane Coffin, Jr.[21] Massive famine caused by civil war and "ethnic cleansing" are likely candidates for military intervention if this is the only way to eliminate them, some argue. Nevertheless, national boundaries and the national right to self-determination also cannot be ignored, so not every seeming injustice may rightly be a candidate for military intervention. Political philosopher Michael Walzer puts it this way: "I think of this in terms of the old international law doctrine of humanitarian intervention. . . . It was always held that in cases of massacre on the other side of the border, you have a right, and maybe an obligation, to go in and stop it if you can."[22] People have certain fundamental rights that states may not override. To what extent, and when, are others obligated to protect these rights?

In a speech to the U.S. Military Academy at West Point on January 5, 1992, President George H. W. Bush put forth the following criteria: "Using military force makes sense as a policy where the stakes warrant, where and when force can be effective, where its application can be limited in scope and time, and where the potential benefits justify the potential costs and sacrifice."[23] These criteria are not new. They have traditionally been part of international law. They are also part of what is known as *just war theory.* Because these principles are still used in the discussions and debates about justified military intervention, it would be well to briefly summarize them here. Some people have preferred the use of the phrase "justified war" instead of "just war" because they believe that in just war theory there is a presumption against the use of military force that must be overcome.

JUST WAR THEORY

As of September 2007, almost 3,800 U.S. soldiers had been killed in Iraq. The numbers of Iraqis killed varies widely with estimates being given between 23,000 and 650,000. The latter figure would amount to 2.5 percent of the population.

Moreover, an estimated 2 million to 4 million Iraqis have fled to Syria and Jordan, and many have been displaced but remain in the country. When one considers not only the deaths and displacements caused by and in war but also the destruction of cities and property, one can rightly ask whether war can ever be justified.[24]

Just war theory has a long history. Its origins can be traced to the writings of St. Augustine, the Bishop of Hippo in North Africa, in approximately 400 A.D. Augustine was concerned about how to reconcile traditional Christian views of the immorality of violence with the necessity of defending the Roman Empire from invading forces.[25] He asked what one should do if one sees an individual attacking an innocent, defenseless victim. His response was that one should intervene and do whatever is necessary (but only so much as was necessary) to protect the victim, even up to the point of killing the aggressor. Further developments of the theory were provided by Thomas Aquinas, the practices of medieval chivalry, and jurists such as Hugo Grotius. In modern times, the theory was given additional detail by the Hague and Geneva Conventions (1901). The first Geneva Conventions were written in 1864 "at the urging of Henri Dunant, founder of the Red Cross, to establish a code for the care and treatment of the sick, wounded and dead in wartime."[26]

There is general agreement that just war theory includes two basic areas: principles that would have to be satisfied for a nation to be justified in using military force, or initiating a war, and principles governing the conduct of the military action or war itself. These have been given the Latin names of *jus ad bellum* (the justness of going to war) and *jus in bello* (justness in war).

Jus ad Bellum

Just Cause The first principle that provides a condition for going to war is the *just cause principle*. To use force against another nation, there must be a serious reason to justify it. In the preceding Bush quotation, the phrase is "when the stakes warrant it." Although according to the just war theory there must be a just cause, the theory itself does not specify what is to count as a just cause. Defense of one's

territory against an invader would seem to be such a cause. However, there may also be other reasons. For example, righting a wrong may be insufficient cause and helping the world's downtrodden too vague, but intervening to prevent another nation from committing genocide on its own people may be a sufficient justification (assuming the other principles are also met). Other causes may sound familiar but may be questionable as justification, including preventing the spread of communism, ridding another country of a despotic and possibly dangerous leader, preventing a nation from obtaining and possibly using nuclear weapons, and protecting the world's oil supply. These may be cases of self-defense, using a broad definition of what is in a nation's vital interest and thus can be defended, but the connection and the seriousness would need to be demonstrated.

Among other related issues is that of preventive and preemptive strikes. A *preventive strike,* as Israel used in 1981 when its air force blew up an Iraqi nuclear reactor that could have been employed to make nuclear weapons materials, seeks to prevent some future harm. Just war theory does not in itself seem to help determine whether this type of strike or attack is ever justifiable, although common sense and notions of proportionality may support it (see below). However, the theory may provide some help with regard to *preemptive strikes.* Say that another nation is about to invade one's territory. Defense against such aggression would seem to be a just response. However, must one wait until the attacker steps across the border or sends planes in order to respond? One would think not. The principle of "only if attacked first" may be too strict. However, the farther one gets from this scenario, the more problematic the justification of preemptive strikes becomes. For example, "They are only now drawing up plans to attack but have not yet even assembled their forces." One might even not be sure that they will put their plans into action. This is not to say that even though remote in connection, such justifications have not been used in recent wars.[27]

The question is more complicated when, for example, there is the possibility of an Israeli or U.S. attack on Iran to prevent it from developing nuclear weapons. Even if it were possible, the benefit–harm comparison might well show that the harm done by the attack would outweigh any prevention of possible development.[28]

Proportionality Not only must the cause be just, according to the theory, but also the probable good to be produced by the intervention must outweigh the likely evil that the war or use of force will cause. This is the second principle, the *proportionality principle.* It requires that, before engaging in such action, we consider the probable costs and benefits and compare them with the probable costs and benefits of doing something else or of doing nothing. Involved in this utilitarian calculation are two elements: One assesses the likely costs and benefits, and the other weighs their relative value. The first requires historical and empirical information, whereas the second involves ethical evaluations. In making such evaluations, we might well compare lives that are likely to be saved with lives lost, for example. But how do we compare the value of freedom and self-determination, or a way of life with the value of a life itself? (Refer to the discussion of cost–benefit analysis in Chapters 4 and 15.)

Last Resort A third requirement for justly initiating a war or military intervention is the *last resort principle.* The idea is that military interventions are extremely costly in terms of suffering, loss of life, and other destruction, so other means must be considered first. They need not all be tried first, for some will be judged useless beforehand. However, this principle may well require that some other means be attempted, at least those that are judged to have a chance of achieving the goal specified by the just cause. Negotiations, threats, and boycotts are such means. When is enough enough? When have these measures been given sufficient trial? There is always something more that could be tried. This is a matter of prudential judgment and therefore always uncertain.[29]

Right Intention A fourth principle in the jus ad bellum part of the just war theory is the *right intention principle.* It requires that the intervention be always directed to the goal set by the cause and to

the eventual goal of peace. Thus, wars fought to satisfy hatreds or to punish others are unjustified. However, this principle also requires that what is done during the conduct of the war is necessary and that it not unnecessarily make peace harder to attain. There should be no gratuitous cruelty, for example. This moves us into discussion of the conduct of a war, the second area covered by the principles of just war theory.[30]

Jus in Bello

Proportionality Even if a war were fought for a just cause, with the prospect of achieving more good than harm, as a last resort only, and with the proper intention, it still would not be fully just if it were not conducted justly or in accordance with certain principles or moral guidelines. The jus in bello part of the just war theory consists of two principles. The first is a principle of *proportionality.* In the conduct of the conflict, this principle requires that to meet the various limited objectives, no more force than necessary be used, and that the force or means used be proportionate to the importance of the particular objective for the cause as a whole.

Discrimination The second principle is that of *discrimination.* This prohibits direct intentional attacks on noncombatants and nonmilitary targets. The principle has two basic elements. One directs us to focus on the issue of what are and are not military targets, and the other on who is and is not a combatant. Are roads and bridges and hospitals that are used in the war effort of the other side to be considered military targets? The general consensus is that the roads and bridges are targets if they contribute directly and in significant ways to the military effort, but that hospitals are not legitimate targets. The principle to be used in making this distinction is the same for the people as for the things. Those people who contribute directly are combatants, and those who do not are not combatants. Obviously, there are gray areas in the middle. One writer puts it this way: Those people who are engaged in doing what they do for persons as persons are noncombatants, and those who are doing what they do specifically for the war effort are combatants.[31] Thus, those who grow and provide food would be noncombatants, whereas those who make or transport the military equipment would be combatants.

Note, too, that although we also hear the term *innocent civilians* in such discussions, it is noncombatants who are supposed to be out of the fight and not people who are judged on some grounds to be innocent. Soldiers fighting unwillingly might be thought to be innocent but are nevertheless combatants. Those behind the lines spending time verbally supporting the cause are not totally innocent, yet they are noncombatants. The danger of using the term *innocents* in place of *noncombatants* is that it also allows some to say that no one living in a certain country is immune because they are all supporters of their country and so not innocent. However, this is contrary to the traditional understanding of the principle of discrimination.

The reason why the terms *combatant* and *noncombatant* are preferable is also related to the second aspect of the principle of discrimination—namely, that noncombatants not be the subject of direct attack. Combatants are not immune because they are a threat. Thus, when someone is not or is no longer a threat, as when they have surrendered or are incapacitated by injury, then they are not to be regarded as legitimate targets. This principle does not require that for a war to be conducted justly no noncombatants be injured or killed, but that they not be the direct targets of attack. Although directly targeting and killing civilians may have a positive effect on a desired outcome, this would nevertheless not be justified according to this principle. It is not a consequentialist principle. The end does not justify use of this type of means. This principle may be grounded in the more basic *principle of double effect,* which we discussed in Chapter 8. If this is true, then the other aspect of the principle of double effect would be relevant; that is, not only must the civilians not be directly targeted, but also the number of them likely to be injured when a target is attacked must not be disproportionately great compared to the significance of the target.

According to just war theory, then, for a war or military intervention to be justified, certain conditions for going to war must be satisfied, and the conduct in the war must follow certain principles or moral guidelines. We could say that if any of the principles are violated, that a war is unjust, or we could say that it was unjust in this regard but not in some other aspects. Some of just war theory has become part of national and international law, including the U.S. Army Rules for Land Warfare and the U.N. Charter. However, some of its principles also appeal to common human reason. As such, you too can judge whether these are valid or reasonable qualifications and whether they can play a useful role in debates about justified use of military force.

When one considers the history of wars and the tradition of just war theory, it can seem inappropriate or more than metaphorical to speak of a "war on terrorism." Today when so-called terrorists are not part of any recognized state, the weapons and rules of war do not apply. One might use military force against supposed terrorists, but that is still not quite a "war on terrorism."

WEAPONS OF MASS DESTRUCTION

According to a 2003 congressional report, the United States was the biggest arms dealer in 2002, "with about $13.3 billion, or 45.5 percent of global conventional weapons deals."[32] Russia came in second with $5 billion and France third with $1 billion. These were conventional weapons. The so-called weapons of mass destruction are purportedly different. This category usually includes biological, chemical, and nuclear weapons. Biological weapons are living microorganisms that can be used as weapons to maim, incapacitate, and kill. Among these weapons is anthrax, which infects either the skin or the lungs. Breathing only a small amount of anthrax causes death in 80 percent to 90 percent of cases. Smallpox, cholera, and bubonic or pneumonic plague are other biological agents that might be used. Genetic engineering may also be used to make more virulent strains. There have been no proven usages of biological weapons in modern wars, although movies such as *The Paradise Virus* and *Outbreak* have dramatized the possibilities. One hundred sixty-two states are signatories to the Biological Weapons Convention (1975), which prohibits the production, stockpiling, and use of such agents as weapons.

Chemical weapons include blister agents such as mustard gas, which is relatively easy and cheap to produce. It produces painful blisters and incapacitates rather than kills. Iraq is said to have used mustard gas in its 1982–87 war with Iran as well as some type of chemical weapon on the Kurdish inhabitants of Halabja in 1988. Through low-level repeated airdrops, as many as 5,000 defenseless people in that town were killed. Phosgene is a choking agent, and hydrogen cyanide "prevents transfer of oxygen to the tissues." Large quantities of the latter, however, would be needed to produce significant effects.[33] Hydrogen cyanide is a deadly poison gas, as is evidenced by its use in executions in the gas chamber. Sarin is called a nerve "gas," but it is actually a liquid. It affects the central nervous system and is highly toxic. In 1995, the Japanese cult group Aum Shinrikyo used many containers of sarin in the Tokyo subway. It sickened thousands and killed twelve people. Chemical weapons were also used somewhat extensively in both world wars. For example, in World War I, the Germans used mustard gas and chlorine, and the French used phosgene. Although it might not be usually classified as the use of a chemical weapon, in 1945 American B-29 bombers "dropped 1665 tons of napalm-filled bombs on Tokyo, leaving almost nothing standing over 16 square miles." One hundred thousand people were killed in this raid, not from napalm directly but from the fires that it caused.[34] One hundred forty-six nations have now signed the Chemical Weapons Convention (1994). Because such weapons can be made by private groups in small labs, however, verifying international compliance with the convention is highly problematic. Furthermore, Egypt, Syria, Lebanon, Libya, and Iraq refused to sign the convention, arguing that they should do this only if all weapons of mass destruction were banned, implying nuclear as well.[35]

Nuclear weapons, including both fission and fusion bombs, are the most deadly because of not only their powerful explosiveness but also their radiation and lingering genetic damage. The effects were well demonstrated by the U.S. bombings of Hiroshima and Nagasaki in August 1945. It is estimated that more than 100,000 people died and another 95,000 were injured. There have been many nuclear weapons treaties—for example, the Nuclear Non-Proliferation Treaty (1968), the Strategic Arms Limitation Treaties (SALT I in 1972 and SALT II in 1993), and the Strategic Offensive Reductions Treaty (2002). Nations known to have nuclear weapons now include China, France, India, Israel, North Korea, Pakistan, Russia, the United Kingdom, and the United States. Although the parties to the 1968 agreement promised to pursue negotiations in good faith and move to a future treaty on general and complete disarmament, none of them has made real efforts in this regard. On the other hand, there has been some progress made regarding the agreement to reduce their stockpiles and the numbers of deployed warheads in the 2002 treaty.[36] There is also a worrisome global black market in nuclear materials and know-how. These weapons are difficult but not impossible to make. A. Q. Kahn, a nuclear scientist now under house arrest in Pakistan, is thought to have given such materials to Libya, Iran, and North Korea. Although Russia agreed to secure its tactical nuclear weapons, many of which were poorly guarded, some are small enough that they could be "carried by one person, put in the back of a truck, and blow up a large part of a city."[37]

In calling these agents *weapons of mass destruction,* we imply that they are of a different order of magnitude than the usual means of modern warfare. It is clear why nuclear weapons are labeled in this way, but it is not so clear why the others are. Even when used somewhat extensively in World War I, "fewer than 1 percent of battle deaths" during that war were caused by gas, and only "2 percent of those gassed during the war died, compared with 24 percent of those struck by bullets, artillery shells, or shrapnel."[38] For gas to work well, there can be no wind or sun, and it must be delivered by an aircraft flying at very low altitude. If delivered by bombs, the weapons would be incinerated before they could become effective. Today's gas masks and antibiotics and other preventives and treatments lessen the lethality of such weapons even more. In 1971, smallpox accidentally got loose in Kazakhstan but killed only three people; and in 1979, a large amount of anthrax was released through the explosion of a Soviet plant, but only sixty-eight people were killed.[39] Nevertheless, the anthrax scare of 2001 in the United States showed that even small amounts can be deadly.

Is the use of biological, chemical, or nuclear weapons unethical, and if so, why? It would at least seem that their use would violate the discrimination and proportionality principles of just war theory. It would be difficult to target them only at those who are directly involved in the fighting and not also involve a disproportionate number of civilians. One wonders, however, whether ordinary bombs and bullets that explode and kill many more people than biological or chemical weapons are less objectionable. Nevertheless, people seem to fear biological and chemical weapons more than conventional weapons. Possibly it is the thought of being killed by something invisible that makes them so feared and is behind the desire to call them weapons of mass destruction with the implication that they are morally abhorrent.

WAR CRIMES AND UNIVERSAL HUMAN RIGHTS

Many of the elements of the laws of war and the nature of war crimes have been developed in the various declarations of the Geneva Conventions. The first convention was formulated in 1864 "to protect the sick and wounded in war time."[40] It was inspired by the founder of the Red Cross, Henri Dunant, and this organization has continued to play a role in its enforcement since then. Other treaties were passed in 1899, 1907, and 1925 relating to the use of poison gas and biological warfare. The convention of 1929 concerned the treatment of prisoners of war and the wounded, while the four agreements of 1949 sought to include protection for sailors and civilians and covered civil wars. A key provision of these conventions was the distinction between *combatants* and *civilians.* Important here was the requirement for combatants to wear uniforms so that they could be distinguished from civilians. The Geneva Conventions and two 1977 "protocols" also determined that "mercenaries," or fighters who do not belong to any state, "are not protected by the Geneva Convention."[41] Those who violate these conventions and protocols may be held guilty of

"war crimes." However, other treaties apply more widely than the Geneva Conventions. For example, the U.N. Convention Against Torture, which was ratified by the United States, requires that all signatory nations "prevent in any territory under its jurisdiction . . . cruel, inhuman, or degrading treatment."[42] In addition, the U.S. Uniform Code of Military Justice makes "cruelty, oppression or maltreatment of prisoners a crime."[43]

War crimes are often equated with "crimes against humanity." The idea is akin to notions espoused by natural law and natural rights theories discussed in Chapter 6. Certain things are violations of the natural value and dignity of persons, and all those who consider them should know this no matter what their own society's views. Thus, those in 1995 who separated the unarmed civilian men from the women and children in Kosovo and who marched them to the river and shot them, as well as those who moved people by force from their homes and burned the buildings because they wanted to cleanse the province from members of that ethnic group, should have known that this was wrong. When called explicitly a "war crime," the implication is also that there are rules of war that have been adopted by the international community over the decades. As noted already, among these is the immunity of civilians or noncombatants during war. Some of these rules were put in place after World War II with its great civilian death toll and the bombings of the cities of London, Dresden, Hiroshima, and Nagasaki. It is also to point out how a number of modern-day practices violate these rules. Among the examples are using civilians as a cover for rebel operations or as human shields against air attacks, as well as terrorizing people and ethnic cleansing. From 2001 to 2003, high-ranking members of the Serbian Yugoslav government and military, most notably Slobodan Milosevic, were put on trial for war crimes at the International Criminal Tribunal in the Hague. Among the crimes of which they were accused were forced expulsions of ethnic Albanians, mass executions and burials of civilians, and sexual assault.

There has recently been a debate about whether the so-called detainees at the U.S. base in

Guantanamo Bay, Cuba, are protected by the Geneva Conventions and whether they are to be considered prisoners of war with the rights guaranteed by these conventions. The denomination of *enemy combatant* is meant to distinguish such prisoners from those covered by these international conventions. Rights to a fair hearing and the ability to be represented by legal counsel to challenge their detention are among the concerns of rights activists. According to Global Rights, an international group, "enemy combatant is an invented classification that is not recognized in international law."[44] Moreover, the Geneva Conventions as well as some other U.S. laws require the humane treatment of prisoners as noted above. Questions have been raised about possible abuses of these detainees as well as others, most notably in the Abu Ghraib prisoner abuse scandals in Iraq that began in 2004.

In an opening address to the U.N. General Assembly on September 20, 1999, Secretary General Kofi Annan said, "nothing in the (U.N.) Charter precludes a recognition that there are rights beyond borders."[45] Although it would be better if a country itself took care to prevent human rights abuses of its citizens, sometimes this does not happen. What, then, is the responsibility of the international community? There is first the question of intervention, whether it can be effective given the conditions; if so, then what kind would be most effective? There is also the question of whether there are other bases for selective international concern about human rights abuses. The lack of intervention to prevent genocide in Rwanda is often cited here as well as the conflict in the Darfur region of Sudan. Others point out that it is too often after the fact of the abuse that international interest is aroused, when there are other means than military intervention that could have prevented it. Among these means are the curbing of the supply of weapons and alleviation of extreme poverty, which is perhaps the main cause of conflict.

There are many politically unstable countries around the world today. According to Robert Kaplan, a correspondent for *The Atlantic Monthly* and author of *The Ends of the Earth,* "More and more it is population growth that threatens stability in the third world."[46] Now more than 6 billion people live on Earth. The proportion of poor people to middle-class people in the third world is growing because their birthrate is higher. Such growth and urban overcrowding makes it difficult for countries to build stable civic institutions and to develop decent standards of living.[47] Combine this with ethnic diversity and conflict and the availability of weapons, and we have a recipe for military conflict. Issues of war and peace are altogether bound up, then, with economic matters.

Furthermore, economist Amartya Sen argues that when people have a say in their government, policies of abuse will not endure. "In any country with a democratic form of government and a relatively free press," he notes, "no substantial famine has ever occurred. People will not stand for it."[48] Among the notions on which the U.N. Declaration of Human Rights is based is that people ought to be able to choose the life that they wish to lead. In fact, this is the ideal of most democratic forms of government. This view is not necessarily an imposition from above of Western ways. Rights movements such as Poland's Solidarity and the National Conference on Soviet Jewry, as well as women's groups in some Muslim countries, are examples of bottom-up efforts to establish human rights. In Afghanistan, for example, the ruling fundamentalist Taliban regime imposed strict prohibitions on women's place in society, but the women did not want to abandon their hard-won freedoms and continued to press for better access to education and health care. What is seemingly needed is an agreement that, although individual nations remain a pillar of the international community, there is a responsibility to intervene that lies somewhere between the extremes of a broad license by which the United States, the United Nations, or NATO becomes the world police force and a narrow interpretation where the rest of the world stands by while observing terror and ethnic cleansing and serious violations of human rights.

It has been more than fifty years since the signing of the Universal Declaration of Human Rights. It was Eleanor Roosevelt who, in her apartment in February 1947, first brought together a committee to draft a human rights document.[49] The final document simply declared that there were universal human rights and then described them. It did not give reasons why we possess these rights. It could not do so because those drafting and signing it had different views on this. For some, it was the dignity given to humans by a divine creator God. For others, it was a recognition of the common humanity that we share and a sympathy for the plight of others like ourselves as well as the ability to imagine the pain or degradation of other human beings and to empathize with them. As a declaration, it appealed to the conscience of peoples and nations because it included no enforcement agency. In fact, the notion of a world tribunal to punish violations is today a controversial issue, one that the United States, for example, opposes. Nongovernmental or-ganizations are said to be the primary enforcers of the rights specified in the declaration: groups such as Amnesty International, which publicizes information on known violations and thus appeals to the moral conscience of others and prompts their moral condemnation of such behaviors.

Sometimes there is conflict between those who believe that political rights are primary—for example, the rights to freedoms of speech, the press, and movement. Others believe that social and economic rights—such as the rights to food, shelter, education, and health care—are more basic. Those who support the latter often insist that the former emphasis is too individualistic. However, it may well be that they each depend on one another. The United Nations has established a Commission on Human Rights to investigate rights abuses. The members meet every year for six weeks to name and thus shame violators. However, more recently the members themselves come from nations that clearly violate the rights of their own citizens—for example, Burma, China, Cuba, Libya, and North Korea—and thus the group has lost some of its power to exercise influence on behalf of human rights. Efforts are currently being made to address this problem.[50]

NOTES

1. Nancy Gibbs, "Darkness Falls: One Troubled Student Rains Down Death on a Quiet Campus," and Jeffrey Keuger, "Why They Kill," *Time,* April 30, 2007, pp. 36–59.
2. Sheryl Gay Stolberg, "War, Murder and Suicide: A Year's Toll Is 1.6 Million," *The New York Times,* Oct. 3, 2002, p. A12.
3. Bob Herbert, "The N.R.A.'s Campaign," *The New York Times,* March 16, 2000, p. A31.
4. Ibid.
5. Lawrie Mifflin, "Evidence Strong for Media Role in Violence," *The New York Times,* May 9, 1999, p. A3.
6. Ibid.
7. Gregg Easterbrook, "Watch and Learn. Yes, the Media Do Make Us More Violent," *New Republic* (May 17, 1999): 22–25.
8. Ibid.
9. www.wiki.media-culture.org.
10. www.esrb.org.
11. http://news.monstersandcritics.com/usa/news/article_1298539.php; www.washingtonpost.com/wp-dyn/content/article/2007/04/30/AR2007043001663.html.
12. Alan B. Krueger and Jitka Maleckova, "Does Poverty Cause Terrorism?" *The New Republic* (June 24, 2002): 27. See also Robert K. Fullinwider, "Terrorism, Innocence, and War," *Philosophy and Public Policy Quarterly, 21,* no. 4 (Fall 2001): 9–16; and www.terrorism.com/terrorism/bpart1.html.
13. Thomas L. Friedman, "A Poverty of Dignity and a Wealth of Rage," *The New York Times,* July 15, 2005, p. A21.
14. Jonathan Curiel, "Terror.com," *San Francisco Chronicle,* July 10, 2005, pp. A1, A11.
15. Peter Bergen and Swati Pandey, "The Madrassa Myth," *The New York Times,* June 14, 2005, p. A19.
16. Ibid.
17. John B. Judis, "Paris Diarist," *New Republic* (Oct. 7, 2002): 42.
18. www.epic.org/privacy/terrorism/usapatriot.
19. Sewell Chan, "U.S. Transit Agencies Turn to Cameras in Terror Fight, but Systems Vary in Effectiveness," *The New York Times,* July 14, 2005, p. A13.
20. William James, "The Moral Equivalent of War," *Popular Science Monthly* (Oct. 1910).
21. Quoted in *The New York Times,* Dec. 21, 1992, p. A1.
22. Ibid.
23. *The New York Times,* Jan. 6, 1993, p. A5.
24. Sarah Boseley, "655,000 Iraqis Killed Since Invasion," *The Guardian,* Oct. 11, 2006 (online at www.guardian.co.uk/Iraq/Story/0,,1892888,00.html).

25. Robert W. Tucker, *The Just War* (Baltimore: Johns Hopkins University Press, 1960): 1.
26. "Swiss Call Meeting on How to Apply Historic War Rules," *San Francisco Chronicle,* Oct. 6, 2002, p. A15.
27. Max Boot, "Who Says We Never Strike First?" *The New York Times,* Oct. 4, 2002, p. A29. See also the review of Boot's book, *The Savage Wars of Peace: Small Wars and the Rise of American Power* (New York: Basic Books, 2002), as well as a review of it by Brian Urguhard, "Is There a Case for Little Wars?" *New York Review of Books, XLIX,* no. 15 (Oct. 10, 2002): 10–13.
28. John Green, "Just How Should We Decide to Strike First?" (a review of *Preemption: The Knife that Cuts Both Ways* by Alan Dershowitz), *San Francisco Chronicle,* March 5, 2006, p. M3.
29. We might consider this particular principle as what is called a *regulative* rather than a *substantive* principle. Instead of telling us when something is enough or the last thing we should try, it can be used to prod us to go somewhat further than we otherwise would.
30. Some versions of the just war theory also note that for a war to be just it must be declared by a competent authority. This was to distinguish not only just wars from battles between individuals but also civil wars and insurrections. These would need to be argued for on other grounds. This principle also would direct the discussion of the justness of a war of nations to whether the proper national authorities had declared the war—with all of the constitutional issues, for example, that this raises.
31. James Childress, "Just-War Theories," *Theological Studies* (1978): 427–445.
32. NYT.com 2003/09/25/international/25ARMS.html?hp.
33. www.fas.org/nuke/intro/cw/intro.htm.
34. Howard W. French, "100,000 People Perished, but Who Remembers?" *The New York Times,* March 14, 2002, p. A4.
35. Daniel J. Kevles, "The Poor Man's Atomic Bomb," *New York Review of Books,* April 12, 2007, pp. 60–63.
36. *Time* (Aug. 1, 2005): 38–39.
37. Ibid.; www.ppionline.org/ppi_ci.cfm?knlgAreaID=124&subsecID=160&contentID=1316.
38. Gregg Easterbrook, "Term Limits, The Meaninglessness of 'WMD'" *New Republic* (Oct. 7, 2002): 23.
39. Ibid.
40. www.globalissuegroup.com/generalhistory.html.
41. Ibid.
42. Anthony Lewis, "Guantanamo's Long Shadow," *The New York Times,* June 21, 2005, p.A23.
43. Ibid.
44. Linda Greenhouse, "Top Court Pits Detainee Rights Against Presidential Powers," *San Francisco Chronicle,* April 18, 2004, p. A10.
45. Barbara Crosette, "U.N. Chief Issues a Call to Speed Interventions and Halt Civil Wars," *The New York Times,* Sept. 21, 1999, p. A1.
46. Robert D. Kaplan, "Weakness in Numbers," *The New York Times,* Oct. 18, 1999, p. A27. Also see Kaplan, *The Ends of the Earth* (New York: Random House, 1996).
47. Ibid.
48. Michael Ignatieff, "Human Rights: The Midlife Crisis," *New York Review of Books* (May 20, 1999): 58–62.
49. Ibid.
50. See Joseph Loconte, "Morality for Sale," *The New York Times,* April 1, 2004, p. A27.

REVIEW EXERCISES

1. What is terrorism? What motivates various types of terrorists?
2. Discuss the problems involved in defining terrorism.
3. Give a consequentialist argument for the use of terrorism. Give one against it.
4. What is pacifism?
5. How would a consequentialist decide whether or not to be a pacifist?
6. How would a nonconsequentialist decide whether to be a pacifist?
7. What is *just war theory,* and how did it come to be developed?
8. List and explain the four basic principles of the jus ad bellum part of just war theory.
9. What is the difference between the proportionality principle as it constitutes part of the jus ad bellum and jus in bello components of just war theory?

10. Explain the two basic elements of the principle of discrimination.
11. What counts as a "war crime" or a "crime against humanity"?
12. How did the U.N. Declaration of Human Rights come about? Why did it not include a rationale?

DISCUSSION CASES

1. Movie and Video Game Violence. Describe the kinds of violence that can be found today in movies. Give examples of particular movies you have seen recently or know about. Do you think that these movies glorify violence? Do you think that these depictions have anything to do with incidents of violence in our society? What about video games? Do you think there should be some sort of legal regulation of this type of entertainment? Why or why not?

2. Terrorism. Do you think that there are any causes or reasons that would justify acts of terrorism? If not, why not? If so, what kinds of terrorist activities do you think would be morally justified?

3. Military Intervention. Suppose you had to write a paper on whether you thought military intervention in some other country was ever justified. What would you write? Do you believe there would ever be any situations under which resort to war would be justified? Knowing the destruction and loss of human life that would be involved, would it still be justified? What if that country's rulers were killing members of certain ethnic groups in their own country? What if they were about to develop weapons of mass destruction? What if their rulers were dangerous madmen? What if they possessed some resource that your country could not do without and could not obtain through trade?

YOU MAKE THE DECISION

Apply the theories and issues discussed in this chapter by accessing this animated simulation on the Ethics Resource Center.

Use the passkey that accompanies your book to gain access. If you do not have a passkey, visit cengage brain.com to purchase instant access to additional study material.

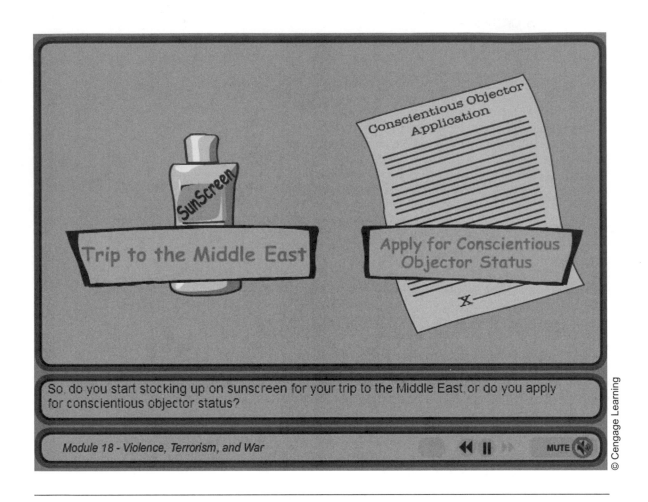

So, do you start stocking up on sunscreen for your trip to the Middle East, or do you apply for conscientious objector status?

Module 18 - Violence, Terrorism, and War

© Cengage Learning

Selected Bibliography

Alonso, Harriet Hyman. *Peace as a Woman's Issue: A History of the U.S. Movement for World Peace and Women's Rights.* Syracuse, NY: Syracuse University Press, 1993.

Bassiouni, M. Cherif. *Crimes Against Humanity in International Criminal Law.* Cambridge, MA: Kluwer Law International, 1999.

Beigbeder, Yves, and Theo Van Boven. *Judging War Criminals: The Politics of International Justice.* New York: St. Martins Press, 1999.

Bell, Linda A. *Rethinking Ethics in the Midst of Violence: A Feminist Approach to Freedom.* Lanham, MD: Rowman & Littlefield, 1993.

Bennett, William J. *Why We Fight: Moral Clarity and the War on Terrorism.* New York: Doubleday, 2002.

Borman, William. *Gandhi and Nonviolence.* Albany: State University of New York Press, 1986.

Brock, Peter. *Varieties of Pacifism: A Survey from Antiquity to the Outset of the Twentieth Century.* Syracuse, NY: Syracuse University Press, 1999.

————, **and Nigel Young.** *Pacifism in the Twentieth Century.* Syracuse, NY: Syracuse University Press, 1999.

Cahill, Lisa Sowle. *Love Your Enemies: Discipleship, Pacifism, and Just War Theory.* Minneapolis, MN: Fortress Press, 1997.

Chesterman, Simon. *Just War or Just Peace? Humanitarian Intervention and International Law.* New York: Oxford University Press, 2002.

Christopher, Paul. *The Ethics of War and Peace: An Introduction to Legal and Moral Issues.* East Rutherford, NJ: Prentice-Hall, 2004.

Cocciardi, Joseph A. *Terrorism Response.* Boston: Jones & Bartlett Publishers, 2008.

Crank, John P., et al. *Counter-Terrorism after 9/11: Justice, Security and Ethics Reconsidered.* Miamisburg, OH: Anderson Publishing, 2005.

Davis, Grady Scott. *Warcraft and the Fragility of Virtue: An Essay in Aristotelian Ethics.* Moscow, ID: University of Idaho Press, 1992.

Donnelly, Jack, and George A. Lopez (Eds.). *International Human Rights.* Boulder: Westview Press, 1997.

Donohooe, Helen. *World Issues: Terrorism.* London: Hodder Publishing, 2008.

Durch, William J., and Barry M. Blechman. *Keeping the Peace: The United Nations in the Emerging World Order.* Washington, DC: Henry L. Stimson Center, 1992.

Dyer, Hugh O. *Moral Order/World Order: The Role of Normative Theory in the Study of International Relations.* New York: St. Martins Press, 1997

Elshtain, Jean Bethke. *Just War against Terror: Ethics and the Burden of American Power in a Violent World.* New York: Basic Books, 2004.

————. *Just War Theory.* New York: New York University Press, 1991.

————. *Women and War.* New York: Basic Books, 1987.

Fletcher, George P. *Romantics at War: Glory and Guilt in the Age of Terrorism.* Princeton, NJ: Princeton University Press, 2002.

Fotion, N. *War and Ethics: A New Just War Theory.* New York: Continuum International Publishing Group, 2007.

French, Peter A., and Jason A. Short. *War and Border Crossings.* New York: Rowman & Littlefield, 2005.

Govier, Trudy. *A Delicate Balance: What Philosophy Can Tell Us about Terrorism.* Boulder, CO: Westview Press, 2002.

Grant, John. *UN Terrorism Convention.* Edinburgh, Scotland: Dunedin Academic Press, 2008.

Guinan, Edward. *Peace and Non-Violence: Basic Writings.* New York: Paulist Press, 1975.

Gutman, Roy (Ed.). *Crimes of War: What the Public Should Know.* New York: W. W. Norton, 1999.

Hashmi, Sohail H., and Steven P. Lee (Eds.). *Ethics and Weapons of Mass Destruction.* New York: Cambridge University Press, 2004.

Heden, C. *Terrorism, Justice and Social Values.* Edwin Mellen Press, 1991.

Holmes, Robert L. *Nonviolence in Theory and Practice.* Belmont, CA: Wadsworth, 1990.

Jinks, Derek. *Rules of War: The Geneva Conventions in the Age of Terror.* New York: Oxford University Press, Incorporated, 2008.

Kaplan, Robert. *The Ends of the Earth.* New York: Random House, 1996.

Kassimeris, George. *Warrior's Dishonour: Barbarity, Morality and Torture in Modern Warfare.* Aldershot, NH: Ashgate Publishing, 2007.

Khatchadourian, Haig. *War, Terrorism, Genocide, and the Quest for Peace: Contemporary Problems in Political Ethics.* Lewiston, NY: Edwin Mellen Press, 2003.

Kinsella, David, et al. *The Morality of War: A Reader.* Boulder, CO: Lynne Rienner, 2007.

Jones, John D., and Mark F. Griesbach. *Just War Theory in the Nuclear Age.* Lanham, MD: University Press of America, 1985.

Jinks, Derek. *Rules of War: The Geneva Conventions in the Age of Terror.* New York: Oxford University Press, 2008.

Lee, Steven P. *Morality, Prudence, and Nuclear Weapons.* New York: Cambridge University Press, 1996.

————. *Intervention, Terrorism, and Torture: Contemporary Challenges to Just War Theory.* New York: Springer, 2007.

Maguire, Daniel C. *The Horrors We Bless: Rethinking the Just-War Legacy.* Kitchner, Ontario, Canada: Castle Quay Books Canada, 2007.

Meggle, Georg. *Ethics of Terrorism and Counter Terrorism.* Somerset, NJ: Transaction Publishers, 2004.

Miller, Richard B. *Interpretations of Conflict: Ethics, Pacifism, and the Just-War Tradition.* Chicago: University of Chicago Press, 1991.

Peden, C. *Terrorism, Justice, and Social Values.* Lewiston, NY: Edwin Mellen Press, 1991.

Ramsey, Paul. *The Just War: Force and Political Responsibility* (foreword by Stanley Hauerwas). Lanham, MD: Rowman & Littlefield, 2002.

Rapoport, D., and Y. Alexander. *The Morality of Terrorism.* New York: Pergamon, 1982.

Reichberg, Gregory M., Henrik Syse, and Endre Begby (Eds.). *The Ethics of War.* Malden, MA: Blackwell Publishers, 2002.

Sorel, Georges. *Reflections on Violence.* Mineola, NY: Dover Publications, 2004.

Steiner, Henry J., and Philip Alston. *International Human Rights in Context: Law, Politics, Morals.* New York: Oxford University Press, 1996.

Steinhoff, Uwe. *On the Ethics of War and Terrorism.* New York: Oxford University Press, 2007.

Suter, Keith. *Teach Yourself Understanding Terrorism.* London: Hodder Publishing, 2008.

Temes, Peter S. *The Just War.* New York: Rowman & Littlefield, 2004.

———. *The Just War: An American Reflection on the Morality of War in Our Time.* Chicago: Ivan R. Dee Publisher, 2004.

Turner, Stansfield. *Terrorism and Democracy.* Boston: Houghton-Mifflin, 1991.

Vaux, Kenneth L. *Ethics and the War on Terrorism.* Eugene, OR: Wipf & Stock, 2002.

Walzer, Michael. *Arguing About War.* New Haven, CT: Yale University Press, 2004.

———. *Just and Unjust Wars.* New York: Basic Books, 1977.

Wardlaw, Grant. *Political Terrorism.* Cambridge, UK: Cambridge University Press, 1982.

Wasserstrom, Richard A. *War and Morality.* Belmont, CA: Wadsworth, 1970.

Wheeler, Charlene Eldridge, and Peggy Chin. *Peace and Power: A Handbook of Feminist Process.* New York: National League for Nursing, 1989.

Wolfendale, Jessica. *Torture and the Military Profession.* New York: Palgrave Macmillan, 2007.

Zawati, Hilmi. *Is Jihad a Just War? War, Peace and Human Rights Under Islamic and Public International Law.* Lewiston, NY: Edwin Mellen Press, 2002.

Zupan, Daniel S. *War, Morality, and Autonomy: An Investigation into Just War Theory.* Aldershot, NH: Ashgate Publishing, 2004.

19

Global Issues and Globalization

As of mid-2007, the world's population was 6.68 billion and growing at the rate of more than 200,000 new humans every day. China had 1,319,000,000 people (19.77 percent of the total), India 1,169,016,000 (17.52 percent), the United States 301,950,000 (4.53 percent), and Indonesia 231,627,000 (3.47 percent).[1]

The most populous metropolitan areas were Tokyo–Yokohama, Japan, with 32 million people; New York, 17.8 million; São Paulo, Brazil, 17.7 million; Seoul–Incheon, South Korea, 17.5 million; and Mexico City, 17.4 million. The next most populous were Osaka–Kobe–Kyoto, Japan; Manila, Philippines; Mumbai (Bombay), India; Jakarta, Indonesia; and Lagos, Nigeria. It was estimated that by the end of 2007, one-half of the world's population would be urban.[2]

RICH AND POOR NATIONS

We have become accustomed to categorizing nations in terms of their economic status and level of development as rich and poor, more affluent and less affluent, developed and developing, and as first, second, third, and possibly fourth world nations. Whichever classification system we use, a tremendous gap clearly exists between the level of economic development of those nations at the top and those at the bottom. According to Gustav Speth of the human development program of the United Nations, "an emerging global elite, mostly urban-based and interconnected in a variety of ways, is amassing great wealth and power, while more than

half of humanity is left out."[3] A 1999 U.N. study reported that technology and Internet access will intensify this difference.[4]

According to World Bank estimates, in 2005 1.1 billion people in the world lived in "extreme poverty" with the greatest number in Asia; however, Africa had the largest portion of its population, nearly one-half, in extreme poverty.[5] *Extreme poverty* means "poverty that kills." Such people live on less than $1 a day and thus are "chronically hungry, unable to get health care, lack safe drinking water and sanitation, cannot afford education for their children, and perhaps lack rudimentary shelter . . . and clothing."[6] More than 8 million people die each year because of poverty, which amounts to 20,000 people each and every day. The poor are also more likely to die of preventable disease. For example, approximately 3 million in Africa die of malaria each year.[7] Improving economies in East Asia have reduced the extent of poverty there "from 58% in 1981 to 15% in 2001, and in South Asia from 52% to 31%," but "the situation is deeply entrenched in Africa, where almost half of the continent's population lives in extreme poverty." Moreover, this situation in Africa has worsened over the last two decades.[8]

In July 2005, the Group of Eight (G8), or heads of eight industrialized nations, held its annual economic summit meeting in a resort in Gleneagles, Scotland. One purpose of the meeting was to discuss how to address the problem of poverty in Africa. In the month before this meeting, a series of "Live 8" concerts were held in major cities around the world with the aim of influencing the G8 members to "double aid sent to the world's poorest countries, fully cancel the debt of developing nations, and revise trade laws in favor of African countries."[9] At their meeting, these world leaders agreed to raise the aid to Africa to $34 billion by 2010 (from the current $23 billion annually). Moreover, in May 2005, the world's richest nations "agreed to write off $40 billion in loans owed by the world's 18 poorest countries, all but four of them in Africa."[10] The United States is the world's richest nation with $10.95 trillion dollars worth of gross domestic product, followed by Japan with 4.3, Germany with 2.4, Britain 1.79, France 1.76, and Italy 1.47 trillion dollars.[11] The United States spent almost $500 billion on the military in 2005, compared to $16 billion on aid to poor countries. This aid amounts to 0.15 percent of U.S. income, compared to Sweden and the Netherlands, for example, which gave 0.5 percent of their GDP, but spent much less on their military.[12]

It is also the case that 358 billionaires in the world control assets larger than the combined annual incomes of those countries that have 45 percent of the world's population.[13] Furthermore, "the ratio of average income of the richest countries in the world to that of the poorest has risen from about 9 to 1 at the end of the nineteenth century to at least 60 to 1 today." For example, "the average family in the United States is 60 times richer than the average family in Ethiopia."[14]

Mexico is among the countries with the largest gap between the rich and poor—in this case, generally between the industrialized north with its Spanish-speaking Mexicans and the rural south with its 10 million Indians.[15] The wealth and income gap in Latin America continues to be the highest in the world and continues to grow despite democratization. Clearly, the status of nations can change, and the rate of change of nations also varies. Some improve, some remain the same, and some fall backward. And some do so faster than others: "70 developing countries [have] incomes lower than they were in the 1960s or 1970s," among them Ghana, Haiti, Liberia, Nicaragua, Rwanda, and Venezuela.[16] Currently, the economies of China and India are growing faster than that of the United States. As these nations advance technologically, this rate is expected to slow.[17] Still, in 2004 the per capita income of people in the United States was eight times greater than that of people in China and eleven times greater than people in India. By the year 2050, the Chinese are expected to reach approximately one-half and Indians approximately one-quarter the income level of people in the United States.[18]

Figures on levels of education, longevity, and health in the world's poorest countries are also depressing. More than half of all children in India are malnourished. In Bangladesh, only one-fourth of adult women can read or write and only one-half of all men. Of the poorest fifty countries in the world, twenty-three had lower average incomes in 1999 than in 1990.[19]

The rich and poor nations differ significantly in life expectancy. Currently, the following microstates have the highest life expectancy: Andorra, 83.5 years old; San Marino, 82.1 years; and Singapore, 81.6 years. Japan as a whole is at 81.5 years. The U.S. average life expectancy is 78 years. Some sub-Saharan African countries average only 33 to 40 years: for example, Swaziland, 33.2 years; Botswana, 33.9 years; and Lesotho, 34.5 years. Unfortunately, one main reason for these low life expectancies is the toll of AIDS in the region. Around the world, women almost always have higher life expectancies than men with worldwide averages for males at 62.7 and females at 66 years; men in Russia, however, live 13 fewer years than Russian women.[20] More than 22 million people worldwide have died from AIDS. Millions more are living with HIV or AIDS: "74 percent of these infected people live in sub-Saharan Africa." There are 14,000 new cases added every day, with 95 percent of these in developing countries.[21] According to a report from a July 2002 United Nations AIDS Conference in Barcelona, if current infection rates continue, AIDS "will kill 68 million people in the 45 most affected countries over the next 20 years." This is more than the 55 million that were killed in all of World War II. "In some of these nations, AIDS could kill half of today's new mothers."[22] Famine is also a killer in many poorer nations. It is estimated that the lack of food is the number one cause of death worldwide, with 3.4 million deaths in 2000. "About 170 million children in poor countries are underweight because of lack of food, while more than a billion adults in North America, Europe and middle income countries are thought to be obese or overweight."[23]

Causes

The causes of extreme poverty and lack of development in a nation are many and complicated. Among them are said to be geographic isolation, epidemic disease, drought and other natural disasters, lack of clean water, poor soil, poor physical infrastructure, lack of education and a decent health care system, civil war and corruption, and the colonial and trade practices of Western nations.[24]

Colonialism In one view, it is colonialism that has been the cause of poverty in many of the world's poorest countries. Among those who hold this to be the case is Franz Fanon in his work *The Wretched of the Earth*.[25] The idea is that the Western nations stole the riches of their colonies, thus enhancing their own wealth while depressing the wealth of the colonies. According to Fanon, "European opulence has been founded on slavery. The well being and progress of Europe have been built up with the sweat and the dead bodies of Negroes, Arabs, Indians and the yellow races."[26] It is true that Western countries took gold from Peru, rubber from Brazil, tea from India, and cocoa from West Africa. However, modern world history is long and complicated and open to different assessments and interpretations. For example, there have been many colonialisms. Before Western colonial rule, there was "the Egyptian empire, the Persian empire, the Macedonian empire, the Islamic empire, the Mongol empire, the Chinese empire and the Aztec and Inca empires of the Americas."[27] Other writers point out that in at least some of the modern cases it was the Western colonizer nations that first helped their colonies develop these resources—which the colonizers then took.

Farm Subsidies and Other Trade Barriers Subsidies for farms of Western countries have also been blamed by some critics for the poverty in developing countries. For example, "the world's wealthiest nations give more than $300 billion of subsidies to their farmers every year."[28] This makes it extremely difficult for poor farmers in sub-Saharan Africa to compete with their Western counterparts. Moreover, in some cases the subsidies go to the biggest industrialized farms, chiefly in the United States, that produce huge surpluses for export. These subsidies originally were intended to help farmers hurt by the Great Depression. In other countries, subsidies are given to small specialty farms—for example, those in the grape-growing or cheese-producing regions of France. According to a representative of the World Bank, "reducing these subsidies and removing agricultural trade barriers is one of the most important things that rich countries can do for millions of people to escape poverty all over the world."[29] Other people, however, argue that the global market demands such movements of foods. Moreover, they point out that eliminating these subsidies may not help poor farmers or be good for the environment. If it leads to the development of industrialized farms in developing nations, then poor people there who otherwise would have worked small farms will migrate to cities where there is often no work for them. Although "high-tech agriculture wastes fossil fuels, it spares land, by growing more food on less acreage."[30]

Cultural and Historical Reasons Another cause or contributing factor may be thought to be cultural or historical. One area of particular interest today is the Arab world. Currently, the combined gross domestic product of all twenty-two Arab nation-states (with a combined population of 280 million people) is less than that of Spain. According to a 2002 report from the U.N. Development Program in coordination with the Arab Fund for Economic and Social Development, there are three main reasons why Arab countries have not advanced economically in modern times: "a shortage of freedom to speak, innovate and affect political life, a shortage of women's rights and a shortage of quality education."[31] The freedoms at issue are "civil liberties, political rights, a voice for the people, independence of the media and government accountability." According to the report, these societies are depriving themselves of the political and economic contributions of half of their citizens. It also points out that education is not as it should be. One indication of this is the lack of translated works. Greece translates fives times more than the mere 300 books that are translated each year in all Arab countries combined. Moreover, "investment in research is less than one-seventh the world average; and Internet connectivity is worse than in sub-Saharan Africa." There are still 65 million Arab adults who are illiterate, two-thirds of them women. These conditions contribute to dissatisfaction and instability.[32] However, there have been some recent improvements. For example, in May 2005, Kuwaiti women won the right to vote. Women could already vote in Oman, Bahrain, Qatar, and Iran.

World Bank and IMF Debate also continues about the role in world development played by international financial institutions. The International Monetary Fund (IMF) and World Bank were both established in 1944 to preserve international financial stability. According to Joseph Stiglitz, a Nobel Prize–winning economist, the key to problems in developing nations has been the financial institutions' ideological support of strict capitalism. He writes, "[F]ree markets left to their own devices, do not necessarily deliver the positive outcomes claimed for them by textbook economic reasoning that assumes that people have full information, can trade in complete and efficient markets, and can depend on satisfactory legal and other institutions."[33] As a result, some IMF and World Bank policies, for example, have harmed rather than helped the development of third world countries. High interest rates harmed fledgling companies, trade liberalization policies made poorer countries unable to compete, and liberalization of capital markets enabled larger foreign banks to drive local banks out of business. Privatization of government-owned enterprises without adequate local regulation also contributed to the increasingly desperate situation of some developing countries. According to Stiglitz, these international financial institutions have ignored some of the consequences of their policies

because of their almost religious belief in unfettered capitalism. He writes:

> Stabilization is on the agenda; job creation is off. Taxation, and its adverse effects, are on the agenda; land reform is off. There is money to bail out banks but not to pay for improved education and health services, let alone to bail out workers who are thrown out of their jobs as a result of the IMF's macroeconomic mismanagement.[34]

Moreover, not all financial aid given to poor countries actually gets directly to the people. Much of it, for example, covers consultants, administrative costs, and debt relief.

Corruption and Other Political Causes In 2005, African countries such as Ghana, Malawi, Mali, Senegal, and Tanzania were relatively well governed and progressing. Others remained problematic because of continuing civil wars and corrupt and unstable governments. Corruption and mismanagement have contributed not only to the poverty of the people but also to the hesitancy of wealthy countries to give aid. On the other hand, corruption is not the sole cause of poverty. Other societies in Asia, for example, are thought to have "extensive corruption, such as Bangladesh, Indonesia and Pakistan," and yet they have enjoyed rapid economic growth.[35]

Some Solutions
Developmental economist Jeffrey Sachs has argued that we should focus on five "development interventions": (1) boosting agriculture, with improvements in fertilizers and seeds; (2) improving basic health, in particular through bed nets and medicines for malaria and treatments for AIDS; (3) investing in education, including meals for primary school children; (4) bringing power; and (5) providing clean water and sanitation.[36] Others argue that money is the solution. As a percentage of the U.S. economy, aid spending "has fallen from nearly 3 percent in 1946 to 0.1 percent today."[37] Since the end of the Cold War, it has remained at approximately $10 billion annually. Those who study the matter differ in their views of whether or how much this aid actually has helped. According to some,

"numerous studies have found no real correlation between aid levels and the economic performance of developing countries." For example, China and India receive little assistance in relation to their impressive economic output, and African nations perform most poorly in spite of their receiving the most aid. On the other hand, there are success stories, according to World Bank representatives. Uganda, Mozambique, Vietnam, and Poland "show that aid can help drive economic growth when developing countries have policies in place like open trade, low inflation, and controlled government spending."[38]

Ethical Considerations

A more basic question is whether richer or Western nations have any moral responsibility or obligation to help poorer ones. Here we examine some ethical principles that can be used as a basis for how we might answer this question.

Self-Interest On the one hand, our own interests may dictate that we should do something to lessen the gap between rich and poor nations and alleviate the conditions of the less fortunate. In terms of trade alone, these nations can contribute much to our economic benefit by the goods they could purchase from us. Moreover, the worldwide problems of migration of desperate people to wealthier countries could be moderated. Furthermore, the present-day problem of terrorism might be dramatically reduced. However, some critics argue that it is not poverty that breeds terrorism but "feelings of indignity and frustration."[39] (See Chapter 18.) One of the consequences of global poverty is stress on the environment. Poor people in the Amazon region, for example, cut down trees to make farms and charcoal to sell. Impoverished people burning wood for cooking and warmth are producing a two-mile-thick blanket of smoke over East Asia. Because we are all affected by damage to the environment, it is in our best interest to find ways to eliminate the poverty that leads to some of this damage. Nevertheless, although there are many self-interested reasons to call for doing something to change things, it is an open question whether these reasons are either practically or ethically sufficient.

Justice On the other hand, it may be that justice requires that we ought to do something about this situation. Justice is not charity. It may well be that *charity* or altruistic concern for the plight of others ought to play a role in our view of ourselves in relation to far-distant peoples. Charity is certainly an ethically important notion, but a more difficult consideration is whether we have any obligation to help those in need in faraway places. Charity, in some sense, is optional. But if we are obligated to help others, then this is not an optional matter. As Kant reminded us, although we may decide not to do what we ought to do, we do not thereby escape the obligation. It is still there. But are we under any obligation to help those faraway persons in need, and why or why not?

Again, justice is not morally optional. It is something whose requirements we are obligated to follow. Recall from Chapter 13 that considerations of justice play a role in evaluating the distribution of goods. In that chapter we discussed this in relation to such a distribution within a society. However, it can also be used to evaluate the distribution of goods in human society as a whole. We can then ask whether or not a particular distribution of goods worldwide is just. As noted in that previous chapter, there are differences of opinion as to how we ought to determine this. One was the *process view,* according to which any distribution can be said to be just if the process by which it comes to be is just. In other words, if there was no theft or fraud or other immoral activity that led to the way things have turned out, then the resulting arrangement is just. In applying this at the global level, we can ask whether the rich nations are rich at least partly because of wrongful past actions. In this case, the issue of whether colonialization played a role in the poverty of poor nations would be relevant.

The other view was called *end state justice.* According to this view, the end state, or how things have turned out, is also relevant. Egalitarians will argue that the gap between rich and poor is something wrong in itself because we are all members of the same human family and share the same planet. On the one hand, some argue that it is morally permissible for some to have more and others less if the difference is a function of something like the greater effort or contributions of the richer nations. Thus, they might point to the sacrifice and invest-ment and savings practices of the newly industrial-ized East Asian nations as justifying their having more. They sacrificed and saved while others did not. On the other hand, if the wealth of some and the poverty of others result instead from luck and fortune, then it does not seem fair that the lucky have so much and the unlucky so little. Is it not luck that one nation has oil and another next to it does not?

Justice is also a matter of *fairness*. For example, people in developing countries in 1992 accounted for only 23 percent of world energy use, even though they had 80 percent of the world's popula-tion.[40] Thus people in the developed world with only 20 percent of the world's population account for about 75 percent of the world's energy use. We could ask whether this represents a fair share. However, this would seem to imply that there was only a set amount of energy and that each nation should withdraw from it only a fair share based on its population, for example. That there is a fixed amount might be true of nonrenewable energy resources such as fossil fuels, but not necessarily true of all energy sources. To address this issue more fully would require complex analysis of the very idea of fair shares of world resources and prob-lems of ownership and distribution.

Other people point out that there is a consi-derable unfairness in some trade practices. Subsidies for exported goods constitute one area of unfairness. The IMF and the World Bank often ask countries to which they give loans and other aid to eliminate subsidies for their exports. However, industrialized countries continue to subsidize their products. For example, James D. Wolfensohn, former World Bank president, has "accused wealthy countries of 'squandering' $1 billion a day on farm subsidies that often have devastating effects on farmers in Latin America and Africa."[41] In 2001, the U.S. Congress passed a bill that authorized more than $100 billion in farm subsidies over eight years. Critics charge that it is hypocritical as well as unfair for wealthy coun-tries to continue such protectionist policies while requiring poor countries to do without. Western

cotton subsidies are said to have hurt Brazilian exports and cost that country $640 million in 2001 alone.[42] In mid-2007, Congress was halfway through approving a new farm bill, this time allot-ting $180 billion for farmers over the next decade. "Although the program began in the 1930s to aid poor family farmers, [now] almost three-quarters of the money goes to the richest 10 percent of American farmers."[43] At the World Summit on Sustainable Development in Johannesburg in the summer of 2002, Oxfam International, a non-governmental organization devoted to helping poor nations, dumped 9,000 sachets of subsidized European sugar near the meeting site to protest the subsidies on sugar and other major commodi-ties that the organization claims are driving poor farmers out of business.[44] However, other people point out that there are other reasons for declin-ing prices of cotton and other third world exports. Nevertheless, the moral ideal of fair competition is certainly relevant in such discussions. Just how to make competition fair is a matter for debate, however.

Rights According to some Westerners, political freedoms, civil rights, and labor standards are not separable from economic progress. They stress that prohibitions on child labor, enforcement of women's rights, prevention of deforestation and pollution, and the enhancement of "intellectual property rights, a free press (and) civil liberties" are essential to any secure development.[45] Asian lead-ers who met with Europeans at a 1996 Bangkok conference on trade and economics responded that this was not their way, and that the welfare of society and economic development ought to come first before political rights. They insisted that hu-man rights should temporarily be put on hold for the sake of economic growth. Thus, it would be better, they say, to give a starving person a loaf of bread than a crate on which to stand and speak his mind. But according to Alex Magno, a political sci-entist at the University of the Philippines, it is not so much an "Asian way" that gives human rights a back seat, but political self-interest on the part of rulers who are spurred on by a growing middle class. The middle class is "not an Islamic or

Buddhist or Catholic middle class," but one that "is intoxicated with growth, whose own personal fortunes depend on the GNP [gross national product] rate." Moreover, a group from Forum Asia insisted that the notion of human rights is not strictly a Western import but also their own concern. It points out that the real Western imports are the economic practices of "consumerism, capitalism, investment, (and) industrialization."[46]

This debate raises the following ethical questions: How important are political and civil rights in comparison with a society's economic development? Should one take precedence over the other? You can get further help in thinking about some of these issues by recalling the distinction between positive and negative rights earlier in this chapter as well as the discussion of natural rights from Chapter 6 and the discussions of utilitarianism in Chapter 4. This is a crucial question asked by Peter Singer.

We can make the general issues of aid to poor countries clearer by considering the issue of famine.

Famine Starvation and famine remain problems around the world. Political corruption and mismanagement of resources are often the cause, but so are uncontrollable events such as earthquakes, famines, and floods. What responsibility do those in other countries have to people suffering starvation? According to Peter Singer, giving to victims of famines, for example, is not charity but duty. In fact, he believes that we have an obligation to help those less well off than ourselves to the extent that helping them does not make us less well off than they are, or require us to sacrifice something of comparable value. This is an ethically demanding position. It implies that I must always justify spending money on myself or my family or friends. Whether I am justified in doing so, in this view, depends on whether anything I do for myself or others is of comparable moral importance to the lives of others who are perhaps starving and lacking in basic necessities.

Of the opposite point of view is Garrett Hardin, who believes that we have no such obligation to give because to do so will do no good.[47] For example, famine relief only postpones the inevitable—death and suffering. According to Hardin, this is because overpopulation produced by famine relief will again lead to more famine and death. However, whether his prediction is correct is an empirical matter. In other words, it needs to be verified or supported by observation and historical evidence. For example, will all forms of famine relief, especially when combined with other aid, necessarily do more harm than good as Hardin predicts? Answering such questions is difficult because it requires knowledge of the effects of aid in many different circumstances. It is worthwhile reflecting, however, on the consequentialist nature of the arguments and asking ourselves whether other nonconsequentialist arguments that rely on notions of justice and fairness are at least as important in determining what we ought to think and do in such matters.

GLOBALIZATION

According to Robert Wright, "globalization dates back to prehistory, when the technologically driven expansion of commerce began."[48] The building of roads and inventions such as wheels and boats led to huge changes in transportation, expanded the world, and at the same time made it smaller. Writing was the new form of information technology, first used for trade to record debts and make contracts. Later, the great empires and merchant leagues played a key role in increasing globalization. Movable print increased the ability of the common person to learn about others, both to increase understanding and sympathy.[49] On the one hand, this would seem to lead to increased tolerance and respect for human equality. The economic integration of isolated communities often brings with it greater peace and understanding as people of different races and cultures trade and rub shoulders with one another, but it can also be the basis of resentment and antipathy.

One can think of globalization in Thomas Friedman's terms, as the world being made flat. People around the world are now connected in ways unimaginable twenty years ago, and the playing field in which they operate is now more even. Provided that they have access to computers, Web connections, and e-mail. This is partly made possible by the invention of the Web and the Web browser and common Internet protocols that allow people with different systems to still connect with one another and transport data around the Internet. It is also made possible by digitization of words, music, and data and the ability to carry more signals more reliably over long distances by fiber-optic cable. "We are now connecting all the knowledge centers on the planet together into a single global network. . . ."[50]

One example of this availability of knowledge is Wikipedia, the online collaborative encyclopedia. Articles are contributed and edited by viewers. The word *wiki* comes from the Hawaiian word for "quick." Started only in 2001, within two years it had more than 20,000 articles, and by 2004 it had 250,000 articles in English and 600,000 in other languages. Another example is Google, the online search engine. Its name is the incorrect spelling of *googol,* or "a play on the word . . . which is sometimes called the largest number and is represented by the numeral 1 followed by 100 zeros."[51]

Outsourcing is one example of how globalization and modern technologies come together and work together. Part of a process—say, one's taxes or call center help—can be farmed out. When you call Dell for help with one of its products, the person answering the phone may be in India, the Philippines, or Panama. One-quarter of a million people in India work in call centers. It makes financial sense for companies such as Dell to hire out this help to India, where the workers at the centers make the equivalent of $200 to $400 a month. Another example of globalization is offshoring. This differs from outsourcing in that rather than taking some specific limited function and hiring it out, one takes the whole factory or operation offshore—for example to Canton, China. Examples might be textiles and auto parts.[52]

One might think that if service and professional jobs and companies go where the lowest priced workers are located, then this would lead to a quick rush to the bottom. However, as will be discussed in the following section on capitalism, this has not happened. In 2003, an information technology company in India "received nearly one million applications from Indian techies for 9,000 software jobs."[53] Although some Americans complain about manufacturing jobs going to Mexico, this country itself is reported to have lost some 500,000 such jobs in 2003–04. Many of these jobs have gone to China. Discount stores in Mexico now have significant quantities of shoes, electronics, and clothing labeled "Made in China."[54] Companies use outsourcing for many reasons. One is the lower cost of labor. Another is the quality of education. For example, Toyota recently decided to build a plant to make its small SUV in Toronto rather than in Mississippi. And the educated middle class in India has significantly better mathematics training than do comparable students in the United States.

To know better what to say about *globalization,* one must first be clear about what the term means. According to one writer, there are at least five different definitions of the term, some of which are overlapping: internationalization, liberalization, universalization, modernization or Westernization, and deterritorialization.[55]

Internationalization According to this version, *globalization* refers to the many types of "cross-border relations between countries." Among these are trade, finance, and communication. From these flow an international interdependence among nations and peoples.

Liberalization A second meaning focuses on the free and "open, borderless world economy." Trade and foreign exchange, as well as travel barriers, are abolished or reduced, making it possible to participate in the world as a whole.

Universalization *Globalization* can also refer to the various ways in which a synthesis of cultures has taken place. This covers such things as having a common calendar and similar methods of manufacturing, farming, and means of transportation.

Modernization or Westernization This is perhaps the most common meaning of *globalization,* namely, the way in which "the social structures of modernity"—capitalism, science, movies, music, and so forth—have spread throughout the world. Among the characteristics of modernity is scientific rational thought. It is the idea that we can know the world as it is and mold it to serve our needs. Technology and technological innovation are among its consequences.

Deterritorialization A final use of the term *globalization* points out that "social space is no longer wholly mapped in terms of territorial places . . . and borders."[56] Thus, corporations as well as non-governmental organizations transcend local groupings. World-governing bodies such as the World Trade Organization, the World Court, and the United Nations also exemplify this.

Values

People disagree about the extent of all of these types of globalization. They point out the ways in which local cultures and law still dominate human interactions. There are also critical reactions to these movements. Some people fear the loss of cultural identities and values and so press for their own ways of doing and being. Some worry about Western imperialism and revolt against it.

With any of its meanings, we can ask whether globalization of that sort is a good thing or bad. For example, how has it affected certain things that are thought to be important for human life? Among these are security, justice, and autonomy.[57]

Security Peace and harmony are thought to be good for humanity and to contribute to security. Has globalization in any of its meanings contributed to peace and harmony or been the cause of conflict and wars? On the one hand, one can find examples of international cooperation. International conferences are held to decide on a global level what to do about global warming or the loss of species or the AIDS epidemic or the condition of women. Some measure of agreement is often reached, and security is enhanced. On the other hand, with the development of modern weaponry, strong and militarily powerful nations can dominate weaker ones, leading to resentment as often as respect. We also have seen the rise of extreme nationalist movements, racism, and terrorism. The extent of the role that globalization has played in these movements, however, is far from clear.

Justice Justice is giving what is due as well as what is fair. Serving justice is a moral imperative. We can also ask whether globalization has promoted justice. The problem of rich and poor countries and the issue of justice were discussed above and can be reconsidered here. Free trade allows corporations to move their factories anywhere. In some

ways, this seems to help the poor who, though they may work in what are labeled "sweat shops," are nevertheless better off there than working in other places or facing their alternatives. Yet the poor do seem to be exploited and often work in unsafe and unhealthy circumstances, conditions that should surely be improved.

Autonomy Finally, if democracy provides a way for people to have a say about what happens to them in their own lives and societies, and if such control over their lives or autonomy is a good, then democracy would seem to be also. However, we can also ask whether globalization has helped spread democracy. One would think that when people see how it works, they would demand democracy. However, powerful interests and fears may and do prevent its development. Local customs and circumstances also influence its forms.

Free-Market Capitalism

There are also other ways to evaluate globalization. Those who hold an economic liberal point of view laud globalization's seeming emphasis on free trade and open markets. Free markets are thought to lead to free minds because they work best under these conditions. The idea is that economic liberty will bring with it political liberty and democracy, which are good things. With U.S. jobs fleeing overseas, what happens to the lesser-skilled but higher-paid U.S. workers? If companies grow by these means, then the number of jobs may overall increase. However, they may be at a higher level of skills. Is protectionism then the answer? There are alternatives. For example, instead of lifetime employment for workers, the switch can be made to providing them with lifetime employability.[58]

Companies may be shamed into being more responsible and providing continuing training for their employees. They may also gain good name by being good stewards—for example, by ensuring that their outsourced jobs follow good labor laws and practices and give due regard for the environment. Parents may also need to teach their children to be adaptable and to work harder if they want to succeed. Among the areas of study for which the United States has lately been found wanting are science and engineering. Ways need to be found to encourage and support students to enter these fields, which are going to be so central to the future. For example, according to Thomas Friedman in *The World Is Flat,* globalization is necessarily free market but will also bring with it peace and human economic fulfillment. Critics, however, point out that the technological advancements that have made the world smaller have not made it flatter. There are still large portions of world populations that are, as earlier described, extremely poor and not benefiting by these advances. Moreover, they argue that globalization characterized by technological advance is entirely compatible with different types of economic systems, including those of less-than-democratic regimes. With other countries such as China and India becoming more powerful in the globalized world, there is also the continued possibility for conflict as much as for peace. Those who believe in the necessary correlation of technological advance and free-market capitalism do not adequately acknowledge the powerful roles of nationalism and religion in history, according to these critics.[59]

Those who hold a more socialist perspective also believe that it is important to keep a so-called safety net of basic goods for those who are not able to compete well in a capitalistic or free-market system. They often blame certain forms of globalization for their inability to compete and sometimes argue that we ought to return to simpler and more localized ways of living. In the middle are those who believe that market economics and cross-border transfers and trade are good but that they also need to be supplemented by measures that help those who fall behind and restrain powerful corporations. Market capitalism also needs to be adapted to the particular conditions of developing countries.[60]

Modernization

Universalization, modernization, and Westernization are often cited as other aspects of globalization. Western-style clothing, advertising, and products are becoming more and more pervasive. Coca-Cola, McDonald's, and Wal-Mart seem to be everywhere. Can it be that this is because this is what many people around the world admire or want? So-called Western values have also been the

cause for antipathy and resentment by people who hold other traditional cultural or religious values. Among the examples cited are the lack of modest dress in women and graphic and sexualized forms of popular entertainment and music. Clearly, there are criticisms to be made of some elements of Western societies that are showing up around the world. On the other hand, we may want to argue that other elements of modern culture ought to become universally accepted. Take, for example, the position of women. Should modern notions of individual rights and freedoms become the norm? There are those who argue against this. They would retain individual cultural and religious practices regarding the position of women. Can we actually judge the practices of another culture? Are one culture and its values as good as any other? This is the issue of ethical relativism discussed in Chapter 2. We surely want to say that even if some culture has a practice of enslaving some of its members, this is not morally acceptable. Which elements of globalization are good and bad is not always an easy matter to judge. Hopefully, however, the ethical signposts, values, and principles discussed here and elsewhere in this text can help determine the way we should go in a world that is, in ever-increasing ways, becoming one.

NOTES

1. www.wikipedia.org/wiki//world_population.
2. http://geography.about.com/od/urbaneconomic-geography/a/agglomerations.htm; Yahoo News.
3. Quoted by Barbara Crosette in "U.N. Survey Finds World Rich-Poor Gap Widening," *The New York Times,* July 15, 1996, p. A3.
4. Judith Miller, "Globalization Widens Rich–Poor Gap, U.N. Report Says," *The New York Times,* July 13, 1999, p. A8.
5. *Time,* March 14, 2005, p.46.
6. Ibid., p. 47.
7. Ibid., p. 46.
8. Ibid., p. 47.
9. *San Francisco Chronicle,* July 3, 2005, p. A13.
10. *The New York Times,* July 6, 2005, p. A1.
11. Ibid.; World Bank figures are from 2003, the most recent available.
12. *Time,* op. cit., p. 46.
13. "U.N. Survey," op. cit.

14. Nancy Birdsall, "Life Is Unfair: Inequality in the World," *Foreign Policy,* no. 111 (Summer 1998): 76.

15. Anthony DePalma, "Mexico's Serious Divisions Getting Wider and Deeper," *The New York Times,* July 20, 1996, p. A8.

16. "U.N. Survey," op. cit.

17. Jeffrey D. Sachs, "Welcome to the Asian Century: By 2050, China and Maybe India Will Overtake the U.S Economy in Size" (http://money.cnn.com/magazines/fortune/fortune_archive/2004/01/12/357912/index.htm).

18. Ibid.

19. Ibid.; Benjamin M. Friedman, "Globalization: Stiglitz's Case," *New York Review of Books, 49,* no. 13 (Aug. 15, 2002). This is a review of *Globalization and Its Discontents* by Joseph F. Stiglitz.

20. http://geography.about.com/od/populationgeography/a/lifeexpectancy.htm; http://en.wikipedia.org/wiki/List_of_countries_by_life_expectancy.

21. www.until.org/statistics.shtml.

22. Peter Piot, "In Poor Nations, a New Will to Fight AIDS," *The New York Times,* July 3, 2002, p. A19.

23. "Agency Puts Hunger No.1 on List of World's Top Health Risks," *The New York Times,* Oct. 31, 2002, p. A11.

24. *Time,* op. cit., pp. 46–48.

25. Franz Fanon, *The Wretched of the Earth* (New York: Grove Press, 1968).

26. Quoted in Dinesh D'Souza, "Two Cheers for Colonialism," *San Francisco Chronicle,* July 7, 2002, p. D6.

27. Ibid.

28. *The New York Times,* Sept. 8, 2003, p. A8.

29. Ibid.

30. Ibid., p. A27.

31. Thomas L. Friedman, "Arabs at the Crossroads," *The New York Times,* July 3, 2002, p. A19.

32. Ibid.

33. Summarized in Benjamin M. Friedman, op. cit., p. 48.

34. Ibid., p. 52.

35. *Time,* op. cit. p. 53.

36. Jeffrey Sachs, *The End of Poverty: Economic Possibilities for Our Time* (New York: Penguin Press, 2005); cited in *Time,* op. cit., pp. 50–51.

37. Joseph Kahn and Tim Weiner, "World Leaders Rethinking Strategy on Aid to Poor," *The New York Times,* March 18, 2002, p. A3.

38. Ibid.

39. Alan B. Krueger and Jitka Maleckova, "Does Poverty Cause Terrorism?" *New Republic* (June 24, 2002): 27.

40. David Ordal, "Energy in the Developing World" (April 28, 1999); U.S. Congress Office of Technology Assessment, "Fueling Development," p. 1; Andrew C. Revkin, "Climate Panel Reaches Consensus on the Need to Reduce Harmful Emissions," *The New York Times,* May 4, 2007, p. A4.

41. Edmund L. Andrews, "Rich Nations Criticized for Barriers to Trade," *The New York Times,* Sept. 20, 2002, p. A7.

42. Ibid.

43. www.commondreams.org/views02/0506-09.htm; www.washingtonpost.com/wp-dyn/content/article/2006/07/01/AR2006070100962.html.

44. "Oxfam Dumps Sugar at WSSD," *Oxfam Exchange* (Fall 2002): 3.

45. Seth Mydans, "Do Rights Come First? Asia and Europe Clash," *The New York Times International,* March 1, 1996, p. A6.

46. Ibid.

47. Garrett Hardin, "Living on a Lifeboat," *Bioscience* (Oct. 1974).

48. Robert Wright, "Two Years Later, a Thousand Years Ago," *The New York Times,* Op-Ed., Sept. 11, 2003.

49. Ibid.

50. Thomas L. Friedman, *The World Is Flat: A Brief History of the Twenty First Century* (New York: Farrar, Straus, and Giroux, 2005), p. 8.

51. Ibid., pp. 94–95, 152. And see www.lrb.co.uk/v28/n02/lanc01_.html.

52. Ibid., pp. 24, 114–115.

53. Thomas L. Friedman, "Small and Smaller," *The New York Times,* March 4, 2004, p. A31.

54. Thomas L. Friedman, "What's That Sound?" *The New York Times,* April 1, 2004, p. A27.

55. Ibid., pp. 15–17.

56. Ibid.

57. Jan Aart Scholte, *Globalization, A Critical Introduction* (New York: St. Martin's Press, 2000), 15–17. Scholte in *Globalization* writes of these as *security, equity,* and *democracy.*

58. Friedman, op. cit, p. 284.

59. See, for example, John Gray, "The World is Round," *New York Review of Books* (August 11, 2005): pp. 13–15; Thomas L. Friedman, *The World is Flat,* op. cit.

60. This is a version of the category system in Scholte, *Globalization.*

REVIEW EXERCISES

1. What are some of the current contrasting conditions between rich and poor nations described in the text?
2. What causes do people give for the inequalities?
3. What self-interested reasons can be given for doing something to remedy the situation of poor countries?
4. What is justice, and what role does it play in determining what ought to be done and why?
5. What is the difference between economic and political rights, and how is this distinction related to Eastern and Western perspectives?
6. Describe the ethical problem concerning responsibility for those far and near.
7. Contrast Singer's and Hardin's views on how we ought to deal with famine.
8. Summarize the five different meanings of *globalization* given in the text.
9. Describe some positive and some negative aspects of globalization.

DISCUSSION CASES

1. Job Flight. For some time, companies in the United States and other Western countries have sought to cut costs by moving some manufacturing jobs to countries where labor is cheaper. Often the working conditions are deplorable and workers have fewer protections than in first world countries. Should these companies have the freedom to do this? Or do these countries have a responsibility to the employees in their own countries?

2. Famine Relief. In a certain African country, the drought has been unusually harsh this year. Many people are starving. The political situation in the country is unstable. Some of the lack of food is the result of government mismanagement. The news media have nevertheless been able to get to the area and broadcast images of people who are clearly malnourished. Do people with so much more have any obligation to help these folks? Why or why not? If we ought to help them, is it a matter of charity or obligation?

3. Global Culture. Sam and Jane have been arguing about the effects of globalization as a form of modernization or Westernization of the world. Sam points out all of globalization's crass and commercialized aspects—including the ubiquitous McDonald's and Levis—that have negative effects on local cultures. Jane argues that Western personal and political freedoms ought to be made universal. With whom do you agree, Sam or Jane? Why?

4. Controlling Global Environmental Threats. Consider the threats to civilization as we know it presented by global warming and newly formed gaps in the protective ozone layer. Consider also the various nations and what each contributes to the threats. Suppose there are no strong international curbs. Each nation, then, must determine its own responsibility for lessening the threats. However, if Nation X lessens its own contribution by controlling emissions and other damaging chemicals, it will be put at a disadvantage economically in comparison with similarly developed nations that do not discipline themselves. It is the problem of the "free rider"—that is, when others do their share, I benefit most by not contributing.

Do problems such as this require some sort of international organizations and agreements or should each nation or region make its own decisions on such matters?

YOU MAKE THE DECISION

Apply the theories and issues discussed in this chapter by accessing this animated simulation on the Ethics Resource Center.

   Use the passkey that accompanies your book to gain access. If you do not have a passkey, visit cengage brain.com to purchase instant access to additional study material.

Just do it? .. Or just say no?

Ethics Module 19 Global Issues and Globalization

Selected Bibliography

Aiken, William, and Hugh LaFollette. *World Hunger and Morality,* 2nd ed. Upper Saddle River, NJ: Prentice Hall, 1996.

Arthur, John, and William Shaw (Eds.). *Justice and Economic Distribution,* 2nd ed. Englewood Cliffs, NJ: Prentice Hall, 1991.

Barrera, Albino. *Globalilzation and Economic Ethics: Distributive Justice in the Knowledge Economy.* New York: Palgrave Macmillan, 2007.

Bauer, P. T. *Equality, the Third World and Economic Delusion.* Cambridge, MA: Harvard University Press, 1981.

Bayles, Michael D. *Morality and Population Policy.* Birmingham: University of Alabama Press, 1980.

Brown, Sherrod, et al. *Myths of Free Trade: How and Why America's Trade Policy Flies in the Face of Reality.* New York: The New Press, 2004.

Caney, Lehning. *International Distributive Justice: Cosmopolitanism and Its Critics.* New York: Routledge, 2003.

Cragg, Wesley. *Ethics Codes, Corporations, and the Challenge of Globalization.* Northampton, MA: Edward Elgar Publishing, 2005.

© Cengage Learning

Dougherty, Peter J. *Who's Afraid of Adam Smith: How the Market Got Its Soul.* Hoboken, NJ: Wiley & Sons, 2005.

Eade, John, et al. *Global Ethics and Civil Society.* Aldershot, NH: Ashgate Publishing, 2005.

Ferguson, Ann. *Sexual Democracy: Women, Oppression, and Revolution.* Boulder, CO: Westview, 1991.

Friedman, Milton. *Capitalism and Freedom.* Chicago: University of Chicago Press, 1962.

Frost, Mervyn. *Ethics in International Relations.* New York: Cambridge University Press, 1996.

Germain, Randall D., et al. *Idea of Global Civil Society: Ethics and Politics in a Globalizing Era.* New York: Routledge, 2005.

Gimlin, Debra, et al. *The Globalization of Food.* Oxford, UK: Berg Publishers, 2008.

Head, Simon. *The New Ruthless Economy: Work and Power in the Digital Age.* New York: Oxford University Press, 2005.

Hertz, Noreena. *The Silent Takeover: Global Capitalism and the Death of Democracy.* New York: Simon & Schuster, 2003.

Kay, John. *Culture and Prosperity: Why Some Nations Are Rich but Most Remain Poor.* New York: HarperCollins Publishers, 2005.

Khan, Shuhrukh R. *Do World Bank and IMF Policies Work?* New York: St. Martin's Press, 1999.

Khorus, Ingrid, and Jamie Bartram (Eds.). *Towards a Fair Global Labour Market: Avoiding the New Slavery.* New York: Routledge, 1999.

Landes, David S. *The Wealth and Poverty of Nations: Why Some Are So Rich and Some So Poor.* New York: W. W. Norton & Company, 1999.

Lappé, Frances Moore. *World Hunger: Twelve Myths.* New York: Grove, 1986.

Leimgruber, Walter. *Between Global and Local, Marginality and Marginal Regions in the Context of Globalization and Deregulation.* Aldershot, NH: Ashgate Publishing, 2004.

Lemons, John, and Donald A. Brown. *Sustainable Development: Science, Ethics, and Public Policy.* Norwell, MA: Kluwer Academic Publishers, 1995.

Little, Daniel. *The Paradox of Wealth and Poverty: Mapping the Ethical Dilemmas of Global Development.* Boulder, CO: Westview Press, 2003.

Luper-Foy, Steven (Ed.). *Problems of International Justice.* Boulder, CO: Westview, 1988.

Marable, Manning. *Race, Globalization, and Empire.* New York: Palgrave Macmillan, 2008.

Poe, Marshall T. *Everyone Knows Everything: Wikipedia and the Globalization of Knowledge.* New York: Random House, 2009.

Postel, Sandra. *Last Oasis: Facing Water Scarcity.* New York: W.W. Norton, 1992.

Reich, Robert B. *The Work of Nations: Preparing Ourselves for 21st Century Capitalism.* New York: Knopf, 1991.

Reichert, Elisabeth. *The Other Human Rights: Perspectives on Economic, Social, and Cultural Rights.* New York: Columbia University Press, 2007.

Rowe, James K., et al. *Globalization, Governmentality and Global Politics: Regulation for the Rest of Us?* New York: Routledge, 2005.

Rupp, George. *Globalization Challenged: Conviction, Conflict, Community.* New York: Columbia University Press, 2008.

Sachs, Jeffrey. *The End of Poverty: Economic Possibilities for Our Time.* New York: Penguin Group Incorporated, 2005.

Saenz, Mario (Ed.). *Latin American Perspectives on Globalization: Ethics, Politics, and Alternative Visions* (foreword by Linda Martin Alcoff). Lanham, MD: Rowman & Littlefield, 2002.

Saxton, Jim (Ed.). *Reform of the IMF and World Bank: Congressional Hearing.* Collingdale, PA: DIANE Publishing Co., 2002.

Schwartz, Peter, and Blair Gibb. *When Good Companies Do Bad Things: Responsibility and Risk in an Age of Globalization.* Somerset, NJ: John Wiley & Sons, 1999.

Scruton, Roger. *The West and the Rest, Globalization and the Terrorist Threat.* New York: Continuum Books, 2002.

Segesvary, Victor. *From Illusion to Delusion: Globalization and the Contradictions of Late Modernity.* Washington, DC: University Press of America, 2001.

Shaw, Martin (Ed.). *Politics and Globalisation: Knowledge, Ethics and Agency.* New York: Routledge, 1999.

Shiva, Vandana. *Close to Home: Women Reconnect Ecology, Health and Development Worldwide.* Atlantic Highlands, NJ: Zed Books, 1994.

Shue, Henry. *Basic Rights: Subsistence, Affluence, and U.S. Foreign Policy.* Princeton, NJ: Princeton University Press, 1980.

van den Anker, Christien. *Distributive Justice in a Global Era.* New York: Palgrave Macmillan, 2004.

Wheeler, Keith A., and Anne Perraca Bijur (Eds.). *Education for a Sustainable Future: A Paradigm of Hope for the 21st Century.* Norwell, MA: Kluwer Academic Publishers, 2000.

Wortman, Sterling, and Ralph Cummings, Jr. *To Feed This World.* Baltimore: Johns Hopkins Press, 1978.

How to Write an Ethics Paper

Writing a paper does not have to be difficult. It can at least be made easier by following certain procedures. Moreover, you want to do more than write a paper—you want to write a *good* paper. You can do several things to improve your paper, changing it from a thing of rags and patches to a paper of which you can be proud. If it is a good paper, then you also will have learned something from producing it. You will have improved your abilities to understand and communicate, and you will have come to appreciate the matters about which you have written.

Writing philosophy papers, in particular, has a value beyond what one learns about the subject matter. As you know, philosophy is a highly rational discipline. It requires us to be clear, precise, coherent, and logical. Skill in doing this can be improved by practice and care. By trying to make your philosophy paper excel in these aspects, you will improve these skills in yourself in ways that should carry over to other areas of your life. Sloppy and careless thinking, speaking, and writing should be diminished.

In what follows, I review general procedures for writing papers and then outline elements that are particularly important for writing ethics papers. By following the suggestions given here, you should be able to produce a good ethics paper and further perfect your reasoning skills.

Several elements are basic to any paper. Among these are its content, the content's structure and format, and correct usage of grammar, spelling, and gender-neutral pronouns.

THE CONTENT OF THE PAPER

Your paper's subject matter is partly determined by the course for which it is assigned. Sometimes the topic will be chosen for you. As detailed in Chapter 1 and exemplified throughout this text, if the paper is for an ethics course, then it will deal with matters of right and wrong, good and bad, or just and unjust. It also probably will be given as a certain type of paper: a summary or critical analysis of some article or other writing, an exploration of a thesis or idea, or a research paper. (More on this below.) At other times, you will choose a topic yourself from a list or be asked to choose something specific from some more general area. You can select something in which you are particularly interested or something you would like to explore. It may be a topic you know something about or one about which you know little but would like to know more. Sometimes you can begin with a tentative list that is the result of brainstorming. Just write down ideas as you think of them. Sometimes you will have to do exploratory reading or library or Internet research to get ideas. In any case, choosing a topic is the first order of business in writing a paper. This is true of papers in general and ethics papers in particular.

THE PAPER'S STRUCTURE

I still recall the good advice of a teacher I had in graduate school. It was two simple bits of advice, but this did not make it less valuable.

1. A paper should have a beginning, a middle, and an end.

2. First you should tell what you are going to do. Then you should do it. Finally, you should tell what you have said or done.

This may seem overly simplistic, but you may be surprised to find out how many papers suffer from not including either or both of these elements. Over the years of writing papers in school and beyond, I have found this simple advice extraordinarily helpful.

You can develop the structure of your paper with an outline. Here is a sample using the advice just discussed.

1. *Beginning paragraph(s).* Tell what you are going to do or say. Explain what the problem or issue is and how you plan to address it. You should make your reader want to go on. One way to do this is by showing why there is a problem. This can be done by giving contrasting views on something, for example. This is a particularly good way to begin an ethics paper.
2. *Middle Paragraph(s).* Do what you said you were going to do. This is the bulk of the paper. It will have a few divisions, depending on how you handle your subject matter. (A more detailed outline of an ethics paper is given at the end of this appendix.)
3. *End Paragraph(s).* Tell what you have done or said or concluded. More often than not, students end their papers without really ending them. Perhaps they are glad to have finished the main part of the paper and then forget to put an ending to it. Sometimes they really have not come to any conclusion and thus feel unable to write one. The conclusion can be tentative. It can tell what you have learned, for example, or it can tell what questions your study has raised for you.

Some word-processing programs provide an outlining function. These are helpful because they provide ways in which to set your main points first and then fill in the details. Parts can be expanded, moved, and reoriented. You can look at your paper as you progress with just the main headings or with as much detail as you like and have. In this way you can keep your focus on the logic of your presentation. If your word processor provides such a program, then you may want to get acquainted with and use it. Or you may stick with the pen-and-paper, write-and-crossout method.

Format

How you arrange and present your ideas is also important. Among the elements that deal with these are the following: size, notes, citing Internet sources, and title page and biography.

Size   This is most often the first, and perhaps the most significant, question asked by students when a paper is assigned: "How long does it have to be?" To pose the question of length in this way may suggest that the student will do no more than the minimum required. Although an excellent paper of the minimum length may fetch a top grade, it is probably a good idea to aim at more than the minimum length. It is also not enough just to know how many pages within a range are expected. If I type with a large print (font), then I will write much less in five pages than if I use a small one. A word-count estimate is more definite. For example, one could be told that the paper should be between eight and ten pages with approximately 250 typed words per page. In some cases, professors have very specific requirements, expecting, for instance, ten pages of Times-style font, point size 12, with one-inch margins all around! You should have definite information as to what is expected in this regard.

Footnotes   Does the instructor expect notes or citations? If so, must they be at the bottom of the page or is it permissible to place them at the end of the paper? Is there a specific format that must be followed for these?[1] Not to document sources that you have used may be a form of *plagiarism*. Plagiarism is not acknowledging the source of ideas you include and attempting to pass them off as your own. This not only is deceitful, but also can even be thought of as a form of stealing. The use of proper citations avoids this.

Footnotes and endnotes have three basic purposes. The first purpose is to give the source of a direct quotation. This gives proper credit to other authors for their ideas and statements. You use quotations to back up or give examples of what you have said. You should always introduce or comment on the quotations that you use. You can introduce a quotation with something like this:

> One example of this position is that of Jack Sprat, who writes in his book, <u>Why One Should Eat No Fat</u>, that ' . . . .'[1]

Sometimes, you will want to follow a quote with your own interpretation of it, such as "I believe that this means. . . ." In other words, you should always put the quotation in a context.

The second purpose is to give credit for ideas that you have used but summarized or put into your own words. Sometimes students think that the instructor will be less pleased if they are using others' ideas and are tempted to treat them as their own without giving a footnote reference. Actually, these attempts are often suspicious. Thus, the student who says that "Nowhere in his writings does Descartes mention x, y, or z" is obviously suspicious; it is unlikely that the student will have read all of the works of Descartes or know this on his or her own. It is one sign of a good paper if it gives credit for such indirect references. It shows that the student has read the source that is cited and has made an attempt to put it into his or her own words. This is a plus for the paper.

The third purpose of footnotes and endnotes is to give further information or clarification. For example, you might want to say that you mean just *this* in the paper and not *that*. You might also want to say something further about a point in the paper but you don't want to markedly interrupt the current line of thought.

Citing Internet Sources   Many people today find help for writing papers from the Internet. Some of these sources are more reliable and suitable for your ethics papers than others. InfoTrac, a source available by subscription through some libraries, for example, has many periodicals available online. It has an encyclopedia and many empirically oriented articles. Another recommended gateway site is Voice of the Shuttle: Web Page for Humanities Research, from the University of California at Santa Barbara.[2] Yahoo, Google, and other search engines can be exceptionally helpful if used correctly. Suppose you type in "cloning." You may find a million entries. You

may then want to narrow your search by typing "human cloning." Even then you will have many entries to choose from. To be more specific, before typing either of these on Google, you can choose "more," which will give you various possibilities. You may want to choose "news" for the latest news on your topic or "scholar" for scholarly papers.

You can learn a lot about your topic this way. However, if you include any of the material in your paper, you need to be sure that you credit your source—otherwise you are plagiarizing the material. You should cite your source and use quotation marks when you make a direct quote. But you should also cite it if you are putting the ideas there in your own words (as noted above on the purposes of notes and citations). You may think you will not be found out, but professors now have ways to check suspicious aspects of any paper. Depending on your instructor's directions for your paper, you probably should not limit your research or sources to the Internet, however, especially if you are doing something in-depth or on historical topics such as the philosophy of Kant. You also should be aware that not all Web sites are equally reliable sources of information. According to Jim Kapoun, a reference and instruction librarian, you should base your "Web evaluation on five criteria . . . accuracy, authority, objectivity, currency and coverage."[3] You should consider who wrote the page, what the author's credentials are, whether the source of publication is a respected institution, whether the presentation is objective or is a mask for advertising, whether it is up to date, and whether the article is whole and intact or has elements that you must find elsewhere.

Using and then showing how you used the Internet itself requires some detail and direction. For example, you probably should supply the *uniform resource locator* (URL) of the site you use. Because these frequently change, you also can use the site's author, date you visited, and title. Giving the URL involves giving the whole reference enclosed in angle brackets as follows.

> <http://www.search.yahoo.com/com/bin/ search?p=justice>

The "http" (hypertext transfer protocol) in the address is the usual method of connecting to information on the World Wide Web (the "www") through linked text and graphics.[4] The rest of the items in the address indicate the path, folders, or directory names that tell where the information can be found. Much of the time, references end with "html," which means "hypertext markup language"; this type of file is the primary type of document on the Internet.[5]

Title Page and Bibliography   You also will want to know whether the instructor expects a title page, a bibliography, and so forth. Even if they are not expected, a title page and a folder are nice touches. A bibliography will be fitting for certain types of papers—namely, research papers—and unnecessary for others. A paper in which you are mainly arguing for a point and developing ideas of your own may not require a bibliography. If a bibliography is required, then just how extensive it should be will depend on the paper's purpose, type, and length.

Grammar, Spelling, and Gender

In many cases, your paper will be graded not only on its content but also on mechanics such as grammar and spelling. It is always advisable to check your paper for grammar before the final version. For example, make sure all of your sentences are complete sentences. In the initial writing or revision, a sentence may lose its verb, the subject and predicate may no longer match, nouns and pronouns may not match, and so forth. You should review the paper to correct such mistakes.

Misspelling often is a sign of carelessness. We know how to spell the words, but we do not take care to do so. Sometimes we are uncertain and do not take the time to look up the word in a dictionary. In using a word processor, the checking of spelling is made much simpler. However, even here spelling mistakes can be missed. For example, a spell checker cannot tell that you mean to say "to" instead of "too" or that you wanted to write "he" rather than "hell."

Today, we are also much more conscious of gender issues and gender bias than in decades past. In writing your ethics paper, you should be careful to avoid gender or sexist bias. For example, you should avoid such terms as *mailman* and *policeman*. Acceptable substitutes are *mail carrier* and *police officer*. You also can avoid gender bias by not using traditional gender roles. You might, for instance, speak of the business executive as a "she" and the nurse as a "he."

In times past, it also may have been acceptable to use the pronoun *he* throughout a paper. Today, this is often less acceptable or even unacceptable. It is not always easy to remedy the situation, however, even when one wants to be fair and nondiscriminatory. If one is referring to a particular male or female, then the proper pronoun is easy. But if the reference can be either male or female, then what should one do with the pronouns? One can say "she" or "he" or "he or she." You can also alternate pronouns throughout the paper, sometimes using "he" and sometimes "she." As I have done in this paragraph, you can also use the gender-neutral "you," "one," or "they," "their," or "them" when possible.

TYPES OF ETHICS PAPERS

There are several basic types of ethics papers that can be described. You should be clear from the beginning which type you have been assigned or which you intend to pursue if you have a choice. According to one writer, there are five types of philosophy papers:[6]

1. thesis defense papers in which one "state(s) a position and give(s) reasons for believing it is true",[7]
2. a paper that compares and contrasts two viewpoints,
3. an analysis paper in which some particular viewpoint is examined more closely,
4. a paper that summarizes an article or a book, and
5. research papers or surveys on a specific topic.[8]

Our division here overlaps this fivefold division. The following sections describe three types of ethics papers. Short examples of each can be found at the end of this appendix.

A Historical Approach

If you have already covered at least part of the beginning of this text, you will have some background in the history of ethics. Writings on ethics go back to the time of Plato in the West and earlier in other cultures. Other major figures in the history of Western ethics are Aristotle, Augustine, Aquinas, Locke, Hume, Kant, Marx, Mill, Nietzsche, Kierkegaard, and Sartre. And innumerable philosophers in the twentieth century have written and are writing on matters of ethics. If you are interested in exploring the ethical views of any of these philosophers, you can start with a general overview of their philosophies as given in some more general historical commentary on philosophy. The *Encyclopedia of Philosophy* (Macmillan and the Free Press, 1967) or the *Stanford Encyclopedia of Philosophy* (at http://plato.stanford.edu) might be an initial starting point. From this, you can determine whether a philosopher's views interest you, and you can see in general what type of ethical theory he or she espouses.

The main point of a historical exposition is to summarize or analyze a philosopher's views. It involves learning and writing down in some structured way your own understanding of those views. Your own views and interpretive comments can be added either as you go along or in some final paragraphs. You also can add your own critical or evaluative comments (positive or negative or both), possibly saving them for the end of the paper. Alternatively, you might make the paper entirely exposition, without adding your own views or critical comments.

A Problem in Ethical Theory

Another type of ethics paper is one that examines some particular issue in ethical theory. Part I of this text addresses several of these. Among these problems are:

- The Nature of Ethical Reasoning
- An Ethics of Rights Versus an Ethics of Care
- Ethical Relativism
- Moral Realism
- Moral Pluralism
- Ethical Egoism

- Why Be Moral?
- The Nature of a Right
- Charity Versus Obligation
- What Is Justice?
- What Is Virtue?

The point of a paper that treats a matter of ethical theory is to examine the problem itself. One approach is to start with a particular view on the issue, either in general or from some philosopher's point of view, and then develop it using your own ideas. Another approach is to contrast two views on the issue and then try to show which one seems more reasonable in your opinion. For example, you could give two views on the nature of justice. One might hold that justice requires some kind of equality. Thus, a just punishment is one that fits the crime, or a just distribution of wealth is one that is equal. Then contrast this with another view and follow that with your own comments. For another approach, you might do a general presentation that simply tries to state the gist of the issue or problem and then give your own position on it. To summarize these, you could:

1. State a view, then develop it with your own ideas.
2. Contrast two views on a subject, then say which, if either, you find more persuasive.
3. Explain the problem, and explain your views on it.

A Contemporary Moral Issue

A third type of ethics paper focuses on some practical moral issue that is currently being debated. Part II of this text presents a selection of such issues. However, in each chapter in Part II, there are several issues from which you could choose. You might, for example, just focus on the issue of active euthanasia or physician-assisted suicide. You might write about the ethical issues that arise in our treatment of endangered species. Both issues are treated as part of chapters in this text. You might want instead to address some ethical issue that is not treated in this text: gun control, for example. However, on this topic as well as the others just mentioned, you should be certain to focus on the ethical issues involved if you are to make this an ethics paper. You can also use the bibliographies found at the end of each chapter in this text to give you ideas on possible sources of material to read when researching your paper. Although incomplete, these bibliographies do give you some possibilities, and they are updated with each edition of this text.

One useful method of approaching a contemporary moral issue is to distinguish conceptual, factual, and ethical matters. *Conceptual matters* are matters of meaning or definition. *Factual matters* refer to what is the case about something. *Ethical matters* are matters of good and bad, better and worse, and they involve evaluation. Thus, regarding pornography, we could distinguish conceptual problems related to the attempt to say what it is as well as categorizing various forms of it. Factual matters would include descriptions of the types of pornography available, where they can be found, the numbers of users or viewers, its cost, and so on. The majority of an ethics paper should be the attempt to evaluate it and give reasons for the evaluation. I have tried to exemplify this approach in the chapters throughout Part II of this text.

IS IT AN ETHICS PAPER?

An ethical problem can be approached in different ways. Not all of them are ethical approaches or would make the basis of an ethics paper. Take problems of violence in this country. Many people believe that this society is too violent. One approach to examining the problem is to focus on questions about the causes of violence. Is it something in our history or our psyche? Does the media cause violence or reflect it or both? To make either of these issues the focus of one's paper, however, is not to do ethics or an ethics paper but a sociological analysis or descriptive account of the situation.

An ethics paper requires that you take a normative approach and ask about what is better or worse, right or wrong, good or bad, just or unjust, and so on. (See Chapter 1 on the distinction between a normative and descriptive approach.) Therefore, regarding violence, an ethics paper might begin with a clarification of what is meant by violence and a description of the different kinds of violence. Next, it should become a discussion of what kinds of violence are justified or unjustified, for example. It might address the question of whether social or legal force is justified to diminish violence. This latter discussion could raise issues of the morality of legal force or the importance of individual liberty. In such discussions, one would be doing ethics, because one would be addressing the ethical issues about just and unjust behavior or the moral justification of some practice or the moral value of liberty.

To be sure that your presentation is one that strictly addresses an ethical issue as an ethical problem, make sure you do not appeal primarily to authorities who are not authorities on ethical matters. For instance, if you are addressing the issue of gun control, then you should not appeal simply to legal sources such as the U.S. Constitution to back up your ideas. You may appeal to ethical values that are part of the Constitution, such as the value of life or freedom of speech, but then you are using them as ethical values apart from whether or not the law values them. If you are considering whether the law ought to permit active euthanasia or physician-assisted suicide, then you may consider whether having such a law would or would not promote certain ethical values. This would be an approach that could be used in an ethics paper.

STRUCTURING OR ANALYZING AN ETHICAL ARGUMENT

Most ethics papers either present or analyze ethical arguments, so you should consider some of the elements and types of ethical arguments. (Review the sections on ethical reasoning and ethical arguments from Chapter 1). Among these are the following:

Reasons and Conclusions

It is important to notice or be clear about what follows from what. Sometimes, key words or phrases will indicate this. For example, consider this statement: "Because X has better results than its alternative Y, we ought thus to adopt X." In this statement, the conclusion is that we ought to adopt some practice. The reason for this is that it has better results than its alternative. The key to knowing what follows from what in this example are the words *thus* and *because*. Being clear about this distinction enables you to make a better argument, for you can then back up your conclusion with other reasons and fill in the conclusions with more details.

Types and Sources of Evidence

As just noted, if you are to make an ethical argument, strictly speaking, you cannot appeal simply to legal sources as such in order to make your case. You also cannot appeal to scientific sources for the ethical values or principles that you want to stress. For instance, although physicians are experts in diagnoses and prognoses, such medical expertise does not make them experts in knowing what kind of life is worthwhile or valuable, or how important are rights or autonomy. So, also, natural scientists can give us valuable information about the results of certain environmental practices, but this information and knowledge does not determine the importance or value of wilderness or endangered species. Sometimes, religious sources or authorities can be used in ethical arguments. When this is acceptable in an ethics or moral philosophy paper, however, it is usually because the values supported by religious sources are ethical values. For example, respect for one's parents might be promoted by a religion, but it also can be reasoned about by those who are not members of that or any religion.

Types of Reasons

As noted throughout this text, one primary distinction in the types of reason given in ethical arguments is the one between the appeal to consequences of some action or practice, and judging acts as right or wrong regardless of the consequences. It is important to be clear about which type of reason you or your source uses or critically evaluates.

Consequentialist Reasoning   Your argument or the argument that you are summarizing or evaluating may be one that appeals to consequences. For example, you or the argument may assert that if we do such and such it will produce certain bad results. The argument can document this from some scientific source. The argument also must show why these results are bad—they may result in loss of life or produce great suffering, for example.

Nonconsequentialist Reasoning   If your argument appeals to some basic moral value or what is alleged to be a moral right, then it is nonconsequentialist. For example, it might be based on the idea that we ought to be honest no matter the consequences. It may appeal to certain basic rights that ought to be protected whatever the consequences. To complete the argument or our evaluation of it, we should show or ask what the basis is for this type of assertion. For example, we might want to ask why autonomy is said to be a value or why liberty of action is a moral right.

Other Types of Reasons   Consequentialist and nonconsequentialist are not the only types of reasons that can be given. One might say that something is just or unjust because all persons, when they think about it in the proper light, would agree that this is just. This is an appeal to something like common moral rationality or a common moral sense. Although this is problematic, the appeals to other types of reasons are also not without their critics.

Some people believe that persons of good character or virtue or of caring temperaments will best be able to judge what is right. To give a moral reason appealing to this sort of belief will also need some explanation. But it will be a start to notice that this is the type of reason that is being given.

Top-to-Bottom or Bottom-to-Top Reasoning?

Another way to construct or analyze ethical arguments is to decide whether the reasoning moves from top to bottom or from bottom to top. In the first approach, we start with a concrete case or situation and our judgment about it, and then we ask what moral value or principle leads us to make this judgment about it.

The top-to-bottom argument starts with a particular moral principle or moral value, and then the argument applies the particular to a specific situation. For example, you might do the following:

1. Start with the assertion that happiness is the most important value, or the principle that we always ought to do whatever promotes the

greatest amount of happiness (the utilitarian moral principle).

2. Then you would ask which alternative among those that you are analyzing would promote the most happiness.

The bottom-to-top argument starts with a situation in which we intuitively feel that a certain course of action is right. For example, one might take the following approach:

1. Start with a case in which we believe that if someone is in great danger of drowning and we can save them, then we ought to do so.
2. Then we proceed to ask why we believe that this is so. What value does it promote or what rights or principles? We ask why we believe that we ought to do so. We might conclude that it flows from a moral principle that says that we always ought to help others in great need when we can do so without much cost to ourselves, and that this is a matter of obligation rather than of charity.

Although one can do a paper that uses one or the other of these types of reasoning, actual moral reasoning often does both. Thus, your ethics paper also could incorporate both types.

Using Analogies

Many writings in ethics today use real or imaginary examples in their arguments. Among the more famous ones are Judith Thomson's violinist analogy (described in Chapter 9 on abortion) and James Rachels's tub example (in the Chapter 8 reading on euthanasia). There are also innumerable lifeboat examples. The method of arguing by analogy is as follows: If I start with some case and reach a certain moral conclusion about it, and if there is another case that is like it in the relevant respects, then I should conclude the same about it. Consider this example:

If we are dividing a pie and one person is hungrier than another, then that person should get the bigger piece. This is only fair. So, also, then we should say that in society at large the fair distribution of wealth is one in which those people who have greater needs should have a greater share of the wealth.

We can critically evaluate an analogy by considering whether the analogy fits. We ask whether the two situations or scenarios are similar in the relevant respects. Thus, in the previous example we might ask whether being hungrier than another is the same as having greater needs. We might also wonder whether there is anything crucially different between what is fair among individuals in sharing some good and what is fair in society with regard to sharing a nation's wealth. We might say that nothing else matters so much in the pie-sharing situation, but that additional things do matter in the situation of sharing a nation's wealth.

Many other considerations go into making an ethical argument a strong argument. However, these few given here should help you construct and critically analyze ethical arguments, which are the heart of an ethics paper.

SAMPLE ETHICS PAPERS

Here follow three shortened versions or outlines of the three types of ethics papers described. The first gives an outline of a historical ethics paper. The other two give examples of papers that address issues in ethical theory and practice. Although there are a few footnotes and endnotes here as examples, other examples of endnotes can be found throughout this text. You also can use the end-of-chapter bibliographies found in this text for examples of one type of bibliographical format.

NOTES

1. See, for example, Joseph Gibaldi, *MLA Handbook for Writers of Research Papers,* 6th ed. (New York: The Modern Language Association of America, 2003), for detailed help on forms of citation.
2. Ibid., 21.
3. Christian Crumlish, *The ABCs of the Internet,* 2nd ed. (Alameda, CA: Sybex, 1997).
4. Jim Kapoun, "Questioning Web Authority: How a Librarian Trains Students to Assess Web Page Credibility," *On Campus* (February 2000): 4.
5. See the *MLA Handbook,* 178–190, for details on types of Web site citations.
6. Zachary Seech, *Writing Philosophy Papers,* 3d ed. (Belmont, CA: Wadsworth, 1997).
7. Ibid., 5.
8. Ibid.

Historical Approach

Kant's Theory of the Good Will

I. The Problem: Is it always good to do what you yourself think is right?

Sometimes people seem to act out of conscience and we like to praise this. However, sometimes they then do things that turn out to hurt others. How can we praise such behavior? Is it enough to have a good intention or a good will?

In this paper I plan to consider this issue from the perspective of the modern philosopher, Immanuel Kant, who is known for his views on the importance of motive in ethics. I will look briefly at who Kant was and then proceed to examine his views on the good will. Finally, I will see whether his views help me to answer the question I have posed in this paper.

II. Kant's Theory of the Good Will

A. Who was Kant?

B. What Kant holds on the good will

1. It is always good

2. To act with a good will is to act out of duty

3. To act with a good will is to act out of respect for the moral law

C. How this position relates to the initial problem

III. In this paper I have described Kant's views on the good will. I have found that, according to Kant, it is always good because the person who acts with a good will acts with the motive to do what morality requires. I then returned to the original questions that I posed to see how Kant answered them.

Finally, in my view Kant does (not) give a reasonable answer to my question, because . . .

A Problem in Ethical Theory

Moral Relativism

Many people today seem to be moral relativists. We tend to believe that what is good for some people is not necessarily also good for others. In some circumstances it seems that it is permissible to lie, and at other times it seems that we ought to tell the truth. On the other hand, we also argue with one another all the time about what actually is right and wrong. We do not seem to always accept the view that there is no better way. Are we then moral relativists or not? What is moral relativism? This paper will address these questions. It will begin with an attempt to determine what ethical relativism is. Then it will look at some of the arguments about whether it is true. Finally it will draw some conclusions about whether we are actually do believe in ethical relativism.

What Ethical Relativism Is

According to the philosopher, Richard Grace, ethical relativism is a theory which holds that " . . . ."[1] He goes on to explain that. . . . As I understand it, this would mean. . .

Two Views of Ethical Relativism

Professor Grace believes that what ethical relativism asserts is not correct. The reasons he gives for his view are. . . .[2]

Notes as Footnotes

----

1. Richard Grace, "What Relativism Is," Journal of Philosophy, vol. 3, no. 2 (June 1987): 5-6.
2. Ibid., 6.

A contrasting view is held by the philosopher Eleanor Brown. She writes that " . . . ."[3] The reasons that Professor Brown believes that ethical relativism is a valid theory are. . . .

My Views

I believe that Professor Grace have given reasonable arguments against ethical relativism. In particular I agree with his argument that. . . . My reason for doing so is that this is true to my experience. For
example. . . .

My Conclusions

In this paper I have looked at two views on ethical relativism, one critical of it and one supporting it. Now that I have become clearer about what relativism is and have looked at opposing views on it, I
conclude that it is (not) a reasonable view. Additionally, I believe that if we understand relativism in the way that these philosophers have explained it, we generally do not behave as thought we were ethical
relativists. For example. . . . On the other hand, there are some things that are still questions in my mind about ethical relativism. Among these are. . . . I look forward sometime to finishing my inquiry into this difficult problem.

Notes as Endnotes

Notes

1. Richard Grace, "What Relativism Is," <u>Journal of Philosophy</u>, vol. 3, no. 2 (June 1987): 5-6.

2. Ibid., 6.

3. Eleanor Brown, <u>Relativism</u> (Cambridge, Mass: Harvard University Press, 1988), 35.

A Contemporary Ethical Issue

The Ethics of Cloning

Just the other day in the newspaper there was a report of a case of the cloning of a human being.[1] According to this report, while we have cloned vegetables and some small animals in the past, there has never before been a published report of a case of a human being being cloned. This case has raised quite a stir. In particular many people have raised ethical questions about this case. There is a diversity of opinion about whether such a practice is right or wrong. In this paper I will examine the ethical debate over the cloning of human beings. I will begin with a description of the process and this case. Next I will summarize the arguments for and against this practice. Finally I will present my own conclusions about the ethics of cloning human beings.

What Is Cloning?

There are two types of cloning.[2] One is. . . . The other is. . . . In this case the second type was used. What these scientists did was. . . .

The Case against Cloning

Many people wonder about the ethics of cloning human beings. Some ex-press fears that it would be abused. For example, Professor . . . is quoted in the news article saying that. . . .[3] The idea seems to be that many people might have themselves cloned so that they could use this clone for organ transplants. Others worry that. . . .

The arguments of Professor . . . seem reasonable. I especially agree with him that. . . .

The Case in Favor of Cloning

On the other hand, Doctor . . . and others argue that with the right kinds of safeguards the cloning of humans would be just as ethically acceptable as the cloning of carrots. Among the safeguards that they list are. . . .[4]

One of the problems that I see with this position is. . . .

My Conclusions

In this paper I have found that the project to clone human beings consists in a process of. . . . I have looked at ethical arguments in support and critical of this procedure when applied to humans. I conclude that while there may be some advantages to be gained from this method of producing babies, what worries me about cloning humans is. . . . I will continue to follow this issue as it develops, for I'm sure that this is not the last time we will hear of the cloning of humans nor the last of the debate about its ethical implications.

Notes

1. The Sue City Daily News, January 17, 1993, C7.

2. Jane Gray, Modern Genetics (New York: The American Press, 1988), 5-10.

3. The Sue City Daily News, C7.

4. See Chapter 4 in Martin Sheen and Sam Spade, Cloning (San Francisco: The Free Press, 1991), 200-248.

Ethics in the News

"CAPITALISM: A LOVE STORY"

On September 19, 2009, in Belleaire, MI, filmmaker Michael Moore gave residents a preview of his new film, "Capitalism: A Love Story," which is based on the idea that U.S. democracy has been undermined by greed and corruption. Michigan has an unemployment rate of 15.2%, which is the highest in the country. It is even higher in northern Michigan, caused by the closing of factories and manufacturers who supplied the auto industry. In the film, Michael Moore blames the economic crisis on deregulation introduced during the Reagan era, as well as the greed of business executives who Moore believes pushed for policies that benefited the richest 1% of the population while hurting the middle classes and the poor. Neither such deregulation nor the policies that the greedy executives pushed for were ethical, Moore believes, since they led to the immoral outcomes that are so evident in Michigan.

The former Republican Governor of Michigan, William Millikin, who watched the film, said that it sent a powerful message about the injustices that still persist in American society. Other viewers were inspired by the film, saying that they had no idea that such wrongs were being perpetrated, and that it led them to think that they and others should become politically active to fight against the injustices that it portrayed.

Discussion Questions

1. Is there anything intrinsically immoral about high unemployment? Do people have a right to work? If so, should jobs be provided for them at taxpayer expense if the free market has failed them?
2. According to this article, is Michael Moore opposed to capitalism, or to government policies that undermine capitalism? Is there a difference between being opposed to big business and being opposed to the free market?
3. Are there any ethical advantages to greed, or is greed always a bad thing? What would a virtue ethicist say here? What would a utilitarian say? What might Kant say? Which view do you think is correct?
4. What sort of regulations should be put in place to curtail the power of businesses to lobby for policies that aid the wealthy at the expense of the poor? Should we restrict government power or increase it to curtail such injustice?
5. What are the injustices that are the focus on this article? Who has perpetrated them? Who has a duty to rectify them?

HEALTH CARE FOR UNDOCUMENTED IMMIGRANTS

In September 2009, religious leaders in Los Angeles began a telephone campaign to press lawmakers to have any health care reform plan cover undocumented immigrants. At a religious service on Friday, September 18 at Our Lady Queen of Angels Catholic Church prayed that any health care reform plan would be all-inclusive, with their leaders saying that this was both a moral and a spiritual imperative. This view was echoed by Father Richard Estrada, who leads the immigrant services organization Joyenes Inc. Father Estrada claims that the inclusion of immigrants in a health care plan is consistent with biblical teaching about aiding the most vulnerable

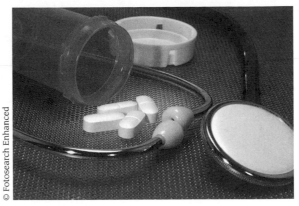

© Fotosearch Enhanced

within society. However, in response to this, religious conservatives have held that the injunction to care for society's most vulnerable people is an injunction that applies only to people of faith, and not to governments.

Discussion Questions

1. Do you believe that U.S. citizens have a moral duty to provide health care to undocumented immigrants? Why, or why not?
2. Does a person's legal status make any difference to his or her moral status or to the moral rights that he or she can claim? Why or why not? How is your answer to this question related to your answer to question 1?
3. Do you believe that U.S. citizens have a moral duty to provide for the health care needs of other U.S. citizens? Why, or why not? If so, how far does this moral duty extend? If not, are there any moral duties incumbent upon people to aid others?
4. Do you believe that moral or religious values should play a role in political decision making? Support your view, making sure that you use moral, rather than legal, arguments to do so.
5. If the religious conservatives whose views are noted above are right that Biblical teachings should apply only to people of faith, not to governments, what does this imply about the relationship between governments and morality? Do you agree with this implied view? Why or why not?

SHOULD TROUBLED FIRMS FAIL?

In September 2009, Larry Summers, the director of President Obama's National Economic Council, argued both that new restrictions should be placed on the nation's largest financial institutions and that the financial industry should not expect to be bailed out again by the government. In particular, Summers argued that Congress should pass new laws that would require financial institutions to have bigger capital reserves to protect them against failure due to risky business practices. Summers condemned the situation the government found itself in, claiming that such measures were necessary in fall 2008. When Lehman Brothers went bankrupt the financial sector experienced tremendous alarm. Soon after, the government provided billions of dollars to prevent American International Group, a large insurance company, from entering bankruptcy, to prevent the same kind of panic, or worse. These options—bankruptcy or bailouts—were insufficient and place an undue burden on the taxpayer, Summers argued, and proposed legislation requiring banks

© Imageshop/PunchStock

to avoid incurring risks that they could not bear. Summers pointed out that this issue one the Obama administration places a heavy emphasis on—right behind health care. Summers had also proposed that a consumer finance protection agency should be created, but Congress, the U.S. Chamber of Commerce, and community banks oppose the creation of such an agency because they believe it will hinder consumers' access to credit.

Discussion Questions

1. Is it morally acceptable for governments to act paternalistically toward firms by requiring them to have cushions of capital to protect them if their risky transactions fail? If it is, then can governments also require the same risk-aversion of private individuals, requiring them to save to protect themselves against risky decisions? If it is not, why not?

2. Is there a moral difference between firms and individuals that might justify governments interfering in the actions of the former but not the latter? Does it matter that a firm's failure might affect more people than an individual's failure?

3. The doctrine of "moral hazard" states that if a person or a firm is insured against the adverse effects of the risks that they take they will be more inclined to engage in risky behavior. Do you believe that government bails out lead to a form of "moral hazard" for firms? If so, does this necessarily mean that they are a bad thing?

4. What does it mean to claim that a firm is "too big to fail"? Does the possibility of such firms existence justify bailouts—or does it justify the government being allowed to break up such firms into smaller, independent units?

5. Do you believe that governments have a role to play in regulating businesses? If not, why not? If so, explain the extent to which you believe that this is justified.

HEALTH CARE PRICE TRANSPARENCY

Bob Hausheer of Chicago, IL, has a $5,000 deductible on his health insurance plan, so he ends up paying for most of his own health care needs. Since this is so, he wants to know how much his care will cost him before he decides to purchase it. He didn't, for example, know how much his $7,500 back surgery would cost him until he received the bill for it. Noting that he knows upfront how much other goods he buys cost—such as coffee at his local coffee shop—Hausheer observes that the health care industry is the only industry where this is not the case.

Hausheer will be pleased to know that the Senate Finance Committee's version of health care reform may lead to such transparency in pricing, requiring that hospitals make public the amounts they charge for many services. The Senate Finance Committee's bill, sponsored by Max Baucus (D-Montana) will also require health plans to report how much of insurance premiums cover administrative costs rather than the cost of health care itself.

Currently, it is very difficult if not impossible for patients to find out how much a procedure will cost. Moreover, the cost of procedures varies according to who is paying for them. Insurance companies make deals with hospitals and doctors about how much they will pay for certain procedures even before any of their clients need them. The prices paid by government agencies such as Medicaid are even lower than those paid for by commercial insurers, for the government simply sets its own schedule of rates. The people who pay the most for their health care are those who pay for it themselves. For example, in Maine, Medicaid pays one hospital $793 for a colonoscopy, while commercial insurers pay between $800 and $950. People who pay out of pocket are required to pay $1,326.

Increasing deductibles are leading health care consumers to become more motivated to shop around for the services that they need so that they can find better deals. But without transparency in health care pricing, this is impossible.

However, even if health care prices were made transparent, this would not necessarily lead to lower prices. This is because if a hospital is powerful in a market, insurance companies might not be able to work out any better deals, while the lack of competition might let prices remain high. Besides, people who need urgent health care aren't in a very good position to negotiate lower

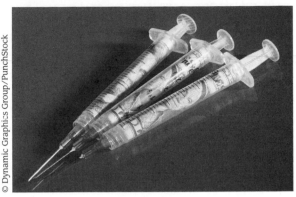

© Dynamic Graphics Group/PunchStock

prices with those who provide it, even if they do know the prices they will be charged.

Discussion Questions

1. Do hospitals have a moral obligation to charge people the same prices for the same treatment? Or do you believe that it is morally acceptable for them to agree to charge less to insurance companies as a way of giving them "bulk discounts"?

2. Should insurance companies pay more than individual patients for the health care that they buy, as they are able to pay more? That is, do you think that insurance companies have a moral obligation to subsidize the uninsured?

3. Do you think that health care is a good like other consumer goods, such as coffee, or do you think that there is something special about it? If you think that it is just another consumer good, why should hospitals be required to disclose their prices if they do not want to? After all, if a coffee shop refused to disclose its prices, it could do so with impunity. If you think that health care is different in some way, explain why it is different, and outline how this difference should lead to health care being treated differently from other goods.

4. Do health care providers exploit their patients? Explain and justify your answer.

5. Is it morally acceptable for a hospital to be run for a profit? In answering this question explain, what you think the advantages of for-profit health care could be, as well as the disadvantages of it.

DUE PROCESS AND THE DEATH PENALTY

Gerald James Holland, who was 71 in 2009, is the oldest prisoner on death row in the state of Mississippi. He was sentenced to death in 1987 after being convicted of raping and murdering a 15-year-old girl. In Mississippi, as in several other states in the 5th circuit U.S. Court of Appeals, capital cases involve two jury trials. The first trial is held to determine whether the defendant is guilty or innocence. If the defendant is found guilty, a second trial is held at which prosecutors present aggravating factors and the defendant presents mitigating factors. After hearing both, the jury must decide whether the defendant should receive a life sentence or should be executed. According to the rules for this procedure, the second trial is not supposed to question the verdict from the first trial.

In 2009, the federal court heard Holland's appeal to the sentencing trial; his lawyers claimed that it was a violation of his rights that he was not allowed to contest the details of the crime as presented by the prosecutors. They asserted that if the prosecution was allowed to describe the crime as a part of their presentation of aggravating factors, the defendant should be allowed to present an argument rebutting the prosecution's description of the crime by claiming that he did not kill the victim while raping her. Lawyers for Holland argued that the current system unjustly requires a jury that does not know the details of the crime to determine the sentence.

The federal court ruled against Holland, asserting that he did not have the right to argue against the decision of the first jury at the sentencing stage of the hearings, although he did have the right to discuss the circumstances of the crime and his own background. Judge Edward Charles Prado, in the decision for the 5th Circuit Panel, said Holland did not "have the right to present evidence at resentencing that is inconsistent with the verdict of the guilt-phase jury."

Discussion Questions

1. Do you believe that this case can be used to object to the death penalty on moral grounds? Explain your answer.

2. How would (a) a rule utilitarian and (b) an act utilitarian respond to the ruling of the federal appeals court panel in this case? Explain your answer.

3. Is the death penalty for cases of rape and murder required by a retributivist justification of punishment? Explain your answer. Do you believe that this approach to justifying punishment in general is a good one? If not, explain why not, and outline an alternative approach to take.

4. In what way is the Mississippi court system supposed to be "unfair" in cases such as this? Do you believe that this charge is justified? Explain your answer.

5. In holding that a convicted defendant can present evidence to mitigate the crime that he has been convicted of the prosecutor makes a certain assumption. What is that assumption, and it is a fair one to make? Does your answer to this question vary according to the actual guilt or innocence of the person convicted of the crime? Argue for your view.

ADVERTISING ETHICS AND INFANT FORMULA

In Vietnam, baby formula is sometimes marketed so relentlessly that the companies selling the product circumvent or even ignore regulations that have been put in place to promote breastfeeding.

It is widely recognized that when it is possible for a mother to breast feed her baby, breast milk is the best choice for an infant's health. However, there is a considerable body of evidence that formula companies in Vietnam utilize suspect or illegal practices to encourage mothers to give up breast feeding and use formula instead. The multinational companies have been accused of paying doctors and health care workers a commission on sales of their products, promoting formula for use with children under the age of twelve months, or marketing directly to mothers and health care workers at or near health care facilities. All of these actions are against Vietnamese law.

The following statistics show a definite change in how infants are fed in Vietnam over the last ten years:

- Companies selling infant formula spent $10 million on advertising in Vietnam in 2008, making the formula industry one of the top five advertisers in Vietnam.
- UNICEF has found that the number of mothers who breastfeed exclusively until their infants are six months old has decreased by half over the last ten years to a current low of 17%.
- Formula sales increased 39% in 2008, according to a study by the market research firm Nielsen.

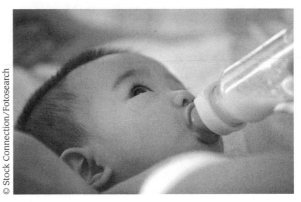

© Stock Connection/Fotosearch

The companies deny any wrong doing. They claim that they utilize only legal tactics in their sales and marketing practices. They point to the increase in the number of working women in Vietnam and say that factors like increased discretionary income and less time at home have led to increased demand for their products.

Aggressive marketing of formula takes place in many developing Asian countries. For example, the formula company Dutch Lady denied that they paid commissions to doctors to sell their product but admitted that they had provided certain goods (such as furniture) to a clinic to which included a large Dutch Lady logo prominently displayed in the waiting room. The director of this clinic, Tran Thi Hanh, said that the clinic had signed an agreement to promote products for pregnant women and nursing mothers, but not infant formula. There are no restrictions on selling powdered milk products for mothers or older children, and brands are often advertised in conjunction with these products; the advertising has been known to suggest that drinking these products will improve a child's intelligence or strength, although there appears to be little or no evidence to support this claim.

While formula cannot be sold in Vietnamese hospitals, outside of the pharmacy, many brands of formula are sold and promoted legally in shops that are located near hospitals. Sales people are not allowed to approach mothers or health care professions, but there are allegations that this law is flouted and that company employees have used unethical practices to try to get patient names for direct contact. Other new mothers receive sales calls from company representatives, and suspect that their names have been passed on to them by their health care providers. The formula companies claim that they only contact women who have provided their contact information through promotions.

Discussion Questions

1. Should there be restrictions on advertising, or should the buyer beware? If there should be restrictions on advertising, what should they be? Should advertisers be allowed to lie or to suggest that their products are better than they are? Or should they be required just to state facts about them? If the latter, can they obscure certain facts about their products or must they state them all? If all, must they state all the facts, or only those that are relevant to a consumer's decision-making? How would one state all the facts in a normal advertisement and how could one know which are relevant to consumers' decision-making processes?

2. Is there anything wrong with health care professionals being paid to provide information about their patients to marketers? Would it make an ethical difference if they received benefits for their hospitals or other patients rather than for themselves?

3. Is it ethically acceptable to make money from other peoples' desire to have their children be as healthy as possible? Why, or why not?

4. Is there anything special about health care or could it be treated as a commodity like anything else that can be bought and sold in the marketplace? What implications does your answer to this question have for your answers to the questions above?

5. In business, we often believe that consumers should look out for their own interests, while we require standards of informed consent when patients are asked to make decisions concerning their health care. Is this dual standard justified, or not?

HEALTH CARE RATIONING

Congresswoman Sue Myrick of North Carolina (R) opposes the Democratic plans for the U.S. health care system on the grounds that a government run system would delay care in life threatening situations. She credits the quick detection of her own breast cancer to her ability to see the specialists of her choice with little or no waiting. Noting that the process of detecting her breast cancer took only a few weeks, Myrick held that under the government run health care systems of both Canada and the UK her recovery would have been threatened because she might have had to wait longer for the tests necessary for her cancer's detection. She cited a study that showed that in those countries three times as many people waited over a month to see a specialist that did in the United States.

The democratic plans for health care reform generally hope to establish competition among private health insurance companies to control the cost of health care. The possible ways of doing this include a government-run insurance option, a trigger to add this option at a later date, or the institution of nonprofit insurance cooperatives.

Myrick claims that all of these proposals are the first steps toward government-run health care. She holds a number of negative results can be expected if we move in that direction in addition to her concern about longer waits for specialist care. She warns that seniors in Medicare, as well as participants in Medicaid could find themselves subject to rationing and small businesses will have to bear the burden of higher taxes.

President Obama has claimed that eliminating waste and abuse in Medicare and Medicaid would be the primary way to help pay for the proposed programs to cover uninsured Americans.

Discussion Questions

1. Is there anything morally wrong with rationing publically-funded health care? If so, what? If not, on what grounds should it be rationed? For example, should it be rationed on the basis of social worth, individual desert, or medical need? Could—and should—all three of these considerations play a role? Justify your answer.
2. Is there an ethical obligation for governments to provide health care options to their citizens? If so, why? If not, why not?
3. Is there a difference between government run health care and government provided health care? Would this difference—if any—make a difference to the debate? If so, in what way? If not, explain why not.
4. Are private insurance companies subject to sufficient competition to ensure that they are efficient? Explain your answer.
5. Is there anything wrong with insurance companies making profits? Should they instead be run for the good of the persons they insure? Justify your answer.
6. Is it fair to allow the wealthy to have better access to health care than the poor? Why or why not? If it is, should we not only provide public health care, but prohibit private health care, to ensure equitable access? Explain your answer.

ETHICAL ISSUES IN IMMIGRATION AND OUTSOURCING

After college, Mikala Reasbeck looked for work for two months and applied to fifty employers nationwide. The only job she could find paid only $7 an hour, so she took the unusual move of flying to Beijing to job hunt. A week after she started looking, she had a full-time job teaching English.

Many young foreigners like Reasbeck are going to China to look for work since the recession has not hit as hard in China as it has in other parts of the world. The Chinese government injected $586 billion in stimulus money into the economy, which helped boost economic growth to 7.9% from a year earlier in the quarter that ended June 30, an increase from the 6.1% of growth the previous year. This stimulus money has helped support the Chinese job market; however, despite this strong economic showing, it is estimated that as many as 12 million job seekers in China will still be unable to find work.

In addition to the relatively strong economic growth that China is experiencing, employment rules for hiring foreigners are less restrictive than in many other countries. (In spite of a tightening of the rules prior to the 2008 Olympics held in Beijing, it was rumored that these restrictions were enacted to keep out possible protestors.) Although employers need government permission to hire foreigners the authorities promise an answer within 15 working days. This compares favorably with a wait of months or longer than might be imposed in other countries. Moreover, although an employer has to justify the need to hire a foreigner, it is usually enough to explain that the worker has special technical or managerial experience. In 2008, seven thousand more foreigners held work permits than in 2007. Many more use temporary business visas in order to work in China legally.

Not all foreigners who seek work in China do so as a refuge from harsh economic conditions in their home countries. Some simply see China as offering better opportunities for them, even though they already have established careers.

Despite this openness, employment rules were tightened ahead of the 2008 Olympics, held in Beijing. It seems that this was owed to the government's desire to keep out possible protestors.

Discussion Questions

1. Is there anything morally wrong with non-Chinese citizens taking jobs from Chinese nationals who would otherwise have them? If not, why not? If so, explain why. Does a person's national origin give her any moral claim on jobs in her own country, vis-à-vis the claims of foreigners?

2. Is it morally wrong to prevent people from taking jobs in countries in which they are foreigners? Similarly, is it wrong to place obstacles to their taking such jobs if they can find them? Explain and justify your answers. Would your answers to these questions change depending on how many foreign workers were coming to

a country to seek jobs? Why or why not? Again, justify your position.

3. Should we, morally, place restrictions on who an employer can hire? If so, would national origin be the only legitimate ground that we could use to do so, or could we place restrictions on who can be hired on other grounds (such as race, age, sex or disability) also? Justify your answers.

4. Is the question of willing employer and willing potential employee the only one that matters, or could have other legitimate interests—such as avoiding protestors or making sure that certain cultures are not overrun?

5. What are the implications of your answers to the questions above for the question of whether it is morally acceptable for American countries to (a) hire foreign workers on temporary work visas, such as the H1B visa? (b) outsource their manufacturing or services offshore?

TOYOTA VEHICLE RECALL

Toyota is recalling 3.8 million vehicles in the United States including some of its most popular models, including the Toyota Camry and the Prius

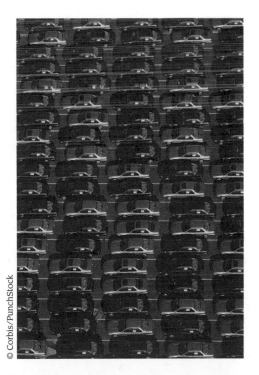

© Corbis/PunchStock

gas-electric hybrid. The recall is necessary because a floor mat in the car can cause accelerators to get stuck, making it impossible for drivers to stop the car, possibly causing a crash. Toyota announced that it was working with the National Highway Traffic Safety Administration to find a solution. Meanwhile, the company said that drivers should be sure that the floor mat be removed from the driver's side of the vehicle.

The National Highway Traffic Safety Administration said that it has received 102 reports of the accelerator getting stuck. Although it is not clear how many of these cases led to crashes, the floor mat is suspected to have caused the problem in at least one fatal crash of a Lexus ES in California. Toyota issued instructions to Toyota owners whose vehicles might be affected by this problem concerning what to do in case the accelerator does become stuck.

In mid-September, Toyota ordered its dealers to check the floor mats in all the Toyota and Lexus models they had under their control.

Discussion Questions

1. Do you think that Toyota should have recalled its vehicles when owners could just be asked to remove the floor mats? How is your answer to this question related to your view of utilitarianism?
2. Do you think that Toyota had a moral obligation to recall the vehicles or do you think that "buyer beware" applies here?
3. Why do you think bears responsibility for any crashes after Toyota has issued information about the floor mats? Toyota or the car owners? Justify your answer.
4. If it would cost Toyota less in compensation payments to the people killed in crashes caused by defective floor mats, or to the heirs of people killed in them, would this justify Toyota failing to issue a recall? Why or why not?
5. Does Toyota have a moral duty to look out for the welfare of its customers? Why or why not?

PACIFIC EARTHQUAKE

On Tuesday, September 29, 2009, a Pacific Ocean earthquake led to tsunami waves that engulfed the islands of Samoa and American Samoa (a U.S. territory with a population of around 65,000). Villages were destroyed, at least 39 people were killed and at least 50 more were injured. Survivors headed to high ground as the waves carried cars and people out to sea. Homes were destroyed by flood waters.

There is a national park in American Samoa which suffered heavy damage, with only 20% of the park's dozen or so employees and 30 to 50 volunteers accounted for in the hours immediately after the quake and subsequent tsunami and flooding. The disaster destroyed the park's visitor center and offices.

Also in American Samoa, a tuna cannery which produced Chicken of the Sea canned tuna was closed, although the tsunami had inflicted no damage on the plant. Before the disaster, the closing of the plant had been announced, and more than 2,100 workers were laid off. Tuna packing makes up 60% of the economy in American Samoa, making it the territory's principle industry.

The initial quake was followed by three aftershocks.

In the nearby island of Samoa coastal areas frequented by tourist as well as villages were destroyed. Landslides and looting were reported as well.

Immediately after the disaster, the Coast Guard was evaluating the territory's need for aid and resources and the U.S. Federal Emergency Management Agency was preparing to send support teams to American Samoa.

Discussion Questions

1. Do you believe that American aid should be sent to Samoa, as well as to American Samoa? Why or why not? If not, why do you think that national borders render some persons with lesser moral claims to aid than others? If you do, why do you believe that there is a duty to provide aid at all?
2. Should the national park be restored or should it be left as it is, since it has been affected by a natural disaster? How does your answer reflect your views concerning what is natural and what is not natural?

3. Does Chicken of the Sea now have a moral duty to keep its plant open to provide work for the workers in the devastated area? Justify your answer.
4. Do you think that the students should be blamed for looting the convenience store? What if they only looted food that would spoil and go to waste? Should they leave this alone, or should they take it? If they take it, are they morally obligated to pay for it at a later date?
5. Do you think that it would be immoral for someone to go to American Samoa with the intent of selling emergency supplies at prices greater than they would fetch before the disaster happened? Do you think that this would be unjust exploitation? Justify your view.

NEW YORK CITY TERRORIST TRIAL
On Tuesday September 29, Najibullah Zazi, a shuttle driver from Colorado who is suspected of being a member of al-Qaida, appeared in court on charges that he purchased products containing hydrogen peroxide and acetone with intention to make a bomb. He pled not guilty. The FBI believes that Zazi attempted to create the explosives in a hotel room in Colorado before driving to New York with intention to and then drove to New York to utilize the explosives in an attack. On September 10, Zazi's apartment was searched, and instructions for making a bomb were found on his computer. Zazi began to suspect that he was under surveillance, so returned to Denver by plane on September 12. He was arrested the next week.

Although Zazi was alleged to have three co-conspirators, the police commissioner in New York, said at the time that there was no longer any threat now that Zazi had been arrested and the plot exposed and that no extra security measures were required or in place. While the commissioner would give no further details, others familiar with investigations of this nature felt that this meant either that the conspirators had fled the United States or might be assisting police in their investigations.

After Zazi pled not guilty to the conspiracy charges, the judge ordered that he be held without bail. His defense attorney said that while his client did purchase beauty supplies in Colorado, "Those acts are not illegal." The attorney denied that he knew of anyone else who allegedly conspired with his client.

Because this case involves national security, classified material is involved which Zazi's lawyer, and other participants will be required to have security clearance before being allowed access.

Discussion Questions
1. Should it be easier for investigators to secure warrants to investigate serious crimes, such as terrorism? Justify your view.
2. Would it be acceptable to torture people suspected of terrorism if it is believed that this could secure information about their plots? Argue for your view. Why might someone object to such a practice? What would Kant say? What would Mill say? Why? Who do you agree with?
3. Is it fair that Zazi's lawyer cannot readily access information about his client's case because it is classified? Why or why not? Is there any way to avoid this difficulty with crimes involving national security? Explain your answer. Do you think that such crimes should be treated differently from other crimes that might involve loss of life? Why?
4. If beauty products are legal to buy, should we prosecute someone for buying them? Would it matter if the person in question owned instructions on how to make a bomb using them? Explain your answer. Should we prosecute the persons who sell such supplies? What if they knew how they could be used?
5. Should it be legal to publish material explaining how to make a bomb from materials that are readily available? Would prohibiting the publication of such material violate the First Amendment? Why or why not?

U.S. TROOP WITHDRAWAL FROM IRAQ
As the American military prepares to reduce its engagement in Iraq, the operation's top general, Gen. Ray Odierno, is reducing the number of soldiers from about 160,000 to about 120,000. The reduction in force is roughly equivalent to the size of one Army brigade.

© SuperStock/Fotosearch

In his statement to the House Armed Services Committee, Odierno said, "As we go forward, we will thin our lines across Iraq in order to reduce the risk and sustain stability through a deliberate transition of responsibilities to the Iraqi security forces."

In remarks prepared for the congressional hearing, Odierno indicated that the last two years have seen a dramatic decrease in the number of attacks each month: there were more than 4,000 in August 2007 and only 600 such attacks in August 2009. The number of foreign combatants and al-Quaida operatives in Iraq has also decreased sharply.

However, Odierno also highlighted problems which are expected to continue. The list included security issues, difficulty in setting up a system of government that allows people from different regions, ethnic and sectarian groups to work together, and friction between Arabs and Kurds.

Among other sectarian issues, the Shiite dominated government has been accused of working too slowly to integrate Sunnis into positions with the police and military. government leaders had for example, while Iraqi leaders had pledged to ensure employment for all members of the Sons of Iraq group. This group was heavily involved in reining in the insurgency in Iraq. In the briefing, Odierno said that it was now unlikely that the Iraqi government's promised time frame for full employment of this mostly Sunni group would be met.

Discussion Questions

1. Do you believe that the Sons of Iraq should be rewarded for aiding the government with government jobs? Would it matter to you if they were awarded such jobs after having had to compete for them against all-comers, with their status as Sons of Iraq acting only as a tie-breaker? Justify your answer.

2. Do you believe that jobs should be allocated on the basis of ethnicity, with the ratio of persons of different ethnic or religious groups in government service reflecting the ratio of those groups in the population? Why, or why not?

3. Should race or ethnicity play any role in hiring decisions? Justify your answer.

4. Do you believe that the United States has a moral obligation to Iraqis to ensure that Iraq is stable? Why or why not? If so, for how long would this obligation exist? If not, why not?

5. If it was a moral obligation to effect regime change in Iraq, should this have been done through the use of government action? What does your answer tell you about your view of the relationship between government and moral enforcement? Do you think that the government should enforce morality, or not? If yes, do you believe that there is an objective morality that can be known? If not, why not—wouldn't this make everyone better off?

NERO'S DINING ROOM AND ECONOMIC INEQUALITY

In late September 2009, archeologists announced that they believe they have discovered the ruins of the banquet hall in the Roman emperor Nero's Golden Place (or Domus Aurea, in Latin). This circular banquet area was built to rotate around the clock in initation of the rotation of the Earth. Archeologists believe that the Golden Palace and the extravagant banquet hall were built so that Nero could entertain government officials and other important guests. The area is only partially excavated, but appears to be 50 feet in diameter; and the mechanism underneath which kept it rotating was probably water powered.

Nero's Palace rose over the ashes of Rome, which burned in 64 AD. It is thought to be Nero's because of references to it in association with him in ancient biographies, including one by the historian Suetonius, which describes a series of ivory panels sliding back and forth to shower roses and perfumes on the guests.

Nero, who was known for living an opulent and indulgent life and inflicting great cruelty during his rule, became emperor when he was 17 and ruled from 54 AD to 68 AD. During a revolt in 86 AD, Nero committed suicide.

Discussion Questions

1. Do you believe that it was immoral of Nero to build the Golden Palace overlooking the ruins of Rome? Why, or why not? If you believe that it was not moral of him so to do because he should have spent the money thus used on rebuilding Rome, what justifies your claim here? Would your response be different if he had used his private funds rather than the public purse? Would it be different if in using the public purse he actually made Rome stronger in the long run by impressing visiting dignitaries with Rome's wealth, thus deterring them from going to war with it?

2. Do you believe that Nero could have built the Golden Palace and still fulfilled his imperfect duty of charity, according to Kant's account of this? Could he have built it and fulfilled a duty of charity according to a utilitarian? Is there a necessary duty of charity, according to a utilitarian? Explain your answer.

3. Imperial Rome was the site of significant inequalities of wealth. Do you believe that this is morally problematic? Why or why not? Would it matter to you how these inequalities came about? If so, in what way?

4. Nero clearly had many more opportunities than other Romans, solely in virtue of his noble birth. Do you believe that this is fair or do you believe that there is a moral obligation incumbent upon persons to ensure equality of opportunity? Explain your answer and justify it. How could such equality be ensured? Provide practical examples to illustrate your position.

5. Is there any moral difference between inherited wealth and earned wealth? Explain and justify your answer.

THE U.S. SUPREME COURT AND GUN CONTROL

On September 28, 2009, the U.S. Supreme Court agreed to decide whether state and local gun control laws violate the Second Amendment. The court said that it would review a lower court ruling that upheld a handgun ban in Chicago.

Gun rights supporters challenged this and other laws after the high court decided in June 2008 to strike down a handgun ban in the District of Columbia. The new case tests whether last year's ruling also applies to local and state laws.

The 7th U.S. Circuit Court of Appeals upheld ordinances barring the ownership of handguns in most cases in Chicago and Oak Park, IL. Judge Frank Easterbrook, said that "the Constitution establishes a federal republic where local differences are to be cherished as elements of liberty rather than extirpated in order to produce a single, nationally applicable rule," claiming that

"Federalism is an older and more deeply rooted tradition than is a right to carry any particular kind of weapon," and that evaluating arguments over the extent of the Second Amendment was for the "justices rather than a court of appeals."

Judges in both courts agreed that only the Supreme Court could decide whether to extent the 2008 ruling throughout the country.

© Rubberball/PunchStock

Discussion Questions

1. Do you think that federalism is a good idea? Do you think that states should be allowed to set their own rules on issues such as gun control? If so, how far are you willing to allow states to go? Are there certain things that should not be legalized in any state? If so, what? Why do you believe this? Justify your answer.
2. Do you think that the Supreme Court should decide what the law is for everyone in the United States? Why or why not?
3. Do you believe that persons have a moral (rather than a legal) right to own guns? If so, are there any limits on the type of weaponry that you would allow people to own? Why or why not? If not, why not? In each case, justify your answer.
4. If the Supreme Court has to interpret the Constitution to apply it, does this mean that Supreme Court judges are making law? Explain your answer. Do you think that it is a problem if they are?
5. If you endorse federalism, does this commit you to holding that states have a moral right to secede? Explain your answer.

ECONOMIC RECOVERY

Analysts predicted a slowing in the economic recovery during the end of 2009 because they expected an increase in unemployment and elusive credit to put pressure on consumers.

Here are some statistics which were known or predicted at that time:

- The overall economy will grow at a rate of 2.5% for the final quarter of 2009. The U.S. economy had contracted by 0.7% in the second quarter of 2009 followed by a 3% increase from July-September.
- The government's Cash for Clunkers program, designed to provide support to the battered auto industry is heavily credited with the strong third quarter performance.
- Consumer spending was expected to be flat or decrease. Consumer spending makes up 70% of the U.S economy.
- From April to June in 2009, wages fell 4.7%.

- The unemployment rate was expected to top 10%, having reached 9.8% in September, with nearly 15 million Americans unemployed at that time.

In September 2009, Ben Bernanke, chairman of the Federal Reserve, stated that the recession which began at the end of 2007 was "very likely over." But he warned that some economic difficulties will continue, especially for the nearly 15 million unemployed Americans. Dennis Lockhart, president of the Federal Reserve Bank of Atlanta said, "In thinking about the recovery, I recommend for now a mindset of measured optimism."

Discussion Questions

1. Does it matter morally whether the economy grows or not? Would your answer be different if you were (a) a utilitarian, (b) a Kantian deontologist, (c) a virtue theorist?
2. Do unemployed persons have a right to unemployment benefit? If so, why? If not, why not? In each case explain and justify your answer.
3. Cars that were turned in under the Cash for Clunkers program were often destroyed, even if they could still be used. Is this a morally acceptable action to take? Explain your answer and place it in the context of the boost to the economy that this program provided.
4. What effect do you think the Cash for Clunkers program had on the used car market? Which section of the population do you think was worst affected by this? Which section of the population do you think was best affected by this program? Do you think that the effects of this program were fair? If not, could they still be justified?
5. Since consumer spending is such a significant proportion of the economy, do you think that people have a moral obligation to spend money? Does it matter that one person's spending would not make much difference to the economy as a whole? In what way might these two questions concerning a possible duty to consume and the lack of effect that any given individual would have on the whole be related to similar questions concerning the ethics of voting in national elections?

DISTRACTED DRIVING

U.S. Transportation Secretary Ray LaHood declared distracted driving 'a menace to society", during a speech launching a two-day meeting designed to stop drivers from using phones, hand-held computers and other mobile devices while behind the wheel of a vehicle.

According to statistics publicized by the White House, driver distraction was a factor in crashes that resulted in the deaths of nearly 6,000 people and half a million injuries in the United States last year.

Congress is paying attention. In July 2009, Sen. Charles Schumer and other Democrats sponsored a bill that would make 25% of federal highway funding incumbent upon state bans of texting or e-mailing while driving. The Obama administration has not expressed support or objection to the legislation.

Some see a ban on the use of mobile devices while driving as a broadening of drunk driving laws and seat belt regulation. LaHood also made this connection, pointing out that the government learned from these prior efforts. "We need a combination of strong laws, tough enforcement and ongoing public education to make a difference," he said.

© Brand X Pictures/Fotosearch

Discussion Questions

1. Do you believe that we should ban people engaging in activities while driving that could be distracting? If so, should we ban people from driving with small children, whose crying or demands for attention could be distracting? If yes, do you think that such a restriction on the movement of families is justified? If no, explain how this case is different from the distractions of texting.

2. Do you believe that we should punish people for driving while texting even when they have not harmed anyone by doing so? Should we punish people merely for placing others at risk? If so, what degree of risk would justify this?

3. Would a utilitarian advocate punishing people for placing others at risk or would she advocate more severe punishments for persons who do place others at risk and that risk transpires? Explain your answer here.

4. Do you believe that seat belt laws are paternalist? Explain your reasoning.

5. One argument in favor of having state laws requiring seat belts is that many persons who would be injured were they to crash while not wearing them lack private insurance and would have their medical bills covered by the state. Thus, seat belt laws can be seen as cost-saving measures for the state. Do you think that it would be better to repeal seat belt laws while also refusing medical treatment to anyone who is injured as a result of not wearing them?

INDEX